POEMS FOR STUDY

A Critical and Historical Introduction

POEMS FOR STUDY

by

Leonard Unger

Associate Professor of English

and

William Van O'Connor

Associate Professor of English

UNIVERSITY OF MINNESOTA

Holt, Rinehart and Winston

New York

to MARY *and* SHERLEY

Preface

■■■■■■■■■■

THE EDITORS would like to make here a few statements about the organization of this text. The editorial comments, general introductions, analyses, and questions after poems bulk larger in some sections than in others. There are a number of reasons why this is so. If certain matters are discussed in relation to Wordsworth, for example, which are also relevant to Coleridge, there is no need to repeat them; and some poems, whether by major or minor figures, invite more commentary than others, because of the need to explain historical or biographical background, or because of the need to illustrate a method of analysis. In other words, the number of pages devoted to a poet is not meant to imply a judgment about his significance or to establish his rank in the hierarchy of English and American poets. In many instances, too, we have not written analyses or asked questions about certain poems, preferring to leave these to the instructor and student. Again, we have for the most part printed short poems rather than long ones for reasons of space and because shorter poems lend themselves better to brief analyses.

A glance at the table of contents will reveal that the poets are arranged in chronological order. It will also be obvious that the poets to whom sections are devoted are, for the most part, the inevitable choices, the "major" poets, from Spenser and Shakespeare to Yeats and Frost. (Chaucer has been omitted for reasons of space and also because of the special problems of language and scholarship involved.) In a few cases the decision to include certain poets and to omit others represents a compromise between the editors' critical attitudes and the limits and purposes of the book. The contents of the individual sections also result from the same kind of compromise. Our basic principles of selection, with regard to poets and poems, have been to illustrate the historical course of poetry in English, to give representative selections of the poets included, and to provide a body of poetry useful for study and for discussion in the classroom.

At the end of the book will be found a section of supplementary poems, also arranged in chronological order. Poets not included in the main body of the book are briefly represented here. The purpose of this section is to give flexibility to the possible uses of the book. It may, where time allows, serve to supplement the historical survey of poetry. It may also serve as a source of exercises to be used in conjunction with a study of the main Introduction.

In each section the student will find a list of recommended readings. The lists have been kept brief, and the items on the lists are, for the most part, short articles and chapters. It is intended that this brevity, in the lists and in the readings, will encourage the student to make use of them. The items are recommended, not always as the definitive or best works on a particular poet, but as suggestions for further reading which will introduce the student to various types of scholarly and critical commentaries as well as help him with the problems or issues under discussion in a particular section.

This text approaches problems of literary history primarily through concrete examples, through analyses of particular poems. We have tried to avoid sweeping generalizations and have deliberately made no attempt to cover all aspects of literary history as it relates to poetry. The poets and poems chosen operate as focal points for the discussion of historical problems. It will be obvious that there is no definitive treatment of any poet in the sense of an extensive and intensive historical and scholarly examination. On the other hand, we have drawn upon such information and wish the student to do so when the occasion calls for it; indeed, the conception and organization of the book imply the need to investigate relevant historical and scholarly considerations.

In the Introduction the student will find discussions of the language and structure of poetry—characteristics, that is, which are likely to be found in some degree in the poetry of all periods. But in addition to the commentaries scattered throughout he will also find a brief section in the Introduction entitled "Shifts in Taste and Sensibility." Here it is observed that the poetry of the late sixteenth century is likely to be different from that of the late nineteenth century because the general beliefs of the two eras differ considerably and because each has a different conception of what good poems should be. Exceptions can, of course, be found to generalizations about the poetry of a period, but the generalizations themselves, if not accepted in a narrow or literal-minded way, may be helpful. No formulas composed of historical and critical considerations will invariably serve a reader. Each poem asks to be read on its own terms.

LEONARD UNGER
WILLIAM VAN O'CONNOR

University of Minnesota
March, 1953

Contents

■ ■ ■ ■ ■ ■ ■ ■ ■ ■

POEMS FOR STUDY

Introduction

....

I. General

It is generally agreed that poetry should be read for pleasure. And it is agreed that there is no final and absolute definition of what poetry is. But behind these widely accepted opinions there is a variety of assumptions as to what the *reading* of poetry actually is and how it should be done. It may therefore be well for the editors to reveal some of the assumptions which have determined the character of this book.

Probably everyone is familiar with the statement, "I don't know anything about art, but I know what I like," and with the attitude it represents. In a sense all of us must be sympathetic to this attitude, for we share it in one respect or another. We may not be experts in certain forms of athletics, in the ballet, or in contract bridge, but we occasionally attend to or engage in one or another of such activities, and we don't hesitate to discuss them, even to make critical comments about them. On the other hand, this attitude is untenable when it implies that there are no differences of quality and intensity in the pleasure which different people derive from a ball game, a ballet performance, or a game of bridge, and that one person's critical comment on these is as valid as another's. That is, the average person does not experience the kind of pleasure and he cannot exercise the kind of critical insight that are possible for the expert or the loyal fan. Actually, he is not seriously interested in these activities; he does not really *follow* them but uses them as a part of his social activity or as a means of passing time pleasantly when his more serious interests are relaxed. In that sense, again, he rightfully knows what he likes.

By reading poetry we mean being seriously interested in it, being a loyal follower, or having gone through a period of being one. It is true that some poems impress us immediately and with no effort on our part. We may feel that we like a poem before we know very much about it. But when we are seriously interested we want to know a good deal about a poem, to get not only the immediate effect but the full effect. We want to read a poem carefully, to examine it closely, in order to decide just how much (or how little) we like it. There are some people who

3

object to such treatment of poetry, who consider a critical analysis or a scholarly explication a violation of the poem. But no poem can continue indefinitely to give us the pleasure of its first impact upon us, and those of us who are seriously interested are entitled to explore the poem for those pleasures and those satisfactions of interest which come only from intimate knowledge. We want, at least, to examine it carefully enough in order to decide whether we wish to explore it further, just as we deliberate and reconsider before buying a recording or a picture. Few poets, moreover, would be satisfied with just a momentary response to their work. They want to be read and reread, to be considered and reconsidered. And few of us care to be unreflective and silent about our serious interests. In the broadest sense, the activity of reading poetry includes thinking about it and talking about it. We test and probe the poem in our thought and talk, and then we return to the poem in order to test our ideas, to see if we have made new strides in exploring the poem. This practice not only makes us better readers of poems that we already know but prepares us for a more perceptive reading of new poems.

With a view toward appropriate vocabulary, familiar and serviceable terms from literary history and literary criticism have been used in the general introduction, in the discussions of particular poets, and in the analyses of individual poems. An attempt has been made to use such special vocabulary, within the limits of its obvious advantages, to provide tools for clarity and economy of expression. The disadvantage of a special vocabulary, either historical or critical, is that it may lead to rigid patterns of thinking and even to thoughtlessness. This is a danger, of course, which always threatens and against which caution must never be relaxed.

Particular attention has been given to frame of reference and to vocabulary in order to combine the two approaches to poetry, the scholarly and the critical. These have often been used with exclusive emphasis on one or the other. With the scholarly approach, poems have been studied in relation to (1) literary history, (2) the social events and intellectual atmosphere of the times in which they were written, (3) the personality, life, and thought of the author. With the critical approach, the tendency has been to isolate individual poems in order to achieve a concentration of attention on these, and thus to examine closely the various details of each poem and their relationship to each other in the poem's total organization and effect. Such specialization, whatever the approach, has the advantages of thoroughness within the chosen limits, but there are also disadvantages. The scholarly approach may use the text of the poem merely as a steppingstone to the consideration of general ideas, historical circumstances, or biographical facts. On the other hand, the critical approach may be misguided or incomplete if it neglects relevant information which the scholarly approach can provide.

11. Concreteness and Particularity

One of the characteristics common to almost all poetry is the use of the *concrete* and the *particular*. Philosophy and science usually attempt to arrive at broad generalizations, at general truths. Their characteristic language is abstract. Poetry is not opposed to generalization or abstraction —and to some extent it employs both—but ordinarily it arrives at a generalization only by implication, the implication being inherent in the situation treated in the poem. It is no accident certainly that much of a people's wisdom comes down in the form of fables or parables. On the other hand, generalizations and abstractions have developed because they enable the mind to grasp significance beyond certain particulars and concrete instances. It is of course necessary to be able to think about human affairs in terms of broad abstractions.

Before we can pursue *these* generalizations any further, however, it is necessary to ask ourselves what we mean by the terms *abstract* and *concrete*. For example, to say, "The soldiers died in the line of duty," or "The country was defeated after enduring a war of attrition for many years," is to state abstractly or generally. The statement about the soldiers suggests little or nothing about them in an individualized way. We know little or nothing of the way they acted—courageously, fearfully, willingly, carelessly—and nothing about them as individual men; therefore we find it impossible to respond to their deaths in an emotional way. Their motives and actions require some form of dramatization to involve our emotions. A similar comment could be made about the other sentence.

Statements that appeal strongly to our emotions contribute to our convictions. Poetry is concerned with insights and generalizations, but it is concerned with them not merely in our minds but in our emotions. The following lines on the inevitability of death by John Webster (1580–1625) affect us in a way that an extended commentary of a more abstract nature never could:

> All the flowers of the spring
> Meet to perfume our burying;
> These have but their growing prime,
> And man does flourish but his time.
> Survey our progress from our birth—
> We are set, we grow, we turn to earth.
> Courts adieu, and all delights,
> All bewitching appetites.
> Sweetest breath and clearest eye
> Like perfumes go out and die;
> Vain the ambition of kings
> Who seek by trophies and dead things

> To leave a living name behind,
> And weave but nets to catch the wind.

This poem appeals to us intellectually, but its appeal is in concrete, sensuous language. Meanings, which can be abstracted, are implied by the images.

Similarly, in the following passage from *Hamlet* we can see how certain meanings are suggested more effectively by concrete terms:

> I prithee, when thou seest that act *a-foot*,
> Even with the very comment of thy soul,
> Observe my uncle: if his occulted guilt
> Do not itself *unkennel* in one speech. . . .

Hamlet is talking about his uncle Claudius, the murderer of Hamlet's father, and about the play within the play which will dramatize the murder. He is telling Horatio, his friend, to watch closely, intently. He does not say that Horatio should watch when the action *begins* but when it is "a-foot," an expression that evokes an image of the movement of the actors. Nor does he say that Claudius' guilt will *suggest itself*; he says it will "unkennel" itself, as though it would creep out of a kennel like a dog, a term which also indicates Hamlet's contempt for Claudius. By enabling us to visualize the scene and by symbolizing the meaning, these two terms involve us much more deeply in the meaning than would two abstract terms.

In poetry we know objects in their colors, sizes, contours, and textures. However, it would be an error to say that the sensory appeal in poetry is primarily visual. There are images in poetry appealing to different senses: gustatory, to our sense of taste; olfactory, to our sense of smell; tactile, to our sense of touch; and auditory, to our hearing. It is interesting to note the extent to which a poet like Keats could go in creating a sense of the physical world as it appeals to our various senses. The following stanzas are from "The Eve of St. Agnes":

> St. Agnes' Eve—Ah, bitter chill it was!
> The owl, for all his feathers, was a-cold;
> The hare limp'd trembling through the frozen grass,
> And silent was the flock in woolly fold:
> Numb were the Beadsman's fingers, while he told
> His rosary, and while his frosted breath,
> Like pious incense from a censor old,
> Seem'd taking flight for heaven, without a death,
> Past the sweet Virgin's picture, while his prayer he saith.

. . . . .

And still she slept an azure-lidded sleep,
In blanched linen, smooth, and lavender'd,
While he from forth the closet brought a heap
Of candied apple, quince, and plum, and gourd;
With jellies soother than the creamy curd,
And lucent syrops, tinct with cinnamon;
Manna and dates, in argosy transferr'd
From Fez; and spiced dainties, every one
From silken Samarcand to cedar'd Lebanon.

Images, however, are not merely verbal references to particular objects. As we saw in the passage from *Hamlet,* they contribute most to a poem when they suggest meanings beyond the mere identity of the specific object.

Perhaps the easiest way to reduce this subject to its common denominator is to say that poetry is concerned with *resemblances.* We see resemblances between one object or situation and another: the ticking of a clock is related to mortality, the hardness of steel to determination, the green lake to a young lady's eyes, a faded photograph to mutability, and so forth. These are commonplaces. The genuine poet is capable of employing them in a complex pattern, and capable of seeing resemblances between dissimilar things. Such terms as *connotation, simile, metaphor,* and *symbol* are easily seen to be aspects of poetry as the expression of resemblances.

II. Denotation and Connotation

As a matter of convenience, we may say a word has both denotative and connotative meanings. Actually it is probably an oversimplification to insist always that *this* meaning is denotative and *that* connotative. The dictionary definition of a word is rarely its full meaning. The full meaning includes both the dictionary definition and the special meanings and associations a word takes on in a given phrase or expression. Here, we will restrict our attention to limited aspects of the problem.

A tiger, for example, is a carnivorous animal belonging to the cat family. (See a dictionary for a definition.) This is the word's denotative meaning. But we have certain associations with the word: sinuous movement, slinkiness, sudden leap, jungle violence, and so forth. These are the connotations around the word. A gem, to take another example, is defined as "any jewel; semiprecious; cut and polished for ornament." A secondary meaning, which is a connotation, is "something to be prized for its great value or beauty."

The poet, concerned as he is with the emotive power in words, is keenly aware of connotative elements. Very often he employs them in such a way that the texture of his statement is enriched and complicated.

In the following passage from Milton's *Samson Agonistes* the Chorus is commenting on the fallen Samson:

> O dearly bought revenge, yet glorious!
> Living or dying thou hast fulfilled
> The work for which thou wast foretold
> To Israel, and now liest victorious
> Among thy slain self-killed
> Not willingly, but tangled in the fold
> Of dire necessity, whose law in death conjoined
> Thee with thy slaughtered foes in number more
> Than all thy life had slain before.
>   (ll. 1660–1668)

Perhaps the meaning which is most immediately evident is that Samson has been caught in an action foreordained by Providence. But "tangled in the fold" also suggests that he has been caught by the fallen pillars and roof. The building has literally folded. Both these meanings are relevant; together they form the total meaning. It is hardly necessary to point out that "tangled" is concrete, suggesting physical involvement. Most of the passage quoted is abstract, causing the particularity and concreteness of the phrase discussed to stand out.

In a poem from a much later period, A. E. Housman's "To an Athlete Dying Young," * we find an instance in which the connotative meaning is primary and the denotative meaning of lesser, perhaps negligible, importance. The lines with which we are especially concerned are italicized:

> The time you won your town the race
> We chaired you through the market-place;
> Man and boy stood cheering by,
> And home we brought you shoulder-high.
>
> To-day, the road all runners come,
> Shoulder high we bring you home,
> And set you at your threshold down,
> Townsman of a stiller town.
>
> Smart lad, to slip betimes away
> From fields where glory does not stay

....

* "To an Athlete Dying Young" is from *A Shropshire Lad*, by A. E. Housman. Used by permission of Henry Holt and Company, Inc.

And early though the laurel grows
It withers quicker than the rose.

It is a natural fact that the laurel matures and withers even more quickly than the rose, but, more important, the poet is also saying that the laurel symbolizes glory and that glory too withers and passes— more quickly, indeed, than the rose, symbolizing mortal beauty, which itself passes quickly enough. Therefore the young athlete is said to be lucky, dying before his glory has passed.

It is necessary, therefore, to be aware of the implications or the connotations of words. In the following poem by William Carlos Williams, if we are not aware of double meanings we miss the entire point:

The Yachts[1]

Contend in a sea which the land partly encloses
shielding them from the too heavy blows
of an ungoverned ocean which when it chooses

tortures the biggest hulls, the best man knows
to pit against its beating, and sinks them pitilessly.
Mothlike in mists, scintillant in the minute

brilliance of cloudless days, with broad bellying sails
they glide to the wind tossing green water
from their sharp prows while over them the crew crawls

ant-like, solicitously grooming them, releasing,   10
making fast as they turn, lean far over and having
caught the wind again, side by side, head for the mark.

In a well guarded arena of open water surrounded by
lesser and greater craft which, sycophant, lumbering
and flittering follow them, they appear youthful, rare

as the light of a happy eye, live with the grace
of all that in the mind is feckless, free and
naturally to be desired. Now the sea which holds them

is moody, lapping their glossy sides, as if feeling
for some slightest flaw but fails completely.   20
Today no race. Then the wind comes again. The yachts

....

1. "The Yachts" is from *The Collected Earlier Poems,* by William Carlos Williams. Copyright, 1938, by William Carlos Williams. Used by permission of New Directions.

move, jockeying for a start, the signal is set and they
are off. Now the waves strike at them but they are too
well made, they slip through, though *they take in canvas.*

Arms with hands grasping seek to clutch at the prows.
Bodies thrown recklessly in the way are cut aside.
It is a sea of faces about them in agony, in despair

until the horror of the *race* dawns staggering the mind,
the whole sea become an entanglement of watery bodies
lost to the world bearing what they cannot hold. Broken,   30

beaten, desolate, reaching from the dead to be taken up
they cry out, failing, failing! their cries rising
in waves still as the *skillful* yachts pass over.

By italicizing certain words we can see more quickly how the poem is
organized. The reader's first impression is that he is reading a description of a yacht race; the race is beginning, the yachts jockey for position, they move ahead more quickly by taking in canvas, etc. But then
the reader discovers that the sea and the waves are imagined to be
masses of people who attempt to hold back the progress of the yachts.
At this point the implication of the poem becomes clearer: the yachts are
those who live well at the expense of vast numbers of people. Sometimes
it is necessary for this small coterie to move a little more slowly, to take
less advantage of other people than they would like to take; they are
forced, as we say, to trim their sails a little, to "take in canvas." The
symbolism of the slight, trim yachts overcoming the waves in the bay
emphasizes the point that merely a few can overcome great masses of
their fellows. A reading of the opening lines suggests that there are
forces which can destroy the skillful yachtsman, too, if they choose.

The feelings of melancholy, sadness, and impersonality associated with the sea are transferred to our thoughts of the sadness and impersonality of masses of unknown people who are defeated in their attempts to achieve success and happiness. In the context of the poem the
word "race" is seen to mean not merely a yacht race but the human
race. And the word "skillful," in terms of the context, takes on connotations like "ruthless" and "practiced in exploitation."

Although these comments are not an exhaustive analysis of the
poem, they suggest that we should not be satisfied with a surface impression of the poem's meaning. It is necessary to recognize that the meanings of the individual words are sometimes multiple. It is also necessary
to recognize that the meaning of the poem inheres in part in its
imagery.

IV. Simile, Metaphor, Symbol

Simile is the rhetorical term used to designate the most elementary form of resemblances. "My love is like a red, red rose" and "The holy time is quiet as a nun, Breathless with adoration" are similes. Most similes are introduced by "like" or "as." But it is not a simile to say, "My hope is like your hope." The comparisons involved are not between objects or situations almost identical but between dissimilar objects or situations that have something in common—the beauty or value of the woman and the rose, or the hushed quiet of the evening and the nun.

A *metaphor*, on the other hand, leaving out "like" or "as," implies a comparison between objects or situations. Simple examples are, "All flesh is grass," and "All the world's a stage, And all the men and women merely players." (It is necessary to distinguish between poetic metaphors and "dead" metaphors, those like the "leg" of the chair, as well as "worn" metaphors, like "pillar of the church.")

Other useful terms are *synecdoche*, a form of metaphor which in mentioning an important part signifies the whole, as the *hands* for laborers; and *metonymy*, allowing an object closely associated with an object or situation to stand for the thing itself, as *scepter* for king.*

It is sometimes said that a *symbol* is a metaphor from which the first term is omitted. "My love is a red, red rose" is a metaphor. If through persistent identification of the rose with the beloved woman we came to associate the rose with her and her particular virtues, then the rose would be a symbol. There are, of course, cultural symbols of long standing like the horseshoe, the flag, and the cross; but poets through constant usage or the evocative power in a particular image sometimes turn images into symbols. Thus, one poet might use a tower to signify dignity, remoteness, loneliness, and the aristocratic virtues of earlier generations. Or he might so employ other objects. Observe that in these

....

* The above definitions are useful, but perhaps they do not suggest the importance of metaphor as a way of expressing new experiences or new ideas. When a precise, denotative term or phrase is lacking we must resort to analogy. Of a fire, we may say, "It burns steadily, only occasionally flaring up." Of a person, we may say, "Usually his anger over that situation burns steadily enough, but occasionally it flares up." The context in the latter sentence tells us that "burns" and "flares up" are being used as analogies. When such analogies are used over and over again, we are likely to forget that originally they were figures of speech, metaphors. Thus if we say, "As I remember, that old road ran for miles and miles over those hills," it is unlikely that we will think of "ran" as having once been used as a metaphor. Such expressions, which we accept as literal and denotative, are called "faded metaphors." Susanne Langer in an interesting chapter on language in *Philosophy in a New Key* (Harvard University Press, 1942), says this about metaphor: "Metaphor is the law [of language]. It is the force that makes it essentially relational, intellectual, forever showing up new, abstractable forms in reality, forever laying down a deposit of old, abstracted concepts in an increasing treasure of general words."

lines from Whittier's "Snowbound" we have neither a simile nor a meta-phor, but rather images—stars and cypress trees—used as symbols:

> Alas for him who never sees
> The stars shine through the cypress trees!
> Who, hopeless, lays his dead away,
> Nor looks to see the breaking day
> Across the mournful marbles play.

In the poem stars symbolize religious faith and survival after death, and cypress trees, common in cemeteries, symbolize man's mortality.

Allegory can be defined as a one-to-one correspondence between a series of abstract ideas and a series of images or pictures presented in the form of a story or narrative. A simple example of an allegorical poem is Longfellow's "Excelsior" (see p. 696), which the author describes in these terms: "[The poem displays] in a series of pictures the life of a man of genius, resisting all temptations, laying aside all fears, heedless of all warnings, and pressing right on to accomplish his purpose. His motto is Excelsior—'higher.'"

V. Poetry as a Language of Indirection

The simplest way of distinguishing between poetry and prose is to say that poetry employs meter and rhyme, devices or usages uncommon in prose. But this is an inadequate distinction, which will not serve for all cases, especially for modern poetry. A less obvious but useful way of distinguishing between the language of poetry and the language of prose is to say that poetry relies more insistently than prose on *indirection*. Per-haps only loose generalizations can be made about the kinds of indirec-tion common to *all* poetry, but examinations of single poems show us that such forms of indirection as metaphor, connotation, and verbal irony are frequent in poetry and usually crucial in creating what we think of as the poetic experience.

To begin, we may consider these four seemingly simple lines, an anonymous early sixteenth-century poem:

> O Western wind, when wilt thou blow
> That the small rain down can rain?
> Christ, that my love were in my arms,
> And I in my bed again!

The center of the poem, of course, is in the lover's desire to be re-united with his beloved. This is explicity stated in lines three and four. But the full meaning of the poem depends on the first two lines also.

Obviously the lover associates his grief with the wind and rain, but the poet leaves to implication, to indirection, just how the lover's situation and the wind and rain are related. Upon analysis, we note that they are related in several ways: The need for experiencing and manifesting love is an inherent need, like nature's need for the rain; in a word, love, like the wind and rain, is natural. Secondly, the lover is living in a kind of drought or arid state which can be slaked only by the soothing presence of the beloved. Thirdly, the rising of the wind and the coming of the rain can be neither controlled nor foretold exactly, and human affairs, like the lover's predicament, are subject to the same sort of chance or fortuitousness.

Undoubtedly too there are associations with specific words, like "Western" or "small rain," that the reader is only half aware of but which nonetheless contribute to the meaning the four lines have for him. These associations or connotations afford a few indirections which enrich the entire poem. For example, "Western" has connotations of mystery and hope, which relate to the lover's situation; "small rain" at once describes the kind of rain that the lover wants to fall and suggests the joy and peace of lovers' tears, and "small" alone might suggest the daintiness or femininity of the beloved. Such connotations tend to be elusive, but some such meanings do hover in the back of the reader's mind. Removing the words from the poem injures more than the rhythm of their respective lines. Other aspects of this poem might be discussed—such as its use of specific detail and its forthrightness—but here we are concerned with the matter of indirection.

Poets in the early seventeenth century frequently employed such forms as paradox, understatement, and overstatement. Andrew Marvell in "Bermudas" praises God's bounty and adds that we should praise Him:

> Oh, let our voice his praise exalt,
> Till it arrive at heaven's vault;
> Which thence, perhaps, rebounding, may
> Echo beyond the Mexic Bay.

The idea is stated in exaggerated terms. We know that the poet does not literally mean that the echo will carry hundreds and hundreds of miles, but we accept such an exaggeration as an appropriate statement.

But this sort of poetry, some will object, is not typical; there is also the language of direct statement. Poetic language can be direct as well as oblique. This objection is undoubtedly valid, but one should not assert it too flatly. First, the poets cited as evidence that there is a poetry of direct statement are merely *less* oblique, less dependent on metaphors or forms of irony than are some of their fellow poets. The poetry of John Dryden, for instance, is simply less dependent, or less startlingly so, on irony than Donne's or Marvell's. Second, as we will illustrate below, the language of direct statement, of a kind of prose commentary or reporting, is frequently used in writing about a situation that *in itself* is ironical or paradoxical.

John Dryden, as we said, is often held to be a poet of "direct statement." If we look at specific lines and poems of his, however, we can discover that he too employs forms of indirection. T. S. Eliot, in a well-known essay on Dryden, quotes the following lines:

> That short dark passage to a future state;
> That melancholy riddle of a breath,
> That something, or that nothing, after death.

Dryden's words, Mr. Eliot says, "are precise, they state immensely." Does this imply that the words are in no sense indirect? The situation being discussed, of course, is the uncertainty of life after death. To evoke a sense of uncertainty Dryden introduces the metaphor of a "short dark passage." He asks us, in other words, to consider the uncertainty indirectly in the form of the metaphor of moving through an unlit passageway. (The word "state" in line one, incidentally, is appropriately abstract because we cannot visualize what, if anything, is beyond the passage.) The second line, which invites us to consider breath or life as a riddle, is also an indirect way of evoking a sense of uncertainty.

In Dryden the reader also finds various forms of wit. In these lines on the Civic Guards of Rhodes we can visualize the soldiers drawn up in ranks and with the serious mien of men engaged in military training:

> Drawn up in rank and file they stood prepared
> Of seeming arms to make a short essay,
> Then hasten to be drunk, the business of the day.

The irony of the final phrase is a form of indirection. "Business" usually carries associations of serious work and effort. And "business of the day" as a military phrase suggests a similar seriousness, but in this context it is used ironically. Again, in these lines from the play *Aurungzebe* there is the paradox that virtue itself when shrill is equally offensive with orthodox sin or vice:

> Such virtue is the plague of human life:
> A virtuous woman, but a cursed wife.
> In vain of pompous chastity y'are proud:
> Virtue's adultery of the tongue, when loud.

Adultery, a serious moral offense, is used to characterize virtue that is offensive because self-satisfied and loud. Paradox, like other forms of verbal irony, is of course a form of indirect statement.

There is, however, a distinction to be made between the paradox as a figure of speech and a paradoxical situation. In paradox that is a figure of speech there is sometimes, although not always, a literal contradiction. In Richard Lovelace's "To Althea, from Prison," the lines

> Stone walls do not a prison make,
> Nor iron bars a cage

are, read literally, untrue. In T. S. Eliot's line, "Liberty is a different kind of pain from prison," there is only a seeming contradiction. Ordinarily we associate the term "liberty" with freedom, being at ease, and so forth; but there is also the fact that liberty implies obligations to make one's own decisions, to use freedom intelligently, to endure whatever pain is necessary in making the best use of liberty. In this sense, liberty *is* a different kind of pain.

There are also paradoxical *situations*, those in which two elements might at first seem mutually contradictory. In Matthew Prior's "Written in the Beginning of Mezeray's History of France" (1709), we find a paradoxical situation. Instead of writing paradoxes of his own, Prior points out the ironical situation which is at the center of the poem. (And in it too of course we find such rhetorical devices as rhyme, metrical shifts, inversion, and ellipsis, ways of evoking and dramatizing the theme.)

> Whate'er thy countrymen have done
> By law and wit, by sword and gun,
>   In thee is faithfully recited:
> And all the living world, that view
> Thy work, give thee the praises due,
>   At once instructed and delighted.
>
> Yet for the fame of all these deeds,
> What beggar in the Invalides,
>   With lameness broke, with blindness smitten,
> Wish'd ever decently to die,
> To have been either Mezeray,
>   Or any monarch he has written?
>
> It strange, dear author, yet it true is,
> That, down from Pharamond to Louis,
>   All covet life, yet call it pain:
> All feel the ill, yet shun the cure:
> Can sense this paradox endure?
>   Resolve me, Cambray, or Fontaine.

The man in graver tragic known
(Though his best part long since was done)
    Still on the stage desires to tarry:
And he who play'd the Harlequin,
After the jest still loads the scene
    Unwilling to retire, though weary.

The theme of the poem is centered in the irony of living in pain and difficulty, and yet clinging to life instead of relinquishing it willingly. Ordinarily, when we reflect about kings, wealthy nobles, and famous and great men, we are likely to think of them as fortunate. They are honored even in death. In contrast, the lives of beggars seem pitiful. But the fortunate and unfortunate shift their respective positions when we consider that the beggars in the Invalides are *alive,* the great ones sung are *dead.*

Having acknowledged that certain poets do not employ metaphors or verbal ironies as frequently as some of their fellows and that other poets comment directly about situations in themselves ironic or paradoxical, we may look at a final example of a poem, from the mid-nineteenth century, which illustrates the tendency of poetic language to be indirect. The poem is Matthew Arnold's "Requiescat":

Strew on her roses, roses,
    And never a spray of yew!
In quiet she reposes;
    Ah, would that I did too!

Her mirth the world required;
    She bathed it in smiles of glee.
But her heart was tired, tired,
    And now they let her be.

Her life was turning, turning,
    In mazes of heat and sound.
But for peace her soul was yearning,
    And now peace laps her round.

Her cabined, ample spirit,
    It fluttered and failed for breath.
Tonight it doth inherit
    The vasty hall of death.

The theme of the poem is that the dead woman has earned the peace that is death and therefore her survivors should not mourn but rejoice for her. From the first and final stanzas we may select examples of the indirections which help evoke the theme. Yew trees are grown in cemeteries and therefore are symbols of sorrow, but roses, of course, are symbols of beauty and life. Because the woman's survivors are to rejoice they are asked to strew roses but not "a spray of yew." Therefore the first two lines are to be read as a symbolic act or gesture. In the final stanza, and by implication in the earlier stanzas, we are told that the woman's spirit was large, or "ample." But her obligations, which she fulfilled dutifully, restrained her, and she wished to be free from them. The physical limitations of her body and her restrictions caused her to be "cabined," but she escaped into a "vasty hall." The metaphors suggest what death meant to her. There are, naturally, further examples of indirections in the poem, but these help to demonstrate that the language of poetry is frequently a language of indirection.

VI. Irony and Sentimentality

Irony, in one sense of the term, is a mode of perception that enables one to express an insight or an attitude without sacrificing its complexities. There are of course a number of phrases that indicate the various forms of irony. The phrase *irony of situation* or *irony of circumstance* bears witness to chance in human affairs—a dropped handkerchief or an unmailed letter may spell sudden defeat or unexpected success. The phrase *dramatic irony* usually suggests an action in which the audience has more information or a greater perspective than the participants in the action, who because they lack it persist or indulge in conduct detrimental to or destructive of their best interests. Many of Hardy's poems and stories may serve as examples of irony of situation, and *Oedipus* or *Othello* as examples of dramatic irony.

The phrase *verbal irony* may include *understatement, overstatement,* and *conscious naïveté*. Mercutio in *Romeo and Juliet* employs understatement when in speaking of his mortal wound he says: "No, 'tis not so deep as a well, nor so wide as a church door; but 'tis enough, 'twill serve."

We find an example of overstatement in these lines from Robert Frost's "To Earthward" *:

> Love at the lips was touch
> As sweet as I could bear;
> And once that seemed too much;
> I lived on air

---

* "To Earthward" is from *The Complete Works of Robert Frost.* Copyright, 1930, 1949, by Henry Holt and Company, Inc. Copyright, 1936, by Robert Frost. Used by permission of the publishers.

Conscious naïveté is suggested by the very title of Stephen Crane's "War is Kind."

There are also various forms of irony suggested by the phrases *romantic irony* and *cosmic irony*. Included among these are attacks upon God as the sponsor of so many ills, awareness of man's ineffectualness or his unimportance in this tremendous universe, and complaints of the mere tedium of existence. Sometimes these forms are merely negative protests, almost a reveling in sadness and despair, but sometimes they are positive expressions, protests against smugness, pompousness, sentimentality, or limited vision. Expressions of these kinds can of course be found in all periods of literature, but they can sometimes be seen as well to be expressions arising from conditions in a particular period. Thus one finds cosmic irony frequently in the Victorian world, which faced the theory of evolution and the conflicts between religion, idealism, and science. Representative poets of the nineteenth century in whose work one finds examples of romantic irony are Shelley, Swinburne, and Hardy.

Irony, then, may be a positive or a negative force. And it will differ in character and quality from poet to poet. It is most valuable as a mode of perception that assists the poet to see around and behind opposed attitudes, to avoid bathos and "microscopic tragedies." But irony is itself open to ridicule when it encourages the pose of superior knowledge or a belief in the futility of any attitude except wry awareness of human stupidity.

Sentimentality, an indulgence in or stress upon emotion that is out of proportion or inappropriate to its cause, is a not uncommon fault among certain poets. The sentimentalist is unable or unwilling to look at the complexities and subtleties of a subject. By way of example, we may look at an early eighteenth-century poem, "Against Idleness and Mischief," by Isaac Watts:

> How doth the little busy bee
>   Improve each shining hour,
> And gather honey all the day
>   From ev'ry op'ning flow'r!
>
> How skillfully she builds her cell!
>   How neat she spreads the wax;
> And labours hard to store it well
>   With the sweet food she makes.
>
> In works of labour or of skill
>   I would be busy too:
> For Satan finds some mischief still
>   For idle hands to do.

> In books, or works, or healthful play
>   Let my first years be past,
> That I may give for ev'ry day
>   Some good account at last.

Ultimately the theme suggested by this poem is a serious and complicated one, namely, in what manner man should conduct himself as a moral being. Watts asserts simply that one can be moral by being busy; he does not consider the alternative, the contemplative way. A more complex view of the subject would lead to a more philosophical tone. The tone and manner which Watts employs are almost coy. (For further discussion of the relation between sentimentality and tone see the section on Tone, p. 30ff.) The poet has greatly oversimplified the life of the bee, which is thoroughly unlike the pleasant domestic scene he presents. The reader may well feel that this sweetness-and-light view of the life of the bee has its parallel in the oversimplification of man's moral problems. The ironic mind finds it rather easy to ridicule such an outlook. In Watt's sentimental moralizing Lewis Carroll found a ready target. The parody of this particular poem is called "The Crocodile":

> How doth the little crocodile
>   Improve his shining tail,
> And pour the waters of the Nile
>   On every shining scale!
>
> How cheerfully he seems to grin,
>   How neatly spreads his claws,
> And welcomes little fishes in
>   With gently smiling jaws!

The sentimentalist is also likely to indulge himself in, as one critic has put it, warm baths of emotion. Often the emotions are sadness and self-pity. Ernest Dowson's "Villanelle of the Poet's Road" works variations on this theme:

> Wine and woman and song,
>   Three things garnish our way:
> Yet is day over long.

And William Ernest Henley has a little poem in which he describes the pleasures he sees about him but concludes:

> When children romp in the surges,
>   And sweethearts wander free,
> And the Firth as with laughter dimples—
>   I would it were deep over me.

Sentimentality, of course, should not be confused with sentiment, without which poetry or any art would be of no moment at all. The point is a simple one: the manner and tone of the poem should be mature and appropriate to their occasion. Ultimately, of course, maturity and appropriateness are matters of taste.

VII. Versification

1. *Metrics and Sound Effects*

English versification has been traditionally described in terms of strong and weak syllables, sometimes called stressed and unstressed, or accented and unaccented. For example, in the word *belief* the first syllable is weak and the second is strong. A technical terminology has been adapted from Greek and Latin prosody for reference to the relationship between strong and weak syllables in the line of English verse. This terminology is theoretically quite simple. The line of verse is considered as containing a number of rhythmical units, which are called *feet*. The feet in a line are distinguished as a recurring pattern of two or three syllables, and the pattern, or foot, is designated according to the number of syllables contained and the relationship in each foot between strong and weak syllables. Thus, in the line

A book/ of vers/es un/derneath/ the bough

the recurring pattern is that of a weak followed by a strong syllable. A foot of this pattern is called an *iamb,* or an *iambic* foot. Other feet common in English verse are

Trochee (trochaic), a strong syllable followed by a weak syllable:

Fairer/ than the/ Mermaid/ Tavern.

Anapest (anapestic), two weak syllables followed by a strong syllable:

On this night/ of all nights/ in the year.

Dactyl (dactylic), a strong syllable followed by two weak syllables:

How shall I/ know whether/ they will come/ back to me.

Spondee (spondaic), two strong syllables. Lines made up entirely of spondaic feet are rare in English poetry. An example of spondee is the

second foot of the line: And no/ birds sing.

When we speak of the meter of a line of verse we mean the number of feet contained in it, and we name the meter according to the number of feet:

One foot: Alas. Iambic *monometer*.

Two feet: Indestruct/able men. Anapestic *dimeter*.

Three feet: The ice/ was all/ between. Iambic *trimeter*.

Four feet: Tell me/ not in/ mournful/ numbers. Trochaic *tetrameter*.

Five feet: What oft/ was thought/ but ne'er/ so well/ expressed. Iambic *pentameter*.

Six feet: Dead cats/ and tur/nip-tops/ come tumb/ling down/ the flood. Iambic *hexameter*. When hexameter is in iambic rhythm, as in this line, it is also called an *alexandrine*.

Seven feet: I saw/ within/ my troub/led head/ a heap/ of thoughts/ appear. Iambic *heptameter*.

Lines of more than six feet are rare in English poetry. The longer lines, including hexameter, when used at all, have usually been set among shorter lines rather than in succession. An obvious reason for the infrequency of the longer line is the difficulty of avoiding a pause within the line and a consequent division into what are, in effect, two short lines. For example, in the heptameter quoted above there is a pause after the word *head* and a rhythmical effect much like that of a tetrameter followed by a trimeter.

Any example of what is generally regarded as traditional English verse may be analyzed for its rhythm, or *scanned*, in terms of feet and meter. Thus the scansion of a stanza from Wordsworth's "Lucy poems" follows:

Strange fits/ of pa/ssion have/ I known

And I/ will dare/ to tell,

But in/ the Lov/er's ear/ alone,

What once/ to me/ befell.

Having scanned the stanza, we can define its rhythm. The first and third lines are iambic tetrameter, and the second and fourth lines are iambic trimeter. The scansion of the stanza and the resulting definition are accurate insofar as they indicate the *basic* rhythm. In this respect, most questions of rhythm are quite simple, since all traditional versification has a basic rhythm that is easily determined.

It is seldom, however, that the lines of any poem adhere consistently to the basic rhythm. There are two chief reasons why this is so. Because of the nature of the language, even a short passage of perfectly regular rhythm is practically impossible. What we call weak and strong syllables are not all equally weak and equally strong, but vary according to sound, meaning, emphasis, context, and other features. Consequently, only an approximate regularity of rhythm is possible. Such regularity is to be found in the line, "But in the Lover's ear alone," for it contains no actual violation of the basic rhythm. Although the line is composed entirely of iambic feet, some variation of rhythm is present. The last syllable of the word "alone" is stronger than "ear," and "ear" is stronger than "in." The first word of the stanza, "strange," although scanned as weak, is relatively strong.

The second reason for the infrequency of perfectly regular rhythm is that, even if it were possible, perfect rhythm is usually undesirable. It is true that close approximations to such regularity are catchy and have an undeniable appeal. This appeal is to be seen in poems for children, which have a steady beat that is easily felt and easily memorized. Consider, for example, the steady beat of the familiar nursery rhyme, "Mary Had a Little Lamb," and the rhythmical use of nonsense syllables in many children's poems. The same appeal counts for much among those inexperienced readers who regard rhyme as an absolutely indispensable feature of poetry, who want both rhyme and the stress of syllables to beat with an unvarying measure. This appeal, however, is subject to the law of diminishing returns. The even beat of a too regular rhythm soon becomes monotonous. The regularity which at first gains our attention eventually distracts us from the meaning of the words and "puts us to sleep." Furthermore, there are few subjects and few poetic purposes for which a steadily beating rhythm is appropriate.

As already mentioned, some variation must enter into even the most strictly regulated rhythm, the variation that derives from the nature of the spoken language. Other kinds of variation are those which are actual departures from the basic rhythm. Attempts have been made to systematize the analysis of such departures and to provide a fixed terminology for this purpose. But such terminology is useful only within limits and varies in its adequacy from verse to verse, poem to poem, and poet to poet. In using these terms it is therefore well to remember that they are merely descriptive conveniences which are suitable for some, but not all, occasions. An example of such terminology is the word *substitution,* which means simply the use of a foot different from the basic rhythm. In the line

How with/ this rage/ shall beauty hold/ a plea

the basic rhythm is iambic, and a trochee is substituted for an iamb.

Irregularities, however, are not always so easily designated. The following line is from a poem of which the basic rhythm is iambic:

$$\cup \; - \; \cup \; - \quad - \; \cup \; \cup \; - \; \cup \; -$$
When most/ I wink,/ then do/ mine eyes/ best see.

We might scan as indicated. We would then say that the line is an iambic pentameter with a trochee substituted in the third foot. But this would not be a complete account of the rhythmical quality of the line, for it might be said that both syllables in the last foot, "best see," should be read as strong. In that case, a spondee would be substituted. And it might also be said that the first and fourth feet are also spondees. If that were so, then we would scan the line in this way:

$$- \; - \; \cup \; - \quad - \; \cup \; - \; - \; - \; -$$
When most/ I wink,/ then do/ mine eyes/ best see.

Scanned thus, the line can no longer be said to have a basic iambic rhythm, since only the second foot is iambic. A way out of this difficulty is to say that there is in the first, fourth, and fifth feet *hovering accent*— that is, a division of accent between both syllables of each foot, but with the second syllable tending (in iambic) to be slightly stronger. (In trochaic, the *first* syllable.) In fact, it might be said that there is hovering accent in every foot of the line, for it may be noticed that the so-called weak syllables of this line are not so unmistakably weak as those in the line, "How with this rage shall beauty hold a plea." Our complete metrical account of the line would then be as follows: iambic pentameter, with trochee substituted in the third foot and hovering accent in every foot. This scansion would then be used:

$$\overset{\cup}{-} \; - \; \overset{\cup}{-} \; - \quad - \; \overset{\cup}{-} \; \overset{\cup}{-} \; - \; \overset{\cup}{-} \; -$$
When most/ I wink,/ then do/ mine eyes/ best see.

Our discussion at this point suggests the possibility that some lines of verse may defy scansion. The fourth line of the following passage may be considered as approaching this condition:

That time of year thou mayst in me behold
When yellow leaves, or none, or few, do hang
Upon those boughs which shake against the cold,

$$- \; - \; \cup \; - \quad \cup \; - \; \cup \; - \; - \; -$$
Bare ru/in'd choirs,/ where late/ the sweet/ birds sang.

Since the line is from a poem of which the basic rhythm is iambic pentameter, it has been scanned as indicated. According to this scansion, spondees are substituted in the first and fifth feet. An interesting feature of the line is that, while it may be considered as basically iambic pentameter, it contains seven strong syllables. It is, however, the division into feet which is most disturbing, since the concept of the foot as a rhythmical unit implies a pause between feet. In this line, however, the conventional scansion is not an accurate indication of how the line is naturally read. The forced and unnatural pause produced by this scansion is especially obvious in the last four words of the line. The pauses which occur in a natural reading may be indicated as follows:

Bare ruin'd choirs,/ where late/ the sweet birds/ sang.

We might further continue our rhythmical analysis of the line by observing that after "sweet birds" there is a slight drop, or weakening, of the accent on the word "sang." And, finally, we may consider the prolonged effect of the line produced by the numerous strong syllables as appropriate to the image and the meaning expressed. In this respect the weakening accent of the last word is a fitting rhythmical accompaniment to the thought that the birds no longer sing.

Our study of the line thus far has emphasized the limitations of the conventional terminology and scansion. Nonetheless, it is likely that our final reading of the line owes something to the basic rhythm of the passage, and therefore to the conventional concepts. For example, if the line occurred in another context, among verses with a pronounced lilting rhythm, we might tend to read it, and scan it, as follows:

Bare ruin'd/ choirs [kwy-ers] where/ late the sweet/ birds sang.

This line will illustrate still another problem in rhythmical analysis. In each reading of the line the word "where" has been treated as a weak syllable. But some readers might contend that it can be read as strong. This would be a valid contention, for it is an important word in the statement and may therefore be read with emphasis. It is possible, then, that in poetry there may at times be alternate readings. In the following line we have another example of two rhythmical possibilities:

Ere you/ were born/ was beau/ty's sum/mer dead

or:

Ere you, etc.

The analysis of rhythm in poetry, like other kinds of literary criticism, is only a means by which a reader may clarify for himself or for another reader certain effects of poetry and the details which contribute to the effects. Despite the term *prosody,* the terminology of feet and meters, and the practice of scansion, there is no science for the analysis of verse rhythm, and probably the soundest view is that there can never be one. The system of scansion can be extremely useful for rhythmical analysis, but it has limitations that must be kept in mind, and it must be supplemented by a "good ear," common sense, and an open mind.

2. Stanzas and Verse Forms

A *stanza* is a series of lines with a specific rhyme scheme and metrical pattern. The term is usually confined to a recurring pattern of rhyme and meter in the same poem. When poems are divided into several series of lines that have no recurring pattern, each group of lines is called an *irregular stanza* or a *verse paragraph* [see Arnold's "Dover Beach" (p. 537)]. *Verse form* is a general term which includes stanzas and all other kinds of linear arrangements in poems. It is useful for referring to arrangements that are not clearly stanzaic. *Verse* may mean poetry in general or the single line of poetry. It is sometimes used as a synonym for stanza, but this practice may result in misunderstanding and is best avoided.

STANZAS: Some stanzaic forms are specifically named because they have become traditional through usage by a number of poets. The more familiar stanzas of this kind are:

Ballad stanza: four lines in iambic rhythm, the first and third lines tetrameter and the second and fourth lines trimeter, rhyme scheme *xaxa*. (Unrhymed line endings are indicated by an *x*.) This stanza occurs frequently in narrative poems of folk origin, or *ballads*. Poets have adopted the tradition and the stanza in the composition of *literary ballads*. [See "Lucy Gray" (p. 361) and "La Belle Dame Sans Merci" (p. 446).] Literary ballads frequently rhyme *abab*.

Ottava rima: eight lines, iambic pentameter, rhyme scheme *abababcc*.

Rime Royal: seven lines, iambic pentameter, rhyme scheme *ababbcc*.

Spenserian stanza: nine lines, the first eight iambic pentameter and the ninth an alexandrine, rhyme scheme *ababbcbcc*. First used by Edmund Spenser in *The Faerie Queene,* and then by poets in the eighteenth and nineteenth centuries.

Sonnet: a poem of fourteen lines, iambic pentameter. There are two rhyme schemes, depending on the kind of sonnet. (1) The *Petrarchan* or *Italian sonnet* is divided into two parts: the *octave* (first eight lines) always rhymes *abbaabba*; the *sestet* (last six lines) frequently rhymes *cdecde* or *cdcdcd*, but is sometimes in other patterns, such as *cdeedc, cdedce, cdcede*. According to traditional practice, the thought is logically adapted to the form. An argument or general idea is developed in the octave, and a conclusion or specific application of the idea is given in the sestet. Poets have sometimes deliberately loosened the form by ending the thought of the octave within the eighth line or by continuing it through part of the first line of the sestet. (2) The *English* or *Shakespearean sonnet* is divided into four parts which are indicated by the rhyme scheme *abab cdcd efef gg*. Usually each four-line stanza, or *quatrain*, completes both a grammatical and a logical stage in the development of the poem, and the last two lines, or *couplet*, summarize or conclude the thought of the preceding stanzas. Fourteen-line poems in iambic pentameter which combine features of both the Italian and Shakespearean sonnets or which depart from these rhyme patterns altogether are called *irregular sonnets*.

VERSE FORMS. The following are terms used for describing versification that is not clearly stanzaic:

Blank verse: unrhymed iambic pentameter.

Free verse: poetry having no rhyme and showing no regular metrical pattern; is not to be confused with blank verse. The general problem of the rhythmical nature of free verse is still unsettled. Many poems in free verse have rhythmical features in common with traditional versification and may be analyzed accordingly; i.e., individual lines may be described in terms of feet and meter.

Couplet: a pair of rhyming lines. *Heroic couplet:* iambic pentameter. Sometimes the term *heroic couplet* is used to mean specifically a *closed couplet*; that is, there is at least a slight grammatical pause at the end of each couplet, as in the poetry of Pope. *Octosyllabic couplet:* iambic tetrameter.

Tercet: lines arranged in groups of three.

Terza rima: tercets rhyming *aba*, with the initial line of each succeeding tercet rhyming with the middle line of the preceding tercet, *aba bcb cdc*, etc. First used by the Italian poet Dante in his *Divina Commedia*.

Quatrain: any stanza of four lines, such as the ballad stanza and the stanza in the Shakespearean sonnet.

OTHER TERMS. The following terms indicate a number of sound effects in poetry and the devices that produce them. The terms are useful for the analysis and discussion of specific sound effects achieved in individual poems and passages.

Masculine rhyme: rhyming of single strong syllables, such as "event" and "consent," "goal" and "bowl," "guess" and "happiness."

Feminine rhyme: rhyming of strong syllables followed by identical weak syllables, such as "wonder" and "asunder," "sleeping" and "weeping."

Internal rhyme: rhyme occurring elsewhere than at line endings. Such rhyme seldom occurs according to a set pattern. It need not occur within a single line, but may, as in "The pain be *mine*, but *thine* shall be the praise."

Pause: any natural delay or rest that occurs in the reading of a passage of poetry, such as those which occur at points of punctuation and according to emphasis and completion of thought. When there is a pause at the end of a line, the line is called *end-stopped.* When there is no pause, the line is called *run-on.* Pauses within the line are one of the main devices for variety in rhythmical effects, since different pauses may be of varying lengths. An especially long pause or an internal pause that recurs in successive lines is called a *caesura.*

Alliteration: the repetition or frequent recurrence of the same consonants, as in "the *r*ivers that *r*estlessly *r*oll."

Assonance: identical vowel sounds within differing consonants, such as m*ee*t and gr*ee*n, br*ea*k and h*a*te.

Consonance: identical consonant sounds accompanying different vowel sounds, such as g*reen* and g*roan*, la*rk* and lu*rk*.

Slant rhyme: identical final consonant sounds accompanying different initial consonant sounds and different but closely related vowel sounds, such as *blood* and *mood, weak* and *pick, map* and *drape.* Among modern poets there has been a usage comparable to slant rhyme but without regard to a close relationship of vowel sounds. It might be called semiconsonance or half-rhyme. Some examples (from W. B. Yeats) are "desire" and "endure," "cloth" and "breath," "soul" and "oil." The use of such irregular rhymes extends the range of rhyming, which is fairly limited in the English language. It is also a means of adhering to a formal pattern while avoiding the insistent beat of exact rhymes when such avoidance is purposeful.

Onomatopoeia: a sound effect which is appropriate to, or imitates, the meaning of the words. Some words are themselves onomatopoeic, such as "murmur," "gulp," "swish." An example of onomatopoeia achieved by a combination of words is Poe's line

And the silken, sad, uncertain, rustling of each purple curtain,

where the sound described is suggested by the complex alliteration of *s, n, r,* and *l,* by the assonance of "uncertain rustling," "purple curtain," and by the internal rhyme. An example of a common error is the view that these sounds independently suggest the meaning of this line, of the rustling curtain. The following line has approximately the same sounds but, if we dissociate it from Poe's line, does not suggest a rustling curtain:

And the sullen man, uncertain, hustling with each dirty burden.

One might say that these sounds suggest a sullen hustling. Actually, no sound, and especially no combination of sounds, is independently suggestive of a specific meaning. In onomatopoeia we have sound that is appropriate to a given meaning, but not productive of meaning apart from the sense of the words.

Verse texture: the total pattern of sound and rhythm in a passage or in a whole poem, including the effects on sound and rhythm produced by the meaning of the words.

Many of the points we have been considering are applied in the following analysis of Shakespeare's Sonnet 65*:

Since brass,/ nor stone,/ nor earth,/ nor bound/less sea,

But sad/ mortal/ity/ o'er-sways/ their power,

How with/ this rage/ shall beau/ty hold/ a plea

Whose ac/tion is/ no strong/er than/ a flower?

O, how/ shall sum/mer's hon/ey breath/ hold out

Against/ the wreck/ful siege/ of bat/tering days,

When rocks/ impreg/nable/ are not/ so stout,

Nor gates/ of steel/ so strong,/ but Time/ decays?

O, fear/ful med/ita/tion! where,/ alack,

Shall Time's/ best jew/el from/ Time's chest/ lie hid?

Or what/ strong hand/ can hold/ his swift/ foot back?

Or who/ his spoil/ of beau/ty can/ forbid?

O, none,/ unless/ this mir/acle/ have might,

That in/ black ink/ my love/ may still/ shine bright.

In this sonnet Shakespeare used both a theme and a form which were common in his own day. The theme is that with the passage of time all things, including men, are lost in oblivion, but that a person may escape this fate by being immortalized in verse, which survives the passage of time. We can see how this theme is developed by stages through each succeeding quatrain and then completed in the final cou-

---

* There are a few possible alternatives to the scansion given, but they would not affect the following discussion of the poem.

plet. Despite the conventionality of both form and theme, the poem has an individual quality resulting from the adaptation of the form and the theme to each other and from the specific application of the theme.

One aspect of the poem's individuality lies in its effects of sound and rhythm, and we shall consider these in detail. As the scansion indicates, frequent departures from iambic rhythm (lines 3, 4, 5, 9, 10, 11, 13, and 14) contribute to the verse texture. Another textural feature, not indicated by the scansion, is the varying pace from line to line resulting from the varying degrees of accent on strong syllables. For example, emphatic accents produce a slow pace in the first line, as compared to the second line, where the pace is quickened by the weaker accents of the word "mortality."

While all the details of sound and rhythm are involved in the verse texture of the poem, some of them are especially significant in that they are peculiarly appropriate to the meanings stated. The varying pace from line to line is one such detail. The slow movement of the opening line is expressive of the enduring character of the things mentioned, and the quicker movement of the next line is part of the statement of their mortality. Lines 3, 4, and 5 contain departures from iambic rhythm, and the regularity of line 6 is thus more striking. The weak syllables in line 6 are all relatively unimportant and lack even the degree of emphasis that may possibly fall on weak syllables, such as "When," "are," and "so" in line 7. As a result the strong syllables follow each other with an insistent beat which is onomatopoeic in its relationship to the idea of "battering." The poem reaches a kind of climax in lines 10 and 11, where the general theme of the poem is applied to the person whom the speaker of the poem has in mind, to "Time's best jewel." The climactic character of these lines is emphasized by their greater length, which is produced by the greater number of strong syllables, seven in each line. And the strong accents are significantly grouped together on the important phrases in the lines. In line 11 the heavily stressed phrases —"what strong hand" and "swift foot back"—are dramatically expressive of the image and idea of resistance.

There are in the poem a number of continuing alliterations. This repetition of emphatic initial consonants produces a *binding effect*— that is, it provides a rhythmical and organizing element comparable to meter and rhyme. Some of the alliterations are significant beyond this binding function. Notice that the things mentioned in the first line are in a meaningful order, each thing being more enduring and impressive than the previous one. There is a rising emphasis throughout the line, and this emphasis reaches a peak with the "boundless sea," the last and most impressive item in the series. The word "boundless" is the only adjective in the line and comes with climactic force. Some of this force derives from the fact that "boundless" alliterates with "brass," the first strong syllable of the line. This alliteration serves as a kind of frame or envelope for the line and occurs at the culmination of the rising emphasis. Moreover, the alliteration of *b*, which falls on the important word "boundless," reverberates throughout the poem and contributes to the effectiveness of the following important words: "beauty" (3), "breath" (5), "battering" (6), "best" (10), "back" (11), "beauty" (12), "forbid" (12), "black" (14), "bright" (14). (The numbers indicate the lines in which the words occur.) Comparable effects are produced by the alliteration of the sound *h* in the words "How" (3), "hold" (3), "Whose" (4), "how" (5), "honey" (5), "hold" (5), "hid" (10), "hand" (11), "hold" (11), "who" (12), "have" (13). The questioning force of *how* in lines 3 and 5 brings the alliteration into prominence throughout the poem. The word "hold" in lines 3, 5, and 11 gains in emphasis by alliterating with previous words in each line, and the recurrence of the aspirant sound participates in the meaning and rhetorical quality of the statements. Still another sound alliterating through the poem is *s*, and especially effective is the alliteration of the double consonant *st* in the words "stone" (1), "stronger" (4), "stout" (7), "steel" (8), "strong" (8), "strong" (11), "still" (14). This alliteration is most effective in lines 7 and 8, where it occurs frequently within just a few words and where, in line 8, it combines with other dental sounds—in "gates," "Time," "decays"—to enforce the meaning of the statement.

Assonance, like alliteration, may also have a binding effect and at times contribute to dramatic and rhetorical quality. The first vowel sound of the emphatic word "boundless" is echoed by the rhyming words "power" and "flower," "out" and "stout," and twice by the word "how." This assonance is not only a textural detail in the versification but also contributes to the quality and effectiveness of the statement. It points up the fact that the important words in which it occurs are related in the developing meaning. For example, the word "how" gains in emphasis and in meaning because the assonance has already been set up and because in each occurrence it immediately follows the words "power" and "flower." This example illustrates also the enrichment of texture and meaning which results from the function in both assonance pattern and rhyme pattern of several important words.

VIII. Tone

Tone is a word commonly used in the critical discussion of literature and especially of poetry. It is, of course, a term originally referring to the quality of a sound—the sound of a bell, of a musical instrument, of the human voice. We are all familiar with it as applied not only to the sound-quality of a voice but also to the psychological quality of the words spoken. We all know what is meant by the expression, "Don't speak to me in that tone of voice." Consider a specific example, the question, "Who are you?" Depending on the tone with which the words are spoken, the question may be humorous, astonished, contemptuous or merely inquisitive. Tone may result not only from the inflection of the voice but also from the nature of the specific words used. The differences between "Shut up" and "Please don't talk right now" are too obvious for comment. It is only in the most general sense that the two statements have the same meaning. The specific meanings are different because in each sentence the meaning includes the tone of the expression. In each there is a quality of feeling and a particular attitude which are parts of the meaning.

It is with this understanding of the word *tone* that we use it in discussions of poetry. The principle that the full meaning of the poem cannot be given in a paraphrase rests on this concept. One value of paraphrase as a critical exercise or as an interpretation lies in the necessity of recognizing and then indicating the tone of the poem. The paraphrase of course cannot reproduce the tone. A paraphrase is accurate if, while restating the poem, it calls attention to the feelings and attitudes expressed by the poem, or if, at least, it does not falsify these feelings and attitudes.

Let us take as an example a passage and a paraphrase of it that troubled Matthew Arnold:*

I once mentioned in a school-report, how a young man in one of our English training colleges having to paraphrase the passage in *Macbeth* beginning,

Can'st thou not minister to a mind diseased?

turned this line into, "Can you not wait upon the lunatic?" And I remarked what a serious state of things it would be, if every pupil of our national schools knew, let us say, that the moon is two thousand and one hundred and sixty miles in diameter, and thought at the same time that a good paraphrase for

Can'st thou not minister to a mind diseased?

was, "Can you not wait upon the lunatic?"

Here we are concerned merely with asking why the student's paraphrase was a falsification or distortion of Shakespeare's line. Macbeth uttered the line when asking a physician about Lady Macbeth's illness (Act V, scene iii, line 41). Naturally he is eager to learn what can be done to help her. He is solicitous about her condition, and his lan-

* "Literature and Science," in *Discourses in America*, 1882.

guage reflects his feeling. He does not use a word like "lunatic," which is a pejorative and suggests the raving madness of a person who has lost his human intelligence and sympathies. Because Macbeth thinks of his wife as one he knows and loves, he sees her madness as illness, thus maintaining his image of her as a beloved person. To "wait on" a person suggests an impersonal act but to "minister" to someone who is ill suggests assistance performed with reverence and love. The two terms "wait upon" and "lunatic" used in the paraphrase distort the meaning because they do not convey the feelings of tenderness and love expressed in Macbeth's own words. The paraphrase belies the tone aroused by Macbeth's language.

Our discussion of Macbeth's line indicates that diction is closely related to the question of tone. And so are rhyme, rhythm, imagery, syntax, logic—indeed, every conceivable aspect of poetry. Considerations of tone are important both for an understanding of poetry and for making judgments on poetry. This may be illustrated by examining a few poems and passages. First, let us look at some examples that have been regarded as defective in respect to tone. One of these is a phrase in Milton's description of the meal which Adam and the angel Raphael take in the Garden of Eden:

> Raised of grassy turf
> Their table was, and mossy seats had round,
> And on her ample square from side to side
> All autumn piled, though spring and autumn here
> Danced hand in hand. A while discourse they hold;
> No fear lest dinner cool; . . . .
>
> (*Paradise Lost,* Book V, ll. 391–396)

This passage, although brief and out of its context, illustrates the prevailing style of *Paradise Lost.* The grammatical inversions, such as "A while discourse they hold," produce a lofty tone that is appropriate to the extraordinary subject of the poem. But the observation, "No fear 'est dinner cool," intrudes distractingly on the grand and idyllic scene hat is being portrayed and on the serious attitude which Milton had naintained up to that point. That Adam and Eve had no worries in Paradise about food cooling, because none was cooked, is a trivial consideration. It is an amusing one, but there is no indication that Milton intended it as such. If we smile, we do so at the poet's expense, because there is a lapse in tone rather than a witty achievement.

When we say that a poem is defective in tone we mean that the poet has adopted an attitude inappropriate to his subject, or else has failed to maintain the proper attitude. An example of defective tone resulting from diction, rhythm, and rhyme is found in "My Garden," by the nineteenth-century poet T. E. Brown:

> A garden is a lovesome thing, God wot!
> Rose plot,
> Fringed pool,
> Ferned grot—
> The veriest school
> Of peace; and yet the fool
> Contends that God is not—
> Not God! in gardens! when the eve is cool?
> Nay, but I have a sign;
> 'Tis very sure God walks in mine.*

In this poem the conspicuous "lovesome" and "God wot," the harsh rhyme of "wot," "plot," "grot," "not," the abrupt rhythm of the short phrases, the exclamatory expressions—all contribute to a tone that is inappropriate to the experience of peacefulness and divine presence which a garden may produce. The subject of the poem has possibilities of sentimentality, and it is clear from the first and the last lines of the poem that the poet has yielded to these, and then attempted in an argumentative and bumptious manner to defend his position. The poem, instead of being a controlled expression of plausible sentiment, is a mixture of sentimentality and strained exuberance.

Ben Jonson's famous song "To Celia" is a good example of tone successfully controlled. Consider this stanza:

> I sent thee late a rosy wreath,
> Not so much honoring thee,
> As giving it a hope that there
> It could not withered be.
> But thou thereon didst only breathe,
> And sent'st it back to me,
> Since when it grows and smells, I swear,
> Not of itself, but thee.

This is neither an earnest declaration of the young lady's extraordinary virtues nor the kind of assinine flattery of which suitors are sometimes capable. It is a graceful, witty, and charming compliment. That it is intended as such is obvious from the melodic quality of the language, from the skillful development of thought that leads to the surprising and witty conclusion. The phrase "I swear," emphasized by its position at the end of the line, heightens both the jesting and sincerity which are blended in the tone of the poem. The thought with which the poem ends is absurd, but because it is a gracious and charming absurdity it is also a compliment to the young lady's taste and intelligence.

* "My Garden" is from *The Collected Poems*, by Thomas Edward Brown. Reprinted by permission of The Macmillan Company.

If she failed to recognize the tone of the poem and the attitude which is a mixture of playfulness and seriousness, she might have concluded that she was being mocked.

It is hardly conceivable that anyone might misinterpret Jonson's poem. There are poems, however, in which the question of tone is more problematic and requires careful consideration. Here, for example, is a poem that might easily be misread, A. E. Housman's "Epitaph on an Army of Mercenaries"*:

> These, in the day when heaven was falling,
>   The hour when earth's foundations fled,
> Followed their mercenary calling
>   And took their wages and are dead.
>
> Their shoulders held the sky suspended;
>   They stood, and earth's foundations stay;
> What God abandoned, these defended,
>   And saved the sum of things for pay.

This poem might at first appear to be a condemnation of the mercenaries, who fought for money rather than for an ideal, who opposed the will of God, and who were therefore punished with death. But this reading, or paraphrase, does not recognize the tone of the poem. The tone is not one of righteous condemnation, but of ironic reflection. The poem seems rather to say something like this: a good cause, which seemed hopelessly lost, was saved by mercenaries, who died while carrying out their professional commitment. The poet's attitude, or implied reflection, is that loyalty and courage may be exercised even in a merely practical calling and that great causes are sometimes served by merely practical motivations. To read the poem correctly one must see that the poet has an ambiguous, or double, attitude toward the mercenaries, and that the phrase "What God abandoned" is an idiomatic expression meaning "what appears hopeless" and not "what is rightfully condemned." For readers familiar with the body of Housman's poetry the phrase might also have overtones of Housman's cynical attitude toward the traditional concept of God.

We have described tone as an indication of the poet's attitude and as the quality of feeling which is a part of the meaning of a poetic statement. Tone is an important consideration in determining the success of a poem and in the accurate reading of a poem. It is, of course, only in the study of poetry that we consciously try to describe the tone of a poem. Often it is difficult to describe clearly and briefly, but even then we must grasp, or respond to, the tone in order to achieve a complete reading of the poem.

....
* From *A Shropshire Lad* by A. E. Housman. By permission of Henry Ho't and Company, and of The Society of Authors, literary representative of the Trustees of the estate of the late A. E. Housman, and Messrs. Jonathan Cape Ltd., publishers of A. E. Housman's *Collected Poems*.

IX. Shifts in Taste and Sensibility

The usual divisions under which English poetry is classified historically are these:

Anglo-Saxon (Old English)	428–1066
Early Middle English (Medieval)	1066–1350
Late Middle English	1350–1500
Early Tudor (Renaissance)	1500–1557
Elizabethan (Renaissance)	1557–1603
Jacobean and Caroline (Renaissance)	1603–1642
Puritan (Commonwealth 1649–1660)	1642–1660
Restoration	1660–1700
Neoclassical (Age of Pope; Age of Queen Anne)	1700–1750
Neoclassical and Beginnings of Romantic (Age of Johnson)	1750–1798
Romantic	1798–1832
Victorian	1832–1870
Late Victorian and *Fin de Siècle*	1870–1900
Modern	1900–

Because of the special language problems involved in reading Anglo-
Saxon and Middle English poetry, none of the poets in this anthology
are earlier than the Renaissance. (Skelton is usually thought of as a
bridge between medieval and modern periods.) Looked at from a distance, each of these periods seems homogeneous, that is, having characteristics common to almost every writer. But, if a period is looked at
more closely, conflicting impulses and characteristics peculiar to the
individual writer appear. In this anthology the work of the individual
poet is stressed, but where it is possible his work is usually related to its
period.

The following paragraphs give some of the characteristics commonly attributed to these periods. If they are not accepted in a
straitened, literal-minded way they may be useful generalizations.

In the Renaissance in England (which was later than the Renaissance in Italy) intellectual life turned outward to a study of the natural
world. There is an individualistic exuberance in much of the poetry
(as in Shakespeare), a high idealism (as in Sidney and Spenser), and a
desire to experiment with literary forms, such as pastorals and sonnets.
With the Jacobeans poetry becomes more analytical (the metaphysical poets) and more classical ("Tribe of Ben"). A half-pleasant melancholy is fairly common in the early seventeenth century. It is typified by
the *carpe diem* ("seize the day") theme; lovers especially were to

> Gather ye rosebuds while ye may,
> Old time is still a-flying.

On the other hand, there is the exuberant baroque style (this is a term
which has been used by various writers to characterize different and

sometimes mutually exclusive styles) in the religious poetry of Crashaw, and the sensuousness, melody, and moral earnestness of the school of Spenser (Giles and Phineas Fletcher, William Browne, and Sir John Davies). This school influenced Milton, thus forming a link between the two great Puritan poets. The restoration of the Stuarts in 1660 gave its name to the latter decades of the seventeenth century. Generally the poets in the period (Dryden was its greatest poet), allied themselves with the spirit of rationality and classicism, especially as these were expressed by French writers, and reacted against Puritan restraints.

After Dryden, poetry was predominantly written in a neoclassical mode. Pope, Swift, and Addison were the leading figures in the first half of the eighteenth century. Their ideals about literature were that it should exhibit restraint, decorum, polish, brilliance, clarity, logic, "correctness," and "good taste." The best poets in this mode were satirists and wits. There was a good deal of didactic verse. And the most successfully employed verse form was the rhymed couplet, which was suitable to epigrammatic barbs and neat summaries:

> The relish of the muse consists in rhyme:
> One verse must meet another like a chime.

Samuel Johnson, the leading literary figure in the second half of the eighteenth century, was conservative and held to neoclassical principles, but the period witnessed the beginnings of romanticism. Sentimentalism, Gothic romance, and love of nature began to compete with the rationalism, restrained imagination, and urban ideals of the earlier decades. The heroic couplet began to give way to blank verse and other forms, rural life and rugged nature were idealized, and interest developed in Celtic and Norse mythology and in the medieval ballad. The triumph of the romantic spirit came in the early years of the nineteenth century with Scott, Wordsworth, Coleridge, Southey, Byron, Shelley, and Keats. Generally speaking, the romantic poets stressed the distant, strange, and mysterious; intuition; the healing power of imagination; individualism; originality; and the emotional and the subjective.

The Victorian period, considered as extending from 1832 (the death of Scott) to 1900 (Victoria's death), saw great industrial changes, tremendous population increases, a considerable extension of suffrage, and a great deal of religious uncertainty, particularly because of the theory of evolution. The work of Tennyson, Browning, and Arnold, the leading poets, exhibits the temper of the age and many of its issues. Tennyson strove, in the face of his religious doubts, to be optimistic and affirmative. Like Ruskin and Carlyle, prose writers, he worked very hard and wrote at great length. It has been suggested that his use of Arthurian

matter as a subject for his poetry was in part a retreat from the intellectual issues of his day. Browning was perhaps constitutionally an optimist,
but his hopefulness and hardy courage in the face of difficulties have
often been taken to typify Victorian ideals. Arnold made the issues of
his day the subject for his best poetry. Like most of his contemporaries
he did not distinguish between solemnity and seriousness.

The closing decades, especially the 1890's, show a mixture of feverish gaiety, a half-submerged eroticism, in the poetry of Dowson, Wilde,
and Beardsley, the harsh determinism of Hardy, and the artistic conscience of Yeats and Hopkins. There was a reaching out for new beginnings and an attempt to break free from the Victorian ethos, insofar as this had meant an uncritical optimism, serving the spirit of utili-
tarianism, and refusing open discussion of such matters as sex.

In the poetry of the twentieth century there is likely to be a strong
emphasis on the actual, physical world. In Eliot or Yeats or Hart Crane
there is a kind of realism, an acceptance of all subjects whether pretty
or ugly, that we rarely find in the nineteenth century. Undoubtedly
there are many good reasons for this shift in taste. Twentieth-century
poets believed that poetry in the latter part of the nineteenth century
had retreated farther and farther from the real world, that among many
readers there was a growing suspicion that in poetry, which was associated with the fanciful and unreal, truly important subjects were
not treated. Prose was considered more "true to life." It seemed necessary, therefore, for poets to introduce what may be called prose elements into their work: meters closer to the rhythms of prose; language
on various levels, whether used for conversational, academic, or other
purposes; and a wider range of subject matter. These prose elements
are among the characteristics of the poetry of our time.

A poet in a given period, then, works inside the preconceptions,
inside the "world view" of his age (even though, like Blake, he may
fight against it). There will be attitudes and literary conventions which
he will accept almost without question. In other words, the poet is
affected by his milieu. It has been suggested, for example, that the
neoclassical poets liked metonymy because it implied clear distinctions
and clear relationships. Thus in these lines:

> Sceptre and crown must tumble down
> And in the dust be equal made
> With the poor crooked scythe and spade

On the other hand, these poets generally disapproved of metaphors
in which nature, the larger category, was subsumed under the domestic
or homely, the smaller category. Dryden, one of the poets who helped
to create the neoclassical taste for order, said that as a boy he had liked
this line: "And periwig with snow the bald-pate woods." Such a line
would not have been written by a neoclassical poet.

Or, to take another example, we can examine this passage from Pope's *Essay on Criticism*:

> First follow Nature, and your judgement frame
> By her just standard, which is still the same:
> Unerring Nature, still divinely bright,
> One clear, unchang'd, and universal light,
> Life, force, and beauty, must to all impart,
> At once the source, and end, and test of Art.

and compare it with these lines by E. E. Cummings:

> my father moved through dooms of love
> through sames of am through haves of give.*

Pope asserts, for his age, the belief in the inexorable laws of the universe, or nature; understanding these laws leads to rational systems of thought and of expression. Language itself, conforming to reason, should be held to rational patterns. Language moves according to logical progression, in carefully balanced or contrasted phrases. One does not feel that Pope attempted to recreate language, though his precision, at its best, gives him his particular inimitableness. Cummings, on the other hand, is much less concerned with conventional thought. He is not concerned with any objective set of laws. He *is* concerned with the importance of the subjective realm, the unique individual. Therefore he is not committed, as was Pope, to laws of syntax or punctuation or conventional word usage. Like many other men of our time, Cummings is not at all certain about the existence of absolute laws governing man, but he is apparently quite certain about the importance of being self-aware and refusing to be caught in molds of habit.

Josephine Miles in *The Primary Language of Poetry in the 1640's* points out that the nineteenth-century critic and poet were uneasy with the metaphysical poets. "The poet," they believed, "would do better to report actual fusions and especially his own feelings of unity, than to create unity out of figures of speech." Another way of putting the matter is to say the metaphysical poet stressed *relationships* and employed figures of speech that pointed them up in vigorous fashion, whereas the nineteenth-century poet was likely, more often than not, to *report* his feelings. Thus, in "A Nocturnal upon Saint Lucy's Day," Donne figuratively objectifies his feelings:

> But I am by her death, which word wrongs her,
> Of the first nothing the elixir grown.

....
* Lines from "my father moved through dooms of love" in *50 Poems*, published by Duell, Sloan & Pearce, Inc. Copyright, 1939, 1940, by E. E. Cummings.

In "She Dwelt among the Untrodden Ways," Wordsworth reports his feelings (he does not dramatize them in a figure of speech):

> But she is in her grave, and, oh,
> The difference to me.

Regardless of the characteristics of the poetry in a given period, however, the poetry written in it will have certain characteristics in common with the poetry of another period. Poetry is, we might say, the expression of insight, in language designed to arouse appropriate emotion. In the poetry of each period we find connotation, images, symbols, understatement, overstatement, paradox, generalization, and so forth. The worth of the individual poem may be decided in terms of the appropriateness of the use of any or all of these means of expression. In reading a poem, therefore, we must be aware of the characteristics it has which are peculiar to poetry as a literary genre, as well as the characteristics it has which are peculiar to its time. Nor should we forget that as the work of an individual it has characteristics peculiar to the writer.*

John Skelton
(c.1460–1529)

■ ■ ■ ■ ■ ■ ■ ■ ■ ■

THE BIRTHPLACE OF John Skelton and most of the facts of his life cannot be set down with any certainty. He probably took a degree from Cambridge in 1484, and was awarded the title of laureate by Cambridge, Oxford, and the continental University of Louvain at various times during his early career. Both Erasmus and Caxton praise him for his learning. He was tutor to Prince Henry, later to be Henry VIII. His life at court conceivably was filled with the problems that his open, imprudent nature must have called into being, and his becoming rector of Diss around 1500, two years after taking orders, has been attributed to these difficulties. It is a matter of record that his great attacks on Cardinal Wolsey were written dur-

....

* The following studies furnish valuable examinations in taste and sensibility: Frederick Pottle, *The Idiom of Poetry* (Ithaca, N. Y.: Cornell University Press, 1941); F. W. Bateson, *English Poetry and English Language* (Oxford: the Clarendon Press, 1934); Cleanth Brooks, *Modern Poetry and the Tradition* (Chapel Hill: University of North Carolina Press, 1939); and Robert Sharp, *From Donne to Dryden* (Chapel Hill: University of North Carolina Press, 1942).

ing the period at Diss, far from the Tudor court. Skelton wrote a morality
play, *Magnyfycence,* and a great deal of poetry. In his work there is much
variety, but it is with "Skeltonics" that his name is most associated. For a
long time neglected by readers of English poetry, Skelton is being read again
and has had an influence on twentieth-century verse.

Suggested Readings

W. H. AUDEN, "John Skelton," in K. Garvin, ed., *The Great Tudors.* New
   York: E. P. Dutton Co., Inc., 1935, pp. 55–67.
IAN GORDON, *John Skelton.* Melbourne: Melbourne University Press, 1943.
E. M. FORSTER, "John Skelton," *Two Cheers for Democracy.* New York:
   Harcourt, Brace and Co., 1951, pp. 135–153.

■■■■■■■■■■

Elynour Rummynge

The tunnyng of Elynour Rummynge per Skelton Laureat

> Tell you I chyll,[1]
> If that ye wyll
> A whyle be styll,
> Of a comely gyll[2]
> That dwelt on a hyll:
> But she is somwhat sage
> And well worne in age;
> For her usage
> It would aswage
> A mannes courage.   10
>   Her lothely lere
> Is nothynge clere,
> But ugly of chere,
> Droupy and drowsy,
> Scurvy and lowsy;
> Her face all bowsy,
> Comely crynkled,
> Woundersly wrynkled,
> Lyke a rost pygges eare,
> Brystled wyth here.   20
>   Her lewde lyppes twayne,
> They slaver, men sayne,

1. Will. Although the remaining poems in this brief selection from the works
of Skelton are for the most part modernized, "Elynour Rummynge" has been left
with its original spellings in order to give the student a sense of the way Skelton's
poetry looked to a sixteenth-century reader.   2. Jill.

Lyke a ropy rayne,
A gummy glayre:
She is ugly fayre;
Her nose somdele hoked,
And camously[3] croked,
Never stoppynge,
But ever droppyng;
Her skynne lose and slacke,   30
Grained lyke a sacke;
With a croked backe.

Her eyen gowndy
Are full unsowndy,
For they are blered;
And she gray hered;
Jawed lyke a jetty;
A man would have pytty
To se how she is gumbed,
Fyngered and thumbed,   40
Gently joynted,
Gresed and annoynted
Up to the knockels;
The bones of her huckels[4]
Lyke as they were with buckels
Togyther made fast:
Her youth is farre past:
Foted lyke a plane,
Legged lyke a crane;
And yet she wyll jet,[5]   50
Lyke a jollyvet,[6]
In her furred flocket,[7]
And gray russet rocket,[8]
With symper the cocket.
Her huke[9] of Lyncole grene,
It had ben hers, I wene,
More than fourty yere;
And so doth it apere,
For the grene bare thredes
Loke lyke sere wedes,   60
Wyddered lyke hay,
The woll worne away;
And yet I dare saye
She thynketh herselfe gaye
Upon the holy daye,

3. Awry.   4. Hips.   5. Strut.   6. A pretty young thing.
7. Loose gown.   8. Tunic.   9. Cloak.

Whan she doth her aray,
And gyrdeth in her gytes[10]
Stytched and pranked with pletes;
Her kyrtel Brystow[11] red,
With clothes upon her hed   70
That wey a sowe of led,
Wrythen[12] in wonder wyse,
After the Sarasyns gyse
With a whym wham,
Knyt with a trym tram,
Upon her brayne pan,
Lyke an Egyptian,
Capped about:
Whan she goeth out
Herselfe for to shewe,   80
She dryveth downe the dewe
Wyth a payre of heles
As brode as two wheles;
She hobles as a gose
With her blanket hose
Over the falowe;
Her shone smered wyth talowe,
Gresed upon dyrt
That baudeth[13] her skyrt.

Primus Passus

And this comely dame,   90
I understande, her name
Is Elynour Rummynge,
At home in her wonnynge[14];
And as men say
She dwelt in Sothray,[15]
In a certayne stede
Bysyde Lederhede.
She is a tonnysh gyb[16];
The devyll and she be syb.[17]
But to make up my tale,   100
She breweth noppy ale,
And maketh therof port sale[18]
To travellars, to tynkers,
To sweters,[19] to swynkers,[20]

....

10. Clothes.   11. Bristol.   12. Wound.   13. Soils.
14. Dwelling.   15. Surrey.   16. Tomcat.   17. Related.
18. Public, or immediate, sale.   19. Sweaters.   20. Laborers.

And all good ale drynkers,
That wyll nothynge spare,
But drynke tyll they stare
And brynge themselfe bare,
With, Now away the mare,[21]
And let us sley care,   110
As wyse as an hare!
 Come who so wyll
To Elynour on the hyll,
Wyth, Fyll the cup, fyll,
And syt there by styll,
Erly and late:
Thyther cometh Kate,
Cysly,[22] and Sare,[23]
With theyr legges bare,
And also theyr fete   120
Hardely full unswete;
Wyth theyr heles dagged,
Theyr kyrtelles all to-jagged,
Theyr smockes all to-ragged,
Wyth titters and tatters,
Brynge dysshes and platters,
Wyth all theyr myght rynnynge
To Elynour Rummynge,
To have of her tunnynge:
She leneth[24] them on the same,   130
And thus begynneth the game.
 Some wenches come unlaced,
Some huswyves come unbrased,
Wuth theyr naked pappes,
That flyppes and flappes;
It wigges and it wagges,
Lyke tawny saffron bagges;
A sorte of foule drabbes
All scurvy with scabbes:
Some be flybytten,[25]   140
Some skewed[26] as a kytten;
Some wyth a sho clout
Bynde theyr heddes about;
Some have no herelace,[27]
Theyr lockes about theyr face,
Theyr tresses untrust,
All full of unlust[28];

21. Away foreboding. 22. Cicely. 23. Sarah. 24. Lends
25. Flea-bitten. 26. Piebald. 27. Hairlace. 28. Unpleasantness.

Some loke strawry,
Some cawry mawry[29];
Full untydy tegges,[30]   150
Lyke rotten egges.
Suche a lewde sorte
To Elynour resorte
From tyde to tyde:
Abyde, abyde,
And to you shall be tolde
Howe hyr ale is solde
To Mawte and to Molde.

Septimus Passus

Soft, quod one, hyght[31] Sybbyll,
And let me wyth you bybyll.[32]   160
She sat downe in the place,
With a sory face
Wheywormed[33] about;
Garnyshed was her snout
Wyth here and there a puscull,
Lyke a scabbyd muscull.
This ale, sayde she, is noppy;
Let us syppe and soppy,
And not spyll a droppy,
For so mote I hoppy,[34]   170
It coleth well my croppy.
    Dame Elynoure, sayde she,
Have here is for me,
A cloute of London pynnes;
And wyth that she begynnes
The pot to her plucke,
And dranke a good lucke;
She swynged up a quarte
At ones for her parte;
Her paunche was so puffed,   180
And so wyth ale stuffed,
Had she not hyed apace,
She had defoyled the place.
    Then began the sporte
Amonge that dronken sorte:
Dame Elynour, sayde they,

---

29. Possibly slatternly.   30. Young sheep.   31. Called.   32. Tipple.
33. Pimpled.   34. So may I hap.

Lende here a cocke of hey,
To make all thynge cleane;
Ye wote well what we meane.
　　But, syr, among all   190
That sat in that hall,
There was a pryckemedenty,[35]
Sat lyke a seynty,[36]
And began to paynty[37]
As thoughe she would faynty[38];
She made it as koy
As a lege de moy[39];
She was not halfe so wyse
As she was pevysshe nyse.
She sayde never a worde,   200
But rose from the borde,
And called for our dame,
Elynour, by name.
We supposed, I wys,
That she rose to pys;
But the very grounde
Was for to compounde
Wyth Elynour in the spence,[40]
To pay for her expence:
I have no penny nor grote   210
To pay, sayde she, God wote,
For washyng of my throte;
But my bedes of amber
Bere them to your chamber.
Then Elynour dyd them hyde
Wythin her beddes syde.
　　But some than sat ryght sad
That nothynge had
There of theyr awne,
Neyther gelt nor pawne;   220
Suche were there menny
That had not a penny,
But, whan they should walke,
Were fayne wyth a chalke
To score on the balke,
Or score on the tayle:
God gyve it yll hayle!
For my fyngers ytche;

....
35.　Simperer.　36.　Saint.　37.　Feign.
38.　Faint.　39.　A dance.　40.　Storeroom.

I have wrytten to mytche
Of this made mummynge   230
Of Elynour Rummynge:
Thus endeth the gest
Of this worthy fest!

QUOD SKELTON, LAUREAT

■ "Elynour Rummynge" is reprinted here only in part, but the poem, which tends to be formless, does not suffer from being excerpted. Elynour Rummynge operates an alehouse at Leatherhead. According to the fiction of the poem, Skelton, visiting there, sits in the corner study-ing and commenting on the various women who frequent the ale-house. They bring all sorts of gifts to pay for their ale. Every detail, however gross, is put down. The poem opens with a long prologue de-scribing Elynour. Then in the succeeding sections each of the custom-ers is given a few lines of description. The detail is crude, often scato-logical, and requires a strong-stomached reader. But there is a mordant directness and honesty in the treatment that gives the poem an unusual strength. Skelton, of course, was deliberately exaggerating his material in order to make more effective the essential qualities which he was faithfully portraying. Thus he concludes, when he feels he has carried his fun far enough:

I have wrytten to mytche
Of this made mummynge
Of Elynour Rummynge.

(ll. 229–231)

Perhaps a word should be said in interpretation of the kind of coarseness we find in this poem. It is about Tudor life on one of its levels. It has the frankness and directness that are a part of life on such a level. If it offends modern ears it will offend because of vulgarity, not because of a suggestive eroticism. Later in the sixteenth century, poetry such as Shakespeare's *Venus and Adonis* would exhibit such an eroticism. And it is more than likely that this later sort of poetry would have seemed immoral to Skelton. Nonetheless, the generations after the Tudors found Skelton too gross for their literary tastes. Pope called him "beastly Skelton." The nineteenth century ignored him. But a number of poets in the twentieth century have found certain virtues in his poetry, some which we may be able to suggest here.

Perhaps a part of the exaggeration in this satire is the result of Skelton's living at the end of the Middle Ages and the beginning of the Renaissance in England. Behind him in the literature of the Middle Ages were three types of literature about women. There were religious hymns to the Virgin. There were the idealistic lyrics and romances of

the courtly love tradition. In these, women were written about in ecstatic and exaggerated terms. And, finally, there were the frequently
bitter satires directed against women as the daughters of Eve, the source
of all evil, and a snare for men. This satirical type, which served the
needs of preachers and moralists, often concentrated not merely on the
lust but on the ugliness of women. It gave rise to a crude kind of realism,
some of which can be found in the prologue to Chaucer's "Wife of
Bath's Tale" or in some of the fabliaux. This third type of literature
about women almost died out in the sixteenth century, being replaced
by the idealizations of the Petrarchan tradition, the satires in some of
the plays and antifeminist literature, and the development of a literature
in which neither idealization nor ridiculous abuse was dominant. But
the crude realism in "Elynour Rummynge" was a part of a literary
tradition that was still thriving in Skelton's time.

Skelton's meter and rhyme scheme, which has been labeled the
"Skeltonic," has given students of Skelton's work grounds for a great
deal of theorizing, particularly about its origins. Two or three scholars
have found its antecedents in French poetry, whereas others have found
it in accentual Latin poetry of the Middle Ages. And a more recent
scholar has found it in rhymed Latin prose. At least two scholars, however, find it to be "the descendant of the Anglo-Saxon alliterative line
through the alliterative revival of Middle English." * Skelton's play
Magnyfycence is in this tradition. The following is a typical passage
from the play:

> I blunder, I bluster, I blowe, and I blother;
> I make one the one day, and I marre on the other;
> Bysy, bysy, and euer bysy,
> I daunce vp and downe tyll I am dyssy;
> I can fynde fantasyes where none is;
> I wyll not haue it so, I wyll haue it this.
>
> (ll. 984–1054)

Professor Robert Ramsay, who edited the play, has noted that these
lines fall naturally into two sections, each one forming a Skeltonic.
In other words, usually the Skeltonic line is marked by brevity. Gordon
has written that the "Skeltonic has normally two (occasionally three)
powerful stresses and a group of unstressed syllables, the whole line containing a total length of four syllables and upwards." Each line, that is,
will usually have two stressed syllables but a variable number of unstressed syllables. We can see that this definition is appropriate by examining, for instance, the five lines that close the prologue to "Elynour
Rummynge":

----
* See Ian Gordon, *John Skelton*, pp. 194ff.

She hobles as a gose	*Six syllables*
With her blanket hose	*Six syllables*
Ouer the falowe;	*Five syllables*
Her shone smered wyth talowe,	*Six syllables*
Gresed vpon dyrt	*Four syllables*
That baudeth her skyrt.	*Five syllables*

A good case can be made out for the naturalness of this metric. In fact, W. H. Auden, an excellent metrist himself, has written: "The skeltonic is such a simple metre that it is surprising that so few poets have used it. The natural unit of speech rhythm seems to be one of four accents, dividing into two half verses of two accents. If one tries to write ordinary conversation in verse, it will fall more naturally into this scheme than into any other. . . . Skelton is said to have spoken as he wrote, and his skeltonics have the natural ease of speech rhythm." Auden goes on to say that this sytem of accents is what we find in many nursery rhymes; for example:

> Little Jack Horner
> Sat in a corner.

There are four accents, two to each line. Skelton, of course, is not the only poet who discovered this conversational meter. He, as we have noted, inherited it from the medieval alliterative poets. In the nineteenth century we also find a poet, Gerard Manley Hopkins, theorizing about accentual metrics, which he called "sprung rhythm," in this fashion: "I had long had haunting my ear the echo of a new rhythm which now I realized on paper. To speak shortly, it consists in scanning by accents or stresses alone, without any account of the number of syllables, so that a foot may be one strong syllable or it may be many light and one strong. I do not say the idea is altogether new; there are many hints of it in music, in nursery rhymes and popular jingles. . . ." * Skelton's lines, however, are usually shorter than Hopkins' and also have a more helter-skelter quality. Skelton observes no regular pattern of rhymes. Sometimes a word rhymes only with the word in the following line, but sometimes the rhyme runs for five or six lines. The helter-skelter quality and the repeated rhyme are seen in these lines:

> This ale, sayde she, is noppy;
> Let us syppe and soppy,
> And not spyll a droppy,
> For so mote I hoppy,
> It coleth well in my croppy.
>
> (ll. 167–171)

....
* C. C. Abbot, ed., *The Correspondence of Gerard Manley Hopkins and Richard Watson Dixon* (London: Oxford University Press, 1935), p. 14.

It is as though the poet were following both his rhyme and exuberance where they listeth.

The diction of Skelton's poetry, out of one of the lower strata of the society, is earthy, direct, and colloquial. Therefore it is appropriate to the anti-romantic temper of Skelton. Thus, for example, when he wishes to suggest some manner of affectedness or pomposity, the context of his poem affords an immediate contrast both in diction and tone:

> But, syr, among all
> That sat in that hall,
> There was a pryckemedenty,
> Sat lyke a seynty,
> And began to paynty,
> As though she would faynty.
>
> (ll. 190–195)

The nicety of the woman he is satirizing here seems far more affected than it would in a less realistic poem. And the affectation of his own diction here affords a similar contrast. (Skelton, incidentally, made his early reputation as a poet by writing in the *termis aureat* or aureate diction and high style of the late fifteenth century.) In his *Magnyfycence* he puts all the statements made to noblemen into the high style he had written himself as a younger poet. The aureate style employed a Latinized vocabulary. Often, as Auden observes, it was dull and smelled of the candle and study. Skelton seems to have realized this and turned toward a language more appropriate to his own genius. Thus in "Philip Sparrow" he writes: "My style as yet direct/ With English words elect."

Occasionally in Skelton's verse, although not especially in "Elynour Rummynge," one finds a line or two with the pith of a folk proverb, but essentially Skelton's poetry is not of an intellectual kind. The satire is rarely subtle innuendo—it is blunt, and abusive. But the bluntness is an essential part of his poetry. His poetry is concerned with the objective and the physical, which he treats in such a way that the effect, as Auden has put it, "is like looking at the human skin through a magnifying glass."

Here folowith divers Balettis and Dities solacious, devised by Master Skelton, Laureate

> With, Lullay, lullay, like a childe,
> Thou sleepest too long, thou art beguiled.
>
> My darling dear, my daisy flower,
> Let me, quod he, lie in your lap.

Lie still, quod she, my paramour,
   Lie still hardily, and take a nap.
His head was heavy, such was his hap,
All drowsy dreaming, drowned in sleep,
That of his love he took no keep,
         With, Hey, lullay, etc.   10

With ba, ba, ba, and bas, bas, bas,
   She cherished him both cheek and chin,
That he wist never where he was;
   He had forgotten all deadly sin.
He wanted with her love to win:
He trusted her payment, and lost all his pray:
She left him sleeping, and stole away,
         With, Hey, lullay, etc.

The rivers wroth, the waters wan,
   She spared not, to wet her feet;   20
She waded over, she found a man
   That halsyd [1] her heartily and kissed her sweet:
Thus after her cold she caught a heat.
My leaf, she said, rooteth in his bed;
I wis he hath an heavy head,
         With, Hey, lullay, etc.

What dreamest thou, drunkard, drowsy pate!
   Thy lust and liking is from thee gone:
Thou blinkered blowboll, thou wakest too late,
   Behold, thou liest, luggard, alone!   30
   Well may thou sigh, well may thou groan,
To deal with her so cowardly:
I wis, powle hachet,[2] she bleared thine I.

         QD. SKELTON, LAUREATE.

   1. Paraphrase the situation of the poem.
   2. What is the attitude of the poet toward the lover?
   3. What is the stanza form employed in this poem?
   4. Compare this poem of Skelton's in theme, structure, and tone
with Keats' "La Belle Dame sans Merci" (p. 446).

....

1. Embraced. To halse is to embrace round the neck.   2. Blockhead.

To Mistress Isabel Pennell

By Saint Mary, my lady,
Your mammy and your dady
Brought forth a goodly baby!
    My maiden Isabel,
Reflaring rosabell,
The flagrant camamell,
    The ruddy rosary,
The sovereign rosemary,
The pretty strawberry,
    The columbine, the nepte,
The jeloffer well set,
The proper violet;
Ennewed your colowre
Is like the daisy flower
After the April shower;
    Star of the morrow gray,
The blossom on the spray,
The freshest flower of May:
    Maidenly demure,
Of womanhood the lure;
Wherefore I make you sure
    It were an heavenly health,
It were an endless wealth,
A life for God himself,
    To hear this nightingale
    Among the birdës smale
Warbeling in the vale,—
Dug, dug, jug, jug,
Good year and good luck,
With chuck, chuck, chuck, chuck!

1. How many major stresses to a line are there in this poem?

2. Do the closing lines suggest that there is a literal seriousness in the statements of the poem?

3. The imagery of the poem identifies the beauties of the girl with those of nature. Explain how this is done.

4. In the context, is the idea, that God would enjoy the natural excellences of the girl, to be read as sacrilege or hyperbole?

Sir Thomas Wyatt

(1503–1542)

■■■■■■■■■

TOGETHER with his young friend Henry Howard, Earl of Surrey, Sir Thomas Wyatt is credited with inaugurating the great period of Tudor poetry. Wyatt lived, in the king's service, in France, Italy, and Spain. Like Chaucer before him, he imported Italian and French poetic forms into England. He used not only the Petrarchan sonnet form and the form that was to become known as the Shakespearean sonnet, but also the terza rima, the ottava rima, and the very intricate rondeau. Yet many critics think the finest poetry of Sir Thomas Wyatt is the series of lyrics written for the lute, native in melody and form and quite apart from any foreign influence.

The son of Sir Henry Wyatt, a loyal follower of Henry VII, the poet was trained from the first for service to the reigning house. Educated at Cambridge, Wyatt early became a successful diplomat, courtier, scholar, and musician. Tradition has it that he was the lover of Anne Boleyn before Henry VIII married her. But Wyatt's brief imprisonment about the time of her fall seems not to have been connected in any way with her but rather to have been due to an affray with the Duke of Norfolk. In 1541, after the fall of his patron Cromwell, Wyatt was again in prison on charges levied by the Bishop of London. He defended himself successfully at his trial and was fully restored to the royal favor. The next year, on a journey for the King, he fell ill and died.

Suggested Readings

A. K. FOXWELL, *A Study of Sir Thomas Wyatt's Poems.* London: University of London Press, 1911, pp. 59–102.

E. K. CHAMBERS, "Sir Thomas Wyatt," *Sir Thomas Wyatt and Some Collected Studies.* London: Sidgwick & Jackson, Ltd., 1933, pp. 96–145.

ALAN SWALLOW, "The Pentameter Lines in Skelton and Wyatt," *Modern Philology,* XLVIII, 1 (August, 1950), 1–11.

■■■■■■■■■

Description of the Contrarious Passions in a Lover

> I find no peace, and all my war is done;
> I fear and hope; I burn, and freeze like ice;
> I fly aloft, yet can I not arise;

And nought I have, and all the world I season.
That locks nor looseth holdeth me in prison,
And holds me not, yet can I 'scape no wise;
Nor lets me live, nor die, at my devise,
And yet of death it giveth me occasion.
Without eye, I see; without tongue, I plain;
I wish to perish, yet I ask for health;
I love another, and thus I hate myself;
I feed me in sorrow, and laugh in all my pain.
Lo, thus displeaseth me both death and life,
And my delight is causer of this strife.

■   There are disagreements about Wyatt's metrical patterns—about how regular his lines are. But George Puttenham, a sixteenth-century critic, called Wyatt and his young contemporary Henry Howard, the Earl of Surrey, the "first reformers of our English numbers." English prosody had fallen into chaos or near chaos in the fifteenth century, and Puttenham undoubtedly meant that Wyatt and Surrey had done much to establish new patterns. In the fifteenth century one can find such metrical crudity as the following:

Sapience bade me marvel nothing
   For she would show me the signification
Why he so sat by short reckoning,
   According to a moralisation.

By Wyatt's time the final e was no longer sounded, and accents had shifted from the second to the first syllable in words like "favour" and "honour." These changes from Middle to modern English caused readers to miss the delicacy of Chaucer's metrical art. Sixteenth-century readers inevitably reduced many of his lines to doggerel, and even Dryden, late in the seventeenth century, believed Chaucer the victim of a barbarous age. Wyatt, it is generally believed, learned a good deal about regularity of metrical patterns from studying the poetry of Petrarch and other Italian poets.

Can the above poem be scanned according to any regular pattern?

The Lover Compareth His State to a Ship[1]

My galley chargèd with forgetfulness
Through sharp seas, in winter nights, doth pass
'Tween rock and rock; and eke my foe, alas,

....
1.   This sonnet is modeled to a considerable extent on Petrarch's one hundred and fifty-ninth sonnet.

That is my lord, steereth with cruelness;
And every oar a thought in readiness,
As though that death were light in such a case.
An endless wind doth tear the sail apace,
Of forcèd sighs and trusty fearfulness;
A rain of tears, a cloud of dark disdain,
Have done the wearied cords great hinderance;
Wreathèd with error and with ignorance,
The stars be hid that led me to this pain;
Drowned is reason, that should be my comfort,
And I remain despairing of the port.

The Lover Complaineth the Unkindness of His Love

My lute, awake, perform the last
Labor that thou and I shall waste,
And end that I have now begun;
And when this song is sung and past,
My lute, be still, for I have done.

As to be heard where ear is none,
As lead to grave in marble stone,
My song may pierce her heart as soon.
Should we then sigh, or sing, or moan?
No, no, my lute, for I have done.   10

The rocks do not so cruelly
Repulse the waves continually,
As she my suit and affection;
So that I am past remedy,
Whereby my lute and I have done.

Proud of the spoil that thou hast got
Of simple hearts, through love's shot;
By whom unkind thou hast them won,
Think not he hath his bow forgot,
Although my lute and I have done.   20

Vengeance shall fall on thy disdain,
That makest but game on earnest pain;
Think not alone under the sun
Unquit to cause thy lovers plain,
Although my lute and I have done.

Perchance thee lie withered and old,
In winter nights that are so cold,
Plaining in vain unto the moon;
Thy wishes then dare not be told.
Care then who list, for I have done.   30

And then may chance thee to repent
The time that thou hast lost and spent
To cause thy lovers sigh and swoon;
Then shalt thou know beauty but lent,
And wish and want as I have done.

Now cease, my lute, this is the last
Labor that thou and I shall waste,
And ended is that we begun,
Now is this song both sung and past,
My lute, be still, for I have done.   40

■ It is believed that Wyatt found further guidance toward metrical regularity in the musical tradition of the popular song descended from the Middle Ages. V. De Sola Pinto has summarized the medieval influence in these words: "Wyatt is the successor of a long line of anonymous medieval minstrels who naturalized in English the short riming stanzas of Latin and medieval lyric poetry. His best work has their sweetness and spontaneity, their perfect command of metrical form, and the freshness of their simple language; and to these qualities Wyatt adds a courtly grace and delicacy, the dignity of a man of learning and culture." *

Comment on the above poem in terms of its "metrical form," "freshness" of language, and "courtly grace and delicacy."

The Lover Showeth How He Is Forsaken of Such as He Sometime Enjoyed

They flee from me, that sometime did me seek,
With naked foot stalking within my chamber.
Once have I seen them gentle, tame, and meek,
That now are wild, and do not once remember
That sometime they have put themselves in danger
To take bread at my hand; and now they range,
Busily seeking in continual change.
Thanked be fortune it hath been otherwise,

---
* V. De Sola Pinto, *The English Renaissance* (New York: The McBride Company, Inc., 1937), pp. 34–35.

Twenty times better; but once especial,
In thin array, after a pleasant guise,
When her loose gown did from her shoulders fall,
And she me caught in her arms long and small,
And therewithal so sweetly did me kiss
And softly said, Dear heart, how like you this?
　　It was no dream, for I lay broad awaking.
But all is turned now, through my gentleness,
Into a bitter fashion of forsaking;
And I have leave to go, of her goodness,
And she also to use newfangleness.
But since that I unkindly so am served,
How like you this? what hath she now deserved?

■ 1. Does "unkindly" in the second from the last line mean (a)
served with generous human sympathy or (b) served in the way one of
her kind or type of being is likely to serve? If one reads the "they" and
"them" of the first stanza to be deer—wild creatures—how is the character of the woman to be interpreted? Is the poet condemning her as a very
immoral and unfaithful woman?

　2. In Wyatt's manuscript the final line is "I would fain know
what she hath deserved." In *Tottel's Miscellany* (1557) it is emended
to read, "How like you this, what hath she now deserved?" Which is
more in keeping with the tone of the rest of the poem?

　3. What is the rhyme scheme?

　4. Are there significant shifts in tone from stanza to stanza?

To a Lady to Answer Directly with Yea or Nay

Madam, withouten many words,
Once I am sure, you will or no;
And if you will, then leave your bordes,
And use your wit, and show it so;
For with a beck you shall me call.
And if of one that burns alway
Ye have pity or ruth at all,
Answer him fair, with yea or nay:
If it be yea, I shall be fain;
If it be nay, friends as before;
You shall another man obtain,
And I mine own, and yours no more.

Edmund Spenser

(1552–1599)

■■■■■■■■■

EDMUND SPENSER was educated, perhaps as a poor man's son, at the Merchant Taylors' School, under Headmaster Richard Mulcaster, and at Cambridge, where he spent seven years in Pembroke, a strongly Calvinistic college. The sympathies Spenser developed there show clearly in *The Shepherd's Calendar* (1579), his first published work. Spenser never changed the basic convictions inspired in him by these early years: devotion to an "ultra-English poetry," with Chaucer as the fountainhead; Low Church religion; and English avoidance of French political entanglements. Appointed secretary to Lord Grey, Spenser took up his residence in Ireland in 1580, and there he wrote *The Faerie Queene*. Upon its publication in England (the first three books appeared in 1589, the last three in 1596) Spenser was assured of Queen Elizabeth's good will. His publisher, William Ponsonby, then brought out Spenser's minor poems: *Daphnaida* (1591) and *Complaints* (1591), the latter volume containing enough political satire offensive to the authorities to cause its suppression. *Colin Clout's Come Home Again* (1595), the *Amoretti* (1595), and *Epithalamion* (1595) apparently had their source in highly personal experiences. *Prothalamion* (1596) and the *Four Hymns* (1596) show that he was equally at ease with subjects in which he was less personally involved. His chief prose work, *A View of the Present State of Ireland* (1598–1633) is a controversial piece, on the one hand showing sympathy for the land, its culture, and its people, and on the other advocating measures for order and reform that have seemed to many readers severe, and even brutal. As sheriff of Cork, Spenser had returned to London on a govenment mission and to plead for the loyal Irish when he suddenly died. He is buried in Westminster Abbey.

Suggested Readings

LILLIAN WINSTANLEY, ed., *Edmund Spenser: The Foure Hymnes*. Cambridge: Cambridge University Press, 1907.

W. L. RENWICK, *Edmund Spenser, an Essay in Renaissance Poetry*. London: Edward Arnold & Co., 1925.

J. B. FLETCHER, *Literature of the Italian Renaissance*. New York: The Macmillan Company, 1934, Chaps. 13–14.

W. B. C. WATKINS, *Shakespeare and Spenser*. Princeton: Princeton University Press, 1950.

■■■■■■■■■

From the Prologue of the Fifth Booke of *The Faerie Queene*

Prologue

So oft as I with state of present time
The image of the antique world compare,
When as mans age was in his freshest prime,
And the first blossome of faire vertue bare,
Such oddes I finde twixt those, and these which are,
As that, through long continuance of his course,
Me seemes the world is runne quite out of square
From the first point of his appointed sourse,
And being once amisse, growes daily wourse and wourse.

Let none then blame me, if in discipline
Of vertue and of civill uses lore,
I doe not forme them to the common line
Of present dayes, which are corrupted sore,
But to the antique use which was of yore,
When good was onely for it selfe desyred,
And all men sought their owne, and none no more;
When Justice was not for most meed outhyred,
But simple Truth did rayne, and was of all admyred.

Dread soverayne goddesse, that doest highest sit
In seate of judgment, in th'Almighties stead,
And with magnificke might and wondrous wit
Doest to thy people righteous doome aread,
That furthest nations filles with awfull dread,
Pardon the boldnesse of thy basest thrall,
That dare discourse of so divine a read,
As thy great justice praysed over all:
The instrument whereof, loe! here thy Artegall.

From *Amoretti*

34

Lyke as a ship that through the Ocean wyde,
  by conduct of some star doth make her way,
  whenas a storme hath dimd her trusty guyde,
  out of her course doth wander far astray.
So I whose star, that wont with her bright ray,
  me to direct, with cloudes is overcast,
  doe wander now in darknesse and dismay,

through hidden perils round about me plast.
Yet hope I well, that when this storme is past
my *Helice* the lodestar of my lyfe
will shine again, and looke on me at last,
with lovely light to cleare my cloudy grief.
Till then I wander carefull comfortlesse,
in secret sorrow and sad pensivenesse.

■   Spenser did not originate all the features of the sonnet form we now call Spenserian. The Italian and the French sonneteers had employed a system of five rhymes. Wyatt and Surrey, who brought the sonnet into English, used the concluding couplet, which in Italy was most infrequent. In studying the pattern of Spenser's rhyme scheme we will see that he uses his rhyme to link one quatrain with the next. (It has been suggested that he took this practice from the French poet Marot.) Two obvious consequences of this scheme are that the linking of quatrains suggests a closer relationship between the units than would otherwise be suggested (this may be a seeming rather than actual linking if the ideas are not themselves related) and that the melodious elements are increased or intensified. There is also the possibility that the development of the idea behind the poem may be slower if the poet is obliged to fulfill his obligations to a complex rhyme scheme at the expense of the forward movement of the idea. In other words, it is difficult for the poet with such a scheme to employ a language notable for its precision. His language, in such a verse form, is more likely to tend toward diffuseness.

It so happens that in Spenser's day there was a theory of poetic usage, inherited from medieval rhetorical theory and practice, that required or at least accommodated itself to a kind of diffuseness. F. W. Bateson, in *English Poetry and the English Language,* has shown in analyzing one of Spenser's sonnets (59) that there is a pattern of repitions in words and phrases, an amplification of (or a gloss upon) certain terms. In other words, there is no attempt to use a minimum number of words, giving each its greatest possible burden of meaning or suggestiveness. (In modern poetry, on the contrary, we find this attempt to make each word carry the greatest possible weight of meaning.) The Elizabethans called this practice of amplification "copie," from the Latin *copia verborum* (abundance of words).

There appears to have been good reason why the Elizabethans would employ such a style. (This is not to imply that none of Spenser's contemporaries opposed diffuseness. Ben Jonson, a younger contemporary who did not think highly of Spenser's art, said in *Timber:* "Now because they speak all they can, however unfitly, they are thought to have the great copy." To Jonson, a greater selectivity and precision were preferable.) The Elizabethans were borrowing a tremendous number of words from other European languages. It may be that the number of words in English doubled during the course of the sixteenth century. There was a controversy among the critics and teachers of rhetoric about the wisdom of borrowing so many words. Nonetheless, the borrowing continued. Consequently many words were new. They had not been in common use long enough to have exact connotations and definite meanings. Some of the words introduced by poets or scholars did not thrive—they died shortly after being introduced. The abundance of new words must have given the poets a sense of great riches to work with in the way of vocabulary. There was not only an opportunity but a need for experiment if the poets were to write at all. And we know that the Elizabethan poets loved words, loved to play with them and exploit them with a kind of exuberance. But, on the other hand, as Bateson suggests, they may have been unsure of their vocabularies, unsure, for example, that a given word would still be in use after a few years. Francis Bacon, warning his fellow writers, said "these modern languages will at one time or other play the bankrupt with books." If the poet could not be sure of the stability of a word, he would be inclined to re-enforce its primary meaning with repetitions, glosses, and amplifications.

Professor Rosamund Tuve, in *Elizabethan and Metaphysical Imagery*, has also discussed the Elizabethan practice of employing "copie." She interprets it, unlike Bateson, as a means of giving delight through variety and a more complex unity. Her generalizations undoubtedly are appropriate to a good deal of Elizabethan poetry. In the preceding sonnet (34) from Spenser's *Amoretti*, however, one finds repetitiousness, or merely very slight variations, rather than genuine variety or complex unity.

In the first quatrain Spenser introduces his figure, the ship that loses its way because the star that guides it is hidden by clouds. The lines tend toward diffuseness in that they might have been compressed a great deal more than they are, but they are not remarkably diffuse. In the succeeding lines, however, there is an unmistakable diffuseness. It might have been sufficient for the poet to identify himself with the ship and the star with his beloved. The implications of the identification would be clear enough. Instead, in the second quatrain, Spenser points up each of the elements in the comparison. And in the phrase "darkness and dismay" there is a suggestion of the amplification about which Bateson comments. In the third quatrain he refers explicitly to the storm and to the star again. The references to the star are multiple. First he identifies his beloved with Helice, a huntress loved by Zeus and turned into a constellation, the Great Bear, by the jealous Hera. Then the poet identifies the beloved with the lodestar, the polestar by which directions are set. It is not beside the point to observe that Spenser first uses for his star a figure out of classical mythology but then follows it by a native, Anglo-Saxon term. In lines 11 and 12 we may note further evidences of amplification. We might assume that if the star was to shine again his griefs would be dissipated, but Spenser not only has the star shine but shine with "lovely light," and on himself, clearing his "cloudy grief." In the first line of the final couplet there is a repetition of words to suggest his troubles meanwhile, "careful" and "comfortless." And in the last line there is a balance of phrases, each of which might suggest the grief he bears, "secret sorrow" and "sad pensiveness."

In terms of the purpose of the poem we may say that this tendency toward diffuseness serves the poet well. Certain forms of grief give rise to pensiveness, in the poetic evoking of which it may be necessary to employ a slow movement and to avoid sharp intellectual thrusts. The poet expresses his grief over some unnamed difficulty that has caused him to be separated from his beloved or at least to be cut off from her favor. In other words, he is attempting to express a grief which hardly needs analyzing in any minute fashion. The repetitious use of detail, on the other hand, suggests the weight and pervasiveness of the grief.

This sonnet must also be examined in terms of the Platonism and neo-Platonism in which Spenser is known to have been steeped. Light is for Spenser, as it was for Plato (*Phaedrus* and *The Republic*), a symbol of eternal beauty and knowledge. Each soul before passing into the form of man saw this light. Imprisoned in the physical world, few recall it, but it may be recalled when one sees certain earthly beauties. (There is a great deal of light imagery in Spenser's *Four Hymns*.) In the imagery of this sonnet light plays an important part. The star is the beloved, a source of beauty and light. The star, like the beloved, apparently is not to be reached. Plato held that particular beauty (although he did not give the beauty of women as an instance) is merely one of the stages upward to eternal light. All the poet asks is "her bright ray," her "lovely light." Without it the ship is directionless and in danger. The lover needs the beauty of the starlight to guide him in the first stage of his journey toward heavenly beauty in another world.

Aware of Platonism and neo-Platonism, Spenser would also have been conscious of the four elements and their degrees of beauty, in this ascending order: earth, water, air, and fire. In the ship, away from earth (the lowest of the elements) and experiencing the cleanliness of water and air, he is able, with the light of the star (suggesting fire?), to proceed on his journey. Certainly some of these meanings would have been present in the minds of Elizabethans.

Such readers would also have been aware of the sonnet in relation to the Renaissance tradition of love sonnets. Plato, as we have noted, had not thought of women as being by their beauty spiritual uplifters of men, but frequenters of Renaissance salons, which were involved with the social and literary aspects of neo-Platonism, did. In the Renaissance, when women had come into far greater social and intellectual freedom than they had either in Plato's world or in the medieval world, the salons were of considerable importance. The Platonic cult of women with which they were associated inspired a considerable part of the prose and verse of the period. The central doctrine, as Professor Fletcher has put it, was this: "Beauty itself unmoved, moves to love, and from love to virtue, and from virtue to holiness." (Spenser in Books III and IV of *The Faerie Queene* allegorizes, using sets of characters, "the rings of the Ladder of Love, from lowest to highest, from lust to love purely spiritual.")

Closely related to the literature of Platonic love was Petrarchanism, the vogue of sonnets treating, in amorous, witty, and often greatly exaggerated fashion, the virtues of a beloved woman. The women of these sonnets usually had golden hair, eyes of topaz, neck and breasts milk white, teeth of pearls, a manner humble yet proud. Petrarch (1304–1374) wrote his sonnets to Laura, said to be the wife of an Italian nobleman. Petrarch had to be satisfied with an idealized, Platonic passion. Thus, quite naturally, the sonnet vogue, which began in Italy but spread to France and England, was readily associated with the Platonic cults spoken of above. In these sequences, as in Shakespeare's, the Platonic elements were sometimes neglected for other themes, including burlesque and caricature of the beloved. Spenser's sequence is more strictly in the mode followed by Petrarch himself. If in the sonnet we have been discussing we think of the poet as aspiring to receive the rather chilly comfort of attention from his beloved, rather than guidance toward eternal beauty, we are simply choosing to stop on a lower rung of the Platonic ladder. Either of the two readings, which complement each other, indicates that the poet is concerned with Platonic, heavenly beauty, not with consummating an ordinary love affair.

46

When my abodes prefixed time is spent,
   my cruell fayre streight bids me wend my way:
   but then from heaven most hideous stormes are sent
   as willing me against her will to stay.
Whom then shall I or heaven or her obay?
   the heavens know best what is the best for me:
   but as she will, whose will my life doth sway,
   my lower heaven, so it perforce must bee.
But ye high heavens, that all this sorrow see,
   sith all your tempests cannot hold me backe:
   aswage your stormes, or else both you and she,
   will both together me too sorely wrack.

Enough it is for one man to sustaine
the stormes, which she alone on me doth raine.

■ Explain the "logic" of the poem. A key to its meaning is in the
phrase "my lower heaven."

70

Fresh spring the herald of loves mighty king,
in whose cote armour richly are displayd
all sorts of flowers the which on earth do spring
in goodly colours gloriously arrayd.
Goe to my love, where she is carelesse layd,
yet in her winters bowre not well awake:
tell her the joyous time wil not be staid
unlesse she doe him by the forelock take.
Bid her therefore her selfe soone ready make,
to wayt on love amongst his lovely crew:
where every one that misseth then her make,
shall be by him amearst with penance dew.
Make hast therefore sweet love, whilest it is prime,
for none can call againe the passed time.

■ 1. Compare the theme of this poem with "Go, Lovely Rose" by
Edmund Waller (p. 194).
2. What is the effect of the two meanings of "spring" (lines 1
and 3)?
3. Discuss also the several uses of "make" (lines 9, 11, and 13).
4. Is there a pun on "lovely" (line 10)?

75

One day I wrote her name upon the strand,
but came the waves and washed it away:
agayne I wrote it with a second hand,
but came the tyde, and made my paynes his pray.
Vayne man, sayd she, that doest in vaine assay,
a mortall thing so to immortalize,
for I my selve shall lyke to this decay,
and eek my name bee wyped out lykewize.
Not so, (quod I) let baser things devize
to dy in dust, but you shall live by fame:
my verse your vertues rare shall eternize,
and in the hevens wryte your glorious name.

Where whenas death shall all the world subdew,
    our love shall live, and later life renew.

■   1. Is the promise the poet makes to "eternize" his lover peculiar to
Spenser, or does one find it in other poets?
    2. Discuss the possible meanings of "vaine" and "vayne" (line 5).

79

Men call you fayre, and you doe credit it,
    for that your selfe ye dayly such doe see:
    but the trew fayre, that is the gentle wit,
    and vertuous mind, is much more praysd of me.
For all the rest, how ever fayre it be,
    shall turne to nought and loose that glorious hew:
    but onely that is permanent and free
    from frayle corruption, that doth flesh ensew.
That is true beautie: that doth argue you
    to be divine and borne of heavenly seed:
    deriv'd from that fayre Spirit, from whom al true
    and perfect beauty did at first proceed.
He onely fayre, and what he fayre hath made,
    all other fayre lyke flowres untymely fade.

■   1. Discuss the Platonic theme in this sonnet.
    2. Discuss elements of "copie" or amplification in this sonnet.
    3. Discuss the use of balanced and antithetical phrasing.
    4. The key word in the poem seems to be "fayre." Discuss the
alliterative effect to be found in the employment of other words beginning with *f*.

Epithalamion

Ye learned sisters which have oftentimes
Beene to me ayding, others to adorne:
Whom ye thought worthy of your gracefull rymes,
That even the greatest did not greatly scorne
To heare theyr names sung in your simple layes,
But joyed in theyr prayse.
And when ye list your owne mishaps to mourne,
Which death, or love, or fortunes wreck did rayse,
Your string could soone to sadder tenor turne,
And teach the woods and waters to lament   10

Your dolefull dreriment.
Now lay those sorrowfull complaints aside,
And having all your heads with girland crownd,
Helpe me mine owne loves prayses to resound;
Ne let the same of any be envide:
So Orpheus did for his owne bride:
So I unto my selfe alone will sing;
The woods shall to me answer, and my eccho ring.

Early, before the worlds light giving lampe
His golden beame upon the hils doth spred, 20
Having disperst the nights unchearefull dampe,
Doe ye awake, and, with fresh lustyhed,
Go to the bowre of my belovèd love,
   My truest turtle dove:
Bid her awake; for Hymen is awake,
And long since ready forth his maske to move,
With his bright tead[1] that flames with many a flake,
And many a bachelor to waite on him,
   In theyr fresh garments trim.
Bid her awake therefore, and soone her dight,[2] 30
For lo! the wishèd day is come at last,
That shall, for al the paynes and sorrowes past,
Pay to her usury of long delight:
   And whylest she doth her dight,
Doe ye to her of joy and solace sing,
That all the woods may answer, and your eccho ring.

Bring with you all the nymphes that you can heare,
Both of the rivers and the forrests greene,
And of the sea that neighbours to her neare,
Al with gay girlands goodly wel beseene. 40
And let them also with them bring in hand
   Another gay girland,
For my fayre love, of lillyes and of roses,
Bound truelove wize with a blew silke riband.
And let them make great store of bridale poses,
And let them eeke bring store of other flowers,
   To deck the bridale bowers.
And let the ground whereas her foot shall tread,
For feare the stones her tender foot should wrong,
Be strewed with fragrant flowers all along, 50
And diapred lyke the discolored mead.

....

1. Torch.   2. Bedeck.

Which done, doe at her chamber dore awayt,
    For she will waken strayt;
The whiles doe ye this song unto her sing
The woods shall to you answer, and your eccho ring.

Ye nymphes of Mulla,[3] which with carefull heed
The silver scaly trouts doe tend full well,
And greedy pikes which use therein to feed,
(Those trouts and pikes all others doo excell)
And ye likewise which keepe the rushy lake,   60
    Where none doo fishes take,
Bynd up the locks the which hang scattered light,
And in his waters, which your mirror make,
Behold your faces as the christall bright,
That when you come whereas my love doth lie,
    No blemish she may spie.
And eke ye lightfoot mayds which keepe the dere
That on the hoary mountayne use to towre,
And the wylde wolves, which seeke them to devoure,
With your steele darts doo chace from comming neer,   70
    Be also present heere,
To helpe to decke her, and to help to sing,
That all the woods may answer, and your eccho ring.

Wake now, my love, awake! for it is time:
The rosy Morne long since left Tithones bed,
All ready to her silver coche to clyme,
And Phoebus gins to shew his glorious hed.
Hark how the cheerefull birds do chaunt theyr laies,
    And carroll of loves praise!
The merry larke hir mattins sings aloft,   80
The thrush replyes, the mavis[4] descant playes,
The ouzell[5] shrills, the ruddock[6] warbles soft,
So goodly all agree, with sweet consent,
    To this dayes merriment.
Ah! my deere love, why doe ye sleepe thus long,
When meeter were that ye should now awake,
T'awayt the comming of your joyous make,
And hearken to the birds love-learnèd song,
    The deawy leaves among?
For they of joy and pleasance to you sing,   90
That all the woods them answer, and theyr eccho ring.

....
3. A river.   4. Song thrush.   5. Blackbird.   6. Robin.

My love is now awake out of her dreame,
And her fayre eyes, like stars that dimmèd were
With darksome cloud, now shew theyr goodly beams
More bright then Hesperus his head doth rere.
Come now, ye damzels, daughters of delight,
   Helpe quickly her to dight.
But first come ye, fayre Houres, which were begot,
In Joves sweet paradice, of Day and Night,
Which doe the seasons of the year allot,   100
And al that ever in this world is fayre
   Do make and still repayre.
And ye three handmayds of the Cyprian Queene,
The which doe still adorne her beauties pride,
Helpe to addorne my beautifullest bride:
And as ye her array, still throw betweene
   Some graces to be seene:
And as ye use to Venus, to her sing,
The whiles the woods shal answer, and your eccho ring.

Now is my love all ready forth to come: 110
Let all the virgins therefore well awayt,
And ye fresh boyes, that tend upon her groome,
Prepare your selves, for he is comming strayt.
Set all your things in seemely good aray,
   Fit for so joyfull day,
The joyfulst day that ever sunne did see.
Faire Sun, shew forth thy favourable ray,
And let thy lifull heat not fervent be,
For feare of burning her sunshyny face,
   Her beauty to disgrace.   120
O fayrest Phoebus, father of the Muse,
If ever I did honour thee aright,
Or sing the thing that mote[7] thy mind delight,
Doe not thy servants simple boone refuse,
But let this day, let this one day be myne,
   Let all the rest be thine.
Then I thy soverayne prayses loud wil sing,
That all the woods shal answer, and theyr eccho ring.

Harke how the minstrels gin to shrill aloud
Their merry musick that resounds from far,   130
The pipe, the tabor, and the trembling croud,
That well agree withouten breach or jar,

---

7. Might.

But most of all the damzels doe delite,
   When they their tymbrels smyte,
And thereunto doe daunce and carrol sweet,
That all the sences they doe ravish quite,
The whyles the boyes run up and downe the street,
Crying aloud with strong confused noyce,
     As if it were one voyce.
"Hymen, Iö Hymen, Hymen," they do shout,   140
That even to the heavens theyr shouting shrill
Doth reach, and all the firmament doth fill;
To which the people, standing all about,
As in approvance doe thereto applaud,
   And loud advaunce her laud,
And evermore they "Hymen, Hymen" sing,
That al the woods them answer, and theyr eccho ring.

Loe! where she comes along with portly pace,
Lyke Phoebe, from her chamber of the east,
Arysing forth to run her mighty race,   150
Clad all in white, that seemes a virgin best.
So well it her beseemes, that ye would weene
   Some angell she had beene.
Her long loose yellow locks lyke golden wyre,
Sprinckled with perle, and perling flowres atweene,
Doe lyke a golden mantle her attyre,
And being crownèd with a girland greene,
   Seeme lyke some mayden queene.
Her modest eyes, abashèd to behold
So many gazers as on her do stare,   160
Upon the lowly ground affixèd are;
Ne dare lift up her countenance too bold,
But blush to heare her prayses sung so loud,
   So farre from being proud.
Nathlesse doe ye still loud her prayses sing,
That all the woods may answer, and your eccho ring.

Tell me, ye merchants daughters, did ye see
So fayre a creature in your towne before,
So sweet, so lovely, and so mild as she,
Adornd with beautyes grace and vertues store?   170
Her goodly eyes lyke saphyres shining bright,
   Her forehead yvory white,
Her cheekes lyke apples which the sun hath rudded,
Her lips lyke cherryes charming men to byte,

Her brest like to a bowle of creame uncrudded,
    Her paps lyke lyllies budded,
Her snowie necke lyke to a marble towre,
And all her body like a pallace fayre,
Ascending uppe, with many a stately stayre,
To honors seat and chastities sweet bowre.   180
Why stand ye still, ye virgins, in amaze,
    Upon her so to gaze,
Whiles ye forget your former lay to sing,
To which the woods did answer, and your eccho ring.

But if ye saw that which no eyes can see,
The inward beauty of her lively spright,
Garnisht with heavenly guifts of high degree,
Much more then would ye wonder at that sight,
And stand astonisht lyke to those which red
    Medusaes mazeful hed.   190
There dwels sweet Love and constant Chastity,
Unspotted Fayth, and comely Womanhood,
Regard of Honour, and mild Modesty;
There Vertue raynes as queene in royal throne,
    And giveth lawes alone,
The which the base affections doe obay,
And yeeld theyr services unto her will;
Ne thought of thing uncomely ever may
Thereto approch to tempt her mind to ill.
Had ye once seene these her celestial threasures,   200
    And unrevealèd pleasures,
Then would ye wondr, and her prayses sing,
That al the woods should answer, and your eccho ring.

Open the temple gates unto my love,
Open them wide that she may enter in,
And all the postes adorne as doth behove,
And all the pillours deck with girlands trim,
For to receyve this saynt with honour dew,
    That commeth in to you.
With trembling steps and humble reverence,   210
She commeth in before th' Almighties view:
Of her, ye virgins, learne obedience,
When so ye come into those holy places,
    To humble your proud faces.
Bring her up to th' high altar, that she may
The sacred ceremonies there partake,
The which do endlesse matrimony make;

And let the roring organs loudly play
The praises of the Lord in lively notes,
   The whiles with hollow throates 220
The choristers the joyous antheme sing,
That al the woods may answere, and their eccho ring.

Behold, whiles she before the altar stands,
Hearing the holy priest that to her speakes,
And blesseth her with his two happy hands,
How the red roses flush up in her cheekes,
And the pure snow with goodly vermill stayne,
   Like crimsin dyde in grayne:
That even th' angels, which continually
About the sacred altare doe remaine, 230
Forget their service and about her fly,
Ofte peeping in her face that seemes more fayre,
The more they on it stare.
But her sad eyes still fastened on the ground,
Are governed with goodly modesty,
That suffers not one looke to glaunce awry,
Which may let in a little thought unsownd.
Why blush ye love to give to me your hand,
The pledge of all our band?
Sing, ye sweet Angels, Alleluya sing, 240
That all the woods may answere and your eccho ring.

Now al is done; bring home the bride againe,
Bring home the triumph of our victory,
Bring home with you the glory of her gaine,
With joyance bring her and with jollity.
Never had man more joyfull day then this,
Whom heaven would heape with blis.
Make feast therefore now all this live long day,
This day for ever to me holy is,
Poure out the wine without restraint or stay, 25
Poure not by cups, but by the belly full,
Poure out to all that wull,
And sprinkle all the postes and wals with wine,
That they may sweat, and drunken be withall.
Crowne ye God Bacchus with a coronall,
And Hymen also crowne with wreathes of vine,
And let the Graces daunce unto the rest;
For they can doo it best:
The whiles the maydens doe theyr carroll sing,
To which the woods shal answer and theyr eccho ring. 26

Ring ye the bels ye yong men of the towne,
And leave your wonted labors for this day:
This day is holy; doe ye write it downe,
That ye for ever it remember may.
This day the sunne is in his chiefest hight,
With Barnaby[8] the bright,
From whence declining daily by degrees,
He somewhat loseth of his heat and light,
When once the Crab behind his back he sees.
But for this time it ill ordained was,   270
To chose the longest day in all the yeare,
And shortest night, when longest fitter weare:
Yet never day so long, but late would passe.
Ring ye the bels, to make it weare away,
And bonefiers make all day,
And daunce about them, and about them sing:
That all the woods may answer, and your eccho ring.

Ah when will this long weary day have end,
And lende me leave to come unto my love?
How slowly do the houres theyr numbers spend?   280
How slowly does sad Time his feathers move?
Hast thee O fayrest Planet to thy home
Within the Westerne fome:
Thy tyred steedes long since have need of rest.
Long though it be, at last I see it gloome,
And the bright evening star with golden creast
Appeare out of the East.
Fayre childe of beauty, glorious lampe of love
That all the host of heaven in rankes doost lead,
And guydest lovers through the nightes dread,   290
How chearefully thou lookest from above,
And seemst to laugh atweene thy twinkling light
As joying in the sight
Of these glad many which for joy doe sing,
That all the woods them answer and their eccho ring.

Now ceasse ye damsels your delights forepast;
Enough is it, that all the day was youres:
Now day is doen, and night is nighing fast:
Now bring the Bryde into the brydall boures.
Now night is come, now soone her disaray,   300
And in her bed her lay;

....
3. June 11, St. Barnabas' day.

Lay her in lillies and in violets,
And silken courteins over her display,
And odourd sheetes, and Arras coverlets.
Behold how goodly my faire love does ly
In proud humility;
Like unto Maia,[9] when as Jove her tooke,
In Tempe, lying on the flowry gras,
Twixt sleepe and wake, after she weary was,
With bathing in the Acidalian brooke.   310
Now it is night, ye damsels may be gon,
And leave my love alone,
And leave likewise your former lay to sing:
The woods no more shal answere, nor your eccho ring.

Now welcome night, thou night so long expected,
That long daies labour doest at last defray,
And all my cares, which cruell love collected,
Hast sumd in one, and cancelled for aye:
Spread thy broad wing over my love and me,
That no man may us see,   320
And in thy sable mantle us enwrap,
From feare of perrill and foule horror free.
Let no false treason seeke us to entrap,
Nor any dread disquiet once annoy
The safety of our joy:
But let the night be calme and quietsome,
Without tempestuous storms or sad afray:
Lyke as when Jove with fayre Alcmena lay,
When he begot the great Tirynthian groome:
Or lyke as when he with thy selfe did lie,   330
And begot Majesty.
And let the mayds and yongmen cease to sing:
Ne let the woods them answer, nor theyr eccho ring.

Let no lamenting cryes, nor dolefull teares,
Be heard all night within nor yet without:
Ne let false whispers, breeding hidden feares,
Breake gentle sleepe with misconceived dout.
Let no deluding dreames, nor dreadful sights
Make sudden sad affrights;
Ne let housefyres, nor lightnings helpelesse harmes,   340
Ne let the Pouke,[10] nor other evill sprights,
Ne let mischivous witches with theyr charmes,

---

9. One of the Pleiades, or seven daughters of Atlas, who formed a con
stellation.   10. In Irish folklore the Pooka, a malicious phantom.

Ne let hob Goblins, names whose sence we see not,
Fray us with things that be not.
Let not the shriech Oule, nor the Storke be heard:
Nor the night Raven that still deadly yels,
Nor damned ghosts cald up with mighty spels,
Nor griesly vultures make us once affeard:
Ne let th'unpleasant Quyre of Frogs still croking
Make us to wish theyr choking.   350
Let none of these theyr drery accents sing;
Ne let the woods them answer, nor theyr eccho ring.

But let stil Silence trew night watches keepe,
That sacred peace may in assurance rayne,
And tymely sleep, when it is tyme to sleepe,
May poure his limbs forth on your pleasant playne,
The whiles an hundred little winged loves,
Like divers fethered doves,
Shall fly and flutter round about your bed,
And in the secret darke, that none reproves,   360
Their prety stealthes shal worke, and snares shal spread
To filch away sweet snatches of delight,
Conceald through covert night.
Ye sonnes of Venus, play your sports at will,
For greedy pleasure, carelesse of your toyes,
Thinks more upon her paradise of joyes,
Then what ye do, albe it good or ill.
All night therefore attend your merry play,
For it will soone be day:
Now none doth hinder you, that say or sing,   370
Ne will the woods now answer, nor your Eccho ring.

Who is the same, which at my window peepes?
Or whose is that faire face, that shines so bright,
Is it not Cinthia, she that never sleepes,
But walkes about high heaven al the night?
A fayrest goddesse, do thou not envy
My love with me to spy:
For thou likewise didst love, though now unthought,
And for a fleece of woll, which privily,
The Latmian[11] shepherd once unto thee brought,   380
His pleasures with thee wrought.
Therefore to us be favorable now;
And sith of wemens labours thou hast charge,

....

11. Endymion, a lovely shepherd boy from Mount Latmos, with whom the
moon goddess, Cinthia, fell in love as he slept.

And generation goodly dost enlarge,
Encline thy will t'effect our wishfull vow,
And the chast wombe informe with timely seed,
    That may our comfort breed:
Till which we cease our hopefull hap to sing,
Ne let the woods us answere, nor our eccho ring.

And thou, great Juno, which with awful might   390
The lawes of wedlock still dost patronize,
And the religion of the faith first plight
With sacred rites hast taught to solemnize,
And eeke for comfort often callèd art
    Of women in their smart,
Eternally bind thou this lovely band,
And all thy blessings unto us in part.
And thou, glad Genius, in whose gentle hand
The bridale bowre and geniall bed remaine,
    Without blemish or staine,   400
And the sweet pleasures of theyr loves delight
With secret ayde doest succour and supply,
Till they bring forth the fruitfull progeny,
Send us the timely fruit of this same night.
And thou, fayre Hebe, and thou, Hymen free,
    Grant that it may so be.
Til which we cease your further prayse to sing,
Ne any woods shal answer, nor your eccho ring.

And ye high heavens, the temple of the gods,
In which a thousand torches flaming bright   410
Doe burne, that to us wretched earthly clods
In dreadful darknesse lend desirèd light,
And all ye powers which in the same remayne,
    More then we men can fayne,
Poure out your blessing on us plentiously,
And happy influence upon us raine,
That we may raise a large posterity,
Which from the earth, which they may long possesse
    With lasting happinesse,
Up to your haughty pallaces may mount,   420
And for the guerdon of theyr glorious merit,
May heavenly tabernacles there inherit,
Of blessed saints for to increase the count.
So let us rest, sweet love, in hope of this,
And cease till then our tymely joyes to sing:
The woods no more us answer, nor our eccho ring.

Song, made in lieu of many ornaments
With which my love should duly have bene dect,
Which cutting off through hasty accidents,
Ye would not stay your dew time to expect,   430
   But promist both to recompens,
Be unto her a goodly ornament,
And for short time an endlesse moniment.

1. See *A Spenser Handbook,* Chapter 27, or some similar reference work, and then characterize briefly Spenser's poem in relation to the marriage hymn genre.

2. This poem, as a marriage hymn, can be thought of as ritualistic because it celebrates the institution of marriage. In what way is Nature, as it were, made to seem to be sponsoring the institution? (Are there any other kinds of literature which you can think of that can be interpreted as serving a ritualistic purpose?)

3. The introduction of classical and English mythological figures would seem, at first thought, to give the substance of the poem an air of unreality. What other elements in the poem serve to offset this effect?

4. Examine the poem up to line 315 in terms of all the imagery which may be related to daylight, and from line 315 to the end in terms of the imagery which may be related to night. Do these instances, which seem to be examples of "copie," appear to be repetitious, or do they genuinely elaborate the subject matter of the poem?

5. At what point is there a significant alteration in the refrain?

6. Does each of the stanzas of "Epithalamion" have a unity of effect of its own? If, in addition, the poem as a whole has unity of effect, what factors contribute to it?

Sir Philip Sidney

(1554–1586)

....

Born at penshurst, which was celebrated in a number of Renaissance poems, Sir Philip Sidney was educated at Shrewsbury School, at Oxford, and, briefly, at Cambridge. To his own time he was known as a model courtier, soldier, scholar, and diplomat. Though little of his work was published during his lifetime, Sidney, together with his sister, the Countess of Pembroke, was an important influence in literature. His prose romance *Arcadia,* which contains a great deal of interspersed poetry, was a part of the experiments in self-conscious prose and poetry that were going on in the Elizabethan world. Sidney was also the author of a famous critical work, *Defense of Poesy,* in reply to a Puritanical attack on poetry and drama by Stephen Gosson, *The School of Abuse.* Sidney's sonnet sequence, *Astrophel and Stella,* published in 1591, apparently influenced other sonnet sequences written during the 1590's. Sidney was killed in a minor engagement before the city of Zutpen in Holland during the war between Catholic Spain and the Protestant Netherlands.

Suggested Readings

L. C. JOHN, *The Elizabethan Sonnet Sequences.* New York: Columbia University Press, 1938.

L. E. PEARSON, *Elizabethan Love Conventions.* Berkeley: University of California Press, 1938.

K. O. MYRICK, *Sir Philip Sidney as a Literary Craftsman.* Cambridge: Harvard University Press, 1935.

■■■■■■■■■

From *Astrophel and Stella*[1]

1

Loving in truth, and fain in verse my love to show,
That she, dear she, might take some pleasure of my pain,
Pleasure might cause her read, reading might make her know,
Knowledge might pity win, and pity grace obtain,—
I sought fit words to paint the blackest face of woe;
Studying inventions fine, her wits to entertain,
Oft turning others' leaves to see if thence would flow
Some fresh and fruitful showers upon my sunburnt brain.
But words came halting forth, wanting invention's stay;
Invention, Nature's child, fled step-dame Study's blows,
And others' feet still seemed but strangers in my way.
Thus, great with child to speak, and helpless in my throes,
    Biting my truant pen, beating myself for spite,
        "Fool," said my muse to me, "look in thy heart and write!"

■   1. What metrical pattern is employed?
    2. What is the rhyme scheme?

....

1. For a discussion of sonnet sequences, see the introductory comments on Shakespeare's sonnets, pp. 28–30.

3. Would a neater, more taut form of expression improve the poem or worsen it?

39

Come sleep! O sleep, the certain knot of peace,
The baiting place of wit, the balm of woe,
The poor man's wealth, the prisoner's release,
Th' indifferent judge between the high and low;
With shield of proof shield me from out the prease[1]
Of those fierce darts despair at me doth throw;
O make in me those civil wars to cease;
I will good tribute pay, if thou do so.
Take thou of me smooth pillows, sweetest bed,
A chamber deaf to noise and blind to light,
A rosy garland and a weary head;
And if these things, as being thine by right,
   Move not thy heavy grace, thou shalt in me,
   Livelier than elsewhere, Stella's image see.

1. Indicate the rhyme scheme.
2. Can the concluding couplet be said to be epigrammatic?

16

Having this day my horse, my hand, my lance
Guided so well that I obtained the prize,
Both by the judgment of the English eyes
And of some sent from that sweet enemy, France;
Horsemen my skill in horsemanship advance,
Town-folks my strength; a daintier judge applies
His praise to sleight which from good use doth rise;
Some lucky wits impute it but to chance;
Others, because of both sides I do take
My blood from them who did excel in this,
Think nature me a man of arms did make.
How far they shot awry! The true cause is,
   Stella looked on, and from her heav'nly face
   Sent forth the beams which made so fair my race.

Paraphrase this poem; then comment on the quality of the conceit.

1. Press, crowd.

69

O joy too high for my low style to show!
O bliss fit for a nobler state than me!
Envy, put out thine eyes, lest thou do see
What oceans of delight in me do flow!
My friend, that oft saw through all masks my woe,
Come, come, and let me pour myself on thee.
Gone is the winter of my misery!
My spring appears, O, see what here doth grow:
For Stella hath, with words where faith doth shine,
Of her high heart giv'n me the monarchy;
I, I, oh I, may say that she is mine!
And though she give but thus conditionly
    This realm of bliss, while virtuous course I take,
    No kings be crown'd but they some covenants make.

■ Is there a development in the thought of this sonnet which justifies the shift in tone?

First Song

Doubt you to whom my Muse these notes intendeth,
Which now my breast o'ercharged to music lendeth?
    To you, to you, all song of praise is due,
Only in you my song begins and endeth.

Who hath the eyes which marry state with pleasure?
Who keeps the key of Nature's chiefest treasure?
    To you, to you, all song of praise is due,
Only for you the heaven forgat all measure.

Who hath the lips where wit in fairness reigneth?
Who womankind at once both decks and staineth?
    To you, to you, all song of praise is due,
Only by you Cupid his crown maintaineth.

Who hath the feet whose step of sweetness planteth?
Who else, for whom Fame worthy trumpets wanteth?
    To you, to you, all song of praise is due,
Only to you her scepter Venus granteth.

Who hath the breast whose milk doth passions nourish?
Whose grace is such that when it chides doth cherish?

To you, to you, all song of praise is due,
Only through you the tree of life doth flourish.

Who hath the hand which without stroke subdueth?
Who long-dead beauty with increase reneweth?
   To you, to you, all song of praise is due,
Only at you all envy hopeless rueth.

Who hath the hair which loosest fastest tieth?
Who makes a man live then glad when he dieth?
   To you, to you all song of praise is due,
Only of you the flatterer never lieth.

Who hath the voice which soul from senses sunders?
Whose force but yours the bolts of beauty thunders?
   To you, to you, all song of praise is due,
Only with you not miracles are wonders.

Doubt you to whom my Muse these notes intendeth,
Which now my breast o'ercharged to music lendeth?
   To you, to you, all song of praise is due,
Only in you my song begins and endeth.

■ 1. In the sequence *Astrophel and Stella* there are also songs and madrigals. The madrigal is in part also a development from the Italian. Its pattern suggests how close the Elizabethan poet felt himself to the spontaneity of actual songs. Usually the rhyme endings are preponderantly feminine, and there is a frequent use of refrains. More formally defined, the madrigal is a polyphonic lyric. With it there was no instrumental accompaniment. The fact that these songs would be set to music gave the poet a sense of structure to be respected.

2. Explain the rhyme scheme of this poem.

3. What is the basic rhythm? Does it harm the spontaneous quality of the song?

Ring Out Your Bells

Ring out your bells, let mourning shows be spread;
     For Love is dead:
  All Love is dead, infected
With plague of deep disdain:
  Worth, as naught worth, rejected,
And Faith fair scorn doth gain.
   From so ungrateful fancy,

From such a female franzy,
From them that use men thus,
Good Lord, deliver us!

Weep, neighbors, weep; do you not hear it said
  That Love is dead?
  His death-bed, peacock's folly,
His winding-sheet is shame,
  His will, false-seeming holy,
His sole exec'tor, blame.
  From so ungrateful fancy, etc.

Let dirge be sung, and trentals rightly read,
  For Love is dead;
  Sir Wrong his tomb ordaineth:
My mistress' marble heart
  Which epitaph containeth,
"Her eyes were once his dart."
  From so ungrateful fancy, etc.

Alas, I lie: rage hath this error bred;
  Love is not dead;
  Love is not dead, but sleepeth
In her unmatched mind,
  Where she his counsel keepeth,
Till due deserts she find.
  Therefore from so vile fancy,
  To call such wit a franzy,
  Who Love can temper thus,
  Good Lord, deliver us!

■ What is the effect on the tone of the use of the ritualistic refrain?
What is the effect of its variation in the final stanza?

William Shakespeare

(1564–1616)

■■■■■■■■■■

SHAKESPEARE was baptized at the Church of Holy Trinity of Stratford-on-Avon on April 26, 1564. He was the son of John Shakespeare, a well-to-do tradesman, and Mary Arden, daughter of a prosperous farmer. It is assumed he attended the grammar school in Stratford. Ben Jonson was to speak of Shakespeare's "small Latin and less Greek," but Shakespearean scholars now are usually of the opinion that in twentieth-century terms Shakespeare knew a good deal of Latin. Stratford was visited by dramatic companies; Coventry, famous for its pageants, was not far away; and Kenilworth Castle, sixteen miles away, witnessed magnificent spectacles in 1575 in honor of Queen Elizabeth.

In 1582 Shakespeare married Anne Hathaway, his senior by eight years. There has been considerable speculation about the success of their marriage, none of it based on actual evidence. Their daughter Susanna was born in May, 1583. It is conjectured that after the birth of Hamnet and Judith, twins, in 1585, Shakespeare went to London. There is also a tradition that he was a schoolmaster for a short period. Those who promote the belief that he taught school point to the Latin influences in *The Comedy of Errors, Titus Andronicus,* and the long Ovidian poem, *Venus and Adonis.* An attack by Robert Green suggests that Shakespeare was a playwright by 1592. Most references to Shakespeare indicate that he was well liked. Financially he was very successful, and he was able in 1597 to buy New Place, the second largest house in Stratford, to which he retired about 1611.

Suggested Readings

E. E. KELLETT, "Some Notes on a Feature of Shakespeare's Style," in *Suggestions: Literary Essays.* Cambridge: Cambridge University Press, 1923, pp. 57–78.

G. H. W. RYLANDS, *Words and Poetry.* New York: Harcourt, Brace, 1928.

L. C. KNIGHTS, "Shakespeare's Sonnets," *Explorations.* New York: George W. Stewart, Publisher, Inc., 1947, pp. 55–81.

■■■■■■■■■■

It is impossible to make Shakespeare share a book with other poets and still give him adequate representation. Even the reasons for this fact constitute a formidable subject. But they are, at the same time, so obvious and familiar that they can be mentioned without the need of further comment. Surely the most obvious of the reasons is that his greatest achievement lies in his many dramatic masterpieces. If we separated the poet from the dramatist, especially when space is limited, we could get only a glimpse of one isolated facet of his work. Short passages excerpted from the plays may show successfully some features of his style, but they can never satisfactorily represent Shakespeare's achievement. Other reasons, besides the bulk and form of Shakespeare's work, are his unique reputation and the vast amount of Shakespearean scholarship and criticism that exist.

But Shakespeare was also a writer of nondramatic poems, and in that respect he may more readily be viewed as related to the course of English poetry. In addition to the songs in the plays, which can be considered out of their contexts, there are also the independent poems. Those which are definitely of Shakespearean authorship were written early in his career. They are the narrative poems *Venus and Adonis* and *The Rape of Lucrece,* and the sequence of 154 sonnets. Of a later period, and probably but not certainly Shakespeare's, is the 67-line poem "The Phoenix and the Turtle," which is terse and cryptic in style, difficult in thought, and not unworthy of Shakespeare.

It is, of course, Shakespeare's sonnets which are the best known, and the fairest example, of his nondramatic work, and which may conveniently be considered apart from the reputation of the plays. In writing a sonnet sequence, Shakespeare was following a fashion of numerous other poets (including Sidney and Spenser) of the late sixteenth and early seventeenth centuries. All of Shakespeare's sonnets are in the form to which he has given his name and which was first used by Wyatt and Surrey. Shakespeare, no less than the other sonneteers, made use of the Petrarchan conventions. Some of these are the faithful but unrequited lover who, in exaggerated terms, praises the lady's beauty and character and laments his own unworthiness; the lover's suffering is described as a paradoxical freezing and burning, as a storm-tossed ship; flowers, precious stones, the sun and stars are all used for comparisons in describing the lady's beauty; the lover calls for the comfort of sleep, speaks of his dreams, humbly insists on the inadequacy of his verses, and also claims that his verses will immortalize the lady's fame and beauty. Reversals and parodies of these conventions had also become conventional.

Despite the fact that many of Shakespeare's sonnets appear to be routine exercises, using strained conceits and adding nothing to the established conventions, they are in some respects quite different from the usual sequences. For one thing, they are not a clear and predetermined sequence. Written in the early and middle years of the 1590's, they were, without Shakespeare's permission or cooperation, arranged by Thomas Thorpe, who published them in 1609. While his arrangement seems adequate for the most part, it is also obvious that he was including some which probably belonged to no series at all. Related to the peculiar nature of the sequence is the fact that the sonnets are addressed to at least two people, a male friend and a "dark lady." Insofar as the sonnets present a story and reflect an actual experience, only this much is clear: Shakespeare was betrayed by both the friend and the lady when they entered into a relationship with each other (see Sonnet 144). The impression given by the sonnets, even those which are clearly in a proper sequence, is that they were not composed according to any plan, but were in many cases written as occasion arose and refer to actual experiences and personal circumstances. Some of the sonnets are less in the nature of addresses intended for a particular person than they are self-expressions of the author directed to no specific reader.

Shakespeare's great distinction lies in those sonnets where he transcends the conventions with which he worked. This he does repeatedly by giving to the traditional themes of beauty, love, and the ravagings of time a melodic eloquence, by using a diction which enriches and refreshes the stock images and conceits, and by making the form seem to yield inevitably the tones of a variety of genuine feelings. (For an analysis of one of Shakespeare's sonnets, see pp. 28-30 in the Introduction.)

Much of the scholarly attention given to Shakespeare's sonnets are centered on the problematic identity of the man to whom most of them are addressed. A clue to this question seems to have been provided by the quaint dedication which Thorpe placed in the 1609 edition: "To the onlie begetter of these insuing sonnets Mr. W. H. all happinesse and that eternity promised by our ever living poet wisheth the well-wishing adventurer in setting forth. T. T." Through several generations of tedious research and contention scholars have been divided as to who was meant by "Mr. W. H.," some favoring William Herbert, Earl of Pembroke, and others Henry Wriothesley (pronounced Rosely), Earl of Southhampton. But the evidence for each case is so slim as to leave open the speculation that it was neither Pembroke nor Southampton. Actually, the mystery is important only because it remains unsolved, and its solution could add nothing to our appreciation and understanding of the artistic failures and successes in Shakespeare's sonnets.

15

When I consider every thing that grows
Holds in perfection but a little moment,
That this huge stage presenteth nought but shows
Whereon the stars in secret influence comment;
When I perceive that men as plants increase,
Cheered and checked even by the self-same sky,

Vaunt in their youthful sap, at height decrease,
And wear their brave state out of memory;
Then the conceit of this inconstant stay
Sets you most rich in youth before my sight,
Where wasteful Time debateth with Decay,
To change your day of youth to sullied night;
    And all in war with Time for love of you,
    As he takes from you, I engraft you new.

■ Are the quatrains repetitious or do they mark a steady development?

18

Shall I compare thee to a summer's day?
Thou art more lovely and more temperate.
Rough winds do shake the darling buds of May,
And summer's lease hath all too short a date.
Sometime too hot the eye of heaven shines,
And often is his gold complexion dimm'd;
And every fair from fair sometime declines,
By chance or nature's changing course untrimm'd;
But thy eternal summer shall not fade
Nor lose possession of that fair thou ow'st;
Nor shall Death brag thou wand'rest in his shade
When in eternal lines to time thou grow'st.
    So long as men can breathe or eyes can see,
    So long lives this, and this gives life to thee.

■ Notice the number of words which are repeated in this sonnet. Are any significant effects produced by the repetitions?

26

Lord of my love, to whom in vassalage
Thy merit hath my duty strongly knit,
To thee I send this written embassage,
To witness duty, not to show my wit:
Duty so great, which wit so poor as mine
May make seem bare, in wanting words to show it,
But that I hope some good conceit of thine
In thy soul's thought, all naked, will bestow it;

Till whatsoever star that guides my moving,
Points on me graciously with fair aspect,
And puts apparel on my tatter'd loving,
To show me worthy of thy sweet respect:
Then may I dare to boast how I do love thee;
Till then not show my head where thou mayst prove me.

1. The humility of the speaker and the praise of the person addressed are conventional. What, if anything, is achieved beyond a use of the convention?

2. Comment on effects of sound and rhythm; relate them, if possible, to the preceding question.

27

Weary with toil, I haste me to my bed,
The dear repose for limbs with travel tired;
But then begins a journey in my head
To work my mind, when body's work's expired:
For then my thoughts, from far where I abide,
Intend a zealous pilgrimage to thee,
And keep my drooping eyelids open wide,
Looking on darkness which the blind do see:
Save that my soul's imaginary sight
Presents thy shadow to my sightless view,
Which, like a jewel hung in ghastly night,
Makes black night beauteous and her old face new.
Lo! thus, by day my limbs, by night my mind,
For thee and for myself no quiet find.

29

When in disgrace with fortune and men's eyes
I all alone beweep my outcast state,
And trouble deaf heaven with my bootless cries,
And look upon myself and curse my fate,
Wishing me like to one more rich in hope,
Featured like him, like him with friends possessed,
Desiring this man's art, and that man's scope,
With what I most enjoy contented least;
Yet in these thoughts myself almost despising,
Haply I think on thee—and then my state,
Like to the lark at break of day arising

From sullen earth, sings hymns at heaven's gate;
For thy sweet love remembered, such wealth brings
That then I scorn to change my state with kings.

■ The language in this sonnet is relatively abstract. What is the effect
of this on the passage about the lark?

30

When to the sessions of sweet silent thought
I summon up remembrance of things past,
I sigh the lack of many a thing I sought,
And with old woes new wail my dear time's waste.
Then can I drown an eye, unused to flow,
For precious friends hid in death's dateless night,
And weep afresh love's long-since cancelled woe,
And moan the expense of many a vanished sight.
Then can I grieve at grievances foregone,
And heavily from woe to woe tell o'er
The sad account of fore-bemoaned moan,
Which I new pay as if not paid before.
    But if the while I think on thee, dear friend,
    All losses are restored, and sorrows end.

■ Consult the analysis on pp. 28–30, and then analyze this sonnet for
effects of rhythm and sound.

51

Thus can my love excuse the slow offense
Of my dull bearer when from thee I speed:
From where thou art why should I haste me thence?
Till I return, of posting is no need.
O, what excuse will my poor beast then find,
When swift extremity can seem but slow?
Then should I spur, though mounted on the wind,
In winged speed no motion shall I know:
Then can no horse with my desire keep pace;
Therefore desire, of perfect'st love being made,
Shall neigh—no dull flesh—in his fiery race;
But love, for love, thus shall excuse my jade;
    Since from thee going he went willful-slow,
    Toward thee I'll run and give him leave to go.

Discuss the effectiveness of the couplet in this and in the preceding sonnets.

64

When I have seen by Time's fell hand defaced
The rich proud cost of outworn buried age;
When sometime lofty towers I see down-razed,
And brass eternal slave to mortal rage;
When I have seen the hungry ocean gain
Advantage on the kingdom of the shore,
And the firm soil win of the watery main,
Increasing store with loss, and loss with store;
When I have seen such interchange of state,
Or state itself confounded to decay;
Ruin hath taught me thus to ruminate—
That Time will come and take my love away.
    This thought is as a death, which cannot choose
    But weep to have that which it fears to lose.

1. Is there anything unusual about the use of the words *eternal* and *mortal* in line 4? Explain fully the meanings of these words in the context.

2. Consider Sonnets 64 and 65 in sequence (see p. 28). Do the sonnets gain anything by being considered together? What irony does the word "boundless" in Sonnet 65 derive from the preceding sonnet?

73

That time of year thou may'st in me behold
When yellow leaves, or none, or few, do hang
Upon those boughs which shake against the cold,
Bare ruined choirs, where late the sweet birds sang.
In me thou seest the twilight of such day
As after sunset fadeth in the west,
Which by and by black night doth take away,
Death's second self, that seals up all in rest:
In me thou seest the glowing of such fire
That on the ashes of his youth doth lie,
As the death-bed whereon it must expire,
Consumed with that which it was nourished by.
    This thou perceiv'st, which makes thy love more strong,
    To love that well which thou must leave ere long.

■ Write a detailed analysis of the meaning of this poem. Try to give each phrase its full weight of meaning.

87

Farewell! thou art too dear for my possessing,
And like enough thou know'st thy estimate:
The charter of thy worth gives thee releasing;
My bonds in thee are all determinate.
For how do I hold thee but by thy granting?
And for that riches where is my deserving?
The cause of this fair gift in me is wanting,
And so my patent back again is swerving.
Thyself thou gav'st, thy own worth then not knowing,
Or me, to whom thou gav'st it, else mistaking;
So thy great gift, upon misprision growing,
Comes home again, on better judgment making.
    Thus have I had thee, as a dream doth flatter,
    In sleep, a king; but waking, no such matter.

■ Discuss the rhymes in this sonnet in their relationship to the tone.

97

How like a winter hath my absence been
From thee, the pleasure of the fleeting year!
What freezings have I felt, what dark days seen!
What old December's bareness every where!
And yet this time removed was summer's time;
The teeming autumn, big with rich increase,
Bearing the wanton burthen of the prime,
Like widowed wombs after their lords' decease:
Yet this abundant issue seem'd to me
But hope of orphans and unfather'd fruit;
For summer and his pleasures wait on thee,
And, thou away, the very birds are mute;
    Or, if they sing, 'tis with so dull a cheer
    That leaves look pale, dreading the winter's near.

106

When in the chronicle of wasted time
I see descriptions of the fairest wights,
And beauty making beautiful old rime,

In praise of ladies dead and lovely knights;
Then, in the blazon of sweet beauty's best,
Of hand, of foot, of lip, of eye, of brow,
I see their antique pen would have express'd
Even such a beauty as you master now.
So all their praises are but prophecies
Of this our time, all you prefiguring;
And, for they look'd but with divining eyes,
They had not skill enough your worth to sing:
 For we, which now behold these present days,
 Have eyes to wonder, but lack tongues to praise.

129

The expense of spirit in a waste of shame
Is lust in action; and till action, lust
Is perjured, murderous, bloody, full of blame,
Savage, extreme, rude, cruel, not to trust;
Enjoyed no sooner but despisèd straight;
Past reason hunted; and no sooner had,
Past reason hated, as a swallowed bait
On purpose laid to make the taker mad:
Mad in pursuit, and in possession so;
Had, having, and in quest to have, extreme;
A bliss in proof, and proved, a very woe;
Before, a joy proposed; behind, a dream.
 All this the world well knows; yet none knows well
 To shun the heaven that leads men to this hell.

■ 1. Discuss the justaposition of the terse, contrasting phrases. What
is the effect on the tone?
 2. Is the first line open to more than one interpretation?

From *Richard II*

Richard II Banishes Bolingbroke

Draw near
And list what with our council we have done.
For that our kingdom's earth should not be soil'd
With that dear blood which it hath fostered;
And for our eyes do hate the dire aspect
Of civil wounds plough'd up with neighbours' sword;
And for we think the eagle-winged pride

Of sky-aspiring and ambitious thoughts,
With rival-hating envy, set on you
To wake our peace, which in our country's cradle
Draws the sweet infant breath of gentle sleep;
Which, so rous'd up with boist'rous untun'd drums,
With harsh resounding trumpets' dreadful bray,
And grating shock of wrathful iron arms,
Might from our quiet confines fright fair peace
And make us wade even in our kindred's blood;
Therefore we banish you our territories.

■   1. Discuss the connotations that hover about "dire aspect," "plough'd
up with neighbours' sword," "eagle-winged pride," and "untun'd drums."
    2. Does the phrase "set on you" mean (a) that the eagle, pride,
rests on Bolingbroke or (b) that pride and ambition cause him to want
to revolt, as though the phrase read "set you on"? Can both meanings be
accepted?

From *Romeo and Juliet*

Queen Mab

She is the fairies' midwife, and she comes
In shape no bigger than an agate-stone
On the fore-finger of an alderman,
Drawn with a team of little atomies
Over men's noses as they lie asleep;
Her wagon-spokes made of long spinners' legs.
The cover of the wings of grasshoppers,
Her traces of the smallest spider web,
Her collars of the moonshine's watery beams,
Her whip of cricket's bone, the lash of film,   10
Her waggoner a small grey-coated gnat,
Not half so big as a round little worm
Prick'd from the lazy finger of a maid;
Her chariot is an empty hazel-nut
Made by the joiner squirrel, or old grub,
Time out o' mind the fairies' coachmakers.
And in this state she gallops night by night
Through lovers' brains, and then they dream of love;
On courtiers' knees, that dream on curtsies straight;
O'er lawyers' fingers, who straight dream on fees;   20
O'er ladies' lips, who straight on kisses dream,
Which oft the angry Mab with blisters plagues,
Because their breath with sweetmeats tainted are.

Sometimes she gallops o'er a courtier's nose,
And then dreams he of smelling out a suit;
And sometime comes she with a tithe-pig's tail
Tickling a parson's nose as 'a lies asleep,
Then dreams he of another benefice.
Sometime she driveth o'er a soldier's neck,
And then dreams he of cutting foreign throats,   30
Of breaches, amubuscadoes, Spanish blades,
Of healths five fathom deep: and then anon
Drums in his ear, at which he starts and wakes,
And being thus frighted, swears a prayer or two
And sleeps again.

From *King Henry the Fifth*
Henry V to His Soldiers

Once more unto the breach, dear friends, once more;
Or close the wall up with our English dead!
In peace there's nothing so becomes a man
As modest stillness and humility:
But when the blast of war blows in our ears,
Then imitate the action of the tiger;
Stiffen the sinews, summon up the blood,
Disguise fair nature with hard-favored rage:
Then lend the eye a terrible aspect;
Let it pry through the portage of the head   10
Like the brass cannon; let the brow o'erwhelm it
As fearfully as doth a galled rock
O'erhang and jutty his confounded base,
Swilled with the wild and wasteful ocean.
Now set the teeth, and stretch the nostril wide;
Hold hard the breath, and bend up every spirit
To his full height!—On, on, you noble English,
Whose blood is fet[1] from fathers of war-proof!—
Fathers that, like so many Alexanders,
Have in these parts from morn till even fought,   20
And sheathed their swords for lack of argument.
Dishonor not your mothers; now attest
That those whom you called fathers did beget you!
Be copy now to men of grosser blood,
And teach them how to war!—And you, good yeomen,
Whose limbs were made in England, show us here

1. Inherited.

The mettle of your pasture; let us swear
That you are worth your breeding: which I doubt not;
For there is none of you so mean and base,
That hath not noble lustre in your eyes.   30
I see you stand like greyhounds in the slips,
Straining upon the start. The game's afoot:
Follow your spirit; and, upon this charge,
Cry "God for Harry, England, and Saint George!"

From *Twelfth Night*

If Music Be the Food of Love

If music be the food of love, play on;
Give me excess of it, that, surfeiting,
The appetite may sicken, and so die.
That strain again! it had a dying fall:
O, it came o'er my ear like the sweet sound,
That breathes upon a bank of violets,
Stealing and giving odor! Enough; no more:
'Tis not so sweet now as it was before.
O spirit of love, how quick and fresh art thou!
That, notwithstanding thy capacity
Receiveth as the sea, nought enters there,
Of what validity and pitch soe'er,
But falls into abatement and low price,
Even in a minute! so full of shapes is fancy,
That it alone is high fantastical.

From *Antony and Cleopatra*

Cleopatra's Barge

The barge she sat in, like a burnished throne,
Burned on the water: the poop was beaten gold;
Purple the sails, and so perfumed that
The winds were love-sick with them; the oars were silver,
Which to the tune of flutes kept stroke, and made
The water which they beat to follow faster,
As amorous of their strokes. For her own person,
It beggared all description: she did lie
In her pavilion—cloth-of-gold of tissue—
O'er-picturing that Venus where we see
The fancy outwork nature: on each side her

Stood pretty dimpled boys, like smiling Cupids,
With divers-colored fans, whose wind did seem
To glow the delicate cheeks which they did cool,
And what they undid did.

Shakespeare used North's translation of the life of Antony from Plutarch's *Lives* as his chief source in writing *Antony and Cleopatra*. The following passage from North is obviously the source of Shakespeare's famous lines: ". . . she disdained to set forward otherwise, but to take her barge into the river of Cydnus, the poop whereof was of gold, the sails of purple, and the oars of silver, which kept stroke in rowing after the sound of the music of flutes, hautboys, citherns, viols, and such other instruments as they played upon in the barge. And now for the person of herself: she was laid under a pavillion of cloth of gold of tissue, apparelled and attired like the goddess Venus commonly drawn in picture: and hard by her, on either hand of her, pretty fair boys apparelled as painters do set forth god Cupid, with little fans in their hands, with the which they fanned wind upon her." Comment on the elements that Shakespeare borrowed or ignored and also upon his additions.

From *Love's Labor's Lost*

Winter

When icicles hang by the wall
　　And Dick the shepherd blows his nail,
And Tom bears logs into the hall,
　　And milk comes frozen home in pail;
When blood is nipped, and ways be foul,
Then nightly sings the staring owl
"To-whit! Tu-whoo!" A merry note,
While greasy Joan doth keel the pot.

When all aloud the wind doth blow,
　　And coughing drowns the parson's saw,
And birds sit brooding in the snow,
　　And Marian's nose looks red and raw;
When roasted crabs hiss in the bowl—
Then nightly sings the staring owl
"To-whit! Tu-whoo!" A merry note,
While greasy Joan doth keel the pot.

1. Comment on the second to the last line in each of the stanzas.
2. Explain the following: "parson's saw," and "keel the pot."

3. Substitute "charming Joan" for "greasy Joan" and discuss the effect upon the tone of the poem.

From *Love's Labor's Lost*

Spring

When daisies pied and violets blue,
   And lady-smocks all silver-white,
And cuckoo-buds of yellow hue
    Do paint the meadows with delight,
The cuckoo then, on every tree,
Mocks married men, for thus sings he:
"Cuckoo! cuckoo!" O word of fear,
Unpleasing to a married ear.

When shepherds pipe on oaten straws,
   And merry larks are ploughmen's clocks,
When turtles tread, and rooks, and daws,
   And maidens bleach their summer smocks,
The cuckoo then, on every tree,
Mocks married men, for thus sings he:
"Cuckoo! cuckoo!" O word of fear,
Unpleasing to a married ear.

From *Twelfth Night*

O Mistress Mine

O Mistress mine, where are you roaming?
O, stay and hear—your true love's coming,
   That can sing both high and low.
Trip no further, pretty sweeting;
Journeys end in lovers' meeting,
   Every wise man's son doth know.

What is love? 'tis not hereafter;
Present mirth hath present laughter;
   What's to come is still unsure:
In delay there lies no plenty—
Then come kiss me, sweet-and-twenty,
   Youth's a stuff will not endure.

From *Cymbeline*

Fear No More

Fear no more the heat o' the sun
   Nor the furious winter's rages;
Thou thy worldly task hast done,
   Home art gone and ta'en thy wages:
Golden lads and girls all must,
As chimney-sweepers, come to dust.

Fear no more the frown o' the great,
   Thou art past the tyrant's stroke;
Care no more to clothe and eat;
   To thee the reed is as the oak:
The sceptre, learning, physic, must
All follow this, and come to dust.

Fear no more the lightning-flash
   Nor the all-dreaded thunder-stone;
Fear not slander, censure rash;
   Thou hast finished joy and moan:
All lovers young, all lovers must
Consign to thee, and come to dust.

No exorciser harm thee!
Nor no witchcraft charm thee!
Ghost unlaid forbear thee!
Nothing ill come near thee!
Quiet consummation have;
And renownèd be thy grave!

1. Which of these stanzas is quite different in tone from the other three? Characterize the nature of the tone in this and the other stanzas.
2. There is an obvious pun at the end of the first stanza. Does it seem appropriate or inappropriate? Justify your answer.

Sir Walter Ralegh

(1552–1618)

■■■■■■■■■

Born at hayes barton, of good Devonshire family, Ra-
legh was educated at Oxford and was later in residence at the Middle Temple. As a young man he fought in both France and Ireland. From 1582 to
1592, Ralegh was the favorite of Queen Elizabeth, who showered wealth,
titles, and honors upon him, but the Earl of Essex's rise to favor in 1589
somewhat threatened Ralegh's position at court, and Ralegh retired to Ireland, where he became a friend and patron of Edmund Spenser. Returning
to England, Ralegh brought with him the first three books of Spenser's *Faerie
Queene* and his own *Bookes of the Ocean's Love to Cynthia,* both of which
helped to restore him to Elizabeth's good graces. However, because he had a
love affair with Elizabeth Throckmorton, a maid of honor whom he afterwards married, he was confined in the Tower for a time. There Ralegh wrote
the eleventh *Book of the Ocean's Love to Cynthia,* the only part of the
work extant.

After Elizabeth's death in 1603, Ralegh was unjustly arrested, con-
victed, and sentenced to death on a treason charge. James reprieved him at
the last moment but kept him in prison for thirteen years. During this time
Ralegh studied much and wrote poems and his *History of the World.* In
1616, James sent Ralegh on an expedition to Guiana, at the same time betraying Ralegh's plans to the Spaniards. After the failure of this voyage, James
had Ralegh beheaded, ostensibly to pacify the Spanish government, using
the sentence of 1603 to effect Ralegh's removal in 1618.

Suggested Readings

E. K. Chambers, "The Disenchantment of the Elizabethans," *Sir Thomas
    Wyatt and Some Collected Studies.* London: Sidgwick & Jackson, Ltd.
    1933, pp. 181–201.
M. C. Bradbrook, *The School of Night, a Study in the Literary Relation-
    ships of Sir Walter Raleigh.* Cambridge: Cambridge University Press,
    1936.
Esther Dunn, "Raleigh and the 'New Poetry,'" in *The Literature of
    Shakespeare's England.* New York: Charles Scribner's Sons, 1936, pp.
    140–163.

■■■■■■■■■

The Lie

Go, soul, the body's guest,
Upon a thankless arrant.
Fear not to touch the best;
The truth shall be thy warrant.
 Go, since I needs must die,
 And give the world the lie.

Say to the court, it glows
And shines like rotten wood;
Say to the church, it shows
What's good, and doth no good: 10
 If church and court reply,
 Then give them both the lie.

Tell potentates, they live
Acting by others' action,
Not loved unless they give,
Not strong but by affection:
 If potentates reply,
 Give potentates the lie.

Tell men of high condition
That manage the estate,   20
Their purpose is ambition,
Their practice only hate:
 And if they once reply,
 Then give them all the lie.

Tell them that brave it most,
They beg for more by spending,
Who, in their greatest cost,
Like nothing but commending:
 And if they make reply,
 Then give them all the lie.   30

Tell zeal it wants devotion;
Tell love it is but lust;
Tell time it meets but motion;
Tell flesh it is but dust:
 And wish them not reply,
 For thou must give the lie.

Tell age it daily wasteth;
Tell honor how it alters;

Tell beauty how she blasteth;
Tell favor how it falters: 40
  And as they shall reply,
  Give every one the lie.

Tell wit how much it wrangles
In tickle points of niceness;
Tell wisdom she entangles
Herself in over-wiseness:
  And when they do reply,
  Straight give them both the lie.

Tell physic of her boldness;
Tell skill it is prevention;   50
Tell charity of coldness;
Tell law it is contention:
  And as they do reply,
  So give them still the lie.

Tell fortune of her blindness;
Tell nature of decay;
Tell friendship of unkindness;
Tell justice of delay:
  And if they will reply,
  Then give them all the lie.   60

Tell arts they have no soundness,
But vary by esteeming;
Tell schools they want profoundness,
And stand too much on seeming:
  If arts and schools reply,
  Give arts and schools the lie.

Tell faith it's fled the city;
Tell how the country erreth;
Tell, manhood shakes off pity,
Tell, virtue least preferreth: 7
  And if they do reply,
  Spare not to give the lie.

So when thou hast, as I
Commanded thee, done blabbing,
Because to give the lie
Deserves no less than stabbing,
  Stab at thee he that will—
  No stab thy soul can kill.

■   In "The Lie" Ralegh has generated an intensity of emotion by the central device of giving example after example of worldly and some-times cynical motives or actions. Almost all the examples are given in the same direct, forthright manner:

> Tell potentates, they live . . .
> Tell them that brave it most
> Tell wit how much it wrangles . . .
> Tell fortune of her blindness

and so on. The refrain also adds to the increasing intensity:

> If church and court reply
> Then give them both the lie
>
> And if they once reply,
> Then give them all the lie
>
> And when they do reply
> Straight give them both the lie.

Largely, it is the persistency of the rhythms rather than imagery or narra-tion or description that enables Ralegh to build up the kind of fury the poem holds. "The Lie" is vituperative, and the lines are delivered like verbal blows, but it is a controlled rather than explosive vituperation. The emotion is intense, but that it is under control is indicated by the way it is varied to suit the meaning. In the first and last stanzas the poet addresses his own soul. In the first we read

Go, soul,/ the bod/y's guest.

The spondee which slows the statement down is appropriate to the rever-ence and respect with which the poet addresses his soul. The pattern of the line contrasts with the persistent trip-hammer blows in the stanzas that follow it.

In the final stanza Ralegh turns, as it were, to speak more directly to his soul. We might expect the same reverence that we saw in the first stanza, but it is not actually present. The accumulated intensity is pres-ent, but with it a kind of self-irony—"done blabbing"—as though he were asking if his vituperation is to be viewed as virtue. Has his attack on worldly vices betrayed him into venomous feeling, a kind of strident moralism that he as a good Christian has no right to enjoy? To give someone the lie will give rise to, even seem to deserve, stabbing. That the soul should expect. To some degree it may be deserved because the enjoyment of anger, even legitimate anger, is perverse. In other words, not even Ralegh's soul can escape some of the vituperation. The realm of the soul, he says by implication, is above that of the flesh. The soul is immortal and therefore should not fear attacks by those it enrages through the pointing out of evil motives or actions. The poet's manner of addressing his soul is therefore more complex in the final than in the opening stanza. There is a measure of irony as well as reverence in the slowness with which the final stanza opens:

> So when thou hast, as I
> Commanded thee, done blabbing. . . .

There are also modifications of the tempo, as in the sixth stanza, justified or demanded by the meaning. In the second stanza, for example, the monosyllabic lines further the intensity (as of course the nature of the imagery does, too):

> Say to the court it glows
> And shines like rotten wood.

The lines end emphatically. But in the sixth stanza neither zeal nor time is deserving of rebuke with the same emphasis or firmness. Therefore the lines may appropriately end more softly.

> Tell zeal it wants devotion;
> Tell love it is but lust
> Tell time it meets but motion
> Tell flesh it is but dust. . . .

A Description of Love

> Now what is love? I pray thee, tell.
> It is that fountain and that well
> Where pleasure and repentance dwell.
> It is perhaps that sauncing[1] bell
> That tolls all into heaven or hell:
> And this is love, as I hear tell.
>
> Yet what is love? I pray thee say.
> It is a work on holy-day;
> It is December matched with May;
> When lusty bloods, in fresh array,
> Hear ten months after of the play:
> And this is love, as I hear say.
>
> Yet what is love? I pray thee sain.
> It is a sunshine mixed with rain;

10

---
1. Sanctus.

It is a tooth-ache, or like pain;
It is a game where none doth gain;
The lass saith no, and would full fain:
And this is love, as I hear sain.

Yet what is love? I pray thee say.
It is a yea, it is a nay,   20
A pretty kind of sporting fray;
It is a thing will soon away;
Then take the vantage while you may:
And this is love, as I hear say.

Yet what is love, I pray thee show.
A thing that creeps, it cannot go;
A prize that passeth to and fro;
A thing for one, a thing for mo;
And he that proves must find it so:
And this is love, sweet friend, I trow.   30

This poem develops its theme by a series of statements that reinforce
the initial statement. Compare it structurally with Spenser's Sonnet 34
(p. 58).

Like to a Hermit

Like to a hermit poor in place obscure
I mean to spend my days of endless doubt,
To wail such woes as time cannot recure,
Where none but love shall ever find me out.

My food shall be of care and sorrow made,
My drink nought else but tears fall'n from mine eyes;
And for my light in such obscured shade
The flames shall serve which from my heart arise.

A gown of gray my body shall attire,
My staff of broken hope whereon I'll stay;
Of late repentance linked with long desire
The couch is framed whereon my limbs I'll lay;

And at my gate despair shall linger still
To let in death when love and fortune will.

1. There is a central paradox in this poem. What is it?
2. The hermit was a familiar medieval figure but not a familiar

Elizabethan figure. Is the reader expected to take the figure of the hermit quite literally?

On Edmund Spenser's *Faerie Queene,* 1590
A Vision upon This Conceit of the Fairy Queen

Methought I saw the grave where Laura lay,
Within that temple where the vestal flame
Was wont to burn; and passing by that way
To see that buried dust of living fame,
Whose tomb fair Love and fairer Virtue kept,
All suddenly I saw the Fairy Queen;
At whose approach the soul of Petrarch wept,
And from thenceforth those graces were not seen,
For they this queen attended; in whose stead
Oblivion laid him down on Laura's hearse.
Hereat the hardest stones were seen to bleed,
And groans of buried ghosts the heaven did pierce;
Where Homer's sprite did tremble all for grief,
And cursed th' access of that celestial thief.

■ Why is Petrarch said to weep? Who is Laura?

The Nymph's Reply to the Shepherd

If all the world and love were young,
And truth in every shepherd's tongue,
These pretty pleasures might me move,
To live with thee and be thy love.

But time drives flocks from field to fold,
When rivers rage, and rocks grow cold;
And Philomel becometh dumb;
The rest complains of cares to come.

The flowers do fade, and wanton fields
To wayward Winter reckoning yields;
A honey tongue, a heart of gall,
Is fancy's spring, but sorrow's fall.

Thy gowns, thy shoes, thy beds of roses,
Thy cap, thy kirtle, and thy posies,

Soon break, soon wither, soon forgotten,
In folly ripe, in reason rotten.

Thy belt of straw and ivy buds,
Thy coral clasps and amber studs,
All these in me no means can move,
To come to thee and be thy love.

But could youth last, and love still breed,
Had joys no date, nor age no need,
Then these delights my mind might move,
To live with thee and be thy love.

Compare the complexity of attitude in this poem with that in Marlowe's "The Passionate Shepherd to His Love" (p. 669).

His Pilgrimage

Give me my scallop-shell of quiet,
　　My staff of faith to walk upon,
My scrip of joy, immortal diet,
　　My bottle of salvation,
My gown of glory, hope's true gage;
And thus I'll take my pilgrimage.

Blood must be my body's balmer;
　　No other balm will there be given;
Whilst my soul, like a quiet palmer,
　　Traveleth toward the land of heaven,　　　　　10
Over the silver mountains,
Where spring the nectar fountains.
　　　　　There will I kiss
　　　　　The bowl of bliss,
And drink mine everlasting fill
Upon every milken hill.
My soul will be a-dry before;
But, after, it will thirst no more.

Then by that happy, blissful day
　　More peaceful pilgrims I shall see,　　　　　20
That have cast off their rags of clay,
　　And walk appareled fresh like me.
　　　　　I'll take them first,
　　　　　To quench their thirst

And taste of nectar suckets,
　　At those clear wells
　　Where sweetness dwells,
Drawn up by saints in crystal buckets.

　And when our bottles and all we
Are filled with immortality,   3
Then the blessed paths we'll travel,
Strowed with rubies thick as gravel;
Ceilings of diamonds, sapphire floors,
High walls of coral, and pearly bowers.
　From thence to heaven's bribeless hall,
Where no corrupted voices brawl;
No conscience molten into gold;
No forged accuser bought or sold;
No cause deferred, no vain-spent journey,
For there Christ is the king's attorney,   4
Who pleads for all, without degrees,
And he hath angels but no fees.
　And when the grand twelve million jury
Of our sins, with direful fury,
Against our souls black verdicts give,
Christ pleads his death; and then we live.

　Be Thou my speaker, taintless pleader!
Unblotted lawyer! true proceeder!
Thou giv'st salvation, even for alms,
Not with a bribèd lawyer's palms.   5
　And this is mine eternal plea
To Him that made heaven and earth and sea:
That since my flesh must die so soon,
And want a head to dine next noon,
Just at the stroke, when my veins start and spread,
Set on my soul an everlasting head!
Then am I ready, like a palmer fit,
To tread those blest paths, which before I writ.

Of death and judgment, heaven and hell,
Who oft doth think, must needs die well.   6

■   1. Pilgrims returning from Palestine sometimes wore on their cap
shells which they had picked up from the seashore in the Holy Land
Does this fact explain the effectiveness of the first line of the poem?
　2. There are two major patterns of imagery in this poem. Discuss
them.

3. There are several significant puns in this poem. Explain how ach functions.

4. There is a shift in the metrical pattern. Where does it occur? Is : a legitimate or appropriate shift?

Sir Walter Ralegh the Night before His Death

Even such is time, that takes in trust
    Our youth, our joys, our all we have,
And pays us but with earth and dust;
    Who, in the dark and silent grave,
When we have wandered all our ways,
Shuts up the story of our days.
But from this earth, this grave, this dust,
My God shall raise me up, I trust!

John Donne
(1573–1631)

■■■■■■■■

JOHN DONNE was born of Roman Catholic parents. He en-
red Oxford in 1584 and transferred to Cambridge three years later. His lack
f a degree from either university probably resulted from his inability, as a
'atholic, to take the required oaths. While still a young man, possibly be-
veen his residences at Oxford and Cambridge, he made a tour of Europe.
Ie entered Lincoln's Inn in 1592 in order to study law, but seems to have
ent most of his time in satisfying an "immoderate desire of humane learning
d languages," and in considering the differences between the Protestant
d Catholic religions. We know little, however, of the course which finally
d him into the Anglican church, although some of his later poetry suggests
at he was not positively at home in it. After a voyage to the Azores in
597, he gained employment with Sir Thomas Egerton, Lord Keeper of the
reat Seal. In 1601 he eloped with Egerton's niece, Anne More, whose fa-
er disapproved of the match. As a result, he lost his position with Eger-
n. The years that followed were difficult, for Donne's family grew rapidly
d, lacking satisfactory employment, he lived in poverty and humiliation.
riends urged him to take orders in the Anglican church, but he was not

prepared to take this step. After much deliberation, he finally decided to en
ter the ministry. He was completely devoted to his calling, preached elo
quent sermons of enduring value, and became dean of St. Paul's in 1621

Donne's best work, his love poems and religious poems, were written
respectively, at the beginning and end of his career. Except for a few oc
casional poems and the long *Anniversaries,* which he was commissioned
to write in commemoration of the death of a young girl, Donne published
nothing during his lifetime; his poems appeared first in 1633. They had, how
ever, circulated widely in manuscript, and their running to seven editions
by 1669 proves their continuing popularity in the seventeenth century.

Suggested Readings

SAMUEL JOHNSON, "Cowley," in *Lives of the English Poets.*
H. J. C. GRIERSON, ed., *The Poems of John Donne.* Oxford: The Clarendon
    Press, 1912.
T. S. ELIOT, "The Metaphysical Poets," in *Selected Essays.* New York
    Harcourt, Brace & Co., 1932, pp. 241–250.
LEONARD UNGER, *Donne's Poetry and Modern Criticism.* Chicago: Henry
    Regnery Co., 1950.

■ ■ ■ ■ ■ ■ ■ ■ ■ ■

The poetry of John Donne has, in a sense, been rediscovered in the
twentieth century, and in the last few decades it has been the subject of
much scholarship and of perhaps even more critical comment and de
bate. Before considering some of the controversial issues raised by modern
critics, it is well to view the poetry as it relates to literary history.

Donne's best known and most frequently discussed works are the
love poems which were collected under the title *Songs and Sonets.*
These poems are clearly different from much of the verse that was pro
duced by Donne's contemporaries and immediate predecessors. They are
different *as* love poems in that they are a departure from the smoothly
flowing complaints and eloquent protestations of the Petrarchan sonnet
eers. The attitudes developed in some of the poems are obvious reversals
of such conventional concepts as woman's purity, lovers' faithfulness
and the value of chastity. In Donne's poems the "psychology of love" has
the quality of real and individual experience rather than of literary con
vention. "Woman's Constancy" illustrates these qualities. The unrequited
lover here is not stricken with love-longing and heartache, is not com
mitted to loving the woman in spite of all, and he is certainly not chival
rous and courtly in his attitude toward woman. His attitude toward
himself is neither ennobling nor degrading.

There is much in Donne's poetry (in the love poems, the religious
poems, the satires, and other kinds) which belongs to both older and

more recent traditions, and even to the mere fashions of his time. But Donne added much to the inherited and given elements. His poems are full of references to human activities which previously had never or seldom found their way into lyric poetry, so that his poems of love and of religious experience have a breadth and variety of reference. Images and details from law, medicine, commerce, geography, philosophy, theology, and the like are profusely and logically employed to give a dramatic presentation of emotional and intellectual experience. Donne's poems show not only learning but a vast amount of information which was common to seventeenth-century minds and which he was the first to use frequently and effectively in lyric poems.

Like his attitudes and references, to which they are closely related, Donne's language and meter are significant in the course of English poetry. They, too, show a departure from literary convention. Donne's language is conversational—it suggests the inflections of the speaking voice, as distinguished from the cadences of a literary style. This conversational quality is produced by the same diction and grammatical structure which produce the tone and idiom of conversation, but not done by these. It derives also from the way in which Donne handled meter.

The iambic foot is the basic pattern of rhythm throughout most of Donne's versification, but he introduced more than the usual amount of irregularity. It is clear that the metrical irregularity is used not only to avoid monotony through the use of appropriate variations in rhythm but also to produce the rhythmical and accentual qualities of the spoken language. In Donne's poems there is a tension between two kinds of rhythm. The first line of "Woman's Constancy" is a good illustration:

Now thou hast loved me one whole day. . .

The underlying metrical rhythm of the poem is iambic, and this line might be read as an iambic pentameter. But such a reading would obviously be forced and unnatural. We have, in fact, no technical terms of meter for referring accurately to the accentual strength of the syllables in this line. If it is to be read naturally, it must be read in the manner of conversation, and each of us might read it somewhat differently. For example, there are three possible readings of the first two words: stronger accent on "Now," stronger accent on "thou," or equally strong accent on both words. In a sense, there is no truly weak syllable in the whole line. This is characteristic of Donne's tendency toward a frequent use of strong (and conversational) accents.

All of these characteristics have figured importantly in the modern revival of Donne's reputation. There are other characteristics, however, which have been of special significance in modern literary criticism. One of these has been the distinctive use of figurative language to be found in metaphysical poetry, and especially in Donne's poetry. An intensive

scholarly study of the subject* has pointed out that English poets of th
sixteenth and seventeenth centuries used imagery in order to commun
cate their ideas by means of analogy, and that this practice was a resu
of the discipline of logic taught in the schools in those times. While th
is true enough, some of the poets of the seventeenth century used image
for analogies in such a way as to be considered a distinct group o
school of poets, and of this school Donne, who came first chronologicall
is considered to be the founder, or at least the most representative

It was Samuel Johnson, in his life of Abraham Cowley, who fir
classified these poets under the term which is now regularly applied t
them: "a race of writers that may be termed the *metaphysical poets*
Since Johnson not only fixed the general name but also first used th
terms and concepts by which the metaphysical poets have been di
cussed in modern criticism, it will be well to look at some of his mo
impressive and influential remarks:

> But wit, abstracted from its effects upon the hearer, may be mo
> rigorously and philosophically considered as a kind of *discordia concor*
> a combination of dissimilar images, or discovery of occult resemblanc
> in things apparently unlike. Of wit, thus defined, they have more tha
> enough. The most heterogeneous ideas are yoked by violence togethe
> nature and art are ransacked for illustrations, comparisons, and allusion
> their learning instructs and their subtlety surprises; but the reader co
> monly thinks his improvement dearly bought, and though he som
> times admires, is seldom pleased. . . . Their attempts were always an
> lytic; they broke every image into fragments . . . Yet great labor, c
> rected by great abilities, is never wholly lost: if they frequently thre
> away their wit upon false conceits, they likewise sometimes struck o
> unexpected truth; if their conceits were far-fetched, they were oft
> worth the carriage. To write on their plan, it was at least necessary
> read and think.

In the twentieth century the metaphysical poets, and especially Donn
have been read with both admiration and pleasure. Modern critics ha
rewritten and elaborated Johnson's observations, with the neoclassical o
jections removed and with a fuller appreciation. What Johnson call
"yoked by violence" and "far-fetched" has come to be regarded as
union and integration by intellect and imagination. This violent yokin
or imaginative integration, refers, of course, to the *metaphysical conce*
a technical device that has been of the greatest interest to contempora
critics and that has been most often discussed in connection with Donn
poetry.

A traditional meaning of *conceit* is a witty or imaginative thoug
(or conception); and *metaphysical conceit,* as used in modern criticis

....
* Rosamund Tuve, *Elizabethan and Metaphysical Imagery* (Chicago: Univ
sity of Chicago Press, 1947).

may be defined as follows: a comparison, in the form of simile or metaphor, which indicates several points of similarity between the things
compared, and which is therefore of sufficient length to embrace, or to
serve as the structure of, a whole passage. By far the most famous example of this device is the comparison of parted lovers to the feet of a compass, through twelve lines of "A Valediction: Forbidding Mourning."
Another example is the comparison of the lover's broken heart to a shattered mirror, in lines 24 through 30 of "The Broken Heart." Sometimes
this device is called the *expanded conceit* to distinguish it from the
condensed conceit, a single and simple statement of comparison in which
the basis of comparison is implied rather than explained within the
conceit. The last line of Holy Sonnet 1 is an example: "And thou like
adamant draw mine iron heart." The condensed conceit as a critical concept and designation is less useful than the expanded conceit, for it is less
readily distinguished from "ordinary" metaphor and simile. It may serve,
however, to indicate the qualities frequently found in the metaphors
and similes of Donne and other metaphysical poets. One of these qualities is "surprise," and it is produced by the originality (that is, the strange-
ness) of the comparison. Another is intellectuality, and this is produced
by the basis of comparison: the things compared are related by some
precise detail of their actual function or constitution rather than by
their general characteristics.

Among present-day critics it is usually the expanded figure that is
meant by *metaphysical conceit,* and it is this device that has been of great
importance in the formulation of modern poetic theory. Among some
critics, particularly John Crowe Ransom, Allen Tate, and Cleanth
Brooks, the metaphysical conceit has been considered the essential characteristic of metaphysical poetry. In the writings of these critics, the term
metaphysical poetry seems at times to be abstracted from its original historical reference, that is, from its strict designation of certain seventeenth-
century poets. While these critics have made a historic contribution to
critical thought and the understanding of poetry, some of their statements may be misleading with respect to the seventeenth-century poetry
in question. Ransom at one time identified the typical metaphysical
poem as one containing a single metaphysical conceit—that is, a single
and uninterrupted metaphor extended from the beginning to the end of
the poem. Tate offered a less exacting definition with the suggestion that
the poem develops, not necessarily as a single conceit, but by one or more,
as a series of metaphors—by the logical extension of imagery, to use his
own terms. Brooks's definition was similar to Tate's. For him, too, the
technique of metaphor, but not necessarily a single metaphor, constituted
the structure of the poem: "The comparison *is* the poem in a structural
sense."

These critics have been tremendously interested in the technical
relationship of imagery and metaphor to poetry and poetic effect, and

this interest has been closely allied with their admiration for the meta
physical poets. Yet if we look at Donne's poetry—for if any poetry i
metaphysical it *must* be Donne's—we find that their definitions are no
wholly borne out, are indeed too limited to imagery and metapho
While a general characterization can hardly be made without taking int
account the importance of metaphysical conceit, that device canno
serve as the essential and exclusive characteristic, and probably n
formula as clear-cut as that which the critics have sought can be devise
to fit Donne's poems. There are other characteristics which are obviou
facets of Donne's style but which have no systematic relationship to eac
other on general and abstract grounds and aside from Donne's practice
T. S. Eliot observed, in the essay so largely responsible for the growth o
interest in Donne, that, while the conceit is one characteristic, another i
"development by rapid association of thought." We may return to "*A*
Valediction: Forbidding Mourning" for an example of such deve
opment. The poem opens with a comparison to a deathbed scene
moves through the incidental metaphors, "melt," "tear-floods" and "sigh
tempests," into the implication that the lovers are sanctified, while othe
persons are "laity." Next, there are references to earthquake, Ptolemai
astronomy, and the theological concept of the soul's substance. This i
followed by an almost literal statement of the lover's attitudes, and the
the poem continues with the conceits of the beaten gold and of th
compasses. These various references are in a meaningful sequence be
cause of their stated correspondence to a central idea and not by an
surface relationship among images. The critics have been much con
cerned with the interesting problem of structure. This poem will illu
trate, as well as any other poem of Donne's, that it is difficult and poss
bly misleading to isolate any one aspect of a poem's development as i
structure. With respect to the imagery, Eliot's term "association" is a les
precise formula of technique than Tate's "logical extension" and
therefore a more accurate account of the poem. While Tate, Ranson
and Brooks have attempted too much in the way of a precise formul.
their insistence on the importance of imagery and metaphor in Donne
poetry is, of course, beyond question.

Like the speculation about imagery and metaphor, another subjee
prominent in modern criticism was first considered in connection wit
Donne's poetry. Sir Herbert Grierson, Donne's modern editor, had sa
that the "blend of passion and thought" was an essential characteristic o
Donne's poetry. This idea was developed by Eliot in his influential essa
on the metaphysical poets, and it is obviously related to his theory tha
the metaphysical poets possessed a unified sensibility but that a "dissoci
tion of sensibility," which has not yet been repaired, was already und
way in the seventeenth century. But we need not explore this theo
here in order to consider Eliot's proposal that Donne's poetry shows
combination, or fusion, of thought and feeling. Both thought and fee

ing are, of course, present in any poem, but in Donne's poetry they are present in an unusually great measure and in a particular relationship to each other. Donne's lyrics are vividly and intensely dramatic, so that we can say they have emotion as feeling; they abound in physical images and particular human situations, and thus they have sensuousness as feeling. The thought in the lyrics is conspicuous in two respects. The kind of meaning that can be paraphrased from the poems is often subtle, complex, difficult. And the means by which both thought and feeling are expressed—the conceits and other technical devices—show an intellectual and imaginative agility. There is thus an impressive intellectuality of both content and technique, as we distinguish these for the convenience of critical discussion. The different kinds of thought and feeling are, moreover, closely related. They develop simultaneously as the poem proceeds. This is achieved in part by the dramatic form of the poems and by the frequent use of images and figures of speech as the means by which feelings and ideas are represented. It also derives from the subject matter and from the approach to the subject matter. In Donne's lyrics his subject matter is either the emotions of love or of religious experience, and his treatment of these subjects is argumentative and analytical. In other words, there is an intellectual approach to feelings, a thoughtfulness about feelings.

There is sufficient justification for critical emphasis on the presence of thought and feeling in Donne's poems. But Eliot, and later other critics, have meant not simply that these elements are present in an unusually great measure and in an unusually close relationship. What they have meant can be briefly indicated by a few phrases that are typical of the critical language they have used at times. These phrases are "felt thought" and "thought feeling," and they are supposed to refer to something that can be found in Donne's poems, something that differentiates those poems in a special way from the poetry that has been written since the seventeenth century. But anyone attempting to read Donne's poems under the guidance of this criticism may run into difficulties and confusions. In the first place there is the assumption that other poets—for example, Pope, Keats, Tennyson, and Frost—do not, each in his own way, combine thought and feeling in their poems. Secondly, here is the difficulty—we might claim, the impossibility—of locating an illustration in Donne's poetry of a thought that is felt, or a feeling that thought. There are, of course, the conceits and the frequency of figurative language, but other poets use metaphors and figurative language. It is true that there are technical differences in metaphor, but here is no satisfactory explanation of how any metaphor, by this technical difference, becomes a felt thought or a thought feeling. And thirdly, one may decide that one does not understand what is meant by these phrases as they are applied to poetry—especially when *feel* and *feeling* are taken to mean physical sensation. We have thoughts, and we have sensations, and we may have them simultaneously, but we are familiar with no experience by which thought and sensation are an identical event. Eliot had said that Tennyson and Browning "do not feel their thought as immediately as the odour of a rose." But if we attempt to take this literally we become confused, for we do not know with which of our physical senses a thought can be felt.

The confusions and difficulties that we have been discussing may be avoided if we bear in mind that the critical statements about thought and feeling are figurative, and not literal. It is likely that there would be no danger of confusion if Eliot and the other critics had said that there is an apparent fusion of thought and feeling in Donne's poetry. Then we would not be tempted to apply their remarks analytically. Their statements are a kind of criticism that is called impressionistic, rather than analytical or technical. In Eliot's statements we have not an analysis or explanation of Donne's poetry, but a response to it. The poetry made him feel *as if* thought and feeling had been fused. This is sufficiently understandable, because we can conceive of the response and we can share it. But our response, our *impression,* is evidence of the effect of a poem. It is not an explanation or a description of it. This effect is indeed quite obvious, and we may surmise that it is intended, in much of Donne's poetry. It has often been observed that surprise is a characteristic effect of Donne, and this apparent fusion is one of the variety of surprises to be found in his poetry. We see it most clearly in certain poems and passages where the fusion is not only an effect but is actually stated or suggested. "A naked thinking heart" in "The Blossom" is such a phrase. Another example is the entire poem "The Ecstasy," which argues that for "pure lovers" spiritual union and physical union are indistinguishable:

> So must pure lovers' souls descend
> T'affections, and to faculties,
> Which sense may reach and apprehend, . . .

Still another example is the oft-quoted passage from "Of the Progress of the Soul: the Second Anniversary":

> her pure and eloquent blood
> Spoke in her cheeks, and so distinctly wrought,
> That one might almost say, her body thought.

This passage clearly shows that Donne considered "felt thought" a daring and surprising notion—at least, it is so considered in the passage. There could hardly be a stronger qualification, a more cautious and self conscious approach to a metaphor, than the words "might almost say." Many other passages achieve the same kind of surprising effect by assuming that an abstraction, generalization, or attitude is a physical object. We have an example of this in the opening lines of "Love's Diet"

To what a cumbersome unwieldiness
And burdenous corpulence my love had grown, . . .

Of course, Donne achieved many witty and surprising effects by other means. But this kind—the identification of physical and nonphysical, the "fusion" of thought and feeling—has been peculiarly impressive and has had a notable influence on modern critical thought.

Woman's Constancy

Now thou hast loved me one whole day,
To-morrow when thou leav'st, what wilt thou say?
Wilt thou then antedate some new-made vow?
 Or say that now
We are not just those persons which we were?
Or, that oaths made in reverential fear
Of love, and his wrath, any may forswear?
Or, as true deaths true marriages untie,
So lovers' contracts, images of those,
Bind but till sleep, death's image, them unloose?
 Or, your own end to justify,
For having purposed change and falsehood, you
Can have no way but falsehood to be true?
Vain lunatic, against these scapes I could
 Dispute and conquer, if I would;
 Which I abstain to do,
For by to-morrow, I may think so too.

A Valediction: Forbidding Mourning

As virtuous men pass mildly away,
 And whisper to their souls to go,
While some of their sad friends do say,
 The breath goes now, and some say, no:

So let us melt, and make no noise,
 No tear-floods, nor sigh-tempests move,
T'were profanation of our joys
 To tell the laity our love.

Moving of th'earth brings harms and fears,
 Men reckon what it did and meant;
But trepidation of the spheres,
 Though greater far, is innocent.

10

Dull sublunary lovers' love
  (Whose soul is sense) cannot admit
Absence, because it doth remove
  Those things which elemented it.

But we by a love, so much refin'd,
  That ourselves know not what it is,
Inter-assurèd of the mind,
  Care less, eyes, lips, and hands to miss.   20

Our two souls therefore, which are one,
  Though I must go, endure not yet
A breach, but an expansion,
  Like gold to airy thinness beat.

If they be two, they are two so
  As stiff twin compasses are two,
Thy soul the fixt foot, makes no show
  To move, but doth, if th' other do.

And though it in the center sit,
  Yet when the other far doth roam,   30
It leans, and hearkens after it,
  And grows erect, as that comes home.

Such wilt thou be to me, who must
  Like th'other foot, obliquely run;
Thy firmness makes my circle just,
  And makes me end, where I begun.

The Good-Morrow

I wonder by my troth, what thou and I
Did, till we loved? Were we not weaned till then,
But sucked on country pleasures, childishly?
Or snorted we in the seven sleepers' den?
'Twas so; but this, all pleasures fancies be.
If ever any beauty I did see,
Which I desired, and got, 'twas but a dream of thee.

And now good morrow to our waking souls,
Which watch not one another out of fear;
For love all love of other sights controls,
And makes one little room an everywhere.

Let sea-discoverers to new worlds have gone,
Let maps to other, worlds on worlds have shown;
Let us possess one world, each hath one, and is one.

My face in thine eye, thine in mine appears,
And true plain hearts do in the faces rest;
Where can we find two better hemispheres
Without sharp north, without declining west?
Whatever dies was not mixed equally;
If our two loves be one, or thou and I
Love so alike that none do slacken, none can die.

The Sun Rising

Busy old fool, unruly sun,
   Why dost thou thus
Through windows and through curtains call on us?
Must to thy motions lovers' seasons run?
   Saucy pedantic wretch, go chide
   Late schoolboys and sour prentices,
Go tell court-huntsmen that the King will ride,
Call country ants to harvest offices;
Love, all alike, no season knows, nor clime,
Nor hours, days, months, which are the rags of time.   10

   Thy beams, so reverend and strong
   Why shouldst thou think?
I could eclipse and cloud them with a wink,
But that I would not lose her sight so long;
   If her eyes have not blinded thine,
   Look, and to-morrow late tell me
Whether both the 'Indias of spice and mine
Be where thou left'st them, or lie here with me.
Ask for those kings whom thou saw'st yesterday,
And thou shalt hear, all here in one bed lay.   20

   She'is all states, and all princes I;
   Nothing else is.
Princes do but play us; compared to this,
All honor's mimic, all wealth alchemy.
   Thou, sun, art half as happy'as we,
   In that the world's contracted thus;
Thine age asks ease, and since thy duties be
To warm the world, that's done in warming us.

Shine here to us, and thou art everywhere;
This bed thy center is, these walls thy sphere.   3(

■   1. Attempt to describe the tone of this poem and explain how var
ious elements (such as diction, rhythm, wit, and figurativeness) con
tribute to the tone.

2. List the surprising effects and analyze each.

3. Consider whether or not a single conceit extends through th
entire poem.

4. The apostrophes in lines 17 and 21 indicate slight rhythmica
elisions.

The Canonization

For God's sake hold your tongue, and let me love;
    Or chide my palsy, or my gout;
    My five gray hairs, or ruined fortune flout;
With wealth your state, your mind with arts improve;
    Take you a course, get you a place,
    Observe his honor, or his grace;
Or the king's real, or his stampèd face
    Contemplate; what you will, approve,
    So you will let me love.

Alas! alas! who's injured by my love?   1(
    What merchant's ships have my sighs drowned?
    Who says my tears have overflowed his ground?
When did my colds a forward spring remove?
    When did the heats which my veins fill
    Add one more to the plaguy bill?
Soldiers find wars, and lawyers find out still
    Litigious men, which quarrels move,
    Though she and I do love.

Call us what you will, we are made such by love;
    Call her one, me another fly;   2(
    We're tapers too, and at our own cost die,
And we in us find the eagle and the dove.
    The phoenix riddle hath more wit
    By us; we two being one, are it.
So, to one neutral thing both sexes fit;
    We die and rise the same, and prove
    Mysterious by this love.

We can die by it, if not live by love,
    And if unfit for tomb or hearse
    Our legend be, it will be fit for verse;   30
And if no piece of chronicle we prove,
    We'll build in sonnets pretty rooms;
    As well a well-wrought urn becomes
The greatest ashes, as half-acre tombs,
    And by these hymns all shall approve
    Us canonized for love;

And thus invoke us: "You, whom reverend love
    Made one another's hermitage;
    You, to whom love was peace, that now is rage;
Who did the whole world's soul contract, and drove   40
    Into the glasses of your eyes—
    So made such mirrors, and such spies,
That they did all to you epitomized,—
    Countries, towns, courts; beg from above
    A pattern of your love."

1. The poem ends with the expanded conceit of the lovers considered as canonized, that is, as saints. Are there any other expanded conceits in the poem?

2. In the third stanza there is this sequence of metaphorical references: burning tapers; the contrasting birds, eagle and dove; and the mythical phoenix bird, which is consumed by fire and reborn from its own ashes. What other examples of development by association are to be found in the poem?

3. Within the conceit of canonization there is the conceit of the lovers as seeing "whole worlds" in each other's eyes. In this conceit, as in "The Good-Morrow" and "The Sun Rising," there is a witty adaptation of the familiar medieval notion of the microcosm and the macrocosm, according to which there is a detailed correspondence between the individual and the universe. By what means earlier in "The Canonization" is the experience of love represented as a world in itself, separate and independent from the rest of the world?

Twicknam Garden

Blasted with sighs, and surrounded with tears,
    Hither I come to seek the spring,
    And at mine eyes, and at mine ears,
Receive such balms as else cure everything;
    But oh, self traitor, I do bring

The spider love, which transubstantiates all,
  And can convert manna to gall;
And that this place may thoroughly be thought
  True paradise, I have the serpent brought.

'Twere wholesomer for me that winter did
  Benight the glory of this place,
  And that a grave frost did forbid
These trees to laugh and mock me to my face;
  But that I may not this disgrace
Endure, nor yet leave loving, Love, let me
  Some senseless piece of this place be;
Make me a mandrake, so I may groan here,
  Or a stone fountain weeping out my year.

Hither with crystal vials, lovers, come
  And take my tears, which are love's wine,
  And try your mistress' tears at home,
For all are false that taste not just like mine;
  Alas, hearts do not in eyes shine,
Nor can you more judge woman's thoughts by tears,
  Than by her shadow what she wears.
O perverse sex, where none is true but she,
  Who's therefore true, because her truth kills me.

■ 1. This poem is a dramatic utterance spoken out of an ironical situation. Explain the irony, avoiding as much as possible terms used in the poem.

2. How are references to the speaker's physical location (his presence in the garden) used to suggest his emotion?

3. Comment on "spider" and "serpent" in the first stanza. Do they function as visual images?

4. State in general terms the emotional conflict uttered in the second stanza.

5. The opening lines of the third stanza are obviously absurd and illogical. Do they provide an acceptable comic effect? Or are they justified by the tone of the poem and as a dramatic indication of the speaker's emotion and attitude? Explain your answer.

Air and Angels

Twice or thrice had I loved thee,
Before I knew thy face or name;
So in a voice, so in a shapeless flame,

Angels affect us oft, and worshipped be;
 Still when, to where thou wert, I came,
Some lovely glorious nothing I did see.
 But since my soul, whose child love is,
 Takes limbs of flesh, and else could nothing do,
 More subtle than the parent is
Love must not be, but take a body too;
 And therefore what thou wert, and who,
 I bid love ask, and now
That it assume thy body I allow,
And fix itself in thy lip, eye, and brow.

Whilst thus to ballast love I thought,
 And so more steadily to have gone,
With wares which would sink admiration,
 I saw I had love's pinnace overfraught;
 Ev'ry thy hair for love to work upon
Is much too much, some fitter must be sought;
 For, nor in nothing, nor in things
Extreme and scatt'ring bright, can love inhere;
 Then as an angel, face and wings
Of air, not pure as it, yet pure doth wear,
 So thy love may be my love's sphere;
 Just such disparity
As is 'twixt air and angels' purity,
'Twixt women's love and men's will ever be.

■ Because of its subject, the manner of development, and the numerous distinctions of ideas made within a poem of moderate length, "Air and Angels" is one of Donne's most complex poems. It may be well, therefore, to paraphrase the poem. A man is speaking to the woman he loves. He tells her that he loved her before he met her, as people worship angels whom they have never seen. It is thus implied that his love was directed toward an *idea* of a woman, for people have only ideas of angels, never having seen them. The woman's first appearance to the man is described as a "lovely glorious nothing." This phrase is deliberately ambiguous. It means that the woman's appearance corresponded with his idea, and she therefore seemed to be an ~~insubstantial~~ vision, or "nothing." Another ~~additional~~ meaning is that she did not become the actual object of his love until he made her so, until he identified her with his idea of the loved object. The process of identification is explained by a conceit: love is the child of his soul, and since his soul has taken a body (his body), love, like the parent, must also take one. This it does when it is urged to discover the identity of the woman: it assumes—identifies itself with —the body of the woman, and in this way the woman becomes the actual object of love, of which the man previously had only an idea. Here the first stanza ends.

Another conceit, by which love is equated with a ship, opens the second stanza. The speaker of the poem says that, in having love assume the body of the woman, he had thought to give it stability and fixation, as one ballasts a ship with weight, but he discovers that he has over-weighted it. This is explained, after the conceit has been dropped, by the statement that the woman, in all her detail, "for love to work upon/ Is much too much." In other words, the woman, as she appears to him and as she represents the ideal object of love, is more than his love can manage to attach itself to. For as his love could not formerly come to rest, when there was no basis on which it might rest, so now it is not able to partake of an extreme and ultimate fulfillment. Consequently, it must abandon this fulfillment of the ideal and adjust itself to the love which the woman offers, not to the woman herself. This adjustment is necessary because woman's love is less than man's, and hence can be the "sphere" of man's love, just as an angel's body, though pure, is less pure than the angel's soul contained therein.

In approaching a consideration of its structural aspects perhaps it will be well to summarize the paraphrase of the poem: Man has a conception of the woman whom he would love before having found the woman, but, when finally an individual woman is accepted as representing this conception, man discovers that his love does not fully measure up to the woman he sees as the loved object, and so an adjustment is made according to the measure—not of the woman—but of the woman's love, which is always less than man's.

It is obvious that the structure of the poem is not determined by a single extended conceit. There is no conceit until the middle of the first stanza, where we have the conceit—extended to the end of the stanza —of love as the child of an embodied soul. Then there is a conceit extended from the beginning of the second stanza through the first four lines, this time of love as a ship that is ballasted. These two conceits are adjacent, but the one does not follow the other by logical extension of imagery or even by obvious association; there is a complete break in figurativeness. The sequence is dependent upon the fact that both are metaphors about love, which is the subject of a discourse that begins before and extends through and beyond both conceits. At the conclusion of the poem there is, not a conceit, but an analogy between the psychological anatomy of angels and the loves of men and of women.

And now let us examine a structural aspect of the poem other than that which would be determined by figurative language. According to the paraphrase that was made, the lover addresses the woman he loves in terms of praise, exalting her above himself, until almost the end of the poem. And then it develops that this discussion leads to a statement that the woman is in a respect lower than the lover. With this surprising reversal, seemingly unprepared for, the poem ends. The reversal is surprising, and a calculated surprise is witty. Moreover, the reversal makes for irony: one attitude is apparently prepared for, and then its opposite is given. Hence the poem is not a straightforward development of a single attitude, but it provides a complexity of attitudes. The argument, or line of thought, by which the complexity of attitudes is developed may be regarded as a structural aspect of the poem.

The Broken Heart

He is stark mad, who ever says,
   That he hath been in love an hour,
Yet not that love so soon decays,
   But that it can ten in less space devour;
Who will believe me, if I swear
That I have had the plague a year?
   Who would not laugh at me, if I should say,
   I saw a flask of powder burn a day?

Ah, what a trifle is a heart,
   If once into love's hands it come!   10
All other griefs allow a part
   To other griefs, and ask themselves but some;
They come to us, but us love draws,
He swallows us, and never chaws;
   By him, as by chain'd shot, whole ranks do die,
   He is the tyrant pike, our hearts the fry.

If 'twere not so, what did become
   Of my heart when I first saw thee!
I brought a heart into the room,
   But from the room I carried none with me;   20
If it had gone to thee, I know
Mine would have taught thine heart to show
   More pity unto me, but love, alas,
   At one first blow did shiver it as glass.

Yet nothing can to nothing fall,
   Nor any place be empty quite;
Therefore I think my breast hath all
   Those pieces still, though they be not unite;
And now as broken glasses show
A hundred lesser faces, so   30
   My rags of heart can like, wish, and adore,
   But after one such love, can love no more.

Love's Diet

To what a cumbersome unwieldiness
And burdenous corpulence my love had grown,
   But that I did, to make it less,
   And keep it in proportion,
Give it a diet, made it feed upon
That which love worst endures, discretion.

Above one sigh a day I 'allow'd him not,
Of which my fortune and my faults had part;
   And if sometimes by stealth he got
   A she sigh from my mistress' heart,   10
And thought to feast on that, I let him see
'Twas neither very sound, nor meant to me.

If he wrung from me 'a tear, I brined it so
With scorn or shame that him it nourish'd not.
   If he sucked hers, I let him know
   'Twas not a tear which he had got;
His drink was counterfeit, as was his meat,
For eyes which roll towards all weep not, but sweat.

Whatever he would dictate, I writ that,
But burnt my letters. When she writ to me,   20
   And that that favor made him fat,
   I said, if any title be
Conveyed by this, ah, what doth it avail
To be the fortieth name in an entail?

Thus I reclaimed my buzzard love, to fly
At what, and when, and how, and where I choose.
   Now negligent of sport I lie,
   And now, as other falc'ners use,
I spring a mistress, swear, write, sigh and weep,
And the game killed or lost, go talk, and sleep.   30

■ In "The Good-Morrow," "The Sun Rising," and "The Canonization" the experience of love is represented as a world or realm of reality separate from the ordinary world of reality. In "Twicknam Garden" the lover is committed to a rivalry of attitudes. In "Air and Angels" the lover adjusts himself to an acknowledged complexity of attitudes by shifting from one attitude to another. Specify the complexity of attitudes and the means by which it is expressed in each of the poems, "The Broken Heart" and "Love's Diet."

The Ecstasy

Where, like a pillow on a bed,
    A pregnant bank swell'd up to rest
The violet's reclining head,
    Sat we two, one another's best.
Our hands were firmly cémented
    With a fast balm, which thence did spring;
Our eye-beams twisted, and did thread
    Our eyes, upon one double string;
So t' intergraft our hands, as yet
    Was all the means to make us one,   10
And pictures in our eyes to get
    Was all our propagation.
As 'twixt two equal Armies, Fate
    Suspends uncertain victory,
Our souls (which to advance their state,
    Were gone out), hung 'twixt her, and me.
And whilst our souls negotiate there,
    We like sepulchral statues lay;
All day, the same our postures were,
    And we said nothing, all the day.   20
If any, so by love refin'd,
    That he soul's language understood,
And by good love were grown all mind,
    Within convenient distance stood,
He (though he knew not which soul spake,
    Because both meant, both spake the same)
Might thence a new concoction take,
    And part far purer than he came.
This Ecstasy doth unperplex
    (We said) and tell us what we love;   30
We see by this, it was not sex,
    We see, we saw not what did move:
But as all several souls contain
    Mixture of things, they know not what,
Love these mix'd souls doth mix again,
    And makes both one, each this and that.
A single violet transplant,
    The strength, the colour, and the size
(All which before was poor, and scant),
    Redoubles still, and multiplies.   40
When love, with one another so
    Interinanimates two souls,
That abler soul, which thence doth flow,

Defects of loneliness controls.
We then, who are this new soul, know,
  Of what we are compos'd, and made,
For, th' Atomies of which we grow,
  Are souls, whom no change can invade.
But O alas, so long, so far
  Our bodies why do we forbear?   50
They are ours, though they are not we, We are
  The intelligences, they the sphere.
We owe them thanks, because they thus,
  Did us, to us, at first convey,
Yielded their forces, sense, to us,
  Nor are dross to us, but allay.
On man heaven's influence works not so,
  But that it first imprints the air,
So soul into the soul may flow,
  Though it to body first repair.   60
As our blood labours to beget
  Spirits, as like souls as it can,
Because such fingers need to knit
  That subtle knot, which makes us man:
So must pure lovers' souls descend
  T'affections, and to faculties,
Which sense may reach and apprehend,
  Else a great Prince in prison lies.
To our bodies turn we then, that so
  Weak men on love reveal'd may look;   70
Love's mysteries in souls do grow,
  But yet the body is his book,
And if some lover, such as we,
  Have heard this dialogue of one,
Let him still mark us, he shall see
  Small change, when we're to bodies gone.

Witchcraft by a Picture

I fix mine eye on thine and there
  Pity my picture burning in thine eye;
My picture drowned in a transparent tear
  When I look lower I espy.
    Hadst thou the wicked skill
  By pictures made and marred, to kill,
How many ways might'st thou perform thy will?

But now I have drunk thy sweet salt tears,
    And though thou pour more, I'll depart.
My picture vanished, vanish fears
    That I can be endamaged by that art.
      Though thou retain of me
One picture more, yet that will be,
Being in thine own heart, from all malice free.

■   The basic reference, or allusion, of this poem is the superstition that a curse can be placed upon a person through some action, such as burning, performed upon the person's picture or effigy. Write an interpretive paraphrase of the poem and in so doing explain the implications of the allusion as it is maintained throughout the poem.

Holy Sonnets

I

Thou hast made me, and shall thy work decay?
Repair me now, for now mine end doth haste;
I run to Death, and Death meets me as fast,
And all my pleasures are like yesterday.
I dare not move my dim eyes any way,
Despair behind, and Death before doth cast
Such terror, and my feeble flesh doth waste
By sin in it, which it towards hell doth weigh:
Only thou art above, and when towards thee
By thy leave I can look, I rise again;
But our old subtle foe so tempteth me,
That not one hour myself I can sustain;
Thy grace may wing me to prevent his art,
And thou like adamant draw mine iron heart.

6

This is my play's last scene; here heavens appoint
My pilgrimage's last mile; and my race,
Idly yet quickly run, hath this last pace;
My span's last inch, my minutes' latest point;
And gluttonous death will instantly unjoint
My body and my soul, and I shall sleep a space;
But my'ever-waking part shall see that face
Whose fear already shakes my every joint.
Then as my soul to'heaven, her first seat, takes flight,
And earth-born body in the earth shall dwell,
So fall my sins, that all may have their right,

To where they'are bred, and would press me,—to hell.
Impute me righteous, thus purged of evil,
For thus I leave the world, the flesh, the devil.

7

At the round earth's imagined corners, blow
Your trumpets, angels; and arise, arise
From death, you numberless infinities
Of souls, and to your scattered bodies go;
All whom the flood did, and fire shall o'erthrow,
All whom war, dearth, age, agues, tyrannies,
Despair, law, chance hath slain, and you whose eyes
Shall behold God and never taste death's woe.
But let them sleep, Lord, and me mourn a space,
For if above all these my sins abound,
'Tis late to ask abundance of thy grace
When we are there; here on this lowly ground
Teach me how to repent; for that's as good
As if thou'hadst sealed my pardon with thy blood.

10

Death, be not proud, though some have callèd thee
Mighty and dreadful, for thou art not so;
For those whom thou think'st thou dost overthrow
Die not, poor Death, nor yet canst thou kill me.
From rest and sleep, which but thy pictures be,
Much pleasure; then from thee much more must flow,
And soonest our best men with thee do go,
Rest of their bones, and soul's delivery.
Thou art slave to fate, chance, kings, and desperate men,
And dost with poison, war, and sickness dwell;
And poppy or charms can make us sleep as well
And better than thy stroke; why swell'st thou then?
One short sleep past, we wake eternally,
And death shall be no more; Death, thou shalt die.

14

Batter my heart, three-personed God, for you
As yet but knock, breathe, shine, and seek to mend;
That I may rise and stand, o'erthrow me; 'and bend
Your force to break, blow, burn, and make me new.
I, like an unsurped tower to 'another due,
Labor to 'admit you, but oh, to no end.
Reason, your viceroy in me, me should defend,
But is captived, and proves weak or untrue.

Yet dearly 'I love you,' and would be loved fain,
But am betrothed unto your enemy;
Divorce me, 'untie or break that knot again;
Take me to you, imprison me, for I,
Except you 'enthrall me, never shall be free,
Nor ever chaste, except you ravish me.

■ Analyze one or more of the sonnets, with special attention to the use
of the sonnet form and to rhythmical effects.

A Hymn to God the Father

Wilt Thou forgive that sin where I begun,
  Which was my sin, though it were done before?
Wilt Thou forgive that sin, through which I run,
  And do run still, though still I do deplore?
    When Thou hast done, Thou hast not done,
      For I have more.

Wilt Thou forgive that sin which I have won
  Others to sin, and made my sin their door?
Wilt Thou forgive that sin which I did shun
  A year or two, but wallowed in a score?
    When Thou hast done, Thou hast not done,
      For I have more.

I have a sin of fear, that when I have spun
  My last thread, I shall perish on the shore;
But swear by Thyself, that at my death Thy Son
  Shall shine as he shines now, and heretofore;
    And, having done that, Thou hast done;
      I fear no more.

Ben Jonson

(1573–1637)

■ ■ ■ ■ ■ ■ ■ ■ ■ ■

THE POSTHUMOUS SON of a minister, Jonson was raised in London and educated briefly at Westminster School. He felt a lifelong debt to its headmaster, William Camden, who stimulated in him an intense love of learning. Besides being a scholar and industrious man of letters Jonson was also a vigorous man of action, winning a reputation for bravery with the English army in the Netherlands and even daring to ridicule King James in *Eastward Ho,* a play written in collaboration with Marston and Chapman. For this indiscretion he was in danger of losing his ears and nose, and only the pleas of eminent men saved him. Jonson was a highly original writer, developing the "comedy of humors" as a new literary form and helping to formulate the neoclassical esthetic. Something of his forthrightness as a person and his position in criticism can be inferred from the following excerpts taken from a record of conversations made by William Drummond, a Scottish poet with whom Jonson visited in 1619: "He cursed Petrarch for redacting verses to sonnets, which he said were like the tyrants bed, where some who were too short were racked, others too long, cut short. . . . He esteemeth John Donne the first poet in the world for some things [but said that] Donne himself, for not being understood, would perish. . . . He [Jonson] was better versed, and knew more in Greek and Latin, than all the poets in England. . . ." But Jonson was also an affectionate and highly respected man. The esteem in which he was held is suggested by the volume, *Jonsonus Viribus,* elegies published in his honor the year after his death.

Suggested Readings

R. S. WALKER, "Ben Jonson's Lyric Poetry," *Criterion,* XII (April, 1934), 430–448.

GEORGE WILLIAMSON, "The Rhetorical Pattern of Neo-classical Wit," *Modern Philology,* XXXIII, 1 (August, 1935), 55–81.

MATTHEW W. BLACK, "Tribe of Ben," *Elizabethan and Seventeenth Century Lyrics.* Philadelphia: J. B. Lippincott Co., 1938, pp. 379–425.

■ ■ ■ ■ ■ ■ ■ ■ ■ ■

To the Memory of My Beloved, Master William Shakespeare

To draw no envy, Shakespeare, on thy name,
Am I thus ample to thy book and fame;
While I confess thy writings to be such
As neither man, nor muse, can praise too much.
'Tis true, and all men's suffrage. But these ways
Were not the paths I meant unto thy praise;
For silliest ignorance on these may light,
Which, when it sounds at best, but echoes right;
Or blind affection, which doth ne'er advance
The truth, but gropes, and urgeth all by chance;   10
Or crafty malice might pretend this praise,
And think to ruin, where it seemed to raise.
These are, as some infamous bawd or whore
Should praise a matron. What could hurt her more?
But thou art proof against them, and, indeed,
Above the ill fortune of them, or the need.
I therefore will begin. Soul of the age!
The applause, delight, the wonder of our stage!
My Shakespeare, rise! I will not lodge thee by
Chaucer, or Spenser, or bid Beaumont lie   20
A little further, to make thee a room;
Thou art a monument without a tomb,
And art alive still while thy book doth live
And we have wits to read and praise to give.
That I not mix thee so, my brain excuses,
I mean with great, but disproportioned Muses;
For if I thought my judgment were of years,
I should commit thee surely with thy peers,
And tell how far thou didst our Lyly outshine,
Or sporting Kyd, or Marlowe's mighty line.   30
And though thou hadst small Latin and less Greek,
From thence to honor thee, I would not seek
For names; but call forth thundering Aeschylus,
Euripides, and Sophocles to us;
Pacuvius, Accius,[1] him of Cordova[2] dead,
To life again, to hear thy buskin tread,
And shake a stage; or, when thy socks were on,
Leave thee alone for the comparison
Of all that insolent Greece or haughty Rome
Sent forth, or since did from their ashes come.   40

1. Early Greek tragedians.   2. Seneca, whose tragedies influenced Elizabethan drama.

Triumph, my Britain, thou hast one to show
To whom all scenes of Europe homage owe.
He was not of an age, but for all time!
And all the Muses still were in their prime,
When like Apollo, he came forth to warm
Our ears, or like a Mercury to charm!
Nature herself was proud of his designs
And joyed to wear the dressing of his lines!
Which were so richly spun, and woven so fit,
As, since, she will vouchsafe no other wit.   50
The merry Greek, tart Aristophanes,
Neat Terence, witty Plautus, now not please,
But antiquated and deserted lie,
As they were not of Nature's family.
Yet must I not give Nature all; thy art,
My gentle Shakespeare, must enjoy a part.
For though the poet's matter nature be,
His art doth give the fashion; and, that he
Who casts to write a living line, must sweat
(Such as thine are) and strike the second heat   60
Upon the Muses' anvil; turn the same
(And himself with it) that he thinks to frame,
Or, for the laurel, he may gain a scorn;
For a good poet's made, as well as born.
And such wert thou! Look how the father's face
Lives in his issue; even so the race
Of Shakespeare's mind and manners brightly shines
In his well turnèd, and true filèd lines;
In each of which he seems to shake a lance,
As brandished at the eyes of ignorance.   70
Sweet Swan of Avon! what a sight it were
To see thee in our waters yet appear,
And make those flights upon the banks of Thames,
That so did take Eliza and our James!
But stay, I see thee in the hemisphere
Advanced, and made a constellation there!
Shine forth, thou Star of poets, and with rage
Or influence chide or cheer the drooping stage,
Which, since thy flight from hence, hath mourn'd like night,
And despairs day, but for thy volume's light.   80

■ By examining the couplets employed by Ben Jonson in this tribute
to Shakespeare, one can see that much of the esthetic that was to be
called neoclassical was being formulated long before the Restoration and
the poetry of John Dryden. Dryden thought of Edmund Waller as his

chief predecessor, but later observers have demonstrated that neoclassical principles can be seen clearly in the work of Jonson. As a matter of fact, the line can be seen to run through a number of poets, such as George Sandys, Sir John Beaumont, Lord Falkland, and Sir John Denham. Here we are concerned merely with stressing that Jonson was a strong exponent of the virtues of classicism, brevity, terseness, and emphasis.

In some of the comments he made to William Drummond, recorded in *Conversations,* Jonson indicated his preference for a tightly knit kind of verse. He said, for example, that he had written an epic "all in couplets, for he detested all other rimes," and that he had written a treatise on poetry in which he proved "couplets to be the bravest sort of verses, especially when they are broken" (that is, when they have a caesura). The couplet, of course, is most closely associated with the neoclassical esthetic.

The couplet, with its caesura, which makes balanced and antithetical statements possible within the brief compass of one or two lines, is a natural vehicle for expository and satiric poetry. It is also highly suitable for panegyric verses. The couplet invites compressed thought. And, because of the relative ease with which parallel, balanced, and antithetical thoughts can be expressed in it, the couplet invites both wit and what the Elizabethans called "sentences" or *sententia,* wise sayings.

Jonson's panegyric on Shakespeare is recognizably in the tradition that reaches a high point in the language of Pope, but one will notice in comparing the couplets of the two poets that Pope's are much more compressed. There are many lines in Jonson's poem that Pope would probably have excluded because the statements in them are implied or directly stated in neighboring lines. Consider, for example, the repetitiousness in these lines:

> These are as some infamous bawd or whore
> Should praise a matron. What could hurt her more?
>
> (ll. 13–14)

Nonetheless, one finds in Jonson's poem much that is associated with the tradition brought to perfection by Pope. In the following we find the balanced phrasing, with the caesura in each line coming after the fifth syllable:

> Or crafty malice   might pretend this praise,
> And think to ruin,   where it seemed to raise.
>
> (ll. 11–12)

And we find neat epigrams:

> Thou are a monument without a tomb
>
> (l. 22)

He was not of an age, but for all time!

(l. 43)

The sententious element is not so evident in this poem as it is in many in the neoclassical tradition, but we can find an illustration of it in the passage wherein Jonson recognizes Shakespeare's native genius but adds that art is needed as well,

For a good poet's made, as well as born.

(l. 64)

Again, we may note turns of phrase, the wit, that point up thought in a memorably sharp fashion. Thus in concluding his panegyric Jonson writes that darkness has descended since Shakespeare's death, that the stage

hath mourn'd like night,
And despairs day, but for thy volume's light.

(ll. 79-80)

There is in Jonson's poem, then, the manner we associate with neoclassicism: effort to achieve precision and brevity, the use of balanced, parallel, and antithetical phrases, a preference for the closed couplet, and a tendency to favor witty, sententious, and didactic statement.

To Penshurst [1]

Thou art not Penshurst built to envious show,
Of touch of marble, nor can boast a row
Of polished pillars, or a roof of gold;
Thou hast no lantern, whereof tales are told,
Or stair, or courts; but stand'st an ancient pile,
And, these grudged at, art reverenced the while.
Thou joy'st in better marks, of soil, of air,
Of wood, of water; therein thou art fair.
Thou hast thy walks for health, as well as sport;
Thy mount, to which the dryads do resort,   10
Where Pan and Bacchus their high feasts have made,
Beneath the broad beech and the chestnut shade;
That taller tree, which of a nut was set
At his great birth where all the Muses met.[2]

....

1. Home of the Sidney family. See p. 191 for Waller's poem on Penshurst.
2. The acorn was planted on the birthday of Sir Philip Sidney.

There in the writhed bark are cut the names
Of many a sylvan, taken with his flames;
And thence the ruddy satyrs oft provoke
The lighter fauns to reach thy Lady's Oak.
Thy copse too, named of Gamage, thou hast there,
That never fails to serve the seasoned deer   20
When thou wouldst feast or exercise thy friends.
The lower land, that to the river bends,
Thy sheep, thy bullocks, kine, and calves do feed;
The middle grounds thy mares and horses breed.
Each bank doth yield thee conies; and the tops,
Fertile of wood, Ashore and Sidney's copse,
To crown thy open table, doth provide
The purpled pheasant with the speckled side;
The painted partridge lies in every field,
And for thy mess is willing to be killed.   30
And if the high-swollen Medway[3] fail thy dish,
Thou hast thy ponds, that pay thee tribute fish,
Fat aged carps that run into thy net,
And pikes, now weary their own kind to eat,
As loth the second draught or cast to stay,
Officiously at first themselves betray;
Bright eels that emulate them, and leap on land
Before the fisher, or into his hand.
Then hath thy orchard fruit, thy garden flowers,
Fresh as the air, and new as are the hours.   40
The early cherry, with the later plum,
Fig, grape, and quince, each in his time doth come;
The blushing apricot and woolly peach
Hang on thy walls, that every child may reach.
And though thy walls be of the country stone,
They are reared with no man's ruin, no man's groan;
There's none that dwell about them wish them down;
But all come in, the farmer and the clown,
And no one empty-handed, to salute
Thy lord and lady, though they have no suit.   50
Some bring a capon, some a rural cake,
Some nuts, some apples; some that think they make
The better cheeses bring them, or else send
By their ripe daughters, whom they would commend
This way to husbands, and whose baskets bear
An emblem of themselves in plum or pear.
But what can this (more than express their love)

----

3. The Medway is the river on which the estate is located.

Add to thy free provisions, far above
The need of such? whose liberal board doth flow
With all that hospitality doth know;   60
Where comes no guest but is allowed to eat,
Without his fear, and of thy lord's own meat;
Where the same beer and bread, and self-same wine,
That is his lordship's shall be also mine,
And I not fain to sit, as some this day
At great men's tables, and yet dine away.
Here no man tells my cups, nor, standing by,
A waiter doth my gluttony envy,
But gives me what I call, and lets me eat;
He knows below he shall find plenty of meat.   70
Thy tables hoard not up for the next day;
Nor, when I take my lodging, need I pray
For fire, or lights, or livery; all is there,
As if thou then wert mine, or I reigned here:
There's nothing I can wish, for which I stay.
That found King James when, hunting late this way
With his brave son, the prince, they saw thy fires
Shine bright on every hearth, as the desires
Of thy Penates had been set on flame
To entertain them; or the country came,   80
With all their zeal, to warm their welcome here.
What great I will not say, but sudden cheer
Didst thou then make 'em! and what praise was heaped
On thy good lady then, who therein reaped
The just reward of her high housewifery;
To have her linen, plate, and all things nigh,
When she was far; and not a room but dressed
As if it had expected such a guest!
These, Penshurst, are thy praise, and yet not all.
Thy lady's noble, fruitful, chaste withal.   90
His children thy great lord may call his own,
A fortune in this age but rarely known.
They are, and have been, taught religion; thence
Their gentler spirits have sucked innocence.
Each morn and even they are taught to pray,
With the whole household, and may, every day,
Read in their virtuous parents' noble parts
The mysteries of manners, arms, and arts.
Now, Penshurst, they that will proportion thee
With other edifices, when they see   100
Those proud, ambitious heaps, and nothing else,
May say their lords have built, but thy lord dwells.

■ 1. This poem is about the "good life" both in moral and material terms. Demonstrate this.

2. Jonson evokes the sense of the abundance and fruitfulness of country life, including plant, animal, and human life. Single out and explain what terms best suggest the similarities between the vitality and bountifulness of human life and the other forms of life.

3. What is the meaning of "tells" in line 67?

4. What is the proportion of closed couplets? Are there any passages in which the development of the sense of the poem might be hindered by a series of closed couplets?

5. Is there any considerable number of sententious statements in this poem?

6. Analyze the final line of the poem for its neoclassical elements.

A Fit of Rhyme against Rhyme

Rhyme, the rack of finest wits,
That expresseth but by fits
    True conceit,
Spoiling senses of their treasure,
Cozening judgment with a measure,
    But false weight;
Wresting words from their true calling,
Propping verse for fear of falling
    To the ground;
Jointing syllables, drowning letters,   10
Fast'ning vowels as with fetters
    They were bound!
Soon as lazy thou wert known,
All good poetry hence was flown,
    And are banished.
For a thousand years together
All Parnassus' green did wither,
    And wit vanished.
Pegasus did fly away,
At the wells no Muse did stay,   20
    But bewailed
So to see the fountain dry,
And Apollo's music die,
    All light failed!
Starveling rhymes did fill the stage;
Not a poet in an age
    Worth crowning;
Not a work deserving bays,

Not a line deserving praise,
      Pallas frowning;   30
Greek was free from rhyme's infection,
Happy Greek by this protection
      Was not spoiled.
Whilst the Latin, queen of tongues,
Is not yet free from rhyme's wrongs,
      But rests foiled.
Scarce the hill again doth flourish,
Scarce the world a wit doth nourish
      To restore
Phoebus to his crown again,   40
And the Muses to their brain,
      As before.
Vulgar languages that want
Words and sweetness, and be scant
      Of true measure,
Tyrant rhyme hath so abusèd,
That they long since have refusèd
      Other caesure.
He that first invented thee,
May his joints tormented be,   50
      Cramped forever.
Still may syllables jar with time,
Still may reason war with rhyme,
      Resting never.
May his sense when it would meet
The cold tumor in his feet,
      Grow unsounder;
And his title be long fool,
That in rearing such a school
      Was the founder.   6

■ 1. Indicate the rhyme scheme in this poem.
    2. What, according to Jonson's opinion, are the difficulties th
poet puts in his own way by an excessive use of rhyme?

To the Immortal Memory and Friendship of That Noble Pair, Sir Lucius Cary and Sir H. Morison

The Turn

Brave infant of Saguntum, clear
Thy coming forth in that great year
When the prodigious Hannibal did crown

His rage with razing your immortal town.
Thou, looking then about,
Ere thou wert half got out,
Wise child, didst hastily return
And mad'st thy mother's womb thine urn.
How summed a circle didst thou leave mankind,
Of deepest lore, could we the center find!   10

The Counter-Turn

Did wiser nature draw thee back
From out the horror of that sack,
Where shame, faith, honor, and regard of right
Lay trampled on? The deeds of death and night
Urged, hurried forth, and hurled
Upon th' affrighted world;
Sword, fire, and famine with fell fury met,
And all on utmost ruin set;
As, could they but life's miseries foresee,
No doubt all infants would return like thee.   20

The Stand

For what is life, if measured by the space,
Not by the act?
Or maskèd man, if valued by his face,
Above his fact?
Here's one outlived his peers,
And told fourscore years;
He vexèd time, and busied the whole state,
Troubled both foes and friends,
But ever to no ends;
What did this stirrer but die late?   30
How well at twenty had he fallen or stood!
For three of his fourscore he did no good.

The Turn

He entered well, but virtuous parts
Got up, and thrived with honest arts;
He purchased friends and fame, and honors then,
And had his noble name advanced with men.
But weary of that flight,
He stooped in all men's sight
To sordid flatteries, acts of strife,
And sunk in that dead sea of life   40
So deep as he did then death's waters sup,
But that the cork of title buoyed him up.

The Counter-Turn

Alas, but Morison fell young!
He never fell,—thou fall'st, my tongue.
He stood, a soldier to the last right end,
A perfect patriot and a noble friend,
But most, a virtuous son.
All offices were done
By him so ample, full, and round,
In weight, in measure, number, sound,   50
As, though his age imperfect might appear,
His life was of humanity the sphere.

The Stand

Go now, and tell out days summed up with fears,
And make them years;
Produce thy mass of miseries on the stage,
To swell thine age;
Repeat of things a throng,
To show thou hast been long,
Not lived, for life doth her great actions spell
By what was done and wrought   60
In season, and so brought
To light; her measures are, how well
Each syllable answered, and was formed how fair;
These make the lines of life, and that's her air.

The Turn

It is not growing like a tree
In bulk, doth make man better be;
Or standing long an oak, three hundred year,
To fall a log at last, dry, bald, and sere;
A lily of a day
Is fairer far in May,   70
Although it fall and die that night,
It was the plant and flower of light.
In small proportions we just beauties see;
And in short measures, life may perfect be.

The Counter-Turn

Call, noble Lucius, then for wine,
And let thy looks with gladness shine;
Accept this garland, plant it on thy head,
And think, nay know, thy Morison's not dead.

He leaped the present age,
Possessed with holy rage,   80
To see that bright eternal day
Of which we priests and poets say
Such truths as we expect for happy men,
And there he lives with memory, and Ben

The Stand

Jonson, who sung this of him, ere he went
Himself to rest,
Or taste a part of that full joy he meant
To have expressed
In this bright asterism,
Where it were friendship's schism,   90
Were not his Lucius long with us to tarry,
To separate these twi-
Lights, the Dioscuri,
And keep the one half from his Harry.
But fate doth so alternate the design,
Whilst that in heav'n, this light on earth must shine.

The Turn

And shine as you exalted are,
Two names of friendship, but one star;
Of hearts the union, and those not by chance
Made, or indenture, or leased out t'advance   100
The profits for a time.
No pleasures vain did chime
Of rhymes, or riots at your feasts,
Orgies of drink, or feigned protests;
But simple love of greatness and of good,
That knits brave minds and manners more than blood.

The Counter-Turn

This made you first to know the why
You liked, then after to apply
That liking; and approach so one the t'other
Till either grew a portion of the other;   110
Each stylèd by his end
The copy of his friend.
You lived to be the great surnames
And titles by which all made claims
Unto the virtue; nothing perfect done
But as a Cary, or a Morison.

The Stand

And such a force the fair example had,
As they that saw
The good, and durst not practise it, were glad
That such a law
Was left yet to mankind,
Where they might read and find
Friendship in deed was written, not in words;
And with the heart, not pen,
Of two so early men,
Whose lines her rolls were, and records;
Who, ere the first down bloomèd on the chin,
Had sowed these fruits, and got the harvest in.

120

■ 1. This poem was written after the death, about 1629, of Sir Henry Morison, who was a friend of Sir Lucius Cary, later Lord Falkland, a member of the Tribe of Ben. What, according to the advice given in the poem, is the attitude one should take toward his premature death? Indeed, what is the advice in general about the way one should live and conduct oneself?

2. Is the image of the half-born child trying to return to the womb an ugly image? Does it have a place in the context of the statements and imagery before and after it?

3. Paraphrase the stanza beginning with line 65 and ending with line 74. Explain the meaning of each image.

4. Is there anything contradictory about the attitudes expressed early in the ode and those expressed toward the end of it? Is Jonson's attitude toward the death a simple one of grief and unhappiness, or does he see it in a more complex way?

An Epitaph on S. P.[1]

Weep with me, all you that read
  This little story:
And know, for whom a tear you shed
  Death's self is sorry.
'Twas a child that so did thrive
  In grace and feature,
As Heaven and Nature seem'd to strive
  Which own'd the creature.
Years he number'd scarce thirteen
  When Fates turn'd cruel,

---

1. One of the child actors.

Yet three fill'd zodiacs had he been
    The stage's jewel;
And did act, what now we moan,
    Old men so duly,
As, sooth, the Parcae[2] thought him one,
    He play'd so truly.
So, by error, to his fate
    They all consented;
But viewing him since, alas, too late!
    They have repented;
And have sought, to give new birth,
    In baths to steep him;
But being so much too good for Earth,
    Heaven vows to keep him.

2.   Three Fates.

On My First Son

Farewell, thou child of my right hand, and joy;
My sin was too much hope of thee, loved boy:
Seven years thou wert lent to me, and I thee pay,
Exacted by thy fate, on the just day.
O could I lose all father now! for why
Will man lament the state he should envy—
To have so soon 'scaped world's and flesh's rage,
And, if no other misery, yet age?
Rest in soft peace, and asked, say, "Here doth lie
Ben Jonson his best piece of poetry;
For whose sake henceforth all his vows be such
As what he loves may never like too much."

To William Camden

Camden,[1] most reverend head, to whom I owe
All that I am in arts, all that I know
(How nothing's that!), to whom my country owes
The great renown and name wherewith she goes;
Than thee the age sees not that thing more grave,
More high, more holy, that she more would crave.
What name, what skill, what faith hast thou in things!
What sight in searching the most antique springs!

1.   Jonson's teacher at Westminster School.

What weight and what authority in thy speech!
Man scarce can make that doubt, but thou canst teach.
Pardon free truth and let thy modesty,
Which conquers all, be once overcome by thee.
Many of thine, this better could than I;
But for their powers, accept my piety.

■ 1. Comment on the word "head" in the first line.
2. Is the repetition of the word "what" tedious or effective?

Still to Be Neat

Still to be neat, still to be drest,
As you were going to a feast;
Still to be powdered, still perfumed—
Lady, it is to be presumed,
Though art's hid causes are not found,
All is not sweet, all is not sound.

Give me a look, give me a face
That makes simplicity a grace.
Robes loosely flowing, hair as free,
Such sweet neglect more taketh me
Than all th' adulteries of art;
They strike mine eyes, but not my heart.

■ Compare the language of this with Herrick's "Delight in Disorder" (p. 147).

On My First Daughter

Here lies, to each her parents' ruth,
Mary, the daughter of their youth;
Yet all heaven's gifts being heaven's due,
It makes the father less to rue.
At six months' end she parted hence
With safety of her innocence;
Whose soul heaven's queen, whose name she bears,
In comfort of her mother's tears,
Hath placed amongst her virgin-train:
Where while that severed doth remain,
This grave partakes the fleshly birth;
Which cover lightly, gentle earth!

Song to Celia

Drink to me only with thine eyes,
    And I will pledge with mine;
Or leave a kiss but in the cup,
    And I'll not look for wine.
The thirst that from the soul doth rise
    Doth ask a drink divine;
But might I of Jove's nectar sup,
    I would not change for thine.

I sent thee late a rosy wreath,
    Not so much honoring thee
As giving it a hope, that there
    It could not withered be.
But thou thereon didst only breathe,
    And sent'st it back to me;
Since when it grows, and smells, I swear,
    Not of itself, but thee.

Robert Herrick

(1591–1674)

■■■■■■■■■

FIRST APPRENTICED to his uncle, a goldsmith, Robert Herrick entered Cambridge late. In the ten years after he left the university he was a member of the group of wits and authors who gathered around Ben Jonson. There is a record of his serving as a chaplain on an expedition against the French in 1627. Two years later he was made vicar at Dean Prior in Devonshire, where he learned the country lore and rituals which he put successfully into a number of his poems. When the Puritans came into power they replaced him, but during the next period of his life in London he did not take part in the political conflict. In 1648 he published *Hesperides*. If he had published the book ten or fifteen years earlier it probably would have been more popular than it was. Literary tastes had begun to shift, and his poetry seemed a little out of date. But apparently it was highly respected, for Herrick was represented in liberal fashion in several editions of *Wit's Recreation,* a popular anthology of the period. In 1662 Charles II returned Herrick to the vicarage at Dean Prior, where he spent the remaining thirteen years of his life.

Suggested Readings

Douglas Bush, *English Literature in the Earlier Seventeenth Century.*
New York: Oxford University Press, 1945, pp. 111–116.

Cleanth Brooks, "What Does Poetry Communicate?" in *The Well Wrought Urn.* New York: Reynal & Hitchcock, 1947, pp. 62–73.

■ ■ ■ ■ ■ ■ ■ ■ ■

The Mad Maid's Song

Good morrow to the day so fair;
    Good morning, sir, to you;
Good morrow to mine own torn hair,
    Bedabbled with the dew.

Good morning to this primrose too;
    Good morrow to each maid
That will with flowers the tomb bestrew
    Wherein my love is laid.

Ah, woe is me, woe, woe is me,
    Alack, and well-a-day!
For pity, sir, find out that bee
    Which bore my love away.

I'll seek him in your bonnet brave;
    I'll seek him in your eyes;
Nay, now I think they've made his grave
    I' th' bed of strawberries.

I'll seek him there; I know, ere this,
    The cold, cold earth doth shake him;
But I will go, or send a kiss
    By you, sir, to awake him.

Pray hurt him not; though he be dead,
    He knows well who do love him,
And who with green turfs rear his head,
    And who do rudely move him.

He's soft and tender: pray take heed;
    With bands of cowslips bind him,
And bring him home. But 'tis decreed
    That I shall never find him.

■   Students of the lyric have discovered that, generally speaking, the well-constructed lyric is divided into three parts. First, the poet gives the situation out of which the lyric is to grow; this is the emotional and intellectual stimulus. Second, as John Erskine in *The Elizabethan Lyric* puts it, "the emotion is developed to its utmost capacity, until as it begins to flag the intellectual element reasserts itself." Third, the poet takes advantage of the reader's aroused emotion by associating in a structural way a resolution or an intellectual evaluation with it.

One of the most skillful of lyric writers is Robert Herrick. His "The Mad Maid's Song" exhibits a dramatic structure—the reconciliation of heartbreak and madness with a sane acceptance of death. In the first two verses (the stimulus) Herrick gives us the situation: the girl's lover is dead, and she is mad. Without specifically asking for our sympathy he wins it by references to the newborn day and the beauty of the living primrose—contrasts, of course, with the dead lover:

> Good morrow to the day so fair;
> > Good morrow, sir, to you;
> Good morrow to mine own torn hair,
> > Bedabbled with the dew.

> Good morrow to the primrose too;
> > Good morrow to each maid
> That will with flowers the tomb bestrew
> > Wherein my love is laid.

Herrick employs ambiguity in the line "good morrow to mine own torn hair," suggesting not only her excessive grief but her madness. The further information, "Bedabbled with the dew," implies the wild nocturnal wanderings of the maid; yet the formality of her manner qualifies her madness. Stanzas 3, 4, 5, and 6 express the pathos inherent in the situation.

The wild grief of the girl is felt through her senseless suggestions for finding her dead lover. Toward the end of the poem her emotional debauch is tempered by her sane recognition of the fact—"though he be dead."

Lastly, there is the resolution of the emotion. The girl, returned to the edge of sanity, continues to talk as though mad, but she does so as a transitional step back to a rational acceptance of her permanent loss:

> He's soft and tender; pray take heed;
> > With band of cowslips bind him,
> And bring him home. But 'tis decreed
> > That I shall never find him.

To Daffodils

Fair daffodils, we weep to see
    You haste away so soon:
As yet the early-rising sun
    Has not attained his noon.
        Stay, stay,
    Until the hasting day
        Has run
    But to the evensong;
And, having prayed together, we
    Will go with you along.

We have short time to stay as you;
    We have as short a spring;
As quick a growth to meet decay,
    As you or anything.
        We die,
    As your hours do, and dry
        Away
    Like to the summer's rain;
Or as the pearls of morning's dew,
    Ne'er to be found again.

To the Virgins, to Make Much of Time

Gather ye rosebuds while ye may,
    Old Time is still a-flying;
And this same flower that smiles today
    Tomorrow will be dying.

The glorious lamp of heaven, the Sun,
    The higher he's a-getting,
The sooner will his race be run,
    And nearer he's to setting.

That age is best which is the first,
    When youth and blood are warmer;
But being spent, the worse and worst
    Times still succeed the former.

Then be not coy, but use your time;
    And while ye may, go marry;

> For having lost but once your prime,
>   You may forever tarry.

■ Discuss the structure of this lyric in terms similar to those employed in the discussion of "The Mad Maid's Song."

Delight in Disorder

> A sweet disorder in the dress
> Kindles in clothes a wantonness.
> A lawn about the shoulders thrown
> Into a fine distraction;
> An erring lace, which here and there
> Enthrals the crimson stomacher;
> A cuff neglectful, and thereby
> Ribbands to flow confusedly;
> A winning wave, deserving note,
> In the tempestuous petticoat;
> A careless shoestring, in whose tie
> I see a wild civility;—
> Do more bewitch me, than when art
> Is too precise in every part.

■ F. W. Bateson, in his *English Poetry and English Language,* comments as follows on the connotations and the levels of meaning in this poem:

> The impression of a surprising richness, and almost grandeur (as of a painting by Titian), with a certain tantalizing quality, that Her-rick's poem leaves, is primarily due to the skill with which he has exploited the ambiguous associations of the epithets. On the surface his subject is the 'Delight in Disorder' of the title—a disorder, that is, of costume. But a second subject is hinted at, though not protruded: a delight in disorder, not of costume but of manners and morals. It is not only the clothes but the wearers too whom he would have *sweet, wanton, distracted, erring, neglectful, winning, tempestuous, wild,* and *bewitching* rather than *precise.* The poem, in fact, instead of being the mere *jeu d'esprit* that it would seem to be, is essentially a plea for paganism. There are three themes: (1) untidiness is becoming; (2) the clothes are the woman; (3) anti-Puritanism. But the success of the poem depends upon the fact that the themes are not isolated and contrasted but grow out of and into each other. The suspension between the various meanings produces a range of reference that none of them would have alone.*

....

* F. W. Bateson, *English Poetry and English Language* (Oxford: The Clarendon Press, 1934). Reprinted by permission of the publishers.

The connotations, or what another critic, William Empson, has called the ambiguities, enable us to read the poem on these three levels. They enrich the experience of reading the poem. Herrick is especially adept at discovering and exploiting these levels of meaning.

Cherry-Ripe

Cherry-ripe, ripe, ripe I cry,
Full and fair ones; come and buy.
If so be you ask me where
They do grow, I answer: There,
Where my Julia's lips do smile;
There's the land, or cherry isle,
Whose plantations full show
All the year where cherries grow.

Upon Julia's Clothes

Whenas in silks my Julia goes,
Then, then, methinks, how sweetly flows
The liquefaction of her clothes.

Next, when I cast mine eyes, and see
That brave vibration, each way free,
Oh, how that glittering taketh me!

The Night Piece, to Julia

Her eyes the glow-worm lend thee;
The shooting stars attend thee;
    And the elves also,
    Whose little eyes glow
Like the sparks of fire, befriend thee.

No will-o'-the-wisp mislight thee,
Nor snake or slow-worm bite thee;
    But on, on thy way
    Not making a stay,
Since ghosts there's none to affright thee.

Let not the dark thee cumber;
What though the moon does slumber?

> The stars of the night
> Will lend thee their light
> Like tapers clear without number.
>
> Then, Julia, let me woo thee,
> Thus, thus to come unto me;
> And when I shall meet
> Thy silv'ry feet,
> My soul I'll pour into thee.

Upon Mistress Susanna Southwell Her Feet

> Her pretty feet
> Like snails did creep
> A little out, and then,
> As if they played at bo-peep,
> Did soon draw in again.

Corinna's Going A-Maying

Get up, get up for shame, the blooming morn
Upon her wings presents the god unshorn.[1]
   See how Aurora throws her fair
   Fresh-quilted colors through the air:
   Get up, sweet slug-a-bed, and see
   The dew bespangling herb and tree.
Each flower has wept and bowèd toward the east
Above an hour since: yet you not dressed;
   Nay! not so much as out of bed?
   When all the birds have matins said   10
   And sung their thankful hymns, 'tis sin,
   Nay, profanation, to keep in,
Whenas a thousand virgins on this day
Spring, sooner than the lark, to fetch in May.

Rise, and put on your foliage, and be seen
To come forth, like the springtime, fresh and green,
   And sweet as Flora. Take no care
   For jewels for your gown or hair:
   Fear not; the leaves will strew
   Gems in abundance upon you: 20

----

1. Apollo.

Besides, the childhood of the day has kept,
Against you come, some orient pearls unwept;
   Come and receive them while the light
   Hangs on the dew-locks of the night:
   And Titan on the eastern hill
   Retires himself, or else stands still
Till you come forth. Wash, dress, be brief in praying:
Few beads are best when once we go a-Maying.

Come, my Corinna, come; and, coming mark
How each field turns a street, each street a park   30
   Made green and trimmed with trees; see how
   Devotion gives each house a bough
   Or branch: each porch, each door ere this
   An ark, a tabernacle is,
Made up of white-thorn, neatly interwove;
As if here were those cooler shades of love.
   Can such delights be in the street
   And open fields and we not see 't?
   Come, we'll abroad; and let's obey
   The proclamation made for May: 40
And sin no more, as we have done, by staying;
But, my Corinna, come, let's go a-Maying.

There's not a budding boy or girl this day
But is got up, and gone to bring in May.
   A deal of youth, ere this, is come
   Back, and with white-thorn laden home.
   Some have dispatched their cakes and cream
   Before that we have left to dream:
And some have wept, and wooed, and plighted troth,
And chose their priest, ere we can cast off sloth: 50
   Many a green-gown has been given;
   Many a kiss, both odd and even:
   Many a glance too has been sent
   From out the eye, love's firmament;
Many a jest told of the keys betraying
This night, and locks picked, yet we're not a-Maying.

Come, let us go while we are in our prime,
And take the harmless folly of the time.
   We shall grow old apace, and die
   Before we know our liberty.   60
   Our life is short, and our days run
   As fast away as does the sun;

And, as a vapor or a drop of rain,
Once lost, can ne'er be found again,
　　So when or you or I are made
　　A fable, song, or fleeting shade,
　　All love, all liking, all delight
　　Lies drowned with us in endless night.
Then while time serves, and we are but decaying,
Come, my Corinna, come let's go a-Maying.　　　　70

■　1. Indicate all the imagery which serves to identify the young with nature.

　2. Explain how the imagery of dew or vapor supports the theme.

　3. What is the purpose and what is the tone evoked by the use of Christian terms ("sin," "ark," "tabernacle," and the like) in the service of a pagan point of view?

　4. This poem has been analyzed in detail by Cleanth Brooks in *The Well Wrought Urn,* pp. 62–73. The student may compare his answers to the above questions with the statements made by Brooks.

To the Water Nymphs, Drinking at the Fountain

Reach with your whiter hands to me
　　Some crystal of the spring,
And I about the cup shall see
　　Fresh lilies flourishing.

Or else, sweet nymphs, do you but this—
　　To the glass your lips incline,
And I shall see by that one kiss
　　The water turned to wine.

■　Discuss the mixture of pagan and Christian elements in this poem.

An Ode for Ben Jonson

Ah, Ben!
Say how or when
Shall we, thy guests,
Meet at those lyric feasts,
Made at the Sun,
The Dog, the Triple Tun;
Where we such clusters had,
As made us nobly wild, not mad?

And yet each verse of thine
Out-did the meat, out-did the frolic wine.

My Ben!
Or come again,
Or send to us
Thy wit's great overplus;
But teach us yet
Wisely to husband it,
Lest we that talent spend;
And having once brought to an end
That precious stock, the store
Of such a wit the world should have no more.

Litany to the Holy Spirit

In the hour of my distress,
When temptations me oppress,
And when I my sins confess,
        Sweet Spirit, comfort me!

When I lie within my bed,
Sick in heart and sick in head,
And with doubts discomforted,
        Sweet Spirit, comfort me!

When the house doth sigh and weep,
And the world is drowned in sleep,   10
Yet mine eyes the watch do keep,
        Sweet Spirit, comfort me!

When the artless doctor sees
No one hope, but of his fees,
And his skill runs on the lees,
        Sweet Spirit, comfort me!

When his potion and his pill,
Has, or none, or little skill,
Meet for nothing but to kill,
        Sweet Spirit, comfort me!   20

When the passing bell doth toll,
And the furies in a shoal
Come to fright a parting soul,
        Sweet Spirit, comfort me!

When the tapers now burn blue,
And the comforters are few,
And that number more than true,
     Sweet Spirit, comfort me!

When the priest his last hath prayed,
And I nod to what is said,
'Cause my speech is now decayed,
     Sweet Spirit, comfort me!

When, God knows, I'm tossed about
Either with despair or doubt;
Yet before the glass be out,
     Sweet Spirit, comfort me!

When the tempter me pursu'th
With the sins of all my youth,
And half damns me with untruth,
     Sweet Spirit, comfort me!   40

When the flames and hellish cries
Fright mine ears and fright mine eyes,
And all terrors me surprise,
     Sweet Spirit, comfort me!

When the Judgment is revealed,
And that opened which was sealed,
When to Thee I have appealed,
     Sweet Spirit, comfort me!

George Herbert

(1593–1633)

. . . .

GEORGE HERBERT was the youngest son of a noble family. His mother, a widowed lady of intelligence and of engaging personality, was a close friend to John Donne, whom the young Herbert knew and whose religious poems he admired. Herbert entered Cambridge in 1609, was graduated Master of Arts in 1616, and stayed on at the university, teaching and preparing himself for the ministry. It was assumed by his mother, as well as by himself, that he would become a clergyman, but when in 1619 he was appointed public orator at Cambridge he changed his plans. This was an attractive and promising position, allowing him to exercise his talents and to participate in the fashionable life of his times. Through this position he gained the favorable attention of James I. But when the king and several influential friends died within a short period, Herbert felt again the attraction of the church and finally chose to abandon his hopes for a public career. He resigned his oratorship in 1627, married Jane Danvers in 1629, and in 1630 was ordained priest and instituted at the little church in Bemerton, near Salisbury. There Herbert lived simply and happily in the years that remained, writing poetry and gaining the enduring reputation of an exemplary priest. Shortly before his death Herbert turned the manuscript of his poems over to the discretion of Nicholas Ferrar, friend of his last years and establisher of the monastic community at Little Gidding. Ferrar aranged the publication of Herbert's poems, *The Temple,* soon after Herbert's death.

Suggested Readings

L. C. KNIGHTS, "George Herbert," in *Explorations.* New York: George W. Stewart, Publisher, 1947, pp. 129–148.

ROSEMOND TUVE, *A Reading of George Herbert.* Chicago: University of Chicago Press, 1952.

AUSTIN WARREN, "George Herbert," in *Rage for Order.* Chicago: University of Chicago Press, 1948, pp. 19–37.

HELEN C. WHITE, *The Metaphysical Poets.* New York: The Macmillan Company, 1936.

■■■■■■■■■

George Herbert was an admirer of John Donne, the man who preached in St. Paul's and who wrote the *Holy Sonnets* and other religious poems. While Herbert is often considered as belonging to the religious branch of "the school of Donne," it would be inaccurate to say that he was *influenced* by Donne. But it may be said that he followed Donne's lead. He did so, generally speaking, by writing religious poetry in the first place. And, more particularly, his work is comparable to Donne's in certain stylistic features. Both poets often use metaphor as an essential device for conveying and developing ideas. Like Donne, Herbert avoids the diction, images, and allusions of older literary traditions. He goes to religious tradition and to whatever will best serve to convey his meaning. And again like Donne, his language has a prosaic and conversational quality, and his versification tends toward the natural rhythms of speech, although not so vigorously as Donne's.

A number of Herbert's poems are explicit testimony of his consciousness of the literary conventions which were operating in his time, and of his rejection of them. In the sonnet addressed to his mother and in the first "Jordan" poem, he opposes the secular literary conventions, especially those of love poetry, with religious attitudes and traditions. In the sonnet he deplores the erotic tradition which celebrates the pagan gods, Venus and Cupid. In "Jordan [1]" he dismisses "veiled" allegory, the pastoral tradition, and celebrations of worldly beauty—"nightingale or spring." Herbert's practice was always consistent with the principles argued in these poems, but "Jordan [2]" is quite another matter. Here the principles are violated by the very phrases with which they are argued. "Curling with metaphors a plain intention" is itself a rather finely curled metaphor, and the "sense" of the whole poem, and of many other poems of Herbert's, is skillfully woven. His aim was, of course, to produce an effect of purity and simplicity of feeling, and in this he succeeded repeatedly, but not by sparing expense of intelligence, imagination, or craftsmanship. Rarely, if ever, did the sincerity of his commitment to religious themes distract him from high literary standards or betray his technical resourcefulness. No less than Donne, or any composer of short poems, Herbert was a master of organization. His themes are usually developed with economy and with a clarity and purposefulness of structure. His control of form is otherwise indicated by the variety of stanzaic patterns used—116 unrepeated patterns in 169 poems.

In Herbert's poetry there are a quietness of tone and a clarity of effect which may obscure the intellectuality of his thought and the subtlety and skillfulness of his technique. Herbert's lyrics, like those of Donne, are often dramatic, but with a difference. Many of Donne's poems, secular and religious, are spoken by a person who is engaged in psychological or spiritual conflict, whereas Herbert's poems are spoken by a person who has passed through the conflict and looks back upon it from a condition of relative tranquillity. These differences may, of course, be validly allied with the differences in the personalities of the two poets and in the courses of their lives. A good illustration of Herbert's quieter tone and more reconciled attitude is the autobiographical poem "Affliction," especially the following stanza:

> Whereas my birth and spirit rather took
>   The way that takes the town,
> Thou didst betray me to a ling'ring book
>   And wrap me in a gown.
> I was entangled in the world of strife
> Before I had the power to change my life.

To His Mother

> My God, where is that ancient heat towards thee
>   Wherewith whole shoals of martyrs once did burn,
>   Besides their other flames? Doth poetry

Wear Venus' livery, only serve her turn?
Why are not sonnets made of thee, and lays
Upon thine altar burnt? Cannot thy love
Heighten a spirit to sound out thy praise
As well as any she? Cannot thy dove
Outstrip their Cupid easily in flight?
Or, since thy ways are deep and still the same,
Will not a verse run smooth that bears thy name?
Why doth that fire, which by thy power and might
Each breast does feel, no braver fuel choose
Than that which one day worms may chance refuse?

■ Discuss the development of this poem with respect to denotation and connotation of the words "heat," "burn," "flames," "fire," "fuel."

Jordan [1]

Who says that fictions only and false hair
Become a verse? Is there in truth no beauty?
Is all good structure in a winding stair?
May no lines pass except they do their duty
　　Not to a true, but painted chair?

Is it no verse except enchanted groves
And sudden arbors shadow coarse-spun lines?
Must purling streams refresh a lover's loves?
Must all be veiled, while he that reads, divines,
　　Catching the sense at two removes?

Shepherds are honest people; let them sing.
Riddle who list for me, and pull for prime;
I envy no man's nightingale or spring,
Nor let them punish me with loss of rhyme,
　　Who plainly say, My God, my King.

■ 1. List the images of the poem in the order of their occurrence. Explain the relationship among the images and the particular meaning which each image derives from its context.

2. How important in this poem is the visual function of the imagery?

3. Which is the antecedent of "who" (in the last line): "them" or "me"? Would a consideration of this grammatical ambiguity be relevant to the meaning of the poem? If it is assumed that Herbert meant "me" as the antecedent, would the possible ambiguity still be relevant and of interest—would it still be part of the poem?

Jordan [2]

When first my lines of heav'nly joys made mention,
Such was their luster, they did so excel,
That I sought out quaint words and trim invention;
My thoughts began to burnish, sprout, and swell,
Curling with metaphors a plain intention,
Decking the sense as if it were to sell.

Thousands of notions in my brain did run,
Off'ring their service, if I were not sped.
I often blotted what I had begun:
This was not quick enough, and that was dead.
Nothing could seem too rich to clothe the sun,
Much less those joys which trample on his head.

As flames do work and wind when they ascend,
So did I weave myself into the sense.
But while I bustled, I might hear a friend
Whisper, How wide is all this long pretense!
There is in love a sweetness ready penned,
Copy out only that, and save expense.

The Altar

A broken altar, Lord, Thy servant rears,
Made of a heart and cemented with tears;
Whose parts are as Thy hand did frame;
No workman's tool hath touched the same.
A   heart   alone
Is such a stone
As nothing but
Thy power doth cut.
Wherefore each part
Of my hard heart
Meets in this frame
To praise Thy name;
That if I chance to hold my peace,
These stones to praise Thee may not cease.
O let thy blessed sacrifice be mine,
And sanctify this altar to be Thine.

■ "The Altar" and "Easter Wings" (below) have stanzaic and typographical shapes which visually represent the titles and subjects (or more

accurately, basic metaphors) of the poems. Herbert's practice here probably owes something to the "emblem literature" of the seventeenth century, in which picture engravings and poems complemented each other in presenting a single thought or moral. It is also possible that Donne, Herbert, and other metaphysical poets, in their use of images or visual situations for metaphor, symbol, and allegory, show the influence of the emblems. These two poems may be considered also as showing aspects of baroque tendency—the representation of an idea by profuse and ingenious detail.

Easter Wings

Lord, who createdst man in wealth and store,
Though foolishly he lost the same,
Decaying more and more
Till he became
Most poor;
With Thee
O let me rise
As larks, harmoniously,
And sing this day Thy victories;
Then shall the fall further the flight in me.

My tender age in sorrow did begin;
And still with sickness and shame
Thou didst so punish sin,
That I became
Most thin.
With Thee
Let me combine,
And feel this day Thy victory;
For if I imp my wing on Thine,
Affliction shall advance the flight in me.

■ Do the varying lengths of the lines serve any purpose besides the pictorial?

The Pulley

When God at first made man,
Having a glass of blessings standing by,
Let us, said he. pour on him all we can.

Let the world's riches, which dispersèd lie,
   Contract into a span.

   So strength first made a way,
Then beauty flowed, then wisdom, honor, pleasure.
When almost all was out, God made a stay,
Perceiving that alone of all his treasure
   Rest in the bottom lay.

   For if I should, said he,
Bestow this jewel also on my creature,
He would adore my gifts instead of me,
And rest in nature, not the God of nature;
   So both should losers be.

   Yet let him keep the rest,
But keep them with repining restlessness.
Let him be rich and weary, that at least,
If goodness lead him not, yet weariness
   May toss him to my breast.

Aaron

   Holiness on the head,
    Light and perfections on the breast,
Harmonious bells below, raising the dead
    To lead them unto life and rest:
     Thus are true Aarons dressed.

   Profaneness in my head,
    Defects and darkness in my breast,
A noise of passions ringing me for dead
    Unto a place where is no rest:
     Poor priest, thus am I dressed.

   Only another head
    I have, another heart and breast,
Another music, making live not dead,
    Without whom I could have no rest:
     In him I am well dressed.

   Christ is my only head,
    My alone only heart and breast,
My only music, striking me ev'n dead,

That to the old man I may rest,
And be in him new dressed.

So holy in my head,
Perfect and light in my dear breast,
My doctrine tuned by Christ, who is not dead,
. But lives in me while I do rest,
Come people! Aaron's dressed.

■   1. Aaron, the brother of Moses, was the first Israelite high priest
and was traditionally regarded as the ancestor of all high priests, whose
office was hereditary and who wore distinctive priestly vestments.
What does this allusion contribute to the poem?

2. What are the effects of the same end words repeated throughout the stanzas?

The Collar

I struck the board and cried, No more!
I will abroad.
What? Shall I ever sigh and pine?
My lines and life are free, free as the road,
Loose as the wind, as large as store.
Shall I be still in suit?
Have I no harvest but a thorn
To let me blood, and not restore
What I have lost with cordial fruit?
Sure there was wine
Before my sighs did dry it; there was corn
Before my tears did drown it.
Is the year only lost to me?
Have I no bays to crown it?
No flowers, no garlands gay? All blasted?
All wasted?
Not so, my heart! But there is fruit,
And thou hast hands.
Recover all thy sigh-blown age
On double pleasures. Leave thy cold dispute
Of what is fit and not. Forsake thy cage,
Thy rope of sands,
Which petty thoughts have made, and made to thee
Good cable, to enforce and draw,
And be thy law,
While thou didst wink and wouldst not see.

Away! Take heed!
I will abroad.
Call in thy death's head there. Tie up thy fears.
He that forbears
To suit and serve his need
Deserves his load.
But as I raved and grew more fierce and wild
At every word,
Me thought I heard one calling, Child!
And I replied, My Lord.

This poem is at once dramatic and allegorical. In what way does each of these aspects affect the tone?

Virtue

Sweet day, so cool, so calm, so bright,
The bridal of the earth and sky;
The dew shall weep thy fall to-night,
For thou must die.

Sweet rose, whose hue angry and brave
Bids the rash gazer wipe his eye;
Thy root is ever in its grave,
And thou must die.

Sweet spring, full of sweet days and roses,
A box where sweets compacted lie;
My music shows ye have your closes,
And all must die.

Only a sweet and virtuous soul,
Like seasoned timber, never gives;
But though the whole world turn to coal,
Then chiefly lives.

Life

I made a posie while the day ran by:
Here will I smell my remnant out, and tie
My life within this band;

But Time did beckon to the flowers, and they
By noon most cunningly did steal away,
    And withered in my hand.

My hand was next to them, and then my heart;
I took, without more thinking, in good part
    Time's gentle admonition;
Who did so sweetly Death's sad taste convey,
Making my mind to smell my fatal day,
    Yet sugaring the suspicion.

Farewell, dear flowers; sweetly your time ye spent,
Fit while ye lived for smell or ornament,
    And after death for cures.
I follow straight, without complaints or grief;
Since if my scent be good, I care not if
    It be as short as yours.

■   The comparison of man's life to a flower is familiar in both literary and religious traditions. What details in Herbert's treatment of this familiar material give it fresh interest and poetic effect?

Discipline

Throw away thy rod,
Throw away thy wrath.
    O my God,
Take the gentle path.

For my heart's desire
Unto thine is bent;
    I aspire
To a full consent.

Not a word or look
I affect to own,
    But by book,
And thy book alone.

Though I fail, I weep.
Though I halt in pace,
    Yet I creep
To the throne of grace.

Then let wrath remove;
Love will do the deed,
For with love
Stony hearts will bleed.   20

Love is swift of foot.
Love's a man of war,
And can shoot,
And can hit from far.

Who can 'scape his bow?
That which wrought on thee,
Brought thee low,
Needs must work on me.

Throw away thy rod.
Though man frailties hath,   30
Thou art God.
Throw away thy wrath.

1. What do the various details of versification in this poem contribute to its tone?

2. In many seventeenth-century poems there is a mingling of elements from pagan classicism and the Christian tradition. Is there much mingling of elements in this poem?

Death

Death, thou wast once an uncouth hideous thing,
Nothing but bones,
The sad effect of sadder groans:
Thy mouth was open, but thou couldst not sing.

For we considered thee as at some six
Or ten years hence,
After the loss of life and sense;
Flesh being turned to dust, and bones to sticks.

We looked on this side of thee, shooting short,
Where we did find
The shells of fledge-souls left behind;
Dry dust, which sheds no tears, but may extort.

But since our Saviour's death did put some blood
Into thy face,

Thou art grown fair and full of grace,
Much in request, much sought for, as a good.

For we do now behold thee gay and glad,
As at doomsday,
When souls shall wear their new array,
And all thy bones with beauty shall be clad.

Therefore we can go die as sleep, and trust
Half that we have
Unto an honest faithful grave,
Making our pillows either down or dust.

1. Discuss imagery, metaphor, wit, and irony in this poem.
2. Compare Herbert's poem with Donne's sonnet which begins "Death, be not proud." What are the similarities and differences?
3. Discuss the two poems (Donne's and Herbert's) as characteristic of the work of the two poets.

The Temper

How should I praise thee, Lord? How should my rhymes
Gladly engrave thy love in steel,
If, what my soul doth feel sometimes,
My soul might ever feel!

Although there were some forty heavens or more,
Sometimes I peer above them all;
Sometimes I hardly reach a score,
Sometimes to hell I fall.

Oh, rack me not to such a vast extent,
Those distances belong to thee;
The world's too little for thy tent,
A grave too big for me.

Wilt thou meet arms with man, that thou dost stretch
A crumb of dust from heaven to hell?
Will great God measure with a wretch?
Shall he thy stature spell?

Oh, let me, when thy roof my soul hath hid,
Oh, let me roost and nestle there;

Then of a sinner thou art rid,
        And I of hope and fear.

Yet take thy way; for sure thy way is best:
        Stretch or contract me, thy poor debter;
    This is but tuning of my breast,
            To make the music better.

Whether I fly with angels, fall with dust,
        Thy hands made both, and I am there;
    Thy power and love, my love and trust,
            Make one place everywhere.

■   What is the significance of the title?

Mortification

    How soon doth man decay!
When clothes are taken from a chest of sweets
    To swaddle infants, whose young breath
            Scarce knows the way,
    Those clouts are little winding-sheets,
Which do consign and send them unto death.

    When boys go first to bed,
They step into their voluntary graves;
    Sleep binds them fast, only their breath
            Makes them not dead: 10
    Successive nights, like rolling waves,
Convey them quickly who are bound for death.

    When youth is frank and free,
And calls for music, while his veins do swell,
    All day exchanging mirth and breath
            In company,
    That music summons to the knell
Which shall befriend him at the house of death.

    When man grows staid and wise,
Getting a house and home, where he may move   20
    Within the circle of his breath,
            Schooling his eyes,
    That dumb inclosure maketh love
Unto the coffin that attends his death.

When age grows low and weak,
Marking his grave, and thawing every year,
Till all do melt and drown his breath
When he would speak,
A chair or litter shows the bier
Which shall convey him to the house of death.   30

Man, ere he is aware,
Hath put together a solemnity,
And dressed his hearse, while he has breath
As yet to spare;
Yet, Lord, instruct us so to die,
That all these dyings may be *life in death*.

Richard Crashaw

(1613?–1649)

■ ■ ■ ■ ■ ■ ■ ■ ■ ■

THE SON of an Anglican clergyman bitterly opposed to Catholicism, Richard Crashaw became, after graduation from Pembroke College, Cambridge University, a Fellow at Peterhouse, the college noted for its Roman Catholic tendencies, and he often visited the ascetic Nicholas Ferrar and his community of Little Gidding.

At Cambridge he spent much time in prayer and in devotions, wrote poetry and had a friendly association with Abraham Cowley and Joseph Beaumont, also poets. Crashaw fled the university when the Puritan forces required the Covenant (an agreement to support Presbyterianism) of all who remained. Just when he left the Anglican fold is not known, but in 1647 he was in the household of Cardinal Palotto at Rome, having been given a recommendation to the prelate by Henrietta Maria, the exiled queen of Charles I. Among the Cardinal's household he saw such licentious behavior that he protested, arousing so much enmity that Palotto had to send him to the church at Loretto, where he died within a month. Two versions of the cause of his death have come down to us: that he easily succumbed to an illness after an exhausting trip to the parish of Loretto; and that he was poisoned by his enemies in the Cardinal's household.

Crashaw's first volume of English verse, *Steps to the Temple, Sacred Poems with other Delights of the Muses,* appeared in 1646, and in 1652 a volume entitled *Carmen Deo Nostro* was published in Paris.

uggested Readings

R. C. WALLERSTEIN, *Richard Crashaw, a Study in Style and Poetic Development.* Madison: University of Wisconsin Press, 1935.

AUSTIN WARREN, *Richard Crashaw, a Study in Baroque Sensibility.* Baton Rouge: Louisiana State University Press, 1939.

■■■■■■■■

A Hymn to the Name and Honor of the Admirable Saint Teresa

Foundress of the Reformation of the Discalced Carmelites, both men and women; a woman of angelical heights of speculation, for masculine courage of performance, more than a woman, who yet a child outran maturity, and durst plot a martyrdom.

Love, thou art absolute sole lord
Of life and death. To prove the word,
We'll now appeal to none of all
Those thy old soldiers, great and tall,
Ripe men of martyrdom, that could reach down
With strong arms their triumphant crown,
Such as could with lusty breath,
Speak loud into the face of death
Their great Lord's glorious name, to none
Of those whose spacious bosoms spread a throne   10
For Love at large to fill; spare blood and sweat,
And see him take a private seat,
Making his mansion in the mild
And milky soul of a soft child.
  Scarce has she learned to lisp the name
Of martyr; yet she thinks it shame
Life should so long play with that breath
Which, spent, can buy so brave a death.
She never undertook to know
What death with Love should have to do;   20
Nor has she e'er yet understood
Why, to show love, she should shed blood;
Yet, though she cannot tell you why,
She can love, and she can die.
  Scarce has she blood enough to make
A guilty sword blush for her sake;
Yet has she a heart dares hope to prove
How much less strong is death than Love.

Be Love but there, let poor six years
Be posed with the maturest fears   30
Man trembles at, you straight shall find
Love knows no nonage, nor the mind;
'Tis Love, not years or limbs, that can
Make the martyr or the man.

Love touched her heart, and, lo, it beats
High, and burns with such brave heats,
Such thirsts to die, as dares drink up
A thousand cold deaths in one cup.
Good reason; for she breathes all fire;
Her white breast heaves with strong desire   40
Of what she may, with fruitless wishes,
Seek for amongst her mother's kisses.

Since 'tis not to be had at home
She'll travel to a martyrdom.
No home for hers confesses she,
But where she may a martyr be.

She'll to the Moors, and trade with them
For this unvalued diadem.
She'll offer them her dearest breath,
With Christ's name in it, in change for death.   50
She'll bargain with them, and will give
Them God; teach them how to live
In Him; or, if they this deny,
For Him she'll teach them how to die.
So shall she leave amongst them sown
Her Lord's blood, or at least her own.

Farewell, then, all the world! Adieu!
Teresa is no more for you.
Farewell, all pleasures, sports, and joys
(Never till now esteemed toys);   60
Farewell, whatever dear may be,
Mother's arms, or father's knee;
Farewell, house, and farewell, home!
She's for the Moors and martyrdom.

Sweet, not so fast! lo, thy fair spouse,
Whom thou seek'st with so swift vows,
Calls thee back, and bids thee come
To embrace a milder martyrdom.

Blest powers forbid thy tender life
Should bleed upon a barbarous knife,   70
Or some base hand have power to raze
Thy breast's chaste cabinet, and uncase
A soul kept there so sweet; O no,

Wise Heaven will never have it so:
Thou art Love's victim, and must die
A death more mystical and high.
Into Love's arms thou shalt let fall
A still-surviving funeral.
His is the dart must make the death
Whose stroke shall taste thy hallowed breath;   80
A dart thrice dipped in that rich flame
Which writes thy spouse's radiant name
Upon the roof of heaven, where aye
It shines, and with a sovereign ray
Beats bright upon the burning faces
Of souls, which in that name's sweet graces
Find everlasting smiles. So rare,
So spiritual, pure, and fair
Must be the immortal instrument
Upon whose choice point shall be sent   90
A life so loved; and that there be
Fit executioners for thee,
The fairest and first-born sons of fire,
Blest seraphim, shall leave their quire,
And turn Love's soldiers, upon thee
To exercise their archery.

   O how oft shalt thou complain
Of a sweet and subtle pain;
Of intolerable joys;
Of a death in which who dies   100
Loves his death, and dies again,
And would forever so be slain,
And lives, and dies, and knows not why
To live, but that he thus may never leave to die.

   How kindly will thy gentle heart
Kiss the sweetly killing dart,
And close in his embraces keep
Those delicious wounds, that weep
Balsam to heal themselves with. Thus
When these thy deaths, so numerous,   110
Shall all at last die into one,
And melt thy soul's sweet mansion,
Like a soft lump of incense, hasted
By too hot a fire, and wasted
Into perfuming clouds, so fast
Shalt thou exhale to heaven at last
In a resolving sigh, and then,—
O what? Ask not the tongues of men.

Angels cannot tell; suffice
Thyself shall feel thine own full joys   120
And hold them fast forever there.
So soon as thou shalt first appear,
The moon of maiden stars, thy white
Mistress, attended by such bright
Souls as thy shining self, shall come,
And in her first ranks make thee room;
Where 'mongst her snowy family
Immortal welcomes wait for thee.

    O what delight, when revealed Life shall stand,
And teach thy lips heaven with His hand;   130
On which thou now may'st to thy wishes
Heap up thy consecrated kisses.
What joys shall seize thy soul when she,
Bending her blessed eyes on thee
(Those second smiles of heaven), shall dart
Her mild rays through thy melting heart!
    Angels, thy old friends, there shall greet thee,
Glad at their own home now to meet thee.
    All thy good works which went before
And waited for thee at the door   140
Shall own thee there; and all in one
Weave a constellation
Of crowns, with which the King, thy spouse,
Shall build up thy triumphant brows.
    All thy old woes shall now smile on thee,
And thy pains sit right upon thee;
All thy sorrows here shall shine,
All thy sufferings be divine.
Tears shall take comfort and turn gems,
And wrongs repent to diadems.   150
Even thy deaths shall live, and new
Dress the soul that erst they slew.
Thy wounds shall blush to such bright scars
As keep account of the Lamb's wars.
    Those rare works where thou shalt leave writ
Love's noble history, with wit
Taught thee by none but Him, while here
They feed our souls, shall clothe thine there.
Each heavenly word by whose hid flame
Our hard hearts shall strike fire, the same   16
Shall flourish on thy brows, and be
Both fire to us and flame to thee,
Whose light shall live bright in thy face

By glory, in our hearts by grace.
    Thou shalt look round about, and see
Thousands of crowned souls throng to be
Themselves thy crown, sons of thy vows,
The virgin-births with which thy sovereign spouse
Made fruitful thy fair soul. Go now,
And with them all about thee, bow
To Him. "Put on," He'll say, "put on,   170
My rosy love, that thy rich zone
Sparkling with the sacred flames
Of thousand souls, whose happy names
Heaven keep upon thy score": thy bright
Life brought them first to kiss the light
That kindled them to stars. And so
Thou with the Lamb, thy Lord, shalt go;
And wheresoe'er He sets His white
Steps, walk with Him those ways of light,   180
Which who in death would live to see,
Must learn in life to die like thee.

■   In order to discuss this poem either in its theme or its techniques it is necessary to relate it to the baroque art which was an important part of the Counter-Reformation in Europe in the late Renaissance. There is in contemporary scholarship a growing tendency to consider the Metaphysical poets as baroque, to label their period the baroque era. Here we are concerned merely with Crashaw's methods.

    Crashaw seems to have had great sympathy with the conviction that religious themes and attitudes are best represented through ritualistic acts and sensuous images. The Protestant reformers held that such representations hindered the soul in coming close to God. This was, of course, opposed to the Catholic teaching, and in the Counter-Reformation the conviction that the senses should be employed to aid in devotions was ardently reaffirmed. For example, humility is held to be aided by genuflection, or pity to be stirred by kissing the crucifix. During the Counter-Reformation, painting, sculpture, poetry, and architecture re-emphasized the Catholic conviction in this matter. Every part of the Christian story and beliefs which could be represented were represented, usually in an exuberant, sensuous, and grandiose style. The effect of conjoining the spiritual and the sensuous was, as Austin Warren has put it, "a strange tension between materiality and spirituality. . . ." We find in the poetry that is a part of this baroque movement a highly sophisticated rhetoric: the pun, oxymoron, paradox, antithesis, highly imaginative metaphors, and a rather gaudy diction.

    In this particular poem Crashaw is, of course, writing about the Spanish mystic, St. Teresa, who had had great influence through a number of her books which dealt with her religious ecstasies. She related how in one of her visions she had been visited by a seraph who plunged a fire-tipped dart of gold into her heart: "The pain of it was so excessive that it forced me to utter those groans; and the suavity, which that extremity of pain gave, was also so very excessive that there was no desiring at all to be rid of it." In other words, the experience was composed equally of pain and joy. The presence of these contradictory elements invites the poet to use special figures of speech in invoking the experience, for example, the oxymoron (a rhetorical device bringing together two contradictory terms). In Crashaw's poem Teresa's experience of this mixture of pain and joy is described in these lines:

> O how oft shalt thou complain
> Of a *sweet* and subtle *pain;*
> Of *intolerable joys*
>
> (ll. 97–99)

> How kindly will thy gentle heart
> Kiss the *sweetly killing* dart,
> And close in his embraces keep
> Those *delicious wounds,* that weep
> Balsam to heal themselves with. . . .
>
> (ll. 105–109)

The oxymoron, like the paradox and antithetical statements, is appropriate to the treating of the subject, "love's wound."

Similarly, the poem employs several paradoxes. Christian teaching, as we know, abounds in the use of paradoxes and antithetical statements. They are to be found, for example, in the Sermon on the Mount: "Blessed are the meek, for they shall inherit the earth," and "Blessed are ye when men shall revile and persecute you and say all manner of evil against you falsely for my sake." Similarly, in other Christian teachings: "The first shall be last, and the last shall be first," and "He that loses his life for my sake shall find it." The opposition between the temporal and eternal invites such antithetical and paradoxical statements. We should expect therefore to find one or more of them in a poem on St. Teresa. The persistent paradoxical theme of the poem is that death is life. Thus her death is

> A still-surviving funeral.
>
> (l. 78)

Because death is so desired by Teresa she would welcome repeated deaths:

> Of a death in which who dies
> Loves his death, and dies again,

> And would forever so be slain,
> And lives, and dies, and knows not why
> To live, but that he thus may never leave to die.
>
> (ll. 100–104)

The repeated "deaths" she died will, as it were, be her attendants for eternity:

> Even thy deaths shall live, and new
> Dress the soul that erst they slew.
>
> (ll. 151–152)

Finally, the central paradox of the poem, and an important Christian teaching, draws all the statements together at the close: Whoever would attain eternal life, says the poet,

> . . . who in death would live to see,
> Must learn in life to die like thee.
>
> (ll. 181–182)

The tension between things temporal and things eternal, as we have said, invites contrasting phrases and statements, as in the oxymoron and paradox. It invites too the contrasts found in antithetical statements. The poet, in this instance, contrasts Teresa's temporal pains with her eternal joys in a series of antithesis:

> All thy old woes shall now smile on thee,
> And thy pains sit bright upon thee;
> All thy sorrows here shall shine,
> All thy sufferings be divine.
>
> (ll. 145–148)

Lines of a similar nature can be found as well in other parts of the poem.

Occasionally, also, there is a pun or an ambiguous use of a word, as in the last of the following lines:

> . . . yet she thinks it shame
> Life should so long play with that breath
> Which, *spent,* can buy so *brave* a death.
>
> (ll. 16–18)

The word "spent" is used in the sense of making a purchase but also in the sense of life's being over, spent. Both are appropriate to the sense. The word "brave" is also used with two meanings: Teresa, the child, is willing to die and is courageous about seeking death, but the death itself will also be exciting and beautiful. (Compare this usage with Shakespeare's "O brave new world,/ That has such people in it.") And the word "brave" in the following passage can be examined in similar fashion:

> Love touched her heart, and, lo, it beats
> High, and burns with such *brave* heats
>
> (ll. 35–36)

To take one more example. The word "blush" in the following lines **is** both an image and an ambiguity; it is also a conceit:

> Scarce has she blood enough to make
> A guilty sword *blush* for her sake.
>
> (ll. 25–26)

We have noted above that the Church encouraged the representation in images of spiritual ideals and beliefs. Various students and critics have commented on this. "The Christianity of the Middle Ages," Walter Pater wrote, "made its way partly by the aesthetic beauty, a thing so profoundly felt by the Latin hymn writers, who for one moral or spiritual sentiment had a hundred sensuous images." The images of the sensible world found their meaning in reference to the Christian drama —"all redness turns into blood, all water into tears." And we have noted that the baroque art with which Crashaw's poetry is associated is a reaffirmation of this principle. Not all of the metaphors are startling or gaudy: God makes his home or "mansion" in the breast of the young child (line 13); a quire of angels as archers shoot love's arrows at the heart of Teresa (lines 91–96). But many of them are startling: the soul of the child is a "milky soul" (line 14); tears "turn gems,/ And wrongs repent to diadems" (lines 149–150). The most carefully worked out of these figures is this:

> Thus
> When these thy deaths, so numerous,
> Shall all at last die into one,
> And melt thy soul's sweet mansion,
> Like a soft lump of incense, hasted
> By too hot a fire, and wasted
> Into perfuming clouds, so fast
> Shalt thou exhale to heaven at last
> In a resolving sigh
>
> (ll. 109–117)

The identification of the body of Teresa with a lump of incense may be rather farfetched, but the poet could rationalize it thus: her life and her body have been devoted to worship, just as incense is used in divine worship; her love is a consuming fire; her death is a gradual process, as though she were going from a solid into a cloudy substance; and, the final bit consumed, the incense breathes its last, as though with a final sigh of release. This extended metaphor is an integral part of the poem, related to it in theme, method, and tone.

The poem as a whole, of course, breaks into three sections. The first section recalls her childhood desire to convert the Moors, if not by her words then eventually through her blood as a martyr. The second section is concerned with God's denying her actual martyrdom but granting her martyrdom in the sense that she would suffer the "wound of love." This latter phenomenon dominates most of the poem. In the third and concluding section we see her welcomed into heaven, where she enjoys a state of pure joy.

Crashaw is sometimes accused of extravagances and lapses in taste. Certainly he is often guilty of both. "St. Mary Magdalene" contains this ludicrous conceit describing the saint's eyes:

> Two walking baths, two weeping motions,
> Portable and compendious oceans.

In the successful conceit there is a common ground on which the compared elements, otherwise incongruous, meet. Eyes might, for example, be compared with oceans on the ground that both have mysterious depths; one can ignore the incongruity of differences in size, literal depth, and so forth. But one cannot accept tears flowing like the waters of the ocean. The congruity is too slight. It is commonly agreed that a number of later seventeenth-century poets, including John Cleveland and Abraham Cowley, were sometimes overingenious in pursuing intricate meanings. Crashaw's lines suggest how farfetched a conceit can be. Yet if one grants Crashaw his right to his beliefs, as, for illustration, his belief in the visions of Teresa and in their value, then one must grant that his rhetoric, which frequently threatens to and sometimes does pass the bounds of normal poetic imaginings, has its own kind of appropriateness.

Saint Mary Magdalene, or the Weeper

> Hail, sister springs!
> Parents of silver-footed rills!
> Ever-bubbling things!
> Thawing crystal! snowy hills,
> Still spending, never spent! I mean
> Thy fair eyes, sweet Magdalene!
>
> Heavens thy fair eyes be,
> Heavens of ever-falling stars;
> 'Tis seed-time still with thee,
> And stars thou sow'st, whose harvest dares   10
> Promise the earth to countershine
> Whatever makes heav'n's forehead fine.

But we're deceived all.
Stars indeed they are, too true,
For they but seem to fall
As heav'n's other spangles do.
It is not for our earth and us
To shine in things so precious.

Upwards thou dost weep;
Heav'n's bosom drinks the gentle stream; 20
Where th' milky rivers creep,
Thine floats above, and is the cream.
Waters above th' heav'n's, what they be
We're best taught by thy tears and thee.

Every morn from hence
A brisk cherub something sips,
Whose sacred influence
Adds sweetness to his sweetest lips;
Then to his music, and his song
Tastes of this breakfast all day long. 30

Not in the evening's eyes,
When they red with weeping are
For the sun that dies,
Sits sorrow with a face so fair;
Nowhere but here did ever meet
Sweetness so sad, sadness so sweet.

When sorrow would be seen
In her brightest majesty,
For she is a queen,
Then is she dressed by none but thee; 40
Then, and only then, she wears
Her proudest pearls: I mean—thy tears.

The dew no more will weep
The primrose's pale cheek to deck,
The dew no more will sleep,
Nuzzled in the lily's neck;
Much rather would it be thy tear,
And leave them both to tremble here.

There's no need at all
That the balsam-sweating bough 50
So coyly should let fall

His med'cinable tears, for now
Nature hath learnt t' extract a dew
More sovereign and sweet from you.

    Yet let the poor drops weep,
    Weeping is the ease of woe,
    Softly let them creep,
    Sad that they are vanquished so;
They, though to others no relief,
Balsam may be for their own grief.   60

    Such the maiden gem
    By the purpling vine put on,
    Peeps from her parent stem
    And blushes at the bridegroom sun;
This wat'ry blossom of thy eyne,
Ripe, will make the richer wine.

    When some new bright guest
    Takes up among the stars a room,
    And heav'n will make a feast,
    Angels with crystal vials come   70
And draw from these full eyes of thine
Their master's water, their own wine.

    Golden though he be,
    Golden Tagus murmurs though;
    Were his way by thee,
    Content and quiet he would go;
So much more rich would he esteem
Thy silver, than his golden stream.

    Well does the May that lies
    Smiling in thy cheeks, confess   80
    The April in thine eyes;
    Mutual sweetness they express:
No April e'er lent kinder showers,
Nor May returned more faithful flowers.

    O cheeks! beds of chaste loves
    By your own showers seasonably dashed;
    Eyes! nests of milky doves
    In your own wells decently washed;
O wit of love! that thus could place
Fountain and garden in one face.   90

O sweet contest, of woes
With loves, of tears with smiles disputing!
O fair and friendly foes,
Each other kissing and confuting!
While rain and sunshine, cheeks and eyes,
Close in kind contrarities.

But can these fair floods be
Friends with the bosom fires that fill thee?
Can so great flames agree
Eternal tears should thus distil thee?   100
O floods, O fires, O suns, O showers!
Mixed and made friends by love's sweet powers.

'Twas his well-pointed dart
That digged these wells and dressed this vine;
And taught the wounded heart
The way into these weeping eyne.
Vain loves, avaunt! bold hands, forbear!
The lamb hath dipped his white foot here.

And now where e'er he strays
Among the Galilean mountains,   110
Or more unwelcome ways,
He's followed by two faithful fountains,
Two walking baths, two weeping motions,
Portable and compendious oceans.

O thou, thy Lord's fair store!
In thy so rich and rare expenses,
Even when he showed most poor,
He might provoke the wealth of princes;
What prince's wanton'st pride e'er could
Wash with silver, wipe with gold?   120

Who is that king, but he
Who call'st his crown to be called thine,
That thus can boast to be
Waited on by a wand'ring mine,
A voluntary mint, that strows
Warm silver showers where e'er he goes?

O precious prodigal!
Fair spendthrift of thyself! thy measure,
Merciless love, is all,

Even to the last pearl in thy treasure;   130
All places, times, and objects be
Thy tears' sweet opportunity.

Does the day-star rise?
Still thy stars do fall and fall.
Does day close his eyes?
Still the fountain weeps for all.
Let night or day do what they will,
Thou hast thy task, thou weepest still.

Does thy song lull the air?
Thy falling tears keep faithful time.
Does they sweet-breathed prayer   140
Up in clouds of incense climb?
Still at each sigh, that is, each stop,
A bead, that is, a tear, does drop.

At these thy weeping gates,
Watching their wat'ry motïon,
Each wingèd moment waits,
Takes his tear and gets him gone;
By thine eye's tinct ennobled thus,
Time lays him up, he's precïous.   150

Not, So long she lived,
Shall thy tomb report of thee;
But, So long she grieved,
Thus must we date thy memory:
Others by monuments, months, and years,
Measure their ages, thou by tears.

So do perfumes expire;
So sigh tormented sweets, oppressed
With proud unpitying fire;
Such tears the suff'ring rose that's vexed   160
With ungentle flames does shed,
Sweating in a too warm bed.

Say, ye bright brothers,
The fugitive sons of those fair eyes,
Your fruitful mothers,
What make you here? What hopes can 'tice
You to be born? What cause can borrow
You from those nests of noble sorrow.

Whither away so fast?
For sure the sordid earth   170
Your sweetness cannot taste,
Nor does the dust deserve your birth.
Sweet, whither haste you then? O say
Why you trip so fast away!

We go not to seek
The darlings of Aurora's bed,
The rose's modest cheek,
Nor the violet's humble head;
Though the field's eyes, too, weeping be
Because they want such tears as we.   180

Much less mean we to trace
The fortune of inferior gems,
Preferred to some proud face,
Or perched upon feared diadems:
Crowned heads are toys. We go to meet
A worthy object, our Lord's feet.

■   Attempt to describe the quality of Crashaw's imagery.

Charitas Nimia,
or The Dear Bargain

Lord, what is man? why should he cost Thee
So dear? what had his ruin lost Thee?
Lord, what is man, that thou hast over-bought
So much a thing of naught?

Love is too kind, I see, and can
Make but a simple merchant-man.
'Twas for such sorry merchandise
Bold painters have put out his eyes.

Alas, sweet Lord! what were't to Thee
If there were no such worms as we?   10
Heaven ne'ertheless still heaven would be,
Should mankind dwell
In the deep hell.
What have his woes to do with Thee?

Let him go weep
O'er his own wounds;

Seraphim will not sleep,
Nor spheres let fall their faithful rounds.

Still would the youthful spirits sing,
And still Thy spacious palace ring;   20
Still would those beauteous ministers of light
    Burn all as bright,
And bow their flaming heads before Thee;
Still thrones and dominations would adore Thee;
Still would those ever-wakeful sons of fire
    Keep warm Thy praise
    Both nights and days,
And teach Thy loved name to their noble lyre.

Let froward dust then do its kind,
And give itself for sport to the proud wind.   30
Why should a piece of peevish clay plead shares
In the eternity of Thy old cares?
Why shouldst Thou bow Thy awful breast to see
What mine own madnesses have done with me?

Should not the king still keep his throne
Because some desperate fool's undone?
Or will the world's illustrious eyes
Weep for every worm that dies?

    Will the gallant sun
    E'er the less glorious run?   40
Will he hang down his golden head,
Or e'er the sooner seek his western bed,
    Because some foolish fly
    Grows wanton, and will die?

If I were lost in misery,
What was it to Thy heaven and Thee?
What was it to Thy precious blood
If my foul heart called for a flood?

What if my faithless soul and I
    Would needs fall in
    With guilt and sin;   50
What did the Lamb that He should die?
What did the Lamb that He should need,
When the wolf sins, Himself to bleed?

>   If my base lust
> Bargained with death and well-beseeming dust,
>   Why should the white
>   Lamb's bosom write
>   The purple name
>   Of my sin's shame?
> Why should His unstained breast make good
> My blushes with His own heart-blood?

60

> O my Savior, make me see
> How dearly Thou hast paid for me;
> That, lost again, my life may prove,
> As then in death, so now in love.

■ 1. Point out some of the baroque elements in this poem.
2. What is the relation of the seraphim to thrones and dominations in the hierarchy of angels?

From The Flaming Heart[1]

> O sweet incendiary! show here thy art,
> Upon this carcass of a hard, cold heart;
> Let all thy scattered shafts of light, that play
> Among the leaves of thy large books of day,
> Combined against this breast, at once break in
> And take away from me myself and sin!
> This gracious robbery shall thy bounty be,
> And my best fortunes such fair spoils of me.
> O thou undaunted daughter of desires!
> By all thy dower of lights and fires,
> By all the eagle in thee, all the dove,
> By all thy lives and deaths of love,
> By thy large draughts of intellectual day,
> And by thy thirsts of love more large than they,
> By all thy brim-filled bowls of fierce desire,
> By thy last morning's draught of liquid fire,
> By the full kingdom of that final kiss,
> That seized thy parting soul and sealed thee His;
> By all the heavens thou hast in Him,
> Fair sister of the seraphim,
> By all of Him we have in thee,
> Leave nothing of myself in me!

....
1. These lines were added to *The Flaming Heart* several years after it was first printed. They compose in effect a separate poem.

Let me so read thy life that I
Unto all life of mine may die!

■ 1. Look up the term *apostrophe* as a figure of speech in some good
reference work and relate it to this passage from "The Flaming Heart."
  2. Point out at least one instance of oxymoron.
  3. Explain the paradoxes that conclude the poem.
  4. What is the meaning of the phrase *"intellectual day"* (line 13)?
Relate this phrase to the early lines of the poem.
  5. Discuss the poem with respect to its rhythmical movement.

Henry Vaughan

(1622–1695)

■ ■ ■ ■ ■ ■ ■ ■ ■

HENRY VAUGHAN was born in Brecknockshire, Wales. About
1638 he entered Oxford but withdrew about 1640 to study law in London,
where he first began to write poetry. With the outbreak of the Civil War, he
dropped his legal studies and returned to Wales, where he studied medicine.
It is possible, but not certain, that he served as an officer with Royalist troops
for a while. He settled in Brecknockshire, where he was a popular physician until his death in 1695.

Although a doctor, Vaughan seems not to have been impressed by the
scientific outlook that was emerging in his lifetime. He was of a mystical
and poetical temperament. He was throughout his life a faithful Anglican,
more mystical than George Herbert, whose career and work were a stimulus
to his own thought and activity. Vaughan began writing in the secular tradition, but his most abundant and best work is religious, published under the
title *Silex Scintillans* (Sparkling Flint) in 1650, and reissued, with additions, in 1655.

Suggested Readings

T. S. ELIOT, "The Silurist," *Dial*, LXXXIII, 3 (September, 1927), 259–
  263.
HELEN C. WHITE, "Vaughan," *Four Metaphysical Poets*. Madison: University of Wisconsin Press, 1936.

■ ■ ■ ■ ■ ■ ■ ■ ■

Man

Weighing the steadfastness and state
Of some mean things which here below reside,
Where birds like watchful clocks the noiseless date
    And intercourse of times divide,
Where bees at night get home and hive, and flowers
        Early, as well as late,
Rise with the sun, and set in the same bowers;

I would, said I, my God would give
The staidness of these things to man! for these
To his divine appointments ever cleave,
    And no new business breaks their peace;
The birds nor sow nor reap, yet sup and dine,
        The flowers without clothes live,
Yet Solomon was never dressed so fine.

Man hath still either toys or care,
He hath no root, nor to one place is tied,
But ever restless and irregular
    About this earth doth run and ride;
He knows he hath a home, but scarce knows where,
        He says it is so far
That he hath quite forgot how to go there.

He knocks at all the doors, strays and roams,
Nay, hath not so much wit as some stones have,
Which in the darkest nights point to their homes
    By some hid sense their maker gave;
Man is the shuttle, to whose winding quest
        And passage through these looms
God ordered motion, but ordained no rest.

■ Compare this poem with Herbert's "The Pulley" with respect to organization and treatment of theme. Which poem shows greater economy in the development of theme? Of what significance is the difference in economy? How do the metaphors of the two poems compare as to logical illustration (denotation) and qualitative suggestion (connotation)?

The Waterfall

With what deep murmurs through time's silent stealth
Doth thy transparent, cool, and wat'ry wealth
        Here flowing fall,

And chide, and call,
As if his liquid, loose retínue stayed
Ling'ring, and were of this steep place afraid,
   The common pass
   Where, clear as glass,
   All must descend—
   Not to an end,   10
But quickened by this deep and rocky grave,
Rise to a longer course more bright and brave.

   Dear stream! dear bank, where often I
   Have sat and pleased my pensive eye,
   Why, since each drop of thy quick store
   Runs thither whence it flowed before,
   Should poor souls fear a shade or night,
   Who came, sure, from a sea of light?
   Or since those drops are all sent back
   So sure to thee, that none doth lack,   20
   Why should frail flesh doubt any more
   That what God takes he'll not restore?

   O useful element and clear!
   My sacred wash and cleanser here,
   My first consigner unto those
   Fountains of life where the Lamb goes!
   What sublime truths and wholesome themes
   Lodge in thy mystical deep streams!
   Such as dull man can never find
   Unless that spirit lead his mind   30
   Which first upon thy face did move,
   And hatched all with his quick'ning love.
   As this loud brook's incessant fall
   In streaming rings restagnates all,
   Which reach by course the bank, and then
   Are no more seen, just so pass men.
   O my invisible estate,
   My glorious liberty, still late!
   Thou art the channel my soul seeks,
   Not this with cataracts and creeks.   40

  1. What effects are achieved by the versification?
  2. How is the development of the poem related to its division into
hree parts?
  3. Compare Vaughan's attitude toward nature with that of Words-
vorth in "Tintern Abbey."

4. In Vaughan's poem what is the relationship between nature imagery, metaphor, and the statement in the final lines?

The Retreat

Happy those early days when I
Shined in my angel-infancy!
Before I understood this place
Appointed for my second race,
Or taught my soul to fancy aught
But a white celestial thought;
When yet I had not walked above
A mile or two from my first love,
And looking back at that short space,
Could see a glimpse of his bright face;   10
When on some gilded cloud or flower
My gazing soul would dwell an hour,
And in those weaker glories spy
Some shadows of eternity;
Before I taught my tongue to wound
My conscience with a sinful sound,
Or had the black art to dispense
A sev'ral sin to ev'ry sense;
But felt through all this fleshly dress
Bright shoots of everlastingness.   20
  Oh, how I long to travel back
And tread again that ancient track!
That I might once more reach that plain
Where first I left my glorious train,
From whence th' enlightened spirit sees
That shady city of palm trees.
But, ah, my soul with too much stay
Is drunk, and staggers in the way.
Some men a forward motion love,
But I by backward steps would move,   30
And when this dust falls to the urn,
In that state I came, return.

The World

I saw eternity the other night
Like a great ring of pure and endless light,
    All calm as it was bright;
And round beneath it, time in hours, days, years,
    Driv'n by the spheres,

Like a vast shadow moved, in which the world
   And all her train were hurled:
The doting lover in his quaintest strain
    Did there complain;
Near him his lute, his fancy, and his flights,   10
    Wit's sour delights,
With gloves and knots, the silly snares of pleasure,
    Yet his dear treasure,
All scattered lay, while he his eyes did pore
    Upon a flower.

The darksome statesman, hung with weights and woe,
Like a thick midnight fog moved there so slow
   He did not stay, nor go;
Condemning thoughts, like sad eclipses, scowl
    Upon his soul,   20
And clouds of crying witnesses without
    Pursued him with one shout;
Yet digged the mole, and lest his ways be found,
    Worked underground,
Where he did clutch his prey, but One did see
    That policy;
Churches and altars fed him; perjuries
    Were gnats and flies;
It rained about him blood and tears, but he
    Drank them as free.   30

The fearful miser on a heap of rust
Sat pining all his life there, did scarce trust
   His own hands with the dust,
Yet would not place one piece above, but lives
    In fear of thieves.
Thousands there were as frantic as himself,
    And hugged each one his pelf:
The downright epicure placed heav'n in sense,
    And scorned pretense;
While others, slipped into a wide excess,   40
    Said little less;
The weaker sort slight trivial wares enslave,
    Who think them brave;
And poor despisèd truth sat counting by
    Their victory.

Yet some, who all this while did weep and sing,
And sing and weep, soared up into the ring;

But most would use no wing.
O fools, said I, thus to prefer dark night
        Before true light,   50
To live in grots and caves, and hate the day
        Because it shows the way,
The way which from this dead and dark abode
        Leads up to God,
A way where you might tread the sun, and be
        More bright than he.
But as I did their madness so discuss,
        One whispered thus:
This ring the bridegroom did for none provide
        But for his bride.   60

■   Does this poem escape the dangers of didacticism? Explain your
answer as fully as possible.

Peace

My soul, there is a country
        Far beyond the stars,
Where stands a wingèd sentry
        All skillful in the wars;
There above noise and danger
    Sweet peace sits crowned with smiles,
And one born in a manger
        Commands the beauteous files;
He is thy gracious friend,
        And (O my soul, awake!)   10
Did in pure love descend
        To die here for thy sake.
If thou canst get but thither,
        There grows the flower of peace,
The rose that cannot wither,
        Thy fortress and thy ease;
Leave then thy foolish ranges,
        For none can thee secure
But one who never changes,
        Thy God, thy life, thy cure.   20

The Night

John 3:2

Through that pure virgin-shrine,
That sacred veil drawn o'er thy glorious noon,
That men might look and live, as glow-worms shine,
    And face the moon,
  Wise Nicodemus saw such light
  As made him know his God by night.

Most blest believer he!
Who in that land of darkness and blind eyes
Thy long-expected healing wings could see
    When thou didst rise,   10
  And what can never more be done,
  Did at midnight speak with the Sun!

Oh, who will tell me where
He found thee at that dead and silent hour!
What hallowed solitary ground did bear
    So rare a flower,
  Within whose sacred leaves did lie
  The fullness of the deity.

No mercy-seat of gold,
No dead and dusty cherub, nor carved stone,   20
But his own living works did my Lord hold
    And lodge alone,
  Where trees and herbs did watch and peep
  And wonder, while the Jews did sleep.

Dear night! this world's defeat;
The stop to busy fools; care's check and curb;
The day of spirits; my soul's calm retreat
    Which none disturb;
  Christ's progress, and his prayer time;
  The hours to which high heaven doth chime;   30

God's silent, searching flight;
When my Lord's head is filled with dew, and all
His locks are wet with the clear drops of night;
    His still, soft call;
  His knocking time; the soul's dumb watch,
  When spirits their fair kindred catch.

Were all my loud, evil days
Calm and unhaunted as is thy dark tent,
Whose peace but by some angel's wing or voice
    Is seldom rent,   40
Then I in heaven all the long year
Would keep, and never wander here.

But living where the sun
Doth all things wake, and where all mix and tire
Themselves and others, I consent and run
    To ev'ry mire,
And by this world's ill-guiding light,
Err more than I can do by night.

There is in God, some say,
A deep but dazzling darkness, as men here   50
Say it is late and dusky, because they
    See not all clear;
Oh, for that night, where I in him
Might live invisible and dim.

Edmund Waller

1606–1687)

∎∎∎∎∎∎∎∎∎∎

IN HIS OWN TIME Edmund Waller was famous as a lyric poet,
a wealthy and witty courtier, a member of Parliament under three kings, and
a participant in the struggle between Charles I and the Puritans. He was born
in Coleshill, educated at Eton and Cambridge and, in law, at Lincoln's Inn
and according to his own account was sitting in Parliament at the age of six
teen. A kinsman of John Hampden and Oliver Cromwell, he was associated
with them and the patriot Pym in their efforts to bring about reform and
to restrict the powers of the monarch. However, in the Civil War, he took the
side of the king, planning with several others to deliver London to Charles.
Upon the discovery of "Waller's plot" several of his accomplices were exe
cuted, but Waller's punishment was a fine and banishment. In France he
associated with men like Cowley, Denham, and Hobbes, who was the tutor
to Waller's son. Pardoned and given the post of commissioner of trade by
Cromwell, Waller wrote Panegyric, which was well received by the Lord

Protector of the Commonwealth. Upon the Restoration in 1660, Waller wrote his *Address of Welcome,* and, when Charles II suspiciously pointed out that the tribute to Cromwell was the better poem, Waller said, "Sir, we poets never succeed so well in writing truth as in writing fiction."

Suggested Readings

SAMUEL JOHNSON, "Waller," *Lives of the Poets.*
R. C. WALLERSTEIN, "The Development of the Rhetoric and Metre of the Heroic Couplet, Especially in 1625–1645," *PMLA,* L, 1 (March, 1935), 166–209.

■ ■ ■ ■ ■ ■ ■ ■ ■ ■

At Penshurst

Had Sacharissa lived when mortals made
Choice of their deities, this sacred shade
Had held an altar to her power, that gave
The peace and glory which these alleys have;
Embroidered so with flowers where she stood,
That it became a garden of a wood.
Her presence has such more than human grace
That it can civilize the rudest place;
And beauty too, and order, can impart,
Where nature ne'er intended it, nor art.   10
The plants acknowledge this, and her admire
No less than those of old did Orpheus' lyre;
If she sit down, with tops all towards her bowed,
They round about her into arbors crowd;
Or if she walk, in even ranks they stand,
Like some well-marshaled and obsequious band.
Amphion so made stones and timber leap
Into fair figures from a confused heap;
And in the symmetry of her parts is found
A power like that of harmony in sound.   20
    Ye lofty beeches, tell this matchless dame
That if together ye fed all one flame,
It could not equalize the hundredth part
Of what her eyes have kindled in my heart!
Go, boy, and carve this passion on the bark
Of yonder tree, which stands the sacred mark
Of noble Sidney's birth; when such benign,
Such more than mortal making stars did shine,

That there they cannot but forever prove
The monument and pledge of humble love;   30
His humble love whose hopes shall ne'er rise higher
Than for a pardon that he dares admire.

■   Edmund Waller was hailed by the Augustans as "the parent of our
verse." Although others, such as Jonson, Drayton, Sir John Beaumont,
and Sandys, were in the tradition that came to full flower with the
Restoration and eighteenth century, it was Waller who was given most
credit, especially for the development of the couplet. Dryden, in the
dedication to *The Rival Ladies,* wrote: "But the excellence and dignity of [rhyme] were never fully known till Mr. Waller taught it; he
first made writing easily an art; first showed us to conclude the sense
most commonly in distichs, which in the verse of those before him, runs
over on for so many lines together, that the reader is out of breath to
overtake it." Samuel Johnson, in *Lives of the Poets,* also viewed Waller
as an innovator, but he was more moderate in his praise. He found
Waller's poetry "rather smooth than strong." Its general character, he
said, "is elegance and gaiety . . . never pathetick and very rarely sublime." Johnson was not much impressed either by Waller's intellectual
gifts or learning. He was careful, nonetheless, to say that Waller's virtues
had so often been repeated that there was a danger of forgetting "who
produced them first."

To discover something of what the Augustans saw and felt in the
work of Waller we can examine "At Penshurst." Penshurst was the home
of the Sidneys in Kent. The Sacharissa of the poem is Lady Dorothy,
daughter of Robert, second Earl of Leicester. According to the biography of Waller his love affair with her was not a very serious one.
Whether it was or not is hardly our problem in reading the poem.
The poem is a graceful compliment to Sacharissa. Since it was primarily from his experiments with metrical form that Waller was said to
have caused a minor revolution in verse, we may examine the pattern
of "At Penshurst." But we should not expect that Waller's couplets, at
least in all his poems, will resemble Pope's more closely than those of
some of the Elizabethans or Jacobeans.

The heroic couplet has certain observable characteristics. It expresses a distinct unity of thought, as Dryden suggests in the passage
quoted above. The most basic unit is the half line, the use of which allows the poet a greater freedom of movement both in thought and meter
than the full line or couplet would allow him; however, units composed
of the single line or the couplet itself are also used. Within the couplet
one finds balanced and antithetical phrases, repetition of a definite metrical pattern (iambic pentameter), and strong end rhymes. These give
the couplet its character and pattern, a neatness and formality that make
for decorum and definiteness of statement.

In the following passage, which is also about Penshurst and Sacharissa although not a part of the poem "At Penshurst," some of these characteristics can be readily observed:

> While in the park I sing,/ the listening deer
> Attend my passion,/ and forget to fear.
> When to the beeches/ I report my flame,
> They bow their heads,/ as if they felt the same.
> To gods appealing,/ when I reach the bowers
> With loud complaints,/ they answer me in showers.
> To thee a wild and cruel soul is given,
> More deaf than trees,/ and prouder than the heavens!

The medial pause or caesura which occurs in all but the seventh line establishes the pattern of balancing one-half of a line against the other. In three instances the pause comes at the end of the first four syllables, in three others it comes at the end of the first five syllables, and in one instance it comes after the first six syllables. Thus there is a basic pattern: a half line is balanced against a half line; the break usually comes at or almost at the center of the line; each couplet is complete in itself; and the metrical pattern is iambic pentameter. The first three couplets state parallel ideas: the deer, the beeches, and the gods attend to the lover's passion. The fourth couplet gathers up the ideas of the first three couplets and comments on them. The pattern is firm but not rigid. The major element in the variation, the fourth couplet, helps to stress that the statement of the final couplet is a variation upon those of the first three. The first line of this couplet, lacking a caesura, breaks the pattern of medial pauses established in the preceding lines, but it has, especially through its stress on the balanced phrase "wild and cruel," a pattern of its own. The feminine rhymes of the last two couplets are a further variation.

These lines, then, have a noticeable degree of formality. Having considered them, even though briefly and not very intensively, we can see a little more readily the pattern employed in "At Penshurst."

There is less strict formality in the structure of the lines of the first poem than in those on Penshurst quoted just above. The initial statement runs for four lines. The lines, however, do have strong end rhymes, are regular iambic pentameter, and are fairly regularly balanced in phrases on either side of the caesura. The next couplet is closed, but in neither line is there a very distinct pause. Similarly, in the following couplets, lines 7–18, the thought is held within the couplet but there is no distinct pattern of half lines. Again, the final couplets are composed of run-on lines.

It seems fair to say, after examining these two poems on Penshurst, that Waller is going in the direction of the Augustans in his tendency to employ the couplet in a neat and formalized way. Perhaps, however, it is in his manner, which is low pitched, and in his avoidance of meanings or images that might be startling that he is more especially a precursor of the Augustans. (Johnson, incidentally, said that the passage on Penshurst in which the deer, beeches, and gods attend the lover's passion was "hyperbolical.") None of Waller's figures are after the fashion of the metaphysicals. They are readily understandable, in the same way that his diction and turns of thought are.

In fact, Francis Atterbury, in a preface to Waller's poems in 1690, gave Waller credit for reforming diction (by which he probably meant that Waller avoided the sometimes difficult or learned words, as well as the ambiguities of some of his predecessors), introducing greater harmonies (Waller's "sweetness" and melodic rhythms), and employing strong rhymes. When poets like Dryden turned back to Waller they saw in him a quality they called "smoothness," and an avoidance of thoughts or expressions that might be called extravagant. Most certainly Waller was incapable of what Pope called "the full resounding line" of Dryden, just as he was of the subtlety of Donne, but he had some of the characteristics the Augustans were to nurture. In Waller's work Dryden could find an example of restraint and decorum and a movement in the direction of clear statements, expressed in a language notable for its design, neatness, and "correctness."

Go, Lovely Rose!

Go, lovely rose!
Tell her that wastes her time and me
That now she knows,
When I resemble her to thee,
How sweet and fair she seems to be.

Tell her that's young,
And shuns to have her graces spied,
That hadst thou sprung
In deserts, where no men abide,
Thou must have uncommended died.

Small is the worth
Of beauty from the light retired;
Bid her come forth,
Suffer herself to be desired,
And not blush so to be admired.

Then die! that she
The common fate of all things rare

May read in thee;
How small a part of time they share
That are so wondrous sweet and fair!

1. Explain in some detail why the poet feels the rose is the right symbol for the theme and the mood of the poem.

2. Explain the function of the word "wastes" (line 2).

3. What is the *carpe diem* theme? (See Thrall and Hibbard, *A Handbook to Literature,* or some such reference work.) Do the wit and elegance in these lines of Waller in any way lessen the sense of conviction in the theme?

To a Very Young Lady

Why came I so untimely forth
Into a world which wanting thee
Could entertain us with no worth,
Or shadow of felicity?
    That time should me so far remove
    From that which I was born to love!

Yet, fairest blossom, do not slight
That eye which you may know so soon.
The rosy morn resigns her light
And milder splendors to the noon:
    If such thy dawning beauty's power,
    Who shall abide its noon-tide hour?

Hope waits upon the flowery prime,
And summer though it be less gay,
Yet is not looked on as a time
Of declination and decay.
    For with a full hand that does bring
    All that was promised by the spring.

The Dancer

Behold the brand of beauty tossed!
See how the motion does dilate the flame!
Delighted love his spoils does boast,
And triumph in this game.
Fire, to no place confined,
Is both our wonder and our fear;

Moving the mind,
As lightning hurled through air.

High heaven the glory does increase
Of all her shining lamps, this artful way;
The sun in figures, such as these,
Joys with the moon to play.
To the sweet strains they all advance,
Which do result from their own spheres,
As this nymph's dance
Moves with the numbers which she hears.

On a Girdle

That which her slender waist confined,
Shall now my joyful temples bind;
No monarch but would give his crown,
His arms might do what this has done.

It was my heaven's extremest sphere,
The pale which held that lovely deer;
My joy, my grief, my hope, my love
Did all within this circle move!

A narrow compass! and yet there
Dwelt all that's good and all that's fair;
Give me but what this ribbon bound,
Take all the rest the sun goes round!

■   1. The circle is the controlling image. Point out the ways in which
this imagery is varied and made to relate to the central idea of the poem.
    2. Explain the use of the pun in "deer" (line 6).
    3. Is the final statement a paradox?

Of the Last Verses in the Book

When we for age could neither read nor write,
The subject made us able to indite;
The soul, with nobler resolutions decked,
The body stooping, does herself erect.
No mortal parts are requisite to raise
Her that, unbodied, can her Maker praise.
    The seas are quiet when the winds give o'er;

So, calm are we when passions are no more!
For then we know how vain it was to boast
Of fleeting things, so certain to be lost.
Clouds of affection from our younger eyes
Conceal that emptiness which age descries.
    The soul's dark cottage, battered and decayed,
Lets in new light through chinks that time has made;
Stronger by weakness, wiser men become,
As they draw near to their eternal home.
Leaving the old, both worlds at once they view,
That stand upon the threshold of the new.

■ 1. Point out the sententious statements in this poem. Is there a connection between them and the choice of the couplet form?
    2. Is the poem composed exclusively of closed couplets?
    3. Are there any examples of balanced phrasing? If so, what is their effect?
    4. Discuss the polished manner and air of reasonableness achieved by the poem, both in terms of statement and structure.

John Milton

(1608–1674)

■■■■■■■■■■

JOHN MILTON was born in London, the son of a successful scrivener and man of some cultivation who recognized the young Milton's precociousness and encouraged him in his eagerness for learning. It is possible that this encouragement contributed to Milton's sense of mission and dedication to a calling, and that his early-formed habits of intense and prolonged study eventually brought on his complete loss of sight in later life. Having studied first with private tutors, Milton went to St. Paul's School in 1620 and then to Christ College, Cambridge, in 1625, where he took his bachelor's (1629) and master's degrees (1632). Although discontented at Cambridge and unpopular among the students (who nicknamed him "the Lady of Christ's"), he was highly successful in his studies. Upon leaving Cambridge, he went to his father's country home in Horton, where for about six years he lived quietly and continued his studies independently. Having successfully produced short poems in English and Latin, he looked forward, ambitiously but patiently, to the composition of a major work. In accordance with the prevailing educational customs for a young man of his class, Milton set forth on a tour of Europe in 1638. While visiting in Italy Milton received news of civil strife in England and gave up his plans of touring Sicily and Greece in order to return home in 1639. In the following years Milton was engaged as a private tutor and in the production of prose pamphlets on political subjects. He supported the Puritan cause in the Civil War, and during the Commonwealth served in Cromwell's government as Latin Secretary, during which period he became totally blind. He was briefly imprisoned after the Restoration and escaped severer punishments through the influence of Andrew Marvell and other friends.

Milton was married three times. In 1642 he married a young girl of a Cavalier family, Mary Powell. She separated from him in about a month and remained with her family for the next three years. It was during this period that Milton wrote his tracts arguing for divorce. The couple were reunited, but it has long been conjectured that this marriage was never a happy one. After giving birth to three daughters, Mary Powell died in 1652. Milton's second marriage, to Catherine Woodcock in 1656, lasted only fifteen months, at the end of which time his wife died in childbirth, as did the child. This unhappy event was the occasion for his sonnet, "On His Deceased Wife." His last marriage, with Elizabeth Minshull in 1663, was one of convenience. She survived him when he died in 1674.

Suggested Readings

E. M. W. TILLYARD, *Milton*. London: Chatto & Windus, 1930.

H. HANFORD, *A Milton Handbook,* 4th ed. New York: Appleton-Century-Crofts, Inc., 1946.

J. E. THORPE, *Milton Criticism*. New York: Rinehart & Co. Inc., 1950. (Contains notable essays by Johnson, Eliot, and others on Milton.)

■■■■■■■■■

■   Milton, like Shakespeare and Spenser, defies adequate representation among other poets and within a limited space. The works that are central to Milton's achievement and reputation are so long that it is physically impossible and logically inappropriate to consider them with the shorter poems of other writers. Some of the most interesting questions which arise from Milton's work and which have been explored by the vast body of Miltonic scholarship and criticism demand, primarily, a full view of his long epic, *Paradise Lost,* and also of his short epic, *Paradise Regained,* and his tragedy in classical form, *Samson Agonistes.*

In contrast to Shakespeare, much of Milton's life and thought lies fully revealed and is closely related to his poetry. One important aspect of Milton's achievement is the way in which he used traditional materials for the dramatic representation of themes that emerged from his personal life, from his commitment to the great events of his time, and from his views on political, moral, philosophical, and religious questions. It is in the long poems, the only poems written in the final phases of his development, that this aspect is to be seen most clearly, and there is no short cut that will bring it fully into view.

There are, of course, Milton's shorter poems, some of which are historically and artistically important in their own right. With these and with excerpts from the longer poems it is possible to illustrate the continuity of Milton's development. *Paradise Lost* especially abounds with passages that can be conveniently excerpted. It is therefore possible to give, in a relatively brief selection, an adequate representation of the Miltonic style. This style is one facet of Milton's eclecticism, for it is produced by the complex organization of a variety of elements. The most prominent features of this style are its allusiveness, the nature of the imagery, the quality produced by a special diction and syntax, and the effects produced by versification. Milton's allusions reflect his extensive familiarity with classical literature, philosophy, and mythology, with the literature of western Europe, with history and geography, with the Bible and the postbiblical religious literature of Judaism and Christianity—indeed with all the intellectual and scholarly lore available in his time. Yet his allusions were not pedantic or deliberately abstruse, for he expected that they would be familiar to educated readers of his time, or, if not, would be acceptable as a proper employment of the poet's knowledge. While it is obvious that Milton's allusions serve a decorative purpose in his poems, they can rarely, if ever, be considered detachable ornaments, for they function in a number of ways. At times they are a series of proper names which by their sound give variety and resonance to the versification. Some of the allusions are justified by the felicity of expression and image with which traditional materials are presented. The allusions are rich in qualities and associations that are appropriate to the tone, theme, and immediate subject of the poetry.

The observation has been made, sometimes as an adverse criticism, that Milton's imagery is vague in its outlines, lacking visual clarity and preciseness of detail. Although there are numerous exceptions, this description of Milton's imagery is valid, but it need not, and probably should not, be considered an adverse criticism. While it may be true that he is limited in the effects he achieves with images and that he rarely evokes real objects in their immediacy and particularity, this does not mean that his imagery is generally inferior. It is, rather, of a special kind and is usually well suited to the purpose for which it is used. Although Milton's style has many baroque qualities and departs from classical models in other respects, the formalizing and idealizing practices of classical literature, and especially of the pastoral tradition, entered into almost all that Milton wrote. The conventional and composite quality of his images combines with his allusiveness, diction, and rhythm to produce an elevated style that is in keeping with his choice of form, theme, and subject. Milton's most characteristic and most brilliant effects are, moreover, of a kind for which a sharp focus on a distinct individual object would be inappropriate, for these effects involve superlative conditions, vast distances, or scenes and situations that are beyond the range of actual human experience. Where Milton's images may lack the clarity and detail of things actually seen, they have the generalized and idealized quality of things seen in the glow of the imagination. In defining this quality of Milton's imagery, T. S. Eliot has said that "no theme and no setting, other than that which he chose in *Paradise Lost*, could have given him such scope for the kind of imagery in which he excelled, or made less demand upon those powers of visual imagination which were in him defective." The imagery in which Milton excelled is also used successfully in some of his best sonnets and in other short poems. An example is the image of sunset which occurs among the closing lines of "Lycidas":

> And now the sun had stretched out all the hills,
> And now was dropped into the western bay.
>
> (ll. 190–191)

What is often called the *grand style* of Milton's poetry results, for the most part, from peculiarities of diction and syntax. These peculiarities are to be seen developing early in Milton's work, emerging clearly in "Lycidas," and reaching a peak in *Paradise Lost*. The language of Milton's poetry, unlike that of Shakespeare's plays and Donne's lyrics, is deliberately removed from the patterns of conversation and prose, and at times even from established English usage. The lofty, rhetorical, and ornate style which Milton sought and achieved cannot be analyzed into a definitive set of devices, but specific devices are involved and some of these can be listed. With respect to diction, they are Latinisms, archaisms, biblical expressions, and the use of one part of speech for another (as in "the great consult began," where the verb "consult" is used as a noun). The peculiarities of syntax, many of them derived from Latin, are probably the most striking features of Milton's style. One of the most frequent devices is inversion: placing an adjective after a noun or reversing the usual noun-verb relationship. Sometimes the inversions produce complicated arrangements of elements in long sentences. Two brief and simple examples are "forced fingers rude" and "this dark world and wide."

Milton's versification is closely related to his syntactical practices. This is especially true of *Paradise Lost*. In a note defending his use of blank verse in that poem, he argued that "musical delight" is produced not by rhyme but by "the sense variously drawn out from one verse into another." According to Milton's practice, this drawing out of the sense involves not merely a consistent use of the run-on line but the creation of grammatical suspense, whereby whole groups of lines are bound together into a single rhythmical pattern. The grammatical suspense is achieved by delaying the completion of the subject-verb relationship, by separating the main words of a sentence with appositives, parentheses, and numerous other subordinate elements. The opening lines of *Paradise Lost* are an excellent illustration of the sweep of language achieved by this means. The first five lines are made up entirely of subordinate elements. The main verb of the sentence, "Sing," does not occur until the sixth line, and then a relative clause prolongs the grammatical flow of the sentence into the middle of the tenth line. And even there the sentence does not actually end, for an alternative statement ("or if Sion hill") with another main verb ("invoke") carries the sentence to the end of the sixteenth line.

Ode on the Morning of Christ's Nativity

1

This is the month, and this the happy morn,
Wherein the Son of Heaven's eternal King,
Of wedded maid and virgin mother born,
Our great redemption from above did bring;
For so the holy Sages once did sing,
    That he our deadly forfeit should release,
And with His Father work us a perpetual peace.

2

That glorious form, that light unsufferable,
And that far-beaming blaze of majesty,
Wherewith He wont at Heav'n's high council-table   10
To sit the midst of Trinal Unity,
He laid aside, and here with us to be,
    Forsook the courts of everlasting day,
And chose with us a darksome house of mortal clay.

3

Say, Heav'nly Muse, shall not thy sacred vein
Afford a present to the Infant God?
Hast thou no verse, no hymn, or solemn strain,
To welcome him to this his new abode,
Now while the heav'n by the Sun's team untrod,
    Hath took no print of the approaching light,   20
And all the spangled host keep watch in squadrons bright?

4

See how from far upon the eastern road
The star-led wizards haste with odors sweet!
O run; prevent them with thy humble ode,
And lay it lowly at his blessed feet;
Have thou the honor first thy Lord to greet,
    And join thy voice unto the Angel choir,
From out his secret altar touched with hallowed fire.

The Hymn

1

It was the winter wild,
While the Heaven-born Child   30
    All meanly wrapped in the rude manger lies;
Nature, in awe to him,
Had doffed her gaudy trim,
    With her great Master so to sympathize:
It was no season then for her
To wanton with the Sun, her lusty paramour.

2

Only with speeches fair
She woos the gentle air
    To hide her guilty front with innocent snow,
And on her naked shame,   40
Pollute with sinful blame,[1]
    The saintly veil of maiden white to throw;
Confounded, that her Maker's eyes
Should look so near upon her foul deformities.

3

But he, her fears to cease,
Sent down the meek-eyed Peace:
    She, crowned with olive green, came softly sliding
Down through the turning sphere,
His ready harbinger,
    With turtle wing the amorous clouds dividing;   50
And, waving wide her myrtle wand,
She strikes a universal peace through sea and land.

....

1. In this conceit Milton alludes to the traditional belief that the fall of man
brought corruption to the whole natural world.

4

No war, or battle's sound,
Was heard the world around;
   The idle spear and shield were high uphung;
The hookèd chariot stood,
Unstained with hostile blood;
   The trumpet spake not to the armed throng;
And kings sat still with awful eye,
As if they surely knew their sovran Lord was by.   60

5

But peaceful was the night
Wherein the Prince of Light
   His reign of peace upon the Earth began.
The winds, with wonder whist,
Smoothly the waters kissed,
   Whispering new joys to the mild Ocëan,
Who now hath quite forgot to rave,
While birds of calm sit brooding on the charmèd wave.[2]

6

The stars, with deep amaze,
Stand fixed in steadfast gaze,   70
   Bending one way their precious influence,[3]
And will not take their flight,
For all the morning light,
   Or Lucifer that often warned them thence;
But in their glimmering orbs did glow,
Until their Lord himself bespake, and bid them go.

7

And, though the shady gloom
Had given day her room,
   The Sun himself withheld his wonted speed,
And hid his head for shame,   80
As his inferior flame
   The new enlightened world no more should need:
He saw a greater Sun appear
Than his bright throne or burning axletree could bear.

....

2. According to classical mythology, calm weather prevailed during the period of the winter solstice, and the halcyon (or kingfisher bird) brooded on the waters at this time.   3. An allusion to astrology, the belief that the stars influence men's lives.

8

The shepherds on the lawn,
Or ere the point of dawn,
   Sat simply chatting in a rustic row;
Full little thought they than
That the mighty Pan[4]
    Was kindly come to live with them below: 90
Perhaps their loves,[5] or else their sheep,
Was all that did their silly thoughts so busy keep.

9

When such music sweet
Their hearts and ears did greet
   As never was by mortal finger strook,
Divinely-warbled voice
Answering the stringèd noise,
   As all their souls in blissful rapture took:
The air, such pleasure loth to lose,
With thousand echoes still prolongs each heavenly close.   100

10

Nature, that heard such sound
Beneath the hollow round
   Of Cynthia's seat[6] the airy region thrilling,
Now was almost won
To think her part was done,
   And that her reign had here its last fulfilling:
She knew such harmony alone
Could hold all Heaven and Earth in happier union.

11

At last surrounds their sight
A globe of circular light,   110
   That with long beams the shame-faced Night arrayed;
The helmèd Cherubim
And sworded Seraphim
   Are seen in glittering ranks with wings displayed,
Harping in loud and solemn choir,
With unexpressive notes, to Heaven's new-born Heir.

....

4. In Renaissance poetry Christ was frequently represented by the Greek god Pan. 5. Here Milton is deliberately confusing classical (literary) and biblical pastoralism. This "confusion" had become a traditional practice. 6. The moon.

12

Such music (as 'tis said)
Before was never made,
   But when of old the Sons of Morning sung,
While the Creator great   120
His constellations set,
   And the well balanced World on hinges hung,
And cast the dark foundations deep,
And bid the weltering waves their oozy channel keep.

13

Ring out, ye crystal spheres,
Once bless our human ears,
   If ye have power to touch our senses so;
And let your silver chime
Move in melodious time;
   And let the bass of Heaven's deep organ blow;   130
And with your ninefold harmony
Make up full consort to the angelic symphony.

14

For, if such holy song
Enwrap our fancy long,
   Time will run back and fetch the Age of Gold;
And speckled Vanity
Will sicken soon and die;
   And leprous Sin will melt from earthly mould;
And Hell itself will pass away,
And leave her dolorous mansions to the peering day.   140

15

Yea, Truth and Justice then
Will down return to men,
   Orbed in a rainbow; and, like glories wearing,
Mercy will sit between,
Throned in celestial sheen,
   With radiant feet the tissued clouds down steering;
And Heaven, as at some festival,
Will open wide the gates of her high palace-hall.

16

But wisest Fate says No,
This must not yet be so;   150
   The Babe lies yet in smiling infancy

That on the bitter cross
Must redeem our loss,
   So both himself and us to glorify:
Yet first, to those ychained in sleep,
The wakeful trump of doom must thunder through the deep,

17

With such a horrid clang
As on mount Sinai rang,[7]
   While the red fire and smouldering clouds out brake:
The agèd earth, aghast,   160
With terror of that blast,
   Shall from the surface to the centre shake,
When at the world's last session,
The dreadful Judge in middle air shall spread his throne.

18

And then at last our bliss
Full and perfect is,
   But now begins; for from this happy day
The old Dragon under ground
In straiter limits bound,
   Not half so far casts his usurpèd sway   170
And, wroth to see his kingdom fail,
Swinges the scaly horror of his folded tail.

19

The oracles are dumb;
No voice or hideous hum
   Runs through the archèd roof in words deceiving.
Apollo from his shrine
Can no more divine,
   With hollow shriek the steep of Delphos leaving.
No nightly trance, or breathèd spell
Inspires the pale-eyed priest from the prophetic cell.   180

20

The lonely mountains o'er,
And the resounding shore,
   A voice of weeping heard and loud lament;
From haunted spring, and dale
Edged with poplar pale,
   The parting Genius[8] is with sighing sent;

7. See Exodus 19:16.   8. The guardian spirit of a locality.

With flower-inwoven tresses torn
The Nymphs in twilight shade of tangled thickets mourn.

21

In consecrated earth,
And on the holy hearth,
   The Lars,[9] and Lemures[10] moan with midnight plaint;   190
In urns, and altars round,
A drear and dying sound
   Affrights the flamens[11] at their service quaint;
And the chill marble seems to sweat,
While each peculiar Power foregoes his wonted seat.

22

Peor and Baälim[12]
Forsake their temples dim,
   With that twice-battered God[13] of Palestine;
And moonèd Ashtaroth,[14]   200
Heaven's queen and mother both,
   Now sits not girt with tapers' holy shine:
The Lybic Hammon[15] shrinks his horn;
In vain the Tyrian maids their wounded Thammuz[16] mourn,

23

And sullen Moloch,[17] fled,
Hath left in shadows dread
   His burning idol all of blackest hue;
In vain with cymbals' ring
They call the grisly king,
   In dismal dance about the furnace blue;   210
The brutish gods[18] of Nile as fast,
Isis, and Orus, and the dog Anubis, haste.

24

Nor is Osiris seen
In Memphian grove or green,
   Trampling the unshowered grass with lowings loud;
Nor can he be at rest
Within his sacred chest;
   Nought but profoundest Hell can be his shroud;

9. Roman household gods.   10. Evil spirits.   11. Priest of ancient Rome.
12. Ancient Semitic gods.   13. Dagon; see I Samuel 5:4.   14. Phoenician
fertility goddess, same as Astarte.   15. Ammon, Egyptian equivalent of Zeus.
16. Babylonian fertility god.   17. A Semitic god to whom children were
sacrificed.   18. Osiris, chief Egyptian deity, and his wife Isis, a fertility goddess, were the parents of Horus and Anubis.

In vain, with timbreled anthems dark
The sable-stolèd sorcerers bear his worshipped ark.   220

25

He feels from Juda's land
The dreaded Infant's hand;
 The rays of Bethlehem blind his dusky eyn;
Nor all the gods beside
Longer dare abide,
 Not Typhon[19] huge ending in snaky twine:
Our Babe, to show his Godhead true,
Can in his swaddling bands control the damnèd crew.

26

So, when the Sun in bed,
Curtained with cloudy red,   230
 Pillows his chin upon an orient wave,
The flocking shadows pale
Troop to th' infernal jail;
 Each fettered ghost slips to his several grave,
And the yellow-skirted fays
Fly after the night-steeds, leaving their moon-loved maze.

27

But see, the Virgin blest
Hath laid her Babe to rest.
 Time is our tedious song should here have ending:
Heaven's youngest-teemèd star[20]   240
Hath fixed her polished car,
 Her sleeping Lord with handmaid lamp attending;
And all about the courtly stable
Bright-harnessed Angels sit in order serviceable.

....

19. A monster in Greek mythology.   20. The star of Bethlehem.

Lycidas

Yet once more, O ye laurels, and once more,
Ye myrtles brown, with ivy never sere,
I come to pluck your berries harsh and crude,
And with forced fingers rude
Shatter your leaves before the mellowing year.
Bitter constraint, and sad occasion dear,[1]

....

1. Grievous.

Compels me to disturb your season due;
For Lycidas is dead, dead ere his prime,
Young Lycidas, and hath not left his peer.
Who would not sing for Lycidas? he knew   10
Himself to sing, and build the lofty rhyme.
He must not float upon his watery bier
Unwept, and welter[2] to the parching wind,
Without the meed of some melodious tear.
    Begin then, sisters of the sacred well[3]
That from beneath the seat of Jove doth spring,
Begin, and somewhat loudly sweep the string.
Hence with denial vain, and coy excuse;
So may some gentle Muse[4]
With lucky words favor my destined urn,   20
And as he passes turn,
And bid fair peace be to my sable shroud.
For we were nursed upon the self-same hill,
Fed the same flock by fountain, shade, and rill.
    Together both, ere the high lawns appeared
Under the opening eyelids of the morn,
We drove afield, and both together heard
What time[5] the gray-fly winds her sultry horn,
Batt'ning our flocks with the fresh dews of night,
Oft till the star that rose, at evening, bright,   30
Toward heav'n's descent had sloped his west'ring wheel.
Meanwhile the rural ditties were not mute,
Tempered to the oaten flute,
Rough Satyrs danced, and Fauns with cloven heel
From the glad sound would not be absent long,
And old Damoetas loved to hear our song.
    But, O the heavy change, now thou art gone,
Now thou art gone, and never must return!
Thee, Shepherd, thee the woods, and desert caves
With wild thyme and the gadding vine o'ergrown,   40
And all their echoes mourn.
The willows, and the hazel copses green,
Shall now no more be seen,
Fanning their joyous leaves to thy soft lays.
As killing as the canker to the rose,
Or taint-worm to the weanling herds that graze,
Or frost to flow'rs, that their gay wardrobe wear,
When first the white-thorn blows;
Such, Lycidas, thy loss to shepherd's ear.

2. Toss about.   3. The nine muses.   4. I.e., poet.
5. At such time as (i.e., mid-day).

Where were ye, Nymphs, when the remorseless deep   50
Closed o'er the head of your loved Lycidas?
For neither were ye playing on the steep,
Where your old Bards, the famous Druids, lie,
Nor on the shaggy top of Mona[6] high,
Nor yet where Deva[6] spreads her wizard stream:
Ay me! I fondly dream!
Had ye been there, for what could that have done?
What could the Muse herself that Orpheus bore,
The Muse herself for her enchanting son,
Whom universal nature did lament,   60
When by the rout that made the hideous roar,
His gory visage down the stream was sent,
Down the swift Hebrus to the Lesbian shore?[7]
    Alas! what boots it with uncessant care
To tend the homely slighted shepherd's trade,
And strictly meditate the thankless Muse?
Were it not better done as other use,
To sport with Amaryllis in the shade,
Or with the tangles of Neaera's hair?
Fame is the spur that the clear spirit doth raise   70
(That last infirmity of noble mind)
To scorn delights, and live laborious days;
But the fair guerdon when we hope to find,
And think to burst out into sudden blaze,
Comes the blind Fury[8] with the abhorrèd shears,
And slits the thin-spun life. "But not the praise,"
Phoebus[9] replied, and touched my trembling ears:
"Fame is no plant that grows on mortal soil,
Nor in the glistering foil
Set off to the world, nor in broad rumor lies,   80
But lives and spreads aloft by those pure eyes
And perfect witness of all-judging Jove;
As he pronounces lastly on each deed,
Of so much fame in Heaven expect thy meed."
    O fountain Arethuse[10] and thou honored flood,
Smooth-sliding Mincius,[10] crowned with vocal reeds,
That strain I heard was of a higher mood.

....

6. Places associated with King's shipwreck.   7.   Calliope bore Orpheus. She
was unable to rescue him from the Thracian women, who tore him to pieces when
he refused to join their Bacchic orgies. They threw his head in the river Hebrus,
whence it floated into the sea and to the island of Lesbos, which was thereafter
blessed with the gifts of song and poetry.   8.   That one of the three Fates who
cuts the thread of life.   9.   Apollo, god of poetry.   10.   Rivers, references
respectively to the birthplaces of Theocritus and Virgil; hence, symbolic of the
pastoral tradition.

But now my oat proceeds,
And listens to the herald of the sea,[11]
That came in Neptune's plea.   90
He asked the waves, and asked the felon winds,
What hard mishap hath doomed this gentle swain?
And questioned every gust of rugged wings
That blows from off each beakèd promontory;
They knew not of his story,
And sage Hippotades[12] their answer brings,
That not a blast was from his dungeon strayed;
The air was calm, and on the level brine
Sleek Panope[13] with all her sisters played.
It was that fatal and perfidious bark,   100
Built in the eclipse, and rigged with curses dark,
That sunk so low that sacred head of thine.

Next Camus,[14] reverend sire, went footing slow,
His mantle hairy, and his bonnet sedge,
Inwrought with figures dim, and on the edge
Like to that sanguine flow'r inscribed with woe.
"Ah! Who hath reft" (quoth he) "my dearest pledge?"
Last came, and last did go,
The pilot of the Galilean lake.[15]
Two massy keys he bore of metals twain,   110
(The golden opes, the iron shuts amain)
He shook his mitred locks, and stern bespake,
"How well could I have spared for thee, young swain,
Enow of such as for their bellies' sake   16
Creep, and intrude, and climb into the fold![16]
Of other care they little reckoning make,
Than how to scramble at the shearers' feast,
And shove away the worthy bidden guest;
Blind mouths! that scarce themselves know how to hold
A sheep-hook, or have learned aught else the least   120
That to the faithful herdman's art belongs!
What recks it them? What need they? They are sped;
And when they list, their lean and flashy songs
Grate on their scrannel pipes of wretched straw;
The hungry sheep look up, and are not fed,
But swoln with wind, and the rank mist they draw,
Rot inwardly, and foul contagion spread;
Besides what the grim wolf[17] with privy paw

11. Triton.   12. Aeolus, god of the winds.   13. A sea nymph.
14. God of the river Cam, and hence symbolic of Cambridge University.
15. St. Peter.   16. Here Milton has shifted the symbolic meaning of *shepherd* from poet to clergyman.   17. Usually interpreted as the Catholic church.

Daily devours apace, and nothing said;
But that two-handed engine at the door   130
Stands ready to smite once, and smite no more."
　　Return, Alpheus,[18] the dread voice is past,
That shrunk thy streams; return, Sicilian Muse,
And call the vales, and bid them hither cast
Their bells, and flow'rets of a thousand hues.
Ye valleys low, where the mild whispers use
Of shades, and wanton winds, and gushing brooks,
On whose fresh lap the swart-star sparely looks:
Throw hither all your quaint enamelled eyes,
That on the green turf suck the honied showers,   140
And purple all the ground with vernal flowers.
Bring the rathe primrose that forsaken dies,
The tufted crow-toe, and pale jessamine,
The white pink, and the pansy freaked with jet,
The glowing violet,
The musk-rose, and the well-attired woodbine,
With cowslips wan that hang the pensive head,
And every flower that sad embroidery wears.
Bid amaranthus all his beauty shed,
And daffadillies fill their cups with tears,   150
To strew the laureate hearse where Lycid lies.
For so to interpose a little ease,
Let our frail thoughts dally with false surmise.
Ay me! whilst thee the shores and sounding seas
Wash far away, where'er thy bones are hurled,
Whether beyond the stormy Hebrides,
Where thou perhaps under the whelming tide
Visit'st the bottom of the monstrous world;
Or whether thou, to our moist vows denied,
Sleep'st by the fable of Bellerus old,[19]   160
Where the great vision of the guarded mount
Looks toward Namancos and Bayona's hold;
Look homeward, Angel, now, and melt with ruth;
And, O ye dolphins, waft the hapless youth.
　　Weep no more, woeful shepherds, weep no more,
For Lycidas, your sorrow, is not dead,
Sunk though he be beneath the watery floor;
So sinks the day-star in the ocean bed,
And yet anon repairs his drooping head,

18. A river that emerges from underground and mingles with Arethuse (see note 10). 19. Following a traditional legend, Milton presents here an image of archangel Michael standing on a mount in Land's End, Cornwell, and gazing across the Atlantic Ocean to points on the Spanish coast.

And tricks his beams, and with new-spangled ore   170
Flames in the forehead of the morning sky:
So Lycidas, sunk low, but mounted high,
Through the dear might of him that walked the waves,
Where, other groves and other streams along,
With nectar pure his oozy locks he laves,
And hears the unexpressive nuptial song,
In the blest kingdoms meek of joy and love.
There entertain him all the saints above,
In solemn troops and sweet societies
That sing, and singing in their glory move,   180
And wipe the tears for ever from his eyes.
Now, Lycidas, the shepherds weep no more;
Henceforth thou art the Genius of the shore,
In thy large recompense, and shalt be good
To all that wander in that perilous flood.

   Thus sang the uncouth swain to the oaks and rills,
While the still morn went out with sandals gray;
He touched the tender stops of various quills,
With eager thought warbling his Doric lay.[20]
And now the sun had stretched out all the hills,   190
And now was dropped into the western bay;
At last he rose, and twitched his mantle blue:
To-morrow to fresh woods, and pastures new.

■ 1. Milton wrote "Lycidas" upon being asked to contribute to a collection of memorial poems for Edward King, a former classmate at Cambridge who had been drowned in the Irish Sea. The poem is not only *in* the tradition of the pastoral elegy, but in its echoes and borrowings from other pastoral elegists is also a conscious survey of the tradition. After you have read the poem and the following questions, explain in what ways the poet shows some detachment from the tradition. (For a brief account of traditional elements in "Lycidas," see Hanford, *A Milton Handbook,* 4th edition, pp. 166–170.)

   2. Samuel Johnson severely criticized "Lycidas," one of his complaints being that the artificiality of the pastoral conventions betrayed a lack of sincerity on Milton's part. Actually, Milton was not a close friend of King's and did not experience the deepest grief at his death, but was proper and decent enough in this formal gesture of respect. If there is little grief in the poem, what feelings and attitudes does it express? Is the pastoral convention merely a transparent allegory throughout the poem, or does it at any points have the function of what in modern criticism is called *indirection*? (See Johnson on "Lycidas" in his *Lives of the English Poets.*)

20. Pastoral poem.

3. Explain the continuity of the poem, giving special attention to interrelationships among the following: (1) the pastoral tradition; (2) the circumstances of King's death; (3) the mixture of pagan and Christian elements; (4) the materials that are personal with respect to Milton; (5) the abundance of water images and allusions.

4. What is the stanzaic form of the concluding lines (186–193)? Since the poem is irregular in its pattern of rhyme and meter, examine it to see whether the irregularities are arbitrary or purposeful in any way.

On His Blindness

When I consider how my light is spent
Ere half my days in this dark world and wide,
And that one talent[1] which is death to hide
Lodged with me useless, though my soul more bent
To serve therewith my Maker, and present
My true account, lest He returning chide;
"Doth God exact day-labor, light denied?"
I fondly ask. But Patience, to prevent
That murmur, soon replies, "God doth not need
Either man's work or his own gifts. Who best
Bear his mild yoke, they serve him best. His state
Is kingly: thousands at his bidding speed,
And post o'er land and ocean without rest;
They also serve who only stand and wait."

....
1.   See Matthew 25:14–30.

On the Late Massacre in Piedmont[1]

Avenge, O Lord, Thy slaughtered saints, whose bones
Lie scattered on the Alpine mountains cold;
Even them who kept Thy truth so pure of old,
When all our fathers worshiped stocks and stones,
Forget not: in Thy book record their groans
Who were Thy sheep, and in their ancient fold
Slain by the bloody Piedmontese, that rolled
Mother with infant down the rocks. Their moans
The vales redoubled to the hills, and they
To heaven. Their martyred blood and ashes sow
O'er all the Italian fields, where still doth sway

....
1.   The Waldensians, a Protestant sect, were attacked by orders of the Catholic Duke of Savoy in 1655.

The triple Tyrant[2]; that from these may grow
A hundredfold, who, having learnt Thy way,
Early may fly the Babylonian woe.[3]

....

2. Pope's tiara, triple crown.   3. Puritan term for Church of Rome.

On His Deceased Wife

Methought I saw my late espoused saint
Brought to me like Alcestis[1] from the grave,
Whom Jove's great son to her glad husband gave,
Rescued from Death by force, though pale and faint.
Mine, as whom washed from spot of child-bed taint
Purification in the Old Law did save,[2]
And such as yet once more I trust to have
Full sight of her in heaven without restraint,
Came vested all in white, pure as her mind.
Her face was veiled; yet to my fancied sight
Love, sweetness, goodness, in her person shined
So clear as in no face with more delight.
But, oh! as to embrace me she inclined,
I waked, she fled, and day brought back my night.

1. How appropriate are Milton's subjects to the sonnet form?
2. How much does imagery contribute to the effect of each sonnet?
3. In which sonnet are the rhyme words most effectively used?
4. What features do the sonnets have in common? To what extent are they stylistically repetitious? To what extent are they not?

....

1. Alcestis offered to sacrifice her life for her husband, Admetus. Hercules forced Death to release her as she was being carried to the tomb.   2. See Leviticus 12.

From *Paradise Lost* (Book I, lines 1–49)

Invocation

Of Man's first disobedience, and the fruit
Of that forbidden tree, whose mortal taste
Brought death into the world, and all our woe,
With loss of Eden, till one greater Man
Restore us and regain the blissful seat,
Sing heav'nly Muse, that on the secret top
Of Oreb, or of Sinai, didst inspire
That shepherd, who first taught the chosen seed,
In the beginning how the heav'ns and earth

Rose out of Chaos: or if Sion hill   10
Delight thee more, and Siloa's brook that flowed
Fast by the oracle of God, I thence
Invoke thy aid to my adventurous song,
That with no middle flight intends to soar
Above th' Aonian mount, while it pursues
Things unattempted yet in prose or rhyme.

  And chiefly thou, O Spirit, that dost prefer
Before all temples the upright heart and pure,
Instruct me, for thou know'st; thou from the first
Wast present, and with mighty wings outspread   20
Dove-like sat'st brooding on the vast abyss,
And mad'st it pregnant: what in me is dark
Illumine, what is low raise and support;
That to the height of this great argument
I may assert eternal Providence,
And justify the ways of God to men.

  Say first, for heav'n hides nothing from thy view
Nor the deep tract of hell; say first, what cause
Moved our grand Parents in that happy state,
Favoured of heav'n so highly, to fall off   30
From their Creator, and transgress His will,
For one restraint, lords of the world besides?
Who first seduced them to that foul revolt?
Th' infernal serpent! he it was, whose guile,
Stirred up with envy and revenge, deceived
The mother of mankind, what time his pride
Had cast him out from heav'n, with all his host
Of rebel Angels, by whose aid aspiring
To set himself in glory above his peers,
He trusted to have equalled the Most High,   40
If he opposed; and with ambitious aim
Against the throne and monarchy of God
Raised impious war in heav'n, and battle proud,
With vain attempt. Him the almighty Power
Hurled headlong flaming from th' ethereal sky,
With hideous ruin and combustion, down
To bottomless perdition, there to dwell
In adamantine chains and penal fire,
Who durst defy th' Omnipotent to arms.

■ 1. Continue the analysis of these lines begun in the last paragraph
of the introduction to this section.

   2. Note that there are four synonyms for God in lines 27–49.
Explain their use. Consider whether the synonyms are interchangeable

or whether, aside from questions of meter, each is peculiarly appropriate to its context.

From *Paradise Lost* (Book I, lines 710–751)

Pandemonium and Its Architect

Anon out of the earth a fabric huge
Rose like an exhalation, with the sound
Of dulcet symphonies and voices sweet,
Built like a temple, where pilasters round
Were set, and Doric pillars overlaid
With golden architrave; nor did there want
Cornice or frieze with bossy sculptures graven;
The roof was fretted gold. Not Babylon,
Nor great Alcairo, such magnificence
Equalled in all their glories, to inshrine
Belus or Serapis their gods, or seat   720
Their kings, when Egypt with Assyria strove
In wealth and luxury. Th' ascending pile
Stood fixt her stately highth, and straight the doors,
Op'ning their brazen folds, discover, wide
Within, her ample spaces o'er the smooth
And level pavement: from the archèd roof,
Pendent by subtle magic, many a row
Of starry lamps and blazing cressets, fed
With Naphtha and Asphaltus, yielded light
As from a sky. The hasty multitude   730
Admiring entered, and the work some praise,
And some the architect: his hand was known
In heav'n by many a towered structure high,
Where sceptred angels held their residence,
And sat as princes, whom the supreme King
Exalted to such power, and gave to rule,
Each in his hierarchy, the orders bright.
Nor was his name unheard or unadored
In ancient Greece; and in Ausonian land
Men called him Mulciber; and how he fell   740
From heav'n they fabled, thrown by angry Jove
Sheer o'er the crystal battlements; from morn
To noon he fell, from noon to dewy eve,
A summer's day; and with the setting sun
Dropt from the zenith like a falling star,
On Lemnos th' Aegean isle; thus they relate,
Erring; for he with this rebellious rout

Fell long before; nor aught availed him now
To have built in heav'n high towers; nor did he 'scape
By all his engines, but was headlong sent   750
With his industrious crew to build in hell.

■ 1. "Ausonian land" is Italy. Mulciber (the same as Vulcan) is the
Roman name for Hephaestus. He is the craftsman and architect among
the Greek gods, for whom he built palaces on Olympus. See the description of his fall in the closing passages of the *Iliad*, I, and explain
whether or not Milton has contributed anything to this borrowed image.
How does Milton manage to introduce this bit of pagan lore while
writing from a biblical point of view?

2. A Judaic-Christian view of the pagan gods was that they were
originally rebellious angels who were cast out of Heaven along with
Satan. Note Milton's use of this explanation to fuse pagan and biblical
materials.

3. To what extent does the entire passage above illustrate characteristics of style mentioned in the introduction to this section?

From *Paradise Lost* (Book IV, lines 598–609)

Night Falls on Eden

Now came still evening on, and twilight grey
Had in her sober livery all things clad;
Silence accompanied; for beast and bird,
They to their grassy couch, these to their nests,
Were slunk, all but the wakeful nightingale;
She all night long her amorous descant sung;
Silence was pleased: now glowed the firmament
With living sapphires; Hesperus that led
The starry host rode brightest, till the moon,
Rising in clouded majesty, at length
Apparent queen unveiled her peerless light,
And o'er the dark her silver mantle threw.

From *Paradise Lost* (Book IV, lines 736–775

Wedded Love

This said unanimous,[1] and other rites
Observing none, but adoration pure
Which God likes best, into their inmost bower

....

1. Adam and Eve have just said their evening prayer.

Handed they went; and, eased the putting off
These troublesome disguises which we wear,   740
Straight side by side were laid; nor turned, I ween,
Adam from his fair spouse; nor Eve the rites
Mysterious of connubial love refused:
Whatever hypocrites austerely talk
Of purity, and place, and innocence,
Defaming as impure what God declares
Pure, and commands to some, leaves free to all.
Our Maker bids increase, who bids abstain
But our destroyer, foe to God and man?
Hail wedded love! mysterious law, true source   750
Of human offspring, sole propriety
In Paradise of all things common else.
By thee adulterous lust was driv'n from men
Among the bestial herds to range; by thee
Founded in reason, loyal, just, and pure,
Relations dear, and all the charities
Of father, son, and brother, first were known.
Far be it, that I should write thee sin or blame,
Or think thee unbefitting holiest place,
Perpetual fountain of domestic sweets,   760
Whose bed is undefiled and chaste pronounced,
Present, or past, as saints and patriarchs used.
Here Love his golden shafts employs, here lights
His constant lamp, and waves his purple wings,
Reigns here and revels; not in the bought smile
Of harlots, loveless, joyless, unendeared,
Casual fruition; nor in court amours,
Mixed dance, or wanton mask, or midnight ball,
Or serenate, which the starved lover sings
To his proud fair, best quitted with disdain.   770
These, lulled by nightingales, embracing slept,
And on their naked limbs the flowery roof
Showered roses, which the morn repaired. Sleep on,
Blest pair; and O yet happiest if ye seek
No happier state, and know to know no more.

1. In this passage Milton is expressing views which were deeply held and which he also expressed in his prose. Does he wholly succeed in making poetry of these views?

2. There are biblical, classical, and contemporary sources of reference in this passage. Indicate each and comment on the associations (i.e., suggestions and connotations) which they introduce.

From *Paradise Lost* (Book IX, lines 445–472)

Satan Beholds Eve

As one who long in populous city pent,
Where houses thick and sewers annoy the air,
Forth issuing on a summer's morn to breathe
Among the pleasant villages and farms
Adjoined, from each thing met conceives delight,
The smell of grain, or tedded grass, or kine,   450
Or dairy, each rural sight, each rural sound;
If chance with nymph-like step fair virgin pass,
What pleasing seemed, for her now pleases more,
She most, and in her look sums all delight:
Such pleasure took the serpent to behold
This flow'ry plat, the sweet recess of Eve
Thus early, thus alone: her heav'nly form
Angelic, but more soft and feminine,
Her graceful innocence, her every air
Of gesture or least action, over-awed   46c
His malice, and with rapine sweet bereaved
His fierceness of the fierce intent it brought.
That space the Evil One abstracted stood
From his own evil, and for the time remained
Stupidly good, of enmity disarmed,
Of guile, of hate, of envy, of revenge.
But the hot hell that always in him burns,
Though in mid heav'n, soon ended his delight,
And tortures him now more, the more he sees
Of pleasure not for him ordained: then soon   470
Fierce hate he recollects, and all his thoughts
Of mischief, gratulating, thus excites: . . . .

Andrew Marvell

(1621–1678)

■■■■■■■■■

AFTER RECEIVING his bachelor's degree from Cambridge in 1639, Marvell continued studying there until 1644, when his father died. He was a clerk in a business house for a brief period, then traveled abroad for several years, and was probably employed as a tutor. By 1651 he had become tutor to the daughter of Lord General Fairfax and lived at the Fairfax residence, Nun Appleton House, in Yorkshire. It was in this quiet and pleasant setting, with its lovely garden, that Marvell composed some of his best lyrics. By 1653 he had left Nun Appleton to become the tutor of William Dutton, a ward of Cromwell. In that same year he was recommended by Milton for the position of assistant to the Latin Secretary but, for some unknown reason, did not receive the appointment until 1657. Two years later he was elected to Richard Cromwell's Parliament as the member from Hull, and he remained a member until his death. Marvell maintained a peculiar detachment from the strife and enmity of his times. Of the Civil War, he said: "I think the cause was too good to have been fought for. Men ought to have trusted God—they ought to have trusted the King with that whole matter." But during the Restoration he turned from lyric poetry to satiric verse, attacking corruption in Parliament and the Court. Although the question of his marital status remained in doubt for some time, it is now generally agreed that he lived and died a bachelor.

Suggested Readings

T. S. ELIOT, "Andrew Marvell," in *Selected Essays*. New York: Harcourt, Brace & Co., 1932.

WILLIAM EMPSON, "Marvell's Garden," in *Some Versions of Pastoral*. London: Chatto & Windus, 1935.

M. C. BRADBROOK and LLOYD THOMAS, *Andrew Marvell*. Cambridge: Cambridge University Press, 1940.

FRANK KERMODE, "The Argument of Marvell's 'Garden,'" *Essays in Criticism*, II, 3 (July, 1952), 225–241.

■■■■■■■■■

Andrew Marvell is easily the most eminent of the later metaphysicals. While the metaphysical style—specifically, the use of conceits

—became less interesting in the work of Abraham Cowley and ran to excesses of the grotesque and superficial in the work of John Cleveland, it was used with great skill and effectiveness by Andrew Marvell. Of seventeenth-century lyric poets whose reputations have been positive and influential in modern times, Marvell is second only to Donne.

Like Donne, Marvell makes analogies with a persuasive aptness and develops conceits with a formidable intellectuality. Although comparable to Donne in the successful use of metaphor, Marvell shows an individuality of achievement in many lyrics. Donne's poems have a greater dramatic intensity and personal immediacy, while Marvell's tend to be reflective and meditative and often have a broader philosophical import. A characteristic difference between the two poets lies in their use of the effect of surprise. Donne frequently surprises through the sudden presentation of the shocking and the unexpected, whereas Marvell's effects of surprise are often less conspicuous and emerge fully only under a close reading of his poems. A good illustration of Marvell's almost elusive wit may be found in these famous lines from "The Garden":

> Annihilating all that's made
> To a green thought in a green shade.

The "green thought" is the most conspicuous and immediately effective detail in the two lines. But there is also a kind of surprise, a meaningful wittiness, to be found in the preceding line. The word "annihilate," in ordinary usage, is limited to the meaning "utterly destroy, reduce to nothingness," and it is never followed by the preposition "to." Marvell has subtly complicated the meaning of the word by adding something positive to its basic negative meaning. Thus the passage says that the mind transcends the natural world not simply by reducing that world to nothingness but by transforming it to a "green thought," to an intellectual and spiritual experience. By including the meaning of transformation—"annihilating *to*"—Marvell implies that the spiritual experience is not simply a negation of natural sensory experience but actually proceeds from it. There is a similar complexity in the rest of the line— "all that's made." This expression may readily be regarded as merely synonymous with "everything," with no further implications. But in the passage the word "made" has an especially precise and appropriate meaning. It signifies the world of *created* objects, the realm of the physical and the material as distinguished from the realm of the metaphysical and the spiritual. The expression "all that's made" has a loose and casual quality but also a strict and precise meaning.

A characteristic aspect of Marvell's work is the brilliance of performance achieved within fairly narrow limitations. For example, much of Marvell's best lyric verse is written in relatively short lines—iambic tetrameter, especially octosyllabic couplet. Despite this confining metrical pattern and the simplest of rhyme schemes, Marvell has produced a variety of rhythmical effects. The same simple pattern has been adapted to differing purposes. Adhering to octosyllabic couplet, Marvell has produced the reflective lyricism of "The Garden," the gentle and evocative lilt of "Bermudas," the dramatic change of pace and shifts of tone of "To His Coy Mistress." Similarly, while Marvell used familiar themes and well-worn literary traditions, he surpassed mere charm and gracefulness by his effective use of language and by his subtle and probing thoughtfulness. His wit derives as much from intellectual insight as from skillful technique.

On a Drop of Dew

See how the orient dew,
Shed from the bosom of the morn
  Into the blowing roses,
Yet careless of its mansion new,
For the clear region where 'twas born
  Round in itself incloses,
  And in its little globe's extent
Frames as it can its native element;
How it the purple flower does slight,
  Scarce touching where it lies,   10
But gazing back upon the skies,
  Shines with a mournful light
    Like its own tear,
Because so long divided from the sphere.
  Restless it rolls and unsecure,
    Trembling lest it grow impure,
  Till the warm sun pity its pain,
And to the skies exhale it back again.
  So the soul, that drop, that ray
Of the clear fountain of eternal day,   20
Could it within the human flower be seen,
  Rememb'ring still its former height,
  Shuns the sweet leaves and blossoms green;
  And recollecting its own light,
Does, in its pure and circling thoughts, express
The greater heaven in an heaven less.
  In how coy a figure wound,
  Every way it turns away;
So the world excluding round,
  Yet receiving in the day;   30
Dark beneath but bright above,

Here disdaining, there in love;
How loose and easy hence to go,
How girt and ready to ascend;
Moving but on a point below,
It all about does upwards bend.
Such did the manna's sacred dew distil,
White and entire, though congealed and chill;
Congealed on earth, but does, dissolving, run
Into the glories of th' almighty sun.   40

■ 1. At what point in the poem does it become apparent that the soul is being compared to a drop of dew?

2. Compare this poem with Herrick's "To Daffodils" for similarities and differences of metaphorical technique.

The Definition of Love

My love is of a birth as rare
As 'tis for object strange and high;
It was begotten by despair
Upon impossibility.

Magnanimous despair alone
Could show me so divine a thing,
Where feeble hope could ne'er have flown,
But vainly flapped its tinsel wing.

And yet I quickly might arrive
Where my extended soul is fixed,   10
But fate does iron wedges drive,
And always crowds itself betwixt.

For fate with jealous eye does see
Two perfect loves, nor lets them close;
Their union would her ruin be,
And her tyrannic power depose.

And therefore her decrees of steel
Us as the distant poles have placed,
Though love's whole world on us doth wheel,
Not by themselves to be embraced;   20

Unless the giddy heaven fall,
And earth some new convulsion tear,

And, us to join, the world should all
Be cramped into a planisphere.

As lines, so loves, oblique may well
Themselves in every angle greet;
But ours so truly parallel,
Though infinite, can never meet.

Therefore the love which us doth bind,
But fate so enviously debars,   30
Is the conjunction of the mind,
And opposition of the stars.

1. Consider the appropriateness of the title.
2. How important in producing the tone of scientific accuracy
are denotative and connotative aspects of the language employed?

Bermudas

Where the remote Bermudas ride
In th' ocean's bosom unespied,
From a small boat that rowed along,
The list'ning winds received this song:
    What should we do but sing his praise
That led us through the wat'ry maze
Unto an isle so long unknown,
And yet far kinder than our own?
Where he the huge sea-monsters wracks,
That lift the deep upon their backs,   10
He lands us on a grassy stage,
Safe from the storms and prelates' rage.
He gave us this eternal spring
Which here enamels everything,
And sends the fowls to us in care,
On daily visits through the air.
He hangs in shades the orange bright,
Like golden lamps in a green night;
And does in the pomegranates close
Jewels more rich than Ormus shows.   20
He makes the figs our mouths to meet
And throws the melons at our feet,
But apples, plants of such a price,
No tree could ever bear them twice.
With cedars, chosen by his hand,

From Lebanon, he stores the land,
And makes the hollow seas that roar
Proclaim the ambergris on shore.
He cast, of which we rather boast,
The Gospel's pearl upon our coast,   30
And in these rocks for us did frame
A temple, where to sound his name.
Oh, let our voice his praise exalt,
Till it arrive at heaven's vault;
Which thence, perhaps, rebounding, may
Echo beyond the Mexic Bay.

    Thus sung they in the English boat
An holy and a cheerful note,
And all the way, to guide their chime,
With falling oars they kept the time.   40

To His Coy Mistress

Had we but world enough, and time,
This coyness, lady, were no crime.
We would sit down and think which way
To walk, and pass our long love's day;
Thou by the Indian Ganges' side
Shouldst rubies find; I by the tide
Of Humber would complain. I would
Love you ten years before the Flood;
And you should, if you please, refuse
Till the conversion of the Jews.   10
My vegetable love should grow
Vaster than empires, and more slow.
An hundred years should go to praise
Thine eyes, and on thy forehead gaze;
Two hundred to adore each breast,
But thirty thousand to the rest;
An age at least to every part,
And the last age should show your heart.
For, lady, you deserve this state,
Nor would I love at lower rate.   20

    But at my back I always hear
Time's wingèd chariot hurrying near;
And yonder all before us lie
Deserts of vast eternity.
Thy beauty shall no more be found,
Nor in thy marble vault shall sound

My echoing song; then worms shall try
That long preserved virginity,
And your quaint honor turn to dust,
And into ashes all my lust.   30
The grave's a fine and private place,
But none, I think, do there embrace.
   Now therefore, while the youthful hue
Sits on thy skin like morning dew,
And while thy willing soul transpires
At every pore with instant fires,
Now let us sport us while we may;
And now, like am'rous birds of prey,
Rather at once our time devour,
Than languish in his slow-chapped power.   40
Let us roll all our strength, and all
Our sweetness, up into one ball;
And tear our pleasures with rough strife
Thorough the iron gates of life.
Thus, though we cannot make our sun
Stand still, yet we will make him run.

■ 1. This poem follows the tradition of using the *carpe diem* theme
in a love lyric. Compare it with Herrick's "To the Virgins, to Make
Much of Time" and Waller's "Go, Lovely Rose!" In what sense may
Marvell's poem be said to transcend the tradition of the love lyric?
  2. How is tone involved in the development of the poem?

A Dialogue between the Soul and Body

Soul

Oh, who shall from this dungeon raise
A soul enslaved so many ways?
With bolts of bones; that fettered stands
In feet, and manacled in hands;
Here blinded with an eye, and there
Deaf with the drumming of an ear;
A soul hung up, as 'twere, in chains
Of nerves and arteries and veins;
Tortured, besides each other part,
In a vain head and double heart.   10

Body

Oh, who shall me deliver whole
From bonds of this tyrannic soul?
Which, stretched upright, impales me so

That mine own precipice I go;
And warms and moves this needless frame,
A fever could but do the same.
And, wanting where its spite to try,
Has made me live to let me die.
A body that could never rest,
Since this ill spirit it possessed.   20

Soul

What magic could me thus confine
Within another's grief to pine?
Where whatsoever it complain,
I feel, that cannot feel, the pain.
And all my care itself employs,
That to preserve which me destroys.
Constrained not only to endure
Diseases, but, what's worse, the cure;
And ready oft the port to gain,
Am shipwrecked into health again.   30

Body

But physic yet could never reach
The maladies thou me dost teach:
Whom first the cramp of hope does tear,
And then the palsy shakes of fear;
The pestilence of love does heat,
Or hatred's hidden ulcer eat.
Joy's cheerful madness does perplex,
Or sorrow's other madness vex;
Which knowledge forces me to know,
And memory will not forgo.   40
What but a soul could have the wit
To build me up for sin so fit?
So architects do square and hew
Green trees that in the forest grew.

1. This poem follows a literary tradition which borrowed its form
and theme from theology and philosophy. Usually, in such dispute
between body and soul the wickedness and weakness of the body's
argument was obvious, and the soul eventually triumphed. Notice Marvell's departure from this practice, the deliberate lack of resolution and
the sympathetic presentation of the body's argument.

2. Analyze the poem as an exercise in irony.

The Garden

How vainly men themselves amaze
To win the palm, the oak, or bays,
And their uncessant labors see
Crowned from some single herb or tree,
Whose short and narrow vergèd shade
Does prudently their toils upbraid;
While all flowers and all trees do close
To weave the garlands of repose.

Fair quiet, have I found thee here,
And innocence, thy sister dear!   10
Mistaken long, I sought you then
In busy companies of men;
Your sacred plants, if here below,
Only among the plants will grow.
Society is all but rude,
To this delicious solitude.

No white nor red was ever seen
So am'rous as this lovely green.
Fond lovers, cruel as their flame,
Cut in these trees their mistress' name;   20
Little, alas, they know or heed
How far these beauties hers exceed!
Fair trees! wheres'e'er your barks I wound,
No name shall but your own be found.

When we have run our passion's heat,
Love hither makes his best retreat.
The gods that mortal beauty chase,
Still in a tree did end their race:
Apollo hunted Daphne so,
Only that she might laurel grow;   30
And Pan did after Syrinx speed,
Not as a nymph, but for a reed.

What wond'rous life is this I lead!
Ripe apples drop about my head;
The luscious clusters of the vine
Upon my mouth do crush their wine;
The nectarine and curious peach
Into my hands themselves do reach;

Stumbling on melons as I pass,
Insnared with flowers, I fall on grass.   40

Meanwhile the mind from pleasure less
Withdraws into its happiness;
The mind, that ocean where each kind
Does straight its own resemblance find
Yet it creates, transcending these,
Far other worlds and other seas,
Annihilating all that's made
To a green thought in a green shade.

Here at the fountain's sliding foot,
Or at some fruit-tree's mossy root,   50
Casting the body's vest aside,
My soul into the boughs does glide;
There like a bird it sits and sings,
Then whets, then combs its silver wings;
And till prepared for longer flight,
Waves in its plumes the various light.

Such was that happy garden-state,
While man there walked without a mate;
After a place so pure and sweet,
What other help could yet be meet!
But 'twas beyond a mortal's share   60
To wander solitary there;
Two paradises 'twere, in one,
To live in paradise alone.

How well the skilful gard'ner drew
Of flowers and herbs this dial new,
Where, from above, the milder sun
Does through a fragrant zodiac run;
And, as it works, th' industrious bee
Computes its time as well as we.
How could such sweet and wholesome hours   70
Be reckoned but with herbs and flowers?

■ 1. A pervasive theme throughout the poem is the neo-Platonic concept of "the great chain of being." (It is especially prominent in stanzas
6 and 7.) Clarify the presence of this theme in the poem. Consult the
library, if necessary.

2. Consider the man in the garden as a metaphor for mankind in
the world. What is the relationship of this metaphor to the neo-Platonic

theme? Is it possible to regard the metaphor as sustained throughout the poem?

3. Consider the function of trees in the organization of the poem.

4. At what points in the poem are devices of wit used to enrich meaning?

John Dryden

(1631–1700)

■■■■■■■■■■

JOHN DRYDEN was educated at Westminster School and Cambridge. Of a Puritan family, he first worked as secretary to the Chamberlain of Oliver Cromwell. He wrote "Heroic Stanzas on the Death of Cromwell," but the confusions which followed the Protector's death made him welcome the re-establishment of the monarchy under Charles II in 1660. Dryden turned to the theater as a means of making money from his writing. With his brother-in-law, Sir Robert Howard, he wrote the *Indian Queen* (1664), an "heroic" play, in rhymed verse, and set the pattern or fashion in dramatic writing for the next decade. One of his most admired plays, *All for Love* (1678), based on the story of Antony and Cleopatra, was written in blank verse. He also wrote successful comedies. His *Essay of Dramatic Poesy* (1668) is remarkable for its lucid and vigorous prose as well as for its insights. His first important poem had been *Annus Mirabilis*, about "the wonderful year," 1666, in which the English defeated the Dutch at sea and rallied from the disaster of the Great Fire. His satires are *Absalom and Achitophel* (1681), *The Medal* (1682), and *MacFlecknoe* (1682). *Religio Laici* (1682) and *The Hind and the Panther* (1687) are concerned with his religious and political convictions. Dryden made his way from Presbyterianism to Anglicanism and finally to Catholicism. In his old age he translated Boccaccio and Vergil and put Chaucer into modern English. Dryden gave to the eighteenth century its dominant literary ideals and the standard of English prose which obtains to our own day.

Suggested Readings

MARK VAN DOREN, *The Poetry of John Dryden.* New York: Harcourt, Brace & Co., 1920.

T. S. ELIOT, "John Dryden," *Selected Essays.* New York: Harcourt, Brace & Co., 1932, pp. 264–274.

E. M. W. TILLYARD, *Five Poems, 1470–1870.* London: Chatto & Windus, 1948.

MacFlecknoe[1]

or A Satire upon the True-Blue Protestant Poet, T. S.

All human things are subject to decay,
And when fate summons, monarchs must obey.
This Flecknoe found, who, like Augustus, young
Was called to empire, and had governed long;
In prose and verse was owned, without dispute,
Through all the realms of Nonsense absolute.
This aged prince, now flourishing in peace,
And blessed with issue of a large increase;
Worn out with business, did at length debate
To settle the succession of the State;   10
And, pondering which of all his sons was fit
To reign, and wage immortal war with wit,
Cried; " 'Tis resolved; for nature pleads, that he
Should only rule, who most resembles me.
Sh—— alone my perfect image bears,
Mature in dullness from his tender years:
Sh—— alone, of all my sons, is he
Who stands confirmed in full stupidity.
The rest to some faint meaning make pretense,
But Sh——never deviates into sense.   20
Some beams of wit on other souls may fall,
Strike through, and make a lucid interval;
But Sh——'s genuine night admits no ray,
His rising fogs prevail upon the day.
Besides, his goodly fabric fills the eye,
And seems designed for thoughtless majesty;
Thoughtless as monarch oaks that shade the plain,
And, spread in solemn state, supinely reign.
Heywood and Shirley[2] were but types of thee,
Thou last great prophet of tautology.   30
Even I, a dunce of more renown than they,
Was sent before but to prepare thy way;
And, coarsely clad in Norwich drugget,[3] came
To teach the nations in thy greater name.
My warbling lute, the lute I whilom strung,
When to King John of Portugal[4] I sung,

1. Richard Flecknoe, a Roman Catholic priest and a dull poet, died in 1678. Thomas Shadwell, a dramatist and once a friend of Dryden, is the subject of the satire; Dryden calls him Mac (that is, son of) Flecknoe. Shadwell, a Whig, had attacked Dryden, a Tory, in "The Medal of John Bayes," a hit at Dryden's "The Medal." Dryden published "MacFlecknoe" in reply.   2. Heywood and Shirley were playwrights.   3. A woolen fabric.   4. Flecknoe said he had enjoyed the patronage of John IV in Portugal.

Was but the prelude to that glorious day,
When thou on silver Thames didst cut thy way,
With well-timed oars before the royal barge,
Swelled with the pride of thy celestial charge;   40
And big with hymn, commander of a host,
The like was ne'er in Epsom blankets[5] tossed.
Methinks I see the new Arion sail,
The lute still trembling underneath thy nail.
At thy well-sharpened thumb from shore to shore
The treble squeaks for fear, the basses roar;
Echoes from Pissing Alley Sh—— call,
And Sh—— they resound from Ashton Hall.
About thy boat the little fishes throng,
As at the morning toast that floats along.   50
Sometimes, as prince of thy harmonious band,
Thou wield'st thy papers in thy threshing hand.
St. André's feet ne'er kept more equal time,
Not e'en the feet of thy own *Psyche's* rime;
Though they in number as in sense excel:
So just, so like tautology, they fell,
That, pale with envy, Singleton forswore
The lute and sword, which he in triumph bore,
And vowed he ne'er would act Villerius more."
Here stopped the good old sire, and wept for joy   60
In silent raptures of the hopeful boy.
All arguments, but most his plays, persuade,
That for anointed dullness he was made.

  Close to the walls which fair Augusta[6] bind
(The fair Augusta much to fears inclined),
An ancient fabric raised t' inform the sight,
There stood of yore, and Barbican[7] it hight:
A watchtower once; but now, so fate ordains,
Of all the pile an empty name remains.
From its old ruins brothel-houses rise,   70
Scenes of lewd loves, and of polluted joys,
Where their vast courts the mother-strumpets keep,
And, undisturb'd by watch, in silence sleep;
Near these a Nursery erects its head [8]
Where queens are form'd, and future heroes bred,
Where unfledg'd actors learn to laugh and cry,

....
5. Reference to a play by Shadwell.   6. A Roman name for London.
7. Literally, an outer fortification.   8. A theatre for the training of boys and girls
for the stage, established under royal letters patent (1662), which prohibited "obscene, scandalous, or offensive passages," and restricted the performances to "what
may consist with harmless and inoffensive delights and recreations" (*Christie*).

Where infant punks their tender voices try,
And little Maximins[9] the gods defy.
Great Fletcher never treads in buskins here,
Nor greater Jonson dares in socks appear;   80
But gentle Simkin[10] just reception finds
Amidst this monument of vanished minds:
Pure clinches[11] the suburbian muse affords,
And Panton[12] waging harmless war with words;
Here Flecknoe as a place to fame well known,
Ambitiously design'd his Shadwell's throne.
For ancient Decker[13] prophesied long since,
That in this pile should reign a mighty prince,
Born for a scourge of wit, and flail of sense,
To whom true dullness should some *Psyches* owe,   90
But worlds of *Misers* from his pen should flow:
Humourists and *Hypocrites* it should produce,
Whole *Raymond* families and tribes of *Bruce*.[14]
    Now empress Fame had publish'd the renown
Of Shadwell's coronation through the town.
Rous'd by report of Fame, the nations meet
From near Bunhill and distant Watling-street.[15]
No Persian carpets spread th' imperial way,
But scattered limbs of mangled poets lay;
From dusty shops neglected authors come   100
Martyrs of pies, and relics of the bum.
Much Heywood, Shirley, Ogleby[16] there lay,
But loads of Sh—— almost choked the way.
Bilked stationers, for yeomen stood prepared,
And Herringman[17] was captain of the guard.
The hoary prince in majesty appeared,
High on a throne of his own labors reared.
At his right hand our young Ascanius[18] sate,
Rome's other hope, and pillar of the State.
His brows thick fogs, instead of glories, grace,   110
And lambent dullness played around his face.
As Hannibal did to the altars come,
Sworn by his sire a mortal foe to Rome;
So Sh—— swore, nor should his vow be vain,

....

9. Maximum, in Dryden's *Tyrannic Love,* defies the gods.   10.   Said to be a
cobbler in a lost play.   11.   Puns.   12.   A celebrated punster.
13.   Thomas Dekker, an earlier dramatist (Elizabethan).   14.   *Psyche, The
Miser,* and *The Humourists* were plays by Shadwell. Raymond is a character in
The Humourists, and Bruce in *The Virtuoso.*   15.   Bunhill and Watling
Street were actually not far apart.   16.   An inferior poet and translator.
17.   Dryden's London bookseller.   18.   Ascanius (that is, Shadwell), son of
Aeneas, in Virgil's *Aeneid,* who is called "the other great hope of Rome."

That he till death true dullness would maintain;
And, in his father's right, and realm's defense,
Ne'er to have peace with wit, nor truce with sense.
The king himself the sacred unction made,
As king by office, and as priest by trade.
In his sinister hand, instead of ball,   120
He placed a mighty mug of potent ale;
Love's Kingdom to his right he did convey,
At once his scepter, and his rule of sway;
Whose righteous lore the prince had practiced young,
And from whose loins recorded *Psyche* sprung.
His temples, last, with poppies were o'erspread,
That nodding seemed to consecrate his head.
Just at that point of time, if fame not lie,
On his left hand twelve reverend owls did fly.
So Romulus, 'tis sung, by Tiber's Brook,   130
Presage of sway from twice six vultures took.
Th' admiring throng loud acclamations make,
And omens of his future empire take.
The sire then shook the honours of his head,
And from his brows damps of oblivion shed
Full on the filial dullness: long he stood,
Repelling from his breast the raging God,
At length burst out in this prophetic mood:
    "Heavens bless my son, from Ireland let him reign
To far Barbadoes on the western main;   140
Of his dominion may no end be known
And greater than his father's be this throne;
Beyond *Love's Kingdom* let him stretch his pen."
He paus'd, and all the people cry'd "Amen."
Then thus continued he: "My son, advance
Still in new impudence, new ignorance.
Success let others teach, learn thou from me,
Pangs without birth, and fruitless industry.
Let *Virtuosos* in five years be writ,
Yet not one thought accuse thy toil of wit.[19]   150
Let gentle George[20] in triumph tread the stage,
Make Dorimant betray, and Loveit rage;
Let Cully, Cockwood, Fopling charm the pit,
And in their folly show the writer's wit.
Yet still thy fools shall stand in thy defence,
And justify their author's want of sense.

....
19. Shadwell bragged about his writing speed.   20. Sir George Etheridge,
author of comedies which Dryden admired. The characters mentioned in the next
two lines appear in Etheridge's comedies.

Let 'em be all by thy own model made
Of dulness; and desire no foreign aid,
That they to future ages may be known,
Not copies drawn, but issue of thine own.   160
Nay, let thy men of wit too be the same,
All full of thee, and diff'ring but in name;
But let no alien Sedley[21] interpose,
To lard with wit thy hungry Epsom prose.
And when false flowers of rhet'ric thou wouldst cull,
Trust nature, do not labour to be dull;
But write thy best, and top, and in each line
Sir Formal's[22] oratory will be thine.
Sir Formal though unsought attends thy quill,
And does thy northern dedications[23] fill.   170
Nor let false friends seduce thy mind to fame,
By arrogating Jonson's hostile name.
Let father Flecknoe fire thy mind with praise,
And uncle Ogleby thy envy raise.
Thou art my blood, where Jonson[24] has no part:
What share have we in nature, or in art?
Where did his wit on learning fix a brand,
And rail at arts he did not understand?
Where made he love in Prince Nicander's[25] vein,
Or swept the dust in *Psyche's* humble strain?   180
Where sold he bargains, 'whip-stitch,[26] kiss my arse,'
Promised a play and dwindled to a farce?
When did his Muse from Fletcher scenes purloin,
As thou whole Eth'rege dost transfuse to thine?
But so transfused as oil on water's flow,
His always floats above, thine sinks below.
This is thy province, this thy wondrous way,
New humors to invent for each new play:
This is that boasted bias of thy mind,
By which one way, to dullness, 'tis inclined;   190
Which makes thy writings lean on one side still,
And, in all changes, that way bends thy will.
Nor let thy mountain-belly make pretense
Of likeness; thine's a tympany[27] of sense.
A tun of man in thy large bulk is writ,

---

21. In his Dedication of *A True Widow* Shadwell thanked Sir Charles Sedley for the Prologue which Sedley had written for Shadwell's *Epsom Wells.* 22. Sir Formal Trifle is a character in Shadwell's *The Virtuoso.*   23. Shadwell had dedicated works to the Duke of Newcastle, whose home was in northern England.   24. Shadwell regarded himself as Jonson's successor.   25. A character in Shadwell's *Psyche.*   26. A tailor.   27. Inflated.

But sure thou'rt but a kilderkin[28] of wit.
Like mine, thy gentle numbers feebly creep;
Thy tragic Muse gives smiles, thy comic sleep.
With whate'er gall thou sett'st thyself to write,
Thy inoffensive satires never bite.   200
In thy felonious heart though venom lies,
It does but touch thy Irish pen, and dies.
Thy genius calls thee not to purchase fame
In keen iambics, but mild anagram.
Leave writing plays, and choose for thy command
Some peaceful province in Acrostic land.
There thou mayst wings display, and altars raise,[29]
And torture one poor word ten thousand ways;
Or, if thou wouldst thy different talents suit,
Set thy own songs, and sing them to thy lute."   210
He said, but his last words were scarcely heard,
For Bruce and Longville had a trap prepar'd
And down they sent the yet declaiming bard.[30]
Sinking, he left his drugget robe behind,
Borne upwards by a subterranean wind.
The mantle fell to the young prophet's part
With double portion of his father's art.[31]

....

28. A small cask.   29. Typographical arrangement resembling altars, wings,
and so forth.   30. A trick played on Sir Formal Trifle in *The Virtuoso*,
Act III, by Bruce and Longville.   31. See II Kings, 2: 12–15.

From *Absalom and Achitophel* (Part I, lines 544–568)

Absalom and Achitophel [1]

In the first rank of these did Zimri[2] stand;
A man so various, that he seemed to be
Not one, but all mankind's epitome:
Stiff in opinions, always in the wrong;
Was everything by starts, and nothing long;
But, in the course of one revolving moon,
Was chemist, fiddler, statesman, and buffoon:
Then all for women, painting, rhyming, drinking,
Besides ten thousand freaks that died in thinking.

....

1. Dryden applied the Biblical story of II Samuel 13–18 to contemporary
politics. The Duke of Monmouth, Absalom, was the handsome and much-loved
illegitimate son of Charles II. Led on by Shaftesbury (Achitophel), who headed
the plot against the Catholic Duke of York, brother of Charles II and heir to the
throne, the Duke of Monmouth attempted to usurp the throne. This satire was
written at the request of the king. Charles II is King David, the English are the
Jews, England is Sion, and so on.   2. This portrait is of George Villiers, Duke
of Buckingham.

Blest madman, who could every hour employ,
With something new to wish, or to enjoy!
Railing and praising were his usual themes;
And both (to show his judgment) in extremes:
So over-violent, or over-civil,
That every man, with him, was God or Devil.
In squand'ring wealth was his peculiar art:
Nothing went unrewarded but desert.
Beggared by fools, whom still he found too late,
He had his jest, and they had his estate.
He laughed himself from court; then sought relief
By forming parties, but could ne'er be chief;
For, spite of him, the weight of business fell
On Absalom and wise Achitophel:
Thus, wicked but in will, of means bereft,
He left not faction, but of that was left.

■   Compare the quality of the irony in this portrait with Pope's of
Addison (p. 262).

To the Pious Memory of the Accomplished Young Lady
Mrs. Anne Killigrew
Excellent in the Two Sister Arts of Poesy and Painting

An Ode

I

Thou youngest virgin-daughter of the skies,
    Made in the last promotion of the blest,
Whose palms, new plucked from paradise,
In spreading branches more sublimely rise,
    Rich with immortal green above the rest;
Whether, adopted to some neighboring star,
Thou roll'st above us in thy wandering race,
    Or in procession fixed and regular,
    Moved with the heaven's majestic pace,
    Or called to more superior bliss,   10
Thou tread'st with seraphim the vast abyss:
Whatever happy region is thy place,
Cease thy celestial song a little space;
Thou wilt have time enough for hymns divine,
    Since heaven's eternal year is thine.
Hear, then, a mortal Muse thy praise rehearse
        In no ignoble verse,
But such as thy own voice did practice here,

When thy first fruits of poesy were given,
To make thyself a welcome inmate there,   20
 While yet a young probationer,
  And candidate of heaven.

   2

 If by traduction came thy mind,
 Our wonder is the less to find
A soul so charming from a stock so good;
Thy father was transfused into thy blood:
So wert thou born into the tuneful strain,
An early, rich, and inexhausted vein.
 But if they pre-existing soul
 Was formed at first with myriads more,   30
It did through all the mighty poets roll
 Who Greek or Latin laurels wore,
And was that Sappho last, which once it was before.
 If so, then cease thy flight, O heaven-born mind!
Thou hast no dross to purge from thy rich ore,
 Nor can thy soul a fairer mansion find
Than was the beauteous frame she left behind:
Return, to fill or mend the quire of thy celestial kind!

   3

 May we presume to say that at thy birth
New joy was sprung in heaven as well as here on earth?   40
 For sure the milder planets did combine
 On thy auspicious horoscope to shine,
 And even the most malicious were in trine.
  Thy brother-angels at thy birth
  Strung each his lyre, and tuned it high,
  That all the people of the sky
 Might know a poetess was born on earth;
  And then, if ever, mortal ears
  Had heard the music of the spheres.
  And if no clustering swarm of bees   50
On thy sweet mouth distilled their golden dew,
  'Twas that such vulgar miracles
  Heaven had not leisure to renew;
 For all the blest fraternity of love
Solemnized there thy birth, and kept thy holiday above.

   4

 O gracious God! how far have we
Profaned thy heavenly gift of poesy!

Made prostitute and profligate the Muse,
Debased to each obscene and impious use,
Whose harmony was first ordained above   60
For tongues of angels and for hymns of love!
O wretched we! why were we hurried down
    This lubric and adulterate age
(Nay, added fat pollutions of our own)
    To increase the steaming ordures of the stage?
What can we say to excuse our second fall?
Let this thy vestal, heaven, atone for all:
Her Arethusian stream remains unsoiled,
Unmixed with foreign filth, and undefiled;
Her wit was more than man; her innocence a child.   70

5

Art she had none, yet wanted none,
    For nature did that want supply;
So rich in treasures of her own,
    She might our boasted stores defy:
Such noble vigor did her verse adorn
That it seemed borrowed where 'twas only born.
Her morals too were in her bosom bred,
    By great examples daily fed,
What in the best of books, her father's life, she read.
    And to be read herself she need not fear;   80
    Each test and every light her Muse will bear,
    Though Epictetus with his lamp were there.
    Even love (for love sometimes her Muse expressed)
Was but a lambent flame which played about her breast,
      Light as the vapors of a morning dream;
    So cold herself, whilst she such warmth expressed,
    'Twas Cupid bathing in Diana's stream.

6

Born to the spacious empire of the Nine,
    One would have thought she should have been content
    To manage well that mighty government;   90
But what can young, ambitious souls confine?
    To the next realm she stretched her sway,
    For Painture near adjoining lay,
A plenteous province and alluring prey:
A chamber of dependences was framed
(As conquerors will never want pretense,
    When armed, to justify the offense),
And the whole fief in right of Poetry she claimed.

The country open lay without defense,
    For poets frequent inroads there had made,   100
        And perfectly could represent
The shape, the face, with every lineament;
And all the large demesnes which the dumb Sister swayed,
    All bowed beneath her government,
    Received in triumph wheresoe'er she went.
Her pencil drew whate'er her soul designed,
And oft the happy draught surpassed the image in her mind:
    The sylvan scenes of herds and flocks
    And fruitful plains and barren rocks;
        Of shallow brooks that flowed so clear   110
    The bottom did the top appear;
    Of deeper too and ampler floods,
        Which, as in mirrors, showed the woods;
    Of lofty trees, with sacred shades
    And perspectives of pleasant glades,
    Where nymphs of brightest form appear,
    And shaggy satyrs standing near,
    Which them at once admire and fear;
The ruins, too, of some majestic piece,
Boasting the power of ancient Rome or Greece,   120
Whose statues, friezes, columns, broken lie,
    And, though defaced, the wonder of the eye.
What nature, art, bold fiction, e'er durst frame,
Her forming hand gave feature to the name;
So strange a concourse ne'er was seen before
But when the peopled ark the whole creation bore.

7

The scene then changed: with bold, erected look
Our martial king the sight with reverence strook,
For, not content to express his outward part,
    Her hand called out the image of his heart;   130
His warlike mind, his soul devoid of fear,
His high designing thoughts were figured there,
    As when by magic, ghosts are made appear.
Our phoenix queen was portrayed, too, so bright
Beauty alone could beauty take so right:
Her dress, her shape, her matchless grace,
Were all observed, as well as heavenly face;
With such a peerless majesty she stands
As in that day she took the crown from sacred hands;
    Before, a train of heroines was seen—   140
In beauty foremost, as in rank, the queen.

Thus nothing to her genius was denied,
　　But, like a ball of fire, the farther thrown,
　　Still with a greater blaze she shone,
And her bright soul broke out on every side.
What next she had designed, heaven only knows:
To such immoderate growth her conquest rose
That fate alone its progress could oppose.

8

　　Now all those charms, that blooming grace,
The well-proportioned shape, and beauteous face,   150
　　Shall never more be seen by mortal eyes;
In earth the much-lamented virgin lies.
Not wit nor piety could fate prevent;
Nor was the cruel destiny content
To finish all the murder at a blow,
To sweep at once her life and beauty too;
But, like a hardened felon, took a pride
　　To work more mischievously slow,
　　And plundered first, and then destroyed.
Oh, double sacrilege on things divine,   160
To rob the relic and deface the shrine!
　　But thus Orinda died:
Heaven, by the same disease, did both translate;
As equal were their souls, so equal was their fate.

9

Meantime her warlike brother on the seas
His waving streamers to the winds displays,
And vows for his return with vain devotion pays.
　　Ah, generous youth, that wish forbear;
　　　The winds too soon will waft thee here!
　　　Slack all thy sails, and fear to come;   170
　　Alas! thou know'st not thou art wrecked at home!
No more shalt thou behold thy sister's face;
Thou hast already had her last embrace.
But look aloft; and if thou ken'st from far,
Among the Pleiads, a new-kindled star,
　　If any sparkles than the rest more bright,
'Tis she that shines in that propitious light.

10

When in mid-air the golden trump shall sound,
　　To raise the nations under ground;
　　When in the Valley of Jehoshaphat   180

The judging God shall close the book of fate,
    And there the last assizes keep
    For those who wake and those who sleep;
    When rattling bones together fly
    From the four corners of the sky;
When sinews o'er the skeletons are spread,
Those clothed with flesh, and life inspires the dead;
The sacred poets first shall hear the sound,
    And foremost from the tomb shall bound,
    For they are covered with the lightest ground,   190
And straight, with inborn vigor, on the wing,
Like mounting larks, to the new morning sing.
There thou, sweet saint, before the quire shalt go,
As harbinger of heaven, the way to show,
The way which thou so well hast learned below.

■ 1. What are the actual details which Dryden tells about the life of Anne Killigrew? Is Dryden really concerned to give his reader a biographical account? If not, with what subject or subjects is he concerned?

2. Dryden, in stanza 1, is giving a supernatural sanction to the high place of poetry. Explain how he does this.

3. Explain how stanza 2 further develops the theme that poetry is a part of the eternal scheme. How does stanza 3 extend this theme?

4. Certain words and phrases in stanza 4 afford an almost violent contrast to the diction of the preceding stanzas. Point these out. Do there seem to be two related meanings to the word "adulterate" (line 63)? Are there also extended meanings to the words "prostitute" and "profligate" (line 58)? From what you know of the literature of the Restoration stage, do you consider Dryden's censure justified?

5. Stanza 5 must be read in the light of neoclassical poetic theory. *Imitation* and *nature* were key terms in this theory. A frequently repeated injunction was to "copy" nature. One of the meanings of the term *imitation* was the use of the best poets as models, since it was assumed that they had copied nature most perfectly. In other words, imitation in this sense is a virtue in the artist. Indeed, perfect imitation can be considered art. Taking these statements about neoclassical poetic theory into account, interpret Dryden's compliment to Anne Killigrew.

6. In stanza 6 Dryden comments on Anne Killigrew's abilities as a painter. (Neoclassical critics frequently talked about the doctrine *ut pictura poesis*. Dryden is not talking about the doctrine, even though he alludes to it. One of these allusions is "dumb Sister," which seems to be an echo of Plutarch's saying that painting is mute poetry. (For information about this doctrine, see *The Dictionary of World Literature* or some literary handbook.) Explain the extended figure in lines 88–105. (Is there a muse, among the nine, for the art of painting?)

7. In stanza 8 Dryden treats Fate and Destiny as though they were active agents in the affairs of men. We know that he did not literally believe them to be so. In St. Augustine and in later medieval writers one can often read that the destiny of men is in the stars, under the providence of God. Obviously Fate and Destiny are used in this stanza, for a decorative effect. Where else in the poem are there passages, which once would have been literally believed, also used for decorative effect?

Alexander Pope

(1688–1744)

■ ■ ■ ■ ■ ■ ■ ■ ■ ■

POPE WAS BORN in London, the son of a successful linen draper. He was made hump-backed by illness as a child. Because his family was Roman Catholic, Pope was educated by private tutors rather than in public schools or at Cambridge or Oxford. He is credited with having written an epic before he was fifteen, but his published work begins with *Pastorals* (1709), which was followed by *Essay on Criticism* (1711), *The Rape of the Lock* (1712–1714), and *Windsor Forest* (1713). These works caused Pope to be accepted as the best poet of his time. Translations of the *Iliad* (1715–1720) and the *Odyssey* (1725–1726) into English heroic couplets engaged Pope for the next twelve years, and the returns from these volumes made him financially independent. In 1719 he left London for a country estate, Twickenham, which he had purchased. Here he wrote his remaining poetry, carried on literary intrigues, and entertained his friends: Arbuthnot, Gay, Bolingbroke, Swift, and other Tories. The important satirical and didactic works of Pope include *The Dunciad* (1728–1742), a merciless lampoon of his literary enemies; *Moral Essays* (1731–1735), five poetic epistles on various subjects; *Epistle to Dr. Arbuthnot* (1735), used as a prologue to *Imitations of Horace;* and the *Essay on Man* (1733), a work which attempted to epitomize the philosophy of the age.

Suggested Readings

GEOFFREY TILLOTSON, *On the Poetry of Pope.* Oxford: The Clarendon Press, 1938.

F. R. LEAVIS, "Pope," in *Revaluations.* New York: George W. Stewart, Publisher, 1947, pp. 68–100.

AUSTIN WARREN, "Alexander Pope," in *Rage for Order.* Chicago: University of Chicago Press, 1948, pp. 37–51.

Ode on Solitude

Happy the man whose wish and care
    A few paternal acres bound,
Content to breathe his native air,
       In his own ground.

Whose herds with milk, whose fields with bread,
    Whose flocks supply him with attire,
Whose trees in summer yield him shade,
       In winter fire.

Blest, who can unconcern'dly find
    Hours, days, and years slide soft away,
In health of body, peace of mind,
       Quiet by day,

Sound sleep by night; study and ease,
    Together mixt; sweet recreation;
And Innocence, which most does please
       With meditation.

Thus let me live, unseen, unknown,
    Thus unlamented let me die,
Steal from the world, and not a stone
       Tell where I lie.

■ Discuss the economy of phrase with which this poem is written.

Selections from

An Essay on Criticism

Those RULES of old discover'd, not devis'd,
Are Nature still, but Nature methodiz'd;
Nature, like liberty, is but restrain'd   90
By the same laws which first herself ordain'd.
    Hear how learn'd Greece her useful rules indites,
When to repress, and when indulge our flights:
High on Parnassus' top her sons she show'd,
And pointed out those arduous paths they trod;
Held from afar, aloft, th' immortal prize,
And urg'd the rest by equal steps to rise.
Just precepts thus from great examples giv'n,
She drew from them what they deriv'd from Heav'n.

       •   •   •   •

When first young Maro[1] in his boundless mind   130
A work t' outlast immortal Rome design'd,
Perhaps he seem'd above the critic's law,
And but from Nature's fountains scorn'd to draw:
But when t' examine ev'ry part he came,
Nature and Homer were, he found, the same.
Convinc'd, amaz'd, he checks the bold design;
And rules as strict his labour'd work confine,
As if the Stagirite[2] o'erlooked each line.

.   .   .

Learn hence for ancient rules a just esteem;
To copy nature is to copy them.   140

.   .   .

A perfect Judge will read each work of Wit
With the same spirit that its author writ:
Survey the Whole, nor seek slight faults to find
Where nature moves, and rapture warms the mind;
Nor lose, for that malignant dull delight,
The gen'rous pleasure to be charm'd with wit.
But in such lays as neither ebb, nor flow,
Correctly cold, and regularly low,   240
That shunning faults, one quiet tenour keep,
We cannot blame indeed—but we may sleep.

.   .   .

In every work regard the writer's End,
Since none can compass more than they intend;
And if the means be just, the conduct true,
Applause, in spite of trivial faults, is due.

.   .   .

Some to *conceit* alone their taste confine,
And glitt'ring thoughts struck out at ev'ry line;   290

.   .   .

True Wit is Nature to advantage dress'd,   297
What oft was thought, but ne'er so well expressed.

.   .   .

Others for *language* all their care express,   305
And value books, as women men, for Dress:
Their praise is still,—the Style is excellent:
The Sense, they humbly take upon content.

.   .   .

Some by old words to fame have made pretence,
Ancients in phrase, mere moderns in their sense;   325

....

1. Virgil.   2. Aristotle.

Such labour'd nothings, in so strange a style,
Amaze th' unlearn'd, and make the learned smile.

.   .   .

In words, as fashions, the same rule will hold;
Alike fantastic, if too new, or old:
Be not the first by whom the new are try'd,
Nor yet the last to lay the old aside.   335
    But most by Numbers judge a Poet's song;
And smooth or rough, with them is right or wrong.

.   .   .

Who haunt Parnassus but to please their ear,   341
Not mend their minds; as some to Church repair,
Not for the doctrine, but the music there.

.   .   .

True ease in writing comes from art, not chance,
As those move easiest who have learn'd to dance.
'Tis not enough no harshness gives offence,
The sound must seem an Echo to the sense.   365

■   After you have read these excerpts from Pope's *An Essay on Criticism* a number of times and considered the meaning of each very carefully, write in your own words a list of the rules you believe Pope is advocating.

From *Moral Essays*

Epistle II:
Of the Characters of Women

Nothing so true as what you once let fall,
"Most women have no characters at all."
Matter too soft a lasting mark to bear,
And best distinguish'd by black, brown, or fair.
How many pictures of one nymph we view,
All how unlike each other, all how true!
Arcadia's countess[1] here, in ermin'd pride,
Is there Pastora by a fountain side;
Here Fannia, leering on her own good man,
And there a naked Leda with a swan.
Let then the fair one beautifully cry,   10
In Magdalen's loose hair and lifted eye,

....
1. Lady Winchelsea. Like many of the ladies portrayed, she had been a
friend with whom he had quarreled.

Or, dress'd in smiles of sweet Cecilia shine,
With simp'ring angels, palms, and harps divine;
Whether the charmer sinner it, or saint it,
If folly grow romantic I must paint it.
    Come then, the colours and the ground prepare!
Dip in the rainbow, trick her off in air;
Choose a firm cloud, before it fall, and in it
Catch, ere she change, the Cynthia of this minute.   20
    Rufa, whose eye quick-glancing o'er the park,
Attracts each light gay meteor of a spark,
Agrees as ill with Rufa studying Locke
As Sappho's[2] di'monds with her dirty smock;
Or Sappho at her toilet's greasy task,
With Sappho fragrant at an ev'ning mask:—
So morning insects that in muck begun
Shine, buzz, and fly-blow in the setting sun.
    How soft is Silia! fearful to offend,
The frail one's advocate, the weak one's friend: 30
To her Calista prov'd her conduct nice,
And good Simplicius asks of her advice.
Sudden, she storms! she raves! You tip the wink,
But spare your censure; Silia does not drink:
All eyes may see from what the change arose,
All eyes may see—a pimple on her nose.
    Papillia, wedded to her am'rous spark,
Sighs for the shades—"How charming is a park!"
A park is purchas'd, but the fair he sees
All bath'd in tears—"Oh, odious, odious trees!"   40
    Ladies, like variegated tulips show;
'Tis to their changes half their charms we owe;
Fine by defect, and delicately weak,
Their happy spots[3] the nice admirer take;
'Twas thus Calypso once each heart alarm'd,
Aw'd without virtue, without beauty charm'd;
Her tongue bewitch'd as oddly as her eyes,
Less wit than mimic, more a wit than wise;
Strange graces still, and stranger flights she had,
Was just not ugly, and was just not mad;   50
Yet ne'er so sure our passion to create,
As when she touch'd the brink of all we hate.
    Narcissa's nature, tolerably mild,
To make a wash, would hardly stew a child;
Has ev'n been prov'd to grant a lover's pray'r,

---

2. Lady Mary Wortley Montagu.   3. Patches, artificial beauty marks.

And paid a tradesman once to make him stare;
Gave alms at Easter, in a Christian trim,
And made a widow happy, for a whim.
Why then declare good-nature is her scorn,
When 'tis by that alone she can be borne?   60
Why pique all mortals, yet affect a name?
A fool to pleasure, yet a slave to fame:
Now deep in Taylor[4] and the Book of Martyrs,
Now drinking citron with his Grace[5] and Chartres:[6]
Now conscience chills her, and now passion burns;
And atheism and religion take their turns;
A very heathen in the carnal part,
Yet still a sad, good Christian at her heart.
  See Sin[7] in state, majestically drunk;
Proud as a peeress, prouder as a punk;   70
Chaste to her husband, frank to all beside,
A teeming mistress, but a barren bride.
What then? let blood and body bear the fault,
Her head's untouch'd, that noble seat of thought:
Such this day's doctrine—in another fit
She sins with poets through pure love of wit.
What has not fir'd her bosom or her brain?
Caesar and Tall-boy,[8] Charles and Charlemagne.
As Helluo, late dictator of the feast,
The nose of *haut-gout,* and the tip of taste,   80
Critiqu'd your wine, and analyz'd your meat,
Yet on plain pudding deign'd at home to eat;
So Philomede, lect'ring all mankind
On the soft passion, and the taste refin'd,
Th' address, the delicacy—stoops at once,
And makes her hearty meal upon a dunce.
  Flavia's a wit, has too much sense to pray;
To toast our wants and wishes, is her way;
Nor asks of God, but of her stars, to give
The mighty blessing, "while we live, to live."   90
Then all for death, that opiate of the soul!
Lucretia's dagger, Rosamonda's bowl.[9]
Say, what can cause such impotence of mind?
A spark too fickle, or a spouse too kind.
Wise wretch! with pleasures too refin'd to please;

4. Author of *Holy Living and Holy Dying.*   5. Perhaps the Duke of
Wharton.   6. A notorious rake of the time.   7. Duchess of Marlborough.
8. A low-comedy character in a minor seventeenth-century play.   9. Lucretia
killed herself because she was dishonored by Tarquin. Rosamond was Henry II's
mistress who, in Addison's opera, asks for poison instead of the dagger offered by
the queen.

With too much spirit to be e'er at ease;
With too much quickness ever to be taught;
With too much thinking to have common thought:
You purchase pain with all that joy can give,
And die of nothing but a rage to live.   100
    Turn then from wits; and look on Simo's mate,
No ass so meek, no ass so obstinate.
Or her, that owns her faults, but never mends,
Because she's honest, and the best of friends.
Or her, whose life the church and scandal share,
Forever in a passion, or a pray'r.
Or her, who laughs at hell, but (like her Grace)
Cries, "Ah! how charming, if there's no such place!"
Or who in sweet vicissitude appears
Of mirth and opium, ratafia and tears,   110
The daily anodyne, and nightly draught,
To kill those foes to fair ones, time and thought.
Woman and fool are two hard things to hit;
For true no-meaning puzzles more than wit.
    But what are these to great Atossa's[10] mind?
Scarce once herself, by turns all womankind!
Who, with herself, or others, from her birth
Finds all her life one warfare upon earth:
Shines in exposing knaves, and painting fools,
Yet is whate'er she hates and ridicules.   120
No thought advances, but her eddy brain
Whisks it about, and down it goes again.
Full sixty years the world has been her trade,
The wisest fool much time has ever made.
From loveless youth to unrespected age,
No passion gratified except her rage.
So much the fury still outran the wit,
The pleasure miss'd her, and the scandal hit.
Who breaks with her, provokes revenge from hell,
But he's a bolder man who dares be well.   130
Her ev'ry turn with violence pursu'd,
No more a storm her hate than gratitude:
To that each passion turns, or soon or late;
Love, if it makes her yield, must make her hate:
Superiors? death! and equals? what a curse!
But an inferior not dependent? worse.
Offend her, and she knows not to forgive;
Oblige her, and she'll hate you while you live:

10. Sarah, another Duchess of Marlborough. Some details of the portrait point
to the Duchess of Buckingham.

But die, and she'll adore you—Then the bust[11]
And temple rise—then fall again to dust.   140
Last night, her lord was all that's good and great;
A knave this morning, and his will a cheat.
Strange! by the means defeated of the ends,
By spirit robb'd of pow'r, by warmth of friends,
By wealth of follow'rs! without one distress,
Sick of herself through very selfishness!
Atossa, curs'd with ev'ry granted pray'r,
Childless with all her children, wants an heir.
To heirs unknown descends th' unguarded store,
Or wanders, Heav'n-directed, to the poor.   150

  Pictures like these, dear Madam, to design,
Asks no firm hand, and no unerring line;
Some wand'ring touches, some reflected light,
Some flying stroke alone can hit 'em right:
For how should equal colours do the knack?
Chameleons who can paint in white and black?

  "Yet Chloe[12] sure was form'd without a spot"—
Nature in her then err'd not, but forgot.
"With ev'ry pleasing, ev'ry prudent part,
Say, what can Chloe want?"—She wants a heart.   160
She speaks, behaves, and acts just as she ought;
But never, never, reach'd one gen'rous thought.
Virtue she finds too painful an endeavour,
Content to dwell in decencies forever.
So very reasonable, so unmov'd,
As never yet to love, or to be lov'd.
She, while her lover pants upon her breast,
Can mark the figures on an Indian chest;
And when she sees her friend in deep despair,
Observes how much a chintz exceeds mohair.   170
Forbid it Heav'n, a favour or a debt
She e'er should cancel—but she may forget.
Safe is your secret still in Chloe's ear;
But none of Chloe's shall you ever hear.
Of all her dears she never slander'd one,
But cares not if a thousand are undone.
Would Chloe know if you're alive or dead?
She bids her footman put it in her head.
Chloe is prudent—Would you too be wise?
Then never break your heart when Chloe dies.   180

....

11. A reference perhaps to the bust of Queen Anne which the Duchess put up at
Blenheim but allowed to fall into ruin. 12. Lady Howard, mistress of George II.

One certain portrait may (I grant) be seen,
Which Heav'n has varnish'd out, and made a queen;
The same forever! and describ'd by all
With truth and goodness, as with crown and ball.
Poets heap virtues, painters gems at will,
And show their zeal, and hide their want of skill.
'Tis well—but, artists! who can paint or write,
To draw the naked is your true delight.
That robe of quality so struts and swells,
None see what parts of nature it conceals: 190
Th' exactest traits of body or of mind,
We owe to models of an humble kind.
If Queensberry[13] to strip there's no compelling,
'Tis from a handmaid we must take a Helen.
From peer or bishop 'tis no easy thing
To draw the man who loves his God, or king:
Alas! I copy (or my draught would fail)
From honest Mah'met,[14] or plain Parson Hale.[15]
    But grant, in public men sometimes are shown,
A woman's seen in private life alone: 200
Our bolder talents in full light display'd;
Your virtues open fairest in the shade.
Bred to disguise, in public 'tis you hide;
There, none distinguish 'twixt your shame or pride,
Weakness or delicacy; all so nice,
That each may seem a virtue, or a vice.
    In men, we various ruling passions find;
In women, two almost divide the kind;
Those, only fix'd, they first or last obey,
The love of pleasure, and the love of sway.   210
    That, Nature gives; and where the lesson taught
Is but to please, can pleasure seem a fault?
Experience, this; by man's oppression curst,
They seek the second not to lose the first.
    Men, some to bus'ness, some to pleasure take;
But ev'ry woman is at heart a rake:
Men, some to quiet, some to public strife;
But ev'ry lady would be queen for life.
    Yet mark the fate of a whole sex of queens!
Pow'r all their end, but beauty all the means: 220
In youth they conquer, with so wild a rage,
As leaves them scarce a subject in their age:
For foreign glory, foreign joy, they roam;

----

13. Wife of the third Duke of Queensberry.   14. Servant of the late
George I.   15. A neighbor and friend of the poet's.

No thought of peace or happiness at home.
But wisdom's triumph is well-tim'd retreat,
As hard a science to the fair as great!
Beauties, like tyrants, old and friendless grown,
Yet hate repose, and dread to be alone,
Worn out in public, weary ev'ry eye,
Nor leave one sigh behind them when they die.   230
  Pleasures the sex, as children birds, pursue,
Still out of reach, yet never out of view;
Sure, if they catch, to spoil the toy at most,
To covet flying, and regret when lost:
At last, to follies youth could scarce defend,
It grows their age's prudence to pretend;
Asham'd to own they gave delight before,
Reduc'd to feign it, when they give no more;
As hags hold sabbaths, less for joy than spite,
So these their merry, miserable night;   240
Still round and round the ghosts of beauty glide,
And haunt the places where their honour died.
  See how the world its veterans rewards!
A youth of frolics, an old age of cards;
Fair to no purpose, artful to no end,
Young without lovers, old without a friend;
A fop their passion, but their prize a sot;
Alive, ridiculous, and dead, forgot!
  Ah! Friend! to dazzle let the vain design;
To raise the thought and touch the heart, be thine!   250
That charm shall grow, while what fatigues the Ring,[16]
Flaunts and goes down, an unregarded thing:
So when the sun's broad beam has tir'd the sight,
All mild ascends the moon's more sober light,
Serene in virgin modesty she shines,
And unobserv'd the glaring orb declines.
  Oh! blest with temper, whose unclouded ray
Can make tomorrow cheerful as today;
She, who can love a sister's charms, or hear
Sighs for a daughter with unwounded ear;   260
She, who ne'er answers till a husband cools,
Or, if she rules him, never shows she rules;
Charms by accepting, by submitting sways,
Yet has her humour most, when she obeys;
Let fops or fortune fly which way they will;
Disdains all loss of tickets, or codille;

16. The fashionable resort in Hyde Park.

Spleen, vapours, or smallpox, above them all,
And mistress of herself, though china fall.
   And yet, believe me, good as well as ill,
Woman's at her best a contradiction still.   270
Heav'n, when it strives to polish all it can
Its last best work, but forms a softer man;
Picks from each sex, to make the fav'rite blest,
Your love of pleasure, our desire of rest:
Blends, in exception to all gen'ral rules,
Your taste of follies, with our scorn of fools:
Reserve with frankness, art with truth allied,
Courage with softness, modesty with pride;
Fix'd principles, with fancy ever new;
Shakes all together, and produces—You.   280
   Be this a woman's fame: with this unblest,
Toasts live a scorn, and queens may die a jest.
This Phoebus promis'd (I forget the year)
When those blue eyes first open'd on the sphere;
Ascendant Phoebus watch'd that hour with care,
Averted half your parents' simple pray'r;
And gave you beauty, but denied the pelf
That buys your sex a tyrant o'er itself.
The gen'rous god, who wit and gold refines,
And ripens spirits as he ripens mines,   290
Kept dross for duchesses, the world shall know it,
To you gave sense, good-humour, and a poet.

■   Alexander Pope is one of the major Augustan poets. The term *Augustan* usually suggests the virtues of polish and refinement and the employment of critical intelligence in the service of good form. There was a good deal of talk in the early eighteenth century about "correctness," "decorum," and "the rules." In the literature itself we find symmetry, regularity, economy, precision, and clarity. In the work of Pope we can discover many of the characteristics which lent themselves to the writing of satire, a kind of poetry associated with the term Augustan. And in "Of the Characters of Women" we find a pre-eminent example of Augustan satire.

   The second of the *Moral Essays* is both an elaborate compliment to Martha Blount, a friend of Pope's, and a venomous satire not only on several women of his time but on womankind. The theme is that most women are not merely fickle or immoral but "have no characters at all." Pope begins his poem by quoting this remark, which had been made to him by Martha Blount, and closes it (lines 249–292) with an extended compliment to her. It remains then to examine some of the techniques which enabled Pope to achieve his satiric effects.

He has a strict control over his language. His meaning is rarely obscure. Nor does he ever allow himself to follow an interest tangential to the main theme. Precision and concentration, which seem to be the keys to his style, exhibit themselves in various ways. There is a precision and a straight line of development in his introducing and investigating the implications in a single statement or body of imagery; he does not introduce a statement or figure only to drop it for another. Hence his suggestion that woman is as changeable as air and that her character is insubstantial as a cloud is worked out in compact detail:

> Come then, the colours and the ground prepare!
> Dip in the rainbow, trick her off in air;
> Choose a firm cloud, before it fall, and in it
> Catch, ere she change, the Cynthia of this minute.
>
> (ll. 17–20)

Similarly, after stating that "ev'ry lady would be queen for life" he investigates the implications of this status:

> Yet mark the fate of a whole sex of queens!
> Pow'r all their end, but beauty all the means:
> In youth they conquer, with so wild a rage,
> As leaves them scarce a subject in their age:
> For foreign glory, foreign joy, they roam;
> No thought of peace or happiness at home.
> But wisdom's triumph is well-tim'd retreat,
> As hard a science to the fair as great!
> Beauties, like tyrants, old and friendless grown,
> Yet hate repose, and dread to be alone,
> Worn out in public, weary ev'ry eye,
> Nor leave one sigh behind them when they die.
>
> (ll. 219–230)

William Empson in *Seven Types of Ambiguity** says that a concentration of meanings is a characteristic of Augustan poetry. "This way of suggesting grasp of mind, ingenuity, and control over things, this use of a word with several extended meanings so as to contract several sentences into one, is the fundamental device of the Augustan style. The word is usually a verb precisely because the process is conceived as an activity, as a work of the digesting and controlling mind." An example of the verb functioning in this way is in the opening couplet of the passage referring to Catherine Hyde, wife of the third Duke of Queensberry:

> One certain portrait may (I grant) be seen,
> Which Heav'n has varnish'd out, and made a queen;
>
> (ll. 181–182)

....

*2nd edition (New York: New Directions, 1947), p. 70.

There is a little cluster of meanings which are relevant to the verb "varnish": Heaven, or chance, has dressed her as a duchess, covered her in glistening robes, in the same way varnish gives a glow to the portrait; she is a duchess in name rather than in spirit; and the verb is appropriate in the sense that Pope, as he says, is sketching and finishing portraits. The pun on "queen" is easily recognized. In line 15 there are two words, ordinarily nouns, "sinner" and "saint," used as verbs; as a consequence, one's interest is held more closely.

There are a number of instances where words are used which have two or more meanings. Rufa is presented as a woman who dabbles in learning. She studies Locke, the author of *Essay on Human Understanding;* we could expect her, therefore, to study astronomy. Her interest in astronomy, however, becomes mixed up with her interest in flirtations:

> Rufa, whose eye quick-glancing o'er the park,
> Attracts each light gay meteor of a spark.
> (ll. 21–22)

This flirtation in the park

> Agrees as ill with Rufa studying Locke
> As Sappho's di'monds with her dirty smock;
> Or Sappho at her toilet's greasy task,
> With Sappho fragrant at an ev'ning mask:
> So morning insects that in muck begun
> Shine, buzz, and fly-blow in the setting sun.
> (ll. 23–28)

In the word "mask" there is also a little cluster of meanings: Lady Mary Montagu, or Sappho, is at a masked ball; she herself has masked or hidden the greasiness attending her toilet; and, as with the very "varnish," there is the suggestion that her innermost self is masked, not allowed to be seen. The couplet about the insects is especially packed with meaning. Sappho, he is saying, takes her existence or life out of the grease and cosmetics necessary to mask her in an attractive fashion. Like the fly, she shines at the ball, talks or buzzes, but as the evening wears toward its close the cosmetic begins to appear fly-blown. The reference to flies may also suggest that she is loose or amoral.

There is a witty ambiguity in his lines on Papillia, who

> wedded to her am'rous spark,
> Sighs for the shades—"How charming is a park!"
> (ll. 37–38)

Papillia is, of course, the sort of woman who is dissatisfied with what she has and who believes that something new or different will make her happy. In this instance, she wants a park, especially for its trees and "shades." But "shades" also means, particularly in eighteenth-century usage, the fancies of the mind. Thus Pope manages to convey not only the specific meaning, the shade in a park, but the generalized meaning, the immaterial and unrealizable fancies of her mind.

Possibly one characteristic that deserves special attention is Pope's wonderful capacity for making precise yet witty statements. One can find many examples in this one poem. Thus the early couplet

> Matter too soft a lasting mark to bear,
> And best distinguished by black, brown, or fair.
>
> (ll. 3–4)

He does not say, as a lesser satirist might, that most women, having no character, are amoral; he says by implication that the usual categories, such as virtue or morality, do not fit. To characterize women one must refer to them as "black, brown, or fair." Again, the entire passage on Narcissa is a series of left-handed compliments, each one precisely put and each one so qualified that the reader feels that in her virtue and vice so run together, given direction by gusts of feeling, she can be said to have no character at all:

> Narcissa's nature, tolerably mild,
> To make a wash, would hardly stew a child;
> Has ev'n been prov'd to grant a lover's pray'r,
> And paid a tradesman once to make him stare;
> Gave alms at Easter, in a Christian trim,
> And made a widow happy, for a whim.
>
> (ll. 53–58)

> Now drinking citron with his Grace and Chartres
> Now conscience chills her, and now passion burns;
> And atheism and religion take their turns;
> A very heathen in the carnal part,
> Yet still a sad, good Christian at her heart.
>
> (ll. 64–68)

In some passages the precision is the result of a deft use of paradox. Pope, in lines 41–44, admits a certain attractiveness in feminine delicacy. They do have charm, but it is the result of their instability and sudden changes. They are

> Fine by defect, and delicately weak.

There is, for example, another paradox of this kind in line 203:

> Bred to disguise, in public 'tis you hide.

The paradox is a form of elliptical statement, but it is not the only form of compressed statement of which Pope is a master. In the passage on the whims of Atossa, who was Sarah, Duchess of Marlborough, we find an excellent example:

> Love, if it makes her yield, must make her hate:
> Superiors? death! and equals? what a curse!
> But an inferior not dependent? worse.
>
> (ll. 134–136)

Another example is found in the passage that follows the famous line which states that women have only two driving forces or controlling motives:

> The love of pleasure, and the love of sway.
>   That, Nature gives; and where the lesson taught
> Is but to please, can pleasure seem a fault?
> Experience, this; by man's oppression curst,
> They seek the second not to lose the first.
>
> (ll. 211–215)

The entire passage is closely written, but the beginning of the second line, "That, Nature gives," and the beginning of the fourth line, "Experience, this," are especially so. Each of them is dependent for understanding on the statements preceding it and on the order in which the two motives are enumerated.

No one except a confirmed misogynist would attempt to justify Pope's treatment of the character of women. Yet one can appreciate the art behind Pope's excesses. And it is interesting to note how Pope himself introduces a strong undertone of pity into a passage, that about dowagers, wherein he is most viciously satiric: these dowagers deny, he says, that they indulged in any follies in their youth, and yet, ironically, they pretend that they still possess the charms they had as young women.

> As hags hold sabbaths, less for joy than spite,
> Still round and round the ghosts of beauty glide,
> And haunt the places where their honour died.
>   See how the world its veterans rewards!
> A youth of frolics, an old age of cards;
> Fair to no purpose, artful to no end,
> Young without lovers, old without a friend;
> A fop their passion, but their prize a sot;
> Alive, ridiculous, and dead, forgot.
>
> (ll. 239–247)

Surely, the bitterness, the venom, and the terror in this final line would not be so intense had it not been written with such economy. It is the taut line of a wonderfully able epigrammatist. But it is not an unqualified irony. The pathos of the lost beauty of the dowagers and the futility that causes their spitefulness precede the line and charge it with added meaning. In fact, this passage is an excellent one for studying Pope's method of qualifying a point of view (in this instance a narrow and cruel one) by furnishing the reader with layers of meaning. He presents the dowagers as old hags, unloved women who pass their time in playing cards and in spiteful acts and gossip that release them, at least momentarily, from the bitterness and frustration they feel. They can never forget the frolics of their youth, symbolized by evenings of dancing. They live with the memories as with ghosts of their younger selves. At least three meanings, each appropriate, can be given to the third line: The former beauty of the women can be thought of as their honor. (Those who are beautiful are honored.) When their beauty faded, so did their honor. Secondly, the ghosts may be thought of as dancing among them now, as they play cards and talk, when they have lost their honor by becoming mean and spiteful. Lastly, there is a possibility that Pope is hinting that the women who lost their honor by submitting themselves to their escorts live with the ghosts of that memory as well. In short, Pope introduces some of the reasons that the women are what they are, and does it with a sympathy that deepens the emotion of the passage by adding a strong element of pathos. But the pathos does not deflect Pope from stating his belief that they deserve their misery. Young, they had passion but not love; in age, they deserve no friends.

Pope is often thought of as a sententious or a gnomic writer, a poet more interested in saying something well than in giving great delight or in stirring the emotions of the reader. Certainly Pope was concerned with what he said, but as a poet he was also concerned with the *way* he said it. Pope avoided vague or loose emotions. He is an intellectual poet. But his intellectual exercises are so intense that they arouse emotions appropriate to themselves. Primarily he relied upon precise, clear statements. But there is variety in his language: ambiguity or layers of meanings in many of his terms, understatement, paradox, sudden turns that provide a sharply phrased qualification, a tight interrelationship of lines, and above all economy of expression. All these characteristics give Pope's language its remarkably concentrated power.

Pope was aware, of course, that the poet must appeal to the reader's emotion, although, as we have said, not at the expense of either the intelligence or adherence to objective truth—what he would call "reason" and "Nature." Not even clear, direct statement was enough. Writing to Dr. Arbuthnot, in 1734, he said that the satirist needed examples or pictures to appeal to the senses or passions of his readers.

To attack Vices in the abstract, without touching Persons, may be safe fighting indeed, but it is fighting with Shadows. General propositions are obscure, misty, and uncertain, compar'd with plain, full and homely examples: Precepts only apply to our Reason, which in most men is but weak: Examples are pictures, and strike the Senses, nay raise the Passions, and call in those (the strongest and most general of all motives) to the aid of reformation. . . .

Pope shares with his contemporaries the doctrine of the kinship of poetry and painting. It is evident in "Of the Characters of Women" (lines 17–20) that Pope thinks of himself as representing in words and rhythms those human actions which the painter might represent in color and line. This doctrine had a classical origin. Horace in *Ars Poetica* had used the phrase *ut pictura poesis* (as is painting so is poetry) in observing that there are forms of painting which can be viewed close up and others which must be viewed at a distance; the same, he said, is true of forms of poetry. Plutarch had said that poetry is a speaking picture (*pictura loquens*) and painting is a mute poem. In making much of the doctrine of the kinship of these two arts the Augustans felt they were following classical doctrine. The identification of the two arts was denied by Gotthold Ephraim Lessing in *Laokoon* in the third quarter of the eighteenth century.

We might observe here briefly that Augustan concern with *imitation* is a part of their emphasis on the objective in art. It is, Joel Spingarn has written, "according to whether the objective or the subjective conception of art is insisted upon that we have the classic spirit or the romantic spirit."

No inconsiderable part of Pope's reputation as a craftsman is due to the ease with which he was able to achieve a fluidity of movement inside the usually restricting form of the heroic couplet. Pope was the most "correct" of poets. By "correct" he would have understood, for one thing, the skillful use of the heroic couplet. Geoffrey Tillotson, in his study, *On the Poetry of Pope,* writes that the couplet was looked upon as the important measure "because of its unpretentious 'elegance,' a quality essential for anything intended to contribute to the pleasure of a cultured society. . . ." And by "correct" he would also have understood his "responsibility syllable by syllable" not merely for appropriate versification and elegant balances but for innumerable modulations in the meter and subtle variations in the balances. It is impossible, of course, to analyze his art line for line, but a few instances should suggest that Pope's art was an extremely conscious one.

The first of Pope's rules* is that sound should supplement sense. To illustrate, his line about Flavia's quickness precluding her being truly thoughtful moves with great rapidity:

> With too much quickness ever to be taught
> (l. 97)

. . . .
* See Tillotson for Pope's list.

His second rule is that the caesura coming after the fourth or sixth syllable cannot be repeated without monotony, but the caesura coming after the fifth is less tiring and therefore can be used more steadily. In this passage we see that he observes his own rule:

2nd	Wise wretch!/with pleasures too refin'd to please;
5th	With too much spirit/to be e'er at ease;
5th	With too much quickness/ever to be taught;
5th	With too much thinking/to have common thought
4th	You purchase pain/with all that joy can give,
5th	And die of nothing/but a rage to live.

(ll. 95–100)

The third of his points—it is hardly a rule—is simply a statement that poets sometimes pad their lines with an extra word or phrase in order to maintain the meter or observe a rhyme. That it is difficult to find many examples of such padding in Pope is proof that he reworked his lines until each word bore a significant part of the meaning. Nor, according to his fourth rule, would he allow, except to accommodate some unusual beauty of expression, the use of Alexandrines (iambic hexameter) or triple rhymes. In several couplets of the poem we have been studying, however, he breaks the pattern of his masculine rhymes by introducing a feminine ending:

> Choose a firm cloud, before it fall, and in it
> Catch, ere she change, the Cynthia of this minute.
>
> (ll. 19–20)

> If Queensberry to strip there's no compelling,
> 'Tis from a handmaid we must take a Helen.
>
> (ll. 193–194)

> Kept dross for duchesses, the world shall know it,
> To you gave sense, good-humour, and a poet.
>
> (ll. 291–292)

The first of these couplets ends one of the paragraphs of the poem, and the third concludes the poem. Perhaps we should say that poets usually introduce feminine endings merely for variation or to help create a comic effect. (For instance, they are used for comic purposes throughout *Don Juan* by Byron, who is an admirer of Pope.) The final couplet, which is serious but yet half-mocking, may be said to employ the feminine ending as a kind of half-flourish, appropriate to the slight self-mockery of the statement.

In his fifth rule, Pope says that a rhyme should not be repeated within four or six lines. Most of us undoubtedly do not have ears so sensitive as Pope's, but it is worth a moment's glance to see if he adheres strictly to his rule. In lines 3 and 4 we find the rhyme bear/fair. This is not repeated until lines 17 and 18 in the rhyme prepare/air.

In his sixth rule Pope states that monosyllabic lines can make for stiffness but, properly written, can help express melancholy. We have already commented on the sadness underlying his vicious attack on the dowagers. These two lines, although they are not strictly monosyllabic, do achieve, through the slow movement of the monosyllabic words, a rhythm appropriate to the melancholy underlying the satiric thrust:

> Still round and round the ghosts of beauty glide,
> And haunt the places where their honour died.
>
> (ll. 241–242)

Pope's final rule is that the poet should try, wherever possible, to avoid hiatus, or the opening of one vowel on another. The pronunciation of the words coming together as a hiatus causes the reader to pause. Consequently, the use of the hiatus would mean a break in the movement, in addition to that caused by the normal caesura. Usually, as Pope indicates, he avoids hiatus. But we do find a conspicuous use of the device in

> No ass so meek, no ass so obstinate.
>
> (l. 102)

The caesura, which one may well expect, comes after "meek." But there are additional pauses enforced by the vowels opening on each other: no/ass (twice used) and so/obstinate. If Pope disapproved in general of the hiatus, why should he employ it here three times? There are, in this same line, two more pauses enforced by the sequence of s sounds: ass/so (twice used). Probably he used the latter device, for which there is no technical word, because he believed that it was an aid to the sense: first, the pause after "*ass*," in each instance, causes one to emphasize the word; and, second, the multiplication of pauses in the single line creates a balkiness suggestive of the obstinancy of the ass.

This examination of Pope's poem should suggest that his is a complex art. His motivating spirit is wit. It is a quality which enables him, like the metaphysicals before him, to be serious without being solemn. And it enables him to achieve ease and freedom and the urbanity so desired by the Augustans.

From

An Epistle to Dr. Arbuthnot

> Peace to all such! but were there One whose fires
> True Genius kindles, and fair Fame inspires;
> Blest with each talent and each art to please,

And born to write, converse, and live with ease:
Shou'd such a man, too fond to rule alone,
Bear, like the Turk, no brother near the throne,
View him with scornful, yet with jealous eyes,
And hate for arts that caus'd himself to rise;   200
Damn with faint praise, assent with civil leer,
And without sneering, teach the rest to sneer;
Willing to wound, and yet afraid to strike,
Just hint a fault, and hesitate dislike;
Alike reserv'd to blame, or to commend,
A tim'rous foe, and a suspicious friend:
Dreading ev'n fools, by Flatterers besieg'd,
And so obliging, that he ne'er oblig'd;
Like Cato, gave his little Senate laws,
And sit attentive to his own applause;   210
While Wits and Templers ev'ry sentence raise,
And wonder with a foolish face of praise—
Who but must laugh, if such a man there be?
Who would not weep, if Atticus were he!

1. Atticus is Pope's contemporary, Joseph Addison. Is the passage
to be read as an absolute condemnation of Addison as a man who acts
only from self-love? Is the portrait complex or simple?

2. Distinguish between the method of the satire in this passage
and in Ralegh's "The Lie!" (p. 97).

The Satires of Dr. John Donne, Versified

Satire II [1]

Yes; thank my stars! as early as I knew
This Town, I had the sense to hate it too;
Yet here; as ev'n in Hell, there must be still
One Giant-Vice, so excellently ill,
That all beside, one pities, not abhors;
As who knows Sappho, smiles at other whores.
   I grant that Poetry's a crying sin;
It brought (no doubt) th' Excise and Army in:
Catch'd like the Plague, or Love, the Lord knows how,
But that the cure is starving, all allow.   10
Yet like the Papist's, is the Poet's state,
Poor and disarm'd, and hardly worth your hate!
   Here a lean Bard, whose wit could never give
Himself a dinner, makes an Actor live:

See opening lines from Donne below, p. 266.

The Thief condemn'd, in law already dead,
So prompts, and saves a rogue who cannot read.
Thus, as the pipes of some carv'd Organ move,
The gilded puppets dance and mount above.
Heav'd by the breath th' inspiring bellows blow:
Th' inspiring bellows lie and pant below   20
   One sings the Fair; but songs no longer move;
No rat is rhym'd to death, nor maid to love:
In love's, in nature's spite, the siege they hold,
And scorn the flesh, the dev'l, and all but gold.
   These write to Lords, some mean reward to get,
As needy beggars sing at doors for meat.
Those write because all write, and so have still
Excuse for writing, and for writing ill.
   Wretched indeed! but far more wretched yet
Is he who makes his meal on others' wit: 30
'Tis chang'd, no doubt, from what it was before;
His rank digestion makes it wit no more:
Sense, past thro' him, no longer is the same;
For food digested takes another name.
   I pass o'er all those Confessors and Martyrs,
Who live like S-tt-n, or who die like Chartres,
Out-cant old Esdras, or out-drink his heir,
Out-usure Jews, or Irishmen out-swear;
Wicked as Pages, who in early years
Act sins which Prisca's Confessor scarce hears.   40
Ev'n those I pardon, for whose sinful sake
Schoolmen new tenements in hell must make;
Of whose strange crimes no Canonist can tell
In what Commandment's large contents they dwell.
   One, one man only breeds my just offence;
Whom crimes gave wealth, and wealth gave Impudence:
Time, that at last matures a clap to pox,
Whose gentle progress makes a calf an ox,
And brings all natural events to pass,
Hath made him an Attorney of an Ass.   50
No young divine, new-benefic'd, can be
More pert, more proud, more positive than he
What further could I wish the fop to do,
But turn a wit, and scribble verses too;
Pierce the soft lab'rinth of a Lady's ear
With rhymes of this per cent. and that per year?
Or court a Wife, spread out his wily parts,
Like nets or lime-twigs, for rich Widows' hearts;
Calls himself Barrister to ev'ry wench,

And woo in language of the Pleas and Bench? 60
Language, which Boreas might to Auster hold
More rough than forty Germans when they scold.

    Curs'd be the wretch, so venal and so vain:
Paltry and proud, as drabs in Drury Lane.
'Tis such a bounty as was never known,
If Peter deigns to help you to your own:
What thanks, what praise, if Peter but supplies,
And what a solemn face if he denies!
Grave, as when pris'ners shake the head and swear
'Twas only Suretyship that brought 'em there. 70
His Office keeps your Parchment fates entire,
He starves with cold to save them from the fire;
For you he walks the streets thro' rain or dust,
For not in Chariots Peter puts his trust;
For you he sweats and labours at the laws,
Takes God to witness he affects your cause,
And lies to ev'ry Lord in ev'rything,
Like a King's Favourite—or like a King.
These are the talents that adorn them all,
From wicked Waters ev'n to godly * * 80
Not more of Simony beneath black gowns,
Not more of bastardy in heirs to Crowns,
In shillings and in pence at first they deal;
And steal so little, few perceive they steal;
Till, like the Sea, they compass all the land,
From Scots to Wight, from Mount to Dover strand:
And when rank Widows purchase luscious nights,
Or when a Duke to Jansen punts at White's,
Or City-heir in mortgage melts away;
Satan himself feels far less joy than they. 90
Piecemeal they win this acre first, then that,
Glean on, and gather up the whole estate.
Then strongly fencing ill-got wealth by law,
Indentures, Cov'nants, Articles they draw,
Large as the fields themselves, and larger far
Than Civil Codes, with all their Glosses, are;
So vast, our new Divines, we must confess,
Are Fathers of the Church for writing less.
But let them write for you, each rogue impairs
The deeds, and dext'rously omits *ses heirs*: 100
No Commentator can more slily pass
O'er a learn'd, unintelligible place;
Or, in quotation, shrewd Divines leave out
Those words, that would against them clear the doubt.

So Luther thought the Pater-noster long,
When doom'd to say his beads and Even-song;
But having cast his cowl, and left those laws,
Adds to Christ's pray'r, the Pow'r and Glory clause.
    The lands are bought; but where are to be found
Those ancient woods, that shaded all the ground?   110
We see no new-built palaces aspire,
No kitchens emulate the vestal fire.
Where are those troops of Poor, that throng'd of yore
The good old landlord's hospitable door?
Well, I could wish, that still in lordly domes
Some beasts were kill'd, tho' not whole hecatombs;
That both extremes were banish'd from their walls,
Carthusian fasts, and fulsome Bacchanals;
And all mankind might that just Mean observe,
In which none e'er could surfeit, none could starve.   120
These as good words, 'tis true, we all allow;
But oh! these works are not in fashion now:
Like rich old wardrobes, things extremely rare,
Extremely fine, but what no man will wear.
    Thus much I've said, I trust, without offence;
Let no Court Sycophant pervert my sense,
Nor sly informer watch these words to draw
Within the reach of Treason, or the Law.

■   It is sometimes said that the play of wit and the admiration of polish and correctness in Dryden, Pope, and Swift result in a certain impoverishment of the verbal texture of poetic language. In the attempt to be more civilized and more intellectual, poets often avoided the gross, and even the immediate or direct expression of the physical. The student by making the following comparative studies may decide for himself to what degree poets in various periods were likely to use words and images that give one a strong sense of the physical world. Compare the diction of this poem by Pope with (a) Donne's "Satire II" (printed below), (b) Skelton's "Elynour Rummynge" (p. 40), (c) Byron's "Southey and Wordsworth" (p. 415), (d) Browning's "The Lost Leader" (p. 500), and (e) Yeats's "Sailing to Byzantium" (p. 588).

From

Donne's "Satire II"

Sir, though (I thank God for it) I do hate
Perfectly all this town, yet there's one state
In all ill things so excellently best

That hate toward them breeds pity towards the rest.
Though poetry indeed be such a sin
As I think that brings dearths and Spaniards in,
Though like the pestilence and old-fashion'd love
Riddlingly it catch men, and doth remove
Never, til it be starv'd out; yet their state
Is poor, disarmed, like Papists, not worth hate.   10
One (like a wretch which at bar judged as dead,
Yet prompts him which stands next and cannot read
And saves his life) gives idiot actors means
(Starving himself) to live by his labored scenes;
As in some organ, puppets dance above
And bellows pant below which them do move.
One would move love by rhythms, but witchcraft's charms
Bring not now their old fears nor their old harms.
Rams and slings now are seely battery,
Pistolets are the best artillery.   20
And they who write to lords rewards to get,
Are they not like singers at doors for meat?
And they who write because all write have still
That excuse for writing and for writing ill.
But he is worse who beggarly doth chaw
Others' wits' fruits, and in his ravenous maw
Rankly digested, doth those things outspew
As his own things; and they are his own, 'tis true,
For if one eat my meat, though it be known
The meat was mine, th' excrement is his own.   30

The Rape of the Lock
Canto I

What dire offense from amorous causes springs,
What mighty contests rise from trivial things,
I sing—This verse to Caryl,[1] Muse! is due:
This, even Belinda[2] may vouchsafe to view:
Slight is the subject, but not so the praise,
If she inspire, and he approve my lays.

Say what strange motive, goddess! could compel
A well-bred lord[3] to assault a gentle belle?
Oh, say what stranger cause, yet unexplored,

1. John Caryl, a friend of Pope.   2. Miss Arabella Fermor, a belle, from
whom the celebrated lock of hair was stolen.   3. Lord Petre, who has stolen
the lock.

Could make a gentle belle reject a lord?   10
In tasks so bold, can little men engage,
And in soft bosoms dwells such mighty rage?

Sol through white curtains shot a timorous ray,
And oped those eyes that must eclipse the day;
Now lap-dogs give themselves the rousing shake,
And sleepless lovers, just at twelve, awake;
Thrice rung the bell, the slipper knocked the ground,[4]

And the pressed watch returned a silver sound.
Belinda still her downy pillow pressed,
Her guardian sylph prolonged the balmy rest: 20
'Twas he had summoned to her silent bed
The morning dream that hovered o'er her head;
A youth more glittering than a birth-night beau
(That e'en in slumber caused her cheek to glow),
Seemed to her ear his winning lips to lay,
And thus in whispers said, or seemed to say:

"Fairest of mortals, thou distinguished care
Of thousand bright inhabitants of air!
If e'er one vision touched thy infant thought,
Of all the nurse and all the priest have taught   30
Of airy elves by moonlight shadows seen,
The silver token, and the circled green,
Or virgins visited by angel powers,
With golden crowns and wreaths of heavenly flowers;
Hear and believe! thy own importance know,
Nor bound thy narrow views to things below.
Some secret truths, from learned pride concealed,
To maids alone and children are revealed;
What though no credit doubting wits may give?
The fair and innocent shall still believe.   40
Know, then, unnumbered spirits round thee fly,
The light militia of the lower sky:
These, though unseen, are ever on the wing,
Hang o'er the box, and hover round the Ring,
Think what an equipage thou hast in air,
And view with scorn two pages and a chair.
As now your own, our beings were of old,
And once enclosed in woman's beauteous mold;
Thence, by a soft transition, we repair
From earthly vehicles to these of air.   50

....

4. Calling a servant.

Think not, when woman's transient breath is fled,
That all her vanities at once are dead;
Succeeding vanities she still regards,
And though she plays no more, o'erlooks the cards.
Her joy in gilded chariots, when alive,
And love of ombre,[5] after death survive.
For when the fair in all their pride expire,
To their first elements their souls retire:
The sprites of fiery termagants in flame
Mount up, and take a salamander's name.   60
Soft yielding minds to water glide away,
And sip, with nymphs, their elemental tea.
The graver prude sinks downward to a gnome,
In search of mischief still on earth to roam.
The light coquettes in sylphs aloft repair,
And sport and flutter in the fields of air.

"Know further yet; whoever fair and chaste
Rejects mankind, is by some sylph embraced;
For spirits, freed from mortal laws, with ease
Assume what sexes and what shapes they please.   70
What guards the purity of melting maids,
In courtly balls, and midnight masquerades,
Safe from the treacherous friend, the daring spark,[6]
The glance by day, the whisper in the dark,
When kind occasion prompts their warm desires,
When music softens, and when dancing fires?
'Tis but their sylph, the wise celestials know,
Though honor is the word with men below.
Some nymphs there are, too conscious of their face,
For life predestined to the gnomes' embrace.   80
These swell their prospects and exalt their pride,
When offers are disdained, and love denied:
Then gay ideas crowd the vacant brain,
While peers, and dukes, and all their sweeping train,
And garters, stars, and coronets appear,
And in soft sounds "Your Grace" salutes their ear.
'Tis these that early taint the female soul,
Instruct the eyes of young coquettes to roll,
Teach infant cheeks a bidden blush to know,
And little hearts to flutter at a beau.   90

"Oft, when the world imagine women stray,
The sylphs through mystic mazes guide their way,

5. A game of cards.   6. A beau.

Through all the giddy circle they pursue,
And old impertinence expel by new.
What tender maid but must a victim fall
To one man's treat, but for another's ball?
When Florio speaks, what virgin could withstand,
If gentle Damon did not squeeze her hand?
With varying vanities, from every part,
They shift the moving toyshop of their heart;   100
Where wigs with wigs, with sword-knots sword-knots strive,
Beaux banish beaux, and coaches coaches drive.
This erring mortals levity may call;
Oh, blind to truth! the sylphs contrive it all.

"Of these am I, who thy protection claim,
A watchful sprite, and Ariel is my name.
Late, as I ranged the crystal wilds of air,
In the clear mirror of thy ruling star
I saw, alas! some dread event impend,
Ere to the main this morning sun descend,   110
But Heaven reveals not what, or how, or where:
Warned by the sylph, O pious maid, beware!
This to disclose is all thy guardian can:
Beware of all, but most beware of man!"

He said; when Shock, who thought she slept too long,
Leaped up, and waked his mistress with his tongue.
'Twas then, Belinda, if report say true,
Thy eyes first opened on a billet-doux;
Wounds, charms, and ardors were no sooner read,
But all the vision vanished from thy head.   120

And now, unveiled, the toilet stands displayed,
Each silver vase in mystic order laid.
First, robed in white, the nymph intent adores,
With head uncovered, the cosmetic powers.
A heavenly image in the glass appears.
To that she bends, to that her eyes she rears;
The inferior priestess, at her altar's side,
Trembling begins the sacred rites of pride.
Unnumbered treasures ope at once, and here
The various offerings of the world appear;   130
From each she nicely culls with curious toil,
And decks the goddess with the glittering spoil.
This casket India's glowing gems unlocks,
And all Arabia breathes from yonder box.

The tortoise here and elephant unite,
Transformed to combs, the speckled, and the white.
Here files of pins extend their shining rows,
Puffs, powders, patches, bibles, billets-doux.
Now awful beauty puts on all its arms;
The fair each moment rises in her charms, 140
Repairs her smiles, awakens every grace,
And calls forth all the wonders of her face;
Sees by degrees a purer blush arise,
And keener lightnings quicken in her eyes.
The busy sylphs surround their darling care,
These set the head, and those divide the hair,
Some fold the sleeve, whilst others plait the gown;
And Betty's praised for labors not her own.

Canto II

Not with more glories, in the ethereal plain,
The sun first rises o'er the purpled main,
Than, issuing forth, the rival of his beams
Launched on the bosom of the silver Thames.
Fair nymphs, and well-dressed youths around her shone,
But every eye was fixed on her alone.
On her white breast a sparkling cross she wore,
Which Jews might kiss, and infidels adore.
Her lively looks a sprightly mind disclose,
Quick as her eyes, and as unfixed as those; 10
Favors to none, to all she smiles extends;
Oft she rejects, but never once offends.
Bright as the sun, her eyes the gazers strike,
And, like the sun, they shine on all alike.
Yet graceful ease, and sweetness void of pride,
Might hide her faults, if belles had faults to hide;
If to her share some female errors fall,
Look on her face, and you'll forget 'em all.

This nymph, to the destruction of mankind,
Nourished two locks, which graceful hung behind 20
In equal curls, and well conspired to deck
With shining ringlets the smooth ivory neck.
Love in these labyrinths his slaves detains,
And mighty hearts are held in slender chains.
With hairy springes,[7] we the birds betray,
Slight lines of hair surprise the finny prey,

7. Snares.

Fair tresses man's imperial race ensnare,
And beauty draws us with a single hair.

The adventurous baron the bright locks admired;
He saw, he wished, and to the prize aspired.   30
Resolved to win, he meditates the way,
By force to ravish, or by fraud betray;
For when success a lover's toil attends,
Few ask, if fraud or force attained his ends.
For this, ere Phoebus rose, he had implored
Propitious Heaven, and every power adored,
But chiefly Love—to Love an altar built,
Of twelve vast French romances, neatly gilt.
There lay three garters, half a pair of gloves;
And all the trophies of his former loves;   40
With tender billets-doux he lights the pyre,
And breathes three amorous sighs to raise the fire.
Then prostrate falls, and begs with ardent eyes
Soon to obtain, and long possess the prize:
The powers gave ear, and granted half his prayer,
The rest, the winds dispersed in empty air.

But now secure the painted vessel glides,
The sunbeams trembling on the floating tides:
While melting music steals upon the sky,
And softened sounds along the waters die;   50
Smooth flow the waves, the zephyrs gently play,
Belinda smiled, and all the world was gay.
All but the sylph—with careful thoughts oppressed,
The impending woe sat heavy on his breast.
He summons straight his denizens of air;
The lucid squadrons round the sails repair:
Soft o'er the shrouds aërial whispers breathe,
That seemed but zephyrs to the train beneath.
Some to the sun their insect wings unfold,
Waft on the breeze, or sink in clouds of gold;   60
Transparent forms, too fine for mortal sight,
Their fluid bodies half dissolved in light.
Loose to the wind their airy garments flew
Thin glittering textures of the filmy dew,
Dipt in the richest tincture of the skies,
Where light disports in ever-mingling dyes,
While every beam new transient colors flings,
Colors that change whene'er they wave their wings.
Amid the circle, on the gilded mast,

Superior by the head, was Ariel placed;   70
His purple pinions opening to the sun,
He raised his azure wand, and thus begun.

"Ye sylphs and sylphids, to your chief give ear!
Fays, fairies, genii, elves, and demons, hear!
Ye know the spheres, and various tasks assigned
By laws eternal to the aërial kind.
Some in the fields of purest ether play,
And bask and whiten in the blaze of day.
Some guide the course of wandering orbs on high,
Or roll the planets through the boundless sky.   80
Some less refined, beneath the moon's pale light
Pursue the stars that shoot athwart the night,
Or suck the mists in grosser air below,
Or dip their pinions in the painted bow,
Or brew fierce tempests on the wintry main,
Or o'er the glebe distil the kindly rain.
Others on earth o'er human race preside,
Watch all their ways, and all their actions guide:
Of these the chief, the care of nations own,
And guard with arms divine the British throne.   90

"Our humbler province is to tend the fair.
Not a less pleasing, though less glorious care;
To save the powder from too rude a gale,
Nor let the imprisoned essences exhale;
To draw fresh colors from the vernal flowers;
To steal from rainbows ere they drop in showers,
A brighter wash; to curl their waving hairs,
Assist their blushes, and inspire their airs;
Nay, oft in dreams, invention we bestow,
To change a flounce, or add a furbelow.   100

"This day, black omens threat the brightest fair
That e'er deserved a watchful spirit's care;
Some dire disaster, or by force, or slight;
But what, or where, the fates have wrapped in night.
Whether the nymph shall break Diana's law,
Or some frail china jar receive a flaw;
Or stain her honor, or her new brocade;
Forget her prayers, or miss a masquerade;
Or lose her heart, or necklace, at a ball;
Or whether Heaven has doomed that Shock must fall.   110
Haste, then, ye spirits! to your charge repair;

The fluttering fan be Zephyretta's care;
The drops[8] to thee, Brillante, we consign;
And, Momentilla, let the watch be thine;
Do thou, Crispissa, tend her favorite lock;
Ariel himself shall be the guard of Shock.

"To fifty chosen sylphs, of special note,
We trust the important charge, the petticoat:
Oft have we known that seven-fold fence to fail,
Though stiff with hoops, and armed with ribs of whale;   120
Form a strong line about the silver bound,
And guard the wide circumference around.

"Whatever spirit, careless of his charge,
His post neglects, or leaves the fair at large,
Shall feel sharp vengeance soon o'ertake his sins,
Be stopped in vials, or transfixed with pins;
Or plunged in lakes of bitter washes lie,
Or wedged whole ages in a bodkin's eye:
Gums and pomatums shall his flight restrain,
While clogged he beats his silken wings in vain;   130
Or alum styptics with contracting power
Shrink his thin essence like a rivelled flower:
Or, as Ixion[9] fixed, the wretch shall feel
The giddy motion of the whirling mill,
In fumes of burning chocolate shall glow,
And tremble at the sea that froths below!"

He spoke; the spirits from the sails descend;
Some, orb in orb, around the nymph extend;
Some thrid the mazy ringlets of her hair;
Some hang upon the pendants of her ear;   140
With beating hearts the dire event they wait,
Anxious, and trembling for the birth of fate.

Canto III

Close by those meads, forever crowned with flowers,
Where Thames with pride surveys his rising towers,
There stands a structure of majestic frame,[10]
Which from the neighboring Hampton takes its name.
Here Britain's statesmen oft the fall of foredoom
Of foreign tyrants and of nymphs at home;

---

8. Earrings.   9. For offense to Zeus he was fastened to an eternally revolving wheel.   10. Hampton Court, a royal residence.

Here thou, great Anna! whom three realms obey,
Dost sometimes counsel take—and sometimes tea.

Hither the heroes and the nymphs resort,
To taste awhile the pleasures of a court;   10
In various talk the instructive hours they passed,
Who gave the ball, or paid the visit last;
One speaks the glory of the British queen,
And one describes a charming Indian screen;
A third interprets motions, looks, and eyes;
At every word a reputation dies.
Snuff, or the fan, supply each pause of chat,
With singing, laughing, ogling, and all that.

Meanwhile, declining from the noon of day,
The sun obliquely shoots his burning ray;   20
The hungry judges soon the sentence sign,
And wretches hang that jurymen may dine;
The merchant from the Exchange returns in peace,
And the long labors of the toilet cease.
Belinda now, whom thirst of fame invites,
Burns to encounter two adventurous knights,
At ombre singly to decide their doom;
And swells her breast with conquests yet to come.
Straight the three bands prepare in arms to join,
Each band the number of the sacred nine.   30
Soon as she spreads her hand, the aërial guard
Descend, and sit on each important card:
First, Ariel perched upon a Matadore,
Then each, according to the rank they bore;
For sylphs, yet mindful of their ancient race,
Are, as when women, wondrous fond of place.

Behold, four kings in majesty revered,
With hoary whiskers and a forky beard;
And four fair queens whose hands sustain a flower,
The expressive emblem of their softer power;   40
Four knaves in garbs succinct, a trusty band,
Caps on their heads, and halberts in their hand;
And parti-colored troops, a shining train,
Draw forth to combat on the velvet plain.

The skillful nymph reviews her force with care:
Let spades be trumps! she said, and trumps they were.

Now moved to war her sable Matadores,[11]
In show like leaders of the swarthy Moors.
Spadillio[12] first, unconquerable lord!
Led off two captive trumps, and swept the board.   50
As many more Manillio[13] forced to yield,
And marched a victor from the verdant field.
Him Basto[14] followed, but his fate more hard
Gained but one trump and one plebeian card.
With his broad saber next, a chief in years,
The hoary majesty of spades appears,
Puts forth one manly leg, to sight revealed,
The rest, his many-colored robe concealed.
The rebel knave, who dares his prince engage,
Proves the just victim of his royal rage.   60
Even mighty Pam,[15] that kings and queens o'erthrew,
And mowed down armies in the fights of Loo,
Sad chance of war! now destitute of aid,
Falls undistinguished by the victor spade!

Thus far both armies to Belinda yield;
Now to the baron fate inclines the field.
His warlike Amazon her host invades,
The imperial consort of the crown of spades,
The club's black tyrant first her victim died,
Spite of his haughty mien, and barbarous pride: 70
What boots the regal circle on his head,
His giant limbs, in state unwieldy spread;
That long behind he trails his pompous robe,
And of all monarchs only grasps the globe?

The baron now his diamonds pours apace;
The embroidered king who shows but half his face,
And his refulgent queen, with powers combined,
Of broken troops an easy conquest find.
Clubs, diamonds, hearts, in wild disorder seen,
With throngs promiscuous strew the level green.   80
Thus when dispersed a routed army runs,
Of Asia's troops, and Afric's sable sons,
With like confusion different nations fly,
Of various habit, and of various dye,
The pierced battalions disunited fall,
In heaps on heaps; one fate o'erwhelms them all.

....
11. The three highest cards in ombre, a card game.
12. Ace of spades.   13. The two of a black, the seven of a red, trump.
14. Ace of clubs.   15. Knave of clubs.

The knave of diamonds tries his wily arts,
And wins (oh, shameful chance!) the queen of hearts.
At this the blood the virgin's cheek forsook,
A livid paleness spreads o'er all her look;   90
She sees, and trembles at the approaching ill,
Just in the jaws of ruin, and codille.[16]
And now (as oft in some distempered state)
On one nice trick depends the general fate,
An ace of hearts steps forth; the king unseen
Lurked in her hand, and mourned his captive queen:
He springs to vengeance with an eager pace,
And falls like thunder on the prostrate ace.
The nymph exulting fills with shouts the sky;
The walls, the wood, and long canals reply.   100

Oh, thoughtless mortals! ever blind to fate,
Too soon dejected, and too soon elate.
Sudden, these honors shall be snatched away,
And cursed forever this victorious day.

For lo! the board with cups and spoons is crowned,
The berries crackle, and the mill turns round;
On shining altars of Japan they raise
The silver lamp; the fiery spirits blaze:
From silver spouts the grateful liquors glide,
While China's earth receives the smoking tide: 110
At once they gratify their scent and taste,
And frequent cups prolong the rich repast.
Straight hover round the fair her airy band;
Some, as she sipped, the fuming liquor fanned,
Some o'er her lap their careful plumes displayed,
Trembling, and conscious of the rich brocade.
Coffee (which makes the politician wise,
And see through all things with his half-shut eyes)
Sent up in vapors to the baron's brain
New stratagems the radiant lock to gain.   120
Ah, cease, rash youth! desist ere 'tis too late,
Fear the just gods, and think of Scylla's fate!
Changed to a bird, and sent to flit in air,
She dearly pays for Nisus' injured hair![17]

16. Failure to win a sufficient number of tricks.
17. When Minos of Crete was besieging Megara, Scylla, daughter of Nisus, fell in love with Minos and, hoping to win his love, cut her father's purple hair, thus betraying Nisus to the enemy. She was changed into the sea bird Ciris, and Nisus into an eagle, which wars on the Ciris.

But when to mischief mortals bend their will,
How soon they find fit instruments of ill!
Just then Clarissa drew with tempting grace
A two-edged weapon from her shining case;
So ladies in romance assist their knight,
Present the spear, and arm him for the fight.   130
He takes the gift with reverence, and extends
The little engine on his fingers' ends;
This just behind Belinda's neck he spread,
As o'er the fragrant steams she bends her head.
Swift to the lock a thousand sprites repair,
A thousand wings, by turns, blow back her hair;
And thrice they twitched the diamond in her ear;
Thrice she looked back, and thrice the foe drew near.
Just in that instant, anxious Ariel sought
The close recesses of the virgin's thought;   140
As on the nosegay in her breast reclined,
He watched the ideas rising in her mind,
Sudden he viewed, in spite of all her art,
An earthly lover lurking at her heart.
Amazed, confused, he found his power expired,
Resigned to fate, and with a sigh retired.

The peer now spreads the glittering forfex wide,
To inclose the lock; now joins it, to divide.
Even then, before the fatal engine closed,
A wretched sylph too fondly interposed;   150
Fate urged the shears, and cut the sylph in twain,
(But airy substance soon unites again)
The meeting points the sacred hair dissever
From the fair head, forever, and forever!

Then flashed the living lightning from her eyes,
And screams of horror rend the affrighted skies.
Not louder shrieks to pitying Heaven are cast,
When husbands, or when lap-dogs breathe their last;
Or when rich China vessels, fallen from high,
In glittering dust and painted fragments lie!   160

"Let wreaths of triumph now my temples twine,"
(The victor cried); "the glorious prize is mine!
While fish in streams, or birds delight in air,
Or in a coach and six the British fair,

As long as Atalantis[18] shall be read,
Or the small pillow grace a lady's bed,
While visits shall be paid on solemn days,
When numerous wax-lights in bright order blaze,
While nymphs take treats, or assignations give,
So long my honor, name, and praise shall live!   170
What Time would spare, from steel receives its date,
And monuments, like men, submit to fate!
Steel could the labor of the gods destroy,
And strike to dust the imperial towers of Troy;
Steel could the works of mortal pride confound,
And hew triumphal arches to the ground.
What wonder then, fair nymph! thy hairs should feel
The conquering force of unresisted steel?"

Canto IV

But anxious cares the pensive nymph oppressed,
And secret passions labored in her breast.
Not youthful kings in battle seized alive,
Not scornful virgins who their charms survive,
Not ardent lovers robbed of all their bliss,
Not ancient ladies when refused a kiss,
Not tyrants fierce that unrepenting die,
Not Cynthia when her manteau's pinned awry,
E'er felt such rage, resentment, and despair,
As thou, sad virgin, for thy ravished hair.   10
For, that sad moment, when the sylphs withdrew
And Ariel weeping from Belinda flew,
Umbriel, a dusky, melancholy sprite,
As ever sullied the fair face of light,
Down to the central earth, his proper scene,
Repaired to search the gloomy cave of Spleen.[19]

Swift on his sooty pinions flits the gnome,
And in a vapor reached the dismal dome.
No cheerful breeze this sullen region knows,
The dreaded east is all the wind that blows.   20
Here in a grotto, sheltered close from air,
And screened in shades from day's detested glare,
She sighs forever on her pensive bed,
Pain at her side, and Megrim[20] at her head.

18. A book of contemporary scandal, *The New Atalantis* (1709) by Mrs. Manley.   19. Ill temper.   20. Weariness.

Two handmaids wait the throne, alike in place,
But differing far in figure and in face.
Here stood Ill-nature like an ancient maid,
Her wrinkled form in black and white arrayed;
With store of prayers, for mornings, nights, and noons,
Her hand is filled; her bosom with lampoons.   30

There Affectation, with a sickly mien,
Shows in her cheek the roses of eighteen,
Practiced to lisp, and hang the head aside,
Faints into airs, and languishes with pride,
On the rich quilt sinks with becoming woe,
Wrapped in a gown, for sickness, and for show.
The fair ones feel such maladies as these,
When each new night-dress gives a new disease.

A constant vapor o'er the palace flies;
Strange phantoms rising as the mists arise;   40
Dreadful, as hermit's dreams in haunted shades,
Or bright, as visions of expiring maids.
Now glaring fiends, and snakes on rolling spires,
Pale specters, gaping tombs, and purple fires:
Now lakes of liquid gold, Elysian scenes,
And crystal domes, and angels in machines.

Unnumbered throngs on every side are seen,
Of bodies changed to various forms by Spleen.
Here living tea-pots stand, one arm held out,
One bent; the handle this, and that the spout: 50
A pipkin there, like Homer's tripod, walks;
Here sighs a jar, and there a goose-pie talks;
Men prove with child, as powerful fancy works,
And maids, turned bottles, call aloud for corks.

Safe passed the gnome through this fantastic band,
A branch of healing spleenwort in his hand.
Then thus addressed the power: "Hail, wayward queen!
Who rule the sex, to fifty from fifteen;
Parent of vapors and of female wit,
Who give the hysteric, or poetic fit,   60
On various tempers act by various ways,
Make some take physic, others scribble plays;
Who cause the proud their visits to delay,
And send the godly in a pet to pray.
A nymph there is, that all thy power disdains,

And thousands more in equal mirth maintains.
But oh! if e'er thy gnome could spoil a grace,
Or raise a pimple on a beauteous face,
Like citron-waters matrons' cheeks inflame,
Or change complexions at a losing game;   70
If e'er with airy horns I planted heads,
Or rumpled petticoats, or tumbled beds,
Or caused suspicion when no soul was rude,
Or discomposed the head-dress of a prude,
Or e'er to costive lap-dog gave disease,
Which not the tears of brightest eyes could ease;
Hear me, and touch Belinda with chagrin,
That single act gives half the world the spleen."

The goddess with a discontented air
Seems to reject him, though she grants his prayer.   80
A wondrous bag with both her hands she binds,
Like that where once Ulysses held the winds;
There she collects the force of female lungs,
Sighs, sobs, and passions, and the war of tongues.
A vial next she fills with fainting fears,
Soft sorrows, melting griefs, and flowing tears.
The gnome rejoicing bears her gifts away,
Spreads his black wings, and slowly mounts to day.

Sunk in Thalestris' arms[21] the nymph he found,
Her eyes dejected and her hair unbound.   90
Full o'er their heads, the swelling bag he rent,
And all the furies issued at the vent.
Belinda burns with more than mortal ire,
And fierce Thalestris fans the rising fire.
"O wretched maid!" she spread her hands, and cried,
(While Hampton's echoes, "Wretched maid!" replied)
"Was it for this you took such constant care
The bodkin, comb, and essence to prepare?
For this your locks in paper durance bound,
For this with torturing irons wreathed around?   100
For this with fillets strained your tender head,
And bravely bore the double loads of lead?
Gods! shall the ravisher display your hair,
While the fops envy, and the ladies stare!
Honor forbid! at whose unrivalled shrine
Ease, pleasure, virtue, all our sex resign.

....

21. A Mrs. Morley.

Methinks already I your tears survey,
Already hear the horrid things they say,
Already see you a degraded toast,
And all your honor in a whisper lost!   110
How shall I, then, your helpless fame defend?
'Twill then be infamy to seem your friend!
And shall this prize, the inestimable prize,
Exposed through crystal to the gazing eyes,
And heightened by the diamond's circling rays,
On that rapacious hand forever blaze?
Sooner shall grass in Hyde Park Circus grow,
And wits take lodgings in the sound of Bow;[22]
Sooner let earth, air, sea, to chaos fall,
Men, monkeys, lap-dogs, parrots, perish all!"   120

She said; then raging to Sir Plume[23] repairs,
And bids her beau demand the precious hairs.
(Sir Plume, of amber snuff-box justly vain,
And the nice conduct of a clouded cane)
With earnest eyes, and round unthinking face,
He first the snuff-box opened, then the case,
And thus broke out—"My lord, why, what the devil?
Z——ds! damn the lock! 'fore Gad, you must be civil!
Plague on't! 'tis past a jest—nay prithee, pox!
Give her the hair," he spoke, and rapped his box.   130
"It grieves me much," replied the peer again,
"Who speaks so well should ever speak in vain.
But by this lock, this sacred lock, I swear,
(Which never more shall join its parted hair;
Which never more its honors shall renew,
Clipped from the lovely head where late it grew)
That while my nostrils draw the vital air,
This hand, which won it, shall forever wear."
He spoke, and speaking, in proud triumph spread
The long-contended honors of her head.   140

But Umbriel, hateful gnome! forbears not so;
He breaks the vial whence the sorrows flow.
Then see! the nymph in beauteous grief appears,
Her eyes half languishing, half drowned in tears;
On her heaved bosom hung her drooping head,
Which, with a sigh, she raised; and thus she said:

....

22. St. Mary Le Bow in the heart of Cheapside, famous for its bells.   23. A
Sir George Brown.

"Forever cursed be this detested day,
Which snatched my best, my favorite curl away!
Happy! ah, ten times happy had I been,
If Hampton Court these eyes had never seen!   150
Yet am not I the first mistaken maid,
By love of courts to numerous ills betrayed.
Oh, had I rather unadmired remained
In some lone isle or distant northern land;
Where the gilt chariot never marks the way,
Where none learn ombre, none l'er taste bohea.[24]
There kept my charms concealed from mortal eye,
Like roses, that in deserts bloom and die.
What moved my mind with youthful lords to roam?
Oh, had I stayed, and said my prayers at home!   160
'Twas this, the morning omens seemed to tell,
Thrice from my trembling hand the patch-box fell;
The tottering china shook without a wind.
Nay, Poll sat mute, and Shock was most unkind!
A sylph, too, warned me of the threats of fate,
In mystic visions, now believed too late!
See the poor remnants of these slighted hairs!
My hands shall rend what e'en thy rapine spares;
These in two sable ringlets taught to break,
Once gave new beauties to the snowy neck;   170
The sister lock now sits uncouth, alone,
And in its fellow's fate foresees its own;
Uncurled it hangs, the fatal shears demands,
And tempts once more, thy sacrilegious hands.
Oh, hadst thou, cruel! been content to seize
Hairs less in sight, or any hairs but these!"

Canto V

She said; the pitying audience melt in tears.
But Fate and Jove had stopped the baron's ears.
In vain Thalestris with reproach assails,
For who can move when fair Belinda fails?
Not half so fixed the Trojan could remain,
While Anna begged and Dido raged in vain.
Then grave Clarissa graceful waved her fan;
Silence ensued, and thus the nymph began:

"Say, why are beauties praised and honored most,
The wise man's passion, and the vain man's toast?   10

---

24. A kind of tea.

Why decked with all that land and sea afford,
Why angels called, and angel-like adored?
Why 'round our coaches crowd the white-gloved beaux,
Why bows the side-box from its inmost rows?
How vain are all these glories, all our pains,
Unless good sense preserve what beauty gains:
That men may say, when we the front-box grace:
'Behold the first in virtue as in face!'
Oh! if to dance all night, and dress all day,
Charmed the smallpox, or chased old age away;   20
Who would not scorn what housewife's cares produce,
Or who would learn one earthly thing of use?
To patch, nay ogle, might become a saint,
Nor could it sure be such a sin to paint.
But since, alas! frail beauty must decay,
Curled or uncurled, since locks will turn to gray;
Since painted, or not painted, all shall fade,
And she who scorns a man must die a maid;
What then remains but well our power to use,
And keep good humor still whate'er we lose?   30
And trust me, dear! good humor can prevail,
When airs, and flights, and screams, and scolding fail.
Beauties in vain their pretty eyes may roll;
Charms strike the sight, but merit wins the soul."

    So spoke the dame, but no applause ensued;
Belinda frowned, Thalestris called her prude.
"To arms, to arms!" the fierce virago cries,
And swift as lightning to the combat flies.
All side in parties, and begin th' attack;
Fans clap, silks rustle, and tough whale-bones crack;   40
Heroes' and heroines' shouts confusedly rise,
And bass and treble voices strike the skies.
No common weapons in their hands are found,
Like gods they fight, nor dread a mortal wound.

    So when bold Homer makes the gods engage,
And heavenly breasts with human passions rage;
'Gainst Pallas, Mars; Latona, Hermes arms;
And all Olympus rings with loud alarms:
Jove's thunder roars, Heaven trembles all around,
Blue Neptune storms, the bellowing deeps resound: 50
Earth shakes her nodding towers, the ground gives way,
And the pale ghosts start at the flash of day!

Triumphant Umbriel on a sconce's height
Clapped his glad wings, and sat to view the fight:
Propped on their bodkin spears, the sprites survey
The growing combat, or assist the fray.

While through the press enraged Thalestris flies,
And scatters death around from both her eyes,
A beau and witling perished in the throng,
One died in metaphor, and one in song.   60
"O cruel nymph! a living death I bear,"
Cried Dapperwit,[25] and sunk beside his chair.
A mournful glance Sir Fopling[26] upwards cast,
"Those eyes are made so killing"—was his last.
Thus on Meander's[27] flowery margin lies
The expiring swan, and as he sings he dies.

When bold Sir Plume had drawn Clarissa down,
Chloe stepped in and killed him with a frown;
She smiled to see the doughty hero slain,
But, at her smile, the beau revived again.   70
Now Jove suspends his golden scales in air,
Weighs the men's wits against the lady's hair;
The doubtful beam long nods from side to side;
At length the wits mount up, the hairs subside.

See, fierce Belinda on the baron flies,
With more than usual lightning in her eyes;
Nor feared the chief the unequal fight to try,
Who sought no more than on his foe to die.
But this bold lord with manly strength endued,
She with one finger and a thumb subdued;   80
Just where the breath of life his nostrils drew,
A charge of snuff the wily virgin threw;
The gnomes direct, to every atom just,
The pungent grains of titillating dust.
Sudden, with starting tears each eye o'erflows,
And the high dome re-echoes to his nose.

"Now meet thy fate," incensed Belinda cried,
And drew a deadly bodkin from her side.
(The same, his ancient personage to deck,

---

25. A character in Wycherley's *Love in a Wood*—a conceited, half-witted town character.   26. Sir Fopling Flutter (?) from Etherege's *Man of Mode*.
27. Winding river in Asia Minor, frequently mentioned in classical poetry.

Her great great grandsire wore about his neck,   90
In three seal-rings; which after, melted down,
Formed a vast buckle for his widow's gown;
Her infant grandame's whistle next it grew,
The bells she jingled, and the whistle blew;
Then in a bodkin graced her mother's hairs,
Which long she wore, and now Belinda wears.)

"Boast not my fall," he cried, "insulting foe!
Thou by some other shalt be laid as low,
Nor think to die dejects my lofty mind;
All that I dread is leaving you behind!   100
Rather than so, ah, let me still survive,
And burn in Cupid's flames—but burn alive."

"Restore the lock!" she cries; and all around
"Restore the lock!" the vaulted roofs rebound.
Not fierce Othello in so loud a strain
Roared for the handkerchief that caused his pain.
But see how oft ambitious aims are crossed,
And chiefs contend till all the prize is lost!
The lock, obtained with guilt, and kept with pain,
In every place is sought, but sought in vain: 110
With such a prize no mortal must be blessed,
So Heaven decrees! with Heaven who can contest?

Some thought it mounted to the lunar sphere,
Since all things lost on earth are treasured there.
There heroes' wits are kept in ponderous vases,
And beaux' in snuff-boxes and tweezer cases.
There broken vows and death-bed alms are found,
And lovers' hearts with ends of riband bound,
The courtier's promises, and sick man's prayers,
The smiles of harlots, and the tears of heirs,   120
Cages for gnats, and chains to yoke a flea,
Dried butterflies, and tomes of casuistry.

But trust the Muse—she saw it upward rise,
Though marked by none but quick, poetic eyes:
(So Rome's great founder to the heavens withdrew,[28]
To Proculus alone confessed in view)
A sudden star, it shot through liquid air,
And drew behind a radiant trail of hair.

....

28. Romulus, a founder of Rome.

Not Berenice's locks first rose so bright,
The heavens bespangling with disheveled light.   130
The sylphs behold it kindling as it flies,
And pleased pursue its progress through the skies.

This the beau monde shall from the Mall survey,
And hail with music its propitious ray.
This the blest lover shall for Venus take,
And send up vows from Rosamonda's[29] lake.
This Partridge[30] soon shall view in cloudless skies.
When next he looks through Galileo's[31] eyes;
And hence the egregious wizard shall foredoom
The fate of Louis[32] and the fall of Rome.   140

Then cease, bright nymph! to mourn thy ravished hair,
Which adds new glory to the shining sphere!
Not all the tresses that fair head can boast,
Shall draw such envy as the lock you lost.
For, after all the murders of your eye,
When, after millions slain, yourself shall die:
When those fair suns shall set, as set they must,
And all those tresses shall be laid in dust,
This lock, the Muse shall consecrate to fame,
And 'midst the stars inscribe Belinda's name.

29. A pond in St. James's Park.   30. An astrologer lampooned by Swift.
31. The telescope.   32. Louis XIV of France.

Jonathan Swift

(1667–1745)

■ ■ ■ ■ ■ ■ ■ ■ ■ ■

JONATHAN SWIFT was born in Ireland of English parents. He
was educated at Kilkenny School, where he was a classmate of Congreve,
and at Trinity College in Dublin. For eleven years he served almost constantly as secretary to Sir William Temple; among his tasks in the Temple
household was the supervision of the education of Esther Johnson, the
famous "Stella." During this period, he had decided upon the church as a
career, had been ordained in the Church of England, and had served

briefly as a priest in a small Irish parish. When Temple died in 1699, Swift returned to full service in the church. For his services to the Tory cause, he was made dean of St. Patrick's in Dublin, where he always felt himself to be an exile.

Swift was the intimate of Dr. Arbuthnot, Pope, Gay, Parnell, and other famous men of letters. *The Drapier's Letters* (1724), written under the masquerade of a linen draper, protesting the use of Wood's half-pence, which the Dean considered debased coinage, is an example of his powerful attacks upon English policy. *Gulliver's Travels* is generally accepted as one of the great satires upon men and society. By 1742 gloom and loss of memory had made the appointment of guardians for the Dean necessary, and from then until his death in 1745 the madness he had so feared made his life a tragic burden.

Suggested Readings

HERBERT DAVIS, "Swift's View of Poetry," in *Studies in English by Members of the University College*. Toronto: University of Toronto Press, 1931, pp. 9–58.
W. B. C. WATKINS, *Perilous Balance*. Princeton: Princeton University Press, 1939.

■ ■ ■ ■ ■ ■ ■ ■ ■ ■

There is an eighteenth-century tradition that Dryden offended Swift by saying of his early poetry, "Cousin Swift, you will never be a poet." Swift then gave up, it is said, any romantic reachings in his poetry. Although it is true that Swift's later poetry does not exhibit multiple types of meter, a wide-ranging imagination, or a variety in tonal effects, in the area in which his imagination did work, it worked with brilliant intensity, with a directness and rigorous honesty that would be difficult to match in any period. Swift had a hard sense of fact and actuality, and he used his imagination to evoke a sense of these in his poetry. If we believe that Swift's prosaic subject matter gives an "unpoetic" quality to his verse then the same criticism would have to be directed against Pope and Johnson. It is not a valid criticism, however, because Swift, like Pope and Johnson, was writing out of a strong sense that he was expressing the *real* and the *actual,* heightening and intensifying them so that the reader not only may feel the tremendous sincerity behind the language but be able to identify himself imaginatively with the scene, experience, person, or motive being treated. In the following poem one can observe some of the characteristics of Swift's verse:

A Description of a City Shower

Careful observers may foretell the hour,
(By sure prognostics) when to dread a shower.
While rain depends, the pensive cat gives o'er
Her frolics, and pursues her tail no more.
Returning home at night, you'll find the sink
Strike your offended sense with double stink.
If you be wise, then go not far to dine:
You'll spend in coach-hire more than save in wine.
A coming shower your shooting corns presage,
Old a-ches throb, your hollow tooth will rage;   10
Saunt'ring in coffeehouse is Dulman seen;
He damns the climate, and complains of spleen.
   Meanwhile the South, rising with dabbled wings,
A sable cloud athwart the welkin flings,
That swill'd more liquor than it could contain,
And like a drunkard, gives it up again.
Brisk Susan whips her linen from the rope,
While the first drizzling shower is born aslope;
Such is that sprinkling which some careless quean
Flirts on you from her mop, but not so clean: 20
You fly, invoke the gods; then, turning, stop
To rail; she singing, still whirls on her mop.
Not yet the dust had shunn'd the unequal strife,
But, aided by the wind, fought still for life,
And wafted with its foe by vi'lent gust,
'Twas doubtful which was rain, and which was dust.
Ah! where must needy poet seek for aid,
When dust and rain at once his coat invade?
Sole coat! where dust, cemented by the rain,
Erects the nap, and leaves a cloudy stain!   30
   Now in contiguous drops the flood comes down,
Threatening with deluge this *devoted* town.
To shops in crowds the draggled females fly,
Pretend to cheapen goods, but nothing buy.
The Templer spruce, while ev'ry spout's abroach,
Stays till 'tis fair, yet seems to call a coach.
The tuck'd-up sempstress walks with hasty strides,
While streams run down her oil'd umbrella's sides.
Here various kinds, by various fortunes led,
Commence acquaintance underneath a shed.   40
Triumphant Tories, and desponding Whigs,
Forget their feuds, and join to save their wigs.
Box'd in a chair the beau impatient sits,

While spouts run clatt'ring o'er the roof by fits,
And ever and anon with frightful din
The leather sounds; he trembles from within.
So when Troy chairmen bore the wooden steed,
Pregnant with Greeks impatient to be freed,
(Those bully Greeks, who, as the moderns do,
Instead of paying chairman, ran them through)   50
Laocoön struck the outside with his spear,
And each imprison'd hero quak'd for fear.
   Now from all parts the swelling kennels flow,
And bear their trophies with them as they go:
Filths of all hues and odours, seem to tell
What streets they sail'd from, by their sight and smell.
They, as each torrent drives with rapid force,
From Smithfield, or St. Pulchre's shape their course,
And in huge confluent join at Snowhill Ridge,
Fall from the conduit prone to Holborn bridge.   60
Sweepings from butchers' stalls, dung, guts, and blood,
Drown'd puppies, stinking sprats, all drench'd in mud,
Dead cats, and turnip-tops, come tumbling down the flood.

■   The opening lines mention in a quick series of scenes various ways in which one may sense the impending storm; each of the scenes is realistic: the sensitivity of the cat to the heavy atmosphere, the stench of the garbage, aching corns or teeth, and the irritability of the man in the coffeehouse. In the second section one is given a sense of the first heavy drops in the image of the water from the wet mop being shaken on a passer-by and in Susan hurrying to take her clothes in from the lines. The image of the sable cloud from the south is precise, but the simile of the drunkard vomiting his liquor is not very apposite or appropriate. The next lines about the conflict between the dust and the rain are easily visualized, as is the image of the mingled rain and dust spots on the poor poet's clothes. Similarly, the feelings, motives, and actions of the Londoners are caught when they hurry to get out of the rain. The women pretend they are shopping; the lawyer, whose dandyism contrasts with the natural flood of rain, merely seems to be awaiting a coach; and Whigs and Tories forget their politics in trying to keep their wigs dry. The city, like the impatient beau in the sedan chair, takes cover from the rain. Then in the final stanza we watch the floods in the streets and ditches carry along the refuse, even drowned puppies and dead cats. There is no restraint at work preventing the mention of anything offensive to delicate sensibilities. From the dandies to the turnip-tops London is seen through the eyes of a poet willing to recognize pretence and ugliness where he sees it—but with these or as a part of these he also sees the vigor of the scenes. He is concerned to give the reader a moving sense of London, and he does, by isolating significant details and avoiding abstractions, exhibit London in the rain in all its sights, sounds, smells, and incongruities.

■ 1. It is said that Swift disliked triple rhymes and employed a triplet in this poem to burlesque the practice. Identify it. Is the triplet harmful or helpful to the effect of the poem?

2. The original version of lines 29 and 30 was

His only coat, where dust confused with rain
Roughen the nap and leave a mingled stain.

Comment on the appropriateness of the change.

A Description of the Morning

Now hardly here and there a hackney-coach
Appearing, show'd the ruddy morn's approach.
Now Betty from her master's bed had flown,
And softly stole to discompose her own;
The slip-shod 'prentice from his master's door
Had par'd the dirt, and sprinkled round the floor.
Now Moll had whirl'd her mop with dextrous airs,
Prepar'd to scrub the entry and the stairs.
The youth with broomy stumps began to trace
The kennel's edge, where wheels had worn the place.
The small-coal man was heard with cadence deep,
Till drown'd in shriller notes of chimney-sweep:
Duns at his lordship's gate began to meet;
And brickdust Moll had screamed through half the street.
The turnkey now his flock returning sees,
Duly let out a-nights to steal for fees:
The watchful bailiffs take their silent stands,
And schoolboys lag with satchels in their hands.

■ 1. Is the satire in this poem light or heavy? Is it, for example, as mordant as that in Pope's "On the Moral Character of Women"?

2. One student of this poem has said it is an attempt to discredit the "*laissez-faire* individualism of urban capitalism, and the moral [Swift] is enforcing is the Christian one that we are members of one another." Comment on this interpretation.

Verses on the Death of Dr. Swift,

*Occasioned by Reading the Following Maxim
in Rochefoucauld*

*Dans l'adversité de nos meilleurs amis nous trouvons toujours quelque
chose, qui ne nous deplait pas.* (In the adversity of our best friends we
always find something that doth not displease us.)

As Rochefoucauld his maxims drew
From nature, I believe them true:
They argue no corrupted mind
In him; the fault is in mankind.
   This maxim more than all the rest
Is thought too base for human breast:
"In all distresses of our friends
We first consult our private ends:
While nature, kindly bent to ease us,
Points out some circumstance to please us."   10
   If this perhaps your patience move,
Let reason and experience prove.
We all behold with envious eyes
Our equal rais'd above our size.
Who would not at a crowded show
Stand high himself, keep others low?
I love my friend as well as you:
But why should he obstruct my view?
Then let me have the higher post;
Suppose it but an inch at most.   20
If in battle you should find
One, whom you love of all mankind,
Had some heroic action done,
A champion kill'd, or trophy won;
Rather than thus be overtopt,
Would you not wish his laurels cropt?
Dear honest Ned is with the gout,
Lies rack'd with pain, and you without:
How patiently you hear him groan!
How glad, the case is not your own!   30

. . .

   Thus much may serve by way of proem;
Proceed we therefore to our poem.
   The time is not remote, when I
Must in the course of nature die;
When, I foresee, my special friends

Will try to find their private ends:
Though it is hardly understood
Which way my death can do them good,
Yet thus methinks, I hear 'em speak:
"See, how the Dean begins to break!   80
Poor gentleman! he drops apace!
You plainly find it in his face.
That old vertigo in his head
Will never leave him, till he's dead.
Besides, his memory decays:
He recollects not what he says;
He cannot call his friends to mind;
Forgets the place where last he din'd:
Plies you with stories o'er and o'er,
He told them fifty times before.   90
How does he fancy, we can sit
To hear his out-of-fashion wit?
But he takes up with younger folks,
Who for his wine will bear his jokes.
Faith, he must make his stories shorter,
Or change his comrades once a quarter:
In half the time he talks them round,
There must another set be found."

            .   .   .

Behold the fatal day arrive!
"How is the Dean?" "He's just alive.
Now the departing pray'r is read;
He hardly breathes"—"The Dean is dead."   150
    Before the passing bell begun,
The news throughout the town has run.
"Oh! may we all for death prepare!
What has he left? and who's his heir?"
"I know no more than what the news is;
'Tis all bequeathed to public uses."
"To public use! a perfect whim!
What had the public done for him?
Mere envy, avarice, and pride:
He gave it all—but first he died.   160
And had the Dean in all the nation
No worthy friend, no poor relation?
So ready to do strangers good,
Forgetting his own flesh and blood."
    Now Grub Street wits are all employ'd;
With elegies the town is cloy'd;
Some paragraph in ev'ry paper

To curse the Dean, or bless the Drapier.
  The doctors, tender of their fame,
Wisely on me lay all the blame.   170
"We must confess his case was nice;
But he would never take advice.
Had he been rul'd, for aught appears,
He might have liv'd these twenty years:
For, when we open'd him, we found,
That all his vital parts were sound."
  From Dublin soon to London spread,
'Tis told at court, "The Dean is dead."
Kind Lady Suffolk, in the spleen,
Runs laughing up to tell the Queen.   180
The Queen, so gracious, mild, and good,
Cries, "Is he gone! 'tis time he should.
He's dead, you say; why, let him rot:
I'm glad the medals were forgot.
I promis'd him, I own; but when?
I only was a princess then;
But now, as consort of a king,
You know, 'tis quite a different thing."

       .   .   .

Here shift the scene, to represent
How those I love my death lament.
Poor Pope will grieve a month, and Gay
A week, and Arbuthnot a day.
  St. John himself will scarce forbear
To bite his pen, and drop a tear.   210
The rest will give a shrug, and cry,
"I'm sorry—but we all must die!"

       .   .   .

  My female friends, whose tender hearts
Have better learn'd to act their parts,
Receive the news in doleful dumps:
"The Dean is dead (and what is trumps?);
Then, Lord, have mercy on his soul!
(Ladies, I'll venture for the vole.)   230
Six deans, they say, must bear the pall.
(I wish I knew what kind to call.)
Madame, your husband will attend
The fun'ral of so good a friend?"
"No, madam, 'tis a shocking sight;
And he's engag'd tomorrow night:
My Lady Club would take it ill,
If he should fail her at quadrille.

He lov'd the Dean—(I lead a heart)
But dearest friends, they say must part.   240
His time was come; he ran his race;
We hope he's in a better place."

.   .   .

Suppose me dead; and then suppose
A club assembled at the Rose;   300
Where, from discourse of this and that,
I grow the subject of their chat.
And while they toss my name about,
With favour some, and some without,
One, quite indiff'rent in the cause,
My character impartial draws:
"The Dean, if we believe report,
Was never ill receiv'd at court.
As for his works in verse and prose
I own myself no judge of those;   310
Nor can I tell what critics thought 'em:
But this I know, all people bought 'em.
As with a moral view design'd
To cure the vices of mankind:
And, if he often miss'd his aim.
The world must own it, to their shame,
The praise is his, and theirs the blame."
"Sir, I have heard another story:
He was a most confounded Tory,
And grew, or he is much belied,   320
Extremely dull, before he died."
"Can we the Drapier then forget?
Is not our nation in his debt?
'Twas he that writ the Drapier letters!—"
"He should have left them to his betters,
We had a hundred abler men,
Nor need depend upon his pen.
Say what you will about his reading,
You never can defend his breeding;
Who in his satires running riot,   330
Could never leave the world in quiet;
Attacking when he took the whim,
Court, city, camp—all one to him."

.   .   .

"His vein, ironically grave,
Expos'd the fool, and lash'd the knave.
To steal a hint was never known,
But what he writ was all his own."

. . .

    "Perhaps I may allow the Dean,
Had too much satire in his vein;
And seem'd determin'd not to starve it,   510
    Because no age could more deserve it.
Yet malice never was his aim;
He lash'd the vice, but spar'd the name;
No individual could resent,
Where thousands equally were meant;
His satire points at no defect,
But what all mortals may correct;
For he abhorr'd that senseless tribe
Who call it humour when they gibe:
He spar'd a hump, or crooked nose,   520
Whose owners set up not for beaux."

. . .

    "He gave the little wealth he had
To build a house for fools and mad;
And show'd by one satiric touch,   540
No nation wanted it so much.
That kingdom he hath left his debtor,
I wish it soon may have a better.
And, since you dread no farther lashes,
Methinks you may forgive his ashes."

1. Does the introductory commentary on human motives seem relevant to the subject developed in the remaining sections?

2. What does Swift state to be his notion of the right function of satire?

3. Compare ten or fifteen of these lines with ten or fifteen lines from Pope's "Essay on the Moral Character of Women." Which poet writes more succinctly?

Samuel Johnson

(1709–1784)

■ ■ ■ ■ ■ ■ ■ ■ ■

JOHNSON WAS the son of a Lichfield bookseller. From infancy he was cursed with scrofula and suffered deficient eyesight as a result. He distinguished himself at Oxford but could not remain because of insufficient funds. He taught school for a few years, and in 1737 he set out for London with a play *Irene*, with which he hoped to make his way. In London he was forced to do hack writing to earn a living. Gradually his learning and literary abilities caused him to be known and to be the center of a circle of friends. He published his *Dictionary of the English Language* in 1755, was made a doctor of laws in 1764, and published his edition of Shakespeare in 1765. He wrote *Rasselas* (1759), a novel; a major critical study, *Lives of the English Poets* (1779–1781); and edited the journal *Rambler* (1750–1752). He also wrote a good many poems and scholarly and moral essays, in addition to doing some translating. In his own time as well as in ours his reputation as a conversationalist has rivaled his reputation as a writer. He is, of course, the subject of one of the most notable biographies in English, that done by his companion James Boswell. Johnson has become a legendary figure as scholar, moralist, man of letters, conversationalist, and critic.

Suggested Readings

T. S. ELIOT, Introduction, *London and the Vanity of Human Wishes*. London: Etchells and Hugh Macdonald, 1930. (Also in *English Critical Essays*. World Classics. London: Oxford University Press, 1933.)

GEORGE SHERBURN, "Dr. Johnson," in *A Literary History of England*, ed. Albert C. Baugh. New York: Appleton-Century-Crofts, Inc., 1948, pp. 989.

■ ■ ■ ■ ■ ■ ■ ■ ■

On the Death of Mr. Robert Levet

Condemn'd to Hope's delusive mine,
    As on we toil from day to day,
By sudden blasts, or slow decline,
    Our social comforts drop away.

Well tried through many a varying year,
    See Levet to the grave descend;
Officious, innocent, sincere,
    Of ev'ry friendless name the friend.

Yet still he fills Affection's eye,
    Obscurely wise, and coarsely kind;   10
Nor, letter'd Arrogance, deny
    Thy praise to merit unrefin'd.

When fainting Nature call'd for aid,
    And hov'ring Death prepar'd the blow,
His vig'rous remedy display'd
    The pow'r of art without the show.

In Misery's darkest cavern known,
    His useful care was ever nigh,
Where hopeless Anguish pour'd his groan,
    And lonely Want retir'd to die.   20

No summons-mock'd by chill delay,
    No petty gain disdain'd by pride,
The modest wants of ev'ry day
    The toil of ev'ry day supplied.

His virtues walk'd their narrow round,
    Nor made a pause, nor left a void;
And sure th' Eternal Master found
    The single talent well employ'd.

The busy day, the peaceful night,
    Unfelt, uncounted, glided by;   30
His frame was firm, his pow'rs were bright,
    Though now his eightieth year was nigh.

Then with no throbbing fiery pain,
    No cold gradations of decay,
Death broke at once the vital chain,
    And freed his soul the nearest way.

■   State the theme of this poem and then explain in detail how each
stanza contributes to the development of it.

The Vanity of Human Wishes

Let observation with extensive view,
Survey mankind, from China to Peru;
Remark each anxious toil, each eager strife,
And watch the busy scenes of crowded life;
Then say how hope and fear, desire and hate,
O'erspread with snares the clouded maze of fate,
Where wavering man, betrayed by venturous pride,
To tread the dreary paths without a guide;
As treacherous phantoms in the mist delude,
Shuns fancied ills, or chases airy good.   10
How rarely reason guides the stubborn choice,
Rules the bold hand, or prompts the suppliant voice.
How nations sink, by darling schemes oppressed,
When vengeance listens to the fool's request.
Fate wings with every wish the afflictive dart,
Each gift of nature, and each grace of art,
With fatal heat impetuous courage glows,
With fatal sweetness elocution flows,
Impeachment stops the speaker's powerful breath,
And restless fire precipitates on death.   20
    But scarce observed, the knowing and the bold,
Fall in the general massacre of gold;
Wide-wasting pest! that rages unconfined,
And crowds with crimes the records of mankind;
For gold his sword the hireling ruffian draws,
For gold the hireling judge distorts the laws;
Wealth heaped on wealth, nor truth nor safety buys,
The dangers gather as the treasures rise.
    Let history tell where rival kings command,
And dubious title shakes the maddened land;   30
When statutes glean the refuse of the sword,
How much more safe the vassal than the lord;
Low skulks the hind beneath the rage of power,
And leaves the wealthy traitor in the Tower,
Untouched his cottage, and his slumbers sound,
Though confiscation's vultures hover round.
    The needy traveller, serene and gay,
Walks the wild heath, and sings his toil away.
Does envy seize thee? crush th' upbraiding joy,
Increase his riches and his peace destroy;   40
New fears in dire vicissitude invade,
The rustling brake alarms, and quiv'ring shade,

Nor light nor darkness bring his pain relief;
One shows the plunder, and one hides the thief.
Once more, Democritus, arise on earth,
With cheerful wisdom and instructive mirth,
See motley life in modern trappings dress'd,
And feed with varied fools th' eternal jest:
Thou who couldst laugh where want enchain'd caprice,
Toil crush'd conceit, and man was of a piece;   50
Where wealth unlov'd without a mourner died;
And scarce a sycophant was fed by pride;
Where ne'er was known the form of mock debate,
Or seen a new-made mayor's unwieldy state;
Where change of fav'rites made no change of laws,
And senates heard before they judg'd a cause;
How wouldst thou shake at Britain's modish tribe,
Dart the quick taunt, and edge the piercing gibe!
Attentive truth and nature to descry,
And pierce each scene with philosophic eye.   60
To thee were solemn toys or empty show
The robes of pleasures and the veils of woe:
All aid the farce, and all thy mirth maintain,
Whose joys are causeless, or whose griefs are vain.
Such was the scorn that fill'd the sage's mind,
Renew'd at ev'ry glance on human kind;
How just that scorn ere yet thy voice declare,
Search ev'ry state, and canvass ev'ry pray'r.
Unnumber'd suppliants crowd Preferment's gate,
Athirst for wealth, and burning to be great;   70
Delusive Fortune hears th' incessant call,
They mount, they shine, evaporate, and fall.
On ev'ry stage the foes of peace attend,
Hate dogs their flight, and insult mocks their end.
Love ends with hope, the sinking statesman's door
Pours in the morning worshiper no more;
For growing names the weekly scribbler lies,
To growing wealth the dedicator flies,
From ev'ry room descends the painted face,
That hung the bright palladium of the place,   80
And smok'd in kitchens, or in auctions sold,
To better features yields the frame of gold;
For now no more we trace in ev'ry line
Heroic worth, benevolence divine:
The form distorted justifies the fall,
And detestation rids th' indignant wall.
But will not Britain hear the last appeal,

Sign her foe's doom, or guard her fav'rite's zeal?
Through Freedom's sons no more remonstrance rings,
Degrading nobles and controlling kings;   90
Our supple tribes repress their patriot throats,
And ask no questions but the price of votes;
With weekly libels and septennial ale,
Their wish is full to riot and to rail.

    In full-blown dignity, see Wolsey stand,
Law in his voice, and fortune in his hand:
To him the church, the realm, their pow'rs consign,
Through him the rays of regal bounty shine,
Turn'd by his nod the stream of honour flows,
His smile alone security bestows: 100
Still to new heights his restless wishes tow'r,
Claim leads to claim, and pow'r advances pow'r;
Till conquest unresisted ceas'd to please,
And rights submitted, left him none to seize.
At length his sov'reign frowns—the train of state
Mark the keen glance, and watch the sign to hate.
Where'er he turns, he meets a stranger's eye,
His suppliants scorn him, and his followers fly;
At once is lost the pride of awful state,
The golden canopy, the glittering plate,   110
The regal palace, the luxurious board,
The liveried army, and the menial lord.
With age, with cares, with maladies oppressed,
He seeks the refuge of monastic rest.
Grief aids disease, remembered folly stings,
And his last sighs reproach the faith of kings.

    Speak thou, whose thoughts at humble peace repine,
Shall Wolsey's wealth, with Wolsey's end be thine?
Or liv'st thou now, with safer pride content,
The wisest justice on the banks of Trent?   120
For why did Wolsey, near the steeps of fate,
On weak foundations raise th' enormous weight?
Why but to sink beneath misfortune's blow,
With louder ruin to the gulfs below?

    What gave great Villiers to th' assassin's knife,
And fix'd disease on Harley's closing life?
What murder'd Wentworth, and what exil'd Hyde,
By kings protected and to kings allied?
What but their wish indulg'd in courts to shine,
And pow'r too great to keep or to resign?   130

    When first the college rolls receive his name,
The young enthusiast quits his ease for fame;

Through all his veins the fever of renown
Spreads from the strong contagion of the gown;
O'er Bodley's dome his future labours spread,
And Bacon's mansion trembles o'er his head.
Are these thy views? proceed, illustrious youth,
And Virtue guard thee to the throne of Truth!
Yet should thy soul indulge the gen'rous heat,
Till captive Science yields her last retreat;   140
Should Reason guide thee with her brightest ray,
And pour on misty Doubt resistless day;
Should no false kindness lure to loose delight,
Nor praise relax, nor difficulty fright;
Should tempting Novelty thy cell refrain,
And Sloth effuse her opiate fumes in vain;
Should Beauty blunt on fops her fatal dart,
Nor claim the triumph of a letter'd heart;
Should no disease thy torpid veins invade,
Nor Melancholy's phantoms haunt thy shade;   150
Yet hope not life from grief or danger free,
Nor think the doom of man revers'd for thee:
Deign on the passing world to turn thine eyes,
And pause a while from letters, to be wise;
There mark what ills the scholar's life assail,
Toil, envy, want, the patron, and the jail.
See nations slowly wise, and meanly just,
To buried merit raise the tardy bust.
If dreams yet flatter, once again attend,
Hear Lydiat's life, and Galileo's end.   160
   Nor deem, when Learning her last prize bestows,
The glitt'ring eminence exempt from foes;
See when the vulgar 'scape, despis'd or aw'd,
Rebellion's vengeful talons seize on Laud.
From meaner minds, though smaller fines content
The plunder'd palace, or sequester'd rent;
Mark'd out by dang'rous parts he meets the shock,
And fatal Learning leads him to the block:
Around his tomb let Art and Genius weep,
But hear his death, ye blockheads, hear and sleep.   170
   The festal blazes, the triumphal show,
The ravish'd standard, and the captive foe,
The senate's thanks, the gazette's pompous tale,
With force resistless o'er the brave prevail.
Such bribes the rapid Greek o'er Asia whirl'd,
For such the steady Romans shook the world;
For such in distant lands the Britons shine,

And stain with blood the Danube or the Rhine;
This pow'r has praise, that virtue scarce can warm,
Till fame supplies the universal charm.   180
Yet Reason frowns on War's unequal game,
Where wasted nations raise a single name,
And mortgag'd states their grandsires' wreaths regret
From age to age in everlasting debt;
Wreaths which at last the dear-bought right convey
To rust on medals, or on stones decay.
   On what foundation stands the warrior's pride,
How just his hopes, let Swedish Charles decide;
A frame of adamant, a soul of fire,
No danger fright him, and no labours tire;   190
O'er love, o'er fear, extends his wide domain,
Unconquer'd lord of pleasure and of pain;
No joys to him pacific sceptres yield,
War sounds the trump, he rushes to the field;
Behold surrounding Kings their pow'rs combine,
And one capitulate, and one resign.
Peace courts his hand, but spreads her charms in vain;
"Think nothing gain'd," he cries, "till naught remain,
On Moscow's walls till Gothic standards fly,
And all be mine beneath the polar sky."   200
The march begins in military state,
And nations on his eye suspended wait;
Stern Famine guards the solitary coast,
And Winter barricades the realms of Frost:
He comes, not want nor cold his course delay;—
Hide, blushing Glory, hide Pultowa's day:
The vanquish'd hero leaves his broken bands,
And shows his miseries in distant lands;
Condemn'd a needy supplicant to wait,
While ladies interpose, and slaves debate.   210
But did not Chance at Length her error mend?
Did no subverted empire mark his end?
Did rival monarchs give the fatal wound?
Or hostile millions press him to the ground?
His fall was destined to a barren strand,
A pretty fortress, and a dubious hand;
He left the name at which the world grew pale,
To point a moral, or adorn a tale.
All times their scenes of pompous woes afford,
From Persia's tyrant to Bavaria's lord.   220
In gay hostility, and barb'rous pride,
With half mankind embattled at his side,

Great Xerxes comes to seize the certain prey,
And starves exhausted regions in his way;
Attendant Flatt'ry counts his myriads o'er,
Till counted myriads soothe his pride no more;
Fresh praise is tried till madness fires his mind,
The waves he lashes, and enchains the wind;
New pow'rs are claim'd, new pow'rs are still bestow'd,
Till rude resistance lops the spreading god;   230
The daring Greeks deride the martial show,
And heap their valleys with the gaudy foe;
Th'insulted sea with humbler thought he gains,
A single skiff to speed his flight remains;
Th'encumber'd oar scarce leaves the dreaded coast
Through purple billows and a floating host.
    The bold Bavarian, in a luckless hour,
Tries the dread summits of Caesarean pow'r,
With unexpected legions bursts away,
And sees defenseless realms receive his sway;   240
Short sway! fair Austria spreads her mournful charms,
The queen, the beauty, sets the world in arms;
From hill to hill the beacon's rousing blaze
Spreads wide the hope of plunder and of praise;
The fierce Croatian, and the wild Hussar,
With all the sons of ravage crowd the war;
The baffled prince, in honour's flatt'ring bloom,
Of hasty greatness finds the fatal doom,
His foes' derision, and his subjects' blame,
And steals to death from anguish and from shame.   250
    Enlarge my life with multitude of days,
In health, in sickness, thus the suppliant prays;
Hides from himself his state, and shuns to know,
That life protracted is protracted woe.
Time hovers o'er, impatient to destroy,
And shuts up all the passages of joy:
In vain their gifts the bounteous seasons pour,
The fruit autumnal, and the vernal flow'r;
With listless eyes the dotard views the store,
He views, and wonders that they please no more;   260
Now pass the tasteless meats, and joyless wines,
And Luxury with sighs her slave resigns.
Approach, ye minstrels, try the soothing strain,
Diffuse the tuneful lenitives of pain:
No sounds, alas, would touch th' impervious ear,
Though dancing mountains witness'd Orpheus near;
Nor lute nor lyre his feeble pow'rs attend,

Nor sweeter music of a virtuous friend,
But everlasting dictates crowd his tongue,
Perversely grave, or positively wrong.   270
The still returning tale, and ling'ring jest,
Perplex the fawning niece and amper'd guest,
While growing hopes scarce awe the gath'ring sneer,
And scarce a legacy can bribe to hear;
The watchful guests still hint the last offense,
The daughter's petulance, the son's expense,
Improve his heady rage with treach'rous skill,
And mold his passions till they make his will.

    Unnumber'd maladies his joints invade,
Lay siege to life and press the dire blockade;   280
But unextinguish'd av'rice still remains,
And dreaded losses aggravate his pains;
He turns, with anxious heart and crippled hands,
His bonds of debt, and mortgages of lands;
Or views his coffers with suspicious eyes,
Unlocks his gold, and counts it till he dies.

    But grant, the virtues of a temp'rate prime
Bless with an age exempt from scorn or crime;
An age that melts with unperceiv'd decay,
And glides in modest innocence away;   290
Whose peaceful day Benevolence endears,
Whose night congratulating Conscience cheers;
The gen'ral fav'rite as the gen'ral friend:
Such age there is, and who shall wish its end?

    Yet ev'n on this her load Misfortune flings,
To press the weary minutes' flagging wings:
New sorrow rises as the day returns,
A sister sickens, or a daughter mourns.
Now kindred Merit fills the sable bier,
Now lacerated Friendship claims a tear.   300
Year chases year, decay pursues decay,
Still drops some joy from writh'ring life away;
New forms arise, and diff'rent views engage,
Superfluous lags the vet'ran on the stage,
Till pitying Nature signs the last release,
And bids afflicted worth retire to peace.

    But few there are whom hours like these await,
Who set unclouded in the gulfs of fate.
From Lydia's monarch should the search descend,
By Solon caution'd to regard his end,   310
In life's last scene what prodigies surprise,
Fears of the brave, and follies of the wise!

From Marlb'rough's eyes the streams of dotage flow,
And Swift expires a driv'ler and a show.

   The teeming mother, anxious for her race,
Begs for each birth the fortune of a face:
Yet Vane could tell what ills from beauty spring
And Sedley curs'd the form that pleas'd a king.
Ye nymphs of rosy lips and radiant eyes,
Whom Pleasure keeps too busy to be wise,   320
Whom joys with soft varieties invite,
By day the frolic and the dance by night;
Who frown with vanity, who smile with art,
And ask the latest fashion of the heart,
What care, what rules your heedless charms shall save,
Each nymph your rival, and each youth your slave?
Against your fame with fondness hate combines,
The rival batters, and the lover mines.
With distant voice neglected Virtue calls,
Less heard and less, the faint remonstrance falls;   330
Tir'd with contempt, she quits the slipp'ry reign,
And Pride and Prudence take her seat in vain.
In crowd at once, where none the pass defend,
The harmless freedom, and the private friend.
The guardians yield, by force superior plied:
To Int'rest, Prudence; and to Flatt'ry, Pride.
Now Beauty falls betray'd, despis'd, distress'd,
And hissing Infamy proclaims the rest.

    Where then shall Hope and Fear their objects find?
Must dull suspense corrupt the stagnant mind?   340
Must helpless man, in ignorance sedate,
Roll darkling down the torrent of his fate?
Must no dislike alarm, no wishes rise,
No cries invoke the mercies of the skies?
Enquirer, cease; petitions yet remain
Which Heaven may hear, nor deem Religion vain.
Still raise for good the supplicating voice,
But leave to Heaven the measure and the choice.
Safe in his power whose eyes discern afar
The secret ambush of a specious prayer;   350
Implore his aid, in his decisions rest,
Secure, whate'er he gives, he gives the best.
Yet, when the sense of sacred presence fires,
And strong devotion to the skies aspires,
Pour forth thy fervors for a healthful mind,
Obedient passions, and a will resign'd
For love, which scarce collective man can fill;

For patience, sovereign o'er transmuted ill;
For faith, that, panting for a happier seat,
Counts death kind Nature's signal of retreat.   360
These goods for man the laws of Heav'n ordain,
These goods he grants, who grants the power to gain;
With these celestial Wisdom calms the mind,
And makes the happiness she does not find.

■ Samuel Johnson is usually considered the last of the Augustans, in
the line that runs from Dryden through Pope to himself. As such he
upheld, ostensibly at least, certain principles characteristic of Augustan
poetic theory. Arthur O. Lovejoy, in "'Nature' as Aesthetic Norm," *
includes the representation "only of the generic character of things"
in a list of *desiderata* in Augustan esthetic theory. In other terms, this
rule means the avoidance of the *particular* in favor of the *general*. In
a famous passage in Johnson's *Rasselas*, for example, the ideal poet says:

> The business of a poet is to examine, not the individual, but the species;
> to remark general properties and large appearances; he does not number
> the streaks of the tulip, or describe the different shades in the verdure
> of the forest. He is to exhibit, in his portraits of nature, such prominent
> and striking features, as recall the original to every mind; and must
> neglect the minuter discriminations, which one may have remarked,
> and another have neglected, for those characteristics which are alike
> obvious to vigilance and carelessness.

A similar statement was made by Johnson's friend Sir Joshua Reynolds
(1723–1792) in *Discourses on Painting*, XI: "It may be remarked,
that the impression which is left on our mind even of things which are
familiar to us, is seldom more than their general effect; beyond which
we do not look in recognizing such objects. To express this in painting,
is to express what is congenial and natural to the mind of man, and
what gives him by reflection his own mode of conceiving." This emphasis upon the general is fairly frequent in the critical commentaries
written in the eighteenth century.†

Certain other characteristics, such as simplicity of statement as well
as the avoidance of ornateness and intricacy of design, would seem to
be implied in the doctrine of the *general*. And we find various writers
in the eighteenth century commenting on the need for plainness, clear-
ness, and "perspicuity" in the use of words. John Locke (1632–1704)
in his *Essay on Human Understanding* (1690) wrote:

> The first and most palpable abuse is, the using of Words, without clear
> and distinct Ideas. Another great abuse of Words, is Inconstancy in

....

* *Modern Language Notes*, XLII, 7 (November, 1927), 444–450.
† William Blake (1757–1827), however, stated an opposite view. Referring
to Reynolds' view of the "general" he wrote, "Minute Discrimination is not
Accidental. All Sublimity is founded on Minute Discrimination."

the use of them. It is hard to find a Discourse wherein one shall not observe, if he read with attention, the same Words used sometimes for one Collection of simple Ideas, and sometimes for another. Another abuse of Language is, an affected Obscurity, by either applying old Words, to new and unusual Significations; or introducing new and ambiguous Terms, without defining either; or else putting them so together, as may confound their ordinary meaning.

And Lord Chesterfield (1694–1773), to take one more example, once wrote to his son that "the easiest books are generally the best," adding that he had given up in disgust trying to read Dante because he found the language too obscure to follow. In Augustan poetry we tend to find an emphasis on logical development, on neatness of expression, on the readily understandable, and on reasonableness in all forms.

We should expect then in examining Johnson's "The Vanity of Human Wishes" to find some of these Augustan doctrines of poetry exemplified. And we do find them. The opening ten lines state what the poem is about, a broad view—from China to Peru, in fact—of man's vain pursuit of ultimate or final satisfaction. The poem illustrates a number of Johnson's dicta, quoted above, about the function of the poet: The poem is dealing with a "species," with all of mankind, not with an individual. The figures he uses to illustrate his theme, such as Cardinal Wolsey, George Villiers, Alexander the Great, and one of the kings of Persia, for instance, are discussed only in the most general way, only insofar as they establish Johnson's thesis that all is vanity. In referring to these men he points merely to the events every reader of history will know; he recalls "the original to every mind." In these respects he is following the theory he himself stated.

He is also observing many of the dicta and rules desired by Reynolds, Locke, and Chesterfield. No reader could complain that the poem does not contain "clear and distinct Ideas." Nothing is obscure as the result of "affected Obscurity" or as the result of obscurity in expression. (It is another matter, of course, when a poet is obscure to a later generation of readers as a result of their not knowing the significance of the names or events the poet mentions or discusses.)

The development of the poem is logical. It begins, as we have said, with a statement of the subject and theme, and everything that follows is a logical development of that statement. The language, to a very great extent, is abstract. In fact, Johnson emphasizes certain abstractions, such as Vengeance, History, Novelty, and Melancholy, by personifying them; they become some of the general factors to which he wants to draw special attention in his consideration of the subject. Johnson, we may infer, would have agreed that in writing in this general fashion he was appealing to what Reynolds said "is congenial and natural to the mind of man." Such a mode of writing, "gives him by reflection his own mode of conceiving."

We all recognize what Reynolds and Johnson were getting at in their emphasis upon the "general"; and we know that under certain circumstances generalizations can have an esthetic effect. But we also recognize that the abstract and the general tend to lift us above emotion and strong feeling. To put it another way, a concrete instance is often far more affecting than a generalized commentary. Thus, as we know, propagandists, whether for good or bad end, will attempt to dramatize their statements in order to involve us emotionally. Modern poetry and criticism have strongly emphasized the value of the concrete. In poetry especially, we stress the imagistic, the symbolic, the concrete detail. We believe that in this way our attention is focused more sharply, our consciousness heightened, and our emotions more deeply engaged. There would seem to be a contradiction between the esthetic stated by Johnson and Reynolds and that commonly held by twentieth-century poets and critics. To some extent there is a contradiction. We may grant that both Johnson and Reynolds in stating the virtues in an abstract vocabulary and in a generalized method are holding to a view that can be justified up to a point. But it is also necessary to recognize that many of the most effective lines in Johnson's poems cannot be accounted for under the Augustan concern with generalization. In many of his most memorable lines we find him compromising with the language of the concrete. The following lines, for example, employ very effectively a technique which has been called the "sunken image":

> Unnumber'd suppliants crowd Preferment's gate
> Athirst for wealth and burning to be great;
> Delusive Fortune hears the incessant call,
> They mount, they shine, evaporate, and fall.
> (ll. 73–76)

> For why did Wolsey, near the steeps of fate,
> On weak foundations raise the enormous weight?
> (ll. 125–26)

Henry W. Wells in *Poetic Imagery** defines a sunken image as "one which powerfully affects the imagination without conveying a definite picture." The suppliants crowding near Preferment's gate cannot be identified as a particular group of suppliants at a particular gate, but we tend somehow at first reading the line to think we can identify them. And line 76 implies the rising, bursting, and falling of a skyrocket. Similarly "steeps of fate" approaches but does "not attain abstraction." It is true, of course, that in each instance Johnson has an abstraction, "Preferment" and "fate," but each is qualified by a sunken image. (It is worth observing that Johnson would have felt his use of "Unnumber'd suppliants" an effective bit of generalization. In fact, Aristotle in

* New York: Columbia University Press, 1924.

Rhetoric [III, vi, 7] mentions this description of an object by negatives, by characteristics it does not possess, as a means of amplifying what could be carried to infinity; it is capable of suggesting sublime effects.)

There are instances in which Johnson has juxtaposed concrete and abstract elements in the same line:

> Love ends with hope, the sinking statesman's door
> Pours in the morning's worshiper no more;
>
> (ll. 79–80)

> See nations slowly wise, and meanly just,
> To buried merit raise the tardy bust.
>
> (ll. 161–162)

> Rebellion's vengeful talons seize on Laud.
>
> (l. 168)

> And fatàl learning leads him to the block:
>
> (l. 172)

> For such the steady Romans shook the world;
>
> (l. 180)

> Roll darkling down the torrent of his fate?
>
> (l. 346)

> The secret ambush of a specious pray'r;
>
> (l. 354)

Each of the concrete terms—"sinking," "buried," "talons," "block," "steady," "torrent," and "ambush"—somehow saves the accompanying abstraction from being either trite, vague, or merely unaffecting. Furthermore, these two lines:

> Through all his veins the fever of renown
> Spreads from the strong contagion of the gown;
>
> (ll. 137–38)

are not abstract statement at all; they contain a metaphor which might have been written by a Jacobean poet, in some of whose poems meanings are conveyed by the metaphor alone, not by a statement plus a metaphor. And in another line Johnson employs an adjective, "indignant," that in modern poetry would be called a "surprise adjective":

> And detestation rids th' indignant wall.
>
> (l. 90)

The usage (which here may not be an especially good one) is hardly in keeping with Locke's rule that old words should not be given "new and unusual Significations."

In other words, Johnson uses techniques which are not an explicit part of, or at least not emphasized in, his general theory. Perhaps we can assert positively that in poetry language should be affecting, that it must not only move us but quicken our consciousness. Generalizations and abstractions can be affecting—but unrelieved by the language of the concrete and the particular they can also be extremely dull, as the poetasters in the Augustan world readily demonstrate. In saying this, however, we should not forget that the Augustan language and esthetic has its own native virtues, beyond those already discussed. It can be a language that is often strong with conviction:

> Yet hope not life from grief or danger free,
> Nor think the doom of man revers'd for thee:
> (ll. 155–156)

And its balanced antitheses can afford sharp contrasts:

> He left the name at which the world grew pale,
> To point a moral, or adorn a tale.
> (ll. 221–222)

Perhaps a special point should be made about the prose quality of this poetry. Matthew Arnold went so far as to say Pope wrote prose rather than poetry. If we were to accept this judgment as true we should have to apply it to Johnson's poetry as well. In fact, Johnson resisted some of the tendencies of his time—sentimental philosophizing and a morbid romanticism—in order to hold to this tradition. T. S. Eliot in an introductory essay to an edition of *London and The Vanity of Human Wishes* says that of all the poets of his time Johnson is "the nearest to a die-hard." Eliot means that Johnson wrote in the tradition of Pope, not as a mere imitator of him, not merely because Pope's idiom was available to him in his time, but because he had an Augustan sensibility and the kind of intelligence necessary to make the most of the virtues inherent in that idiom.

Eliot comments on some of the virtues of this idiom by saying, as Ezra Pound had said about the writing of poetry in the twentieth century, that poetry to be good must be as well written as good prose, that it must have some of the flexibility and precision of good prose. He means that poetry must avoid sheer mistiness, a kind of cotton-candy substance, that dissolves and disappears when subjected to analysis. The Augustan age had a special need to write in this fashion because the men who gave their stamp to the age felt their beliefs and convictions strongly (e.g., that the world was explicable in rational terms) and needed an idiom to express them. (Eliot goes on to say that the age changed, as every age does, and that new conditions and new ways of seeing demanded new ways of expression, a new idiom. Lesser men than Johnson, however, sometimes attempted to write in the Augustan tradition despite the fact that they did not think in the way Dryden

or Pope or Johnson thought and as a consequence their poetic forms
were inappropriate to their feelings and their beliefs.) Johnson felt
very strongly about the theme and subject of his poem. In fact, Joseph
Wood Krutch, one of his most recent biographers, says that Johnson felt
in the deepest part of his being that "All is Vanity." He felt too that his
age needed to be convinced that this was so. For this purpose he needed
an idiom that was precise, as in these lines:

> There mark what ills the scholar's life assail,
> Toil, envy, want, the patron, and the jail.
> (ll. 159–160)

In the language of the Augustan tradition he found such an idiom. And
he had the moral earnestness, the perception, and the genius for expression that enabled him to use the language of his time.

Prologue

*Spoken by Mr. Garrick at the Opening of the
Theatre Royal, Drury Lane, 1747*

> When Learning's triumph o'er her barb'rous foes
> First rear'd the stage, immortal Shakespeare rose;
> Each change of many-colour'd life he drew,
> Exhausted worlds, and then imagin'd new:
> Existence saw him spurn her bounded reign,
> And panting Time toil'd after him in vain.
> His pow'rful strokes presiding Truth impress'd,
> And unresisted Passion storm'd the breast.
>   Then Jonson came, instructed from the school,
> To please in method, and invent by rule;   10
> His studious patience and laborious art,
> By regular approach essay'd the hart:
> Cold Approbation gave the ling'ring bays;
> For those who durst not censure, scarce could praise.
> A mortal born, he met the gen'ral doom,
> But left, like Egypt's kings, a lasting tomb.
>   The wits of Charles found easier ways to fame,
> Nor wish'd for Jonson's art, or Shakespeare's flame,
> Themselves they studied; as they felt, they writ:
> Intrigue was plot, obscenity was wit.   20
> Vice always found a sympathetic friend;
> They pleas'd their age, and did not aim to mend.
> Yet bards like these aspir'd to lasting praise,
> And proudly hop'd to pimp in future days.
> Their cause was gen'ral, their supports were strong,

Their slaves were willing, and their reign was long:
Till Shame regain'd the post that Sense betray'd,
And Virtue call'd Oblivion to her aid.

    Then, crush'd by rules, and weaken'd as refin'd,
For years the pow'r of tragedy declin'd;   30
From bard to bard the frigid caution crept,
Till Declamation roar'd whilst Passion slept;
Yet still did Virtue deign the stage to tread,
Philosophy remain'd though Nature fled.
But forc'd, at length, her ancient reign to quit,
She saw great Faustus lay the ghost of wit;
Exulting Folly hail'd the joyful day,
And Pantomime and Song confirm'd her sway.

    But who the coming changes can presage,
And mark the future periods of the stage?   40
Perhaps if skill could distant times explore,
New Behns, new Durfeys,[1] yet remain in store;
Perhaps where Lear has rav'd, and Hamlet died,
On flying cars new sorcerers may ride;
Perhaps (for who can guess th' effects of chance)
Here Hunt may box, or Mahomet[2] may dance.

    Hard is his lot that here by fortune plac'd,
Must watch the wild vicissitudes of taste;
With ev'ry meteor of caprice must play,
And chase the new-blown bubbles of the day.   50
Ah! let not censure term our fate our choice,
The stage but echoes back the public voice;
The drama's laws, the drama's patrons give,
For we that live to please, must please to live.

    Then prompt no more the follies you decry,
As tyrants doom their tools of guilt to die;
'Tis yours, this night, to bid the reign commence
Of rescued Nature and reviving Sense;
To chase the charms of Sound, the pomp of Show,
For useful Mirth and salutary Woe;   60
Bid scenic Virtue from the rising age,
And truth diffuse her radiance from the stage.

■   Write an essay on this poem in which you consider the following:
(a) Johnson's view of English drama; (b) his view of "the rules"; (c) his
view of morality in relation to the stage; and (d) the extent to which his
own verse reflects his literary theory.

1. Mrs. Aphra Behn (1640–1689), a novelist and dramatist, sometimes bawdy
in her writing; Tom Durfey (1653–1723), a writer of plays and poems.   2. Edward Hunt was a lightweight pugilist, and Mahomet a rope dancer.

Thomas Gray

(1716–1771)

■ ■ ■ ■ ■ ■ ■ ■ ■ ■

THOMAS GRAY spent his youth at Eton and Cambridge, where he was educated by means his mother earned as a milliner. His mature years were spent as a scholar and professor at Cambridge. His early poetry, such as "On a Distant Prospect of Eton College," shows the influence of classical poets and Dryden. It has little or none of the experimental or revolutionary spirit that was to appear in such poems as "The Progress of Poesy," "The Fatal Sisters," and "The Bard," work that came out of his interest in the literature and religion of Celtic antiquity. As a person Gray was shy and retiring. Offered the laureateship, he declined it, remaining professor of modern history at Cambridge until his death.

Suggested Readings

SAMUEL JOHNSON, "The Life of Gray," in Lives of the English Poets.
MATTHEW ARNOLD, "Gray," in Essays in Criticism, Second Series. New York: The Macmillan Company, 1891, pp. 69–99.
A. L. REED, The Background of Gray's Elegy. New York: Columbia University Press, 1924.

■ ■ ■ ■ ■ ■ ■ ■ ■ ■

Elegy
Written in a Country Churchyard

The Curfew tolls the knell of parting day,
    The lowing herd wind slowly o'er the lea,
The plowman homeward plods his weary way,
    And leaves the world to darkness and to me.

Now fades the glimmering landscape on the sight,
    And all the air a solemn stillness holds,
Save where the beetle wheels his droning flight,
    And drowsy tinklings lull the distant folds;

Save that from yonder ivy-mantled tower
   The moping owl does to the moon complain   10
Of such, as wand'ring near her secret bower,
   Molest her ancient solitary reign.

Beneath those rugged elms, that yew-tree's shade,
   Where heaves the turf in many a mold'ring heap,
Each in his narrow cell forever laid,
   The rude Forefathers of the hamlet sleep.

The breezy call of incense-breathing Morn,
   The swallow twitt'ring from the straw-built shed,
The cock's shrill clarion, or the echoing horn,
   No more shall rouse them from their lowly bed.   20

For them no more the blazing hearth shall burn,
   Or busy housewife ply her evening care:
No children run to lisp their sire's return,
   Or climb his knees the envied kiss to share.

Oft did the harvest to their sickle yield,
   Their furrow oft the stubborn glebe has broke;
How jocund did they drive their team afield!
   How bowed the woods beneath their sturdy stroke!

Let not Ambition mock their useful toil,
   Their homely joys, and destiny obscure;   30
Nor Grandeur hear with a disdainful smile,
   The short and simple annals of the poor.

The boast of heraldry, the pomp of pow'r,
   And all that beauty, all that wealth e'er gave,
Awaits alike th' inevitable hour.
   The paths of glory lead but to the grave.

Nor you, ye Proud, impute to These the fault,
   If Mem'ry o'er their Tomb no Trophies raise,
Where through the long-drawn isle and fretted vault
   The pealing anthem swells the note of praise.   40

Can storied urn or animated bust
   Back to its mansion call the fleeting breath?
Can Honor's voice provoke the silent dust,
   Or Flatt'ry sooth the dull cold ear of Death?

Perhaps in this neglected spot is laid
  Some heart once pregnant with celestial fire;
Hands, that the rod of empire might have swayed,
  Or waked to ecstasy the living lyre.

But Knowledge to their eyes her ample page
  Rich with the spoils of time did ne'er unroll;   50
Chill Penury repressed their noble rage,
  And froze the genial current of the soul.

Full many a gem of purest ray serene,
  The dark unfathomed caves of ocean bear:
Full many a flower is born to blush unseen,
  And waste its sweetness on the desert air.

Some village Hampden, that with dauntless breast
  The little Tyrant of his fields withstood;
Some mute inglorious Milton here may rest,
  Some Cromwell guiltless of his country's blood.   60

Th' applause of listening senates to command,
  The threats of pain and ruin to despise,
To scatter plenty o'er a smiling land,
  And read their history in a nation's eyes,

Their lot forbade: nor circumscribed alone
  Their growing virtues, but their crimes confined;
Forbade to wade through slaughter to a throne,
  And shut the gates of mercy on mankind;

The struggling pangs of conscious truth to hide,
  To quench the blushes of ingenuous shame,   70
Or heap the shrine of luxury and pride
  With incense kindled at the Muse's flame.

Far from the madding crowd's ignoble strife,
  Their sober wishes never learned to stray;
Along the cool sequestered vale of life
  They kept the noiseless tenor of their way.

Yet e'en these bones from insult to protect
  Some frail memorial still erected nigh,
With uncouth rhymes and shapeless sculpture decked
  Implores the passing tribute of a sigh.   80

Their name, their years, spelt by th' unletter'd Muse,
    The place of fame and elegy supply:
And many a holy text around she strews,
    That teach the rustic moralist to die.

For who to dumb Forgetfulness a prey,
    This pleasing anxious being e'er resign'd,
Left the warm precincts of the cheerful day,
    Nor cast one longing lingering look behind?

On some fond breast the parting soul relies,
    Some pious drops the closing eye requires;   90
Ev'n from the tomb the voice of Nature cries,
    Ev'n in our Ashes live their wonted Fires.

For thee, who mindful of the unhonour'd Dead
    Dost in these lines their artless tale relate,
If chance, by lonely Contemplation led,
    Some kindred spirit shall inquire thy fate,

Haply some hoary-headed Swain may say,
    "Oft have we seen him at the peep of dawn
Brushing with hasty steps the dews away
    To meet the sun upon the upland lawn.   100

"There at the foot of yonder nodding beech
    That wreathes its old fantastic roots so high,
His listless length at noontide would he stretch,
    And pore upon the brook that babbles by.

"Hard by yon wood, now smiling as in scorn,
    Mutt'ring his wayward fancies he would rove,
Now drooping, woeful wan, like one forlorn,
    Or crazed with care, or crossed in hopeless love.

"One morn I missed him on the customed hill,
    Along the heath and near his fav'rite tree;   110
Another came; nor yet beside the rill,
    Nor up the lawn, nor at the wood was he;

"The next with dirges due in sad array
    Slow through the church-way path we saw him borne.
Approach and read (for thou canst read) the lay
    Graved on the stone beneath yon agèd thorn."

The Epitaph

Here rests his head upon the lap of Earth
  A youth, to Fortune and to Fame unknown;
Fair Science frown'd not on his humble birth
  And Melancholy mark'd him for her own.   120

Large was his bounty, and his soul sincere;
  Heav'n did a recompense as largely send:
He gave to Mis'ry all he had, a tear,
  He gain'd from Heav'n ('twas all he wish'd) a friend.

No farther seek his merits to disclose,
  Or draw his frailties from their dread abode
(There they alike in trembling hope repose),
  The bosom of his Father and his God.

■ "Elegy in a Country Churchyard" is one of the most commonly read poems in English literature. The poem, to speak generally, is about the pathos one feels in considering the unfulfilled promise or potentialities of the poor. This is not to say that the poet ignores the lesser pathos inherent in all men, however great, fading into death and usually into obscurity. These notions are commonplaces. If we think as we do, that the "Elegy" is a great statement of these ideas, the reason must lie in the poem's being a moving presentation of them. The difference between the abstract statement and the poetic is that the poetic one is dramatized.

The questions which follow are intended to suggest the nature of the dramatic elements in this poem.

■   1. The narrator, or poet, is not, in the usual sense, outside the subject. He feels his own involvement in the general fate. What are the lines in which he brings himself into the poem?

2. In what way does the poet suggest the terrible poignancy one feels in the stillness of those in their graves?

3. The poet introduces an element of complexity into his comments on the wealthy and the great who lie in Abbey tombs. What purpose is served by this?

4. Explain "storied urn" and "animated bust" in line 41.

5. How does the use of the allegorical figures extend the idea that rich and poor alike come to the same end? How do these allegorical figures at the same time serve to point up the differences in their lives of rich and poor?

6. In the fourteenth stanza the poet introduces an aspect of the theme to be developed in several of the following stanzas. We should note that the statement is made in terms of two images. Comment on

the meaning of these images, including the associations aroused by them. (In what sense is an imagistic statement a dramatization of an idea?)

7. We may say that the poet has introduced Hampden, Milton, and Cromwell as three symbolic figures to signify potential, but unrealized, roles which one or another of the villagers might have played. To have introduced merely Milton or Hampden would have intensified the pathos of the frustrations of the village poor. Explain how the figure of Cromwell brings in an element that complicates the statement.

8. Lines 66 and 67 (which are reminiscent of the technique used by Samuel Johnson in "The Vanity of Human Wishes") possess elements both general and concrete. Comment on these elements.

9. Each of the vices that "Their lot forbade" (lines 66–72) is stated in terms of an image. Explain the meaning of each.

10. In stanza 20 the poet introduces a specific contrast between the Abbey and the churchyard. Explain.

11. Stanzas 22 and 23 are built upon contrasting ideas. What are they?

12. Does the introduction of *thee* and *thy* in stanza 24 harm the congruity of the dramatic structure? (Remember that the poet is the narrator.)

13. It is sometimes said that this poem, despite its looking forward to romantic poetry, has neoclassical elements. Point out, for example, sententious statements; point out also the conscious use of balanced and antithetical phrases and statements.

14. It is also said that a "sentimental movement" began as a reaction against certain aspects of neoclassicism. To what extent, if any, can this poem be characterized as sentimental?

The Progress of Poesy

I. 1[1]

> Awake, Aeolian lyre, awake,
> And give to rapture all thy trembling strings.
> From Helicon's[2] harmonious springs
> A thousand rills their mazy progress take;
> The laughing flowers, that round them blow,
> Drink life and fragrance as they flow.
> Now the rich stream of music winds along,
> Deep, majestic, smooth, and strong,
> Through verdant vales, and Ceres'[3] golden reign;

1. Gray's note: "The various sources of poetry, which gives life and luster to all it touches, are here described."   2. A mountain sacred to the Muses.
3. Ceres, goddess of fields.

Now rolling down the steep amain,   10
Headlong, impetuous, see it pour;
The rocks and nodding groves rebellow to the roar.

I. 2⁴

O! Sovereign of the willing soul,
Parent of sweet and solemn-breathing airs,
Enchanting shell! the sullen Cares
And frantic Passions hear thy soft control.
On Thracia's hills the Lord of War
Has curbed the fury of his car,
And dropped his thirsty lance at thy command.
Perching on the sceptered hand   20
Of Jove, thy magic lulls the feathered king
With ruffled plumes and flagging wing;
Quenched in dark clouds of slumber lie
The terror of his beak, and lightings of his eye.

I. 3⁵

Thee the voice, the dance, obey,
Tempered to thy warbled lay.
O'er Idalia's⁶ velvet-green
The rosy-crownèd Loves are seen,
    On Cytherea's day⁷
With antic Sports and blue-eyed Pleasures,   30
Frisking light in frolic measures;
Now pursuing, now retreating,
    Now in circling troops they meet;
To brisk notes in cadence beating
    Glance their many-twinkling feet.
Slow melting strains their Queen's approach declare;
Where'er she turns the Graces homage pay.
With arms sublime, that float upon the air,
In gliding state she wins her easy way;
O'er her warm cheek, and rising bosom, move   40
The bloom of young Desire, and purple light of Love.

I. 1⁸

Man's feeble race what ills await!
Labor, and Penury, the racks of Pain,

----

4. Gray's note: "The power of harmony to calm the turbulent sallies of the soul."
5. Gray's note: "The power of harmony to produce all the graces of motion in the body."   6. Sacred to Venus.   7. Day for worshipping Venus.
8. Gray's note: "To compensate the real and imaginary ills of life, the Muse was given to mankind by the same Providence that sends day by its cheerful presence to dispel the gloom and terrors of the night."

Disease, and Sorrow's weeping train,
And Death, sad refuge from the storms of Fate!
The fond complaint, my song, disprove,
And justify the laws of Jove.
Say, has he given in vain the heavenly Muse?
Night, and all her sickly dews,
Her specters wan, and birds of boding cry,
He gives to range the dreary sky;
Till down the eastern cliffs afar
Hyperion's[9] march they spy, and glittering shafts of war.

50

II. 2[10]

In climes beyond the solar road,
Where shaggy forms o'er icebuilt mountains roam,
The Muse has broke the twilight gloom
To cheer the shivering native's dull abode.
And oft, beneath the odorous shade
Of Chili's boundless forest laid,
She deigns to hear the savage youth repeat,
In loose numbers wildly sweet,
Their feather-cinctured chiefs and dusky loves.
Her track, where'er the goddess roves,
Glory pursue, and generous Shame,
Th' unconquerable Mind, and Freedom's holy flame.

60

II. 3[11]

Woods, that wave o'er Delphi's[12] steep,
Isles, that crown the Aegean deep,
Fields, that cool Ilissus[13] laves,
Or where Maeander's[14] amber waves
In lingering labyrinths creep,
How do your tuneful echoes languish,
Mute, but to the voice of Anguish!
Where each old poetic mountain
Inspiration breathed around;
Every shade and hallowed fountain
Murmured deep a solemn sound;
Till the sad Nine[15] in Greece's evil hour
Left their Parnassus for the Latian[16] plains.
Alike they scorn the pomp of tyrant Power,

70

9. Sun god.   10. Gray's note: "Extensive influence of poetic genius over the remotest and most uncivilized nations; its connection with liberty, and the virtues that naturally attend to it."   11. Gray's note: "Progress of poetry from Greece to Italy, and from Italy to England."   12. The Greek oracle.   13. Athenian stream.   14. River in Asia Minor.   15. The Muses.   16. Roman.

And coward Vice, that revels in her chains.   80
When Latium had her lofty spirit lost,
They sought, oh Albion![17] next thy sea-encircled coast.

III. 1

Far from the sun and summer-gale,
In thy green lap was Nature's darling[18] laid,
    What time, where lucid Avon strayed,
To him the mighty Mother did unveil
    Her awful face. The dauntless child
    Stretched forth his little arms, and smiled.
This pencil take (she said) whose colors clear
    Richly paint the vernal year;   90
Thine too these golden keys, immortal boy!
    This can unlock the gates of Joy,
    Of Horror that, and thrilling Fears,
Or ope the sacred source of sympathetic tears.

III. 2

Nor second he,[19] that rode sublime
Upon the seraph-wings of Ecstasy,
    The secrets of the Abyss to spy.
He passed the flaming bounds of Place and Time;
    The living throne, the sapphire blaze,
    Where angels tremble, while they gaze,   100
He saw; but, blasted with excess of light,
    Closed his eyes in endless night.
Behold, where Dryden's less presumptuous car
    Wide o'er the fields of Glory bear
    Two coursers of ethereal race,
With necks in thunder clothed, and long-resounding pace.

III. 3

Hark, his hands the lyre explore!
Bright-eyed Fancy hovering o'er
Scattered from her pictured urn
Thoughts that breathe, and words that burn.   110
    But, ah! 'tis heard no more—
Oh! Lyre divine, what daring spirit
Wakes thee now? Though he inherit
Nor the pride, nor ample pinion,
    That the Theban Eagle[20] bear
Sailing with supreme dominion

....
17. England.   18. Shakespeare.   19. Milton.   20. Pindar.

Through the azure deep of air;
Yet oft before his infant eyes would run
    Such forms as glitter in the Muse's ray,
With orient hues unborrowed of the sun;   120
    Yet shall he mount, and keep his distant way
Beyond the limits of a vulgar fate,
Beneath the good how far—but far above the great.

■ Compare the theme, subject matter, method of development of this
poem with "Ode on the Poetical Character" by William Collins (p. 324).

William Collins
(1721–1759)

■■■■■■■■■

COLLINS WAS educated at Winchester College, where he
was a school-fellow of Joseph Warton. Here he wrote *Persian Eclogues,* which
he later published anonymously. Some years later he entered Oxford, in-
tending to take orders. But his growing familiarity with London coffeehouses
and theaters and his acquaintance with eminent figures like David Garrick
and Samuel Johnson stimulated his desire to be a man of letters. In 1764 Collins and Warton submitted manuscripts to Dodsley, a famous publisher.
Dodsley, shrewdly appraising the literary fashion, rejected Collins' poems
but took Warton's. Warton's collection succeeded, but Collins, brought out
by another publisher, failed. His sole consolation was praise from James
Thomson, author of *The Seasons.* He was frequently in financial difficulties,
and once Samuel Johnson intervened for him in the matter of a small debt.
In 1751, a mild mental disorder began, which gradually increased in violence
until his death.

Suggested Readings

SAMUEL JOHNSON, "Collins," in *Lives of the English Poets.*
A. S. WOODHOUSE, "Collins and the Creative Imagination," in *Studies in
    English.* Toronto: University of Toronto Press, 1931, pp. 59–130.
F. R. LEAVIS, "'The Ode to Evening' and Milton," in *Revaluation.* New
    York: George W. Stewart, Publisher, 1947, pp. 131–133.

■■■■■■■■■■

Ode on the Poetical Character

I

As once, if not with light regard,
I read aright that gifted bard
(Him whose school above the rest
His loveliest Elfin Queen has blest),
One, only one, unrival'd fair,
Might hope the magic girdle wear,
At solemn tourney hung on high,
The wish of each love-darting eye;
Lo! to each other nymph in turn applied,
    As if, in air unseen, some hov'ring hand,   10
Some chaste and angel-friend to virgin-fame,
    With whisper'd spell had burst the starting band,
It left unblest her loath'd dishonour'd side;
    Happier, hopeless fair, if never
    Her baffled hand with vain endeavour
Had touch'd that fatal zone to her denied!
Young Fancy thus, to me divinest name,
    To whom, prepar'd and bath'd in Heav'n
    The cest of amplest pow'r is giv'n:
    To few the godlike gift assigns,   20
    To gird their blest, prophetic loins,
And gaze her visions wild, and feel unmix'd her flame!

2

The band, as fairy legends say,
Was wove on that creating day,
When He, who call'd with thought to birth
Yon tented sky, this laughing earth,
And dress'd with springs, and forests tall,
And pour'd the main engirting all,
Long by the lov'd Enthusiast woo'd,
Himself in some diviner mood,   30
Retiring, sate with her alone,
And plac'd her on his sapphire throne;
The whiles, the vaulted shrine around,
Seraphic wires were heard to sound,
Now sublimest triumph swelling,
Now on love and mercy dwelling;
And she, from out the veiling cloud,
Breath'd her magic notes aloud:
And thou, thou rich-hair'd youth of morn,
And all thy subject life was born!   40

The dang'rous passions kept aloof,
Far from the sainted growing woof:
But near it sate ecstatic Wonder,
List'ning the deep applauding thunder:
And Truth, in sunny vest array'd,
By whose the tarsel's eyes were made;
All the shad'wy tribes of Mind,
In braided dance their murmurs join'd,
And all the bright uncounted pow'rs
Who feed on Heav'n's ambrosial flow'rs.   50
Where is the bard, whose soul can now
Its high presuming hopes avow?
Where he who thinks, with rapture blind,
This hallow'd work for him design'd?

3

High on some cliff, to Heav'n up-pil'd,
Of rude access, of prospect wild,
Where, tangled round the jealous steep,
Strange shades o'erbrow the valleys deep,
And holy Genii guard the rock,
Its glooms embrown, its springs unlock,   60
While on its rich ambitious head,
An Eden, like his own, lies spread:
I view that oak, the fancied glades among,
By which as Milton lay, his ev'ning ear,
From many a cloud that dropp'd ethereal dew,
Nigh spher'd in Heav'n its native strains could hear:
On which that ancient trump he reach'd was hung;
    Thither oft, his glory greeting,
    From Waller's myrtle shades retreating,
With many a vow from Hope's aspiring tongue,   70
My trembling feet his guiding steps pursue;
    In vain—such bliss to one alone,
    Of all the sons of soul was known,
    And Heav'n, and Fancy, kindred pow'rs,
    Have now o'erturn'd th' inspiring bow'rs,
Or curtain'd close such scene from ev'ry future view.

■ William Collins represents a line of development in eighteenth-
century poetry which is divergent from, if not a repudiation of, the neoclassical school. Literary historians treat him as a disciple of Spenser,
Shakespeare, and Milton, as well as the introducer, along with Joseph
and Thomas Warton and Thomas Gray, of certain romantic tendencies
and elements in eighteenth-century poetry. His "Ode on the Poetical

Character," which critics and students have found to be his most obscure work, indicates a number of points in which his views differ from those of many of his contemporaries. We may examine the poem as an important example of eighteenth-century poetry, but it is necessary, first, to interpret its meaning line by line.

Collins opens the poem by recalling an episode in the *Faerie Queene,* Book IV, Canto V, in which there is a tourney held to test the chastity of a number of ladies. Only one, Amoret, is able to wear a magic girdle, Cestus, which in classical mythology belonged to Aphrodite (Venus) and had the power to awaken love. In the *Faerie Queene,* Spenser makes the girdle a test of chastity. The unchaste are not able to put it on or wear it, despite their efforts to do so. Collins refers to the girdle as "cest." His references in the strophe to "chaste" and "virgin-fame" show he knows Spenser's treatment, but as the poem progresses it becomes evident that Collins is using the girdle as a symbol of the endowment of the true poet. The poet uses it to gird his "prophetic loins." It is the gift of Fancy. His understanding of the role of the poet is evident in his calling the gift of poetic speech "the godlike gift." It is, like that of the prophet, the gift of seeing visions.

The mythology which Collins uses in explaining the poetical character is pagan, although some aspects of it, such as the comparison of the imagination and the creations of the poet to the mind of God and his acts of creation, had been assimilated into the commentaries on poetry written by Renaissance critics like Sidney and Tasso. In the antistrophe he says that the magic girdle, the "band," according to legend was woven on the same day Zeus took thought and thereby created the sky, the earth, the streams, forests, and ocean (the "main," line 28). The Creator placed Fancy, by whom He had been woo'd (line 29), upon "his sapphire throne." Thereafter in the vaults of heaven, swelling sounds, apparently musical, signifying "love" and "mercy" were heard. (In these lines there is a strong suggestion of the Christian concept of heaven and Deity: the sapphire throne, the indirect reference to seraphim, and the attributes of love and mercy. This mixing of Christian and pagan stories is, of course, common in English poetry, as, for example, the *Faerie Queene* and *Paradise Lost.* It was opposed, however, by many neoclassical poets and critics.) Then Fancy herself, on this same day of creation, breathed her magic notes from the sky, and the poet, with his innate gift for creating further life, was born.

The reference to the "rich-hair'd youth of morn" (line 39) has been interpreted in different ways: as the sun or as the poet. Actually, there is no need for choosing either; both meanings are acceptable. Apollo, who was celebrated in Greek legend for his manly beauty and golden locks, was, among his many functions, god of the sun, of prophecy, of poetry, and of music. The poet, like the sun and like Apollo, nurtures life. In the next few lines (41–50), Collins mentions the characteristics he associates with inspired poetry. The magic girdle, "the sainted growing woof," keeps the poet from "dang'rous passions," but not from "ecstatic Wonder." Indeed, it brings him close to "Truth" and the mysterious, "the shad'wy tribes of Mind." "Truth" gave the "tarsel's eyes" (the tarsel is the falcon) their sharp vision. There is the suggestion, certainly, that Truth has given similar powers to the poet. Furthermore, there are divine powers, "bright uncounted pow'rs," on which the poet draws. The role of poet, he is saying, is tremendous, but where now, he asks (lines 51–53), is the poet capable of undertaking it?

In the epode he says there is a region wherein poets have dwelt. It is a kind of Eden, close to heaven, but filled with strange glooms, wild prospects in which springs of water begin. Again there is a mixture of Christian and pagan story. To follow the implications in many of these lines (especially lines 55–67) it is necessary to recall a little of the classical mythology associated with Pegasus, the winged horse of the Muses. In *A Handbook of Classical Mythology** we read that on the occasion that the Muses "were contesting in song with the daughters of Pierus, streams stood still and Helicon lifted his height to the heavens. [Helicon, who was of gentle nature, had been changed into a mountain by the gods and had become the home of the Muses.] To check Helicon's growth Poseidon commanded Pegasus to strike the mountain, and where his hoof struck the fountain Hippocrene sprang forth, source of inspiration to all who drank of its waters. The springs Aganippe and Pirene also owed their origin to the hoof of Pegasus. Thus in later times he came to be regarded as the source of poetic inspiration." Collins refers to this region where the poets live as Eden, but the phrases "to Heav'n up-pil'd" and "springs unlock" suggest that he is thinking of Helicon. He adds, by implication in the latter part of the epode, that this Eden is not the home of neoclassical poets, who began with Waller (see pages 192–194), but of poets like Milton, who could himself create such "fancied glades." Milton is an "oak" and belongs among these glades, but Waller, whose poetic imagination was slighter, lived among the "myrtle shades." Phrases like "glooms embrown" and "ev'ning ear" suggest that poetry at least approaches the regions of the occult. Poets are "sons of soul." In the final lines (71–76) he does not conclude, as the reader might expect, that poets should attempt to repossess the "fancied glades." He says rather that he himself has attempted to follow Milton's steps but has attempted it in vain. "Heav'n and Fancy," the two sources or powers behind poetry, having recognized that Milton had achieved the ultimate, have denied their powers to later poets. This great tribute to Milton has caused at least one scholar to say that the poem is an ode "on the poetical character of Milton." It is probably closer to the truth to say that the poem is about what the title indicates, "Ode on the Poetical

* New York: F. S. Crofts and Co., 1942, pp. 206–207.

Character." Milton is Collins' supreme example of that character, but if Collins had held at the end to what is evidently the theme of his poem he would more appropriately have concluded, as Woodhouse has put it, with a statement of "his belief in the primacy of the imagination and in its creative activity."

That Collins was primarily preoccupied with this subject is evident from the fact that so much in his poetry is concerned, at least by implication, with the art of poetry. His view of poetry, as we should expect, is to be found in his poems. The nature of his poetry has been excellently although not altogether sympathetically, characterized by Samuel Johnson in *Lives of the English Poets*:

> He had employed his mind chiefly upon works of fiction and subjects of fancy, and by indulging some peculiar habits of thought, was *eminently delighted with those flights of imagination which pass the bounds of nature* and to which the mind is reconciled only by a passive acquiescence in popular traditions. He loved fairies, genii, giants, and monsters; he delighted to rove through the meanders of enchantment, to gaze on the magnificence of golden palaces, to repose by the waterfalls of Elysian gardens. . . . The grandeur of wildness and the novelty of extravagance were always desired by him. . . . This idea which he had formed of excellence led him to oriental fictions and *allegorical imagery*.

We have, in examining "Ode on the Poetical Character," seen that Collins in this poem at least did employ his mind with a subject of "fancy," that he passed beyond the "bounds of nature" or the everyday world to which the Augustan poets held close, that he delighted in the regions and creatures "of enchantment," that his enchanted world was wild and rugged, and that he did use, as with "Eden," "cest," and "Young Fancy," what Johnson called "allegorical imagery." And that he used "popular tradition" is also evident in his allusions to the *Faerie Queene*, classical myth and Christian symbolism.

Johnson's qualified approval of Collins' poetry and his singling out certain characteristics that fall outside the point of view and esthetic he himself accepts suggest that to some considerable extent Collins was moving in a direction counter to the major tendency of his time. No era can be explained in a few neat tags, of course, but a few generalizations can be made. (Such generalizations can be qualified in the light of the actual practice and theory of any figure in the given period.) Most scholars and critics would probably agree with Mr. Woodhouse that the "Neoclassical age in England exhibits a singular absence of the idealizing impulse: its realism extends from subject to thought and tone. . . . but it also escapes the sentimentality and pseudo-idealism of the next age." Woodhouse means that in Dryden or Pope or Johnson we find a strong tendency to stay close to the actual, everyday world. It is no

accident that so much satire was written in the neoclassical period. But
the period also had a tendency "to exalt the thinking head at the expense of the feeling heart." And it is quite understandable, although not
laudable, that a "sentimental movement" would begin in the same period as a reaction against the satire and the cynicism that developed in
those who were too narrowly preoccupied with their everyday world. Accompanying the sentimental poetry was a poetry in which a great emphasis was put upon strong feelings or passion. (Notice in "Ode on the
Poetical Character" how Collins includes references to "rapture" and
"passions." The entire poem is conceived in terms of grandeur and strong
feelings.) This emphasis on strong feeling in Collins' poetry is one of the
germs of romanticism.

The emphasis on imagination, which is of course the center of "Ode
on the Poetical Character," was another augury of romanticism. Actually, neither of these emphases can be considered separately: they are
both a part of the reaction against the neoclassical preoccupation with
reason and "nature" and the avoidance of flights of fancy or imagination. The neoclassicists did not allow the imagination to create forms
of passionate idealism. (As a consequence, incidentally, there is no great
tragic vision in the poetry of the eighteenth century.) In the literary
criticism of the period we can find certain tenets which explain these
emphases.

The word *nature* in the eighteenth century was used as a kind of
talisman, a word of all work and many meanings. Whereas we in the
twentieth century pride ourselves on "facing the facts," those in the
eighteenth century tended to be proud of being "in accord with nature."
This could mean innumerable things, some of which were mentioned in
our comments on the doctrine of generalization in the discussion of "The
Vanity of Human Wishes." Nature was understood, by many at least, as
transcending anything the imagination might conceive. Thus in James
Thomson's "Spring" we find:

> But who can paint
> Like Nature? Can imagination boast,
> Amid its gay creation, hues like hers?

We in the twentieth century might ask why imagination, which is
certainly a part of nature, was not given a more important role in systems
of critical thought that developed around the term *nature*. An adequate
answer to the question would entail a large-scale study of the intellectual climate of the neoclassical period and of periods before it, but
quite possibly an important part of the answer would be that the neoclassical world had a great faith in the power of reason and the methods of science. Another part of the answer might be that the neoclassical world was suspicious of the kinds of thought and literary expression

that produced myth and what they viewed as frenzied or nonrational language. The imagination had produced or had been responsible for these myths and this frenzied language. Therefore it should be held in check. Other aspects of the mind, such as reason and judgment, should be stressed. In a famous piece of criticism, *Answer to Davenant*, by the philosopher Thomas Hobbes we read: "Judgement begets the strength and structure, and Fancy begets the ornaments of a poem." * There was also a strong tendency to associate imagination with the memory and with the making of images rather than with the creation of large concepts. Quite often, then, the word *imagination* or *fancy* was used in a pejorative sense; and sometimes the terms *wit* and *invention* were used in contexts where we should employ the term *imagination*. The use of the term *imagination* in the sense of the creation of large visions or systems of belief seems to have been most infrequent. It is, the neoclassicists would say, the poet's role to "copy nature," to discover the archetypal patterns in nature. Thus the emphasis is on a term like *invention* rather than one like *imagination*.

The attitudes of the neoclassical poets are fairly clear: reason and judgment should be stressed. As a consequence, they emphasized the employment of a language and a view of the world that was ordered, rational, unmysterious, and rather commonplace. In the light of these brief comments on the neoclassical mind certain elements in the work of Collins can, in contrast, be seen more clearly. He stresses the creative power of the imagination rather than the doctrine of imitation. He would have the poet body forth a world of fancy quite unlike the everyday world. He would readmit strong feeling into poetry. And he would have poets strive to conceive a realm filled with symbols of ideal beauties. (Compare Collins' "Ode" with Coleridge's "Dejection: An Ode," (p. 403.)

Collins' own poetry, however, has only a subdued and sober kind of feeling, not the kind of passion that was to appear in Shelley's and Byron's poetry. His tone and mood tend to be pensive and elegiac. There is a kind of decorum informing and partly counteracting his literal profession about the need for poetry to be highly imaginative and passionate. One feels often that Collins comes perilously close to being artificial or "literary" in the pejorative sense. He is perceptive enough to see and desire to achieve those virtues in poetry that lie outside the Augustan esthetic, but he does not achieve them as they had been achieved by Shakespeare or Milton or as they would be achieved by later romantics. Nor does he have the strong, if restricted, virtues of the Augustans. Perhaps it is fair to say there is distinction and skill but no great strength in Collins.

....

* See *Critical Essays of the Seventeenth Century*, Joel E. Spingarn, ed. (New York: Oxford University Press, 1908), II, 59.

Ode to Evening

If aught of oaten stop, or pastoral song,
May hope, chaste Eve, to soothe thy modest ear,
   Like thy own solemn springs,
   Thy springs and dying gales,

O nymph reserved, while now the bright-haired sun
Sits in yon western tent, whose cloudy skirts,
   With brede ethereal wove,
   O'erhang his wavy bed:

Now air is hushed, save where the weak-eyed bat,
With short shrill shriek, flits by on leathern wing,   10
   Or where the beetle winds
   His small but sullen horn,

As oft he rises 'midst the twilight path,
Against the pilgrim borne in heedless hum:
   Now teach me, maid composed,
   To breathe some softened strain,

Whose numbers, stealing through thy dark'ning vale,
May not unseemly with its stillness suit,
   As, musing slow, I hail
   Thy genial loved return!   20

For when thy folding-star arising shows
His paly circlet, at his warning lamp
   The fragrant Hours, and elves
   Who slept in flowers the day,

And many a nymph who wreaths her brows with sedge,
And sheds the fresh'ning dew, and, lovelier still,
   The pensive Pleasures sweet,
   Prepare thy shadowy car.

Then lead, calm vot'ress, where some sheety lake
Cheers the lone hearth, or some time-hallowed pile   30
   Or upland fallows gray
   Reflect its last cool gleam.

But when chill blust'ring winds, or driving rain,
Forbid my willing feet, be mine the hut

That from the mountain's side
Views wilds, and swelling floods,

And hamlets brown, and dim-discovered spires,
And hears their simple bell, and marks o'er all
    Thy dewy fingers draw
    The gradual dusky veil.   40

While Spring shall pour his show'rs, as oft he wont,
And bathe thy breathing tresses, meekest Eve;
    While Summer loves to sport
    Beneath thy ling'ring light;

While sallow Autumn fills thy lap with leaves;
Or Winter, yelling through the troublous air,
    Affrights thy shrinking train,
    And rudely rends thy robes;

So long, sure-found beneath the sylvan shed,
Shall Fancy, Friendship, Science, rose-lipped Health,   50
    Thy gentlest influence own,
    And hymn thy fav'rite name!

■   1. Are there in "Ode to Evening" any verbal echoes from "Lyci-das" (page 209)?

2. Does the poet's response to evening seem exaggerated? (You may want to compare your comment with that of Yvor Winter's in his *Defense of Reason*, [New York, Swallow-Morrow, 1947], pp. 50–51.)

Ode

Written in the Beginning of the Year 1746

How sleep the brave who sink to rest
By all their country's wishes bless'd!
When Spring, with dewy fingers cold,
Returns to deck their hallow'd mould,
She there shall dress a sweeter sod
Than Fancy's feet have ever trod.

By fairy hands their knell is rung;
By forms unseen their dirge is sung;
There Honour comes, a pilgrim gray,
To bless the turf that wraps their clay;
And Freedom shall awhile repair,
To dwell a weeping hermit there!

1. Are the symbolic figures in this poem easily visualized?

2. Compare the imagery in this poem with Blake's in "Holy Thursday" (p. 344). Which of the two leaves you with the greater sense of the actuality of the themes treated? Why?

Dirge in *Cymbeline*

Sung by Guiderus and Arviragus over Fidele,
Supposed to Be Dead

To fair Fidele's grassy tomb
    Soft maids and village hinds shall bring
Each opening sweet, of earliest bloom,
    And rifle all the breathing spring.

No wailing ghost shall dare appear,
    To vex with shrieks this quiet grove;
But shepherd lads assemble here,
    And melting virgins own their love.

No withered witch shall here be seen,
    No goblins lead their nightly crew;   10
The female fays shall haunt the green,
    And dress thy grave with pearly dew.

The red-breast oft at evening hours
    Shall kindly lend his little aid,
With hoary moss, and gathered flowers,
    To deck the ground where thou art laid.

When howling winds, and beating rain,
    In tempests shake the sylvan cell,
Or 'midst the chase on every plain,
    The tender thought on thee shall dwell.   20

Each lonely scene shall thee restore,
    For thee the tear be duly shed;
Beloved till life can charm no more,
    And mourned, till pity's self be dead.

Ode to Simplicity

O thou, by Nature taught
To breathe her genuine thought,
In numbers warmly pure, and sweetly strong;

Who first, on mountains wild,
    In Fancy, loveliest child,
Thy babe, or Pleasure's, nursed the powers of song!

    Thou, who, with hermit heart,
    Disdain'st the wealth of art,
And gauds, and pageant weeds, and trailing pall;
    But com'st a decent maid,   10
    In Attic robe arrayed,
O chaste, unboastful nymph, to thee I call;

    By all the honeyed store
    On Hybla's thymy shore;
By all her blooms, and mingled murmurs dear;
    By her whose lovelorn woe
    In evening musings slow
Soothèd sweetly sad Electra's poet's ear:

    By old Cephisus deep,
    Who spread his wavy sweep,   20
In warbled wanderings, round thy green retreat;
    On whose enameled side,
    When holy Freedom died,
No equal haunt allured thy future feet.

    O sister meek of Truth,
    To my admiring youth,
Thy sober aid and native charms infuse!
    The flowers that sweetest breathe,
    Though Beauty culled the wreath,
Still ask thy hand to range their ordered hues.   30

    While Rome could none esteem
    But virtue's patriot theme,
You loved her hills, and led her laureat band:
    But stayed to sing alone
    To one distinguished throne;
And turned thy face, and fled her altered land.

    No more, in hall or bower,
    The passions own thy power;
Love, only love, her forceless numbers mean;
    For thou hast left her shrine;   40
    Nor olive more, nor vine,
Shall gain thy feet to bless the servile scene.

Though taste, though genius, bless
  To some divine excess,
Faints the cold work till thou inspire the whole;
  What each, what all supply,
  May court, may charm, our eye;
Thou, only thou, canst raise the meeting soul!

  Of these let others ask,
  To aid some mighty task,   50
I only seek to find thy temperate vale;
  Where oft my reed might sound
  To maids and shepherds round,
And all thy sons, O Nature, learn my tale.

William Blake

(1757–1827)

■■■■■■■■■■

WILLIAM BLAKE was the son of a London hosier of comfortable means. Stories are told of the angelic visions he said he had as a child. He attended a drawing school when he was ten years old, and a few years later served an apprenticeship to an engraver. His marriage to Catherine Boucher, an uneducated woman, was very happy. In 1783, the year after the marriage, he published his first volume, *Poetical Sketches*. In 1787 he and his wife designed and engraved *Songs of Innocence*, which had been rejected by a number of publishers. About this time he became associated with political and religious radicals like Priestly, Tom Paine, Godwin, and Mary Wollstonecraft. *Songs of Experience* appeared in 1794. His art was exhibited at the Royal Academy for the first time in 1780 and for the last time in 1808. After that Blake was intent upon illustrations for his prophetic books and for the *Divine Comedy*.

Suggested Readings

MAX PLOWMAN, *An Introduction to the Study of Blake* (New York: E. P. Dutton & Co., Inc., 1927).

ALFRED KAZIN, "Introduction," in *The Portable Blake*. New York: The Viking Press, Inc., 1946.

MARK SCHORER, "The Source and Use of Metaphor," in *William Blake*. New York: Henry Holt & Co., pp. 93–148.

336   POEMS FOR STUDY

The scientific movement of the seventeenth and eighteenth centuries as reflected in the writing of men like Sir Francis Bacon, René Descartes, Sir Isaac Newton, Thomas Hobbes, John Locke, David Hume, and others may be said to have given rise to a climate of opinion in which many poets found it difficult to thrive. To state the matter generally, poets like Shakespeare or Marlowe could feel themselves to be living in a universe in which man and his ideals—his belief in an inherent order or hierarchy of being,* as in the obedience a wife owed her husband or a citizen his king, or the primary and inherent importance of love as a force for good in the universe—played a central role. Man could feel somewhat at home or at ease in such a world. But it is true that certain beliefs, such as that man's fate might be read in the stars or that such heavenly bodies as the stars were incorruptible, were sometimes rationalized or deduced from certain metaphysical assumptions. Such beliefs were, thanks to scientific observations, proved false. The new scientific discoveries, which were quite naturally applauded, gave rise to a somewhat uncritical faith in the scientific method, which unfortunately, was not without certain limitations in the seventeenth and eighteenth centuries.

Perhaps one of the keys to this discussion can be stated this way: The medieval world, concerned with man's mind and moral being, fell into the error of believing the external world or the universe to be quite in accord with certain of his desires or needs. The primary focus of medieval knowledge may be said to be *subjective*. The primary emphasis of modern knowledge, beginning with the scientific movements of the seventeenth century, has tended to be *objective,* focused on the laws of the external universe and somewhat indifferent to man's feelings about the world. If the focus either way is held in too rigorous a fashion certain limitations will become apparent.

We have already noted the inclination of the medieval mind to distort the nature of the physical universe. It is also true, however, that the ideal of many a scientific-minded philosopher in the seventeenth or eighteenth century was to play down or disregard anything that might be labeled *subjective*. Physics, for example, emphasized the objective qualities of matter, weight, size, shape, but it ignored the subjective qualities, color, smell, feel. The objective qualities were called "primary," the subjective "secondary." Physicists looked upon *their* view of the world as philosophical knowledge. There is no question at all about the efficiency of this method for treating the objective, the quantitative, and the measurable. The trouble began as a consequence of devaluating the subjective, the personally imagined, the qualitative, and the immeasurable. The real world was held to be the material outer realm of the functioning universe, with its laws that could

* See, for example, E. M. W. Tillyard, *The Elizabethan World Picture* (New York: The Macmillan Company, 1944).

be stated mathematically and neatly. This view was looked upon as the sole truth or a superior brand of truth. The claims of personal imagination, art, religion, and other forms of philosophy were often denied any strong validity. One student of these developments, E. A. Burtt, has stated the history in these terms:

> It was of the greatest consequence for succeeding thought that now the great Newton's authority was squarely behind that view of the cosmos which saw in man a puny, irrelevant spectator (so far as a being wholly imprisoned in a dark room can be called such) of the vast mathematical system whose regular motions according to mechanical principles constituted the world of nature. . . . The world that people had thought themselves living in—a world rich with colour and sound . . . speaking everywhere of purposive harmony and creative ideals— was crowded now into minute corners in the brains of scattered organic beings. The really important world outside was a world, hard, cold, colourless, silent and dead—a world of quantity, a world of mathematically computable motions in mechanical regularity. The world of qualities as immediately perceived by man became just a curious and quite minor effect of that infinite machine, beyond. In Newton, the Cartesian metaphysics, ambiguously interpreted and stripped of its distinctive claim for serious philosophical consideration, finally overthrew Aristotelianism, and became the predominant world-view of modern times.*

Many of the poems of Blake, who looked upon Bacon and Newton as destructive agents, can be understood more easily against the background of this account.

To the Muses

Whether on Ida's shady brow,
  Or in the chambers of the East,
The chambers of the sun that now
  From ancient melody have ceased;

Whether in Heaven ye wander fair,
  Or the green corners of the earth,
Or the blue regions of the air,
  Where the melodious winds have birth;

Whether on crystal rocks ye rove,
  Beneath the bosom of the sea

---

* *The Metaphysical Foundations of Modern Science* (New York: Harcourt, Brace and Co., pp. 236–237).

Wandering in many a coral grove,
    Fair Nine, forsaking Poetry;

How have you left the ancient love
    That bards of old enjoyed in you!
The languid strings do scarcely move;
    The sound is forced, the notes are few!

■   1. Does this poem suggest that Blake approved of most eighteenth-century poetic fashions?
    2. What elements did he want to see restored to poetry?

Auguries of Innocence

To see a world in a grain of sand
And a Heaven in a wild flower,
Hold Infinity in the palm of your hand
And Eternity in an hour.

A robin redbreast in a cage
Puts all Heaven in a rage.
A dove-house filled with doves and pigeons
Shudders Hell through all its regions.
A dog starved at his master's gate
Predicts the ruin of the state.   10
A horse misused upon the road
Calls to Heaven for human blood.
Each outcry of the hunted hare
A fibre from the brain does tear.
A skylark wounded in the wing,
A cherubim does cease to sing.
The game cock clipped and armed for fight
Does the rising sun affright.
Every wolf's and lion's howl
Raises from Hell a human soul.   20
The wild deer wandering here and there
Keeps the human soul from care.
The lamb misused breeds public strife
And yet forgives the butcher's knife.
That bat that flits at close of eve
Has left the brain that won't believe.
The owl that calls upon the night
Speaks the unbeliever's fright.

He who shall hurt the little wren
Shall never be beloved by men. 30
He who the ox to wrath had moved
Shall never be by woman loved.
The wanton boy that kills the fly
Shall feel the spider's enmity.
He who torments the chafer's sprite
Weaves a bower in endless night.
The caterpillar on the leaf
Repeats to thee thy mother's grief.
Kill not the moth nor butterfly
For the Last Judgment draweth nigh. 40
He who shall train the horse for war
Shall never pass the polar bar.
The beggar's dog and widow's cat,
Feed them and thou wilt grow fat.
The gnat that sings his summer's song
Poison gets from slander's tongue.
The poison of the snake and newt
Is the sweat of envy's foot.
The poison of the honey bee
Is the artist's jealousy. 50
The prince's robes and beggar's rags
Are toadstools on the miser's bags.
The truth that's told with bad intent
Beats all the lies you can invent.
It is right it should be so;
Man was made for joy and woe;
And when this we rightly know
Through the world we safely go.
Joy and woe are woven fine,
A clothing for the soul divine; 60
Under every grief and pine
Runs a joy with silken twine.
The babe is more than swaddling bands
Throughout all human lands.
Tools were made, and born were hands
Every farmer understands.
Every tear from every eye
Becomes a babe in eternity.
This is caught by females bright
And returned to its own delight. 70
The bleat, the bark, bellow and roar
Are waves that beat on heaven's shore.
The babe that weeps the rod beneath

Writes revenge in realms of death.
The beggar's rags, fluttering in air
Does the rags of heaven tear.
The soldier, armed with sword and gun,
Palsied strikes the summer's sun.
The poor man's farthing is worth more
Than all the gold on Afric's shore.   80
One mite wrung from the lab'rer's hands
Shall buy and sell the miser's lands,
Or if protected from on high
Does that whole nation sell and buy.
He who mocks the infant's faith
Shall be mocked in age and death.
He who shall teach the child to doubt
The rotting grave shall ne'er get out.
He who respects the infant's faith
Triumphs over hell and death.   90
The child's toys and the old man's reasons
Are the fruits of the two seasons.
The questioner who sits so sly
Shall never know how to reply.
He who replies to words of doubt
Doth put the light of knowledge out.
The strongest poison ever known
Came from Caesar's laurel crown.
Naught can deform the human race
Like to the arm'rer's iron brace.   100
When gold and gems adorn the plow
To peaceful arts shall envy bow.
A riddle or a cricket's cry
Is to doubt a fit reply.
The emmet's inch and eagle's mile
Make lame philosophy to smile.
He who doubts from what he sees
Will ne'er believe, do what you please.
If the sun and moon should doubt,   110
They'd immediately go out.
To be in a passion you good may do,
But no good if a passion is in you.
The whore and gambler, by the state
Licenced, build that nation's fate.
The harlot's cry from street to street
Shall weave Old England's winding sheet.
The winner's shout, the loser's curse,
Dance before dead England's hearse.

Every night and every morn
Some to misery are born.   120
Every morn and every night
Some are born to sweet delight.
Some are born to sweet delight,
Some are born to endless night.
We are led to believe a lie
When we see *with,* not *through,* the eye,
Which was born in a night, to perish in a night,
When the soul slept in beams of light.
God appears, and God is Light
To those poor souls who dwell in night,   130
But does a human form display
To those who dwell in realms of day.

■ "Auguries of Innocence," an unfinished poem, may be read as
Blake's denial of the impersonal mechanical view of the world held by
the physicist and a reassertion of the older view whereby the great universe finds itself reflected in a miniature way in a small object, such as a
leaf or a grain of sand, and whereby man finds his own views and moral
principles symbolized or verified in various parts of the universe. Blake
wanted to see man as the center of the world and involved in its processes,
not separate and divorced from it.

Blake, as many students of his work have pointed out, seems indebted to the teachings of Emanuel Swedenborg (1688–1772). One of
Swedenborg's doctrines, called "correspondences" (which, incidentally,
later influenced symbolist poets in France and their followers in England
and the United States) was as follows: "The whole natural world corre-
sponds to the spiritual world, and not merely the natural world in general, but also every particular of it." Blake said it was the function of
the poet's imagination to perceive such correspondences. The opening
four lines of "Auguries of Innocence" state the belief that man's con-
cerns with heaven, eternity, and infinity may be seen to be reflected in
physical objects, just as the world itself is reflected in a grain of sand.
These four lines then may be said to be a metaphorical and somewhat
generalized statement of the older view of the world and of the doctrine
of correspondences.

Then the subject matter shifts to a more specialized aspect of the
older view. It shifts, with some lapses and perhaps irrelevancies, to what
has been called "a sacramental view" of the universe. This view, which
is also implicit in "The Rime of the Ancient Mariner," suggests that the
universe is held together in the harmony of love and of goodness. It pre-
supposes an over-all force in the universe that sponsors and is itself love
and goodness. Any immorality, such as wanton destruction of a part of

the universe or unnecessary interfering with the freedom of living creatures, is an offense against the harmony of the universe and therefore against love and law themselves. Thus the wanton killing of the moth or fly is an offense against the nature of things, but the killing of the fly by the spider, or the lamb by the butcher is in the nature of things and therefore neither wanton nor immoral. To cage the robin or dove is to interfere with its natural freedom and therefore to offend the entire universe with which, in freedom, they would be in harmonious relationship.

Interwoven, in a somewhat jerky manner, with this subject in "Auguries of Innocence," are statements about the necessity for faith in the "sacramental view." This again may be read as the poet's opposition to the new faith, which gives credence only to scientifically demonstrated facts. To disbelieve in the "sacramental view" is to offend against the moral order. The skeptic, the constant questioner, never has the important answers. The answers, according to the context of the poem, one may assume to be related to an awareness of the moral order and the harmonious interrelationship of all nature.

The couplet about using passion but not being used by it (lines 111–112) obviously relates to the principal theme of the poem. To be caught up in a passion is an offense against the harmonies of the universe.

In the six lines about the evils sponsored or permitted by England (lines 113–118) there is an exploration of the interrelationship of all things but circumscribed here by national boundaries. If the wounding of a skylark causes the cherubim in heaven to cease singing, so too does the countenancing of the harlot or the gambler kill the spiritual life of all England.

The lines on the misery to which some are born in contrast to the joy that is the lot of others (lines 119–124) do not seem, at first, to tie in very neatly with the general subject of the poem. They serve to enlarge the reader's awareness of the complexity of Blake's view of the world. They make it clear, that is, that Blake is not presenting a sentimental, simplified view of the world—he is not saying that a renewal of faith would, by renewing the harmony of the universe, make every life a "sweet delight."

The presence of evil in the universe, however, does not prevent Blake's condemning the acceptance of a mechanical view of the universe. The eye should not be used to give us mere pictures of the universe but to present to the mind and imagination suggestions that enable us to see the correspondences between one part of the universe and another. The man who sees himself as separate from or uninvolved in the rest of the universe lives in darkness. For the contemporary of Blake the references to light would have aroused associations with the works of Sir Isaac Newton, the great physicist, who had written *Principia* and *Opticks* (1704). The latter book especially influenced greatly the thinking and the imagery of poets writing during the eighteenth century.* And most of these poets, as Englishmen generally, all but deified Newton. Pope, for example, wrote, "God said, 'Let Newton be!' and all was Light!" Blake, of course, said he despised Newton, along with Bacon, Locke, and others like them, because as a scientist Newton saw the world as mechanical, impersonal, and indifferent to man. In Newton's frame of reference, for example, light was outside of man and could be measured objectively, and therefore to speak of light as colored, he said, was to speak subjectively, "grossly," like "vulgar people." To Blake, the only significance light had was the way it appeared to man. In this poem he used light to symbolize the knowledge that men of faith have. His comment that

> God is Light
> To those poor souls who dwell in night,

would seem to be an ironical reference to those who looked upon the Newtonian physics and world view as the ultimate truth. In Blake's view, they lived in ignorance, "in night." Those who were willing to see man involved in the universe could envision God as a "human form." They, not the Newtonians, lived in the light of truth, "in realms of day."

To the Evening Star

Thou fair-haired angel of the evening,
Now, whilst the sun rests on the mountains, light
Thy bright torch of love; thy radiant crown
Put on, and smile upon our evening bed!
Smile on our loves, and, while thou drawest the
Blue curtains of the sky, scatter thy silver dew
On every flower that shuts its sweet eyes
In timely sleep. Let thy west wind sleep on
The lake; speak silence with thy glimmering eyes,
And wash the dusk with silver. Soon, full soon,
Dost thou withdraw; then the wolf rages wide,
And the lion glares through the dun forest:
The fleeces of our flocks are covered with
Thy sacred dew: protect them with thine influence.

■ 1. Is there anything about the structure of this poem that relates it to Collins' "Ode to Evening" (p. 331)?

  2. Are the manner and tone of this poem closer to "Ode to Evening" than to Blake's own "Auguries of Innocence"?

....

* See, for example, Marjorie Nicolson, *Newton Demands the Muse* (Princeton: Princeton University Press, 1946).

3. Scan this poem. Is it metrically regular or not?

4. Why is the reader forced to pause in reading "speak silence with thy glimmering eyes"?

The Lamb

Little lamb, who made thee?
Dost thou know who made thee?
Gave thee life, and bid thee feed,
By the stream and o'er the mead;
Gave thee clothing of delight,
Softest clothing, wooly, bright;
Gave thee such a tender voice,
Making all the vales rejoice?
Little lamb, who made thee?
Dost thou know who made thee?

Little lamb, I'll tell thee,
Little lamb, I'll tell thee:
He is callèd by thy name,
For he calls himself a Lamb.
He is meek and he is mild;
He became a little child.
I a child, and thou a lamb,
We are callèd by his name.
Little lamb, God bless thee!
Little lamb, God bless thee!

Holy Thursday

'Twas on a Holy Thursday, their innocent faces clean,
The children walking two and two, in red and blue and green,
Grey-headed beadles walk'd before, with wands as white as snow;
Till into the high dome of Paul's they like Thames' waters flow.

O what a multitude they seem'd, these flowers of London town!
Seated in companies they sit with radiance all their own.
The hum of multitudes was there, but multitudes of lambs,
Thousands of little boys and girls raising their innocent hands.

Now like a mighty wind they raise to heaven the voice of song,
Or like harmonious thunderings the seats of Heaven among.
Beneath them sit the agèd men, wise guardians of the poor;
Then cherish pity, lest you drive an angel from your door.

■ 1. This poem is concerned with the charity children singing in St. Paul's in London. Blake in many of his poems, as in this one, shows his tremendous concern with social reforms. It has been said that this poem, "Holy Thursday," wears an ironic guise. In what sense is this true? How does the imagery support it?

2. Write a detailed account of the imagery. Why is the nature imagery as appropriate as the religious imagery?

A Cradle Song

Sleep, Sleep, beauty bright
Dreaming o'er the joys of night.
Sleep, Sleep: in thy sleep
Little sorrows sit and weep.

Sweet Babe, in thy face
Soft desires I can trace,
Secret joys and secret smiles,
Little pretty infant wiles.

As thy softest limbs I feel
Smiles as of the morning steal
O'er thy cheek and o'er thy breast
Where thy little heart does rest.

O, the cunning wiles that creep
In thy little heart asleep.
When thy little heart does wake,
Then the dreadful lightnings break.

From thy cheek and from thy eye
O'er the youthful harvests nigh
Infant wiles and infant smiles
Heaven and Earth of peace beguiles.

■ Is this a sentimental account of the innocence of infants?

Nurse's Song

When the voices of children are heard on the green
And whisperings are in the dale,
The days of my youth rise fresh in my mind,
My face turns green and pale.

Then come home, my children, the sun is gone down,
And the dews of night arise;
Your spring and your day are wasted in play,
And your winter and night in disguise.

■   Is this poem addressed to children? If not, to whom is it addressed?

The Sick Rose

O rose, thou art sick:
The invisible worm
That flies in the night,
In the howling storm,

Has found out thy bed
Of crimson joy,
And his dark secret love
Does thy life destroy.

■   It would seem that jealousy is the "invisible worm." Why is the imagery of this poem effective?

The Tiger

Tiger! Tiger! burning bright
In the forests of the night,
What immortal hand or eye
Could frame thy fearful symmetry?

In what distant deeps or skies
Burnt the fire of thine eyes?
On what wings dare he aspire?
What the hand dare seize the fire?

And what shoulder, and what art,
Could twist the sinews of thy heart?
And when thy heart began to beat,
What dread hand? and what dread feet?

What the hammer? what the chain?
In what furnace was thy brain?
What the anvil? what dread grasp
Dare its deadly terrors clasp?

When the stars threw down their spears,
And watered heaven with their tears,
Did he smile his work to see?
Did he who made the Lamb make thee?

Tiger! Tiger! burning bright
In the forests of the night,
What immortal hand or eye
Dare frame thy fearful symmetry?

1. One of the students of Blake's work, Mark Schorer, says this poem is to be read as a conflict between innocence and experience. The lamb, or innocence, is forced to turn into a tiger, or experience. Keeping this statement in mind, paraphrase this poem.

2. Interpret the poem also as the antithesis of spirit and matter, good and evil, love and wrath.

3. Why does the poet wonder about the Creator's attitude toward these conflicts?

4. Professor Schorer also says that in Blake's symbolism the stars signify eighteenth-century rationalism. Why should Blake consider rationalism to be in conflict with energy or experience?

The Sunflower

Ah, Sunflower! weary of time,
Who countest the steps of the Sun,
Seeking after that sweet golden clime
Where the traveler's journey is done:

Where the Youth pined away with desire,
And the pale Virgin shrouded in snow,
Arise from their graves, and aspire
Where my Sunflower wishes to go.

Can this poem be read as a protest against conventional restraints imposed on love? What is the significance of the sunflower?

The Garden of Love

I went to the Garden of Love,
And saw what I never had seen:
A chapel was built in the midst,
Where I used to play on the green.

And the gates of this chapel were shut,
And "Thou shalt not" writ over the door;
So I turned to the Garden of Love
That so many sweet flowers bore;

And I saw it was fillèd with graves,
And tombstones where flowers should be;
And priests in black gowns were walking their rounds,
And binding with briars my joys and desires.

1. Is this poem about the danger of hedging love in with too many restrictions? Justify your answer.

2. Is the poem complex enough, does it have enough detail, to justify the above statement? Do you feel, that is, that the poet not merely states his belief but establishes or proves it?

London

I wander through each chartered street,
Near where the chartered Thames does flow,
And mark in every face I meet
Marks of weakness, marks of woe.

In every cry of every man,
In every infant's cry of fear,
In every voice, in every ban,
The mind-forged manacles I hear.

How the chimney-sweeper's cry
Every blackening church appalls;
And the hapless soldier's sigh
Runs in blood down palace walls.

But most through midnight streets I hear
How the youthful harlot's curse
Blasts the new-born infant's tear,
And blights with plagues the marriage hearse.

1. This poem may be read as an attack on the social structure of London which blights lives and loves. What institutions are attacked?

2. Explain carefully the following: "mind-forged manacles," the soldier's sigh turning to blood, and the "marriage hearse."

A Poison Tree

I was angry with my friend:
I told my wrath, my wrath did end.
I was angry with my foe:
I told it not, my wrath did grow.

And I watered it in fears
Night and morning with my tears,
And I sunnèd it with smiles
And with soft deceitful wiles.

And it grew both day and night,
Till it bore an apple bright,
And my foe beheld it shine,
And he knew that it was mine—

And into my garden stole
When the night had veiled the pole;
In the morning, glad, I see
My foe outstretched beneath the tree.

■ Of the above poems, "Holy Thursday" and "The Lamb" are from *Songs of Innocence* and the rest through this poem are from *Songs of Experience.* Comment on the appropriateness of the inclusive titles.

Love's Secret

Never seek to tell thy love,
    Love that never told can be;
For the gentle wind does move
    Silently, invisibly.

I told my love, I told my love,
    I told her all my heart;
Trembling, cold, in ghastly fears,
    Ah! she did depart!

Soon as she was gone from me,
    A traveler came by,
Silently, invisibly:
    He took her with a sigh.

■ Attempt to set down what the poem implies.

Infant Sorrow

My mother groaned, my father wept;
Into the dangerous world I leapt,
Helpless, naked, piping loud,
Like a fiend hid in a cloud.

Struggling in my father's hands
Striving against my swaddling bands,
Bound and weary, I thought best
To sulk upon my mother's breast.

When I saw that rage was vain,
And to sulk would nothing gain,
Turning many a trick and wile,
I began to soothe and smile.

And I soothed day after day
Till upon the ground I stray;
And I smiled night after night,
Seeking only for delight.

And I saw before me shine
Clusters of the wandering vine,
And many a lovely flower and tree
Stretched their blossoms out to me.

My father then with holy look,
In his hands a holy book,
Pronounced curses on my head
And bound me in a mirtle shade.

Mock On

Mock on, mock on, Voltaire, Rousseau,
    Mock on, mock on; 'tis all in vain;
You throw but dust against the wind
    And the wind blows it back again.

And every stone becomes a gem
    Reflected in the beams divine;
Blown back, they blind the mocking eye,
    But still in Israel's paths they shine.

The atoms of Democritus
  And Newton's particles of light
Are sands upon the Red Sea shore,
  Where Israel's tents do shine so bright.

1. Compare the subject treated in this poem to that treated in "Auguries of Innocence."

2. Explain the development of the imagery, noting the way in which the "atoms" are used in different perspectives or with different emphases.

Milton

And did those feet in ancient time
  Walk upon England's mountains green?
And was the holy Lamb of God
  On England's pleasant pastures seen?

And did the Countenance Divine
  Shine forth upon our clouded hills?
And was Jerusalem builded here
  Among these dark Satanic mills?

Bring me my bow of burning gold!
  Bring me my arrows of desire!
Bring me my spear! O clouds, unfold!
  Bring me my chariot of fire!

I will not cease from mental fight,
  Nor shall my sword sleep in my hand,
Till we have built Jerusalem
  In England's green and pleasant land.

1. Judging from this poem, what do you believe Blake's opinion of the Industrial Revolution was?

2. Scan this poem, then discuss the effects of the metrical changes introduced in lines 2, 9, 10, 11, and 12.

William Wordsworth

(1770–1850)

■ ■ ■ ■ ■ ■ ■ ■ ■ ■

WILLIAM WORDSWORTH was born in the Lake Country of northern England, in the village of Cockermouth. His father, an attorney, belonged to the landed gentry. Wordsworth became an orphan while still a boy, having lost his mother when he was eight years old and his father five years later. Like so many other English poets, he studied at Cambridge, which he entered in 1787. He toured France, Switzerland, and northern Italy in the summer of 1790, and after being graduated from Cambridge in 1791 he went to live in France for about a year. At this time the French Revolution was in a turbulent phase, and Wordsworth was deeply impressed by the events and ideas he encountered. He was won over to revolutionary doctrines and the cause of France. During this same period his personal life was complicated by an affair with a French girl, Annette Vallon, who bore him a child, Caroline. He returned home in 1793, just before England's declaration of war on France. There followed a troubled, restless, and unhappy period, until in 1795 he settled with his sister Dorothy in Somersetshire, where his association with Coleridge soon began. After visiting in Germany for eight months (1798–1799), he settled in Grasmere, in the Lake Country. In 1802 he married a friend of his sister's, Mary Hutchinson. In 1814 he moved to Rydal Mount, where he remained the rest of his life. The years 1797 to 1807 had been the period of Wordsworth's most successful poetic activity, although he continued to write for many years. In the latter half of his life he became increasingly conservative in both politics and religion. Wordsworth was poet laureate of England from 1843, when he succeeded Robert Southey, until his death in 1850.

Suggested Readings

BASIL WILLEY, "On Wordsworth and the Locke Tradition," in *The Seventeenth Century Background*. London: Chatto & Windus, 1934, pp. 296–309.

F. R. LEAVIS, "Wordsworth," in *Revaluation*. New York: George W. Stewart, Publisher, 1947, pp. 154–202.

HERBERT READ, "Wordsworth's Philosophical Faith," *The Sewanee Review*, LVIII, 4 (Autumn, 1950), 564–585.

LIONEL TRILLING, "The Immortality Ode," in *The Liberal Imagination*. New York: Viking Press, 1950, pp. 129–153.

■ ■ ■ ■ ■ ■ ■ ■ ■

Despite the work of the eighteenth-century precursors of romanticism, Wordsworth, like Blake, deserves to be regarded as a revolutionary poet. His criticism of the practice and taste that prevailed when he began writing poetry, and especially his intentions and methods for writing a different kind of poetry, are set forth in his famous Preface to the 1800 edition of *Lyrical Ballads*. A reading of that prose testament is indispensable for an understanding of Wordsworth's poetry, as it relates to the literary and intellectual situation during which it appeared and reflects the poet's response to that situation. The way in which the Preface bears upon the poetry may be illustrated by this brief quotation:

> The principal object, then, proposed in these poems was to choose incidents and situations from common life, and to relate or describe them, throughout, as far as was possible in a selection of language really used by men, and, at the same time, to throw over them a certain coloring of imagination, whereby ordinary things should be presented to the mind in an unusual aspect; and further, and above all, to make these incidents and situations interesting by tracing in them, truly, though not ostentatiously, the primary laws of our nature: chiefly, as far as regards the manner in which we associate ideas in a state of excitement.

Here, as throughout the Preface, we can distinguish some of the issues with which Wordsworth was concerned in his reaction against neoclassical poetry and which we should therefore keep in mind in an examination of his own poetry. These issues may be listed as follows:

1. Language
2. Subject matter
3. A view of human nature
4. The relationship of the human being to the external world

A reading of the Preface, as well as of the poetry, shows that Wordsworth's views on each of these issues were logically related to each other. For example, he chose as his subject matter the life of people in "rural occupations" because such people "hourly communicate with the best objects [the beautiful and permanent forms of nature] from which the best part of language is originally derived; and because, from their rank in society and the sameness and narrow circle of their intercourse, being less under the influence of social vanity, they convey their feelings and notions in simple and unelaborated expressions." It would be a mistake and an oversimplification, however, to conclude that Wordsworth thought that he should write or that he was writing poetry in the language of rural folk, although in some of the poems he does approach such language. While rural folk appealed to him for a number of reasons, he emphasized the value of their language because it was a living language uncontaminated by fashions or literary influence or "the influence of social vanity." Throughout the Preface Wordsworth expresses his dissatisfaction with the language of the neoclassical poets, whose style and works were still in vogue when Wordsworth began writing. The term *poetic diction* had already appeared, and Wordsworth used it disparagingly in the Preface. For example, he claimed that in the *Lyrical Ballads* there could be found "little of what is usually called poetic diction; as much pains has been taken to avoid it as is ordinarily taken to produce it; this has been done for the reason already alleged, to bring my language near to the language of men." Wordsworth's "reason" was not only to bring his style near to one kind of language but to remove it from another kind.

Although the fact was not yet generally admitted, neoclassicism had already run its course, and its conventions of poetic composition were worn out and on the point of being abandoned. It is obvious that Wordsworth, at the end of the eighteenth century, was fully aware of the situation and was resolved to escape from it, among other ways, by resorting to a new kind of language—new with respect to the immediate past. His awareness that a poet writes at a stage in the tradition is indicated by his announced purpose of abstaining "from the use of many expressions, in themselves proper and beautiful, but which have been foolishly repeated by bad poets, till such feelings of disgust are connected with them as it is scarcely possible by any art to overpower." By "the language of men" as contrasted with poetic diction, Wordsworth meant not only the spoken language, and certainly not just the spoken language of a particular class, but also the language of "good prose." It is interesting to note that T. S. Eliot has praised Dryden for restoring to poetry the quality of the spoken language (more than a century before Wordsworth), and to recall that modern poetry began, in some respects, as a revolution against the poetic diction of the nineteenth century by restoring to poetry conversational and prosaic characteristics (more than a century after Wordsworth). The dissatisfaction with a poetic diction is a kind of realism, and it is well to remember that the romantic movement "began" with one of its principles being a return to realistic language. In the Preface Wordsworth argues that "poetry sheds no tears 'such as angels weep,' but natural human tears; she can boast of no celestial ichor that distinguishes her vital juices from that of prose; the same human blood circulates through the veins of them both."

The passage first quoted from the Preface states that Wordsworth's subject matter, at least in the *Lyrical Ballads,* was "incidents and situations from common life." In the same passage Wordsworth said that it was his intention to trace "the primary laws of our nature" in these incidents and situations. The primary laws refer to an account of human nature, a psychology which goes by the term *associationalism.* English associationalism derives from the philosophical teachings of Thomas Hobbes and John Locke. Despite certain large differences, both philosophers held that all aspects of human consciousness were, for each individual, developed from physical sensations. David Hartley, writing toward the middle of the eighteenth century and borrowing particularly from Locke, gave this theory the formulation with which Wordsworth was to become familiar and which remained the basis of his views on poetry and human nature. Wordsworth took from Hartley the belief that all thought derives from physical sensations. There are first the sensations and then, as a result of these, there are feelings which they produce. These feelings leave an impression on the organism; that is, the memory of them remains. From the accumulated memories the first ideas, or simple ideas, are developed. For example, after a number of repeated feelings of cold have become associated with each other in the memory, the idea of coldness is developed. Similarly, the ideas of pain and pleasure emerge, and eventually, through the association of simple ideas, complex ideas are developed—ideas such as those which underlie sentiments, moral attitudes, rational explanation, and creative and imaginative experience. For example, the ideas of love, beauty, truth, virtue, and knowledge are all complex ideas. References to this doctrine recur throughout the Preface. It is explicit in Wordsworth's statement that "our continued influxes of feeling are modified and directed by our thoughts, which are indeed the representatives of all our past feelings."

A likely reason for Wordsworth's sympathy with associationalism, in addition to his accepting it as fact, was that the doctrine accorded nicely with his attitude toward nature. Some of the eighteenth-century "forerunners" of romanticism—Gray, Collins, Thomson—had found nature an appropriate subject for poetry, or at least a usable material, and for Wordsworth nature was of central importance. With the Renaissance and the development of scientific thought, the here-and-now, this world as distinguished from a supernatural hereafter, had become of increasing importance in man's outlook. More and more the physical universe, nature, was accepted as the basic reality. In other words, a philosophical materialism developed alongside traditional Christianity. Wordsworth accepted materialism as the truth and, with the help of associationalism, interpreted it according to his own tendencies of thought and his needs as a poet. Man's mental and emotional experiences derived from physical sensations, and the sensations were produced by the objects of the external world. And thus man's experiences, both the earliest and the most mature, were ultimately linked with nature. Nature was, moreover, not simply a mechanism or so much inanimate matter but was, in its various forms, a living organism, and *living* in the sense that it was vitalized by a spirit or soul that inhered in all things. By analogy with the traditional body-soul concept, God had come to be considered as the soul of the physical universe. Consequently, to "commune with nature" was a kind of religious or spiritual experience, while at the same time it was dependent on physical sensation. Thus, for Wordsworth, sensationalism was consistent with a mystical attitude toward nature.

Implicit in Wordsworth's pantheistic naturalism was an emphasis on nature in its beautiful aspects and the belief that nature was essentially good in terms of human values. Although Wordsworth recommended a passive receptiveness before the forms of nature, he also insisted that man contributes something to the relationship between himself and the external world. Man is himself spiritual and it is only from the human point of view that nature has spiritual significance. Man and nature are complementary, and it is by interaction with each other, an interaction that begins with sensation, that the spirituality of each is made operative and realized:

> . . . I remember well
> That in life's every-day appearances
> I seemed about this time to gain clear sight
> Of a new world—a world, too, that was fit
> To be transmitted, and to other eyes
> Made visible; as ruled by those fixed laws
> Whence spiritual dignity originates,
> Which do both give it being and maintain
> A balance, an ennobling interchange
> Of action from without and from within;
> The excellence, pure function, and best power
> Both of the objects seen, and eye that sees.
>
> (*The Prelude*, XIII, ll. 367–379)

Wordsworth's Preface was admittedly an attempt to orient his audience to the kind of poetry he was writing, a poetry that was "new" not only in its language but also in the general outlook it reflected. He could hope to succeed in this attempt because his outlook was not really a break with established notions but rather a shift in emphasis. Unlike Blake, he accepted the scientific account of the universe and even admitted that the "remotest" scientific discoveries might some day become "proper objects of the poet's art." Whereas for most of the eighteenth century nature meant those physical laws by which the universe operated as a vast mechanism, for Wordsworth it meant the various forms of the universe as a physical organism. The well-ordered external mechanism was less important to him than internal associationalism. If the general temper of the neoclassicists is rationalism, an emphasis on logic and intellect, Wordsworth's may be called psychologism, an emphasis on feeling and sensibility. He would have agreed with Pope's statement that the proper study of mankind is man, but where Pope meant man in the light of social values and institutions, Wordsworth would have insisted also on the individual's psychological constitution and even on his isolation from his fellows:

Points have we all of us within our souls
Where all stand single.
                    (*The Prelude*, III, ll. 185–186)

Lines

*Composed a few miles above Tintern Abbey, on
revisiting the banks of the Wye during a tour.
July 13, 1798.*

Five years have past; five summers, with the length
Of five long winters! and again I hear
These waters, rolling from their mountain-springs
With a soft inland murmur.—Once again
Do I behold these steep and lofty cliffs,
That on a wild secluded scene impress
Thoughts of more deep seclusion; and connect
The landscape with the quiet of the sky.
The day is come when I again repose
Here, under this dark sycamore, and view   10
These plots of cottage-ground, these orchard-tufts,
Which at this season, with their unripe fruits,
Are clad in one green hue, and lose themselves
'Mid groves and copses. Once again I see
These hedge-rows, hardly hedge-rows, little lines
Of sportive wood run wild: these pastoral farms,
Green to the very door; and wreaths of smoke
Sent up, in silence, from among the trees!
With some uncertain notice, as might seem
Of vagrant dwellers in the houseless woods,   20
Or of some Hermit's cave, where by his fire
The Hermit sits alone.
                        These beauteous forms,
Through a long absence, have not been to me
As is a landscape to a blind man's eye:
But oft, in lonely rooms, and 'mid the din
Of towns and cities, I have owed to them,
In hours of weariness, sensations sweet,
Felt in the blood, and felt along the heart;
And passing even into my purer mind,   30
With tranquil restoration:—feelings too
Of unremembered pleasure: such, perhaps,
As have no slight or trivial influence
On that best portion of a good man's life,

His little, nameless, unremembered, acts
Of kindness and of love. Nor less, I trust,
To them I may have owed another gift,
Of aspect more sublime; that blessed mood,
In which the burthen of the mystery,
In which the heavy and the weary weight   40
Of all this unintelligible world,
Is lightened:—that serene and blessed mood,
In which the affections gently lead us on,—
Until, the breath of this corporeal frame
And even the motion of our human blood
Almost suspended, we are laid asleep
In body, and become a living soul:
While with an eye made quiet by the power
Of harmony, and the deep power of joy,
We see into the life of things.   50

                         If this
Be but a vain belief, yet, oh! how oft—
In darkness and amid the many shapes
Of joyless daylight; when the fretful stir
Unprofitable, and the fever of the world,
Have hung upon the beatings of my heart—
How oft, in spirit, have I turned to thee,
O sylvan Wye! thou wanderer thro' the woods,
How often has my spirit turned to thee!

    And now, with gleams of half-extinguished thought   60
With many recognitions dim and faint,
And somewhat of a sad perplexity,
The picture of the mind revives again:
While here I stand, not only with the sense
Of present pleasure, but with pleasing thoughts
That in this moment there is life and food
For future years. And so I dare to hope,
Though changed, no doubt, from what I was when first
I came among these hills; when like a roe
I bounded o'er the mountains, by the sides   70
Of the deep rivers, and the lonely streams,
Wherever nature led: more like a man
Flying from something that he dreads than one
Who sought the thing he loved. For nature then
(The coarser pleasures of my boyish days,
And their glad animal movements all gone by)
To me was all in all.—I cannot paint

What then I was. The sounding cataract
Haunted me like a passion: the tall rock,
The mountain, and the deep and gloomy wood,   80
Their colours and their forms, were then to me
An appetite; a feeling and a love,
That had no need for a remoter charm,
By thought supplied, nor any interest
Unborrowed from the eye.—That time is past,
And all its aching joys are now no more,
And all its dizzy raptures. Not for this
Faint I, nor mourn nor murmur; other gifts
Have followed; for such loss, I would believe,
Abundant recompense. For I have learned   90
To look on nature, not as in the hour
Of thoughtless youth; but hearing oftentimes
The still, sad music of humanity,
Nor harsh nor grating, though of ample power
To chasten and subdue. And I have felt
A presence that disturbs me with the joy
Of elevated thoughts; a sense sublime
Of something far more deeply interfused,
Whose dwelling is the light of setting suns,
And the round ocean and the living air,   100
And the blue sky, and in the mind of man:
A motion and a spirit, that impels
All thinking things, all objects of all thought,
And rolls through all things. Therefore am I still
A lover of the meadows and the woods,
And mountains; and of all that we behold
From this green earth; of all the mighty world
Of eye, and ear,—both what they half create,
And what perceive; well pleased to recognise
In nature and the language of the sense   110
The anchor of my purest thoughts, the nurse,
The guide, the guardian of my heart, and soul
Of all my moral being.

                  Nor perchance,
If I were not thus taught, should I the more
Suffer my genial spirits to decay:
For thou art with me here upon the banks
Of this fair river; thou my dearest Friend,
My dear, dear Friend; and in thy voice I catch
The language of my former heart, and read   120
My former pleasures in the shooting lights

Of thy wild eyes. Oh! yet a little while
May I behold in thee what I was once,
My dear, dear Sister! and this prayer I make,
Knowing that Nature never did betray
The heart that loved her; 'tis her privilege,
Through all the years of this our life, to lead
From joy to joy: for she can so inform
The mind that is within us, so impress
With quietness and beauty, and so feed   130
With lofty thoughts, that neither evil tongues,
Rash judgments, nor the sneers of selfish men,
Nor greetings where no kindness is, nor all
The dreary intercourse of daily life,
Shall e'er prevail against us, or disturb
Our cheerful faith, that all which we behold
Is full of blessings. Therefore let the moon
Shine on thee in thy solitary walk;
And let the misty mountain-winds be free
To blow against thee: and, in after years,   140
When these wild ecstasies shall be matured
Into a sober pleasure; when thy mind
Shall be a mansion for all lovely forms,
Thy memory be as a dwelling-place
For all sweet sounds and harmonies; oh! then,
If solitude, or fear, or pain, or grief
Should be thy portion, with what healing thoughts
Of tender joy wilt thou remember me,
And these my exhortations! Nor, perchance—
If I should be where I no more can hear   150
Thy voice, nor catch from thy wild eyes these gleams
Of past existence—wilt thou then forget
That on the banks of this delightful stream
We stood together; and that I, so long
A worshipper of Nature, hither came
Unwearied in that service: rather say
With warmer love—oh! with far deeper zeal
Of holier love. Nor wilt thou then forget
That after many wanderings, many years
Of absence, these steep woods and lofty cliffs,   160
And this green pastoral landscape, were to me
More dear, both for themselves and for thy sake!

■ This poem ends with an address to the poet's sister. The whole poem is a statement of Wordsworth's beliefs at the time he wrote it and is not far different from the kind of prose statement he might have made. Is the poem ever actually prosaic in the bad sense? Does the poem, in whole or in part, achieve a special tone and produce a distinctive poetic effect? Answer these questions by analyzing passages of your own choice.

Lucy Gray,
or Solitude

Oft I had heard of Lucy Gray:
And, when I crossed the wild,
I chanced to see at break of day
The solitary child.

No mate, no comrade Lucy knew;
She dwelt on a wide moor,
—The sweetest thing that ever grew
Beside a human door!

You yet may spy the fawn at play,
The hare upon the green;   10
But the sweet face of Lucy Gray
Will never more be seen.

"To-night will be a stormy night—
You to the town must go;
And take a lantern, Child, to light
Your mother through the snow."

"That, Father! will I gladly do:
'Tis scarcely afternoon—
The minster-clock has just struck two,
And yonder is the moon!"   20

At this the Father raised his hook,
And snapped a faggot-band;
He plied his work;—and Lucy took
The lantern in her hand.

Not blither is the mountain roe:
With many a wanton stroke
Her feet disperse the powdery snow,
That rises up like smoke.

The storm came on before its time:
She wandered up and down;   30

And many a hill did Lucy climb:
But never reached the town.

The wretched parents all that night
Went shouting far and wide;
But there was neither sound nor sight
To serve them for a guide.

At day-break on a hill they stood
That overlooked the moor;
And thence they saw the bridge of wood,
A furlong from their door.   40

They wept—and, turning homeward, cried,
"In heaven we all shall meet";
—When in the snow the mother spied
The print of Lucy's feet.

Then downwards from the steep hill's edge
They tracked the footmarks small;
And through the broken hawthorn hedge,
And by the long stone-wall;

And then an open field they crossed;
The marks were still the same;   50
They tracked them on, nor ever lost;
And to the bridge they came.

They followed from the snowy bank
Those footmarks, one by one,
Into the middle of the plank;
And further there were none!

—Yet some maintain that to this day
She is a living child;
That you may see sweet Lucy Gray
Upon the lonesome wild.   60

O'er rough and smooth she trips along,
And never looks behind;
And sings a solitary song
That whistles in the wind.

■   "Lucy Gray" was composed in 1799 and was published in the second
edition of *Lyrical Ballads* (1800). Wordsworth wrote this note about the
poem:

Written at Goslar in Germany. It was founded on a circumstance told me by my Sister, of a little girl who, not far from Halifax in Yorkshire, was bewildered in a snow-storm. Her footsteps were traced by her parents to the middle of the lock of a canal, and no other vestige of her, backward or forward, could be traced. The body however was found in the canal. The way in which the incident was treated and the spiritualising of the character might furnish hints of contrasting the imaginative influences which I have endeavoured to throw over common life with Crabbe's matter of fact style of treating subjects of the same kind. This is not spoken to his disparagement, far from it, but to direct the attention of thoughtful readers, into whose hands these notes may fall, to a comparison that may both enlarge the circle of their sensibilities, and tend to produce in them a catholic judgment.

The appropriateness of the subtitle, "Solitude," is not immediately apparent. Since it is an alternate title—"Lucy Gray, or Solitude"—we are led to consider the central character and the situation as embodying and hence suggesting both the concept and the quality of solitude. Every human being of course is *alone,* but in a poem it is necessary to dramatize or evoke a realization and feeling of that fact. A child naturally has a strong sense of and frequently a fear of solitude, and therefore gives a more dramatic instance of solitude than an adult would give. The drama itself, that of a child lost on "the lonesome wild" on a cold, wintry day, with the wind whistling, is obviously designed to evoke such a realization in the reader. In the first stanza she is the "solitary child," and in the final stanza she is shown wandering the moors. Wordsworth has allowed an actual incident to be transmuted by the folk imagination into an image of solitude. Throughout his poetry the acceptance of nature implies the acceptance of solitude. If we learn to accept both, we shall be filled, as we read in the lines on Tintern Abbey (1798),

> With quietness and beauty, and so feed
> With lofty thoughts, that neither evil tongues,
> Rash judgments, nor the sneers of selfish men,
> Nor greetings where no kindness is, nor all
> The dreary intercourse of daily life,
> Shall e'er prevail against us. . . .

That Lucy Gray conveys this awareness of and acceptance of nature is evidenced from line 20: "And yonder is the moon!" Crabb Robinson recorded in his Diary that Wordsworth had singled out this line in conversation; the object was "to exhibit poetically entire solitude, and he represents the child as observing the day-moon, which no town or village girl would ever notice." Despite the girl's experiences, nature is not evil or malevolent. Lucy almost becomes identified with it. In this sense, then, Lucy Gray is more than a realistic representation of a lost child.

Wordsworth's use of the ballad stanza (a quatrain in iambic meter in which the first and third lines have eight syllables and the second and fourth have six each) allows him to realize some of the simplicities of subject matter and language he discusses approvingly in the Preface. The family of Lucy Gray are rustics, who speak a plain language. And the loss of the child in the storm generates "elementary feelings." The occupation of the father is given in his raising a hook to snap a "faggot band," and their elemental feelings are perfectly clear from their having shouted "far and wide" throughout the night. Again, their passions are "incorporated with the beautiful and permanent forms of nature," the solitariness of the wind, moor, and storm.

We must be on our guard, however, in attributing the poetic quality of the poem exclusively to the language of people who, not being under the "influence of social vanity," "convey their feelings and notions in simple and unelaborated expressions." Lines like " 'In heaven we all shall meet,' " and " 'Tonight will be a stormy night,' " and " 'That, Father, will I gladly do,' " can be thought trite or commonplace with more justice than "purified" or philosophical. The lines are effective enough in the poem because they function dramatically, giving us a sense of the girl and her family. They participate in the excitement of the narrative and are carried along by the ballad rhythms. The description of the girl walking in the snow is, especially in its economy, a language of conscious artistry:

> With many a wanton stroke
> Her feet disperse the powdery snow,
> That rises up like smoke.

The image of snow like smoke suggests of course that the day was so cold that little puffs rose behind her heels. The description is not one that would have come naturally from the mouth of Lucy's father.

Wordsworth achieves the quality of pathos by ironical indirection. The death of the girl is never stated outright but is suggested at three different times by these lines:

> Will never more be seen.
> (l. 12)

> But never reached the town.
> (l. 32)

> And further there were none!
> (l. 56)

It is only in one respect that these statements are suggestive, for in another respect they are simply statements of fact. No one saw Lucy die, and "some maintain" that she is alive and can be seen "Upon the lonesome wild." The three lines, then, have a fairly complex function. They have an incidental, a local, effect, and are also related to the conclusion toward which the poem develops. The speaker of the poem says that popular imagination has created the belief that Lucy is still alive and to be seen. This is done in the next-to-last stanza. And then with no positive transition, no indication that the speaker denies or affirms the belief, the final stanza presents a striking image of the girl, still alive and wandering in the wild. The possibility that the speaker shares the popular belief and has actually seen the girl adds to the imaginative force of the final image, and yet this possibility is so slightly suggested that the frame of the poem, the point of view from which it is spoken, remains within the realm of plausibility.

On returning to the opening stanzas of the poem, we may find, if we have not noticed before, that the poem opens with the same ambiguity with which it ends. When the speaker says he has seen Lucy Gray, does he mean that he has seen her *before* or *after* she has disappeared in the storm? That he may have seen her *after* is suggested in the first two stanzas. She was seen when the speaker crossed the wild at break of day. Both the place and the time are appropriate for such a preternatural vision, or for such working of the imagination. The punctuation, the dash, in the second stanza indicates an ambiguity in the tense of the verbs. We may read the stanza in this way: the girl *dwelt* solitary "on the wide moor" after her disappearance in the storm, and previously she "*grew*/ Beside a human door." Lest the ambiguity of the first two stanzas be resolved in the impression that a vision is definitely meant, in the third stanza the statement is made that "the sweet face of Lucy Gray/ Will never be seen." Thus the ambiguity of the first two stanzas is sustained. The statement says in one sense, perhaps the more obvious, that Lucy is dead and gone. And yet, when we know the whole story, including the popular legend, we may take it to mean that her face will not be seen because she appears only at a distance as "she trips along" on the wild and "never looks behind." If this were *all* that is meant, the remarks, in the third stanza, about Lucy's face would be rather pointless, but they are justified by the ambiguity which results from the way in which the statement is made—that is, by the more immediate suggestion, with its shock and pathos, that Lucy is gone, although the fawn and the hare are still to be seen.

The fourth stanza starts immediately with the action that leads to Lucy's disappearance, and the story is told in a manner that is characteristic of the folk ballad: rapid development of the narrative, the use of implication, and the omission of the usual transitions. Wordsworth's literary ballad is elliptical in the same way as the folk ballad, and this elliptical method serves to produce the unresolved ambiguity which is related to the effect of the poem. Thus we see that Wordsworth has chosen a form which is not only appropriate for his subject from "common life," but also for his purpose of spiritualizing the subject.

Three Years She Grew in Sun
and Shower

Three years she grew in sun and shower,
Then Nature said, "A lovelier flower
On earth was never sown;
This Child I to myself will take;
She shall be mine, and I will make
A Lady of my own.

"Myself will to my darling be
Both law and impulse: and with me
The Girl, in rock and plain,
In earth and heaven, in glade and bower,   10
Shall feel an overseeing power
To kindle or restrain.

"She shall be sportive as the fawn
That wild with glee across the lawn,
Or up the mountain springs;
And hers shall be the breathing balm,
And hers the silence and the calm
Of mute insensate things.

"The floating clouds their state shall lend
To her; for her the willow bend;   20
Nor shall she fail to see
Even in the motions of the Storm
Grace that shall mold the Maiden's form
By silent sympathy.

"The stars of midnight shall be dear
To her; and she shall lean her ear
In many a secret place
Where rivulets dance their wayward round,
And beauty born of murmuring sound
Shall pass into her face.   30

"And vital feelings of delight
Shall rear her form to stately height,
Her virgin bosom swell;
Such thoughts to Lucy I will give
While she and I together live
Here in this happy dell."

Thus Nature spake.—The work was done.—
How soon my Lucy's race was run!
She died, and left to me
This heath, this calm, and quiet scene;   40
The memory of what has been,
And never more will be.

A Slumber Did My Spirit Seal

A slumber did my spirit seal;
    I had no human fears;
She seemed a thing that could not feel
    The touch of earthly years.

No motion has she now, no force;
    She neither hears nor sees;
Rolled round in earth's diurnal course,
    With rocks, and stones, and trees.

Strange Fits of Passion Have I Known

Strange fits of passion have I known:
And I will dare to tell,
But in the Lover's ear alone,
What once to me befell.

When she I loved looked every day
Fresh as a rose in June,
I to her cottage bent my way,
Beneath an evening-moon.

Upon the moon I fixed my eye,
All over the wide lea;
With quickening pace my horse drew nigh
Those paths so dear to me.

And now we reached the orchard-plot;
And, as we climbed the hill,
The sinking moon to Lucy's cot
Came near, and nearer still.

In one of those sweet dreams I slept,
Kind Nature's gentlest boon!
And all the while my eyes I kept
On the descending moon.

My horse moved on; hoof after hoof
He raised, and never stopped:
When down behind the cottage roof,
At once, the bright moon dropped.

What fond and wayward thoughts will slide
Into a Lover's head!
"O mercy!" to myself I cried,
"If Lucy should be dead!"

She Dwelt among the Untrodden Ways

She dwelt among the untrodden ways
    Beside the springs of Dove,
A Maid whom there were none to praise
    And very few to love:

A violet by a mossy stone
    Half hidden from the eye!
Fair as a star, when only one
    Is shining in the sky.

She lived unknown, and few could know
    When Lucy ceased to be;
But she is in her grave, and, oh,
    The difference to me!

I Travelled among Unknown Men

I travelled among unknown men,
    In lands beyond the sea;
Nor, England! did I know till then
    What love I bore to thee.

'Tis past, that melancholy dream!
    Nor will I quit thy shore
A second time; for still I seem
    To love thee more and more.

Among thy mountains did I feel
   The joy of my desire;
And she I cherished turned her wheel
   Beside an English fire.

Thy mornings showed, thy nights concealed,
   The bowers where Lucy played;
And thine too is the last green field
   That Lucy's eyes surveyed.

1. The five poems immediately above are considered as a group and are called the "Lucy Poems." What elements do they have in common?

2. To what extent do the poems show Wordsworth's views on nature and associationalism?

3. To what extent do the individual poems depend on metaphor? on imagery? on total organization?

4. Make a comparative evaluation among the poems.

The Simplon Pass

      —Brook and road
Were fellow-travellers in this gloomy Pass,
And with them did we journey several hours
At a slow step. The immeasurable height
Of woods decaying, never to be decayed,
The stationary blasts of waterfalls,
And in the narrow rent, at every turn,
Winds thwarting winds bewildered and forlorn,
The torrents shooting from the clear blue sky,
The rocks that muttered close upon our ears,
Black drizzling crags that spake by the wayside
As if a voice were in them, the sick sight
And giddy prospect of the raving stream,
The unfettered clouds and region of the heavens,
Tumult and peace, the darkness and the light—
Were all like workings of one mind, the features
Of the same face, blossoms upon one tree,
Characters of the great Apocalypse,
The types and symbols of Eternity,
Of first, and last, and midst, and without end.

1. Consider the means by which human sensibility and the picture of natural scenery are combined in this descriptive poem.

2. Does the description, in addition to being evocative of the scene

itself, contribute anything to the development of the theme? For example, is such a detail as "stationary blasts of waterfalls" related in any way to the statement in the last six lines?

3. The Apocalypse is the only allusion in the poem. What does it contribute?

4. Analyze the rhythmic development of the poem.

I Wandered Lonely as a Cloud

I wandered lonely as a cloud
That floats on high o'er vales and hills.
When all at once I saw a crowd,
A host, of golden daffodils,
Beside the lake, beneath the trees,
Fluttering and dancing in the breeze.

Continuous as the stars that shine
And twinkle on the milky way,
They stretched in never-ending line
Along the margin of a bay;
Ten thousand saw I at a glance,
Tossing their heads in sprightly dance.

The waves beside them dance, but they
Outdid the sparkling waves in glee—
A poet could not but be gay
In such a jocund company.
I gazed—and gazed—but little thought
What wealth the show to me had brought.

For oft when on my couch I lie
In vacant or in pensive mood,
They flash upon that inward eye
Which is the bliss of solitude:
And then my heart with pleasure fills,
And dances with the daffodils.

The Solitary Reaper

Behold her, single in the field,
Yon solitary Highland Lass!
Reaping and singing by herself;
Stop here, or gently pass!

Alone she cuts and binds the grain,
And sings a melancholy strain;
O listen! for the Vale profound
Is overflowing with the sound.

No nightingale did ever chaunt
More welcome notes to weary bands   10
Of travellers in some shady haunt,
Among Arabian sands.
A voice so thrilling ne'er was heard
In springtime from the cuckoo-bird,
Breaking the silence of the seas
Among the farthest Hebrides.

Will no one tell me what she sings?—
Perhaps the plaintive numbers flow
For old, unhappy, far-off things,
And battles long ago.   20
Or is it some more humble lay,
Familiar matter of today?
Some natural sorrow, loss, or pain,
That has been, and may be again?

Whate'er the theme, the maiden sang
As if her song could have no ending;
I saw her singing at her work,
And o'er the sickle bending—
I listened, motionless and still;
And, as I mounted up the hill,   30
The music in my heart I bore
Long after it was heard no more.

■   "I Wandered Lonely as a Cloud" and "The Solitary Reaper" have
an obvious similarity. Compare the two poems in terms of treatment of
subject.

Ode to Duty

Stern Daughter of the Voice of God!
O Duty! if that name thou love
Who art a light to guide, a rod
To check the erring, and reprove;
Thou, who art victory and law
When empty terrors overawe;

From vain temptations dost set free;
And calm'st the weary strife of frail humanity!

There are who ask not if thine eye
Be on them; who, in love and truth,   10
Where no misgiving is, rely
Upon the genial sense of youth:
Glad Hearts! without reproach or blot
Who do thy work, and know it not:
Oh! if through confidence misplaced
They fail, thy saving arms, dread Power! around them cast.

Serene will be our days and bright,
And happy will our nature be,
When love is an unerring light,   20
And joy its own security.
And they a blissful course may hold
Even now, who, not unwisely bold,
Live in the spirit of this creed;
Yet seek thy firm support, according to their need.

I, loving freedom, and untried,
No sport of every random gust,
Yet being to myself a guide,
Too blindly have reposed my trust:
And oft, when in my heart was heard   30
Thy timely mandate, I deferred
The task, in smoother walks to stray;
But thee I now would serve more strictly, if I may.

Through no disturbance of my soul,
Or strong compunction in me wrought,
I supplicate for thy control;
But in the quietness of thought:
Me this uncharted freedom tires;
I feel the weight of chance-desires:
My hopes no more must change their name,   40
I long for a repose that ever is the same.

Stern Lawgiver! yet thou dost wear
The Godhead's most benignant grace;
Nor know we anything so fair
As is the smile upon thy face:
Flowers laugh before thee on their beds
And fragrance in thy footing treads;

Thou dost preserve the stars from wrong;
And the most ancient heavens, through Thee, are fresh and strong.   50

To humbler functions, awful Power!
I call thee: I myself commend
Unto thy guidance from this hour;
Oh, let my weakness have an end!
Give unto me, made lowly wise,
The spirit of self-sacrifice;
The confidence of reason give;
And in the light of truth thy Bondman let me live!

Elegiac Stanzas [1]

*Suggested by a picture of Peele Castle, in a storm,
painted by Sir George Beaumont*

I was thy neighbour once, thou rugged Pile!
Four summer weeks I dwelt in sight of thee:
I saw thee every day; and all the while
Thy Form was sleeping on a glassy sea.

So pure the sky, so quiet was the air!
So like, so very like, was day to day!
Whene'er I looked, thy Image still was there;
It trembled, but it never passed away.

How perfect was the calm! it seemed to sleep;
No mood, which season takes away, or brings: 10
I could have fancied that the mighty Deep
Was even the gentlest of all gentle Things.

Ah! then, if mine had been the Painter's hand,
To express what then I saw; and add the gleam,
The light that never was, on sea or land,
The consecration, and the Poet's dream;

I would have planted thee, thou hoary Pile
Amid a world how different from this!
Beside a sea that could not cease to smile;
On tranquil land, beneath a sky of bliss.   20

Thou shouldst have seemed a treasure-house divine
Of peaceful years; a chronicle of heaven;—

----

1. The stanzas are elegiac with reference to Wordsworth's brother, a sea captain who went down with his ship.

Of all the sunbeams that did ever shine
The very sweetest had to thee been given.

A picture had it been of lasting ease,
Elysian quiet, without toil or strife;
No motion but the moving tide, a breeze,
Or merely silent Nature's breathing life.

Such, in the fond illusion of my heart,
Such Picture would I at that time have made: 30
And seen the soul of truth in every part,
A steadfast peace that might not be betrayed.

So once it would have been,—'tis so no more;
I have submitted to a new control:
A power is gone, which nothing can restore;
A deep distress hath humanised my Soul.

Not for a moment could I now behold
A smiling sea, and be what I have been:
The feeling of my loss will ne'er be old;
This, which I know, I speak with mind serene.   40

Then, Beaumont, Friend! who would have been the Friend,
If he had lived, of him whom I deplore,
This work of thine I blame not, but commend;
This sea in anger, and that dismal shore.

O 'tis a passionate Work!—yet wise and well,
Well chosen is the spirit that is here;
That Hulk which labours in the deadly swell,
This rueful sky, this pageantry of fear!

And this huge Castle, standing here sublime,
I love to see the look with which it braves,   50
Cased in the unfeeling armour of old time,
The lightning, the fierce wind, and trampling waves.

Farewell, farewell the heart that lives alone,
Housed in a dream, at distance from the Kind!
Such happiness, wherever it be known,
Is to be pitied; for 'tis surely blind.

But welcome fortitude, and patient cheer,
And frequent sights of what is to be borne!

Such sights, or worse, as are before me here.—
Not without hope we suffer and we mourn.   60

  ■   1. State the similarity of theme in "Ode to Duty" and "Elegiac Stanzas."

     2. How is the theme of "Elegiac Stanzas" related to its organization?

     3. The poet raises the painter's treatment above his own former concept of Peele Castle. Is there any element of remorse in his present attitude?

     4. Does the poem, in addition to being a personal statement, have any dramatic and symbolic force?

Composed upon Westminster Bridge
September 3, 1802

Earth has not anything to show more fair:
Dull would he be of soul who could pass by
A sight so touching in its majesty:
This City now doth, like a garment, wear
The beauty of the morning; silent, bare,
Ships, towers, domes, theatres, and temples lie
Open unto the fields, and to the sky;
All bright and glittering in the smokeless air.
Never did sun more beautifully steep
In his first splendour, valley, rock, or hill;
Ne'er saw I, never felt, a calm so deep!
The river glideth at his own sweet will:
Dear God! the very houses seem asleep;
And all that mighty heart is lying still!

It Is a Beauteous Evening, Calm and Free

It is a beauteous evening, calm and free,
The holy time is quiet as a Nun
Breathless with adoration; the broad sun
Is sinking down in its tranquillity;
The gentleness of heaven broods o'er the Sea:
Listen! the mighty Being is awake,
And doth with his eternal motion make
A sound like thunder—everlastingly.
Dear Child! dear Girl! that walkest with me here,
If thou appear untouched by solemn thought,
Thy nature is not therefore less divine:

Thou liest in Abraham's bosom all the year;
And worshipp'st at the Temple's inner shrine,
God being with thee when we know it not.

London, 1802

Milton! thou shouldst be living at this hour:
England hath need of thee: she is a fen
Of stagnant waters: altar, sword, and pen,
Fireside, the heroic wealth of hall and bower,
Have forfeited their ancient English dower
Of inward happiness. We are selfish men;
Oh! raise us up, return to us again;
And give us manners, virtue, freedom, power.
Thy soul was like a Star, and dwelt apart;
Thou hadst a voice whose sound was like the sea:
Pure as the naked heavens, majestic, free,
So didst thou travel on life's common way,
In cheerful godliness; and yet thy heart
The lowliest duties on herself did lay.

To Sleep

A flock of sheep that leisurely pass by,
One after one; the sound of rain, and bees
Murmuring; the fall of rivers, winds and seas,
Smooth fields, white sheets of water, and pure sky;
I have thought of all by turns, and yet do lie
Sleepless! and soon the small birds' melodies
Must hear, first uttered from my orchard trees;
And the first cuckoo's melancholy cry.
Even thus last night, and two nights more, I lay
And could not win thee, Sleep! by any stealth:
So do not let me wear to-night away:
Without Thee what is all the morning's wealth?
Come, blessed barrier between day and day,
Dear mother of fresh thoughts and joyous health!

The World Is Too Much with Us

The world is too much with us; late and soon,
Getting and spending, we lay waste our powers:
Little we see in Nature that is ours;

We have given our hearts away, a sordid boon!
The Sea that bares her bosom to the moon;
The winds that will be howling at all hours,
And are up-gathered now like sleeping flowers;
For this, for everything, we are out of tune;
It moves us not.—Great God! I'd rather be
A Pagan, suckled in a creed outworn,
So might I, standing on this pleasant lea,
Have glimpses that would make me less forlorn;
Have sight of Proteus rising from the sea;
Or hear old Triton blow his wreathèd horn.

Ode

Intimations of Immortality from Recollections of Early Childhood

To that dream-like vividness and splendour which invests objects of sight in childhood, every one, I believe, if he would look back, could bear testimony, and I need not dwell upon it here: but having in the poem regarded it as presumptive evidence of a prior state of existence, I think it right to protest against a conclusion, which has given pain to some good and pious persons, that I meant to inculcate such a belief. It is far too shadowy a notion to be recommended to faith, as more than an element in our instincts of immortality. But let us bear in mind that, though the idea is not advanced in revelation, there is nothing there to contradict it, and the fall of Man presents an analogy in its favour. Accordingly, a pre-existent state has entered into the popular creeds of many nations; and, among all persons acquainted with classic literature, is known as an ingredient in Platonic philosophy. Archimedes said that he could move the world if he had a point whereon to rest his machine. Who has not felt the same aspirations as regards the world of his own mind? Having to wield some of its elements when I was impelled to write this poem on the Immortality of the Soul, I took hold of the notion of pre-existence as having sufficient foundation in humanity for authorising me to make for my purpose the best use of it I could as a poet. [Wordsworth's note]

> The Child is father of the Man;
> And I could wish my days to be
> Bound each to each by natural piety.

I

There was a time when meadow, grove, and stream,
The earth, and every common sight,
        To me did seem
        Apparelled in celestial light,
The glory and the freshness of a dream.
It is not now as it hath been of yore;—
        Turn whereso'er I may,
        By night or day,
The things which I have seen I now can see no more.

10

2

The Rainbow comes and goes,
And lovely is the Rose,
The Moon doth with delight
Look round her when the heavens are bare,
Waters on a starry night
Are beautiful and fair;
The sunshine is a glorious birth;
But yet I know, where'er I go,   20
That there hath past away a glory from the earth.

3

Now, while the birds thus sing a joyous song,
And while the young lambs bound
As to the tabor's sound,
To me alone there came a thought of grief:
A timely utterance gave that thought relief,
And I again am strong:
The cataracts blow their trumpets from the steep;
No more shall grief of mine the season wrong;
I hear the Echoes through the mountains throng,   30
The Winds come to me from the fields of sleep,
And all the earth is gay;
Land and sea
Give themselves up to jollity,
And with the heart of May
Doth every Beast keep holiday;—
Thou Child of Joy,
Shout round me, let me hear thy shouts, thou happy Shepherd-boy!

4

Ye blessèd Creatures, I have heard the call   40
Ye to each other make; I see
The heavens laugh with you in your jubilee;
My heart is at your festival,
My head hath its coronal,
The fulness of your bliss, I feel—I feel it all.
Oh evil day! if I were sullen
While Earth herself is adorning,
This sweet May-morning,
And the Children are culling
On every side,   50
In a thousand valleys far and wide,
Fresh flowers; while the sun shines warm,

And the Babe leaps up on his Mother's arm:—
    I hear, I hear, with joy I hear!
    —But there's a Tree, of many, one,
A single Field which I have looked upon,
Both of them speak of something that is gone:
      The Pansy at my feet
      Doth the same tale repeat:
Whither is fled the visionary gleam?   60
Where is it now, the glory and the dream?

5

Our birth is but a sleep and a forgetting:
The Soul that rises with us, our life's Star,
    Hath had elsewhere its setting,
      And cometh from afar:
    Not in entire forgetfulness,
    And not in utter nakedness,
But trailing clouds of glory do we come
    From God, who is our home:
Heaven lies about us in our infancy!   70
Shades of the prison-house begin to close
    Upon the growing Boy,
But he beholds the light, and whence it flows,
    He sees it in his joy;
The Youth, who daily farther from the east
    Must travel, still is Nature's Priest,
    And by the vision splendid
    Is on his way attended;
At length the Man perceives it die away,
And fade into the light of common day.   80

6

Earth fills her lap with pleasures of her own;
Yearnings she hath in her own natural kind,
And, even with something of a Mother's mind,
    And no unworthy aim,
    The homely Nurse doth all she can
To make her Foster-child, her Inmate Man,
    Forget the glories he hath known,
And that imperial palace whence he came.

7

Behold the Child among his new-born blisses,
A six years' Darling of a pigmy size!   90

See, where 'mid work of his own hand he lies,
Fretted by sallies of his mother's kisses,
With light upon him from his father's eyes!
See, at his feet, some little plan or chart,
Some fragment from his dream of human life,
Shaped by himself with newly-learnèd art;
  A wedding or a festival,
  A mourning or a funeral;
   And this hath now his heart,
  And unto this he frames his song: 100
   Then will he fit his tongue
Tc dialogues of business, love, or strife;
  But it will not be long
  Ere this be thrown aside,
  And with new joy and pride
The little Actor cons another part;
Filling from time to time his "humorous stage"
With all the Persons, down to palsied Age,
That Life brings with her in her equipage;   110
  As if his whole vocation
  Were endless imitation.

8

Thou, whose exterior semblance doth belie
  Thy Soul's immensity;
Thou best Philosopher, who yet dost keep
Thy heritage, thou Eye among the blind,
That, deaf and silent, read'st the eternal deep,
Haunted forever by the eternal mind,—
  Mighty Prophet! Seer blest!
  On whom those truths do rest,
Which we are toiling all our lives to find,   120
In darkness lost, the darkness of the grave;
Thou, over whom thy Immortality
Broods like the Day, a Master o'er a Slave,
A Presence which is not to be put by;
Thou little Child, yet glorious in the might
Of heaven-born freedom on thy being's height,
Why with such earnest pains dost thou provoke
The years to bring the inevitable yoke,
Thus blindly with thy blessedness at strife?
Full soon thy Soul shall have her earthly freight, 130
And custom lie upon thee with a weight,
Heavy as frost, and deep almost as life!

9

O joy! that in our embers
Is something that doth live,
That nature yet remembers
What was so fugitive!
The thought of our past years in me doth breed
Perpetual benediction: not indeed
For that which is most worthy to be blest;
Delight and liberty, the simple creed
Of Childhood, whether busy or at rest, 140
With new-fledged hope still fluttering in his breast:—
        Not for these I raise
        The song of thanks and praise;
    But for those obstinate questionings
    Of sense and outward things,
    Fallings from us, vanishings;
    Blank misgivings of a Creature
Moving about in worlds not realised,
High instincts before which our mortal Nature 150
Did tremble like a guilty Thing surprised:
        But for those first affections,
        Those shadowy recollections,
    Which, be they what they may,
Are yet the fountain-light of all our day,
Are yet a master-light of all our seeing;
    Uphold us, cherish, and have power to make
Our noisy years seem moments in the being
Of the eternal Silence: truths that wake,
        To perish never: 160
Which neither listlessness, nor mad endeavour,
        Nor Man nor Boy,
Nor all that is at enmity with joy,
Can utterly abolish or destroy!
    Hence in a season of calm weather
        Though inland far we be,
Our Souls have sight of that immortal sea
        Which brought us hither,
    Can in a moment travel thither,
And see the Children sport upon the shore, 170
And hear the mighty waters rolling evermore.

10

Then sing, ye Birds, sing, sing a joyous song!
        And let the young Lambs bound
        As to the tabor's sound!

We in thought will join your throng,
     Ye that pipe and ye that play,
     Ye that through your hearts today
     Feel the gladness of the May!
What though the radiance which was once so bright
Be now forever taken from my sight,   180
     Though nothing can bring back the hour
Of splendour in the grass, of glory in the flower;
     We will grieve not, rather find
     Strength in what remains behind;
     In the primal sympathy
     Which having been must ever be;
     In the soothing thoughts that spring
     Out of human suffering;
     In the faith that looks through death,
In years that bring the philosophic mind.   190

11

And O, ye Fountains, Meadows, Hills, and Groves,
Forebode not any severing of our loves!
Yet in my heart of hearts I feel your might;
I only have relinquished one delight
To live beneath your more habitual sway.
I love the Brooks which down their channels fret,
Even more than when I tripped lightly as they;
The innocent brightness of a new-born Day
     Is lovely yet;
The Clouds that gather round the setting sun   200
Do take a sober colouring from an eye
That hath kept watch o'er man's mortality;
Another race hath been, and other palms are won.
Thanks to the human heart by which we live,
Thanks to its tenderness, its joys, and fears,
To me the meanest flower that blows can give
Thoughts that do often lie too deep for tears.

    1. To what extent are Wordsworth's views on nature and sensation involved in the development of the "Ode"?

    2. Wordsworth says in his note that pre-existence, although a "shadowy notion," was useful to him as a poet. If pre-existence is not meant to be "recommended to faith," what is its use in the poem? Does the notion have too much *literal* force in the poem and therefore fail as a device?

    3. Would you agree with J. W. Beach that the poem "is virtually a recantation of the earlier doctrine of nature"? Give your reasons.

    4. Would you agree with Trilling that the poem is not, as often

claimed, a sad farewell to poetic powers, but rather a "dedication to new powers"?

5. To what extent are the "Ode" and "Elegiac Stanzas" comparable?

Samuel Taylor Coleridge

(1772–1834)

■■■■■■■■■■

COLERIDGE WAS the last of thirteen children born to Rev. John Coleridge, a vicar and headmaster of a boarding school in Devonshire. Samuel's father died when he was nine, and friends arranged for him to be educated at Christ's Hospital School in London. Here he lived a lonely life, but his education, although narrow and severe, gave him training in scholarship and a chance to read widely. As a student at Cambridge he became discouraged over his lack of interest in college and suddenly enlisted in the dragoons, but his inability to perform his tasks as a soldier caused him to reveal his whereabouts to his friends, who secured his discharge and his readmission to Cambridge.

In 1794 he met Southey and discovered that they held radical ideas in common. Together they planned to found a cooperative society in America, to be called Pantisocracy. Twelve gentlemen and their wives were to embark for America the following April. Southey and Lovell, another of the utopians, were engaged to marry two sisters named Fricker. Coleridge, in need of a wife, addressed himself to Sarah, the third sister. The marriage was unfortunate despite the fact that the first year or so was happy for both of them. The Pantisocracy idea was given up, and Coleridge was faced with the task of earning a living. The liberal paper, *The Watchman,* which he edited collapsed after ten issues. A man named Thomas Poole undertook to support Coleridge in return for intellectual companionship. And it was during this period, the latter part of the 1790's, that Coleridge began his close friendship and collaboration with the Wordsworths. The principal result of the association was *Lyrical Ballads.*

To the first edition he contributed "The Ancient Mariner." With the Wordsworths he visited Germany, where he learned a great deal about German poetry and philosophy. In the fall of 1899 he met Sarah Hutchinson (the sister of Mary Hutchinson, who was shortly to marry Wordsworth) and fell deeply in love with her. His inability to marry Sarah Hutchinson contributed to his profound dejection. He was also an acute sufferer from rheumatism and as a consequence took to opium. A John Morgan took him into his family for a while after 1810, and in 1816 Dr. Gillman and his wife took care of him. With them he spent his last eighteen years, during which he published "Christabel," "Kubla Khan," *Biographia Literaria,* and other prose works. Despite his inability to be systematic or comprehensive, Coleridge had a tremendous influence on the later nineteenth century. John Stuart Mill later said that Coleridge and Jeremy Bentham were the two great seminal minds of the century. In the twentieth century he has had a great influence on literary criticism.

Suggested Readings

ERNEST DE SELINCOURT, "Coleridge's 'Dejection: An Ode,'" in *Essays and Studies.* Oxford: Clarendon Press, 1937, XXII, 7–25.

ROBERT PENN WARREN, "A Poem of Pure Imagination: An Experiment in Reading," *The Rime of the Ancient Mariner.* New York: Reynal & Hitchcock, 1946, pp. 61–117.

■ ■ ■ ■ ■ ■ ■ ■ ■ ■

Kubla Khan,
or *A Vision in a Dream*

In the summer of the year 1797, the author, then in ill health, had retired to a lonely farmhouse between Porlock and Linton, on the Exmoor confines of Somerset and Devonshire. In consequence of a slight indisposition, an anodyne had been prescribed, from the effects of which he fell asleep in his chair at the moment he was reading the following sentence, or words of the same substance, in *Purchas's Pilgrimage:* 'Here the Khan Kubla commanded a palace to be built, and a stately garden thereunto. And thus ten miles of fertile ground were inclosed with a wall.' The author continued for about three hours in a profound sleep, at least of the external senses, during which time he has the most vivid confidence that he could not have composed less than from two to three hundred lines; if that indeed can be called composition in which all the images rose up before him as *things,* with a parallel production of the correspondent expressions, without any sensation or consciousness of effort. On awaking he appeared to himself to have a distinct recollection of the whole, and taking his pen, ink, and paper, instantly and eagerly wrote down the lines that are here preserved. At this moment he was unfortunately called out by a person on business from Porlock, and detained by him above an hour, and on his return to his room, found, to his no small surprise and mortification, that though he still retained some vague and dim recollection of the general purport of the vision, yet, with the exception of some eight or ten scattered lines and images, all the rest had passed away like the images on the surface of a stream into which a stone had been cast, but, alas! without the after restoration of the latter! [Coleridge's note]

> In Xanadu did Kubla Khan
> A stately pleasure-dome decree:
> Where Alph, the sacred river, ran
> Through caverns measureless to man
>   Down to a sunless sea.
> So twice five miles of fertile ground
> With walls and towers were girdled round:

And here were gardens bright with sinuous rills,
Where blossomed many an incense-bearing tree;
And here were forests ancient as the hills,   10
Enfolding sunny spots of greenery.
But oh! that deep romantic chasm which slanted
Down the green hill athwart a cedarn cover!
A savage place! as holy and enchanted
As e'er beneath a waning moon was haunted
By woman wailing for her demon-lover!
And from this chasm, with ceaseless turmoil seething,
As if this earth in fast thick pants were breathing
A mighty fountain momently was forced;
Amid whose swift half-intermitted burst   20
Huge fragments vaulted like rebounding hail,
Or chaffy grain beneath the thresher's flail:
And 'mid these dancing rocks at once and ever
It flung up momently the sacred river.
Five miles meandering with a mazy motion
Through wood and dale the sacred river ran,
Then reached the caverns measureless to man,
And sank in tumult to a lifeless ocean:
And 'mid this tumult Kubla heard from far
Ancestral voices prophesying war!   30

    The shadow of the dome of pleasure
    Floated midway on the waves;
    Where was heard the mingled measure
    From the fountain and the caves.
  It was a miracle of rare device,
  A sunny pleasure-dome with caves of ice!

    A damsel with a dulcimer
    In a vision once I saw:
    It was an Abyssinian maid,
    And on her dulcimer she played,   40
    Singing of Mount Abora.
    Could I revive within me,
    Her symphony and song,
    To such a deep delight 'twould win me,
That with music loud and long,
I would build that dome in air,
That sunny dome! those caves of ice!
And all who heard should see them there,
And all should cry, Beware! Beware!
His flashing eyes, his floating hair!   50
Weave a circle round him thrice,

And close your eyes with holy dread,
For he on honey-dew hath fed,
And drunk the milk of Paradise.

■ 1. According to Coleridge's note, this poem is incomplete. But can it, from a reader's point of view, be regarded as unified and complete?
2. Consider the poem as an example of romantic expression.

The Rime of the Ancient Mariner
In Seven Parts

Argument

How a Ship having passed the Line was driven by storms to the cold Country towards the South Pole; and how from thence she made her course to the tropical Latitude of the Great Pacific Ocean; and of the strange things that befell: and in what manner the Ancyent Marinere came back to his own Country.

Part 1

An ancient Mariner meeteth three Gallants bidden to a wedding-feast, and detaineth one.

It is an ancient Mariner,
And he stoppeth one of three.
"By thy long gray beard and glittering eye,
Now wherefore stopp'st thou me?

"The Bridegroom's doors are opened wide,
And I am next of kin,
The guests are met, the feast is set:
May'st hear the merry din."

He holds him with his skinny hand;
"There was a ship," quoth he.   10
"Hold off! unhand me, gray-beard loon!"
Eftsoons his hand dropt he.

He holds him with his glittering eye—
The Wedding-Guest stood still,
And listens like a three years' child.
The Mariner hath his will.

The Wedding-Guest is spellbound by the eye of the old seafaring man and constrained to hear his tale.

The Wedding-Guest sat on a stone:
He cannot choose but hear;
And thus spake on that ancient man,
The bright-eyed Mariner.   20

"The ship was cheered, the harbor cleared,
Merrily did we drop
Below the kirk, below the hill,
Below the light-house top.

*The Mariner tells how
the ship sailed south-
ward with a good wind
and fair weather, till it
reached the Line.*

"The sun came up upon the left,
Out of the sea came he!
And he shone bright, and on the right
Went down into the sea.

"Higher and higher every day,
Till over the mast at noon—"   30
The Wedding-Guest here beat his breast,
For he heard the loud bassoon.

*The Wedding-Guest
heareth the bridal
music; but the Mariner
continueth his tale.*

The bride hath paced into the hall,
Red as a rose is she;
Nodding their heads before her goes
The merry minstrelsy.

The Wedding-Guest he beat his breast,
Yet he cannot choose but hear;
And thus spake on that ancient man,
The bright-eyed Mariner.   40

*The ship driven by a
storm toward the
south pole.*

"And now the Storm-blast came, and he
Was tyrannous and strong:
He struck with his o'ertaking wings,
And chased us south along.

"With sloping masts and dipping prow,
As who pursued with yell and blow
Still treads the shadow of his foe,
And forward bends his head,
The ship drove fast, loud roared the blast,
And southward aye we fled.   50

"And now there came both mist and snow,
And it grew wondrous cold:
And ice, mast-high, came floating by,
As green as emerald.

*The land of ice, and
of fearful sounds
where no living thing
was to be seen.*

"And through the drifts the snowy clifts
Did send a dismal sheen:
Nor shapes of men nor beasts we ken—
The ice was all between.

"The ice was here, the ice was there,
The ice was all around: 60
It cracked and growled, and roared and howled,
Like noises in a swound!

Till a great sea-bird,
called the Albatross,
came through the
snow-fog, and was re-
ceived with great joy
and hospitality.

"At length did cross an Albatross,
Thorough the fog it came;
As if it had been a Christian soul,
We hailed it in God's name.

"It ate the food it ne'er had eat,
And round and round it flew.
The ice did split with a thunder-fit;
The helmsman steered us through!   70

And lo! the Albatross
proveth a bird of good
omen, and followeth
the ship as it returned
northward through fog
and floating ice.

"And a good south wind sprung up behind;
The Albatross did follow,
And every day, for food or play,
Came to the mariners' hollo!

"In mist or cloud, on mast or shroud,
It perched for vespers nine;
Whiles all the night, through fog-smoke white,
Glimmered the white moon-shine."

The ancient Mariner
inhospitably killeth the
pious bird of good
omen.

"God save thee, ancient Mariner!
From the fiends, that plague thee thus!—   80
Why look'st thou so?"—"With my cross-bow
I shot the Albatross!"

Part 2

"The Sun now rose upon the right:
Out of the sea came he,
Still hid in mist, and on the left
Went down into the sea.

"And the good south wind still blew behind,
But no sweet bird did follow,
Nor any day for food or play
Came to the mariners' hollo!   90

His shipmates cry out
against the ancient
Mariner, for killing
the bird of good luck.

"And I had done a hellish thing,
And it would work 'em woe:
For all averred, I had killed the bird
That made the breeze to blow.

Ah, wretch! said they, the bird to slay,
That made the breeze to blow!

*But when the fog
cleared off they justify
the same, and thus
make themselves ac-
complices in the crime.*

"Nor dim nor red, like God's own head,
The glorious Sun uprist:
Then all averred, I had killed the bird
That brought the fog and mist.   100
'Twas right, said they, such birds to slay,
That bring the fog and mist.

*The fair breeze con-
tinues; the ship enters
the Pacific Ocean, and
sails northward, even
till it reaches the Line.*

"The fair breeze blew, the white foam flew,
The furrow followed free;
We were the first that ever burst
Into that silent sea.

*The ship hath been
suddenly becalmed.*

"Down dropt the breeze, the sails dropt down,
'Twas sad as sad could be;
And we did speak only to break
The silence of the sea!   110

"All in a hot and copper sky,
The bloody Sun, at noon,
Right up above the mast did stand,
No bigger than the Moon.

"Day after day, day after day,
We stuck, nor breath nor motion;
As idle as a painted ship
Upon a painted ocean.

*And the Albatross
begins to be avenged.*

"Water, water, everywhere,
And all the boards did shrink;   120
Water, water, everywhere,
Nor any drop to drink.

"The very deep did rot: O Christ!
That ever this should be!
Yea, slimy things did crawl with legs
Upon the slimy sea.

*A Spirit had followed
them; one of the in-
visible inhabitants of
this planet, neither de-
parted souls nor angels;
concerning whom the
learned Jew, Josephus,
and the Platonic*

"About, about, in reel and rout
The death-fires danced at night;
The water, like a witch's oils,
Burnt green, and blue and white.   130

*Constantinopolitan,
Michael Psellus, may
be consulted. They are
very numerous, and
there is no climate or
element without one
or more.*

"And some in dreams assured were
Of the Spirit that plagued us so;
Nine fathom deep he had followed us
From the land of mist and snow.

*The shipmates, in
their sore distress,
would fain throw the
whole guilt on the an-
cient Mariner: in sign
whereof they hang the
dead sea-bird round
his neck.*

"And every tongue, through utter drought,
Was withered at the root;
We could not speak, no more than if
We had been choked with soot.

"Ah! well-a-day! what evil looks
Had I from old and young!   140
Instead of the cross, the Albatross
About my neck was hung."

Part 3

"There passed a weary time. Each throat
Was parched, and glazed each eye.
A weary time! a weary time!
How glazed each weary eye,
When looking westward, I beheld
A something in the sky.

*The ancient Mariner
beholdeth a sign in the
element afar off.*

"At first it seemed a little speck,
And then it seemed a mist;   150
It moved and moved, and took at last
A certain shape, I wist.

"A speck, a mist, a shape, I wist!
And still it neared and neared:
As if it dodged a water-sprite,
It plunged and tacked and veered.

*At its nearer approach,
it seemeth him to be
a ship; and at a dear
ransom he freeth his
speech from the bonds
of thirst.*

"With throats unslaked, with black lips baked,
We could nor laugh nor wail;
Through utter drought all dumb we stood!
I bit my arm, I sucked the blood,   160
And cried, A sail! a sail!

A flash of joy;

"With throats unslaked, with black lips baked,
Agape they heard me call:
Gramercy! they for joy did grin,
And all at once their breath drew in,
As they were drinking all.

And horror follows.
For can it be a ship
that comes onward
without wind or tide?

"See! see! (I cried) she tacks no more!
Hither to work us weal—
Without a breeze, without a tide,
She steadies with upright keel!   170

"The western wave was all aflame,
The day was well nigh done!
Almost upon the western wave
Rested the broad bright Sun;
When that strange shape drove suddenly
Betwixt us and the Sun.

It seemeth him but the
skeleton of a ship.

"And straight the Sun was flecked with bars,
(Heaven's Mother send us grace!)
As if through a dungeon-grate he peered
With broad and burning face.   180

"Alas! (thought I, and my heart beat loud)
How fast she nears and nears!
Are those her sails that glance in the Sun,
Like restless gossameres?

And its ribs are seen
as bars on the face of
the setting Sun.
The Specter-Woman
and her Deathmate,
and no other on board
the skeleton-ship.

"Are those her ribs through which the Sun
Did peer, as through a grate?
And is that Woman all her crew?
Is that a Death? and are there two?
Is Death that woman's mate?

Like vessel, like crew!

"Her lips were red, her looks were free,   190
Her locks were yellow as gold:
Her skin was as white as leprosy,
The Night-mare Life-in-Death was she,
Who thicks man's blood with cold.

Death and Life-in-
Death have diced for
the ship's crew, and
she (the latter) win-
neth the ancient
Mariner.

"The naked hulk alongside came,
And the twain were casting dice;
'The game is done! I've won! I've won!'
Quoth she, and whistles thrice.

No twilight within the
courts of the Sun.

"The Sun's rim dips; the stars rush out:
At one stride comes the dark;   200
With far-heard whisper, o'er the sea,
Off shot the specter-bark.

At the rising of the Moon,

"We listened and looked sideways up!
Fear at my heart, as at a cup,
My life-blood seemed to sip!
The stars were dim, and thick the night,
The steersman's face by his lamp gleamed white;
From the sails the dew did drip—
Till clomb above the eastern bar
The hornèd Moon, wtih one bright star   210
Within the nether tip.

One after another,

"One after one, by the star-dogged Moon,
Too quick for groan or sigh,
Each turned his face with a ghastly pang,
And cursed me with his eye.

His shipmates drop down dead.

"Four times fifty living men,
(And I heard nor sigh nor groan)
With heavy thump, a lifeless lump,
They dropt down one by one.

But Life-in-Death begins her work on the ancient Mariner.

"The souls did from their bodies fly—   220
They fled to bliss or woe!
And every soul, it passed me by
Like the whizz of my cross-bow!"

Part 4

The Wedding-Guest feareth that a Spirit is talking to him;

"I fear thee, ancient Mariner!
I fear thy skinny hand!
And thou art long, and lank, and brown,
As is the ribbed sea-sand.

But the ancient Mariner assureth him of his bodily life, and proceedeth to relate his horrible penance.

"I fear thee and thy glittering eye,
And thy skinny hand, so brown."—
"Fear not, fear not, thou Wedding-Guest!   230
This body dropt not down.

"Alone, alone, all, all alone,
Alone on a wide, wide sea!
And never a saint took pity on
My soul in agony.

He despiseth the creatures of the calm.

"The many men, so beautiful!
And they all dead did lie:
And a thousand thousand slimy things
Lived on; and so did I.

"I looked upon the rotting sea,   240
And drew my eyes away;
I looked upon the rotting deck,
And there the dead men lay.

"I looked to heaven, and tried to pray;
But or ever a prayer had gusht,
A wicked whisper came, and made
My heart as dry as dust.

"I closed my lids, and kept them close,
And the balls like pulses beat;
For the sky and the sea, and the sea
              and the sky   250
Lay like a load on my weary eye,
And the dead were at my feet.

"The cold sweat melted from their limbs,
Nor rot nor reek did they:
The look with which they looked on me
Had never passed away.

"An orphan's curse would drag to hell
A spirit from on high;
But oh! more horrible than that
Is a curse in a dead man's eye!   260
Seven days, seven nights, I saw that curse,
And yet I could not die.

"The moving Moon went up the sky,
And nowhere did abide:
Softly she was going up,
And a star or two beside—

"Her beams bemocked the sultry main,
Like April hoar-frost spread;
But where the ship's huge shadow lay,
The charmèd water burnt alway   270
A still and awful red.

"Beyond the shadow of the ship,
I watched the water-snakes:
They moved in tracks of shining white,
And when they reared, the elfish light
Fell off in hoary flakes.

"Within the shadow of the ship
I watched their rich attire:
Blue, glossy green, and velvet black,
They coiled and swam; and every track   280
Was a flash of golden fire.

Their beauty and
their happiness.

"O happy living things! no tongue
Their beauty might declare:
A spring of love gushed from my heart,

He blesseth them in
his heart.
The spell begins to
break.

And I blessed them unaware;
Sure my kind saint took pity on me,
And I blessed them unaware.

"The selfsame moment I could pray;
And from my neck so free
The Albatross fell off, and sank   290
Like lead into the sea."

Part 5

"Oh sleep! it is a gentle thing,
Beloved from pole to pole!
To Mary Queen the praise be given!
She sent the gentle sleep from Heaven,
That slid into my soul.

By grace of the holy
Mother, the ancient
Mariner is refreshed
with rain.

"The silly buckets on the deck,
That had so long remained,
I dreamt that they were filled with dew;
And when I awoke, it rained.   300

"My lips were wet, my throat was cold,
My garments all were dank;
Sure I had drunken in my dreams,
And still my body drank.

"I moved, and could not feel my limbs:
I was so light—almost
I thought that I had died in sleep,
And was a blessed ghost.

He heareth sounds and
seeth strange sights
and commotions in the
sky and the elements.

"And soon I heard a roaring wind:
It did not come anear;   310
But with its sound it shook the sails,
That were so thin and sere.

"The upper air burst into life!
And a hundred fire-flags sheen,
To and fro they were hurried about!
And to and fro, and in and out,
The wan stars danced between.

"And the coming wind did roar more loud,
And the sails did sigh like sedge;
And the rain poured down from one
    black cloud;   320
The Moon was at its edge.

"The thick black cloud was cleft, and still
The Moon was at its side:
Like waters shot from some high crag,
The lightning fell with never a jag,
A river steep and wide.

The bodies of the "The loud wind never reached the ship,
ship's crew are in- Yet now the ship moved on!
spired and the ship Beneath the lightning and the Moon
moves on; The dead men gave a groan.   330

"They groaned, they stirred, they all uprose,
Nor spake, nor moved their eyes;
It had been strange, even in a dream,
To have seen those dead men rise.

"The helmsman steered, the ship moved on;
Yet never a breeze up blew;
The mariners all 'gan work the ropes,
Where they were wont to do;
They raised their limbs like lifeless tools—
We were a ghastly crew.   340

"The body of my brother's son
Stood by me, knee to knee:
The body and I pulled at one rope,
But he said nought to me."

But not by the souls "I fear thee, ancient Mariner!"
of the men, nor by "Be calm, thou Wedding-Guest!
demons of earth or 'Twas not those souls that fled in pain,
middle air, but by a Which to their corses came again,
blessed troop of angelic But a troop of spirits blest:
spirits, sent down by
the invocation of the
guardian saint.

"For when it dawned—they dropped
        their arms,   350
And clustered round the mast;
Sweet sounds rose slowly through their mouths,
And from their bodies passed.

"Around, around, flew each sweet sound,
Then darted to the Sun;
Slowly the sounds came back again,
Now mixed, now one by one.

"Sometimes a-dropping from the sky
I heard the skylark sing;
Sometimes all little birds that are,   360
How they seemed to fill the sea and air
With their sweet jargoning!

"And now 'twas like all instruments,
Now like a lonely flute;
And now it is an angel's song,
That makes the heavens be mute.

"It ceased; yet still the sails made on
A pleasant noise till noon,
A noise like of a hidden brook
In the leafy month of June,   370
That to the sleeping woods all night
Singeth a quiet tune.

"Till noon we quietly sailed on,
Yet never a breeze did breathe:
Slowly and smoothly went the ship,
Moved onward from beneath.

The lonesome Spirit from the South Pole carries on the ship as far as the Line, in obedience to the angelic troop, but still requireth vengeance.

"Under the keel nine fathom deep,
From the land of mist and snow,
The Spirit slid: and it was he
That made the ship to go.   380
The sails at noon left off their tune,
And the ship stood still also.

"The Sun, right up above the mast,
Had fixed her to the ocean:
But in a minute she 'gan stir,
With a short uneasy motion—

Backwards and forwards half her length
With a short uneasy motion.

"Then like a pawing horse let go,
She made a sudden bound: 390
It flung the blood into my head,
And I fell down in a swound.

*The Polar Spirit's fel-
low demons, the in-
visible inhabitants of
the element, take part
in his wrong; and two
of them relate, one to
the other, that penance
long and heavy for the
ancient Mariner hath
been accorded to the
Polar Spirit, who re-
turneth southward.*

"How long in that same fit I lay,
I have not to declare;
But ere my living life returned,
I heard, and in my soul discerned,
Two voices in the air.

" 'Is it he?' quoth one, 'Is this the man?
By Him who died on cross,
With his cruel bow he laid full low   400
The harmless Albatross.

" 'The Spirit who bideth by himself
In the land of mist and snow,
He loved the bird that loved the man
Who shot him with his bow.'

"The other was a softer voice,
As soft as honey-dew:
Quoth he, 'The man hath penance done,
And penance more will do.' "

Part 6

First Voice

" 'But tell me, tell me! speak again,   410
Thy soft response renewing—
What makes that ship drive on so fast?
What is the ocean doing?'

Second Voice

" 'Still as a slave before his lord,
The ocean hath no blast;
His great bright eye most silently
Up to the Moon is cast—

" 'If he may know which way to go;
For she guides him smooth or grim.

See, brother, see! how graciously   420
She looketh down on him.'

First Voice

The Mariner hath been cast into a trance; for the angelic power causeth the vessel to drive northward faster than human life could endure.

" 'But why drives on that ship so fast,
Without or wave or wind?'

Second Voice

" 'The air is cut away before,
And closes from behind.'
" 'Fly, brother, fly! more high, more high!
Or we shall be belated:
For slow and slow that ship will go,
When the Mariner's trance is abated.'

The supernatural motion is retarded; the Mariner awakes, and his penance begins anew.

"I woke, and we were sailing on   430
As in a gentle weather:
'Twas night, calm night, the moon was high;
The dead men stood together.

"All stood together on the deck,
For a charnel-dungeon fitter:
All fixed on me their stony eyes,
That in the Moon did glitter.

"The pang, the curse, with which they died,
Had never passed away:
I could not draw my eyes from theirs,   440
Nor turn them up to pray.

The curse is finally expiated.

"And now this spell was snapt: once more
I viewed the ocean green,
And looked far forth, yet little saw
Of what had else been seen—

"Like one, that on a lonesome road
Doth walk in fear and dread,
And having once turned round, walks on,
And turns no more his head;
Because he knows, a frightful fiend   450
Doth close behind him tread.

"But soon there breathed a wind on me,
Nor sound nor motion made:
Its path was not upon the sea,
In ripple or in shade.

"It raised my hair, it fanned my cheek
Like a meadow-gale of spring—
It mingled strangely with my fears,
Yet it felt like a welcoming.

"Swiftly, swiftly flew the ship,   460
Yet she sailed softly too:
Sweetly, sweetly blew the breeze—
On me alone it blew.

*And the ancient
Mariner beholdeth his
native country.*

"Oh! dream of joy! is this indeed
The light-house top I see?
Is this the hill? Is this the kirk?
Is this mine own countree?

"We drifted o'er the harbor-bar,
And I with sobs did pray—
O let me be awake, my God!   470
Or let me sleep alway.

"The harbor-bay was clear as glass,
So smoothly it was strewn!
And on the bay the moonlight lay,
And the shadow of the Moon.

"The rock shone bright, the kirk no less,
That stands above the rock:
The moonlight steeped in silentness
The steady weathercock.

"And the bay was white with silent light   480
Till, rising from the same,

*The angelic spirits
leave the dead bodies,*

Full many shapes, that shadows were,
In crimson colors came.

"A little distance from the prow
Those crimson shadows were:
I turned my eyes upon the deck—
Oh, Christ! what saw I there!

"Each corse lay flat, lifeless and flat,
And, by the holy rood!

*And appear in their
own forms of light.*

A man all light, a seraph-man,   490
On every corse there stood.

"This seraph-band, each waved his hand:
It was a heavenly sight!
They stood as signals to the land,
Each one a lovely light;

"This seraph-band, each waved his hand,
No voice did they impart—
No voice; but oh! the silence sank
Like music on my heart.

"But soon I heard the dash of oars,   500
I heard the Pilot's cheer;
My head was turned perforce away,
And I saw a boat appear.

"The Pilot and the Pilot's boy,
I heard them coming fast:
Dear Lord in Heaven! it was a joy
The dead men could not blast.

"I saw a third—I heard his voice:
It is the Hermit good!
He singeth loud his godly hymns   510
That he makes in the wood.
He'll shrieve my soul, he'll wash away
The Albatross's blood."

Part 7

The Hermit of the wood,

"This Hermit good lives in that wood
Which slopes down to the sea.
How loudly his sweet voice he rears!
He loves to talk with marineres
That come from a far countree.

"He kneels at morn, and noon, and eve—
He hath a cushion plump: 520
It is the moss that wholly hides
The rotted old oak-stump.

"The skiff-boat neared: I heard them talk,
'Why, this is strange, I trow!
Where are those lights so many and fair,
That signal made but now?'

Approacheth the ship with wonder.

" 'Strange, by my faith!' the Hermit said—
'And they answered not our cheer!

The planks looked warped! and see those sails,
How thin they are and sere!   530
I never saw aught like to them,
Unless perchance it were

" 'Brown skeletons of leaves that lag
My forest-brook along;
When the ivy-tod is heavy with snow,
And the owlet whoops to the wolf below,
That eats the she-wolf's young.'

" 'Dear Lord! it hath a fiendish look—
(The Pilot made reply)
I am a-feared'—'Push on, push on!'   540
Said the Hermit cheerily.

"The boat came closer to the ship,
But I nor spake nor stirred;
The boat came close beneath the ship,
And straight a sound was heard.

The ship suddenly
sinketh.

"Under the water it rumbled on,
Still louder and more dread:
It reached the ship, it split the bay;
The ship went down like lead.

The ancient Mariner
is saved in the Pilot's
boat.

"Stunned by that loud and dreadful sound,   550
Which sky and ocean smote,
Like one that hath been seven days drowned
My body lay afloat;
But swift as dreams, myself I found
Within the Pilot's boat.

"Upon the whirl, where sank the ship,
The boat spun round and round;
And all was still, save that the hill
Was telling of the sound.

"I moved my lips—the Pilot shrieked   560
And fell down in a fit;
The holy Hermit raised his eyes,
And prayed where he did sit.

"I took the oars: the Pilot's boy,
Who now doth crazy go,

Laughed loud and long, and all the while
His eyes went to and fro.
'Ha! ha!' quoth he, 'full plain I see,
The Devil knows how to row.'

"And now, all in my own countree,   570
I stood on the firm land!
The Hermit stepped forth from the boat,
And scarcely he could stand.

*The ancient Mariner
earnestly entreateth
the Hermit to shrieve
him; and the penance
of Life falls on him.*

" 'O shrieve me, shrieve me, holy man!'
The Hermit crossed his brow.
'Say quick,' quoth he, 'I bid thee say—
What manner of man art thou?'

"Forthwith this frame of mine was wrenched
With a woful agony,
Which forced me to begin my tale;   580
And then it left me free.

*And ever and anon
throughout his future
life an agony con-
straineth him to travel
from land to land,*

"Since then, at an uncertain hour,
That agony returns;
And till my ghastly tale is told,
This heart within me burns.

"I pass, like night, from land to land;
I have strange power of speech;
That moment that his face I see,
I know the man that must hear me:
To him my tale I teach.   590

"What loud uproar bursts from that door!
The wedding-guests are there:
But in the garden-bower the bride
And bride-maids singing are:
And hark the little vesper bell,
Which biddeth me to prayer!

"O Wedding-Guest! this soul hath been
Alone on a wide, wide sea:
So lonely 'twas, that God himself
Scarce seemèd there to be.   600

"Oh sweeter than the marriage-feast,
'Tis sweeter far to me,

To walk together to the kirk
With a goodly company!—

"To walk together to the kirk,
And all together pray,
While each to his great Father bends,
Old men, and babes, and loving friends,
And youths and maidens gay!

And to teach by his
own example love and
reverence to all things
that God made and
loveth.

"Farewell, farewell! but this I tell   610
To thee, thou Wedding-Guest!
He prayeth well, who loveth well
Both man and bird and beast.

"He prayeth best, who loveth best
All things both great and small;
For the dear God who loveth us,
He made and loveth all."

The Mariner, whose eye is bright,
Whose beard with age is hoar,
Is gone: and now the Wedding-Guest   620
Turned from the bridegroom's door.

He went like one that hath been stunned,
And is of sense forlorn:
A sadder and a wiser man,
He rose the morrow morn.

1. One often hears that literature written in a given period *mirrors* that period. Does the surface action of this poem reflect the actual life of Coleridge's period? of any period?

2. The Ancient Mariner implies that the statement made in lines 612–617 is the theme, or lesson, of the story he has told. Explain.

Dejection: An Ode

Late, late yestreen I saw the new Moon,
With the old Moon in her arms;
And I fear, I fear, my master dear!
We shall have a deadly storm.
                    Ballad of Sir Patrick Spence

I

Well! If the Bard was weather-wise, who made
The grand old ballad of Sir Patrick Spence,

This night, so tranquil now, will not go hence
Unroused by winds, that ply a busier trade
Than those which mould yon cloud in lazy flakes,
Or the dull sobbing draft, that moans and rakes
    Upon the strings of this Aeolian lute,
    Which better far were mute.
For lo! the New-moon winter-bright!
And overspread with phantom light,   10
(With swimming phantom light o'erspread
But rimmed and circled by a silver thread)
I see the old Moon in her lap, foretelling
    The coming-on of rain and squally blast.
And oh! that even now the gust were swelling,
    And the slant night-shower driving loud and fast!
Those sounds which oft have raised me, whilst they awed,
    And sent my soul abroad,
Might now perhaps their wonted impulse give,
Might startle this dull pain, and make it move and live!   20

2

A grief without a pang, void, dark, and drear,
    A stifled, drowsy, unimpassioned grief,
    Which finds no natural outlet, no relief,
        In word, or sigh, or tear—
O Lady! in this wan and heartless mood,
To other thoughts by yonder throstle woo'd,
    All this long eve, so balmy and serene,
Have I been gazing on the western sky,
    And its peculiar tint of yellow green;
And still I gaze—and with how blank an eye!   30
And those thin clouds above, in flakes and bars,
That give away their motion to the stars;
Those stars, that glide behind them or between,
Now sparkling, now bedimmed but always seen;
Yon crescent Moon, as fixed as if it grew
In its own cloudless, starless lake of blue;
I see them all so excellently fair,
I see, not feel, how beautiful they are!

3

    My genial spirits fail;
    And what can these avail   40
To life the smothering weight from off my breast?
    It were a vain endeavor,
    Though I should gaze for ever

On that green light that lingers in the west;
I may not hope from outward forms to win
The passion and the life, whose fountains are within.

4

O Lady! we receive but what we give,
And in our life alone does Nature live;
Ours is her wedding-garment, ours her shroud!
    And would we aught behold, of higher worth,   50
Than that inanimate cold world allowed
To the poor loveless ever-anxious crowd,
    Ah! from the soul itself must issue forth
A light, a glory, a fair luminous cloud
      Enveloping the Earth—
And from the soul itself must there be sent
    A sweet and potent voice, of its own birth,
Of all sweet sounds the life and element!

5

O pure of heart! thou need'st not ask of me
What this strong music in the soul may be!   60
What, and wherein it doth exist,
This light, this glory, this fair luminous mist,
This beautiful and beauty-making power.
    Joy, virtuous Lady! Joy that ne'er was given,
Save to the pure, and in their purest hour,
Life, and Life effluence, cloud at once and shower
Joy, Lady! is the spirit and the power,
Which wedding Nature to us gives in dower
    A new Earth and new Heaven,
Undreamt of by the sensual and the proud—   70
Joy is the sweet voice, Joy the luminous cloud—
      We in ourselves rejoice!
And thence flows all that charms or ear or sight,
    All melodies the echoes of that voice,
All colours a suffusion from that light.

6

There was a time when, though my path was rough,
    This joy within me dallied with distress,
And all misfortunes were but as the stuff
    Whence Fancy made me dreams of happiness:
For hope grew round me, like the twining vine,   80
And fruits, and foliage, not my own, seemed mine.
But now afflictions bow me down to earth:

Nor care I that they rob me of my mirth;
　　But oh! each visitation
Suspends what nature gave me at my birth,
　　My shaping spirit of Imagination.
For not to think of what I needs must feel,
　　But to be still and patient, all I can;
And haply by abstruse research to steal
　　From my own nature all the natural man—   90
　　This was my sole resource, my only plan:
Till that which suits a part infects the whole,
And now is almost grown the habit of my soul.

7

Hence, viper thoughts, that coil around my mind,
　　　　Reality's dark dream!
I turn from you, and listen to the wind,
　　Which long has raved unnoticed. What a scream
Of agony by torture lengthened out
That lute sent forth! Thou Wind, that rav'st without,
　　Bare crag, or mountain-tairn, or blasted tree,   100
Or pine-grove whither woodman never clomb,
Or lonely house, long held the witches' home,
　　Methinks were fitter instruments for thee,
Mad Lutanist! who in this month of showers,
Of dark-brown gardens, and of peeping flowers,
Mak'st Devils' yule, with worse than wintry song,
The blossoms, buds, and timorous leaves among.
　　Thou Actor, perfect in all tragic sounds!
Thou mighty Poet, e'en to frenzy bold!
　　　　What tell'st thou now about?   110
　　　　'Tis of the rushing of an host in rout,
　　With groans, of trampled men, with smarting wounds—
At once they groan with pain, and shudder with the cold!
But hush! there is a pause of deepest silence!
　　And all that noise, as of a rushing crowd,
With groans, and tremulous shudderings—all is over—
　　It tells another tale, with sounds less deep and loud!
　　　　A tale of less affright,
　　　　And tempered with delight,
As Otway's[1] self had framed the tender lay,—   120
　　　　'Tis of a little child
　　　　Upon a lonesome wild,

....

　　1. This was originally a reference to Wordsworth, addressed as "Edmund."
The "little child" is obviously "Lucy Gray."

Not far from home, but she hath lost her way:
And now moans low in bitter grief and fear,
And now screams loud, and hopes to make her mother hear.

8

'Tis midnight, but small thoughts have I of sleep:
Full seldom may my friend such vigils keep!
Visit her, gentle Sleep! with wings of healing,
   And may this storm be but a mountain-birth,
May all the stars hang bright above her dwelling,   130
   Silent as though they watched the sleeping Earth!
     With light heart may she rise,
     Gay fancy, cheerful eyes,
Joy lift her spirit, joy attune her voice;
To her may all things live, from pole to pole,
Their life the eddying of her living soul!
   O simple spirit, guided from above,
Dear Lady! friend devoutest of my choice,
Thus mayest thou ever, evermore rejoice.

■ 1. Write a detailed paraphrase of this poem. Also state its theme.

2. Compare Coleridge's beliefs about the nature of the imagination with Wordsworth's (pp. 353–356) and Collins' (pp. 324–330). What similarities and what differences do there seem to be?

3. Is there any evidence that Coleridge makes the power of imagination dependent upon moral character?

4. Is there any similarity in statement between stanza 4 of Wordsworth's "Intimations of Immortality" (p. 378) and stanza 4 of "Dejection"?

5. Is there any way (by internal evidence, that is, information available from the poem itself) of identifying the "Lady"? She is addressed frequently throughout the poem. If you cannot identify her, does her lack of identity hinder your understanding and appreciation?

6. Ernest de Selincourt in "Coleridge's 'Dejection: An Ode'" prints the original version, sent to Sarah Hutchinson on April 4, 1802. The original version of the poem differs in a number of lines from the version (published in Sybilline Leaves, 1817) you have just read. Most notably, the "Lady" is addressed as "Sarah" Hutchinson, with whom the already married Coleridge was in love. In other words, the frustration he feels has caused his loss of joy and therefore his loss of imaginative power. Does this added biographical information make the poem more meaningful to you? Would your appreciation and understanding of the poem be as satisfactory if you did not know about Sarah Hutchinson? Justify your answer.

George Gordon, Lord Byron

(1788–1824)

■■■■■■■■■■

Wɪᴛʜ ᴀ ғᴀᴛʜᴇʀ reputedly profligate and a mother who in twentieth-century terms would be called neurotic, Byron faced a stormy early life. Although crippled from birth Byron was attractive in appearance and active in physical games. From a great-uncle he inherited a title and estate when he was eleven years old. At Cambridge he published *Hours of Idleness* (1807). *English Bards and Scotch Reviewers* (1809) was a stinging reply to the criticism his first book had received in *The Edinburgh Review*. The publication of *Childe Harold* (1812) made him famous. Byron was a passionate social reformer in the House of Lords, but he was forced to leave England in 1816 when the scandal over his affair with his half-sister Augusta Leigh became too strong to endure. Byron's subsequent affairs were passionate, frequent, and often scandalous. On the continent he completed several long poems, among them the great satire *Don Juan* (1819–1823). In Italy he associated with Shelley and members of Shelley's circle. After volunteering his services and resources in the Greek fight for independence from the Turks, Byron contracted a fever and died.

Suggested Readings

T. S. Eʟɪᴏᴛ, "Byron," in *Anne to Victoria,* ed. Bonamy Dobrée. London: Cassell & Company, Ltd., 1937, pp. 601–619.

Bᴇʀᴛʀᴀɴᴅ Rᴜssᴇʟʟ, "Byron and the Modern World," *Journal of the History of Ideas*, I (1940), 24–37.

Sᴀᴍᴜᴇʟ C. Cʜᴇᴡ, "Lord Byron," in *A Literary History of England*. ed. Albert C. Baugh. New York: Appleton-Century-Crofts, Inc., 1948, pp. 1219–1229.

■■■■■■■■■■

The differences between the poetic theory of the neoclassical and romantic periods are usually stated in some such fashion as the following. The facts of nature or experience or moral sentiments were "embellished" or stated as succinctly and as beautifully as possible by a poet like Pope. The neoclassical poet, in other words, thought of himself as holding to the facts of the objective world. But the romantic poet, as typified by Wordsworth, thought of himself as communicating his *own* reactions and his *own* emotions. The poet was held to have some penetrative power greater than that given to other men, and his interpretations therefore were significant and valuable.

The romantics emphasized, then, individual feeling and insight. As reflected in Wordsworth's commentaries (see, for example, *The Prelude*, Book 13) the doctrine is something like this: The poet is stirred by a noble cause; he commits his feelings—"emotion recollected in tranquillity"—to his verse; and the reader in turn is free to experience something of the poet's own experiences. Wordsworth is not often explicit about the nature of the knowledge or insight the poet makes available, but he does insist that the emotions be aroused by honorable experiences and "important subjects." The reader's affections are thus to be "strengthened" and "purified."

Emotion as a good is often associated also with the power of the poet's imagination. Shelley, for instance, said, "The great instrument of moral good is the imagination." And Coleridge speaks of the "idealizing" power of the imagination. The neoclassic poets, on the other hand, tended to be a little suspicious of the emotions and to want to hold them in check. For them moral wisdom was not the creation of the individual poet so much as it was traditional, conventional wisdom of long standing. And for them the imagination was not the tremendous power and force it was for Coleridge or Wordsworth.

This thumbnail account of the differences between neoclassical and romantic doctrine may serve to make clear the somewhat anomalous position into which Byron falls as, on the one hand, an admirer of Pope and, on the other, as a practicing poet contemporary with Wordsworth, Coleridge, Shelley, and the others. Byron's admiration for the neoclassical poets is stated in his "Letter to John Murray, Esq., on the Rev. W. L. Bowles's Strictures on the Life and Writings of Pope." About the concern with imagination he said this: "It is the fashion of the day to lay great stress upon what they call 'imagination' and 'invention,' the two commonest of qualities: an Irish peasant with a little whiskey in his head will imagine and invent more than would furnish forth a modern poem." And about Pope as the poet best able to express inherited moral wisdom, this: "He is the moral poet of all civilization; and as such, let us hope that he will one day be the national poet of mankind." But Byron made his own reputation as a romantic egoist or individualist, not as one expressing inherited, traditional, or fixed moral values. What he did have in common with Pope was a gift for satire, although his own was more boisterous than Pope's.

Keeping these general points in mind we may, in looking at some of Byron's poems, be able to see his work in relation to that of his predecessors and contemporaries.

Sonnet on Chillon [1]

Eternal Spirit of the chainless Mind!
   Brightest in dungeons, Liberty! thou art:
   For there thy habitation is the heart—
The heart which love of thee alone can bind;
And when thy sons to fetters are consigned—
   To fetters, and the damp vault's dayless gloom,
   Their country conquers with their martyrdom,
And Freedom's fame finds wings on every wind.
Chillon! thy prison is a holy place,
   And thy sad floor an altar—for 'twas trod,
Until his very steps have left a trace
   Worn, as if thy cold pavement were a sod,
By Bonnivard!—May none those marks efface!
   For they appeal from tyranny to God.

....

1. For trying to make Geneva a free republic, François de Bonnivard (1493–1570) was confined for six years in the dungeon of the Castle of Chillon near Geneva.

She Walks in Beauty

She walks in beauty, like the night
Of cloudless climes and starry skies,
And all that's best of dark and bright
Meet in her aspect and her eyes;
Thus mellow'd to that tender light
Which heaven to gaudy day denies.

One shade the more, one ray the less,
Had half impair'd the nameless grace
Which waves in every raven tress
Or softly lightens o'er her face,
Where thoughts serenely sweet express
How pure, how dear their dwelling-place.

And on that cheek and o'er that brow
So soft, so calm, yet eloquent,
The smiles that win, the tints that glow
But tell of days in goodness spent,
A mind at peace with all below,
A heart whose love is innocent.

■   Is this an idealized, highly imaginative statement? Explain.

When We Two Parted

When we two parted
  In silence and tears,
Half broken-hearted
  To sever for years,
Pale grew thy cheek and cold,
  Colder thy kiss;
Truly that hour foretold
  Sorrow to this.

The dew of the morning
  Sunk chill on my brow—   10
It felt like the warning
  Of what I feel now.
Thy vows are all broken,
  And light is thy fame;
I hear thy name spoken,
  And share in its shame.

They name thee before me,
  A knell to mine ear;
A shudder comes o'er me—
  Why wert thou so dear?   20
They know not I knew thee,
  Who knew thee too well:—
Long, long shall I rue thee,
  Too deeply to tell.

In secret we met—
  In silence I grieve
That thy heart could forget,
  Thy spirit deceive.
If I should meet thee
  After long years,   30
How should I greet thee?—
  With silence and tears.

■   What is the effect of the final lines if one considers them in relation to a meeting of actual former lovers?

We'll Go No More A-Roving

So, we'll go no more a-roving
    So late into the night,
Though the heart be still as loving,
    And the moon be still as bright.

For the sword outwears its sheath,
    And the soul wears out the breast,
And the heart must pause to breathe,
    And love itself have rest.

Though the night was made for loving,
    And the day returns too soon,
Yet we'll go no more a-roving
    By the light of the moon.

■   Does Byron in this poem (or in any of his poems you have read thus far) appear to believe that the emotion generated by a poem is ennobling or purifying, as Wordsworth believed? Does he, on the other hand, so far as one can judge from this poem (or his poetry generally), seem to conceive of the poet as one expressing the moral wisdom of his race?

Stanzas for Music

There be none of Beauty's daughters
    With a magic like thee;
And like music on the waters
    Is thy sweet voice to me:
When, as if its sound were causing
The charmèd Ocean's pausing,
The waves lie still and gleaming,
And the lulled winds seem dreaming:

And the midnight moon is weaving
    Her bright chain o'er the deep;
Whose breast is gently heaving,
    As an infant's asleep:
So the spirit bows before thee,
To listen and adore thee;
With a full but soft emotion,
Like the swell of summer's ocean.

1. Is Byron here reporting on his emotion, or is he trying to evoke emotion through the instrumentality of his poem—through its symbols, meter, and so forth?

2. What is the effect of the repeated -ing sounds?

When a Man Hath No Freedom to Fight for at Home

When a man hath no freedom to fight for at home,
    Let him combat for that of his neighbors;
Let him think of the glories of Greece and of Rome,
    And get knocked on the head for his labors.

To do good to Mankind is the chivalrous plan,
    And is always as nobly requited;
Then battle for Freedom wherever you can,
    And, if not shot or hanged, you'll get knighted.

Byron is likely to be indifferent to decorum, conventions, and forms which the neoclassical poet would have observed carefully. What is there in this poem that you would not expect to find in a poem, say, by Pope?

Stanzas Written on the Road between Florence and Pisa

Oh, talk not to me of a name great in story;
The days of our youth are the days of our glory;
And the myrtle and ivy of sweet two-and-twenty
Are worth all your laurels, though ever so plenty.

What are garlands and crowns to the brow that is wrinkled?
'Tis but as a dead-flower with May-dew besprinkled.
Then away with all such from the head that is hoary!
What care I for the wreaths that can *only* give glory!

Oh Fame!—if I e'er took delight in thy praises,
'Twas less for the sake of thy high-sounding phrases,
Than to see the bright eyes of the dear one discover,
She thought that I was not unworthy to love her.

There chiefly I sought thee, *there* only I found thee;
Her glance was the best of the rays that surround thee;

When it sparkled o'er aught that was bright in my story,
I knew it was love, and I felt it was glory.

■   There is in most neoclassical verse an air of impersonality, objectivity, and propriety. Does this poem illustrate these characteristics? Consider it in terms of its meter, tone, and diction.

Stanzas for Music

There's not a joy the world can give like that it takes away,
When the glow of early thought declines in feeling's dull decay;
'Tis not on youth's smooth cheek the blush alone, which fades so fast,
But the tender bloom of heart is gone, ere youth itself be past.

Then the few whose spirits float above the wreck of happiness
Are driven o'er the shoals of guilt or ocean of excess:
The magnet of their course is gone, or only points in vain
The shore to which their shivered sail shall never stretch again.

Then the mortal coldness of the soul like death itself comes down;
It cannot feel for others' woes, it dare not dream its own;
That heavy chill has frozen o'er the fountain of our tears,
And though the eye may sparkle still, 'tis where the ice appears.

Though wit may flash from fluent lips, and mirth distract the breast,
Through midnight hours that yield no more their former hope of rest;
'Tis but as ivy-leaves around the ruined turret wreath,
All green and wildly fresh without, but worn and gray beneath.

Oh, could I feel as I have felt—or be what I have been,
Or weep as I could once have wept, o'er many a vanished scene;
As springs, in deserts found, seem sweet, all brackish though they be,
So, midst the withered waste of life, those tears would flow to me.

■   It is sometimes said that a reader can discover a good deal about a
poet's interests and the temper of his mind by studying the persistent or
recurrent imagery in his poetry. What pattern of imagery in this poem
seems to be echoed in the other Byron poems you have read?

From *Don Juan*[1]

Dedication

Bob Southey! You're a poet—Poet laureate,
  And representative of all the race;
Although 'tis true that you turned out a Tory at
  Last—yours has lately been a common case;
And now, my Epic Renegade! what are ye at?
  With all the Lakers,[2] in and out of place?
A nest of tuneful persons, to my eye
Like "four and twenty Blackbirds in a pye[3];

"Which pye being opened they began to sing"
  (This old song and new simile holds goods),   10
"A dainty dish to set before the King,"
  Or Regent, who admires such kind of food;—
And Coleridge, too, has lately taken wing,
  But like a hawk encumbered with his hood—
Explaining metaphysics to the nation—
I wish he would explain his Explanation.

You, Bob! are rather insolent, you know,
  At being disappointed in your wish
To supersede all warblers here below,
  And be the only Blackbird in the dish;   20
And then you overstrain yourself, or so,
  And tumble downward like the flying fish
Gasping on deck, because you soar too high, Bob,
And fall for lack of moisture quite a-dry, Bob!

And Wordsworth, in a rather long "Excursion"
  (I think the quarto holds five hundred pages),
Has given a sample from the vasty version
  Of his new system to perplex the sages;
'Tis poetry—at least by his assertion,

---

1. Byron took the name of his hero, Don Juan, from the Spanish legends concerning a gallant known as Don Juan Tenorio. He used little of the Spanish story save the name. "I meant," says Byron in a letter to Murray, his publisher, "to take him the tour of Europe, with a proper mixture of siege, battle, and adventure. . . . I meant to have him a Cavalier Servente in Italy, and a cause for a divorce in England, and a Sentimental 'Werther-faced man' in Germany, so as to show the different ridicules of the society in each of those countries, and to have displayed him gradually *gâté* and *blasé* as he grew older, as is natural. But I had not quite fixed whether to make him end in Hell, or in an unhappy marriage, not knowing which would be the severest. The Spanish traditon says Hell: but it is probably only an Allegory of the other state."   2. Coleridge, Shelley, Wordsworth, the Lake poets.   3. Pun on Henry James Pye, made laureate in 1790.

And may appear so when the dog-star rages— 30
And he who understands it would be able
To add a story to the Tower of Babel.

You—Gentlemen! by dint of long seclusion
    From better company, have kept your own
At Keswick, and through still continued fusion
    Of one another's minds, at last have grown
To deem as a most logical conclusion,
    That poesy has wreaths for you alone;
There is a narrowness in such a notion,
Which makes me wish you'd change your lakes for ocean. 40

I would not imitate the petty thought,
    Nor coin my self-love to so base a vice,
For all the glory your conversion brought,
    Since gold alone should not have been its price,
You have your salary; wasn't for that you wrought?
    And Wordsworth has his place in the Excise.
You're shabby fellows—true—but poets still,
And duly seated on the Immortal Hill.

■   Compare the opening lines of Pope's "Of the Characters of Women"
with these lines from *Don Juan* in respect to the following: precision of
statement, sharpness of wit, employment of caesura, and tone.

Canto 4[4]

Nothing so difficult as a beginning
    In poesy, unless perhaps the end;
For oftentimes, when Pegasus seems winning
    The race, he sprains a wing, and down we tend,
Like Lucifer, when hurled from heaven for sinning;
    Our sin the same, and hard as his to men,
Being pride, which leads the mind to soar too far,
Till our own weakness shows us what we are.

But Time, which brings all beings to their level,
    And sharp Adversity, will teach at last   10
Man, and—as we would hope—perhaps the devil,
    That neither of their intellects are vast:
While youth's hot wishes in our red veins revel,

4.   Cantos 2, 3, and 4 contain episodes in which Don Juan is shipwrecked and
then nursed back to health by Haidée, daughter of Lambro, a pirate.

We know not this—the blood flows on too fast;
But as the torrent widens towards the ocean,
We ponder deeply on each past emotion.

As boy, I thought myself a clever fellow,
   And wished that others held the same opinion;
They took it up when my days grew more mellow,
   And other minds acknowledged my dominion: 20
Now my sere fancy "falls into the yellow
   Leaf," and Imagination droops her pinion,
And the sad truth which hovers o'er my desk
Turns what was once romantic to burlesque.

And if I laugh at any mortal thing,
   'Tis that I may not weep; and if I weep,
'Tis that our nature cannot always bring
   Itself to apathy, for we must steep
Our hearts first in the depth of Lethe's spring,
   Ere what we least wish to behold will sleep: 30
Thetis baptized her mortal son in Styx;
A mortal mother would on Lethe fix.

Some have accused me of a strange design
   Against the creed and morals of the land,
And trace it in this poem every line:
   I don't pretend that I quite understand
My own meaning when I would be *very* fine;
   But the fact is, that I have nothing planned
Unless it were to be a moment merry,
A novel word in my vocabulary.   40

To the kind reader of our sober clime,
   This way of writing will appear exotic:
Pulci was sire of the half-serious rhyme,
   Who sang when chivalry was more Quixotic,
And reveled in the fancies of the time,
   True knights, chaste dames, huge giants, kings despotic;
But all these, save the last, being obsolete,
I chose a modern subject as more meet.

How I have treated it, I do not know;
   Perhaps no better than they have treated me   50
Who have imputed such designs as show
   Not what they saw, but what they wished to see:
But if it gives them pleasure, be it so·

This is a liberal age, and thoughts are free:
Meantime Apollo plucks me by the ear,
And tells me to resume my story here.

. . .

Now pillowed cheek to cheek, in loving sleep,
 Haidée and Juan their siesta took,
A gentle slumber, but it was not deep,
 For ever and anon a something shook
Juan, and shuddering o'er his frame would creep;
 And Haidée's sweet lips murmured like a brook 230
A wordless music, and her face so fair
Stirred with her dream, as rose-leaves with the air;

Or as the stirring of a deep clear stream
 Within an Alpine hollow, when the wind
Walks o'er it, was she shaken by the dream,
 The mystical usurper of the mind—
O'erpowering us to be whate'er may seem
 Good to the soul which we no more can bind:
Strange state of being! (for 'tis still to be)
Senseless to feel, and with sealed eyes to see. 240

She dreamed of being alone on the seashore,
 Chained to a rock; she knew not how, but stir
She could not from the spot, and the loud roar
 Grew, and each wave rose roughly, threatening her;
And o'er her upper lip they seemed to pour,
 Until she sobbed for breath, and soon they were
Foaming o'er her lone head, so fierce and high—
Each broke to drown her, yet she could not die.

Anon—she was released; and then she strayed
 O'er the sharp shingles with her bleeding feet, 250
And stumbled almost every step she made:
 And something rolled before her in a sheet,
Which she must still pursue, howe'er afraid;
 'Twas white and indistinct, nor stopped to meet
Her glance or grasp, for still she gazed and grasped,
And ran, but it escaped her as she clasped.

The dream changed:—in a cave she stood, its walls
 Were hung with marble icicles: the work
Of ages on its water-fretted halls,
 Where waves might wash, and seals might breed and
  lurk; 260

Her hair was dripping, and the very balls
    Of her black eyes seemed turned to tears, and mirk
The sharp rocks looked below each drop they caught,
    Which froze to marble as it fell—she thought.

And wet, and cold, and lifeless, at her feet,
    Pale as the foam that frothed on his dead brow,
Which she essayed in vain to clear (how sweet
    Were once her cares, how idle seemed they now!)
Lay Juan, nor could aught renew the beat
    Of his quenched heart; and the sea-dirges low   270
Rang in her sad ears like a mermaid's song,
And that brief dream appeared a life too long.

And gazing on the dead, she thought his face
    Faded, or altered into something new—
Like to her father's features, till each trace
    More like and like to Lambro's aspect grew—
With all his keen worn look and Grecian grace;
    And starting, she awoke, and what to view?
O Powers of Heaven! what dark eye meets she there?
'Tis—'tis her father's—fixed upon the pair!   280

Then shrieking, she arose, and shrieking fell,
    With joy and sorrow, hope and fear, to see
Him whom she deemed a habitant where dwell
    The ocean buried, risen from death, to be
Perchance the death of one she loved too well:
    Dear as her father had been to Haidée,
It was a moment of that awful kind—
I have seen such—but must not call to mind.

Up Juan sprang to Haidée's bitter shriek,
    And caught her falling, and from off the wall   290
Snatched down his sabre, in hot haste to wreak
    Vengeance on him who was the cause of all;
Then Lambro, who till now forbore to speak,
    Smiled scornfully, and said, "Within my call,
A thousand scimitars await the word;
Put up, young man, put up your silly sword."

And Haidée clung around him: "Juan, 'tis—
    'Tis Lambro—'tis my father! Kneel with me—
He will forgive us—yes—it must be—yes,
    Oh, dearest father, in this agony   300

Of pleasure and of pain—even while I kiss
    Thy garment's hem with transport, can it be
That doubt should mingle with my filial joy?
Deal with me as thou wilt, but spare this boy."

High and inscrutable the old man stood,
    Calm in his voice, and calm within his eye—
Not always signs with him of calmest mood:
    He looked upon her, but gave no reply;
Then turned to Juan, in whose cheek the blood
    Oft came and went, as there resolved to die   310
In arms, at least, he stood in act to spring
On the first foe whom Lambro's call might bring.

"Young man, your sword!" So Lambro once more said;
    Juan replied, "Not while this arm is free!"
The old man's cheek grew pale, but not with dread,
    But drawing from his belt a pistol, he
Replied, "Your blood be then on your own head."
    Then looked close at the flint, as if to see
'Twas fresh—for he had lately used the lock—
And next proceeded quietly to cock.   320

It has a strange, quick jar upon the ear,
    That cocking of a pistol, when you know
A moment more will bring the sight to bear
    Upon your person, twelve yards off, or so;
A gentlemanly distance, not too near,
    If you have got a former friend for foe;
But after being fired at once or twice,
The ear becomes more Irish, and less nice.

Lambro presented, and one instant more
    Had stopped this canto, and Don Juan's breath,   330
When Haidée threw herself her boy before;
    Stern as her sire, "On me," she cried, "let death
Descend—the fault is mine; this fatal shore
    He found—but sought not. I have pledged my faith;
I love him—I will die with him: I knew
Your nature's firmness—know your daughter's too."

A minute past, and she had been all tears,
    And tenderness, and infancy; but now
She stood as one who championed human fears—
    Pale, statue-like, and stern, she wooed the blow;   340

And tall beyond her sex, and their compeers,
   She drew up to her height, as if to show
A fairer mark; and with a fixed eye scanned
Her father's face—but never stopped his hand.

He gazed on her, and she on him; 'twas strange
   How like they looked! the expression was the same,
Serenely savage, with a little change
   In the large dark eye's mutual-darted flame;
For she, too, was as one who could avenge,
   If cause should be—a lioness, though tame.   350
Her father's blood before her father's face
Boiled up, and proved her truly of his race.

I said they were alike, their features and
   Their stature differing but in sex and years;
Even to the delicacy of their hand
   There was resemblance, such as true blood wears;
And now to see them, thus divided, stand
   In fixed ferocity, when joyous tears
And sweet sensations should have welcomed both,
Show what the passions are in their full growth.   360

The father paused a moment, then withdrew
   His weapon, and replaced it; but stood still,
And looking on her, as to look her through,
   "Not I," he said, "have sought this stranger's ill;
Not I have made this desolation; few
   Would bear such outrage, and forbear to kill;
But I must do my duty—how thou hast
Done thine, the present vouches for the past.

"Let him disarm; or, by my father's head,
   His own shall roll before you like a ball!"   370
He raised his whistle, as the word he said,
   And blew; another answered to the call,
And, rushing in disorderly, though led,
   And armed from boot to turban, one and all,
Some twenty of his train came, rank on rank;
He gave the word—"Arrest or slay the Frank!"

Then, with a sudden movement, he withdrew
   His daughter; while compressed within his clasp,
'Twixt her and Juan interposed the crew;
   In vain she struggled in her father's grasp—   380

His arms were like a serpent's coil: then flew
    Upon their prey, as darts an angry asp,
The file of pirates; save the foremost, who
Had fallen, with his right shoulder half cut through.

The second had his cheek laid open; but
    The third, a wary, cool old sworder, took
The blows upon his cutlass, and then put
    His own well in; so well, ere you could look,
His man was floored, and helpless at his foot,
    With the blood running like a little brook,   390
From two smart sabre gashes, deep and red—
One on the arm, the other on the head.

And then they bound him where he fell, and bore
    Juan from the apartment: with a sign,
Old Lambro bade them take him to the shore,
    Where lay some ships which were to sail at nine.
They laid him in a boat, and plied the oar
    Until they reached some galliots, placed in line;
On board of one of these, and under hatches,
They stowed him, with strict orders to the watches.   400

The world is full of strange vicissitudes,
    And here was one exceedingly unpleasant:
A gentleman so rich in the world's goods,
    Handsome and young, enjoying all the present,
Just at the very time when he least broods
    On such a thing, is suddenly to sea sent,
Wounded and chained, so that he cannot move,
And all because a lady fell in love.

Here I must leave him, for I grow pathetic,
    Moved by the Chinese nymph of tears, green tea!   410
Than whom Cassandra was not more prophetic;
    For if my pure libations exceed three,
I feel my heart become so sympathetic,
    That I must have recourse to black Bohea[5]:
'Tis pity wine should be so deleterious,
For tea and coffee leave us much more serious,

Unless when qualified with thee, Cogniac!
    Sweet Naiad of the Phlegethontic[6] rill!

---

5.   A kind of black tea.   6.   Phlegethon, river of fire in Hades.

Ah! why the liver wilt thou thus attack,
    And make, like other nymphs, thy lovers ill?   420
I would take refuge in weak punch, but *rack*
    (In each sense of the word), whene'er I fill
My mild and midnight beakers to the brim,
Wakes me next morning with its synonym.

I leave Don Juan for the present, safe—
    Not sound, poor fellow, but severely wounded;
Yet could his corporal pangs amount to half
    Of those with which his Haidée's bosom bounded!
She was not one to weep, and rave, and chafe,
    And then give way, subdued, because surrounded;   430
Her mother was a Moorish maid, from Fez,
Where all is Eden, or a wilderness.

There the large olive rains its amber store
    In marble fonts; there grain, and flower, and fruit,
Gush from the earth, until the land runs o'er:
    But there, too, many a poison tree has root,
And midnight listens to the lion's roar,
    And long, long deserts scorch the camel's foot,
Or heaving, whelm the helpless caravan:
And as the soil is, so the heart of man.   440

Afric is all the sun's, and as her earth
    Her human clay is kindled: full of power
For good or evil, burning from its birth.
    The Moorish blood partakes the planet's hour,
And like the soil beneath, it will bring forth:
    Beauty and love were Haidée's mother's dower;
But her large dark eye showed deep Passion's force
Though sleeping like a lion near a source.

Her daughter, tempered with a milder ray,
    Like summer's clouds all silvery smooth and fair,   450
Till slowly charged with thunder, they display
    Terror to earth, and tempest to the air,
Had held till now her soft and milky way,
    But, overwrought with passion and despair,
The fire burst forth from her Numidian veins,
Even as the Simoom sweeps the blasted plains.

The last sight which she saw was Juan's gore,
    And he himself o'ermastered, and cut down;

His blood was running on the very floor,
  Where late he trod, her beautiful, her own;   460
Thus much she viewed an instant, and no more—
  Her struggles ceased with one convulsive groan;
On her sire's arm, which, until now, scarce held
Her, writhing, fell she, like a cedar felled.

A vein had burst, and her sweet lips' pure dyes
  Were dabbled with the deep blood which ran o'er;
And her head drooped, as when the lily lies
  O'ercharged with rain: her summoned handmaids bore
Their lady to her couch, with gushing eyes;
  Of herbs and cordials they produced their store,   470
But she defied all means they could employ,
Like one life could not hold, nor death destroy.

Days lay she in that state, unchanged, though chill—
  With nothing livid, still her lips were red:
She had no pulse, but death seemed absent still;
  No hideous sign proclaimed her surely dead;
Corruption came not, in each mind to kill
  All hope; to look upon her sweet face, bred
New thoughts of life, for it seemed full of soul—
She had so much, earth could not claim the whole.   480

The ruling passion, such as marble shows
  When exquisitely chiseled, still lay there,
But fixed as marble's unchanged aspect throws
  O'er the fair Venus, but forever fair;
O'er the Laocoön's all eternal throes,
  And ever-dying Gladiator's air,
Their energy, like life, forms all their fame,
Yet looks not life, for they are still the same.

She woke at length, but not as sleepers wake,
  Rather the dead, for life seemed something new,   490
A strange sensation which she must partake
  Perforce, since whatsoever met her view
Struck not on memory, though a heavy ache
  Lay at her heart, whose earliest beat, still true,
Brought back the sense of pain without the cause,
For, for a while, the furies made a pause.

She looked on many a face with vacant eye,
  On many a token, without knowing what;

She saw them watch her, without asking why,
   And recked not who around her pillow sat: 500
Not speechless, though she spoke not; not a sigh
   Relieved her thoughts; dull silence and quick chat
Were tried in vain by those who served; she gave
No sign, save breath, of having left the grave.

Her handmaids tended, but she heeded not;
   Her father watched, she turned her eyes away;
She recognized no being, and no spot,
   However dear, or cherished in their day;
They changed from room to room, but all forgot,
   Gentle, but without memory, she lay;   510
At length those eyes, which they would fain be weaning
Back to old thoughts, waxed full of fearful meaning.

And then a slave bethought her of a harp;
   The harper came and tuned his instrument.
At the first notes, irregular and sharp,
   On him her flashing eyes a moment bent,
Then to the wall she turned, as if to warp
   Her thoughts from sorrow through her heart re-sent;
And he began a long low island song
Of ancient days, ere tyranny grew strong.   520

Anon her thin wan fingers beat the wall,
   In time to his old tune; he changed the theme,
And sung of love; the fierce name struck through all
   Her recollection; on her flashed the dream
Of what she was, and is, if ye could call
   To be so being: in a gushing stream
The tears rushed forth from her o'erclouded brain,
Like mountain mists, at length dissolved in rain.

Short solace, vain relief!—thought came too quick,
   And whirled her brain to madness; she arose,   530
As one who ne'er had dwelt among the sick,
   And flew at all she met, as on her foes;
But no one ever heard her speak or shriek,
   Although her paroxysm drew towards its close:—
Hers was a frenzy which disdained to rave,
Even when they smote her, in the hope to save.

Yet she betrayed at times a gleam of sense;
   Nothing could make her meet her father's face,

Though on all other things with looks intense
  She gazed, but none she ever could retrace.   540
Food she refused, and raiment; no pretence
  Availed for either; neither change of place,
Nor time, nor skill, nor remedy, could give her
Senses to sleep—the power seemed gone forever.

Twelve days and nights she withered thus; at last,
  Without a groan, or sigh, or glance, to show
A parting pang, the spirit from her past;
  And they who watched her nearest, could not know
The very instant, till the change that cast
  Her sweet face into shadow, dull and slow,   550
Glazed o'er her eyes—the beautiful, the black—
Oh! to possess such luster—and then lack!

She died, but not alone; she held, within,
  A second principle of life, which might
Have dawned a fair and sinless child of sin;
  But closed its little being without light,
And went down to the grave unborn, wherein
  Blossom and bough lie withered with one blight;
In vain the dews of Heaven descend above
The bleeding flower and blasted fruit of love.   560

Thus lived—thus died she; never more on her
  Shall sorrow light, or shame. She was not made
Through years or moons the inner weight to bear,
  Which colder hearts endure till they are laid
By age in earth; her days and pleasures were
  Brief but delightful—such as had not stayed
Long with her destiny; but she sleeps well
By the sea-shore, whereon she loved to dwell.

The isle is now all desolate and bare,
  Its dwellings down, its tenants passed away;   570
None but her own and father's grave is there,
  And nothing outward tells of human clay:
Ye could not know where lies a thing so fair,
  No stone is there to show, no tongue to say
What was: no dirge, except the hollow sea's,
Mourns o'er the beauty of the Cyclades.

But many a Greek maid in a loving song
  Sighs o'er her name; and many an islander

With her sire's story makes the night less long;
    Valor was his, and beauty dwelt with her: 580
If she loved rashly, her life paid for wrong—
    A heavy price must all pay who thus err,
In some shape; let none think to fly the danger,
For soon or late Love is his own avenger.

.   .   .   .

Percy Bysshe Shelley

(1792–1822)

■■■■■■■■■■

PERCY BYSSHE SHELLEY was the eldest son and heir of a well-to-do Sussex family. A sensitive boy who balked at all restraint, Shelley suffered keenly as a student at Eton and at Oxford, being sent down from that university after the anonymous publication of a pamphlet, *The Necessity of Atheism*, had been traced to him. He made an early and unfortunate marriage with Harriet Westbrook, whom he left when he eloped with Mary Godwin, to the Continent, in 1814. After the suicide of his wife, Shelley married Mary and, except for a brief sojourn in England, the couple lived in Italy until Shelley was drowned on a boating trip in the Gulf of Spezia. His body was burned and his ashes placed in the Protestant cemetery in Rome. Shelley was the friend of Byron, Keats, and Leigh Hunt.

A radical in his social principles, Shelley was also a passionate believer in the perfectibility of mankind, and his poetry is colored with this fervent idealism. Even his love poems tend to express a striving for universal and spiritual love.

Suggested Readings

B. IFOR EVANS, "Shelley," in *Tradition and Romanticism*. New York: Longmans, Green Co., Inc., 1940, pp. 139–155.

WILLIAM EMPSON, *Seven Types of Ambiguity*. New York: New Directions, 1947, pp. 156–161.

F. R. LEAVIS, "Shelley," in *Revaluation*. New York: George W. Stewart, Publisher, 1947, pp. 203–235.

■■■■■■■■■■

Sonnet: England in 1819

An old, mad, blind, despised, and dying king,—
Princes, the dregs of their dull race, who flow
Through public scorn,—mud from a muddy spring,—
Rulers who neither see, nor feel, nor know,
But leech-like to their fainting country cling,
Till they drop, blind in blood, without a blow,—
A people starved and stabbed in the untilled field,—
An army, which liberticide and prey
Makes as a two-edged sword to all who wield,—
Golden and sanguine laws which tempt and slay;
Religion Christless, Godless—a book sealed;
A Senate,—Time's worst statute unrepealed,—
Are graves, from which a glorious Phantom may
Burst, to illumine our tempestuous day.

■ Consider some of the differences between irony and satire. Is this
poem satiric or ironic, or, if it is both satiric and ironic, which predomi-
nates? Compare it in these terms with Swift's "A City Shower" (p. 289).

Songs from Hellas
Worlds on Worlds Are Rolling
Ever

Worlds on worlds are rolling ever
    From creation to decay,
Like the bubbles on a river
    Sparkling, bursting, borne away.
    But they are still immortal
    Who, through birth's orient portal
And death's dark chasm hurrying to and fro,
    Clothe their unceasing flight
    In the brief dust and light
Gathered around their chariots as they go;   10
    New shapes they still may weave,
    New gods, new laws receive,
Bright or dim are they as the robes they last
    On Death's bare ribs had cast.

A power from the unknown God,
    A Promethean conqueror, came;
Like a triumphal path he trod
    The thorns of death and shame.

A mortal shape to him
Was like the vapor dim   20
Which the orient planet animates with light;
Hell, Sin, and Slavery came,
Like bloodhounds mild and tame,
Nor preyed, until their lord had taken flight;
The moon of Mahomet
Arose, and it shall set:
While blazoned as on Heaven's immortal noon
The cross leads generations on.

Swift as the radiant shapes of sleep
From one whose dreams are Paradise,   30
Fly, when the fond wretch wakes to weep,
And Day peers forth with her blank eyes;
So fleet, so faint, so fair,
The Powers of earth and air
Fled from the folding-star of Bethlehem:
Apollo, Pan, and Love,
And even Olympian Jove
Grew weak, for killing Truth had glared on them;
Our hills and seas and streams,
Dispeopled of their dreams,   40
Their waters turned to blood, their dew to tears,
Wailed for the golden years.

Final Chorus

The world's great age begins anew,
The golden years return,
The earth doth like a snake renew
Her winter weeds outworn;
Heaven smiles, and faiths and empires gleam,
Like wrecks of a dissolving dream.

A brighter Hellas rears its mountains
From waves serener far;
A new Peneus rolls his fountains
Against the morning star.   130
Where fairer Tempes bloom, there sleep
Young Cyclads on a sunnier deep.

A loftier Argo cleaves the main,
Fraught with a later prize;
Another Orpheus sings again,
And loves, and weeps, and dies.

A new Ulysses leaves once more
Calypso for his native shore.

Oh, write no more the tale of Troy,
　If earth Death's scroll must be!   140
Nor mix with Laian rage the joy
　Which dawns upon the free;
Although a subtler Sphinx renew
Riddles of death Thebes never knew.

Another Athens shall arise,
　And to remoter time
Bequeath, like sunset to the skies,
　The splendor of its prime;
And leave, if nought so bright may live,
All earth can take or Heaven can give.   150

Saturn and Love their long repose
　Shall burst, more bright and good
Than all who fell, than One who rose,
　Than many unsubdued;
Not gold, not blood, their altar dowers,
But native tears and symbol flowers.

Oh, cease! must hate and death return?
　Cease! must men kill and die?
Cease! drain not to its dregs the urn
　Of bitter prophecy.   160
The world is weary of the past,
Oh, might it die or rest at last!

■　1. Compare these two songs on the coming of a golden world—according to the ancients the sun and moon would return to their original places and history would begin again, that is, the golden age would repeat itself—with Yeats's presentation of a cyclical view of history in his "Two songs" (p. 590).

2. "Compare the quality of Shelley's language with that of Yeats.

Hymn to Intellectual Beauty

The awful shadow of some unseen Power
　Floats though unseen among us—visiting
　This various world with as inconstant wing
As summer winds that creep from flower to flower—

Like moonbeams that behind some piny mountain shower,
    It visits with inconstant glance
    Each human heart and countenance;
Like hues and harmonies of evening—
    Like clouds in starlight widely spread—
    Like memory of music fled—   10
    Like aught that for its grace may be
Dear, and yet dearer for its mystery.

Spirit of Beauty, that dost consecrate
    With thine own hues all thou dost shine upon
    Of human thought or form—where art thou gone?
Why dost thou pass away and leave our state,
This dim vast vale of tears, vacant and desolate?
    Ask why the sunlight not forever
    Weaves rainbows o'er yon mountain-river,
Why aught should fail and fade that once is shown,   20
    Why fear and dream and death and birth
    Cast on the daylight of this earth
    Such gloom—why man has such a scope
For love and hate, despondency and hope?

No voice from some sublimer world hath ever
    To sage or poet these responses given—
    Therefore the names of Demon,[1] Ghost, and Heaven,
Remain the records of their vain endeavor,
Frail spells—whose uttered charm might not avail to sever,
    From all we hear and all we see,   30
    Doubt, chance, and mutability.
Thy light alone—like mist o'er mountains driven,
    Or music by the night-wind sent
    Through strings of some still instrument,
    Or moonlight on a midnight stream,
Gives grace and truth to life's unquiet dream.

Love, Hope, and Self-Esteem, like clouds depart
    And come, for some uncertain moments lent,
    Man were immortal, and omnipotent,
Didst thou, unknown and awful as thou art,   40
Keep with thy glorious train firm state within his heart.
    Thou messenger of sympathies,
    That wax and wane in lovers' eyes—
Thou—that to human thought art nourishment,

1. Demon, a supernatural being conceived as holding a position between gods and men.

Like darkness to a dying flame!
Depart not as thy shadow came,
Depart not—lest the grave should be,
Like life and fear, a dark reality.

While yet a boy I sought for ghosts, and sped
    Through many a listening chamber, cave and ruin,   50
    And starlight wood, with fearful steps pursuing
Hopes of high talk with the departed dead.
I called on poisonous names with which our youth is fed;
    I was not heard—I saw them not—
    When musing deeply on the lot
Of life, at that sweet time when winds are wooing
    All vital things that wake to bring ·
    News of birds and blossoming—
    Sudden, thy shadow fell on me;
I shrieked, and clasped my hands in ecstasy!   60

I vowed that I would dedicate my powers
    To thee and thine—have I not kept the vow?
    With beating heart and streaming eyes, even now
I called the phantoms of a thousand hours
Each from his voiceless grave: they have in visioned bowers
    Of studious zeal or love's delight
    Outwatched with me the envious night—
They know that never joy illumed my brow
    Unlinked with hope that thou wouldst free
    This world from its dark slavery,   70
    That thou—O awful Loveliness,
Wouldst give whate'er these words cannot express.

The day becomes more solemn and serene
    When noon is past—there is a harmony
    In autumn, and a luster in its sky,
Which through the summer is not heard or seen,
As if it could not be, as if it had not been!
    Thus let thy power, which like the truth
    Of nature on my passive youth
Descended, to my onward life supply   80
    Its calm—to one who worships thee,
    And every form containing thee,
    Whom, Spirit fair, thy spells did bind
To fear himself, and love all human kind.

When the Lamp Is Shattered

When the lamp is shattered,
The light in the dust lies dead;
 When the cloud is scattered,
The rainbow's glory is shed;
 When the lute is broken,
Sweet tones are remembered not;
 When the lips have spoken,
Loved accents are soon forgot.

 As music and splendor
Survive not the lamp and the lute,
 The heart's echoes render   10
No song when the spirit is mute:—
 No song but sad dirges,
Like the wind through a ruined cell,
 Or the mournful surges
That ring the dead seaman's knell.

 When hearts have once mingled,
Love first leaves the well-built nest;
 The weak one is singled
To endure what it once possessed.   20
 O Love! who bewailest
The frailty of all things here,
 Why choose you the frailest
For your cradle, your home, and your bier?

 Its passions will rock thee,
As the storms rock the ravens on high;
 Bright reason will mock thee,
Like the sun from a wintry sky.
 From thy nest every rafter
Will rot, and thine eagle home   30
 Leave thee naked to laughter,
When leaves fall and cold winds come.

■ Joseph Warren Beach and F. R. Leavis have written commentaries on "When the Lamp is Shattered" which are in direct contradiction about the worth of the poem. In his *A Romantic View of Poetry* Mr. Beach calls it "a poem of universally acknowledged beauty and power." In his *Revaluation* Mr. Leavis says only the final stanza of "the poem has any distinction, and its personal quality, characteristically Shelleyan, stands out against the sentimental conventionality of the rest."

Both critics are agreed on the theme of the poem. In Mr. Beach's terms it is about "the poet's private disillusionment"—"the fatal decay of the sentiment of love, leaving the erstwhile lover to 'endure what he once possesst.'" The student should write an analysis of the poem which will include considerations of the following points: (1) Is the point of view sentimental, as Mr. Leavis suggests, or does the final stanza, as Mr. Beach maintains, avoid a romantic sentimentality by passing a severe judgment on his own romanticism? (2) Are the figures of speech "comparisons of classic simplicity and familiar power—lamp, rainbow, broken lute, and bird's nest," as Mr. Beach suggests, or are some of them, at least, incongruous, as Mr. Leavis suggests?

Ode to the West Wind

1

O wild West Wind, thou breath of Autumn's being,
Thou, from whose unseen presence the leaves dead
Are driven, like ghosts from an enchanter fleeing,

Yellow, and black, and pale, and hectic red,
Pestilence-stricken multitudes: O thou,
Who chariotest to their dark wintry bed

The wingèd seeds, where they lie cold and low,
Each like a corpse within its grave, until
Thine azure sister of the Spring shall blow

Her clarion o'er the dreaming earth, and fill   10
(Driving sweet buds like flocks to feed in air)
With living hues and odors plain and hill:

Wild Spirit, which art moving everywhere;
Destroyer and preserver; hear, oh, hear!

2

Thou on whose stream, 'mid the steep sky's commotion,
Loose clouds like earth's decaying leaves are shed,
Shook from the tangled boughs of Heaven and Ocean,

Angels of rain and lightning: there are spread
On the blue surface of thine aery surge,
Like the bright hair uplifted from the head   20

Of some fierce Maenad, even from the dim verge
Of the horizon to the zenith's height,
The locks of the approaching storm. Thou dirge

Of the dying year, to which this closing night
Will be the dome of a vast sepulchre,
Vaulted with all thy congregated might

Of vapors, from whose solid atmosphere
Black rain, and fire, and hail will burst: oh, hear!

3

Thou who didst waken from his summer dreams
The blue Mediterranean, where he lay,   30
Lulled by the coil of his crystàlline streams,

Beside a pumice isle in Baiae's bay,
And saw in sleep old palaces and towers
Quivering within the wave's intenser day,

All overgrown with azure moss and flowers
So sweet, the sense faints picturing them! Thou
For whose path the Atlantic's level powers

Cleave themselves into chasms, while far below
The sea-blooms and the oozy woods which wear
The sapless foliage of the ocean, know   40

Thy voice, and suddenly grow gray with fear,
And tremble and despoil themselves: oh, hear!

4

If I were a dead leaf thou mightest bear;
If I were a swift cloud to fly with thee;
A wave to pant beneath thy power, and share

The impulse of thy strength, only less free
Than thou, O uncontrollable! If even
I were as in my boyhood, and could be

The comrade of thy wanderings over Heaven,
As then, when to outstrip thy skiey speed   50
Scarce seemed a vision; I would ne'er have striven

As thus with thee in prayer in my sore need.
Oh, lift me as a wave, a leaf, a cloud!
I fall upon the thorns of life! I bleed!

A heavy weight of hours has chained and bowed
One too like thee: tameless, and swift, and proud.

5

Make me thy lyre, even as the forest is:
What if my leaves are falling like its own!
The tumult of thy mighty harmonies

Will take from both a deep, autumnal tone,   60
Sweet though in sadness. Be thou, Spirit fierce,
My spirit! Be thou me, impetuous one!

Drive my dead thoughts over the universe
Like withered leaves to quicken a new birth!
And, by the incantation of this verse,

Scatter, as from an unextinguished hearth
Ashes and sparks, my words among mankind!
Be through my lips to unawakened earth

The trumpet of a prophecy! O, Wind,
If Winter comes, can Spring be far behind?   70

■ 1. How does this stanza, a variation on terza rima, differ from the Shakespearean sonnet?

2. There are certain thematic relationships between the opening and closing sections of the poem. Comment on these relationships. Throughout the poem there are recurrent patterns of imagery concerned with leaves, clouds, and waves. Demonstrate how they are related, or unrelated if you believe they are, to the wind.

3. F. R. Leavis in his essay on Shelley states that in Section 2 the imagery is loose and vague, lacking in a "grasp upon the actual." Does this criticism seem tenable or not?

4. Does the line "I fall upon the thorns of life! I bleed!" (line 54) seem to you appropriate to or justified by the context?

5. Do the colors employed in the poem have any thematic function?

6. Point out several words that bear a heavy rhythmic stress, and comment on the appropriateness of the stress.

7. One critic has said that in this poem Shelley is writing, partly unconsciously perhaps, about his desire for free love. Comment on this interpretation.

Ozymandias

I met a traveler from an antique land
Who said: Two vast and trunkless legs of stone
Stand in the desert. Near them, on the sand,
Half sunk, a shattered visage lies, whose frown,
And wrinkled lip, and sneer of cold command,
Tell that its sculptor well those passions read
Which yet survive (stamped on these lifeless things),
The hand that mocked them and the heart that fed;
And on the pedestal these words appear:
"My name is Ozymandias, king of kings;
Look on my works, ye Mighty, and despair!"
Nothing beside remains. Round the decay
Of that colossal wreck, boundless and bare
The lone and level sands stretch far away.

■ 1. What is the nature of the irony implicit in "Ozymandias"?
2. Compare the dramatic effect of this poem with that of Yeats's "Second Coming," (see p. 437).

To Night

Swiftly walk o'er the western wave,
    Spirit of Night!
Out of the misty eastern cave,
Where, all the long and lone daylight,
Thou wovest dreams of joy and fear,
Which make thee terrible and dear—
    Swift be thy flight!

Wrap thy form in a mantle gray,
    Star-inwrought!
Blind with thine hair the eyes of day;   10
Kiss her until she be wearied out,
Then wander o'er city, and sea, and land,
Touching all with thine opiate wand—
    Come, long-sought!

When I arose and saw the dawn,
    I sighed for thee;
When light rode high, and the dew was gone,
And noon lay heavy on flower and tree,
And the weary day turned to his rest,

Lingering like an unloved guest,   20
    I sighed for thee.

Thy brother Death came, and cried,
    Wouldst thou me?
Thy sweet child Sleep, the filmy-eyed,
Murmured like a noontide bee,
Shall I nestle near thy side?
Wouldst thou me?—And I replied,
    No, not thee!

Death will come when thou art dead,
    Soon, too soon—   30
Sleep will come when thou art fled;
Of neither would I ask the boon
I ask of thee, beloved Night—
Swift be thine approaching flight,
    Come soon, soon!

■   Comment on the appropriateness of the imagery in this poem.

Love's Philosophy

The fountains mingle with the river
    And the rivers with the Ocean,
The winds of Heaven mix for ever
    With a sweet emotion;
Nothing in the world is single;
    All things by a law divine
In one spirit meet and mingle.
    Why not I with thine?—

See the mountains kiss high Heaven
    And the waves clasp one another;
No sister-flower would be forgiven
    If it disdained its brother;
And the sunlight clasps the earth
    And the moonbeams kiss the sea:
What is all this sweet work worth
    If thou kiss not me?

■   Comment on the tone of this poem.

A Dirge

Rough wind, that moanest loud
  Grief too sad for song;
Wild wind, when sullen cloud
Knells all the night long;
Sad storm, whose tears are vain,
Bare woods, whose branches strain,
Deep caves and dreary main,—
  Wail, for the world's wrong!

■ 1. Does the abstractness of the final line, the failure of the poet to furnish particulars about the wrongs of the world, affect the value of the poem for you?

2. Scan the poem. Comment on the appropriateness of the metrical pattern to the subject.

From *Prometheus Unbound*

Asia

My soul is an enchanted boat,
  Which, like a sleeping swan, doth float
Upon the silver waves of thy sweet singing;
  And thine doth like an angel sit
  Beside a helm conducting it,
Whilst all the winds with melody are ringing.
  It seems to float ever, for ever,
  Upon that many-winding river,
  Between mountains, woods, abysses,   80
A paradise of wildernesses!
Till, like one in slumber bound,
Borne to the ocean, I float down, around,
Into a sea profound, of ever-spreading sound:

  Meanwhile thy spirit lifts its pinions
  In music's most serene dominions;
Catching the winds that fan that happy heaven.
  And we sail on, away, afar,
  Without a course, without a star,
But, by the instinct of sweet music driven;   90
  Till through Elysian garden islets
  By thee, most beautiful of pilots,
  Where never mortal pinnace glided,
  The boat of my desire is guided:

Realms where the air we breathe is love,
Which in the winds and on the waves doth move,
Harmonizing this earth with what we feel above.

We have passed Age's icy caves,
  And Manhood's dark and tossing waves,
And Youth's smooth ocean, smiling to betray: 100
  Beyond the glassy gulfs we flee
  Of shadow-peopled Infancy,
Through Death and Birth, to a diviner day;
  A paradise of vaulted bowers,
  Lit by downward-gazing flowers,
  And watery paths that wind between
  Wildernesses calm and green,
Peopled by shapes too bright to see,
And rest, having beheld; somewhat like thee;
Which walk upon the sea, and chant melodiously!   110

■   I. A. Richards, in his *Principles of Literary Criticism,* distinguishes
between two general types of poetry: first, the poetry which avoids contradictory or discordant elements, and second, the poetry in which the
discordant and contradictory are considered and resolved. "The structures of these two kinds of experience are different, and the difference is
not one of subject but of the relations *inter se* of the several impulses
active in the experience. A poem of the first group is built out of sets of
impulses which run parallel, which have the same direction. In a poem
of the second group the most obvious feature is the extraordinary heterogeneity of the distinguishable impulses. But they are more than het-
erogeneous, they are opposed. They are such that in ordinary, non-
poetic, nonimaginative experience, one or the other set would be sup-
pressed to give as it might appear freer development to the others."
Shelley in his *Defense of Poetry* acknowledges that poetry can transform
the ugly or commonplace into the beautiful, but he does not treat the
matter of resolving heterogeneity or contradictions. To which type of
poetry, as characterized by Richards, does this poem belong? Answer in
some detail.

To a Skylark

Hail to thee, blithe spirit!
  Bird thou never wert,
That from heaven, or near it,
  Pourest thy full heart
In profuse strains of unpremeditated art.

Higher still and higher
   From the earth thou springest
Like a cloud of fire;
   The blue deep thou wingest,
And singing still dost soar, and soaring ever singest.   10

In the golden lightning
   Of the sunken sun,
O'er which clouds are bright'ning,
   Thou dost float and run;
Like an unbodied joy whose race is just begun.

The pale purple even
   Melts around thy flight;
Like a star of heaven
   In the broad daylight
Thou art unseen, but yet I hear thy shrill delight,   20

Keen as are the arrows
   Of that silver sphere,
Whose intense lamp narrows
   In the white dawn clear,
Until we hardly see, we feel that it is there.

All the earth and air
   With thy voice is loud,
As, when night is bare,
   From one lonely cloud
The moon rains out her beams, and Heaven is overflowed.   30

What thou art we know not;
   What is most like thee?
From rainbow clouds there flow not
   Drops so bright to see
As from thy presence showers a rain of melody.

Like a poet hidden
   In the light of thought,
Singing hymns unbidden,
   Till the world is wrought
To sympathy with hopes and fears it heeded not;   40

Like a high-born maiden
   In a palace-tower,
Soothing her love-laden

Soul in secret hour
With music sweet as love, which overflows her bower;

Like a glowworm golden
    In a dell of dew,
Scattering unbeholden
    Its aëreal hue
Among the flowers and grass which screen it from the view;   50

Like a rose embowered
    In its own green leaves,
By warm winds deflowered,
    Till the scent it gives
Makes faint with too much sweet those heavy-wingèd thieves.

Sound of vernal showers
    On the twinkling grass,
Rain-awakened flowers,
    All that ever was
Joyous, and clear, and fresh, thy music doth surpass.   60

Teach us, sprite or bird,
    What sweet thoughts are thine;
I have never heard
    Praise of love or wine
That panted forth a flood of rapture so divine.

Chorus Hymeneal,
    Or triumphal chaunt,
Matched with thine, would be all
    But an empty vaunt,
A thing wherein we feel there is some hidden want.   70

What objects are the fountains
    Of thy happy strain?
What fields, or waves, or mountains?
    What shapes of sky or plain?
What love of thine own kind? what ignorance of pain?

With thy clear keen joyance
    Languor cannot be—
Shadow of annoyance
    Never came near thee—
Thou lovest—but ne'er knew love's sad satiety.   80

Waking or asleep,
  Thou of death must deem
Things more true and deep
  Than we mortals dream,
Or how could thy notes flow in such a crystal stream?

We look before and after,
  And pine for what is not;
Our sincerest laughter
  With some pain is fraught;
Our sweetest songs are those that tell of saddest thought.   90

Yet if we could scorn
  Hate, and pride, and fear;
If we were things born
  Not to shed a tear,
I know not how thy joy we ever should come near.

Better than all measures
  Of delightful sound—
Better than all treasures
  That in books are found—
Thy skill to poet were, thou scorner of the ground!   100

Teach me half the gladness
  That thy brain must know,
Such harmonious madness
  From my lips would flow
The world should listen then—as I am listening now.

■   Reread the question and statement under the poem "Asia" from *Prometheus Unbound* (p. 440). To which type of poetry does "To a Skylark" belong? Answer this question in some detail also.

John Keats

(1795–1821)

▼ ■ ■ ■ ■ ■ ■ ■ ■ ■

JOHN KEATS was born in London. His father, a livery-stable keeper, died when he was nine, and his mother when he was fifteen. As a boy he studied at a private school in Enfield (near London), but when his mother died his guardians removed him from school and apprenticed him to a surgeon in Edmonton (also near London). Keats was, however, always more interested in poetry than in medicine. In London he had met Leigh Hunt, Wordsworth, Shelley, Hazlitt, and the artist Haydon. After finishing his apprenticeship in 1815, he abandoned medicine in order to turn fully to the writing of poetry. His first volume of poems, dedicated to Leigh Hunt, was published in 1817. By this time Keats was already in very poor health and was persuaded by friends to go to the Isle of Wight in order to recuperate. There he continued to write poetry. In 1818 he published another volume, called *Endymion* after the title poem. This volume was criticized harshly in *The Quarterly Review* and *Blackwood's Magazine*, and the latter derided not only the literary shortcomings and immaturities of Keats's poetry but also his humble background and circumstances. It is no longer generally believed, as it once was, that these attacks were the main cause of Keats's physical decline and early death. At this time he was already seriously ill. A more likely cause was the depression brought upon him by the death of his brother Thomas and by the hopelessness of his love for Fanny Brawne. However, he continued to write without interruption and with a rapid development of craftsmanship. In 1820 his greatest and best-known work appeared in a volume called *Lamia, Isabella, The Eve of Saint Agnes, and Other Poems.* His letters of this period show him confident of his powers but fearful about his health. Indeed, by this time he was in such poor condition that in November, 1820, following the doctor's advice, he left England for Rome, accompanied by his friend, the artist Severn. But it was too late. A brief rally was followed by a relapse, and he died on February 23, 1821. Keats is buried in the Protestant cemetery in Rome.

Suggested Readings

JOHN MIDDLETON MURRAY, *Keats and Shakespeare.* London: Oxford University Press, 1925.

M. R. RIDLEY, *Keats' Craftsmanship.* Oxford: The Clarendon Press, 1933.

J. R. CALDWELL, *John Keats' Fancy.* Ithaca: Cornell University Press, 1945.

ALLEN TATE, "A Reading of Keats," in *On the Limits of Poetry.* New York: Alan Swallow, Publisher, 1948, pp. 164–185.

The Mermaid Tavern

Souls of Poets dead and gone,
What Elysium have ye known,
Happy field or mossy cavern,
Choicer than the Mermaid Tavern?
Have ye tippled drink more fine
Than mine host's Canary wine?
Or are fruits of Paradise
Sweeter than those dainty pies
Of venison? O generous food!
Dressed as though bold Robin Hood
Would, with his maid Marian
Sup and bowse from horn and can.

I have heard that on a day
Mine host's sign-board flew away,
Nobody knew whither, till
An astrologer's old quill
To a sheepskin gave the story,
Said he saw you in your glory,
Underneath a new old sign
Sipping beverage divine,
And pledging with contented smack
The Mermaid in the Zodiac!

Souls of Poets dead and gone,
What Elysium have ye known,
Happy field or mossy cavern,
Choicer than the Mermaid Tavern?

When I Have Fears

When I have fears that I may cease to be
Before my pen has glean'd my teeming brain,
Before high piled books, in charact'ry,
Hold like rich garners the full-ripen'd grain;
When I behold, upon the night's starr'd face,
Huge cloudy symbols of a high romance,
And think that I may never live to trace
Their shadows, with the magic hand of chance;
And when I feel, fair creature of an hour!
That I shall never look upon thee more,
Never have relish in the faery power

Of unreflecting love!—then on the shore
Of the wide world I stand alone, and think
Till Love and Fame to nothingness do sink.

La Belle Dame sans Merci
Ballad

O what can ail thee, knight-at-arms,
   Alone and palely loitering!
The sedge has wither'd from the lake,
   And no birds sing.

O what can ail thee, knight-at-arms!
   So haggard and so woe-begone?
The squirrel's granary is full,
   And the harvest's done.

I see a lily on thy brow
   With anguish moist and fever dew,   10
And on thy cheeks a fading rose
   Fast withereth too.

"I met a lady in the meads,
   Full beautiful—a faery's child,
Her hair was long, her foot was light,
   And her eyes were wild.

"I made a garland for her head,
   And bracelets too, and fragrant zone;
She look'd at me as she did love,
   And made sweet moan.   20

"I set her on my pacing steed,
   And nothing else saw all day long.
For sidelong would she bend, and sing
   A faery's song.

"She found me roots of relish sweet,
   And honey wild, and manna dew,
And sure in language strange she said—
   'I love thee true.'

"She took me to her elfin grot,
   And there she wept, and sigh'd full sore,   30

And there I shut her wild wild eyes
　　With kisses four.

"And there she lulled me asleep,
　　And there I dream'd—Ah! woe betide!
The latest dream I ever dream'd
　　On the cold hill's side.

"I saw pale kings and princes too,
　　Pale warriors, death-pale were they all;
They cried—'La Belle Dame sans Merci
　　Hath thee in thrall!'   40

"I saw their starv'd lips in the gloom,
　　With horrid warning gaped wide,
And I awoke and found me here,
　　On the cold hill's side.

"And this is why I sojourn here,
　　Alone and palely loitering,
Though the sedge is wither'd from the lake
　　And no birds sing."

■　In what way has Keats departed from the metrical pattern of ballad stanza? What is the effect of this departure and how is it related to the tone and subject of the poem?

To One Who Has Been Long in City Pent

To one who has been long in city pent,
'Tis very sweet to look into the fair
And open face of heaven,—to breathe a prayer
Full in the smile of the blue firmament.

Who is more happy, when, with heart's content,
Fatigued he sinks into some pleasant lair
Of wavy grass, and reads a debonair
And gentle tale of love and languishment?

Returning home at evening, with an ear
Catching the notes of Philomel,—an eye
Watching the sailing cloudlet's bright career,
He mourns that day so soon has glided by:
E'en like the passage of an angel's tear
That falls through the clear ether silently.

■   1. What is the function of the simile of the angel's tear? How do you like it simply as an image? Explain your taste. Is it any more, or less, characteristic of Keats and his period than the images in the sonnet on Chapman's Homer?

2. Compare this sonnet with the passage from Milton's *Paradise Lost* beginning "As one who long in populous city pent" (see p. 220).

On First Looking into Chapman's Homer

Much have I travell'd in the realms of gold,
And many goodly states and kingdoms seen;
Round many western islands have I been
Which bards in fealty to Apollo hold.
Oft of one wide expanse had I been told
That deep-browed Homer ruled as his demesne;
Yet did I never breathe its pure serene
Till I heard Chapman speak out loud and bold:
Then felt I like some watcher of the skies
When a new planet swims into his ken;
Or like stout Cortez when with eagle eyes
He star'd at the Pacific—and all his men
Look'd at each other with a wild surmise—
Silent, upon a peak in Darien.

■   It is interesting to recall that Homer was available, and probably familiar, to Keats in Pope's translation.

Bright Star, Would I Were
Steadfast As Thou Art

Bright star, would I were steadfast as thou art—
Not in lone splendor hung aloft the night,
And watching, with eternal lids apart,
Like Nature's patient sleepless Eremite,
The moving waters at their priestlike task
Of pure ablution round earth's human shores,
Or gazing on the new soft fallen mask
Of snow upon the mountains and the moors—
No—yet still steadfast, still unchangeable,
Pillowed upon my fair love's ripening breast
To feel for ever its soft fall and swell,
Awake for ever in a sweet unrest,

Still, still to hear her tender-taken breath,
And so live ever—or else swoon to death.

Ode on Melancholy

No, no! go not to Lethe, neither twist
   Wolf's-bane, tight-rooted, for its poisonous wine;
Nor suffer thy pale forehead to be kissed
   By nightshade, ruby grape of Proserpine;
Make not your rosary of yew-berries,
   Nor let the beetle, nor the death-moth be
     Your mournful Psyche, nor the downy owl
A partner in your sorrow's mysteries;
   For shade to shade will come too drowsily,
     And drown the wakeful anguish of the soul.   10

But when the melancholy fit shall fall
   Sudden from heaven like a weeping cloud,
That fosters the droop-headed flowers all,
   And hides the green hill in an April shroud;
Then glut thy sorrow on a morning rose,
   Or on the rainbow of the salt sand-wave,
     Or on the wealth of globèd peonies;
Or if thy mistress some rich anger shows,
   Emprison her soft hand, and let her rave,
     And feed deep, deep upon her peerless eyes.   20

She dwells with Beauty—Beauty that must die;
   And Joy, whose hand is ever at his lips
Bidding adieu; and aching Pleasure nigh,
   Turning to poison while the bee-mouth sips:
Ay, in the very temple of Delight
   Veiled Melancholy has her sovran shrine,
     Though seen of none save him whose strenuous tongue
Can burst Joy's grape against his palate fine;
   His soul shall taste the sadness of her might,
     And be among her cloudy trophies hung.

■ 1. What is the poet's attitude toward melancholy—is it desirable or
not?

   2. Identify the "she" of line 21.

   3. Write an analysis of the poem, with special attention to the relationship between diction and theme.

Ode to a Nightingale

My heart aches, and a drowsy numbness pains
    My sense, as though of hemlock I had drunk,
Or emptied some dull opiate to the drains
    One minute past, and Lethe-wards had sunk:
'Tis not through envy of thy happy lot,
    But being too happy in thine happiness,—
        That thou, light wingèd Dryad of the trees,
            In some melodious plot
    Of beechen green, and shadows numberless,
        Singest of summer in full-throated ease.   10

O, for a draught of vintage! that hath been
    Cool'd a long age in the deep-delvèd earth,
Tasting of Flora and the country green,
    Dance, and Provençal song, and sunburnt mirth!
O for a beaker full of the warm South,
    Full of the true, the blushful Hippocrene,
        With beaded bubbles winking at the brim,
            And purple-stainèd mouth;
    That I might drink, and leave the world unseen,
        And with thee fade away into the forest dim: 20

Fade far away, dissolve, and quite forget
    What thou among the leaves hast never known,
The weariness, the fever, and the fret
    Here, where men sit and hear each other groan;
Where palsy shakes a few, sad, last gray hairs,
    Where youth grows pale, and spectre-thin, and dies;
        Where but to think is to be full of sorrow
            And leaden-eyed despairs,
    Where Beauty cannot keep her lustrous eyes,
        Or new Love pine at them beyond to-morrow.   30

Away! away! for I will fly to thee,
    Not charioted by Bacchus and his pards,
But on the viewless wings of Poesy,
    Though the dull brain perplexes and retards:
Already with thee! tender is the night,
    And haply the Queen-Moon is on her throne,
        Cluster'd around by all her starry Fays;
            But here there is no light,
    Save what from heaven is with the breezes blown
        Through verdurous glooms and winding mossy ways.   40

I cannot see what flowers are at my feet,
   Nor what soft incense hangs upon the boughs,
But, in embalmèd darkness, guess each sweet
   Wherewith the seasonable month endows
The grass, the thicket, and the fruit-tree wild;
   White hawthorn, and the pastoral eglantine;
      Fast fading violets cover'd up in leaves;
         And mid-May's eldest child,
   The coming musk-rose, full of dewy wine,
      The murmurous haunt of flies on summer eves.   50

Darkling I listen; and, for many a time
   I have been half in love with easeful Death,
Call'd him soft names in many a musèd rhyme,
   To take into the air my quiet breath;
Now more than ever seems it rich to die,
   To cease upon the midnight with no pain,
      While thou art pouring forth thy soul abroad
         In such an ecstasy!
   Still wouldst thou sing, and I have ears in vain—
      To thy high requiem become a sod.   60

Thou wast not born for death, immortal Bird!
   No hungry generations tread thee down;
The voice I hear this passing night was heard
   In ancient days by emperor and clown:
Perhaps the self-same song that found a path
   Through the sad heart of Ruth, when, sick for home,
      She stood in tears amid the alien corn;
         The same that oft-times hath
   Charm'd magic casements, opening on the foam
      Of perilous seas, in faery lands forlorn.   70

Forlorn! the very word is like a bell
   To toll me back from thee to my sole self!
Adieu! the fancy cannot cheat so well
   As she is fam'd to do, deceiving elf.
Adieu adieu! thy plaintive anthem fades
   Past the near meadows, over the still stream,
      Up the hill-side; and now 'tis buried deep
         In the next valley-glades:
   Was it a vision, or a waking dream?
      Fled is that music:—Do I wake or sleep?

■ 1. Which of the following words do you consider to be the best one-word description of the poem: *descriptive, meditative, dramatic,* or *philosophic?* Explain your answer.

2. At what point in the poem does the nightingale shift from being an actual bird to being a symbol? Does the symbolic function of the bird continue to the end of the poem?

Ode on a Grecian Urn

Thou still unravish'd bride of quietness,
   Thou foster-child of silence and slow time,
Sylvan historian, who canst thus express
   A flowery tale more sweetly than our rhyme:
What leaf-fring'd legend haunts about thy shape
   Of deities or mortals, or of both,
      In Tempe or the dales of Arcady?
What men or gods are these? What maidens loth?
   What mad pursuit? What struggle to escape?
      What pipes and timbrels? What wild ecstacy?   10

Heard melodies are sweet, but those unheard
   Are sweeter; therefore, ye soft pipes, play on;
Not to the sensual ear, but, more endear'd,
   Pipe to the spirit ditties of no tone:
Fair youth, beneath the trees, thou canst not leave
   Thy song, nor ever can those trees be bare;
      Bold Lover, never, never canst thou kiss
Though winning near the goal—yet, do not grieve;
   She cannot fade, though thou hast not thy bliss,
      For ever wilt thou love, and she be fair!   20

Ah, happy, happy boughs! that cannot shed
   Your leaves, nor ever bid the Spring adieu;
And, happy melodist, unwearied,
   Forever piping songs forever new;
More happy love! more happy, happy love!
   Forever warm and still to be enjoy'd,
      Forever panting, and forever young;
All breathing human passion far above,
   That leaves a heart high-sorrowful and cloy'd,
      A burning forehead, and a parching tongue.   30

Who are these coming to the sacrifice?
   To what green altar, O mysterious priest,
Lead'st thou that heifer lowing at the skies,

And all her silken flanks with garlands dressed?
What little town by river or sea shore,
 Or mountain-built with peaceful citadel,
  Is emptied of this folk, this pious morn?
And, little town, thy streets forevermore
 Will silent be; and not a soul to tell
  Why thou art desolate, can e'er return.   40

charact by
beauty   *classic Plurity simplicty*

O Attic shape! Fair attitude! with brede
 Of marble men and maidens over wrought,
With forest branches and the trodden weed;
 Thou, silent form, dost tease us out of thought
As doth eternity: Cold Pastoral!
 When old age shall this generation waste,
  Thou shalt remain, in midst of other woe
Than ours, a friend to man, to whom thou say'st,
 "Beauty is truth, truth beauty,"—that is all
  Ye know on earth, and all ye need to know.   50

■   Compare your analysis of this poem with that in Kenneth Burke's
"Symbolic Action in a Poem by Keats," *Accent,* IV, 1 (Autumn, 1943),
30–42. (The same essay appears in Burke's *A Grammar of Motives,*
New York: Prentice-Hall, Inc., 1945).

To Autumn

Season of mists and mellow fruitfulness,
 Close bosom-friend of the maturing sun;
Conspiring with him how to load and bless
 With fruit the vines that round the thatch-eaves run;
To bend with apples the moss'd cottage-trees,
 And fill all fruit with ripeness to the core;
  To swell the gourd, and plump the hazel shells
With a sweet kernel; to set budding more,
 And still more, later flowers for the bees,
 Until they think warm days will never cease,   10
  For Summer has o'er-brimmed their clammy cells.

Who hath not seen thee oft amid thy store?
 Sometimes whoever seeks abroad may find
Thee sitting careless on a granary floor,
 Thy hair soft-lifted by the winnowing wind;
Or on a half-reap'd furrow sound asleep,
 Drows'd with the fume of poppies, while thy hook

Spares the next swath and all its twined flowers:
And sometimes like a gleaner thou dost keep
Steady thy laden head across a brook;   20
Or by a cider-press, with patient look,
Thou watchest the last oozings hours by hours.

Where are the songs of Spring? Ay, where are they?
Think not of them, thou hast thy music too,—
While barred clouds bloom the soft-dying day,
And touch the stubble-plains with rosy hue;
Then in a wailful choir the small gnats mourn
Among the river sallows, borne aloft
Or sinking as the light wind lives or dies;
And full-grown lambs loud bleat from hilly bourn;   30
Hedge-crickets sing; and now with treble soft
The red-breast whistles from a garden-croft;
And gathering swallows twitter in the skies.

■ "To Autumn" is a rich and vivid description of nature, expertly achieved within a fairly intricate stanzaic pattern. The words are successfully descriptive (or evocative) in their phonetic qualities and rhythmical arrangement, as well as in their imagistic references. If we are familiar with Keats's other work, however, we can discover that the poem is not only rich in pictorial and sensuous details but that it has a depth of meaning and a characteristic complexity of structure. "To Autumn" is allied especially to the odes on melancholy, on a Grecian urn, and to a nightingale. The four poems are various treatments presenting differing aspects of a single theme.

Insofar as the theme is "stated" in any of the poems, it is most clearly stated in the "Ode on Melancholy." In fact, if we want a general formulation of the theme, we need only quote the last stanza—especially these lines:

Ay, in the very temple of Delight
Veiled melancholy has her sovran shrine,
Though seen of none save him whose strenuous tongue
Can burst Joy's grape against his palate fine.

Keats was obviously preoccupied with the consideration that beauty and melancholy are closely related: true melancholy is to be found only in the fullness of living, in beauty, joy, and delight, for these experiences make most poignant the passage of time, through which such experiences and then life itself must come to an end.

All this is clear enough in the "Ode on Melancholy." There is, however, the implication that the relationship between beauty and melancholy is a mutual one. That is, either joy or sadness is most intensely felt when it is attended by a consciousness of the experience which is opposite and yet so closely related to it. The theme, then, is more complex and subtle than the aspect of it which appears on the surface in "Ode on Melancholy." Other implications of the theme may be found throughout the four poems, which illuminate and clarify each other. This is not to say that the poems are merely repetitions of the same theme, which Keats had in mind before he wrote any of them. When we understand the poems, we might find it more accurate to say that each is an exploration of a certain theme.

With so much of its context in mind, let us examine closely "To Autumn." The poem opens with an apostrophe to the season and with a description of natural objects at their richest and ripest stage. The details about the fruit, the flowers, and the bees constitute a lush and colorful picture of autumn and the effects of the "maturing sun." In the final lines of the first stanza, however, slight implications about the passage of time begin to operate. The flowers are called "later," the bees are assumed to think that "warm days will never cease," and there is a reference to the summer which has already passed.

In the second stanza an imaginative element enters the description, and we get a personification of the season in several appropriate postures and settings. As this stanza proceeds, the implications of the descriptive details become increasingly strong. For example, autumn is now seen, not as setting the flowers to budding, but as already bringing some of them to an end, although it "spares the next swath." Autumn has become a "gleaner." The whole stanza presents the paradoxical qualities of autumn, its aspects both of lingering and passing. This is especially true of the final image of the stanza. Autumn is the season of dying as well as of fulfilling. Hence it is with *patient* look" that she (or he?) watches "the last oozings hours by hours." Oozing, or a steady dripping, is, of course, not unfamiliar as a symbol of the passage of time.

It is in the last stanza that the theme emerges most conspicuously. The opening question implies that the season of youth and rebirth, with its beauties of sight and sound, has passed, and that the season of autumn is passing. But autumn, too, *while* it lasts—"While barred clouds bloom the soft-dying day"—has its beauties, its music, as Keats's poem demonstrates. The imagery of the last stanza contrasts significantly with that of the first, and the final development of the poem adds meaning to its earlier portions. The slight implications are confirmed. We may recall that *maturing* means aging and ending as well as ripening. The earlier imagery is, of course, that of ripeness. But the final imagery is more truly autumnal. The first words used to describe the music of autumn are "wailful" and "mourn." The opening stanza suggests the height of day, when the sun is strong and the bees are gathering honey from the open flowers. But in the last stanza, after the passing of "hours and hours," we have "the soft-dying day," the imagery of sunset and deepening twilight, when the clouds impart their glow to the day and the plains. The transitive, somewhat rare use of the verb "bloom," with its springlike associations, is perhaps surprising, and certainly appropriate and effective in suggesting the tensions of the theme, in picturing a beauty that is lingering, but *only* lingering. The conjunction of "rosy hue" and "stubble-plains" has the same significant incongruity, although the image is wholly convincing and actual in its reference. While the poem is more descriptive and suggestive than dramatic, its latent theme of transitoriness and mortality is symbolically dramatized by the passing course of the day. All these characteristics of the poem are to be found in its final image: "And gathering swallows twitter in the skies." Here we have the music of autumn. And our attention is directed toward the darkening skies. Birds habitually gather in flocks toward nightfall, particularly when they are preparing to fly south at the approach of winter. But they are still gathering. The day, the season, are "soft-dying" and are both the reality and the symbol of life as most intensely and poignantly beautiful when viewed from this melancholy perspective.

The poem has an obvious structure insofar as it is a coherent description. Its structure, however, is not simple in the sense of being merely continuous. For example, the course of the day parallels the development of the poem. And an awareness of the theme gives even greater significance to the structure, for the theme emerges with increasing clarity and fullness throughout the poem until the very last line. Because the theme is always in the process of emerging without ever shaking off the medium in which it is developed, the several parts of the poem have a relationship to each other beyond their progression in a single direction. The gathering swallows return some borrowed meaning to the soft-dying day with substantial interest, and the whole last stanza negotiates with the first in a similar relationship.

We have observed the descriptive, temporal (course of day), and thematic aspects of the structure. Another aspect of structure appears when, once more, we consider the poem within the context of Keats's work. "To Autumn" shares a feature of development with the nightingale and Grecian urn odes. Each of these poems begins with the presentation of realistic circumstances, then moves into an imagined realm, and ends with a return to the realistic. In "Ode to a Nightingale," the most clearly dramatic of the poems, the speaker, hearing the song of the nightingale, wishes to fade with it "into the forest dim" and to forget the painful realities of life. This wish is fulfilled in the fourth stanza— the speaker exclaims "Already with thee!" As the poem proceeds and while the imagined realm is maintained, the unpleasant realities come back into view. From the transition that begins with the desire for "easeful Death" and through the references to "hungry generations" and "the sad heart of Ruth," the imagined and the real, the beautiful and the melancholy, are held balanced against each other. Then, on the word "forlorn," the speaker turns away from the imagined, back to the real and his "sole self."

"Ode on a Grecian Urn" opens with an apostrophe to the actual urn. In the second stanza the imagined realm, the "ditties of no tone," is invoked, and the "leaf-fring'd legend" comes to life. And here, too, the imagined life and real life are set in contrast to each other—the imagined is the negation of the real. It is in the fourth stanza that the imagined life is most fully developed and at the same time collapses into the real. The urn is left behind and the people are considered not only in the scenes depicted on the urn, but as having left some little town. With the image of the town, desolate and silent, the imagination has completed its course. The people can never return to the town. In the final stanza they are again "marble men and maidens" and the urn is a "Cold Pastoral." The statement about truth and beauty with which the poem ends is famous and much debated. It is conceivable that Keats is saying here what he has said elsewhere and in another way—in the "Ode" that begins

> Bards of Passion and of Mirth,
> Ye have left your souls on earth!
> Have ye souls in heaven too,
> Double-lived in regions new?

Toward the end of the poem there are these lines:

> Here, your earth-born souls still speak
> To mortals, of their little week;
> Of their sorrows and delights;
> Of their passions and their spites;
> Of their glory and their shame;
> What doth strengthen and what maim.
> Thus ye teach us every day
> Wisdom, though fled far away.

Keats is not didactic here, nor does he claim didacticism for the bards. Their earth-born souls, their works, teach wisdom in speaking of the lives of men, and in bringing to men, generation after generation, an intensified awareness of being alive. It is the same wisdom which the urn will continue to teach "in midst of other woe." Keats believed that man's life, though rounded by a little sleep, is the stuff of which "a thing of beauty" is made. Art takes its truth from life, and then returns it to life as beauty. The paradox that "teases us out of thought" is that in a work of art there is a kind of life which is both dead and immortal. But—a melancholy truth—*only* the dead are immortal. If there is a heaven, Keats wanted it to be very much like earth, with a Mermaid Tavern where poets could bowse "with contented smack." Delight is inseparable from melancholy because it is not conceivable apart from the mortal predica-

ment. The answer to the question at the end of "Ode to a Nightingale"
—"Do I wake or sleep?"—is, "Both." In the structural imaginative arc of
the poem, the speaker is returned to the "drowsy numbness" wherein he
is awake to his own mortal lot and no longer awake to the vision of
beauty. Yet he knows that it is the same human melancholy which is
in the beauty of the bird's "plaintive anthem" and in the truth of his
renewed depression. His way of stating this knowledge is to ask the question. Such considerations may clarify the truth-beauty passage. Whether
they justify artistically Keats's use of these clichés of Platonic speculation
is another matter. Keats was no Platonist, and if he had avoided those
terms or if he had indicated more obviously, within the poem, that he
was using the word "truth" in a sense close to the materialism of his own
times, "Ode on a Grecian Urn" would have had a different career in the
history of literary criticism. It is unlikely that any amount of exegesis can
rescue those last lines of the poem from associations with Platonic pie-
tism, for Keats was not enough of a witty and conscious ironist to exploit
successfully the philosophical ambiguities of "truth." His romanticism
was neither reactionary nor modernist in that way, and he may not even
have been clearly aware of the ambiguity involved. If it could be proved
that he was innocent of the ambiguity, and wanted only the philosophical prestige of the Platonic associations, then from his point of view
the poem would not suffer from the difficulties which the merest sophisti-
cation can ascribe to it. Whether or not such ignorance of the law
would be too outrageous to merit critical exoneration is a nice problem
for critical theory.

In considering the arc of imagination as an aspect of structure, we
have noticed that "Ode to a Nightingale" approaches general statement
and that "Ode on a Grecian Urn" arrives at it. "To Autumn" is obviously
less explicit, although it shows the same structural aspect. The lush and
realistic description of the first stanza is followed by the imagined picture
of autumn as a person who, while a lovely part of a lovely scene, is also
intent upon destroying it. The personification is dropped in the final
stanza, and there is again a realistic description, still beautiful but no
longer lush, and suggesting an approaching bleakness.

The imaginative aspect of structure which the three odes have in
common illustrates opinions which are in accord with the thought of
Keats's times and which he occasionally expressed in his poetry. The romantic poets' preoccupation with nature is proverbial, and there are a
number of studies (e.g., Caldwell's on Keats) relating their work and
thought to the associationalist psychology which was current in their
times. According to this psychology, all complex ideas and all products
of the imagination were, by the association of remembered sensations,
evolved from sensory experiences. Keats found this doctrine interesting
and important, not because it led back to the mechanical functioning
of the brain and the nervous system, but because sensations led to the

imagination and finally to myth and poetry and because the beauty of nature was thus allied with the beauty of art. In the early poem which begins, "I stood tip-toe upon a little hill," Keats suggests that the legends of classical mythology were created by poets responding to the beauties of nature:

> For what has made the sage or poet write
> But the fair paradise of Nature's light?
> In the calm grandeur of a sober line,
> We see the waving of the mountain pine;
> And when a tale is beautifully staid,
> We feel the safety of a hawthorn glade: . . .
> While at our feet, the voice of crystal bubbles
> Charms us at once away from all our troubles:
> So that we feel uplifted from the world,
> Walking upon the white clouds wreathed and curled.
> So felt he, who first told, how Psyche went
> On the smooth wind to realms of wonderment: . . .
> What first inspired a bard of old to sing
> Narcissus pining o'er the untainted spring?
> In some delicious ramble, he had found
> A little space with boughs all woven round;
> And in the midst of all, a clearer pool. . . .

In the "Ode to Psyche," which was written during the same period as the other odes (spring of 1819), Keats claims a similar experience for himself and contrasts it with those of the "bards of old." He has come upon Cupid and Psyche while he "wander'd in a forest thoughtlessly." Although the times are "too late for antique vows" and the "fond believing lyre," he is still by his "own eyes inspired." If he cannot celebrate this symbolic deity with rites and shrine, then he proposes to do so with the services of the imagination, with "the wreathèd trellis of a working brain, . . . all the gardener Fancy e'er could feign" and with all that "shadowy thought can win." Conspicuous throughout Keats' work, blended and adjusted according to his own temperament and for his own purposes, are these three elements: a theory of the imagination, the romantic's preoccupation with nature, and the refreshed literary tradition of classical mythology. These are reflected by the structure of his most successful poems, and are an element in their interrelatedness.

"To Autumn" is shorter than the other odes, and simpler on the surface in several respects. The nightingale sings "of summer in full-throated ease," and the boughs in the flowery tale on the urn cannot shed their leaves "nor ever bid the Spring adieu." The world in which the longer odes have their setting is either young or in its prime, spring or summer. Consequently, in these poems some directness of statement and a greater complexity are necessary in order to develop the paradoxical theme, in order to penetrate deeply enough the temple of Delight and arrive at the sovran shrine of Melancholy. The urn's "happy melodist" plays a song of spring, and the "self-same song" of the nightingale is of summer. One of these songs has "no tone," and the other is in either "a vision or a waking dream," for the voice of the "immortal Bird" is finally symbolized beyond the "sensual ear." But the music of autumn, the twittering of the swallows, remains realistic and literal, because the tensions of Keats's theme are implicit in the actual conditions of autumn, when beauty and melancholy are merging on the very surface of reality. If "To Autumn" is shorter than the other odes and less complex in its materials, it has the peculiar distinction of great compression achieved in simple terms.

Edgar Allan Poe

(1809–1849)

■■■■■■■■■■

BORN IN BOSTON to parents who were itinerant actors, Edgar Allan Poe was an orphan before he was three. Mr. and Mrs. John Allan, of Richmond, Virginia, adopted him, sending him to good schools. At the University of Virginia, Poe's drinking and gambling were heavy enough to cause his foster father to remove him from college. Poe then enlisted in the Coast Guard in Boston, at the same time publishing *Tamerlane and Other Poems,* "by a Bostonian," in 1827. Poe advanced in the Coast Guard and continued to write poetry, publishing his second volume in 1829. Recommended to a cadetship at West Point, he was there less than a year before his disinheritance by his foster father forced him to resign. From that time on he had to support himself by his writing. He spent the years 1831–1835 in Baltimore, making what meager income he could from poems and stories. In 1835 he became editor of the *Southern Literary Messenger* in Richmond. The following year he married his cousin, Virginia Clemm, a sickly girl of thirteen years. After losing his editorship because of time missed through drinking, Poe became, in succession, editor of *Graham's Magazine* in Philadelphia and *The Broadway Journal* in New York, and a literary contributor to *Godey's Lady's Book.* Publication of "The Raven" in 1844 brought fame but only ten dollars in money. His invalid wife died in 1847. In 1849, on a visit to Richmond, he became engaged to a wealthy widow who had been one of his childhood sweethearts. On his way to the wedding from New York, he celebrated with friends in Baltimore, was found unconscious on the streets of that city, and died four days later.

312412222313134243423423434242312122122323123121241242423423423423423423434343434343434343434343434234223423423423423423434234342323434323434234234234342

Suggested Readings

EDGAR ALLAN POE, *The Poetic Principle*, 1848.

YVOR WINTERS, "Edgar Allan Poe," in *In Defense of Reason*. Alan Swallow, Publisher, 1947, pp. 234–261.

ROY BASLER, "Poe's Dream Imagery," in *Sex, Symbolism, and Psychology in Literature*. New Brunswick, N. J.: Rutgers University Press, 1948, pp. 143–176.

■ ■ ■ ■ ■ ■ ■ ■ ■ ■

The Sleeper

At midnight, in the month of June,
I stand beneath the mystic moon.
An opiate vapor, dewy, dim,
Exhales from out her golden rim,
And, softly dripping, drop by drop,
Upon the quiet mountain top,
Steals drowsily and musically
Into the universal valley.
The rosemary nods upon the grave;
The lily lolls upon the wave;   10
Wrapping the fog about its breast,
The ruin moulders into rest;
Looking like Lethe, see! the lake
A conscious slumber seems to take,
And would not, for the world, awake.
All Beauty sleeps!—and lo! where lies
Irene, with her Destinies!

Oh, lady bright can it be right—
This window open to the night?
The wanton airs, from the tree-top,   20
Laughingly through the lattice drop—
The bodiless airs, a wizard rout,
Flit through thy chamber in and out,
And wave the curtain canopy
So fitfully—so fearfully—
Above the closed and fringèd lid
'Neath which thy slumb'ring soul lies hid,
That, o'er the floor and down the wall,
Like ghosts the shadows rise and fall!
Oh, lady dear, hast thou no fear?   30

Why and what art thou dreaming here?
Sure thou art come o'er far-off seas,
A wonder to these garden trees!
Strange is thy pallor! strange thy dress!
Strange, above all, thy length of tress,
And this all solemn silentness!

The lady sleeps! Oh, may her sleep
Which is enduring, so be deep!
Heaven have her in its sacred keep!
This chamber changed for one more holy,   40
This bed for one more melancholy,
I pray to God that she may lie
Forever with unopened eye,
While the pale sheeted ghosts go by!
My love, she sleeps. Oh, may her sleep,
As it is lasting, so be deep!
Soft may the worms about her creep!
Far in the forest, dim and old,
For her may some tall vault unfold:
Some vault that oft hath flung its black   50
And wingèd panels fluttering back,
Triumphant, o'er the crested palls,
Of her grand family funerals—
Some sepulchre, remote, alone,
Against whose portal she hath thrown,
In childhood, many an idle stone—
Some tomb from out whose sounding door
She ne'er shall force an echo more,
Thrilling to think, poor child of sin!
It was the dead who groaned within.   60

■ Compare this poem with "The Exequy" by Henry King (p. 674).
Discuss the effect upon the expression of grief of the setting Poe uses in
contrast with that King uses.

To Helen

Helen, thy beauty is to me
    Like those Nicéan barks of yore,
That gently, o'er a perfumed sea,
    The weary, way-worn wanderer bore
    To his own native shore.

On desperate seas long wont to roam,
   Thy hyacinth hair, thy classic face,
Thy Naiad airs have brought me home
   To the glory that was Greece,
   And the grandeur that was Rome.

Lo! in yon brilliant window-niche
   How statue-like I see thee stand,
The agate lamp within thy hand!
   Ah, Psyche, from the regions which
   Are Holy-Land!

■   This poem, Poe said, was written in memory of Mrs. Jane Stith Stanard, who became "the first purely ideal love of my soul." Poe's conception of her is stated in classical terms. Explain how the imagery is developed from stanza to stanza.

The City in the Sea

Lo! Death has reared himself a throne
In a strange city lying alone
Far down within the dim West,
Where the good and the bad and the worst and the best
Have gone to their eternal rest.
There shrines and palaces and towers
(Time-eaten towers that tremble not!)
Resemble nothing that is ours.
Around, by lifting winds forgot,
Resignedly beneath the sky   10
The melancholy waters lie.

No rays from the holy heaven come down
On the long night-time of that town;
But light from out the lurid sea
Streams up the turrets silently—
Gleams up the pinnacles far and free—
Up domes—up spires—up kingly halls—
Up fanes—up Babylon-like walls—
Up shadowy long-forgotten bowers
Of sculptured ivy and stone flowers—   20
Up many and many a marvellous shrine
Whose wreathèd friezes intertwine
The viol, the violet, and the vine.
Resignedly beneath the sky

The melancholy waters lie.
So blend the turrets and shadows there
That all seem pendulous in air,
While from a proud tower in the town
Death looks gigantically down.

There open fanes and gaping graves   30
Yawn level with the luminous waves;
But not the riches there that lie
In each idol's diamond eye—
Not the gayly jewelled dead
Tempt the waters from their bed;
For no ripples curl, alas!
Along that wilderness of glass—
No swellings tell that winds may be
Upon some far-off happier sea—
No heavings hint that winds have been   40
On seas less hideously serene.

But lo, a stir is in the air!
The wave—there is a movement there!
As if the towers had thrust aside,
In slightly sinking, the dull tide—
As if their tops had feebly given
A void within the filmy Heaven.
The waves have now a redder glow—
The hours are breathing faint and low—
And when, amid no earthly moans,   50
Down, down that town shall settle hence,
Hell, rising from a thousand thrones,
Shall do it reverence.

■   Is this poem merely description or is it an allegorical statement? If
it is allegorical, is the meaning easily explicable?

Dream-Land

By a route obscure and lonely,
Haunted by ill angels only,
Where an Eidolon, named Night,
On a black throne reigns upright,
I have reached these lands but newly
From an ultimate dim Thule—

From a wild weird clime that lieth, sublime,
    Out of Space—out of Time.

Bottomless vales and boundless floods,
And chasms, and caves, and Titan woods,   10
With forms that no man can discover
For the tears that drip all over;
Mountains toppling evermore
Into seas without a shore;
Seas that restlessly aspire,
Surging, unto skies of fire;
Lakes that endlessly outspread
Their lone waters—lone and dead,—
Their still waters—still and chilly
With the snows of the lolling lily.   20

By the lakes that thus outspread
Their lone waters, lone and dead,—
Their sad waters, sad and chilly
With the snows of the lolling lily,—
By the mountains—near the river
Murmuring lowly, murmuring ever,—
By the grey woods,—by the swamp
Where the toad and the newt encamp,—
By the dismal tarns and pools
    Where dwell the Ghouls,—   30
By each spot the most unholy—
In each nook most melancholy,—
There the traveller meets, aghast,
Sheeted Memories of the Past—
Shrouded forms that start and sigh
As they pass the wanderer by—
White-robed forms of friends long given,
In agony, to the Earth—and Heaven.

For the heart whose woes are legion
'Tis a peaceful, soothing region—   40
For the spirit that walks in shadow
'Tis—oh 'tis an Eldorado!
But the traveller, travelling through it,
May not—dare not openly view it;
Never its mysteries are exposed
To the weak human eye unclosed;
So wills its King, who hath forbid
The uplifting of the fringèd lid;

And thus the sad Soul that here passes
Beholds it but through darkened glasses.   50

By a route obscure and lonely,
Haunted by ill angels only,
Where an Eidolon, named Night,
On a black throne reigns upright,
I have wandered home but newly
From this ultimate dim Thule.

1. Is there a perceptible theme in this poem? Are there any similarities between this poem and "Ulalume"?

Ulalume

The skies they were ashen and sober;
    The leaves they were crispèd and sere—
    The leaves they were withering and sere;
It was night in the lonesome October
    Of my most immemorial year;
It was hard by the dim lake of Auber,
    In the misty mid region of Weir—
It was down by the dank tarn of Auber,
    In the ghoul-haunted woodland of Weir.

Here once, through an alley Titanic,   10
    Of cypress, I roamed with my Soul—
    Of cypress, with Psyche, my Soul.
These were days when my heart was volcanic
    As the scoriac rivers that roll—
    As the lavas that restlessly roll
Their sulphurous currents down Yaanek
    In the ultimate climes of the pole—
That groan as they roll down Mount Yaanek
    In the realms of the boreal pole.

Our talk had been serious and sober,   20
    But our thoughts they were palsied and sere—
    Our memories were treacherous and sere—
For we knew not the month was October,
    And we marked not the night of the year—
    (Ah, night of all nights in the year!)
We noted not the dim lake of Auber—
    (Though once we had journeyed down here)—

Remembered not the dank tarn of Auber,
    Nor the ghoul-haunted woodland of Weir.

And now, as the night was senescent   30
    And star-dials pointed to morn—
    As the star-dials hinted of morn—
At the end of our path a liquescent
    And nebulous lustre was born,
Out of which a miraculous crescent
    Arose with a duplicate horn—
Astarte's bediamonded crescent
    Distinct with its duplicate horn.

And I said—"She is warmer than Dian:
    She rolls through an ether of sighs—   40
    She revels in a region of sighs:
She has seen that the tears are not dry on
    These cheeks, where the worm never dies
And has come past the stars of the Lion
    To point us the path to the skies—
    To the Lethean peace of the skies—
Come up, in despite of the Lion,
    To shine on us with her bright eyes—
Come up through the lair of the Lion,
    With love in her luminous eyes."   50

But Psyche, uplifting her finger,
    Said—"Sadly this star I mistrust—
    Her pallor I strangely mistrust:—
Oh, hasten!—oh, let us not linger!
    Oh, fly!—let us fly!—for we must."
In terror she spoke, letting sink her
    Wings until they trailed in the dust—
In agony sobbed, letting sink her
    Plumes till they trailed in the dust—
    Till they sorrowfully trailed in the dust. 60

I replied—"This is nothing but dreaming:
    Let us on by this tremulous light!
    Let us bathe in this crystalline light!
Its Sibyllic splendor is beaming
    With Hope and in Beauty to-night:—
See!—it flickers up the sky through the night!
Ah, we safely may trust to its gleaming,
    And be sure it will lead us aright—

We safely may trust to a gleaming
   That cannot but guide us aright,   70
   Since it flickers up to Heaven through the night."

Thus I pacified Psyche and kissed her,
   And tempted her out of her gloom—
   And conquered her scruples and gloom;
And we passed to the end of the vista,
   But were stopped by the door of a tomb—
   By the door of a legended tomb;
And I said—"What is written, sweet sister,
   On the door of this legended tomb?"
She replied—"Ulalume—Ulalume—   80
   'Tis the vault of thy lost Ulalume!"

Then my heart it grew ashen and sober
   As the leaves that were crispèd and sere—
   As the leaves that were withering and sere,
And I cried—"It was surely October
   On *this* very night of last year
   That I journeyed—I journeyed down here—
   That I brought a dread burden down here—
   On this night of all nights in the year,
   Ah, what demon has tempted me here?   90
Well I know, now, this dim lake of Auber—
   This misty mid region of Weir—
Well I know, now, this dank tarn of Auber,
   This ghoul-haunted woodland of Weir."

■   We may read "Ulalume" objectively, asking, for example, whether
there is an appropriate relationship between the theme and the imagery, rhythms, diction, and so forth. We may read it, on the other hand,
in relation to Poe's own life, his theory of poetry, and the period in
which it was written. In other words, we may read it not only to discover
whether it is self-sufficient, coherent, and meaningful, when read without the help of biographical or historical information, but to see also
some of the ways in which biographical and historical knowledge may
assist us in reading certain poems.

   The poem begins with a description that is a kind of Gothic stage
set: ashen skies, sere leaves, "lonely October," "dank tarn," "ghoul-
haunted woodland," and so forth. This is not a real world. It is a never-
never world of romantic mysteries. The second stanza gives an account
of excruciatingly painful feelings: the heart of the protagonist, as he
roams with Psyche, is volcanic or melting like burning slag. The occasion of this grief, however, is not at first given. (When we eventually

learn that the grief is caused by the death of Ulalume we are not told in such a way that we feel these grotesque expressions of grief are justified.) In the third stanza we are told that the couple's memories and their powers of observation, for a reason not yet given, are dim. In the next four stanzas we learn that night is fading, and Astarte, as the moon, appears in order to guide them. Psyche is afraid to follow Astarte, but the protagonist insists and Psyche yields. We are not told why the two should argue about their guide, or why Psyche should behave in such a pathetic manner when she argues about it. They follow Astarte, who leads them to the door of Ulalume's tomb. Once there, they recall the burial of Ulalume exactly a year before. In the final stanza, which is none too clear, we learn that the ghouls, who are merciful rather than like ordinary ghouls, have raised the specter of Astarte to lead them to the tomb and therefore prevent their further wanderings in the wolds. (If the "secret that lies in these wolds" is Ulalume's tomb, then the ghouls are hardly "merciful." We must assume therefore that they brought the protagonist and Psyche to the tomb to prevent their being terrified by the "secret," whatever that may be.) The theme of the poem seems to be that grief for the dead beloved draws one toward the tomb. The subject matter, as we have seen, is the Gothic setting, the journey toward the tomb, the expression of terrible grief and dismay.

Is there an appropriate relationship between the theme and the subject matter? Insofar as the reader can tell from examining the poem itself, the setting and the grotesque emotion are greatly in excess of anything suggested by the theme. Every lover undoubtedly would experience pain and melancholy at losing his beloved, but he would not experience them in this larger-than-life fashion, with this volcanic feeling and this loss of memory. Grief can, of course, be terrible in ordinary human terms. It does not require a Gothic setting as a background. Seen against such a background it may seem forced and unnatural. Normal grief of this kind can make ordinary experiences seem eerie and unreal. The separation of grief from commonplace settings and ordinary modes of expression makes it seem fantastic. The place names—Auber, Weir, Yaanek, and so on—are not genuine place names. The ghoul is a robber of graves, but the ghouls in this poem are not sinister. The word "wold," which means an unwooded region in the uplands, is used by Poe to suggest an area with great towering cypress. The diction generally is exaggerated. The night, for example, is not waning, it is "senescent." Why Astarte, Dian, and Psyche have certain roles, or why they are presented as they are (Astarte as a specter of the moon and Psyche as a winged creature), is never made clear in the context of the poem. In other words, the weird subject matter is not appropriate to the theme as we grasp it in reading the poem.

Nor, to follow the question of appropriateness a bit further, is the metrical pattern of "Ulalume" appropriate. Properly employed rhythm supports the sense, slows down or hurries the movement, and assists in evoking an appropriate tone. Ordinarily we expect grief to be expressed haltingly, with some difficulty, but grief in this poem is set to a music that is fast paced and excessively melodious. Aldous Huxley, in *Vulgarity in Literature,** has commented on "Ulalume" in this fashion: "These lines protest too much (and with what a variety of voices!) that they are poetical, and, protesting, are therefore vulgar. Poetry ought to be musical, but musical with tact, subtly and variously. Meters whose rhythms, as in this case, are strong, insistent and practically invariable offer the poet a kind of short cut to musicality. They provide him (my subject calls for a mixture of metaphors) with a ready-made, reach-me-down music. He does not create a music appropriately modulated to his meaning; all he has to do is to shovel the meaning into the moving stream of the meter and allow the current to carry it along on waves. . . ." Neither the subject matter nor the metrical pattern, then, seems to be very appropriate to the conception behind the poem.

Looked at in these ways the poem seems confused, obscure, and self-consciously poetic. Students are sometimes advised not to go outside a poem for information about it. By and large, this may be good advice. Much biographical and historical data are quite irrelevant to a poem, but certain items are relevant in that they enable us to read the poem more clearly (certain meanings are *in* the poem *if* we can see them) or enable us to perceive the esthetic or critical theory in terms of which it was written. No over-all rule excluding biographical and historical information will stand up.

Certain information about Poe helps us to see "Ulalume" in a larger context. Some of the "information" is guesswork and should therefore be used tentatively, but in this instance even the guesswork enables us, regardless of its being literally true or not, to see the principle of organization behind the poem.

In a number of his poems Poe writes about dead maidens. In "The Poetic Principle," he states that the death of beautiful women is the ideal subject matter of poetry. Throughout his work, both in his stories and poems, the heroines have an unearthly beauty and an unearthly purity. His heroes are victims of a heavy melancholy. The fanciful and phantomlike world of his stories and an outstanding fact of his life, his marriage to Virginia Clemm, childlike and a kind of embodiment of the heroines of his imagination, are stressed in Joseph Wood Krutch's *Edgar Allan Poe,*† a psychological interpretation of Poe's life and art. One of the key passages in Krutch's interpretation is this: "That sense of melancholy, foreboding, and horror which, even though its exact meaning is disputed, is generally recognized as the usual accompaniment

* (London: Chatto and Windus, 1930).
† Joseph Wood Krutch, *Edgar Allan Poe* (New York: Alfred A. Knopf, 1926). By permission of the publishers.

of deeply inhibited sexual desires, made his life one long misery, and a similar cloud of horror hung over his stories. Perverse fancies of a usually sadistic character flitted through his mind accompanied by a sickening revulsion against their horror, and these too found a place in his tales alongside all manner of nightmare fears." Krutch goes on to say that psychiatrists will differ in their opinion about the cause of the deeply rooted sex inhibitions from which Poe apparently suffered; the cause might be organic or the result of some experience. According to Krutch, "Poe could not love in the usual fashion and the reason lay, or at least seemed to him to lie, in the death of some woman upon whom his desire had irrevocably fixed itself. If we knew who lay behind the doors of that tomb in the ghoul haunted woodland of Weir, we should know the answer to the greatest riddle of Poe's life." Krutch is saying that Poe's weird marriage to Virginia Clemm, a child rather than a woman, was not really a marriage. In Virginia he found the person who came closest to being the embodiment of the pale figure of his dreams. She "perfectly met the needs of his morbid imagination because her undeveloped mind and pale unhealthy face, with the high forehead characteristic of the family, satisfied his conception of an unearthly purity." She was a part of the fiction by which he lived. And Krutch is also saying that the frequent use in Poe's poems of lost Lenores or a Ulalume is a consequence of his fixation upon a dead woman he had once loved.

If we look at "Ulalume" we see that Astarte, who in many poems has symbolized fleshly love, plays an important role. She leads the protagonist, despite the protests of Psyche, to the tomb, to the closed doors that "shut him forever from the possibility of further love."

Our awareness of the frequency with which Poe wrote of dead women as well as the melancholy and fanciful world of his imagination enables us to relate "Ulalume" to the rest of his work. The reader's knowledge of these other poems or stories enables him to see more clearly what is being said in the individual poem. A knowledge of these other works and of Poe's biography convinces us, for one thing, that this eerie, melancholy world is Poe's private world. The Gothic stage setting may be partly claptrap and artificiality, but the melancholy mood and the preoccupation with morbid subjects are genuinely part of Poe's own mind and being.

If one accepts Krutch's interpretation of Poe's life, then "Ulalume" becomes not merely a kind of Gothic tale in verse but a pathetic statement of a diseased mind. But if one accepts this account of Poe's mental disorders—or some disorder akin to them—one must see how much of the problem, as the poet must have seen it in himself and have faced it, is not put *inside* the poem. There is a conflict in the poem, in that Psyche objects to following Astarte, but it is a meaningless conflict because we as readers are not given any reason why they should not follow

Astarte If Poe's fixation on a dead woman was the subject he was working with, then there was a genuine conflict: should the protagonist allow the dead woman to dominate his mind and draw him toward a continual preoccupation with the eerie and abnormal, or should he struggle to live in a normal, everyday world? The struggle would be between these two forces: the normal and the abnormal. If he had treated his subject in these terms the conflict would seem real and not artificial. The intensity of the poem would be far greater if the everyday world of Poe's life in Baltimore or New York were set against the pull he felt toward this unnatural, weird world of his imagination. By denying the real world and putting his poem inside this fanciful world, he causes the reader to feel that nothing serious or genuine is at stake. Therefore the potential drama of the poem is left undeveloped, and the reader is left unconvinced.

If Poe had written "Ulalume" out of his own actual experience, had put this experience or some part of it inside the poem—in terms that would enable us to perceive the actual problem involved—he probably would have written a better poem. The fuzziness of the whole conception puts the reader off. The dream world, the excessive diction, the meter that bears little relationship to the sense, and so forth—all these make the poem vague and difficult for the reader to accept either as a sincere or a meaningful statement.

Annabel Lee

It was many and many a year ago,
    In a kingdom by the sea,
That a maiden there lived whom you may know
    By the name of Annabel Lee;
And this maiden she lived with no other thought
    Than to love and be loved by me.

I was a child and *she* was a child,
    In this kingdom by the sea,
But we loved with a love that was more than love—
    I and my Annabel Lee—
With a love that the wingèd seraphs of heaven
    Coveted her and me.

And this was the reason that, long ago,
    In this kingdom by the sea,
A wind blew out of a cloud, chilling
    My beautiful Annabel Lee;
So that her high-born kinsmen came

10

And bore her away from me,
To shut her up in a sepulchre
    In this kingdom by the sea.   20

The angels, not half so happy in heaven,
    Went envying her and me—
Yes!—that was the reason (as all men know,
    In this kingdom by the sea)
That the wind came out of the cloud by night,
    Chilling and killing my Annabel Lee.

But our love it was stronger by far than the love
    Of those who were older than we—
    Of many far wiser than we—
And neither the angels in heaven above,   30
    Nor the demons down under the sea,
Can ever dissever my soul from the soul
    Of the beautiful Annabel Lee:

For the moon never beams, without bringing me dreams
    Of the beautiful Annabel Lee;
And the stars never rise, but I feel the bright eyes
    Of the beautiful Annabel Lee:
And so, all the night-tide, I lie down by the side
Of my darling—my darling—my life and my bride,
    In the sepulchre there by the sea—   40
    In her tomb by the sounding sea.

■   In our discussion of "Ulalume," we quoted from Aldous Huxley,
On Vulgarity in Literature. Is the metrical pattern of "Annabel Lee"
"vulgar" in the sense in which Huxley uses the word?

Alfred Tennyson

(1809–1892)

■■■■■■■■■■

TENNYSON'S FATHER was a clergyman, a somber-minded man with bookish inclinations, at Somersby in Lincolnshire. From his father Tennyson may have inherited some of his early melancholia. At Cambridge the young poet was a member of a literary group known as the Apostles. He was friendly with Edward Fitzgerald, who later wrote *The Rubaiyat of Omar Khayyam,* and especially with Arthur Henry Hallam. That during this period he was influenced considerably by the poetry of Keats is evident from the rich texture of *Poems, Chiefly Lyrical* (1830). Knowing as a young man that his gifts were considerable, he worked very hard to perfect himself as a craftsman and to face the problems of his intellectual world. In "Locksley Hall" (1842) Tennyson's social protest is first seen. *The Princess* (1847) established him as a conservative with mildly liberal sympathies. Certainly one of the most important influences on his work was the early death of Hallam. *In Memoriam,* the elegy inspired by Hallam's death, took seventeen years of intermittent work and was published in 1850. In subject it moves from the poet's grief to attempts to reconcile science and religion. In 1850 Tennyson married and was made Laureate, succeeding Wordsworth. Later works include *Idylls of the King* (1859), *Enoch Arden* (1860), and *Lucretius* (1868). After 1864, when he had to compete with Browning, Swinburne, Meredith, and others, there was a reaction against Tennyson. Another reaction against him as a "typical Victorian" came when the "new poetry" movements were beginning in the twentieth century. But Tennyson survived these periods of unpopularity and is generally considered a major English poet.

Suggested Readings

G. K. CHESTERTON, "Tennyson," in *The Uses of Diversity*. London: Methuen and Co., Ltd., 1920.

W. H. AUDEN, Introduction, in *A Selection from the Poems of Alfred Lord Tennyson*. Garden City, N. Y.: Doubleday & Company, Inc., 1944.

T. S. ELIOT, "In Memoriam," in *Selected Essays*. New York: Harcourt, Brace & Co., 1950.

■■■■■■■■■■

Temperamentally the young Tennyson felt a strong kinship with Keats, and his earlier work contains echoes from the great romantic poet. But Tennyson, along with many of his contemporaries, felt impelled to break with the movement sponsored by the romantics, and he disclaimed the charge that his lyrics were similar to the music of Keats. According to one study, *Keats and the Victorians** by George H. Ford, Keats was little read in the years immediately after his death and was known as an escapist, an unsocial, esthetic-minded young man who hungered after sensation. Tennyson felt obliged therefore to disparage his indebtedness to Keats and to find his way in a world that asked the poet to be more deliberately serious, to face the issues of his intellectual world. During the 1830's Tennyson strove to minimize Keats's influence, and he wrote "The Palace of Art" to show that the esthete shrinks in vain from the realm of reality.

It was from his fellow Apostles at Cambridge that Tennyson initially heard a strong plea for a "serious" art. R. C. Trench warned, "Tennyson, we cannot live in art," and his friend Hallam argued that a poet should be more concerned with the good than with the beautiful. Ironically, it was in Hallam's death that Tennyson early suffered a profound sense of evil, of man's being caught in a condition of mortality.

After Hallam's death Tennyson dedicated himself to a period of study of history, sciences, and languages. He directed himself to writing the kind of poetry that would have interest and value for a large audience, not merely for a select group able to admire his virtuosity with language. In one poem, for example, "The Golden Year," he wrote about such current issues and attitudes as a broadened Christianity, free trade, and Carlyle's gospel of work.

Tennyson is usually called the most representative poet of the Victorian world, pursuing the questions that most concerned his large middle-class audience. And he is held up as the poet who best exemplifies the Victorian attitude of compromise. The Victorians were greatly troubled by the conflict between science and religion, and by the social and economic consequences of the broadening base of suffrage. *In Memoriam,* the long poem in which he posed the problem of maintaining faith in God and in a moral order in the face of what seemed the brute facts of man's origins, was an excellent statement of the question which most troubled his age. Tennyson accepted the evolutionary hypothesis but nonetheless retained his faith in God:

> And one far-off divine event,
> To which the whole creation moves.

In respect to enfranchisement of the masses, Tennyson was hardly of the liberal party, although he occasionally spoke of the "warrens of the

* (New Haven: Yale University Press, 1944).

poor" and of the reform bills. He strongly disapproved of the French Revolution, finding it a part of the "falsehood of extremes." He did, however, warn that England would maintain its historic greatness only if those in power remembered the needs of the poor. Nor did the liberalism of feminine emancipation stir him greatly. In *The Princess* he admitted the justice of some of the arguments for woman's emancipation, but he insisted that woman's primary function was rearing children and keeping the home. Perhaps the question of Tennyson's conservatism or liberalism is best seen in these lines:

> Where Freedom slowly broadens down
> From precedent to precedent.

He was willing to ignore certain inequalities and injustices if they threatened to upset the even tenor of things. In our generation there is less talk about Tennyson's being a seer than there was in his own day. He posed many problems, but he was not conspicuously successful in solving any of them.

Mariana

Mariana in the moated grange.

MEASURE FOR MEASURE

With blackest moss the flower plots
    Were thickly crusted, one and all:
The rusted nails fell from the knots
    That held the pear to the gable-wall.
The broken sheds look'd sad and strange:
    Unlifted was the clinking latch;
    Weeded and worn the ancient thatch
Upon the lonely moated grange.
        She only said, "My life is dreary,
            He cometh not," she said;   10
        She said, "I am aweary, aweary,
            I would that I were dead!"

Her tears fell with the dews at even;
    Her tears fell ere the dews were dried:
She could not look on the sweet heaven,
    Either at morn or eventide.
After the flitting of the bats,
    When thickest dark did trance the sky,
    She drew her casement-curtain by,
And glanced athwart the glooming flats.   20
        She only said, "The night is dreary,

He cometh not," she said;
She said, "I am aweary, aweary,
I would that I were dead!"

Upon the middle of the night,
Waking she heard the night-fowl crow:
The cock sung out an hour ere light:
From the dark fen the oxen's low
Came to her: without hope of change,
In sleep she seem'd to walk forlorn,   30
Till cold winds woke the gray-eyed morn
About the lonely moated grange.
She only said, "The day is dreary,
He cometh not," she said;
She said, "I am aweary, aweary,
I would that I were dead!"

About a stone-cast from the wall
A sluice with blacken'd waters slept,
And o'er it many, round and small,
The cluster'd marish-mosses crept.   40
Hard by a poplar shook alway,
All silver-green with gnarled bark:
For leagues no other tree did mark
The level waste, the rounding gray.
She only said, "My life is dreary,
He cometh not," she said;
She said, "I am aweary, aweary,
I would that I were dead!"

And ever when the moon was low,
And the shrill winds were up and away,   50
In the white curtain, to and fro,
She saw the gusty shadow sway.
But when the moon was very low,
And wild winds bound within their cell,
The shadow of the poplar fell
Upon her bed, across her brow.
She only said, "The night is dreary,
He cometh not," she said;
She said, "I am aweary, aweary,
I would that I were dead!"   60

All day within the dreamy house,
The doors upon their hinges creak'd;

The blue fly sung in the pane; the mouse
   Behind the mouldering wainscot shriek'd,
Or from the crevice peer'd about.
     Old faces glimmer'd thro' the doors,
     Old footsteps trod the upper floors,
Old voices called her from without.
      She only said, "My life is dreary,
        He cometh not," she said;   70
      She said, "I am aweary, aweary,
        I would that I were dead!"

The sparrow's chirrup on the roof,
   The slow clock ticking, and the sound
Which to the wooing wind aloof
   The poplar made, did all confound
Her sense; but most he loathed the hour
   When the thick-moted sunbeam lay
   Athwart the chambers, and the day
Was sloping toward his western bower.   80
      Then, said she, "I am very dreary,
        He will not come," she said;
      She wept, "I am aweary, aweary,
        Oh God, that I were dead!"

■   How does the employment of nature imagery contribute to the mood of dejection which Mariana (in Shakespeare's play she is deserted by Angelo and lives in a lonely house) feels?

The Lotos-Eaters

"Courage!" he said, and pointed toward the land,
"This mounting wave will roll us shoreward soon."
In the afternoon they came unto a land
In which it seemèd always afternoon.
All round the coast the languid air did swoon,
Breathing like one that hath a weary dream.
Full-faced above the valley stood the moon;
And, like a downward smoke, the slender stream
Along the cliff to fall and pause and fall did seem.

A land of streams! some, like a downward smoke,   10
Slow-dropping veils of thinnest lawn, did go;
And some through wavering lights and shadows broke,
Rolling a slumbrous sheet of foam below.

They saw the gleaming river seaward flow
From the inner land; far off, three mountain-tops,
Three silent pinnacles of aged snow,
Stood sunset-flushed; and, dewed with showery drops,
Up-clomb the shadowy pine above the woven copse.

The charmèd sunset lingered low adown
In the red west; through mountain clefts the dale
Was seen far inland, and the yellow down   20
Bordered with palm, and many a winding vale
And meadow, set with slender galingale;
A land where all things always seemed the same!
And round about the keel with faces pale,
Dark faces pale against that rosy flame,
The mild-eyed melancholy Lotos-eaters came.

Branches they bore of that enchanted stem,
Laden with flower and fruit, whereof they gave
To each, but whoso did receive of them
And taste, to him the gushing of the wave   30
Far, far away did seem to mourn and rave
On alien shores; and if his fellow spake,
His voice was thin, as voices from the grave;
And deep-asleep he seemed, yet all awake,
And music in his ears his beating heart did make.

They sat them down upon the yellow sand,
Between the sun and moon upon the shore;
And sweet it was to dream of fatherland,
Of child, and wife and slave; but evermore
Most weary seemed the sea, weary the oar,   40
Weary the wandering fields of barren foam.
Then someone said, "We will return no more";
And all at once they sang, "Our island home
Is far beyond the wave; we will no longer roam."

Choric Song

I

There is sweet music here that softer falls
Than petals from blown roses on the grass,
Or night-dews on still waters between walls
Of shadowy granite, in a gleaming pass;
Music that gentlier on the spirit lies,
Than tired eyelids upon tired eyes;   50

Music that brings sweet sleep down from the blissful skies.
Here are cool mosses deep,
And thro the moss the ivies creep,
And in the stream the long-leaved flowers weep,
And from the craggy ledge the poppy hangs in sleep.

2

Why are we weigh'd upon with heaviness,
And utterly consumed with sharp distress,
While all things else have rest from weariness?
All things have rest: why should we toil alone,   60
We only toil, who are the first of things,
And make perpetual moan,
Still from one sorrow to another thrown:
Nor ever fold our wings,
And cease from wanderings,
Nor steep our brows in slumber's holy balm;
Nor hearken what the inner spirit sings,
"There is no joy but calm!"
Why should we only toil, the roof and crown of things?

3

Lo! in the middle of the wood,   70
The folded leaf is woo'd from out the bud
With winds upon the branch, and there
Grows green and broad, and takes no care,
Sun-steep'd at noon, and in the moon
Nightly dew-fed; and turning yellow
Falls, and floats adown the air.
Lo! sweeten'd with the summer light,
The full-juiced apple, waxing over-mellow,
Drops in a silent autumn night.
All its allotted length of days,   80
The flower ripens in its place,
Ripens and fades, and falls, and hath no toil,
Fast-rooted in the fruitful soil.

4

Hateful is the dark-blue sky,
Vaulted o'er the dark-blue sea.
Death is the end of life; ah, why
Should life all labor be?
Let us alone. Time driveth onward fast,
And in a little while our lips are dumb.
Let us alone. What is it that will last?   90

All things are taken from us, and become
Portions and parcels of the dreadful Past.
Let us alone. What pleasure can we have
To war with evil? Is there any peace
In ever climbing up the climbing wave?
All things have rest, and ripen toward the grave
In silence; ripen, fall and cease:
Give us long rest or death, dark death, or dreamful ease.

5

How sweet it were, hearing the downward stream,
With half-shut eyes ever to seem   100
Falling asleep in a half-dream!
To dream and dream, like yonder amber light,
Which will not leave the myrrh-bush on the height;
To hear each other's whisper'd speech;
Eating the Lotos day by day,
To watch the crisping ripples on the beach,
And tender curving lines of creamy spray;
To lend our hearts and spirits wholly
To the influence of mild-minded melancholy;
To muse and brood and live again in memory,   110
With those old faces of our infancy
Heap'd over with a mound of grass,
Two handfuls of white dust, shut in an urn of brass!

6

Dear is the memory of our wedded lives,
And dear the last embraces of our wives
And their warm tears: but all hath suffer'd change;
For surely now our household hearths are cold:
Our sons inherit us: our looks are strange:
And we should come like ghosts to trouble joy.
Or else the island princes over-bold   120
Have eat our substance, and the minstrel sings
Before them of the ten-years' war in Troy,
And our great deeds, as half-forgotten things.
Is there confusion in the little isle?
Let what is broken so remain.
The Gods are hard to reconcile:
'Tis hard to settle order once again.
There is confusion worse than death,
Trouble on trouble, pain on pain,
Long labor unto aged breath,   130

Sore task to hearts worn out by many wars
And eyes grown dim with gazing on the pilot stars.

7

But, propped on beds of amaranth and moly,
How sweet—while warm airs lull us, blowing lowly—
With half-dropped eyelid still,
Beneath a heaven dark and holy,
To watch the long bright river drawing slowly
His waters from the purple hill—
To hear the dewy echoes calling
From cave to cave through the thick-twined vine—   140
To watch the emerald-colored water falling
Through many a woven acanthus-wreath divine!
Only to hear and see the far-off sparkling brine,
Only to hear were sweet, stretched out beneath the pine.

8

The Lotos blooms below the barren peak,
The Lotos blows by every winding creek;
All day the wind breathes low with mellower tone;
Through every hollow cave and alley lone
Round and round the spicy downs the yellow Lotos-dust is blown.
We have had enough of action, and of motion we,   150
Rolled to starboard, rolled to larboard, when the surge was seething free,
Where the wallowing monster spouted his foam-fountains in the sea.
Let us swear an oath, and keep it with an equal mind,
In the hollow Lotos-land to live and lie reclined
On the hills like gods together, careless of mankind.
For they lie beside their nectar, and the bolts are hurled
Far below them in the valleys, and the clouds are lightly curled
Round their golden houses, girdled with the gleaming world;
Where they smile in secret, looking over wasted lands,
Blight and famine, plague and earthquake, roaring deeps and fiery
              sands,   160
Clanging fights, and flaming towns, and sinking ships, and praying hands
But they smile, they find a music centered in a doleful song
Steaming up, a lamentation and an ancient tale of wrong,
Like a tale of little meaning though the words are strong;
Chanted from an ill-used race of men that cleave the soil,
Sow the seed, and reap the harvest with enduring toil,
Storing yearly little dues of wheat, and wine and oil;
Till they perish and they suffer—some, 'tis whispered—down in hell
Suffer endless anguish, others in Elysian valleys dwell,
Resting weary limbs at last on beds of asphodel.   170

Surely, surely, slumber is more sweet than toil, the shore
Than labor in the deep mid-ocean, wind and wave and oar;
Oh, rest ye, brother mariners, we will not wander more.

■   Does this poem, in theme, subject matter, imagery, or tone, seem
reminiscent of any of Keats's odes?

Ulysses

It little profits that an idle king,
By this still hearth, among these barren crags,
Matched with an aged wife, I mete and dole
Unequal laws unto a savage race,
That hoard, and sleep, and feed, and know not me.
I cannot rest from travel; I will drink
Life to the lees. All times I have enjoyed
Greatly, have suffered greatly, both with those
That loved me, and alone; on shore, and when
Through scudding drifts the rainy Hyades   10
Vexed the dim sea. I am become a name;
For always roaming with a hungry heart
Much have I seen and known—cities of men,
And manners, climates, councils, governments,
Myself not least, but honored of them all—
And drunk delight of battle with my peers,
Far on the ringing plains of windy Troy.
I am a part of all that I have met;
Yet all experience is an arch wherethrough
Gleams that untraveled world whose margin fades   20
Forever and forever when I move.
How dull it is to pause, to make an end,
To rust unburnished, not to shine in use!
As though to breathe were life! Life piled on life
Were all too little, and of one to me
Little remains; but every hour is saved
From that eternal silence, something more,
A bringer of new things; and vile it were
For some three suns to store and hoard myself,
And this gray spirit yearning in desire   30
To follow knowledge like a sinking star,
Beyond the utmost bound of human thought.
    This is my son, mine own Telemachus,
To whom I leave the scepter and the isle—
Well-loved of me, discerning to fulfill
This labor, by slow prudence to make mild

A rugged people, and through soft degrees
Subdue them to the useful and the good.
Most blameless is he, centered in the sphere
Of common duties, decent not to fail   40
In offices of tenderness, and pay
Meet adoration to my household gods,
When I am gone. He works his work, I mine.
    There lies the port; the vessel puffs her sail;
There gloom the dark, broad seas. My mariners,
Souls that have toiled, and wrought, and thought with me—
That ever with a frolic welcome took
The thunder and the sunshine, and opposed
Free hearts, free foreheads—you and I are old;
Old age hath yet his honor and his toil;   50
Death closes all. But something ere the end,
Some work of noble note, may yet be done,
Not unbecoming men that strove with Gods.
The lights begin to twinkle from the rocks;
The long day wanes; the slow moon climbs; the deep
Moans round with many voices. Come, my friends.
'Tis not too late to seek a newer world.
Push off, and sitting well in order smite
The sounding furrows; for my purpose holds
To sail beyond the sunset, and the baths   60
Of all the western stars, until I die.
It may be that the gulfs will wash us down;
It may be we shall touch the Happy Isles,
And see the great Achilles, whom we knew.
Though much is taken, much abides; and though
We are not now that strength which in old days
Moved earth and heaven, that which we are, we are—
One equal temper of heroic hearts,
Made weak by time and fate, but strong in will
To strive, to seek, to find, and not to yield.   70

■   1. Identify Ulysses and Achilles.
    2. Do any of the sentiments expressed in the poem seem pecu-
liarly Victorian?
    3. State the theme of the poem.
    4. Scan the first fifteen lines. Is the metrical pattern suitable to a
dramatic monologue? Justify your answer.
    5. Indicate the use of assonance and alliteration in the poem, and
discuss their effect on the tone.
    6. Are there similarities in subject and manner between this and
Browning's "Rabbi Ben Ezra" (p. 505)?

Break, Break, Break

Break, break, break,
  On thy cold gray stones, O Sea!
And I would that my tongue could utter
  The thoughts that arise in me.

O well for the fisherman's boy,
  That he shouts with his sister at play!
O well for the sailor lad,
  That he sings in his boat on the bay!

And the stately ships go on
  To their haven under the hill;
But O for the touch of a vanished hand,
  And the sound of a voice that is still!

Break, break, break,
  At the foot of thy crags, O Sea!
But the tender grace of a day that is dead
  Will never come back to me.

1. What is the relationship between theme and imagery in this poem?

2. Why does the poet use "and" in line 3 and "but" in line 15?

Tears, Idle Tears

Tears, idle tears, I know not what they mean,
Tears from the depth of some divine despair
Rise in the heart, and gather to the eyes,
In looking on the happy autumn-fields,
And thinking of the days that are no more.

Fresh as the first beam glittering on a sail,
That brings our friends up from the underworld,
Sad as the last which reddens over one
That sinks with all we love below the verge;
So sad, so fresh, the days that are no more.

Ah, sad and strange as in dark summer dawns
The earliest pipe of half-awakened birds
To dying ears, when unto dying eyes
The casement slowly grows a glimmering square;
So sad, so strange, the days that are no more.

Dear as remembered kisses after death,
And sweet as those by hopeless fancy feigned
On lips that are for others; deep as love,
Deep as first love, and wild with all regret;
O Death in Life, the days that are no more!

1. Comment on the word "idle."
2. In what sense are past days "fresh"?
3. Why are the pipings of the birds "strange"?
4. Are the images of the ship and of the casement related?
5. Compare this poem with "Break, Break, Break" and with Keats's "To Autumn" (p. 453).

Now Sleeps the Crimson Petal

Now sleeps the crimson petal, now the white;
Nor waves the cypress in the palace walk;
Nor winks the gold fin in the porphyry font:
The fire-fly wakens; waken thou with me.

Now droops the milk-white peacock like a ghost,
And like a ghost she glimmers on to me.

Now lies the Earth all Danaë[1] to the stars,
And all thy heart lies open unto me.

Now slides the silent meteor on, and leaves
A shining furrow, as thy thoughts in me.

Now folds the lily all her sweetness up,
And slips into the bosom of the lake.
So fold thyself, my dearest, thou, and slip
Into my bosom and be lost in me.

....

1. The Greek princess who was visited by Zeus as a shower of gold, even though she had been locked up in a tower by her father.

In Memoriam A. H. H.[1]

Strong Son of God, immortal Love,
        Whom we, that have not seen thy face,

....

1. Arthur Henry Hallam died in Vienna, in September, 1833. The "elegies," as they were called, which made up In Memoriam, were composed at various times during the seventeen years which intervened between Hallam's death and their publication in 1850.

By faith, and faith alone, embrace,
Believing where we cannot prove;

Thine are these orbs of light and shade;
Thou madest Life in man and brute;
Thou madest Death; and lo, thy foot
Is on the skull which thou hast made.

Thou wilt not leave us in the dust;
Thou madest man, he knows not why,
He thinks he was not made to die;
And thou hast made him: thou art just.

10

Thou seemest human and divine,
The highest, holiest manhood, thou:
Our wills are ours, we know not how;
Our wills are ours, to make them thine.

Our little systems have their day,
They have their day and cease to be;
They are but broken lights of thee,
And thou, O Lord, art more than they.

20

We have but faith: we cannot know;
For knowledge is of things we see;
And yet we trust it comes from thee,
A beam in darkness: let it grow.

Let knowledge grow from more to more,
But more of reverence in us dwell;
That mind and soul, according well,
May make one music as before,

But vaster. We are fools and slight;
We mock thee when we do not fear:
But help thy foolish ones to bear;
Help thy vain worlds to bear thy light.

30

Forgive what seemed my sin in me;
What seemed my worth since I began;
For merit lives from man to man,
And not from man, O Lord, to thee.

Forgive my grief for one removed,
Thy creature, whom I found so fair.

I trust he lives in thee, and there
I find him worthier to be loved.   40

Forgive these wild and wandering cries,
    Confusions of a wasted youth;
        Forgive them where they fail in truth,
And in thy wisdom make me wise.

■ Write a paraphrase of these lines.

11

Calm is the morn without a sound,
    Calm as to suit a calmer grief,
    And only through the faded leaf
The chestnut pattering to the ground;

Calm and deep peace on this high wold,
    And on these dews that drench the furze,
    And all the silvery gossamers
That twinkle into green and gold;

Calm and still light on yon great plain
    That sweeps with all its autumn bowers,
    And crowded farms and lessening towers,
To mingle with the bounding main;

Calm and deep peace in this wide air,
    These leaves that redden to the fall—
    And in my heart, if calm at all,
If any calm, a calm despair;

Calm on the seas, and silver sleep,
    And waves that sway themselves in rest,
    And dead calm in that noble breast
Which heaves but with the heaving deep.

15

Tonight the winds begin to rise
    And roar from yonder dropping day;
    The last red leaf is whirled away,
The rooks are blown about the skies;

The forest cracked, the waters curled,
   The cattle huddled on the lea;
   And wildly dashed on tower and tree
The sunbeam strikes along the world.

And but for fancies, which aver
   That all thy motions gently pass
   Athwart a plane of molten glass,
I scarce could brook the strain and stir

That makes the barren branches loud;
   And but for fear it is not so,
   The wild unrest that lives in woe
Would dote and pore on yonder cloud

That rises upward always higher,
   And onward drags a laboring breast,
   And topples round the dreary west,
A looming bastion fringed with fire.

■   Which of these sections, 11 or 15, seems more successful as a poem?
Justify your answer carefully.

50

Be near me when my light is low,
   When the blood creeps, and the nerves prick
   And tingle; and the heart is sick,
And all the wheels of Being slow.

Be near me when the sensuous frame
   Is rack'd with pangs that conquer trust;
   And Time, a maniac scattering dust,
And Life, a Fury slinging flame.

Be near me when my faith is dry,
   And men the flies of latter spring,
   That lay their eggs, and sting and sing
And weave their petty cells and die.

Be near me when I fade away,
   To point the term of human strife,
   And on the low dark verge of life
The twilight of eternal day.

54

Oh yet we trust that somehow good
  Will be the final goal of ill,
  To pangs of nature, sins of will,
Defects of doubt, and taints of blood;

That nothing walks with aimless feet;
  That not one life shall be destroy'd,
  Or cast as rubbish to the void,
When God hath made the pile complete;

That not a worm is cloven in vain;
  That not a moth with vain desire
  Is shrivell'd in a fruitless fire,
Or but subserves another's gain.

Behold, we know not anything;
  I can but trust that good shall fall
  At last—far off—at last, to all,
And every winter change to spring.

So runs my dream: but what am I?
  An infant crying in the night:
  An infant crying for the light:
And with no language but a cry.

55

The wish, that of the living whole
  No life may fail beyond the grave,
  Derives it not from what we have
The likest God within the soul?

Are God and Nature then at strife,
  That Nature lends such evil dreams?
  So careful of the type she seems,
So careless of the single life,

That I, considering everywhere
  Her secret meaning in her deeds,
  And finding that of fifty seeds
She often brings but one to bear,

I falter where I firmly trod,
 And falling with my weight of cares
 Upon the great world's altar-stairs
That slope through darkness up to God,

I stretch lame hands of faith, and grope,
 And gather dust and chaff, and call
 To what I feel is Lord of all,
And faintly trust the larger hope.

118

Contemplate all this work of Time,
 The giant laboring in his youth;
 Nor dream of human love and truth,
As dying Nature's earth and lime;

But trust that those we call the dead
 Are breathers of an ampler day
 For ever nobler ends. They say,
The solid earth whereon we tread

In tracts of fluent heat began,
 And grew to seeming-random forms,
 The seeming prey of cyclic storms,
Till at the last arose the man;

Who throve and branched from clime to clime,
 The herald of a higher race,
 And of himself in higher place,
If so he type this work of time

Within himself, from more to more;
 Or, crowned with attributes of woe
 Like glories, move his course, and show
That life is not an idle ore,

But iron dug from central gloom,
 And heated hot with burning fears,
 And dipped in baths of hissing tears,
And battered with the shocks of doom

To shape and use. Arise and fly
 The reeling Faun, the sensual feast;

Move upward, working out the beast,
And let the ape and tiger die.

■ 1. Why was the subject treated in this section especially close to the Victorian mind?

2. Is the rhyme scheme appropriate to the attitude expressed; that is, does it allow the poet to evoke the sense of rigor and struggle he is commenting about?

3. Does the "reeling Faun" suggest the satyr of Greek legend? What, then, is the meaning of the final stanza, and do the preceding stanzas about the evolutionary developments justify the admonition to sobriety and hard work? It is conceivable another poet might have concluded differently, saying, for example, that man is *in* nature, a sensuous part of it, and therefore he should not try to lift himself above it. Does this possibility suggest that Tennyson's imagery and argument are not well considered?

130

Thy voice is on the rolling air;
    I hear thee where the waters run;
    Thou standest in the rising sun,
And in the setting thou art fair.

What art thou then? I cannot guess;
    But though I seem in star and flower
    To feel thee some diffusive power,
I do not therefore love thee less.

My love involves the love before;
    My love is vaster passion now;
    Though mixed with God and Nature thou,
I seem to love thee more and more.

Far off thou art, but ever nigh;
    I have thee still, and I rejoice;
    I prosper, circled with thy voice;
I shall not lose thee though I die.

From *Maud, A Monodrama*

O That 'Twere Possible

O that 'twere possible
After long grief and pain
To find the arms of my true love
Round me once again!

When I was wont to meet her
In the silent woody places
By the home that gave me birth,
We stood tranced in long embraces
Mixed with kisses sweeter, sweeter
Than anything on earth.   10

A shadow flits before me,
Not thou, but like to thee.
Ah, Christ, that it were possible
For one short hour to see
The souls we loved, that they might tell us
What and where they be!

It leads me forth at evening,
It lightly winds and steals
In a cold white robe before me,
When all my spirit reels   20
At the shouts, the leagues of lights,
And the roaring of the wheels.

Half the night I waste in sighs,
Half in dreams I sorrow after
The delight of early skies;
In a wakeful doze I sorrow
For the hand, the lips, the eyes,
For the meeting of the morrow,
The delight of happy laughter,
The delight of low replies.   30

'Tis a morning pure and sweet,
And a dewy splendor falls
On the little flower that clings
To the turrets and the walls;
'Tis a morning pure and sweet,
And the light and shadow fleet.

She is walking in the meadow,
And the woodland echo rings;
In a moment we shall meet.
She is singing in the meadow,   40
And the rivulet at her feet
Ripples on in light and shadow
To the ballad that she sings.

Do I hear her sing as of old,
My bird with the shining head,
My own dove with the tender eye?
But there rings on a sudden a passionate cry,
There is someone dying or dead,
And a sullen thunder is rolled;
For a tumult shakes the city,   50
And I wake, my dream is fled.
In the shuddering dawn, behold,
Without knowledge, without pity,
By the curtains of my bed
That abiding phantom cold!

Get thee hence, nor come again,
Mix not memory with doubt,
Pass, thou deathlike type of pain,
Pass and cease to move about!
'Tis the blot upon the brain   60
That *will* show itself without.

Then I rise, the eave-drops fall,
And the yellow vapors choke
The great city sounding wide;
The day comes, a dull red ball
Wrapped in drifts of lurid smoke
On the misty river-tide.

Through the hubbub of the market
I steal, a wasted frame;
It crosses here, it crosses there,   70
Through all that crowd confused and loud,
The shadow still the same;
And on my heavy eyelids
My anguish hangs like shame.

Alas for her that met me,
That heard me softly call,

Came glimmering through the laurels
At the quiet evenfall,
In the garden by the turrets
Of the old manorial hall!

80

Would the happy spirit descend
From the realms of light and song,
In the chamber of the street,
As she looks among the blest,
Should I fear to greet my friend
Or to say, "Forgive the wrong,"
Or to ask her, "Take me, sweet,
To the regions of thy rest"?

But the broad light glares and beats,
And the shadow flits and fleets
And will not let me be;
And I loathe the squares and streets,
And the faces that one meets,
Hearts with no love for me.
Always I long to creep
Into some still cavern deep,
There to weep, and weep, and weep
My whole soul out to thee.

90

■ Too frequently perhaps, Victorian poetry treats a kind of vague melancholy, a grief or sorrow that seems diffuse and amorphous because the reader is at a loss to discover the origins of it. Point out how Tennyson has avoided, to a considerable extent, such defects in this poem.

Tithonus

The woods decay, the woods decay and fall,
The vapors weep their burthen to the ground,
Man comes and tills the field and lies beneath,
And after many a summer dies the swan.
Me only cruel immortality
Consumes; I wither slowly in thine arms,
Here at the quiet limit of the world,
A white-haired shadow roaming like a dream
The ever-silent spaces of the East,
Far-folded mists, and gleaming halls of morn.
    Alas! for this gray shadow, once a man—
So glorious in his beauty and thy choice,

10

Who madest him thy chosen, that he seemed
To his great heart none other than a God!
I asked thee, "Give me immortality."
Then didst thou grant mine asking with a smile,
Like wealthy men who care not how they give.
But thy strong Hours indignant worked their wills,
And beat me down and marred and wasted me,
And though they could not end me, left me maimed   20
To dwell in presence of immortal youth,
Immortal age beside immortal youth,
And all I was, in ashes. Can thy love,
Thy beauty, make amends, though even now,
Close over us, the silver star, thy guide,
Shines in those tremulous eyes that fill with tears
To hear me? Let me go; take back thy gift.
Why should a man desire in any way
To vary from the kindly race of men,
Or pass beyond the goal of ordinance   30
Where all should pause, as is most meet for all?

    A soft air fans the cloud apart; there comes
A glimpse of that dark world where I was born.
Once more the old mysterious glimmer steals
From thy pure brows, and from thy shoulders pure,
And bosom beating with a heart renewed.
Thy cheek begins to redden through the gloom,
Thy sweet eyes brighten slowly close to mine,
Ere yet they blind the stars, and the wild team
Which love thee, yearning for thy yoke, arise,   40
And shake the darkness from their loosened manes,
And beat the twilight into flakes of fire.

    Lo! ever thus thou growest beautiful
In silence, then before thine answer given
Departest, and thy tears are on my cheek.

    Why wilt thou ever scare me with thy tears,
And make me tremble lest a saying learnt,
In days far-off, on that dark earth, be true?
"The Gods themselves cannot recall their gifts."

    Ay me! ay me! with what another heart   50
In days far-off, and with what other eyes
I used to watch—if I be he that watched—
The lucid outline forming round thee; saw
The dim curls kindle into sunny rings;
Changed with thy mystic change, and felt my blood
Glow with the glow that slowly crimsoned all
Thy presence and thy portals, while I lay,

Mouth, forehead, eyelids, growing dewy-warm
With kisses balmier than half-opening buds
Of April, and could hear the lips that kissed   60
Whispering I knew not what of wild and sweet,
Like that strange song I heard Apollo sing,
While Ilion like a mist rose into towers.

    Yet hold me not forever in thine East;
How can my nature longer mix with thine?
Coldly thy rosy shadows bathe me, cold
Are all thy lights, and cold my wrinkled feet
Upon thy glimmering thresholds, when the steam
Floats up from those dim fields about the homes
Of happy men that have the power to die,   70
And grassy barrows of the happier dead.
Release me, and restore me to the ground.
Thou seest all things, thou wilt see my grave;
Thou wilt renew thy beauty morn by morn;
I earth in earth forget these empty courts,
And thee returning on thy silver wheels.

■ 1. Tithonus, a figure in Greek legend, was granted the gift of immortality on earth but not eternal youth. After he had grown aged and feeble he asked to die, but Aurora, who had granted him immortal life, could not release him. She did, however, turn Tithonus into a grasshopper. How much of this legend is evident in Tennyson's poem?
    2. Explain the use of color (gray and red) imagery.
    3. What is the theme Tennyson develops?
    4. Is the image of the swan (line 4) unexpected? Is it effective?
    5. Point out instances of spondees in the metrical pattern. Why were they introduced into the regular iambic movement? Point out any other metrical variations. Are they appropriate or not?
    6. Point out instances of alliteration and assonance and discuss their relation to the tone of the poem.

Milton
(Alcaics)[1]

O mighty-mouthed inventor of harmonies,
O skilled to sing of Time or Eternity
   God-gifted organ-voice of England,
      Milton, a name to resound for ages:

1. In classical verse an alcaic is a four-strophe poem, with four lines to the strophe and four stresses to the line.

Whose Titan angels, Gabriel, Abdiel,
Starred from Jehovah's gorgeous armories,
Tower, as the deep-domed empyrean
    Rings to the roar of an angel onset!

Me rather all that bowery loneliness,
The brooks of Eden mazily murmuring,
And bloom profuse and cedar arches
    Charm, as a wanderer out in ocean,

Where some refulgent sunset of India
Streams o'er a rich ambrosial ocean isle,
And crimson-hued the stately palm-woods
    Whisper in odorous heights of even.

To Virgil

Roman Virgil, thou that singest Ilion's lofty temples robed in fire,
Ilion falling, Rome arising, wars, and filial faith, and Dido's pyre;

Landscape-lover, lord of language more than he that sang the "Works
    and Days,"
All the chosen coin of fancy flashing out from many a golden phrase;

Thou that singest wheat and woodland, tilth and vineyard, hive and
    horse and herd;
All the charm of all the Muses often flowering in a lonely word;

Poet of the happy Tityrus piping underneath his beechen bowers;
Poet of the poet-satyr whom the laughing shepherd bound with flowers;

Chanter of the Pollio, glorying in the blissful years again to be,
Summers of the snakeless meadow, unlaborious earth and oarless sea;

Thou that seest Universal Nature moved by Universal Mind;
Thou majestic in thy sadness at the doubtful doom of human kind;

Light among the vanished ages; star that gildest yet this phantom shore;
Golden branch amid the shadows, kings and realms that pass to rise no
    more;

Now thy Forum roars no longer, fallen every purple Caesar's dome—
Though thine ocean-roll of rhythm sound forever of Imperial Rome—

Now the Rome of slaves hath perished, and the Rome of freemen holds
       her place,
I, from out the Northern Island sundered once from all the human race

I salute thee, Mantovano, I that loved thee since my day began,
Wielder of the stateliest measure ever molded by the lips of man.

Robert Browning

(1812–1889)

■ ■ ■ ■ ■ ■ ■ ■ ■ ■

            B<small>ROWNING WAS</small> the son of well-to-do parents. His father
shared the son's interest in ancient tales of intrigue and crime, and his
mother instructed him in the austerities of Evangelical worship. Browning
began to write very early, with "Ossian" and Byron, and later Shelley, as
his first masters. His poem *Paracelsus* (1835) brought him some reputation
and recognition among poets but no public. The general public was made
aware of *Sordello* (1840) because it was singled out as an example of
deliberate obscurity. The story of Browning's romance and marriage with
Elizabeth Barrett, the semi-invalid poetess, is well known. Much of his pro-
lific body of poetry was written in Italy before her death in 1861. *Bells and
Pomegranates* (1841–1846), *Men and Women* (1855), *Dramatis Personae*
(1864), *The Ring and the Book* (1868–1869), *Dramatic Idyls* (1879),
and his last volume, *Assolando: Fancies and Facts* (1889) contain most
of the work by which his reputation continues. As a widower Browning
returned to England to educate his son. By this time he had become a
popular poet. Browning clubs were common both in England and America.
His last two years were spent in Italy. To the end of his life he wrote
with vigor and enthusiasm.

Suggested Readings

G<small>EORGE</small> S<small>ANTAYANA</small>, "The Poetry of Barbarism," in *Interpretations of Poetry
    and Religion*. New York: Charles Scribner's Sons, 1900.
P<small>AUL</small> E<small>LMER</small> M<small>ORE</small>, "Why is Browning Popular?" in *Shelburne Essays*,
    Third Series. New York: G. P. Putnam's Sons, 1905.
H<small>UGH</small> W<small>ALKER</small>, "Browning," in *The Literature of the Victorian Era*. Cam-
    bridge: Cambridge University Press, 1921.

■ ■ ■ ■ ■ ■ ■ ■ ■ ■

The Lost Leader [1]

Just for a handful of silver he left us,
　　Just for a riband to stick in his coat—
Found the one gift of which fortune bereft us,
　　Lost all the others she lets us devote;
They, with the gold to give, doled him out silver,
　　So much was theirs who so little allowed:
How all our copper had gone for his service!
　　Rags—were they purple, his heart had been proud!
We that had loved him so, followed him, honored him,
　　Lived in his mild and magnificent eye,　　　　　　　　　10
Learned his great language, caught his clear accents,
　　Made him our pattern to live and to die!
Shakespeare was of us, Milton was for us,
　　Burns, Shelley, were with us,—they watch from their graves!
He alone breaks from the van and the freemen,
　　He alone sinks to the rear and the slaves!

We shall march prospering,—not thro' his presence;
　　Songs may inspirit us,—not from his lyre;
Deeds will be done,—while he boasts his quiescence,
　　Still bidding crouch whom the rest bade aspire:　　　　20
Blot out his name, then, record one lost soul more,
　　One task more declined, one more footpath untrod,
One more triumph for devils and sorrow for angels,
　　One wrong more to man, one more insult to God!
Life's night begins: let him never come back to us!
　　There would be doubt, hesitation and pain,
Forced praise on our part—the glimmer of twilight,
　　Never glad confident morning again!
Best fight on well, for we taught him,—strike gallantly,
　　Menace our heart ere we master his own;　　　　　　　30
Then let him receive the new knowledge and wait us,
　　Pardoned in Heaven, the first by the throne!

■　Discuss the appropriateness of the metrical pattern of this poem.

1.　William Wordsworth is the lost leader. Browning is bewailing his defection
from the liberal cause.

Life in a Love

Escape me?
Never—
Beloved!

While I am I, and you are you,
  So long as the world contains us both,
  Me the loving and you the loth,
While the one eludes, must the other pursue.
My life is a fault at last, I fear:
  It seems too much like a fate, indeed
  Though I do my best I shall scarce succeed.
But what if I fail of my purpose here?
It is but to keep the nerves at strain,
  To dry one's eyes and laugh at a fall,
And baffled, get up and begin again,—
  So the chase takes up one's life, that's all.
While, look but once from your farthest bound
  At me so deep in the dust and dark,
No sooner the old hope drops to ground
  Than a new one, straight to the self-same mark,
          I shape me—
          Ever
          Removed!

■ Does this poem have one theme consistently developed?

Meeting at Night

The grey sea and the long black land;
And the yellow half-moon large and low;
And the startled little waves that leap
In fiery ringlets from their sleep,
As I gain the cove with pushing prow,
And quench its speed i' the slushy sand.

Then a mile of warm sea-scented beach;
Three fields to cross till a farm appears;
A tap at the pane, the quick sharp scratch
And blue spurt of a lighted match,
And a voice less loud, through its joys and fears,
Than the two hearts beating each to each!

■ Give a detailed account of the appropriateness of the imagery and
symbolism of this poem.

Home-Thoughts, from Abroad

Oh, to be in England
Now that April's there,
And whoever wakes in England
Sees, some morning, unaware,
That the lowest boughs and the brushwood sheaf
Round the elm-tree bole are in tiny leaf,
While the chaffinch sings on the orchard bough
In England—now!

And after April, when May follows,
And the whitethroat builds, and all the swallows!
Hark, where my blossomed pear-tree in the hedge
Leans to the field and scatters on the clover
Blossoms and dewdrops—at the bent spray's edge—
That's the wise thrush; he sings each song twice over,
Lest you should think he never could recapture
The first fine careless rapture!
And though the fields look rough with hoary dew,
All will be gay when noontide wakes anew
The buttercups, the little children's dower
—Far brighter than this gaudy melon-flower!

1. There is an interesting pattern of vowel sounds in this poem. Explain their function.

2. Compare the poem's manner and tone, considering the appropriateness of each, with the manner and tone of "The Lost Leader" (p. 500).

My Last Duchess
Ferrara

That's my last Duchess painted on the wall,
Looking as if she were alive. I call
That piece a wonder, now; Frà Pandolf's hands
Worked busily a day, and there she stands.
Will 't please you sit and look at her? I said
"Frà Pandolf" by design, for never read
Strangers like you that pictured countenance,
The depth and passion of its earnest glance,
But to myself they turned (since none puts by
The curtain I have drawn for you, but I)
And seemed as they would ask me, if they durst,

10

How such a glance came there; so, not the first
Are you to turn and ask thus. Sir, 'twas not
Her husband's presence only, called that spot
Of joy into the Duchess' cheek; perhaps
Frà Pandolf chanced to say, "Her mantle laps
Over my lady's wrist too much," or "Paint
Must never hope to reproduce the faint
Half-flush that dies along her throat." Such stuff
Was courtesy, she thought, and cause enough   20
For calling up that spot of joy. She had
A heart—how shall I say?—too soon made glad,
Too easily impressed; she liked whate'er
She looked on, and her looks went everywhere.
Sir, 'twas all one! My favor at her breast,
The dropping of the daylight in the West,
The bough of cherries some officious fool
Broke in the orchard for her, the white mule
She rode with round the terrace—all and each
Would draw from her alike the approving speech,   30
Or blush, at least. She thanked men,—good! but thanked
Somehow—I know not how—as if she ranked
My gift of a nine-hundred-years-old name
With anybody's gift. Who'd stoop to blame
This sort of trifling? Even had you skill
In speech—(which I have not)—to make your will
Quite clear to such an one, and say, "Just this
Or that in you disgusts me; here you miss,
Or there exceed the mark"—and if she let
Herself be lessoned so, nor plainly set   40
Her wits to yours, forsooth, and made excuse,
—E'en then would be some stooping; and I choose
Never to stoop. Oh sir, she smiled, no doubt,
Whene'er I passed her; but who passed without
Much the same smile? This grew; I gave commands;
Then all smiles stopped together. There she stands
As if alive. Will't please you rise? We'll meet
The company below, then. I repeat,
The Count your master's known munificence
Is ample warrant that no just pretense   50
Of mine for dowry will be disallowed;
Though his fair daughter's self, as I avowed
At starting, is my object. Nay, we'll go
Together down, sir. Notice Neptune, though,
Taming a sea-horse, thought a rarity,
Which Claus of Innsbruck cast in bronze for me!

■   Explain in detail how the poem depends on the ironic contrast between the Duke's statements and the interpretation his listener (or you as reader) puts on them. Is it a complex irony?

The Laboratory

Ancient Régime

Now that I, tying thy glass mask tightly,
May gaze through these faint smokes curling whitely,
As thou pliest thy trade in this devil's-smithy—
Which is the poison to poison her, prithee?

He is with her, and they know that I know
Where they are, what they do; they believe my tears flow
While they laugh, laugh at me, at me fled to the drear
Empty church, to pray God in, for them!—I am here.

Grind away, moisten and mash up thy paste,
Pound at thy powder—I am not in haste!   10
Better sit thus, and observe thy strange things,
Than go where men wait me and dance at the King's.

That in the mortar—you call it a gum?
Ah, the brave tree whence such gold oozings come!
And yonder soft phial, the exquisite blue,
Sure to taste sweetly—is that poison too?

Had I but all of them, thee and thy treasures,
What a wild crowd of invisible pleasures!
To carry pure death in an earring, a casket,
A signet, a fan-mount, a filigree basket!   20

Soon, at the King's, a mere lozenge to give,
And Pauline should have just thirty minutes to live!
But to light a pastile, and Elise, with her head
And her breast and her arms and her hands, should drop dead!

Quick—is it finished? The color's too grim!
Why not soft like the phial's, enticing and dim?
Let it brighten her drink, let her turn it and stir,
And try it and taste, ere she fix and prefer!

What a drop! She's not little, no minion like me!
That's why she ensnared him; this never will free   30

The soul from those masculine eyes—say "no!"
To that pulse's magnificent come-and-go.

For only last night, as they whispered, I brought
My own eyes to bear on her so, that I thought
Could I keep them one half minute fixed, she would fall
Shriveled; she fell not; yet this does it all!

Not that I bid you spare her the pain;
Let death be felt and the proof remain;
Brand, burn up, bite into its grace—
He is sure to remember her dying face!   40

Is it done? Take my mask off! Nay, be not morose;
It kills her, and this prevents seeing it close:
The delicate droplet, my whole fortune's fee!
If it hurts her, beside, can it ever hurt me?

Now, take all my jewels, gorge gold to your fill,
You may kiss me, old man, on my mouth if you will!
But brush this dust off me, lest horror it brings
Ere I know it—next moment I dance at the King's!

■   Is the irony of this poem more or less subtle than that of "My Last Duchess"?

Rabbi Ben Ezra

Grow old along with me!
The best is yet to be,
The last of life, for which the first was made.
Our times are in His hand
Who saith, "A whole I planned,
Youth shows but half; trust God; see all, nor be afraid!"

Not that, amassing flowers,
Youth sighed, "Which rose make ours,
Which lily leave and then as best recall?"
Not that, admiring stars,   10
It yearned, "Nor Jove, nor Mars;
Mine be some figured flame which blends, transcends them all!"

Not for such hopes and fears
Annulling youth's brief years,

Do I remonstrate—folly wide the mark!
Rather I prize the doubt
Low kinds exist without,
Finished and finite clods, untroubled by a spark.

Poor vaunt of life indeed,
Were man but formed to feed   20
On joy, to solely seek and find and feast.
Such feasting ended, then
As sure an end to men;
Irks care the crop-full bird? Frets doubt the maw-crammed beast?

Rejoice we are allied
To That which doth provide
And not partake, effect and not receive!
A spark disturbs our clod;
Nearer we hold of God
Who gives, than of His tribes that take, I must believe.   30

Then, welcome each rebuff
That turns earth's smoothness rough,
Each sting that bids nor sit nor stand but go!
Be our joys three-parts pain!
Strive, and hold cheap the strain;
Learn, nor account the pang; dare, never grudge the throe!

For thence—a paradox
Which comforts while it mocks—
Shall life succeed in that it seems to fail:
What I aspired to be,   40
And was not, comforts me;
A brute I might have been, but would not sink i' the scale.

What is he but a brute
Whose flesh has soul to suit,
Whose spirit works lest arms and legs want play?
To man, propose this test—
Thy body at its best,
How far can that project thy soul on its lone way?

Yet gifts should prove their use.
I own the Past profuse   50
Of power each side, perfection every turn;
Eyes, ears took in their dole,

Brain treasured up the whole;
Should not the heart beat once, "How good to live and learn"?

Not once beat, "Praise be thine!
I see the whole design,
I, who saw power, see now Love perfect too;
Perfect I call thy plan.
Thanks that I was a man!
Maker, remake, complete—I trust what thou shalt do!"   60

For pleasant is this flesh;
Our soul, in its rose-mesh
Pulled ever to the earth, still yearns for rest.
Would we some prize might hold
To match those manifold
Possessions of the brute—gain most, as we did best!

Let us not always say,
"Spite of this flesh today
I strove, made head, gained ground upon the whole!"
As the bird wings and sings,
Let us cry, "All good things   70
Are ours, nor soul helps flesh more, now, than flesh helps soul!"

Therefore I summon age
To grant youth's heritage,
Life's struggle having so far reached its term.
Thence shall I pass, approved
A man, for aye removed
From the developed brute—a god, though in the germ.

And I shall thereupon
Take rest, ere I be gone   80
Once more on my adventure brave and new;
Fearless and unperplexed,
When I wage battle next,
What weapons to select, what armor to indue.

Youth ended, I shall try
My gain or loss thereby;
Leave the fire ashes, what survives is gold.
And I shall weigh the same,
Give life its praise or blame.
Young, all lay in dispute; I shall know, being old.   90

For note, when evening shuts,
A certain moment cuts
The deed off, calls the glory from the gray;
A whisper from the west
Shoots—"Add this to the rest,
Take it and try its worth; here dies another day."

So, still within this life,
Though lifted o'er its strife,
Let me discern, compare, pronounce at last,
"This rage was right i' the main,   100
That acquiescence vain;
The Future I may face now I have proved the Past."

For more is not reserved
To man, with soul just nerved
To act tomorrow what he learns today;
Here, work enough to watch
The Master work, and catch
Hints of the proper craft, tricks of the tool's true play.

As it was better, youth
Should strive, through acts uncouth,   110
Toward making, than repose on aught found made;
So, better, age, exempt
From strife, should know, than tempt
Further. Thou waitedst age; wait death nor be afraid!

Enough now, if the Right
And Good and Infinite
Be named here, as thou callest thy hand thine own,
With knowledge absolute,
Subject to no dispute
From fools that crowded youth, nor let thee feel alone.   120

Be there, for once and all,
Severed great minds from small,
Announced to each his station in the Past!
Was I, the world arraigned,
Were they, my soul disdained,
Right? Let age speak the truth and give us peace at last!

Now, who shall arbitrate?
Ten men love what I hate,
Shun what I follow, slight what I receive;

Ten, who in ears and eyes   130
Match me: we all surmise,
They this thing, and I that: whom shall my soul believe?

Not on the vulgar mass
Called "work," must sentence pass,
Things done, that took the eye and had the price;
O'er which, from level stand,
The low world laid its hand,
Found straightway to its mind, could value in a trice:

But all the world's coarse thumb
And finger failed to plumb,   140
So passed in making up the main account;
All instincts immature,
All purposes unsure,
That weighed not as his work, yet swelled the man's amount:

Thoughts hardly to be packed
Into a narrow act,
Fancies that broke through language and escaped;
All I could never be,
All, men ignored in me,
This, I was worth to God, whose wheel the pitcher shaped.   150

Ay, note that Potter's wheel,
That metaphor! and feel
Why time spins fast, why passive lies our clay,—
Thou, to whom fools propound,
When the wine makes its round,
"Since life fleets, all is change; the Past gone, seize to-day!"

Fool! All that is, at all,
Lasts ever, past recall;
Earth changes, but thy soul and God stand sure:
What entered into thee,   160
That was, is, and shall be:
Time's wheel runs back or stops: Potter and clay endure.

He fixed thee 'mid this dance
Of plastic circumstance,
This Present, thou, forsooth, wouldst fain arrest:
Machinery just meant
To give thy soul its bent,
Try thee and turn thee forth, sufficiently impressed.

What though the earlier grooves,
Which ran the laughing loves   170
Around thy base, no longer pause and press?
What though, about thy rim,
Skull-things in order grim
Grow out, in graver mood, obey the sterner stress?

Look not thou down but up!
To uses of a cup,
The festal board, lamp's flash and trumpet's peal,
The new wine's foaming flow,
The Master's lips aglow!
Thou, heaven's consummate cup, what needst thou with Earth's
                    wheel?   180

But I need, now as then,
Thee, God, who mouldest men,
And since, not even while the whirl was worst,
Did I—to the wheel of life
With shapes and colors rife,
Bound dizzily—mistake my end, to slake thy thirst:

So, take and use thy work,
Amend what flaws may lurk,
What strain o' the stuff, what warpings past the aim!
My times be in thy hand!   190
Perfect the cup as planned!
Let age approve of youth, and death complete the same!

■   One of the admirers of Browning admits that at his worst he suffers
certain defects: "from literariness, and excessive facility," from "an entire
lack of the 'magical' quality and of that penetrative force, that 'X–
radiance,' which only a concentrated aptness of stylistic beauty can
give. . . ." To what extent—mention specific lines and specific words
—is Browning guilty of these defects in "Rabbi Ben Ezra"? Is he
guilty of these same defects in the poem printed below?

A Toccata of Galuppi's

O Galuppi, Baldassare, this is very sad to find!
I can hardly misconceive you; it would prove me deaf and blind;
But although I take your meaning, 'tis with such a heavy mind!

Here you come with your old music, and here's all the good it brings.
What, they lived once thus at Venice where the merchants were the
       kings,
Where St. Mark's is, where the Doges used to wed the sea with rings?

Aye, because the sea's the street there; and 'tis arched by—what you
       call—
Shylock's bridge with houses on it, where they kept the carnival.
I was never out of England—it's as if I saw it all.

Did young people take their pleasure when the sea was warm in
       May?   10
Balls and masks begun at midnight, burning ever to midday,
When they made up fresh adventures for the morrow, do you say?

Was a lady such a lady, cheeks so round and lips so red—
On her neck the small face buoyant, like a bell-flower on its bed,
O'er the breast's superb abundance where a man might base his head?

Well, and it was graceful of them—they'd break talk off and afford—
She, to bite her mask's black velvet—he, to finger on his sword,
While you sat and played Toccatas, stately at the clavichord?

What? Those lesser thirds so plaintive, sixths diminished, sigh on sigh,
Told them something? Those suspensions, those solutions—"Must we
       die?"   20
Those commiserating sevenths—"Life might last! we can but try!"

"Were you happy?"—"Yes."—"And are you still as happy?"—"Yes. And
       you?"—
"Then, more kisses!"—"Did I stop them, when a million seemed so
       few?"
Hark, the dominant's persistence till it must be answered to!

So, an octave struck the answer. Oh, they praised you, I dare say!
"Brave Galuppi! that was music! good alike at grave and gay!
I can always leave off talking when I hear a master play!"

Then they left you for their pleasure; till in due time, one by one,
Some with lives that came to nothing, some with deeds as well undone,
Death stepped tacitly and took them where they never see the sun.   30

But when I sit down to reason, think to take my stand nor swerve,
While I triumph o'er a secret wrung from nature's close reserve,
In you come with your cold music till I creep through every nerve.

Yes, you, like a ghostly cricket, creaking where a house was burned:
"Dust and ashes, dead and done with, Venice spent what Venice
      earned.
The soul, doubtless, is immortal—where a soul can be discerned.

"Yours for instance; you know physics, something of geology,
Mathematics are your pastime; souls shall rise in their degree;
Butterflies may dread extinction—you'll not die, it cannot be!

"As for Venice and her people, merely born to bloom and drop,   40
Here on earth they bore their fruitage, mirth and folly were the crop;
What of soul was left, I wonder, when the kissing had to stop?"

"Dust and ashes!" So you creak it, and I want the heart to scold.
Dear dead women, with such hair, too—what's become of all the gold
Used to hang and brush their bosoms? I feel chilly and grown old.

Herman Melville

(1819–1881)

■■■■■■■■■■

MELVILLE WAS BORN in New York City to parents in
comfortable circumstances, but by the time the boy was fifteen his father
had died and he had to find small jobs. Finally he went to sea, and it was
mainly out of his experiences as a seaman that he wrote his fiction and
poetry. The earliest of Melville's books, *Typee* (1846), *Oomoo* (1847), and
Mardi (1849) were popular enough to support him and his family, but
most of his later work was poorly received. "Though I wrote the Gospels
in this century," he said while at work on *Moby Dick*, "I should die in
the gutter." In our own century, however, Melville's reputation has risen
greatly, and he is commonly looked upon as a major American writer. His
poetry has not received the attention given his fiction, but there have been a
few studies of it, and it seems to be winning a place in the canon of
nineteenth-century American poetry.

Suggested Readings

F. O. MATTHIESSEN, *American Renaissance: Art and Expression in the Age
    of Emerson and Whitman.* New York: Oxford University Press, 1941,
    pp. 371–514.
ROBERT PENN WARREN, "Melville the Poet," *Kenyon Review,* VIII, 2
    (Spring, 1946), 208–223.

The Maldive Shark

About the Shark, phlegmatical one,
Pale sot of the Maldive sea,
The sleek little pilot fish, azure and slim,
How alert in attendance be.
From his saw-pit mouth, from his charnel of maw
They have nothing of harm to dread,
But liquidly glide on his ghastly flank
Or before his Gorgonian head;
Or lurk in the port of serrated teeth
In white triple tiers of glittering gates,
And there find a haven when peril's abroad,
An asylum in jaws of the Fates!
They are friends; and friendly they guide him to prey,
Yet never partake of the treat—
Eyes and brains to the dotard lethargic and dull,
Pale ravener of horrible meat.

■   This poem can be read simply as a description of the shark and the
pilot fish. Can it also be read as the life of sycophants around a tyrant?

The Portent

Hanging from the beam,
    Slowly swaying (such the law),
Gaunt the shadow on your green,
    Shenandoah!
The cut is on the crown
(Lo, John Brown),
And the stabs shall heal no more.

Hidden in the cap
    Is the anguish none can draw;
So your future veils its face,
    But the streaming beard is shown
(Weird John Brown)
The meteor of the war.

■   1. In this poem the hanged figure of John Brown symbolizes the
oncoming war. Indicate how the various details of the symbol operate.
    2. Why is the word "weird" appropriate both to John Brown
and to the context of the poem? If necessary, look at the dictionary
meanings of the word.

Shiloh

A Requiem

Skimming lightly, wheeling still,
  The swallows fly low
Over the field in clouded days,
  The forest field of Shiloh—
Over the field where April rain
Solaced the parched one stretched in pain
  Through the pause of night
That followed the Sunday flight
  Around the church of Shiloh—
The church so lone, the log-built one,
That echoed to many a parting groan
    And natural prayer
Of dying foemen mingled there—
  Foemen at morn, but friends at eve—
    Fame or country least their care:
  (What like a bullet can undeceive!)
    But now they lie low,
While over them the swallows skim,
    And all is hushed at Shiloh.

■ 1. There is a central irony controlling the theme of the poem.
What is it? Are there any incidental ironies?

2. R. P. Warren in his essay on Melville's poems says, "Nature and
history provide the chief terms of resolution in *Battle-Pieces*." "Shiloh"
is from *Battle-Pieces*. Discuss Mr. Warren's comment in relation to the
poem.

In a Bye-Canal

A swoon of noon, a trance of tide,
The hushed siesta brooding wide
  Like calms far off Peru;
No floating wayfarer in sight
Dumb noon, and haunted like the night
  When Jael the wild one slew.
A languid impulse from the car
Plied by my indolent gondolier
Tinkles against a palace hoar!
  And hark, response I hear!
A lattice clicks; and io, I see
Between the slats, mute summoning me,

10

What loveliest eyes of scintillation,
What basilisk glance of conjuration!

Fronted I have, part taken the span
Of portent in nature and peril in man.
I have swum—I have been
'Twixt the whale's black fluke and the white shark's fin;
The enemy's desert have wandered in,
And there have turned, have turned and scanned,   20
Following me how noiselessly,
Envy and Slander, lepers hand in hand.

All this. But at the latticed eye—
"Hey, Gondolier, you sleep, my man;
Wake up!" And shooting by, we ran;
The while I mused, This surely now,
Confutes the Naturalists, allow!
Sirens, true sirens verily be,
Sirens, waylayers in the sea.
Well, wooed by these same deadly misses,   30
Is it shame to run?
No! Flee them did divine Ulysses,
Brave, wise, and Venus' son.

■ 1. Two of the three sections are similar to each other in meter and tone but different from the third sections. Discuss these differences in detail.

2. Do these differences seem to be the result of inability on the part of the poet to make the poem all of a piece, or does there seem to be a reason behind the differences?

Time's Long Ago

Time's Long Ago! Nor coral isles
In the blue South Sea more serene
When the lagoons unruffled show,
There Fates and Furies change their mien.
Though strewn with wreckage to the shore,
The halcyon haunts it; all is green,
And wins the heart that hope can lure no more.

■ 1. Explain the significance of the title.
2. Identify the "Furies." Why is this reference introduced?
3. What is the meaning of "the halcyon haunts it"?

4. Comment on the alliteration and the imagery of the poem.
5. Restate the final line in your own terms.

Art

In placid hours well-pleased we dream
Of many a brave unbodied scheme.
But form to lend, pulsed life create,
What unlike things must meet and mate:
A flame to melt—a wind to freeze;
Sad patience—joyous energies;
Humility—yet pride and scorn;
Instinct and study; love and hate;
Audacity—reverence. These must mate,
And fuse with Jacob's mystic heart,
To wrestle with the angel—Art.

■ Write a brief essay in which you explain Melville's understanding of the nature of art as suggested in this poem. Refer to any of the poems you have read in this text which may serve to illustrate your points.

The Berg
A Dream

I saw a ship of martial build
(Her standards set, her brave apparel on)
Directed as by madness mere
Against a stolid iceberg steer,
Nor budge it, though the infatuate ship went down.
The impact made huge ice-cubes fall
Sullen, in tons that crashed the deck;
But that one avalanche was all—
No other movement save the foundering wreck.

Along the spurs of ridges pale,
Not any slenderest shaft and frail,
A prism over glass-green gorges lone,
Toppled; nor lace of traceries fine,
Nor pendant drops in grot or mine
Were jarred, when the stunned ship went down.

Nor sole the gulls in cloud that wheeled
Circling one snow-flanked peak afar,

10

But nearer fowl the floes that skimmed
And crystal beaches, felt no jar
No thrill transmitted stirred the lock   20
Of jack-straw needle ice at base;
Towers undermined by waves—the block
A tilt impending— kept their place.
Seals, dozing sleek on sliddery ledges
Slipt never, when by loftier edges
Through very inertia overthrown,
The impetuous ship in bafflement went down.

Hard berg (methought) so cold, so vast,
With mortal damps, self-overcast,
Exhaling still thy dankish breath—   30
Adrift dissolving, bound for death;
Though lumpish thou, a lumbering one—
A lumbering lubbard loitering slow,
Impingers rue thee and go down,
Sounding thy precipice below,
Nor stir the slimy slug that sprawls
Along thy dead indifference of walls.

■   1. Insofar as one may judge from this poem, what is Melville saying about man's relationship with the nature external to him?
    2. Is the foundering of the ship more stirring, in terms of the
theme, in its setting close to land than it would be far out at sea?

Walt Whitman
(1819–1892)

■■■■■■■■■■

WHITMAN'S WAS a highly original voice in American poetry.
He was contemporary with James Russell Lowell, but he wrote as though
he belonged to a different world from Lowell's New England. Whitman,
whose ancestry was Dutch and English, was born in Westhills, Long Island,
was sent to Brooklyn and New York schools, and trained as a carpenter and
typesetter. Later he did newspaper work in Brooklyn and New Orleans.
When *Leaves of Grass* appeared in 1855, it received favorable attention only
from Emerson. During the Civil War Whitman served as a nurse, and for

many years thereafter he worked as a clerk in the Treasury Department. Throughout his life he considered himself the poet of democracy and the common man. In the New England tradition of Lowell, poetry observed all the proprieties of manner and form; in the tradition begun by Whitman, poetry was free to experiment with the unconventional in subject matter and form.

As could be expected, Whitman has been a highly controversial figure. His has been called a "poetry of barbarism," but, on the other hand, it has been hailed as the true expression of things American, and he became the forerunner of those poets who have written of the growing and expanding America, of the West, the great cities, the melting pot.

In addition to the eleven editions of *Leaves of Grass*, Whitman published *Drum Taps* (1865), *Specimen Days and Collect*, a prose volume (1882), and *Good-bye, My Fancy* (1891).

Suggested Readings

SCULLEY BRADLEY, "The Fundamental Metrical Pattern in Whitman's Poetry," *American Literature*, X, 1938, 437–459.

F. O. MATTHIESSEN, "Whitman," in *American Renaissance*. New York: Oxford University Press, 1941, pp. 517–646.

ROBERT SPILLER, *et al.*, eds., "Walt Whitman," in *Literary History of the United States*, New York: The Macmillan Company, 1948, I, pp. 472–498.

■■■■■■■■■■

Historians of American poetry usually observe that there are two general lines in American literature, one running from Hawthorne and Melville through James and Eliot, and one running from Whitman through Robinson Jeffers, Carl Sandburg, Edgar Lee Masters, and Stephen Vincent Benét. As usual in such a generalization, one finds figures who do not fit readily on one side or the other. Hart Crane, for example, was deeply involved with both lines or traditions. Again, Whitman's breaking with strict metrical forms influenced almost all modern poets, even those not consciously indebted to him.

American poets and critics have quarreled over the value of the Whitman tradition, over such issues as whether or not his figures—his dramatis personae—are too generalized to be convincing; whether he sees America in any real complexity and multiplicity; whether his optimistic vision of American brotherhood is another form of sentimentality, an unwillingness to look closely at the manifestations of self-interest, exploitation, or greed; and, finally, whether his notions of poetic form are too relaxed.

For our purposes here we may center attention on the final point of argument, Whitman's notions of form. The following statement is Whitman's justification of "free verse":

> The want for something finished, completed, and technically beautiful will certainly not be supplied by this writer, as it is by existing esthetic works. For the best poems both the old and the later ones now accepted as first class are polished, rhymed regular, with all the elegance of fine conceits, carefully elaborated, showing under all the restraints of art, language and phrase chosen after very much has been rejected, and only the best admitted, and then all joined and cemented together, and finally presenting the beauty of some architectural temple—some palace, proudly rising in proportions of marble, entered from superb porticos and adorned with statuary satisfying the art sense and that of form, fulfilling beauty and inviting criticism. Not so his poetry. Its likeness is not the solid stately palace, nor the sculpture that adorns it, nor the paintings on its walls. Its analogy is *the Ocean*. Its verses are the liquid, billowy waves, ever rising and falling, perhaps wild with storm, always moving, always alike in their nature as rolling waves, but hardly any two exactly alike in size or measure (meter), never having the sense of something finished and fixed, always suggesting something beyond.

Whitman, one may want to observe, has not been quite fair to the poetry written inside standard metrical and stanzaic forms. The image of the palace implies a fixed, a static, even a "dead" art, whereas the concept of organic art, which Whitman is taking over for himself, included, as in Coleridge's discussions, variety and multiplicity *inside* the "fixed" forms. Similarly, one might say that the ocean's waves as an analogy of the best poetic form are not quite satisfactory, that they can suggest formlessness as much as form.

Perhaps a better generalization about "free verse" is to be found in T. S. Eliot's saying that actually there is no such thing as *free* verse, that even in the "freest" of free verse there should lurk the ghost of some simple meter, which "should advance menacingly as we doze, and withdraw as we arouse." Eliot is saying, of course, that the poet should avoid a "tom tom" beat and the mechanics of the metronome, on the one hand, but that the other extreme, the complete absence of a pattern, invites looseness, disorder, formlessness. Finally, precision of form makes for precision of statement. The appropriate rhythm, whether in the individual line or throughout the poem as a whole, is idea or insight in its appropriate form of expression.

If Eliot is correct, the question for the student of Whitman is how, and to what extent—his critical manifesto aside—he achieved sufficient rhythmical control to bring his work inside the realm of the esthetic.

Song of Myself

1

I celebrate myself, and sing myself,
And what I assume you shall assume,
For every atom belonging to me as good belongs to you.

I loafe and invite my soul,
I lean and loafe at my ease observing a spear of summer grass.

My tongue, every atom of my blood, form'd from this soil, this air,
Born here of parents born here from parents the same, and their parents
    the same,
I, now thirty-seven years old in perfect health begin,
Hoping to cease not till death.
Creeds and schools in abeyance,   10
Retiring back a while sufficed at what they are, but never forgotten,
I harbor for good or bad, I permit to speak at every hazard,
Nature without check with original energy.

8

The little one sleeps in its cradle,
I lift the gauze and look a long time, and silently brush away flies
    with my hand.

The youngster and the red-faced girl turn aside up the bushy hill,
I peeringly view them from the top.

The suicide sprawls on the bloody floor of the bedroom,
I witness the corpse with its dabbled hair, I note where the pistol
    has fallen.

The blab of the pave, tires of carts, sluff of boot-soles, talk of the
    promenaders,   20
The heavy omnibus, the driver with his interrogating thumb, the clank
    of the shod horses on the granite floor,
The snow-sleighs, clinking, shouted jokes, pelts of snow-balls,
The hurrahs for popular favorites, the fury of rous'd mobs,
The flap of the curtain'd litter, a sick man inside borne to the hospital,
The meeting of enemies, the sudden oath, the blows and fall,
The excited crowd, the policeman with his star quickly working his
    passage to the center of the crowd,
The impassive stones that receive and return so many echoes,
What groans of over-fed or half-starv'd who fall sunstruck or in fits,

What exclamations of women taken suddenly who hurry home and
     give birth to babes,
What living and buried speech is always vibrating here, what howls
     restrain'd by decorum,   30
Arrests of criminals, slights, adulterous offers made, acceptances,
     rejections with convex lips,
I mind them or the show or resonance of them—I come and I depart.

31

I believe a leaf of grass is no less than the journeywork of the stars,
And the pismire is equally perfect, and a grain of sand, and the egg
     of the wren
And the tree-toad is a chef-d'oeuvre for the highest,
And the running blackberrry would adorn the parlors of heaven,
And the narrowest hinge in my hand puts to scorn all machinery,
And the cow crunching with depress'd head surpasses any statue,
And a mouse is miracle enough to stagger sextillions of infidels.

I find I incorporate gneiss, coal, long-threaded moss, fruits, grains,
     esculent roots,   40
And am stucco'd with quadrupeds and birds all over,
And have distanced what is behind me for good reasons,
But call any thing back again when I desire it.

In vain the speeding or shyness,
In vain the plutonic rocks send their old heat against my approach,
In vain the mastodon retreats beneath its own powder'd bones,
In vain objects stand leagues off and assume manifold shapes,
In vain the ocean settling in hollows and the great monsters lying low,
In vain the buzzard houses herself with the sky,
In vain the snake slides through the creepers and logs,   50
In vain the elk takes to the inner passes of the woods,
In vain the razor-bill'd auk sails far north to Labrador,
I follow quickly, I ascend to the nest in the fissure of the cliff.

32

I think I could turn and live with animals, they are so placid and
     self-contain'd,
I stand and look at them long and long.

They do not sweat and whine about their condition,
They do not lie awake in the dark and weep for their sins,
They do not make me sick discussing their duty to God,
Not one is dissatisfied, not one is demented with the mania of owning
     things,

Not one kneels to another, nor to his kind that lived thousands of
        years ago,   60
Not one is respectable or unhappy over the whole earth.

So they show their relations to me and I accept them,
They bring me tokens of myself, they evince them plainly in their
        possession.

I wonder where they get those tokens,
Did I pass that way huge times ago and negligently drop them?
Myself moving forward then and now and forever,
Gathering and showing more always and with velocity,
Infinite and omnigenous, and the like of these among them,
Not too exclusive toward the reachers of my remembrancers,
Picking out here one that I love, and now go with him on brotherly
        terms.   70

A gigantic beauty of a stallion, fresh and responsive to my caresses,
Head high in the forehead, wide between the ears,
Limbs glossy and supple, tail dusting the ground,
Eyes full of sparkling wickedness, ears finely cut, flexibly moving.
His nostrils dilate as my heels embrace him,
His well-built limbs tremble with pleasure as we race around and
        return.

I but use you a minute, then I resign you, stallion,
Why do I need your paces when I myself out-gallop them?
Even as I stand or sit passing faster than you.

48

I have said that the soul is not more than the body,   80
And I have said that the body is not more than the soul,
And nothing, not God, is greater to one than one's self is,
And whoever walks a furlong without sympathy walks to his own
        funeral drest in his shroud,
And I or you pocketless of a dime may purchase the pick of the earth,
And to glance with an eye or show a bean in its pod confounds the
        learning of all times,
And there is no trade or employment but the young man following
        it may become a hero,
And there is no object so soft but it makes a hub for the wheel'd
        universe,
And I say to any man or woman, Let your soul stand cool and
        composed before a million universes.

And I say to mankind, Be not curious about God,
For I who am curious about each am not curious about God,   90
(No array of terms can say how much I am at peace about God and
        about death.)

I hear and behold God in every object, yet understand God not in
        the least,
Nor do I understand who there can be more wonderful than myself.

Why should I wish to see God better than this day?
I see something of God each hour of the twenty-four, and each
        moment then,
In the faces of men and women I see God, and in my own face in
        the glass,
I find letters from God dropt in the street, and every one is sign'd
        by God's name,
And I leave them where they are, for I know that wheresoe'er I go,
Others will punctually come for ever and ever.

▪   After equally careful study of these passages from "Song of Myself"
and Poe's "Dream-land" (p. 464), write an essay in which you attempt
to infer the notions each poet held about the kind of subject matter a
poet should treat. Include in your paper discussions of diction, rhyme,
and meter.

When Lilacs Last in the Door-yard Bloom'd

1

When lilacs last in the dooryard bloom'd,
And the great star early droop'd in the western sky in the night,
I mourn'd, and yet shall mourn with ever-returning spring.

Ever-returning spring, trinity sure to me you bring,
Lilac blooming perennial and drooping star in the west,
And thought of him I love.

2

O powerful western fallen star!
O shades of night—O moody, tearful night!
O great star disappear'd—O the black murk that hides the star!
O cruel hands that hold me powerless—O helpless soul of me!   10
O harsh surrounding cloud that will not free my soul.

3

In the dooryard fronting an old farmhouse near the white-wash'd
    palings,
Stands the lilac-bush tall-growing with heart-shaped leaves of rich
    green,
With many a pointed blossom rising delicate, with the perfume
    strong I love,
With every leaf a miracle—and from this bush in the dooryard,
With delicate-color'd blossoms and heart-shaped leaves of rich green,
A sprig with its flower I break.

4

In the swamp in secluded recesses,
A shy and hidden bird is warbling a song.

Solitary the thrush,   20
The hermit withdrawn to himself, avoiding the settlements,
Sings by himself a song.
Song of the bleeding throat,
Death's outlet song of life, (for well dear brother I know,
If thou wast not granted to sing thou would'st surely die.)

5

Over the breast of the spring, the land, amid cities,
Amid lanes and through old woods, where lately the violets peep'd
    from the ground, spotting the gray debris,
Amid the grass in the fields each side of the lanes, passing the endless
    grass,
Passing the yellow-spear'd wheat, every grain from its shroud in the
    dark-brown fields uprisen,
Passing the apple-tree blows of white and pink in the orchards,   30
Carrying a corpse to where it shall rest in the grave,
Night and day journeys a coffin.

6

Coffin that passes through lanes and streets,
Through day and night with the great cloud darkening the land,
With the pomp of the inloop'd flags with the cities draped in black,
With the show of the States themselves as of crape-veil'd women
    standing,
With processions long and winding and the flambeaus of the night,
With the countless torches lit, with the silent sea of faces and the
    unbared heads,
With the waiting depot, the arriving coffin, and the somber faces,

With dirges through the night, with the thousand voices rising
        strong and solemn,
With all the mournful voices of the dirges pour'd round the coffin,   40
The dim-lit churches and the shuddering organs—where amid these
        you journey,
With the tolling tolling bells' perpetual clang,
Here, coffin that slowly passes,
I give you my sprig of lilac.

7

(Nor for you, for one alone,
Blossoms and branches green to coffins all I bring,
For fresh as the morning, thus would I chant a song for you O sane
        and sacred death.

All over bouquets of roses,
O death, I cover you over with roses and early lilies,   50
But mostly and now the lilac that blooms the first,
Copious I break, I break the sprigs from the bushes,
With loaded arms I come, pouring for you,
For you and the coffins all of you O death.)

8

O western orb sailing the heaven,
Now I know what you must have meant as a month since I walk'd,
As I walk'd in silence the transparent shadowy night,
As I saw you had something to tell as you bent to me night after night,
As you droop'd from the sky low down as if to my side, (while the
        other stars all look'd on,)
As we wander'd together the solemn night, (for something I know
        not what kept me from sleep,)   60
As the night advanced, and I saw on the rim of the west how full
        you were of woe,
As I stood on the rising ground in the breeze in the cool transparent
        night,
As I watch'd where you pass'd and was lost in the netherward black
        of the night,
As my soul in its trouble dissatisfied sank, as where you sad orb,
Concluded, dropt in the night, and was gone.

9

Sing on there in the swamp,
O singer bashful and tender, I hear your notes, I hear your call,
I hear, I come presently, I understand you,

But a moment I linger, for the lustrous star has detain'd me,
The star my departing comrade holds and detains me.   70

10

O how shall I warble myself for the dead one there I loved?
And how shall I deck my song for the large sweet soul that has gone?
And what shall my perfume be for the grave of him I love?

Sea-winds blown from east and west,
Blown from the Eastern sea and blown from the Western sea, till
          there on the prairies meeting,
These and with these and the breath of my chant,
I'll perfume the grave of him I love.

11

O what shall I hang on the chamber walls?
And what shall the pictures be that I hang on the walls,
To adorn the burial-house of him I love?   80

Pictures of growing spring and farms and homes,
With the Fourth-month eve at sundown, and the gray smoke lucid
          and bright,
With floods of the yellow gold of the gorgeous, indolent, sinking
          sun, burning, expanding the air,
With the fresh sweet herbage under foot, and the pale green leaves
          of the trees prolific,
In the distance the flowing glaze, the breast of the river, with a
          wind-dapple here and there,
With ranging hills on the banks, with many a line against the sky,
          and shadows,
And the city at hand with dwellings so dense, and stacks of chimneys,
And all the scenes of life and the workshops, and the workmen
          homeward returning.

12

Lo, body and soul—this land,
My own Manhattan with spires, and the sparkling and hurrying
          tides, and the ships,   90
The varied and ample land, the South and the North in the light,
          Ohio's shores and flashing Missouri,
And ever the far-spreading prairies cover'd with grass and corn.

Lo, the most excellent sun so calm and haughty,
The violet and purple morn with just-felt breezes,
The gentle soft-born measureless light,

The miracle spreading bathing all, the fulfill'd noon,
The coming eve delicious, the welcome night and the stars,
Over my cities shining all, enveloping man and land.

13

Sing on, sing on you gray-brown bird,
Sing from the swamps, the recesses, pour your chant from the
              bushes,   100
Limitless out of the dusk, out of the cedars and pines.

Sing on dearest brother, warble your reedy song,
Loud human song, with voice of uttermost woe.

O liquid and free and tender!
O wild and loose to my soul—O wondrous singer!
You only I hear—yet the stars hold me, (but will soon depart,)
Yet the lilac with mastering odor holds me.

14

Now while I sat in the day and look'd forth,
In the close of the day with its light and the fields of spring, and
              the farmers preparing their crops,
In the large unconscious scenery of my land with its lakes and
              forests,   110
In the heavy aerial beauty, (after the perturbed winds and the
              storms,)
Under the arching heavens of the afternoon swift passing, and the
              voices of children and women,
The many-moving sea-tides, and I saw the ships how they sail'd,
And the summer approaching with richness, and the fields all busy
              with labor,
And the infinite separate houses, how they all went on, each with
              its meals and minutia of daily usages,
And the streets how their throbbings throbb'd, and the cities pent—
              lo, then and there,
Falling upon them all and among them all, enveloping me with
              the rest,
Appear'd the cloud, appear'd the long black trail,
And I knew death, its thought, and the sacred knowledge of death.

Then with the knowledge of death as walking one side of me,   120
And the thought of death close-walking the other side of me,
And I in the middle as with companions, and as holding the hands
              of companions,
I fled forth to the hiding receiving night that talks not,

Down to the shores of the water, the path by the swamp in the
        dimness,
To the solemn shadowy cedars and ghostly pines so still.

And the singer so shy to the rest receiv'd me,
The gray-brown bird I know receiv'd us comrades three,
And he sang the carol of death, and a verse for him I love.

From deep secluded recesses,
From the fragrant cedars and the ghostly pines so still,   130
Came the carol of the bird.

And the charm of the carol rapt me
As I held as if by their hands my comrades in the night,
And the voice of my spirit tallied the song of the bird.

Come lovely and soothing death,
Undulate round the world, serenely arriving, arriving,
In the day, in the night, to all, to each,
Sooner or later delicate death.

Prais'd be the fathomless universe,
For life and joy, and for objects and knowledge curious,   140
And for love, sweet love—but praise! praise! praise!
For the sure-enwinding arms of cool-enfolding death.

Dark mother always gliding near with soft feet,
Have none chanted for thee a chant of fullest welcome?
Then I chant it for thee, I glorify thee above all,
I bring thee a song that when thou must indeed come, come
        unfalteringly.

Approach strong deliveress,
When it is so, when thou hast taken them I joyously sing the dead,
Lost in the loving floating ocean of thee,
Laved in the flood of thy bliss O death.   150

From me to thee glad serenades,
Dances for thee I propose saluting thee, adornments and feastings
        for thee,
And the sights of the open landscape and the high-spread sky are
        fitting,
And life and the fields, and the huge and thoughtful night.

The night in silence under many a star,
The ocean shore and the husky whispering wave whose voice I know,

And the soul turning to thee O vast and well-veil'd death,
And the body gratefully nestling close to thee.

Over the tree-tops I float thee a song,
Over the rising and sinking waves, over the myriad fields and the
   prairies wide,   160
Over the dense-pack'd cities all and the teeming wharves and ways,
I float this carol with joy, with joy to thee O death.

15

To the tally of my soul,
Loud and strong kept up the gray-brown bird,
With pure deliberate notes spreading filling the night.

Loud in the pines and cedars dim,
Clear in the freshness moist and the swamp-perfume.
And I with my comrades there in the night.

While my sight that was bound in my eyes unclosed,
As to long panoramas of visions.   170

And I saw askant the armies,
I saw as in noiseless dreams hundreds of battle-flags,
Borne through the smoke of the battles and pierc'd with missiles I
   saw them,
And carried hither and yon through the smoke, and torn and bloody,
And at last but a few shreds left on the staffs, (and all in silence,)
And the staffs all splinter'd and broken.

I saw battle-corpses, myriads of them,
And the white skeletons of young men, I saw them,
I saw the debris and debris of all the slain soldiers of the war,
But I saw they were not as was thought,   180
They themselves were fully at rest, they suffer'd not,
The living remain'd and suffer'd, the mother suffer'd,
And the wife and the child and the musing comrade suffer'd,
And the armies that remain'd suffer'd.

16

Passing the visions, passing the night,
Passing, unloosing the hold of my comrades' hands,
Passing the song of the hermit bird and the tallying song of my soul,
Victorious song, death's outlet song, yet varying ever-altering song,
As low and wailing, yet clear the notes, rising and falling, flooding
   the night,

Sadly sinking and fainting, as warning and warning, and yet again
          bursting with joy,   190
Covering the earth and filling the spread of the heaven,
As that powerful psalm in the night I heard from recesses,
Passing, I leave thee lilac with heart-shaped leaves,
I leave thee there in the dooryard, blooming, returning with spring.

I cease from my song for thee,
From my gaze on thee in the west, fronting the west, communing
          with thee,
O comrade lustrous with silver face in the night.

Yet each to keep and all, retrievements out of the night,
The song, the wondrous chant of the gray-brown bird,
And the tallying chant, the echo arous'd in my soul,   200
With the lustrous and drooping star with the countenance full of
          woe,
With the holders holding my hand nearing the call of the bird,
Comrades mine and I in the midst, and their memory ever to keep,
          for the dead I loved so well,
For the sweetest, wisest soul of all my days and lands—and this for
          his dear sake,
Lilac and star and bird twined with the chant of my soul,
There in the fragrant pines and the cedars dusk and dim.

■   Is the metrical pattern in this poem more or less successful than that in "Song of Myself"? Justify your answer.

I Hear America Singing

I hear America singing, the varied carols I hear,
Those of mechanics, each one singing his as it should be blithe
          and strong,
The carpenter singing his as he measures his plank or beam,
The mason singing his as he makes ready for work, or leaves off work,
The boatman singing what belongs to him in his boat, the deckhand
          singing on the steamboat deck,
The shoemaker singing as he sits on his bench, the hatter singing as
          he stands,
The wood-cutter's song, the plowboy's on his way in the morning, or
          at the noon intermission or at sundown,
The delicious singing of the mother, or of the young wife at work,
          or of the girl sewing or washing,
Each singing what belongs to him or her and to none else.

The day what belongs to the day—at night the party of young
      fellows, robust, friendly,
Singing with open mouths their strong melodious songs.

■ Discuss the tone in relation to the diction of this poem.

To a Locomotive in Winter

Thee for my recitative,
Thee in the driving storm even as now, the snow, the winter-day
      declining,
Thee in thy panoply, thy measur'd dual throbbing and thy beat
      convulsive,
Thy black cylindric body, golden brass and silvery steel,
Thy ponderous side-bars, parallel and connecting rods, gyrating,
      shuttling at thy sides,
Thy metrical, now swelling pant and roar, now tapering in the
      distance,
Thy great protruding head-light fix'd in front,
Thy long, pale, floating vapor-pennants, tinged with delicate purple,
The dense and murky clouds out-belching from thy smoke-stack,
Thy knitted frame, thy springs and valves, the tremulous twinkle
      of thy wheels,
Thy train of cars behind, obedient, merrily following,
Through gale or calm, now swift, now slack, yet steadily careering;
Type of the modern—emblem of motion and power—pulse of the
      continent,
For once come serve the Muse and merge in verse, even as here I
      see thee,
With storm and buffeting gusts of wind and falling snow,
By day thy warning ringing bell to sound its notes,
By night thy silent signal lamps to swing.

Fierce-throated beauty!
Roll through my chant with all thy lawless music, thy swinging
      lamps at night,
Thy madly-whistled laughter, echoing, rumbling like an earthquake,
      rousing all,
Law of thyself complete, thine own track firmly holding,
(No sweetness debonair of tearful harp or glib piano thine,)
Thy trills of shrieks by rocks and hills return'd,
Launch'd o'er the prairies wide, across the lakes,
To the free skies unpent and glad and strong.

■   1. Is the locomotive a well-developed symbol?
   2. Does the intrusion of the author in lines 1 and 14 diminish or increase the effectiveness of the locomotive as a symbol?

Darest Thou Now, O Soul

Darest thou now, O soul,
Walk out with me toward the unknown region,
Where neither ground is for the feet nor any path to follow?

No map there, nor guide,
Nor voice sounding, nor touch of human hand,
Nor face with blooming flesh, nor lips, nor eyes, are in that land.

I know it not, O soul,
Nor dost thou; all is a blank before us;
All waits undreamed of in that region, that inaccessible land.

Till when the ties loosen,
All but the ties eternal, Time and Space,
Nor darkness, gravitation, sense, nor any bounds bounding us.

Then we burst forth, we float,
In Time and Space, O soul, prepared for them,
Equal, equipped at last (O joy! O fruit of all!) them to fulfill, O soul.

Matthew Arnold

(1822–1888)

■■■■■■■■■

THOMAS ARNOLD, Matthew's father, was a notable historian, an early member of the Oxford Movement (he wanted a more liberal Anglican church), and the distinguished headmaster of Rugby. Mary Penrose Arnold, the poet's mother, came from a well-known clerical family. Young Matthew was encouraged in his writing by William Wordsworth, a friend of the Arnold family and the subject of one of Arnold's most famous critical essays. At Rugby he was a close friend of Arthur Clough, who was also to write a considerable body of poetry about his loss of religious faith. Arnold studied at Balliol College, Oxford, where he heard Newman preach, and in 1845 he was elected to a Fellowship at Oriel College. In 1851 he married Francis Lucy Wrightman. Among his earlier volumes are *The Strayed Reveller and Other Poems* (1849), *Empedocles on Etna and Other Poems* (1852) and *Poems* (1853). A large part of Arnold's adult life was spent as an inspector of schools, but in 1857 he was elected professor of poetry at Oxford. Much of Arnold's reputation and influence derive from his work as a critic.

Suggested Readings

H. W. GARROD, *Poetry and the Criticism of Life*. Oxford: Oxford University Press, 1931.

LIONEL TRILLING, *Matthew Arnold*. New York: Columbia University Press, reissued 1949, pp. 77–141.

■■■■■■■■■

The Buried Life

Light flows our war of mocking words, and yet,
Behold, with tears mine eyes are wet!
I feel a nameless sadness o'er me roll.
Yes, yes, we know that we can jest,
We know, we know that we can smile!
But there's a something in this breast,
To which thy light words bring no rest,
And thy gay smiles no anodyne.
Give me thy hand, and hush awhile,
And turn those limpid eyes on mine,   10
And let me read there, love! thy inmost soul.

Alas! is even love too weak
To unlock the heart, and let it speak?
Are even lovers powerless to reveal
To one another what indeed they feel?
I knew the mass of men concealed
Their thoughts, for fear that if revealed
They would by other men be met
With blank indifference, or with blame reproved;
I knew they lived and moved   20
Tricked in disguises, alien to the rest
Of men, and alien to themselves—and yet
The same heart beats in every human breast!

534   POEMS FOR STUDY

But we, my love!—doth a like spell benumb
Our hearts, our voices?—must we too be dumb?

Ah! well for us, if even we,
Even for a moment, can get free
Our heart, and have our lips unchained;
For that which seals them hath been deep-ordained!

Fate, which foresaw   30
How frivolous a baby man would be—
By what distractions he would be possessed,
How he would pour himself in every strife,
And well-nigh change his own identity—
That it might keep from his capricious play
His genuine self, and force him to obey
Even in his own despite his being's law,
Bade through the deep recesses of our breast
The unregarded river of our life
Pursue with indiscernible flow its way;   40
And that we should not see
The buried stream, and seem to be
Eddying at large in blind uncertainty,
Though driving on with it eternally.

But often, in the world's most crowded streets,
But often, in the din of strife,
There rises an unspeakable desire
After the knowledge of our buried life;
A thirst to spend our fire and restless force
In tracking out our true, original course;   50
A longing to inquire
Into the mystery of this heart which beats
So wild, so deep in us—to know
Whence our lives come and where they go.
And many a man in his own breast then delves,
But deep enough, alas! none ever mines.
And we have been on many thousand lines,
And we have shown, on each, spirit and power;
But hardly have we, for one little hour,
Been on our own line, have we been ourselves—   60
Hardly had skill to utter one of all
The nameless feelings that course through our breast,
But they course on forever unexpressed.
And long we try in vain to speak and act
Our hidden self, and what we say and do

Is eloquent, is well—but 'tis not true!
And then we will no more be racked
With inward striving, and demand
Of all the thousand nothings of the hour
Their stupefying power;   70
Ah yes, and they benumb us at our call!
Yet still, from time to time, vague and forlorn,
From the soul's subterranean depth upborne
As from an infinitely distant land,
Come airs, and floating echoes, and convey
A melancholy into all our day.

Only—but this is rare—
When a beloved hand is laid in ours,
When, jaded with the rush and glare
Of the interminable hours,   80
Our eyes can in another's eyes read clear,
When our world-deafened ear
Is by the tones of a loved voice caressed—
A bolt is shot back somewhere in our breast,
And a lost pulse of feeling stirs again.
The eye sinks inward, and the heart lies plain,
And what we mean, we say, and what we would, we know.
A man becomes aware of his life's flow,
And hears its winding murmur; and he sees
The meadows where it glides, the sun, the breeze.   90

And there arrives a lull in the hot race
Wherein he doth forever chase
That flying and elusive shadow, rest.
An air of coolness plays upon his face,
And an unwonted calm pervades his breast.
And then he thinks he knows
The hills where his life rose,
And the sea where it goes.

■ 1. Why does the symbolism of the river dominate the poem?
   2. Is the symbol of the river explored as successfully or as fully as
that of the sea in "Dover Beach" (p. 537)?
   3. Are there passages in "The Buried Life" which could be removed without destroying the meaning or power of the poem?

Austerity of Poetry

That son of Italy who tried to blow,
Ere Dante came, the trump of sacred song,
In his light youth amid a festal throng
Sate with his bride to see a public show.
Fair was the bride, and on her front did glow
Youth like a star; and what to youth belong—
Gay raiment, sparkling gauds, elation strong.
A prop gave way! crash fell a platform! lo,
'Mid struggling sufferers, hurt to death, she lay!
Shuddering, they drew her garments off—and found
A robe of sackcloth next the smooth, white skin.
Such, poets, is your bride, the Muse! young, gay,
Radiant, ordorned outside; a hidden ground
Of thought and of austerity within.

■   Does the anecdote treated in this poem convince you of the austerity of poetry? Answer in some detail.

The Last Word

Creep into thy narrow bed,
Creep, and let no more be said!
Vain thy onset! all stands fast.
Thou myself must break at last.

Let the long contention cease!
Geese are swans, and swans are geese.
Let them have it how they will!
Thou art tired; best be still.

They outtalked thee, hissed thee, tore thee?
Better men fared thus before thee;
Fired their ringing shot and passed,
Hotly charged—and sank at last.

Charge once more, then, and be dumb!
Let the victors, when they come,
When the forts of folly fall,
Find thy body by the wall.

Dover Beach

The sea is calm tonight,
The tide is full, the moon lies fair
Upon the straits—on the French coast the light
Gleams and is gone; the cliffs of England stand,
Glimmering and vast, out in the tranquil bay.
Come to the window, sweet is the night-air!
Only, from the long line of spray
Where the ebb meets the moon-blanched land,
Listen! you hear the grating roar
Of pebbles which the waves draw back, and fling   10
At their return, up the high strand,
Begin, and cease, and then again begin,
With tremulous cadence slow, and bring
The eternal note of sadness in.

Sophocles long ago
Heard it on the Aegean, and it brought
Into his mind the turbid ebb and flow
Of human misery; we
Find also in the sound a thought,
Hearing it by this distant northern sea.   20

The Sea of Faith
Was once, too, at the full, and round earth's shore
Lay like the folds of a bright girdle furled.
But now I only hear
Its melancholy, long, withdrawing roar,
Retreating, to the breath
Of the night-wind, down the vast edges drear
And naked shingles of the world.

Ah, love, let us be true
To one another! for the world, which seems   30
To lie before us like a land of dreams,
So various, so beautiful, so new,
Hath really neither joy, nor love, nor light,
Nor certitude, nor peace, nor help for pain;
And we are here as on a darkling plain
Swept with confused alarms of struggle and flight,
Where ignorant armies clash by night.

■ Write a short essay on this poem. Include in it discussions of the following points: the appropriateness of the sea as a symbol of faith; the diversified references to the "moon-blanch'd sand," the "Aegean," "naked shingles," "ignorant armies," and so forth; and the interrelated themes.

Philomela

Hark! ah, the nightingale—
The tawny-throated!
Hark, from that moonlit cedar what a burst!
What triumph! hark—what pain!

O wanderer from a Grecian shore,
Still, after many years, in distant lands,
Still nourishing in thy bewildered brain
That wild, unquenched, deep-sunken, old-world pain—
Say, will it never heal?
And can this fragrant lawn   10
With its cool trees, and night,
And the sweet, tranquil Thames,
And moonshine, and the dew,
To thy racked heart and brain
Afford no balm?

Dost thou tonight behold,
Here, through the moonlight on this English grass,
The unfriendly palace in the Thracian wild?
Dost thou again peruse
With hot cheeks and seared eyes   20
The too clear web, and thy dumb sister's shame?
Dost thou once more assay
Thy flight, and feel come over thee,
Poor fugitive, the feathery change
Once more, and once more seem to make resound
With love and hate, triumph and agony,
Lone Daulis, and the high Cephissian vale?
Listen, Eugenia—
How thick the bursts come crowding through the leaves!
Again—thou hearest?   30
Eternal passion!
Eternal pain!

■   Why is it important in the development of the theme to juxtapose England and Greece?

The Scholar-Gipsy

The poem is based on the following passage abbreviated from Glan-vil's *Vanity of Dogmatizing*, 1661; cf. ll. 31, 133, 159.

There was very lately a lad in the University of Oxford, who was by his poverty forced to leave his studies there; and at last to join himself to a company of vagabond gipsies. Among these extravagant people, by the insinuating subtilty of his carriage he quickly got so much of their love and esteem as that they discovered to him their mystery. After he had been a pretty while exercised in the trade, there chanced to ride by a couple of scholars, who had formerly been of his acquaint-ance. They quickly spied out their old friend among the gipsies; and he gave them an account of the necessity which drove him to that kind of life, and told them that the people he went with were not such im-postors as they were taken for, but that they had a traditional kind of learning among them, and could do wonders by the power of imagina-tion, their fancy binding that of others; that himself had learned much of their art, and when he had compassed the whole secret, he intended, he said, to leave their company, and give the world an account of what he had learned. [Arnold's note]

Go, for they call you, shepherd, from the hill;
   Go, shepherd, and untie the wattled cotes;
      No longer leave thy wistful flock unfed,
   Nor let thy bawling fellows rack their throats,
      Nor the cropped herbage shoot another head.
         But when the fields are still,
   And the tired men and dogs all gone to rest,
      And only the white sheep are sometimes seen
      Cross and recross the strips of moon-blanched green,
Come, shepherd, and again begin the quest!   10

Here, where the reaper was at work of late—
   In this high field's dark corner, where he leaves
      His coat, his basket, and his earthen cruse,
   And in the sun all morning binds the sheaves,
      Then here, at noon, comes back his stores to use—
         Here will I sit and wait,
   While to my ear from uplands far away
      The bleating of the folded flocks is borne,
      With distant cries of reapers in the corn—
All the live murmur of a summer's day.   20

Screened is this nook o'er the high, half-reaped field,
   And here till sun-down, shepherd! will I be.
      Through the thick corn the scarlet poppies peep

And round green roots and yellowing stalks I see
    Pale pink convolvulus in tendrils creep;
        And air-swept lindens yield
Their scent, and rustle down their perfumed showers
    Of bloom on the bent grass where I am laid,
    And bower me from the August sun with shade;
And the eye travels down to Oxford's towers.   30

And near me on the grass lies Glanvil's book—
    Come, let me read the oft-read tale again!
        The story of that Oxford scholar poor,
Of pregnant parts and quick inventive brain,
    Who, tired of knocking at preferment's door,
        One summer-morn forsook
His friends, and went to learn the gipsy lore,
    And roamed the world with that wild brotherhood,
    And came, as most men deemed, to little good,
But came to Oxford and his friends no more.   40

But once, years after, in the country-lanes,
    Two scholars, whom at college erst he knew,
    Met him, and of his way of life inquired;
Whereat he answered, that the gipsy-crew,
    His mates, had arts to rule as they desired
        The workings of men's brains,
And they can bind them to what thoughts they will.
    "And I," he said, "the secret of their art,
        When fully learned, will to the world impart;
But it needs heaven-sent moments for this skill."   50

This said, he left them, and returned no more.—
    But rumors hung about the countryside,
    That the lost Scholar long was seen to stray,
Seen by rare glimpses, pensive and tongue-tied,
    In hat of antique shape, and cloak of gray,
        The same the gipsies wore.
Shepherds had met him on the Hurst[1] in spring;
    At some lone alehouse in the Berkshire moors,
    On the warm ingle-bench,[2] the smock-frocked boors
Had found him seated at their entering.   60

But, 'mid their drink and clatter, he would fly.
    And I myself seem half to know thy looks,

----

1. One of the Cumner hills south of Oxford in Berkshire.   2. Fireside bench

And put the shepherds, wanderer, on thy trace;
And boys who in lone wheat fields scare the rooks
  I ask if thou hast passed their quiet place; ·
    Or in my boat I lie
Moored to the cool bank in the summer heats,
  'Mid wide grass meadows which the sunshine fills,
  And watch the warm, green-muffled Cumner hills,
And wonder if thou haunt'st their shy retreats.   70

For most, I know, thou lov'st retirèd ground!
  Thee at the ferry Oxford riders blithe,
    Returning home on summer-nights, have met
  Crossing the stripling Thames at Bablockhithe,[3]
    Trailing in the cool stream thy fingers wet,
      As the punt's[4] rope chops round:
    And leaning backward in a pensive dream,
    And fostering in thy lap a heap of flowers
    Plucking in shy fields and distant Wychwood[5] bowers,
  And thine eyes resting on the moonlit stream.   80

And then they land, and thou art seen no more.
  Maidens, who from the distant hamlets come
    To dance around the Fyfield elm in May,
  Oft through the darkening fields have seen thee roam,
    Or cross a stile into the public way.
      Oft thou hast given them store
    Of flowers—the frail-leafed, white anemone,
    Dark bluebells drenched with dews of summer eves,
    And purple orchises with spotted leaves—
  But none hath words she can report of thee.   90

And, above Godstow[6] Bridge, when haytime's here
  In June, and many a scythe in sunshine flames,
    Men who through those wide fields of breezy grass
  Where black-winged swallows haunt the glittering Thames,
    To bathe in the abandoned lasher[7] pass,
      Have often passed thee near,
    Sitting upon the river bank o'ergrown;
    Marked thine outlandish garb, thy figure spare,
    Thy dark vague eyes, and soft abstracted air—
  But, when they came from bathing, thou wast gone.   100

....

3. Ferry above Oxford.   4. Long, flat-bottomed boat.   5. Forest north of
Oxford.   6. Site of a ruined nunnery on the Thames above Oxford.   7. Originally, the turbulent water running through an opening in a weir; then applied
to the weir itself, or to the pool below the weir into which the lasher empties.

At some lone homestead in the Cumner hills,
  Where at her open door the housewife darns,
    Thou hast been seen, or hanging on a gate,
  To watch the threshers in the mossy barns.
    Children, who early range these slopes and late
      For cresses from the rills,
  Have known thee eying, all an April day,
    The springing pastures and the feeding kine;
    And marked thee, when the stars come out and shine,
  Through the long dewy grass move slow away.   110

In Autumn, on the skirts of Bagley Wood—
  Where most the gipsies by the turf-edged way
    Pitch their smoked tents, and every bush you see
  With scarlet patches tagged and shreds of gray,
    Above the forest-ground called Thessaly—
      The blackbird picking food
  Sees thee, nor stops his meal, nor fears at all;
    So often has he known thee past him stray,
    Rapt, twirling in thy hand a withered spray,
  And waiting for the spark from heaven to fall.   120

And once, in winter, on the causeway chill
  Where home through flooded fields foot-travelers go,
    Have I not passed thee on the wooden bridge
  Wrapt in thy cloak and battling with the snow,
    Thy face toward Hinskey and its wintry ridge?
      And thou hast climbed the hill,
  And gained the white brow of the Cumner range,
    Turned once to watch, while thick the snowflakes fall,
    The line of festal light in Christ Church hall—
  Then sought thy straw in some sequestered grange.   130

But what—I dream! Two hundred years are flown
  Since first thy story ran through Oxford halls,
    And the grave Glanvil did the tale inscribe
  That thou wert wandered from the studious walls
    To learn strange arts, and join a gipsy tribe:
      And thou from earth art gone
  Long since, and in some quiet churchyard laid;
    Some country nook, where o'er thy unknown grave
    Tall grasses and white flowering nettles wave—
  Under a dark red-fruited, yew-tree's shade.   140

—No, no, thou hast not felt the lapse of hours,
  For what wears out the life of mortal men?

'Tis that from change to change their being rolls:
'Tis that repeated shocks, again, again,
　　Exhaust the energy of strongest souls,
　　　And numb the elastic powers.
　Till having used our nerves with bliss and teen,
　　And tired upon a thousand schemes our wit,
　　To the just-pausing Genius we remit
Our worn-out life, and are—what we have been.　　150

Thou hast not lived, why shoud'st thou perish so?
　Thou had'st *one* aim, *one* business, *one* desire;
　　Else wert thou long since numbered with the dead—
Else hadst thou spent, like other men, thy fire.
　　The generations of thy peers are fled,
　　　And we ourselves shall go;
　But thou possessest an immortal lot,
　　And we imagine thee exempt from age,
　　And living as thou liv'st on Glanvil's page,
Because thou hadst—what we, alas, have not!　　160

For early didst thou leave the world, with powers
　Fresh, undiverted to the world without,
　　Firm to their mark, not spent on other things;
　Free from the sick fatigue, the languid doubt,
　　Which much to have tried, in much been baffled, brings.
　　　O life unlike to ours!
　Who fluctuate idly without term or scope,
　　Of whom each strives, nor knows for what he strives,
　　And each half lives a hundred different lives;
Who wait like thee, but not, like thee, in hope.　　170

Thou waitest for the spark from heaven: and we,
　Light half-believers of our casual creeds,
　　Who never deeply felt, nor clearly willed,
　Whose insight never has borne fruit in deeds,
　　Whose vague resolves never have been fulfilled;
　　　For whom each year we see
　Breeds new beginnings, disappointments new;
　　Who hesitate and falter life away,
　　And lose to-morrow the ground won to-day—
Ah, do not we, wanderer, await it too?　　180

Yes, we await it, but it still delays,
　And then we suffer; and amongst us one,
　　Who most has suffered, takes dejectedly

His seat upon the intellectual throne;
    And all his store of sad experience he
        Lays bare of wretched days;
Tells us his misery's birth and growth and signs,
    And how the dying spark of hope was fed,
    And how the breast was soothed, and how the head,
And all his hourly varied anodynes.   190

This for our wisest: and we others pine,
    And wish the long unhappy dream would end,
        And waive all claim to bliss, and try to bear
With close-lipped patience for our only friend,
    Sad patience, too near neighbor to despair,
        But none has hope like thine.
Thou through the fields and through the woods dost stray,
    Roaming the country side, a truant boy,
    Nursing thy project in unclouded joy,
And every doubt long blown by time away.   200

O born in days when wits were fresh and clear,
    And life ran gaily as the sparkling Thames;
        Before this strange disease of modern life,
With its sick hurry, its divided aims,
    Its heads o'ertaxed, its palsied hearts, was rife—
        Fly hence, our contact fear!
Still fly, plunge deeper in the bowering wood!
    Averse, as Dido[8] did with gesture stern
    From her false friend's approach in Hades turn,
Wave us away, and keep thy solitude.   210

Still nursing the unconquerable hope,
    Still clutching the inviolable shade,
        With a free onward impulse brushing through,
By night, the silvered branches of the glade—
    Far on the forest skirts, where none pursue,
        On some mild pastoral slope
Emerge, and resting on the moonlit pales,
    Freshen thy flowers, as in former years,
    With dew, or listen with enchanted ears,
From the dark dingles, to the nightingales.   220

But fly our paths, our feverish contact fly,
    For strong the infection of our mental strife,

----

8. Aeneas on a journey through Hades met the shade of Dido, who had killed herself for love of him. The shade turns away in aversion.

Which, though it gives no bliss, yet spoils for rest;
And we should win thee from thy own fair life,
Like us distracted, and like us unblest.
Soon, soon thy cheer would die,
Thy hopes grow timorous, and unfixed thy powers,
And thy clear aims be cross and shifting made:
And then thy glad perennial youth would fade,
Fade, and grow old at last, and die like ours.   230

Then fly our greetings, fly our speech and smiles!
—As some grave Tyrian trader, from the sea,
Descried at sunrise an emerging prow
Lifting the cool-haired creepers stealthily,
The fringes of a southward-facing brow
Among the Aegean isles;
And saw the merry Grecian coaster come,
Freighted with amber grapes, and Chian wine,
Green bursting figs, and tunnies steeped in brine;
And knew the intruders on his ancient home,   240

The young light-hearted masters of the waves—
And snatched his rudder, and shook out more sail,
And day and night held on indignantly
O'er the blue Midland waters with the gale,
Betwixt the Syrtes and soft Sicily,
To where the Atlantic raves
Outside the western straits; and unbent sails
There, where down cloudy cliffs, through sheets of foam,
Shy traffickers, the dark Iberians come;
And on the beach undid his corded bales.   250

Emily Dickinson

(1830–1886)

·········

EMILY DICKINSON was the daughter of a prominent citizen
of Amherst, Massachusetts, the treasurer of Amherst College, and a United
States Congressman for two terms. She was educated at Mount Holyoke
Female Seminary and Amherst Institute. When she was twenty-three she
visited her father in Washington, and enroute home met in Philadelphia
a minister named Charles Wadsworth, a very effective preacher and a

dynamic personality. Although he was married and she saw him only three times, it seems clear that he figured strongly in her thoughts for many years. Only four of Miss Dickinson's poems were published during her lifetime. She led a secluded life in the family home in Amherst. Her first volume was published in 1890 and went through a number of editions, but then her work was neglected for another generation. In 1924 three volumes of letters and further poems were published, and since that time her reputation has grown steadily.

Suggested Readings

ALLEN TATE, "Emily Dickinson," in *Reactionary Essays*. New York: Charles Scribner's Sons, 1936, pp. 3–26.

R. E. SPILLER, *et al.*, eds., *Literary History of the United States,* New York: The Macmillan Company, 1948, II, 899–916.

· · · · · · · · · ·

The Chariot

Because I could not stop for Death,
He kindly stopped for me;
The carriage held but just ourselves
And Immortality.

[handwritten: quickness of motion]

We slowly drove, he knew no haste,
And I had put away
My labour, and my leisure too, *[handwritten: work   free time]*
For his civility. *[handwritten: politeness]*

We passed the school where children played
Their lessons scarcely done;
We passed the fields of gazing grain,
We passed the setting sun.

We paused before a house that seemed
A swelling on the ground;
The roof was scarcely visible,
The cornice but a mound.

Since then 'tis centuries; but each
Feels shorter than the day
I first surmised the horses' heads
Were toward eternity.

548

I Heard A Fly Buzz When I Died

I heard a Fly buzz – when I died –
The Stillness in the Room
Was like the Stillness in the Air –
Between the Heaves of Storm –

The Eyes around – had wrung them dry –
And Breaths were gathering firm

For that last onset, when the king
   Be witnessed in his power.

I willed my keepsakes, signed away
   What portion of me I
Could make assignable,—and then
   There interposed a fly,

With blue, uncertain, stumbling buzz,
   Between the light and me;
And then the windows failed, and then
   I could not see to see.

■ 1. What is it that the fly symbolizes? What is the effect of juxtaposing the death scene with the description of the fly?
   2. What is the effect of the double use of the word "see" in the final line?

A Light Exists in Spring [1]

A light exists in spring
Nor present in the year
At any other period.
When March is scarcely here

A color stands abroad
On solitary hills
That science cannot overtake,
But human nature feels.

It waits upon the lawn;
It shows the furthest tree
Upon the furthest slope we know;
It almost speaks to me.

Then, as horizons step,
Or noons report away,
Without the formula of sound,
It passes, and we stay:

A quality of loss
Affecting our content,

As trade had suddenly encroached
Upon a sacrament.

■ 1. Explain the various figures in the poem.
   2. Compare the "lyric structure" of this poem with the structure
of Herrick's "A Mad Maid's Song" (p. 144).

As Imperceptibly as Grief

As imperceptibly as grief
The Summer lapsed away,—
Too imperceptible, at last,
To seem like perfidy.

A quietness distilled,
As twilight long begun,
Or Nature, spending with herself
Sequestered afternoon.

The dusk drew earlier in,
The morning foreign shone,—
A courteous, yet harrowing grace,
As guest who would be gone.

And thus, without a wing,
Or service of a keel,
Our summer made her light escape
Into the beautiful.

■ Paraphrase this poem carefully, line by line.

There's a Certain Slant of Light

There's a certain slant of light,
On winter afternoons,
That oppresses, like the weight
Of cathedral tunes.

Heavenly hurt it gives us;
We can find no scar,
But internal difference
Where the meanings are.

None may teach it anything,
'Tis the seal, despair,—
An imperial affliction
Sent us of the air.

When it comes, the landscape listens,
Shadows hold their breath;
When it goes, 'tis like the distance
On the look of death.

■ 1. What is the meaning of "Heavenly hurt"?
   2. Comment on the syntax and the diction of this poem. Compare it, in these terms, with Poe's "Dream-Land" (p. 464).

The Brain Is Wider Than the Sky [1]

The brain is wider than the sky,
    For, put them side by side,
The one the other will include
    With ease, and you beside.

The brain is deeper than the sea,
    For, hold them, blue to blue,
The one the other will absorb,
    As sponges, buckets do.

The brain is just the weight of God,
    For, lift them, pound for pound,
And they will differ, if they do,
    As syllable from sound.

■ Explain the essential paradox on which this poem is built.

....

Algernon Charles Swinburne
(1837–1909)

■■■■■■■■■■

A LONDONER, educated at Eton and Oxford, Algernon Charles Swinburne was a brilliant, unstable man whose poetic interests were counterbalanced in his youth by his radical leanings in politics and philosophy. Although he had published two dramas as early as 1860, it was not until 1866, upon the publication of the first series of *Poems and Ballads*, that the reviewers, notably John Morley, attacked Swinburne as the "laureate of libidinousness and the apostle of despair." They thus created the notoriety which drove Swinburne farther into his "Art for Art's sake" position. Swinburne's literary tastes led him to write the tribute to Baudelaire *Ave atque Vale* (1867), an elegiac poem of great beauty, and a prose criticism of William Blake (1868), which is a pioneer work in the study of that poet. On the other hand, Swinburne's continuing passion for political liberty engaged him, as it had many English poets before him, in the cause of Italian independence. For this cause he wrote *A Song of Italy* (1867) and *Songs before Sunrise* (1871). The defeat of Italian libertarian hopes disillusioned Swinburne and led him at last into a conservative political position. In 1879, to recover from a serious illness brought on by alcoholism, Swinburne went to live with W. T. Watts at Putney. Under Watts's influence he became more reactionary politically and wrote a kind of nature poetry not particularly suited to his talents. He also completed several closet dramas of rather melodramatic quality. The bulk of Swinburne's writings is considerable, for he wrote much literary criticism as well as poetry and poetic drama.

Suggested Readings

T. S. ELIOT, "Swinburne as Poet," in *Selected Essays*. New York: Harcourt Brace and Co., 1932.

SAMUEL C. CHEW, "Algernon Charles Swinburne," in *A Literary History of England*, ed. by Albert C. Baugh. New York: Appleton-Century Crofts, Inc., 1948.

■■■■■■■■■■

When the Hounds of Spring [1]

When the hounds of spring are on winter's traces,
 The mother of months in meadow or plain
Fills the shadows and windy places
 With lisp of leaves and ripple of rain;
And the brown bright nightingale amorous
Is half assuaged for Itylus,
For the Thracian ships and the foreign faces,
 The tongueless vigil, and all the pain.

Come with bows bent and with emptying of quivers,
 Maiden most perfect, lady of light,   10
With a noise of winds and many rivers,
 With a clamor of waters, and with might;
Bind on thy sandals, O thou most fleet,
Over the splendor and speed of thy feet;
For the faint east quickens, the wan west shivers,
 Round the feet of the day and the feet of the night.

Where shall we find her, how shall we sing to her,
 Fold our hands round her knees, and cling?
Oh, that man's heart were as fire and could spring to her,
 Fire, or the strength of the streams that spring!   20
For the stars and the winds are unto her
As raiment, as songs of the harp-player;
For the risen stars and the fallen cling to her,
 And the southwest-wind and the west-wind sing.

For winter's rains and ruins are over,
 And all the season of snows and sins;
The days dividing lover and lover,
 The light that loses, the night that wins;
And time remembered is grief forgotten,
And frosts are slain and flowers begotten,   30
And in green underwood and cover
 Blossom by blossom the spring begins.

The full streams feed on flower of rushes,
 Ripe grasses trammel a traveling foot,
The faint fresh flame of the young year flushes
 From leaf to flower and flower to fruit;
And fruit and leaf are as gold and fire,

. From *Atalanta in Calydon.*

And the oat is heard above the lyre,
And the hoofèd heel of a satyr crushes
   The chestnut-husk at the chestnut-root.   40

And Pan by noon and Bacchus by night,
   Fleeter of foot than the fleet-foot kid,
Follows with dancing and fills with delight
   The Maenad and the Bassarid;
And soft as lips that laugh and hide
The laughing leaves of the trees divide,
And screen from seeing and leave in sight
   The god pursuing, the maiden hid.

The ivy falls with the Bacchanal's hair
   Over her eyebrows hiding her eyes;   50
The wild vine slipping down leaves bare
   Her bright breast shortening into sighs;
The wild vine slips with the weight of its leaves,
But the berried ivy catches and cleaves
To the limbs that glitter, the feet that scare
   The wolf that follows, the fawn that flies.

One of the keys to Swinburne's poetry is his interest in words for their own sake. Perhaps we should say that he was interested in words, not because they can point up a meaning, but because they can contribute to a dream-world effect of luminousness, glitter, and dazzle.

A number of critics have spoken of the tendency of poets in the Victorian world to write as though they lived in and were trying to create an emotional mist. Arthur O'Shaughnessy, a few years younger than Swinburne, wrote the following lines, which must have seemed the ideal toward which many poets were striving:

We are the music-makers,
   And we are the dreamers of dreams,
Wandering by lone sea-breakers,
   And sitting by desolate streams;
World-losers and world-forsakers,
   On whom the pale moon gleams.

Swinburne was a far abler poet than O'Shaughnessy, but he too seems to have thought of the poet as a dreamer. William Butler Yeats as a young man in the late Victorian world said, "All art is dream." Dante Gabriel Rossetti and Christina Rossetti, with many others, wrote in a somewhat similar manner.

In reading Swinburne one is often at a loss to know just what i being said. We have elsewhere indicated that a given word in any poem can have several connotations, each of which contributes to the meaning. Usually there is a primary meaning which the connotative meanings either supplement or qualify. (See, for example, the discussion of William Carlos Williams' "The Yachts.") This use of multiple meanings has been labeled *ambiguity*. In Swinburne we often find it difficult to tell which, if any, meaning is primary and which is secondary. Consider, for example, the italicized words in the following passage:

> When the hounds of spring are on winter's *traces*
> > *The mother of months* in meadow or plain
> Fills the shadows and windy places
> > With lisp of leaves and ripple of rain.

The word "traces" suggests *reins* (the hounds drawing winter away) and *remains* (the patches of snow or dirt from winter). Neither seems to dominate the meaning. The phrase "mother of months" is difficult to understand with any precision; it might be the year, or spring, or Artemis (the goddess of the moon, the seasons, earth, fruitfulness, and so on), or change, or time. Again there is no dominant or primary meaning.

We are not able to visualize the "hounds of spring" because we are not sure of their connection with "winter's traces." We might, in order to emphasize the way in which a poet may effectively evoke visual images, quote from the hunting scene in *A Midsummer Night's Dream*:

> My hounds are bred out of the Spartan kind,
> So flew'd, so sanded, and their heads are hung
> With ears that sweep away the morning dew;
> Crook-knee'd and dew-lapped like Thessalian bulls;
> Slow in pursuit, but match'd in mouth like bells,
> Each under each.

Hounds might seem a commonplace, unromantic sort of subject matter for a poet. The subject, however, suggested images and associations to Shakespeare that enabled him to write of them in such a way that we see them, hear them, and accept the contagion of their excitement. There can, of course, be effective lines in poetry that are not visual. Here we may look at two lines by T. S. Eliot:

> The awful daring of a moment's surrender
> Which an age of prudence can never retract.

The conflict between "moment's surrender" and "age of prudence" dramatizes an idea. Even though there is no specific image to be visualized, one understands the nature of the conflict.) Swinburne's line is neither dramatic nor visual. We cannot understand the intention of the line, and the image dissolves as we try to perceive its significance.

Some of the lines are not very meaningful. This, for example, does not seem, in terms of the poem, to make sense at all: "And time remembered is grief forgotten." Or this: "The full streams feed on flower of rushes." Such lines have an air or tone of meaningfulness, but they do not make a coherent statement, however much we may try to discover their significance. The poem itself, echoing though it does the Greek legends of Philomela, Pan, and Bacchus, does not make a clear statement. The meaning is vague, and the associations aroused are dim and blurred. The usual effect of Swinburne's poetry is a *feeling*, not an *idea* strongly *felt*.

Since feelings cannot exist without a cause, one may suggest at least two general reasons for the feelings one experiences on reading Swinburne. First, the manner in which the lines are expressed is impressive, as though tremendous statements were being made. Their very vagueness suggests a wisdom that is above the commonplace and therefore not readily perceived. Secondly, the language is consciously rich, with such poetic devices as internal rhyme ("brown bright nightingale"), alliteration ("The faint fresh flame of the young year flushes"), and the consciously musical rhythms. T. S. Eliot has said that Swinburne, in such a poem as the one under discussion, does not communicate in the usual sense, that he creates a "state of mind—the state of mind of a dreamer. The value of that state of mind is, of course, another question." The point, then, is that frequently Swinburne consciously used techniques that enabled him to create a diffuse, vague language. He managed to employ words that seem to, but actually do not, evoke images, and to make statements that seem to say more than they do. Almost of necessity one must admire Swinburne's genius for language. It does not follow that one should admire the uses to which he put his genius.

Before the Beginning of Years

Before the beginning of years
  There came to the making of man
Time, with a gift of tears;
  Grief, with a glass that ran;
Pleasure, with pain for leaven;
  Summer, with flowers that fell;
Remembrance fallen from heaven,
  And madness risen from hell;

Strength without hands to smite;
　　Love that endures for a breath;   10
Night, the shadow of light,
　　And life, the shadow of death.

And the high gods took in hand
　　Fire, and the falling of tears,
And a measure of sliding sand
　　From under the feet of the years;
And froth and drift of the sea;
　　And dust of the laboring earth;
And bodies of things to be
　　In the houses of death and of birth;   20
And wrought with weeping and laughter,
　　And fashioned with loathing and love,
With life before and after
　　And death beneath and above,
For a day and a night and a morrow,
　　That his strength might endure for a span
With travail and heavy sorrow,
　　The holy spirit of man.

From the winds of the north and the south
　　They gathered as unto strife;   30
They breathed upon his mouth,
　　They filled his body with life;
Eyesight and speech they wrought
　　For the veils of the soul therein,
A time for labor and thought,
　　A time to serve and to sin;
They gave him light in his ways,
　　And love, and a space for delight,
And beauty and length of days,
　　And night, and sleep in the night.   40
His speech is a burning fire;
　　With his lips he travaileth;
In his heart is a blind desire,
　　In his eyes foreknowledge of death;
He weaves, and is clothed with derision;
　　Sows, and he shall not reap;
His life is a watch or a vision
　　Between a sleep and a sleep.

Are any of the critical comments made about "When the Hounds
f Spring" relevant to this poem? Answer in some detail.

A Forsaken Garden

In a coign of the cliff between lowland and highland,
    At the sea-down's edge between windward and lee,
Walled round with rocks as an inland island,
    The ghost of a garden fronts the sea.
A girdle of brushwood and thorn encloses
    The steep square slope of the blossomless bed
Where the weeds that grew green from the graves of its roses
    Now lie dead.

The fields fall southward, abrupt and broken,
    To the low last edge of the long lone land.   10
If a step should sound or a word be spoken,
    Would a ghost not rise at the strange guest's hand?
So long have the gray bare walks lain guestless,
    Through branches and briers if a man make way,
He shall find no life but the sea-wind's, restless
    Night and day.

The dense hard passage is blind and stifled
    That crawls by a track none turn to climb
To the strait waste place that the years have rifled
    Of all but the thorns that are touched not of time.   20
The thorns he spares when the rose is taken;
    The rocks are left when he wastes the plain;
The wind that wanders, the weeds wind-shaken,
    These remain.

Not a flower to be pressed of the foot that falls not;
    As the heart of a dead man the seed-plots are dry;
From the thicket of thorns whence the nightingale calls not,
    Could she call, there were never a rose to reply.
Over the meadows that blossom and wither,
    Rings but the note of a sea-bird's song;   30
Only the sun and the rain come hither
    All year long.

The sun burns sear, and the rain dishevels
    One gaunt bleak blossom of scentless breath.
Only the wind here hovers and revels,
    In a round where life seems barren as death.
Here there was laughing of old, there was weeping,
    Haply, of lovers none ever will know,

Whose eyes went seaward a hundred sleeping
    Years ago.   40

Heart handfast in heart as they stood, "Look thither,"
    Did he whisper? "Look forth from the flowers to the sea;
For the foamflowers endure when the rose-blossoms wither,
    And men that love lightly may die—but we?"
And the same wind sang, and the same waves whitened,
    And or ever the garden's last petals were shed,
In the lips that had whispered, the eyes that had lightened,
    Love was dead.

Or they loved their life through, and then went whither?
    And were one to the end—but what end who knows?   50
Love deep as the sea as a rose must wither,
    As the rose-red seaweed that mocks the rose.
Shall the dead take thought for the dead to love them?
    What love was ever as deep as a grave?
They are loveless now as the grass above them
    Or the wave.

All are at one now, roses and lovers,
    Not known of the cliffs and the fields and the sea.
Not a breath of the time that has been hovers
    In the air now soft with a summer to be.   60
Not a breath shall there sweeten the seasons hereafter
    Of the flowers or the lovers that laugh now or weep,
When as they that are free now of weeping and laughter
    We shall sleep.

Here death may deal not again forever;
    Here change may come not till all change end.
From the graves they have made they shall rise up never,
    Who have left naught living to ravage and rend.
Earth, stones, and thorns of the wild ground growing,
    While the sun and the rain live, these shall be;   70
Till a last wind's breath, upon all these blowing,
    Roll the sea.

Till the slow sea rise, and the sheer cliff crumble,
    Till terrace and meadow the deep gulfs drink,
Till the strength of the waves of the high tides humble
    The fields that lessen, the rocks that shrink,
Here now in his triumph where all things falter,

Stretched out on the spoils that his own hands spread
   As a god self-slain on his own strange altar,
      Death lies dead.

■   1. State the theme of the poem.
   2. Does the detail (the imagery, the diction, rhythms, and so on)
cause you, as the reader, to feel or sense any dread or terror of death?

The Garden of Proserpine

Here, where the world is quiet;
   Here, where all trouble seems
Dead winds' and spent waves' riot
   In doubtful dreams of dreams;
I watch the green field growing
For reaping folk and sowing
For harvest-time and mowing,
   A sleepy world of streams.

I am tired of tears and laughter,
   And men that laugh and weep;   10
Of what may come hereafter
   For men that sow to reap;
I am weary of days and hours,
Blown buds of barren flowers,
Desires and dreams and powers
   And everything but sleep.

Here life has death for neighbor,
   And far from eye or ear
Wan waves and wet winds labor,
   Weak ships and spirits steer;   20
They drive adrift, and whither
They wot not who make thither;
But no such winds blow hither,
   And no such things grow here.

No growth of moor or coppice,
   No heather-flower or vine,
But bloomless buds of poppies,
   Green grapes of Proserpine,
Pale beds of blowing rushes,
Where no leaf blooms or blushes   30
Save this whereout she crushes
   For dead men deadly wine.

Pale, without name or number,
  In fruitless fields of corn,
They bow themselves and slumber
  All night till light is born;
And like a soul belated,
In hell and heaven unmated,
By cloud and mist abated
  Comes out of darkness morn.   40

Though one were strong as seven,
  He too with death shall dwell,
Nor wake with wings in heaven,
  Nor weep for pains in hell;
Though one were fair as roses,
His beauty clouds and closes;
And well though love reposes,
  In the end it is not well.

Pale, beyond porch and portal,
  Crowned with calm leaves, she stands   50
Who gathers all things mortal
  With cold immortal hands;
Her languid lips are sweeter
Than love's who fears to greet her
To men that mix and meet her
  From many times and lands.

She waits for each and other,
  She waits for all men born;
Forgets the earth her mother,
  The life of fruits and corn;   60
And spring and seed and swallow
Take wing for her and follow
Where summer song rings hollow
  And flowers are put to scorn.

There go the loves that wither,
  The old loves with wearier wings;
And all dead years draw thither,
  And all disastrous things;
Dead dreams of days forsaken,
Blind buds that snows have shaken,   70
Wild leaves that winds have taken,
  Red strays of ruined springs.

We are not sure of sorrow,
  And joy was never sure;
Today will die tomorrow;
  Time stoops to no man's lure;
And love, grown faint and fretful,
With lips but half regretful
Sighs, and with eyes forgetful
  Weeps that no loves endure.   80

From too much love of living,
  From hope and fear set free,
We thank with brief thanksgiving
  Whatever gods may be
That no life lives forever;
That dead men rise up never;
That even the weariest river
  Winds somewhere safe to sea.

Then star nor sun shall waken,
  Nor any change of light;   90
Nor sound of waters shaken,
  Nor any sound or sight;
Nor wintry leaves nor vernal,
Nor days nor things diurnal—
Only the sleep eternal
  In an eternal night.

■   1. State the theme of this poem.
    2. Compare the theme and the effectiveness of the way it is
stated (imagery, diction, rhythm, and so on) with the theme and statement of "A Forsaken Garden."

In Memory of Walter Savage Landor

Back to the flower-town, side by side,
  The bright months bring,
Newborn, the bridegroom and the bride,
  Freedom and spring.

The sweet land laughs from sea to sea,
  Filled full of sun;
All things come back to her, being free;
  All things but one.

In many a tender wheaten plot
   Flowers that were dead   10
Live, and old suns revive; but not
   That holier head.

By this white wandering waste of sea,
   Far north, I hear
One face shall never turn to me
   As once this year—

Shall never smile and turn and rest
   On mine as there,
Nor one most sacred hand be pressed
   Upon my hair.   20

I came as one whose thoughts half linger,
   Half run before;
The youngest to the oldest singer
   That England bore.

I found him whom I shall not find
   Till all grief end,
In holiest age our mightiest mind,
   Father and friend.

But thou, if anything endure,
   If hope there be,   30
O spirit that man's life left pure,
   Man's death set free,

Not with disdain of days that were
   Look earthward now;
Let dreams revive the reverend hair,
   The imperial brow;

Come back in sleep, for in the life
   Where thou art not
We find none like thee. Time and strife
   And the world's lot   40

Move thee no more; but love at least
   And reverent heart
May move thee, royal and released,
   Soul, as thou art.

And thou, his Florence, to try trust
   Receive and keep,
Keep safe his dedicated dust,
   His sacred sleep.

So shall thy lovers, come from far,
   Mix with thy name   50
As morning star with evening star
   His faultless fame.

■ Is the detail and manner of this poem appropriate to its subject
matter?

Nephelidia

From the depth of the dreamy decline of the dawn through a notable
   nimbus of nebulous noonshine,
   Pallid and pink as the palm of the flag-flower that flickers with fear of
      the flies as they float,
Are they looks of our lovers that lustrously lean from a marvel of mystic
   miraculous moonshine,
   These that we feel in the blood of our blushes that thicken and
      threaten with throbs through the throat?
Thicken and thrill as a theatre thronged at appeal of an actor's appalled
   agitation,
   Fainter with fear of the fires of the future than pale with the promise
      of pride in the past;
Flushed with the famishing fullness of fever that reddens with radiance
   of rathe recreation,
   Gaunt as the ghastliest of glimpses that gleam through the gloom of
      the gloaming when ghosts go aghast?
Nay, for the nick of the tick of the time is a tremulous touch on the
   temples of terror,
   Strained as the sinews yet strenuous with strife of the dead who is
      dumb as the dust-heaps of death;   10
Surely no soul is it, sweet as the spasm of erotic emotional exquisite
   error,
   Bathed in the balms of beatified bliss, beatific itself by beatitude's
      breath.
Surely no spirit or sense of a soul that was soft to the spirit and soul of
   our senses
   Sweetens the stress of suspiring suspicion that sobs in the semblance
      and sound of a sigh;

Only this oracle opens Olympian, in mystical moods and triangular
    tenses—
    "Life is the lust of a lamp for the light that is dark till the dawn of
      the day when we die."
Mild is the mirk and monotonous music of memory, melodiously mute
    as it may be,
    While the hope in the heart of a hero is bruised by the breach of
      men's rapiers, resigned to the rod;
Made meek as a mother whose bosom-beats bound with the bliss-
    bringing bulk of a balm-breathing baby,
    As they grope through the graveyard of creeds, under skies growing
      green at a groan for the grimness of God.   20
Blank is the book of his bounty beholden of old, and its binding is
    blacker than bluer;
    Out of blue into black is the scheme of the skies, and their dews are
      the wine of the bloodshed of things;
Till the darkling desire of delight shall be free as a fawn that is freed
    from the fangs that pursue her,
    Till the heartbeats of hell shall be hushed by a hymn from the hunt
      that has harried the kennel of kings.

1. Is Swinburne parodying his own style here? In what way does a parody allow you to understand or feel the distinctive qualities and characteristics of a poet's work?

2. The title of this poem means "cloudlets." Is the title related to the subject matter and development of the poem?

Thomas Hardy

(1840–1928)

■ ■ ■ ■ ■ ■ ■ ■

HARDY WAS BORN in Dorsetshire, was educated in a somewhat irregular manner, and was apprenticed to an architect for six years before definitely turning to writing in 1865. Hardy's peculiar quality, both in his fiction and his poetry, frequently depends upon the irony which derives from the disparity between chance and human will. Because of his views Hardy was often attacked by his contemporaries. *Jude the Obscure* (1896), for example, was banned from circulating libraries and was publicly burned by a clergyman. Thereafter Hardy turned largely to writing poetry. *Collected Poems* appeared in 1919 and was followed by *Poetical*

Works of Thomas Hardy, 1920–1924 and *Winter Words in Various Moods and Metres* in 1928.

Suggested Readings

A special Hardy issue of the *Southern Review* in Summer, 1940, Vol. I, No. 1. Especially interesting for students of Hardy's poetry are the articles by Blackmur, Ransom, Zabel, and Schwartz.

■■■■■■■■■■

It is almost a rule that historical accounts of modern poetry and chronological groupings of modern poets should begin with Thomas Hardy. This practice is justified for more reasons than the fact that Hardy was born before the middle of the nineteenth century and continued to write poetry well into the modern period. His poetry, including much that was written before 1900, stands in sharp contrast to that of Tennyson, Browning, Arnold, and Swinburne.

While Hardy used traditional forms and meters with great versatility, he enlarged, like Wordsworth before him, the common ground existing between prose and poetry. In his work, even when it is decidedly lyrical, we do not find the smoothness of Tennyson, the vigorous rhythm of Browning, or the lilting musicality of Swinburne. Hardy' lyricism, even the quality of song, is often achieved in the manner of conversational or prosaic language. Sometimes the plainness of tone and the simplicity of statement are sufficiently striking to contribute a dramatic and lyrical quality. In "Nobody Comes" the line "It has nothing to do with me" is of this kind. Frequently the prosaic effect is produced not only by the diction and word order but by the irregularity of the meter. Each stanza of "Neutral Tones" (written in 1867) has three four-stress lines with a final three-stress line, and the recurring rhythm is felt from stanza to stanza, but most of the lines cannot be characterized by a single kind of metrical foot. Probably we can be no more precise in technical description than to say that the rhythm hovers between anapestic and iambic; that is, the rhythm approaches a prosaic irregularity. The prosaic (or conversational) quality results even when anapestic usually an impelling rhythm, is an apt description, as in the line "They had fallen from an ash, and were gray." The line

$$\overset{/}{\text{And}}\ \text{some}\ \overset{/}{\text{words}}\ \overset{/}{\text{played}}\ \overset{/}{\text{between}}\ \text{us}\ \overset{/}{\text{to}}\ \text{and}\ \text{fro}$$

is peculiarly illustrative. Out of its context, it seems to incline toward five stresses, as indicated. But in the poem it is read as a four-stress line

$$\overset{/}{\text{And}}\ \text{some}\ \overset{/}{\text{words}}\ \text{played}\ \overset{/}{\text{between}}\ \text{us}\ \overset{/}{\text{to}}\ \text{and}\ \text{fro,}$$

a reading which is closer to the inflection of the speaking voice.

Closely related to the conversational quality of the language is the special way in which Hardy's poems are at times dramatic. Many are dramatic in conventional ways, because they are narratives, or dialogues between two or more speakers. Some of them, however, are "spoken" by the poet or an implied character, and these are expressed with a realistic personal note and relate to a particular situation. For example, many of Hardy's poems are comparable in theme to Tennyson's "Break, Break, Break" and "Tears, Idle Tears," but Tennyson's poems are less dramatic in that they are not spoken from an immediate circumstantial and realistic situation. While personal poetry abounds in the nineteenth century, it usually has the quality of public statement. The personal but declamatory style is found in poems from Wordsworth through Arnold. The odes of Keats and Shelley are personal, but their drama is that of ritual, of public performance rather than that of immediate and particular experience.

A striking illustration of the way in which Hardy's "personal" poetry differs may be had by comparing "Neutral Tones" with Byron's "When We Two Parted." The poems are similar in subject, are spoken in first person singular, and are addressed by a man to a woman. But where Byron's poem is general, rhetorical, and declamatory, Hardy's is specific, conversational, and dramatic. These latter qualities do not necessarily make for superior poetry, but they are significant in that they place Hardy among the modern poets in contrast with those of the nineteenth century. Hardy differs in style from Eliot, Frost, and Auden, just as these poets differ among themselves; and yet all of them, including Hardy, differ in a common way from the prevailing rhetoric of the nineteenth century. Perhaps this difference may be indicated by observing that the rhetorical quality of modern poetry is closer to that of contemporary prose. (And, it might be added, contemporary prose is drier and less ornate than that of the nineteenth century.)

Critics of Hardy's poetry have been in general agreement about its defects and virtues. It is a common opinion that his word coinages, archaisms and grammatical inversions often appear to be stylistic eccentricities, although they are sometimes fresh and effective devices. Even more important in the critical comment has been the relationship between Hardy's poetry and his beliefs. He accepted the scientific account of the universe and of man's origin, and rejected traditional religious faith. Other poets, from Wordsworth and Blake on, struggled for optimistic or otherwise consoling interpretations of scientific "truth" or sought refuge from it in antirationalism or devotion to art, or they succumbed to melancholy. Hardy, however, took a positive satisfaction in his acceptance of scientific views and implications, but he also vehemently admitted that they were cheerless and unconsoling. For Hardy, the scientific account meant that life was meaningless, but he also insisted that man, by his nature, needs to find a meaning in life, and hence he arrived at an impressive and universal irony. Man must hope for what is hopeless.

This pattern of irony runs through much of Hardy's poetry, and in terms of it the success or failure of the poems has been measured. It seems that Hardy was so impressed with the irony and tragedy of the human predicament that he considered almost any general formulation or specific illustration of it to be effective and acceptable verse. Of almost nine hundred short poems, written over a span of sixty years, many are, in whole or in part, mechanical formulations of the ironical pattern. Reading through his poems, one finds endless repetitions of certain themes, such as human faithlessness, the irony of fate, the inevitability of misfortune, and the certainty of death and oblivion. As Blackmur has observed, the successful poems (and there are many) have the same themes but escape the mechanically applied *formula* and achieve a distinctive *form*.

The formula is apparent in "The Newcomer's Wife," even if one is not familiar with other Hardy poems that resemble it closely in theme and organization. The particular experience of the newcomer is obviously contrived to illustrate the general principle of irony. Through the first four stanzas, this poem, to use a phrase from "Neutral Tones," teaches the "lesson that love deceives." The lesson is wholly detachable from the particular experience, just as a moral is detachable from its didactic illustration. "Neutral Tones" contains the same lesson, but it has a far different poetic effect because the lesson is presented as dramatically experienced in particular details. The poetic effect of "Neutral Tones" derives, obviously, not from the lesson, but from the persuasiveness with which a human experience is presented— a persuasiveness which involves the total organization of many elements: images, rhythm, tone, theme, and the like. The final stanza of "The Newcomer's Wife" does, of course, produce an effect that is an addition to the lesson and the pointed irony—an effect that derives from the image in which the suicide is described. But the effective details of the image do not relieve the triteness of the language, the narrative coincidence, and the crude ironical contrast of the rest of the poem.

The poems by Thomas Hardy are from The Collected Poems of Thomas Hardy. *Reprinted with the permission of the publishers, The Macmillan Company, and The Macmillan Company of Canada Ltd.*

Neutral Tones

We stood by a pond that winter day,
And the sun was white, as though chidden of God,
And a few leaves lay on the starving sod;
    They had fallen from an ash, and were gray.

Your eyes on me were as eyes that rove
Over tedious riddles of years ago;
And some words played between us to and fro
    On which lost the more by our love.

The smile on your mouth was the deadest thing
Alive enough to have strength to die;
And a grin of bitterness swept thereby
    Like an ominous bird a-wing. . . .

Since then, keen lessons that love deceives,
And wrings with wrong, have shaped to me
Your face, and the God-curst sun, and a tree,
    And a pond edged with grayish leaves.

Nature's Questioning

When I look forth at dawning, pool,
    Field, flock, and lonely tree,
    All seem to gaze at me
Like chastened children sitting silent in a school;

Their faces dulled, constrained, and worn,
    As though the master's ways
    Through the long teaching days
Had cowed them till their early zest was overborne.

Upon them stirs in lippings mere
    (As if once clear in call,
    But now scarce breathed at all)—
"We wonder, ever wonder, why we find us here!

"Has some Vast Imbecility,
    Mighty to build and blend,
    But impotent to tend,
Framed us in jest, and left us now to hazardry?

"Or come we of an Automaton
    Unconscious of our pains? . . .
    Or are we live remains
Of Godhead dying downwards, brain and eye now gone?

"Or is it that some high Plan betides,
    As yet not understood,

Of Evil stormed by Good,
We the Forlorn Hope over which Achievement strides?"

Thus things around. No answerer I . . .
        Meanwhile the winds, and rains,
        And Earth's old glooms and pains
Are still the same, and Life and Death are neighbours nigh.

■   1. Would a familiarity with the romantic concept of nature be
relevant for a reading of this poem? (See the chapter on Hardy in
Joseph Warren Beach's *The Concept of Nature in Nineteenth Century
English Poetry*, pp. 503–527.)

2. Analyze the metaphor in the last two lines of the fifth stanza.
How successful is the integration of Hardy's beliefs and other materials in the poem? (See Allen Tate's "Hardy's Philosophic Metaphors,"
in *On the Limits of Poetry*, pp. 185–196, or in *The Southern Review*,
VI [Summer, 1940], 99–108.)

Channel Firing

That night your great guns, unawares,
Shook all our coffins as we lay,
And broke the chancel window-squares,
We thought it was the Judgment-day

And sat upright. While drearisome
Arose the howl of wakened hounds:
The mouse let fall the altar-crumb,
The worms drew back into the mounds,

The glebe cow drooled. Till God Called, "No;
It's gunnery practice out at sea   10
Just as before you went below;
The world is as it used to be:

"All nations striving strong to make
Red war yet redder. Mad as hatters
They do no more for Christés sake
Than you who are helpless in such matters.

"That this is not the judgment-hour
For some of them's a blessed thing,
For if it were they'd have to scour
Hell's floor for so much threatening. . . .   20

"Ha, ha. It will be warmer when
I blow the trumpet (if indeed
I ever do; for you are men,
And rest eternal sorely need)."

So down we lay again. "I wonder,
Will the world ever saner be,"
Said one, "than when He sent us under
In our indifferent century!"

And many a skeleton shook his head.
"Instead of preaching forty year,"
My neighbour Parson Thirdly said,   30
"I wish I had stuck to pipes and beer."

Again the guns disturbed the hour,
Roaring their readiness to avenge,
As far inland as Stourton Tower,
And Camelot, and starlit Stonehenge.

1. What is the relationship between the tone of the poem, particularly of the language used by God, and its implausibility?

2. Assume first that the poem ends before the final stanza, and then consider what the final stanza contributes to the development of the poem.

The Newcomer's Wife

He paused on the sill of a door ajar
That screened a lively liquor-bar,
For the name had reached him through the door
Of her he had married the week before.

"We called her the Hack of the Parade;
But she was discreet in the games she played;
If slightly worn, she's pretty yet,
And gossips, after all, forget:

"And he knows nothing of her past;
I am glad the girl's in luck at last;
Such ones, though stale to native eyes,
Newcomers snatch at as a prize."

"Yes, being a stranger he sees her blent
Of all that's fresh and innocent,

Nor dreams how many a love-campaign
She had enjoyed before his reign!"

That night there was the splash of a fall
Over the slimy harbour-wall:
They searched, and at the deepest place
Found him with crabs upon his face.

Last Words to a Dumb Friend

Pet was never mourned as you,
Purrer of the spotless hue,
Plumy tail, and wistful gaze
While you humoured our queer ways,
Or outshrilled your morning call
Up the stairs and through the hall—
Foot suspended in its fall—
While, expectant, you would stand
Arched, to meet the stroking hand;
Till your way you chose to wend   10
Yonder, to your tragic end.

Never another pet for me!
Let your place all vacant be;
Better blankness day by day
Than companion torn away.
Better bid his memory fade,
Better blot each mark he made,
Selfishly escape distress
By contrived forgetfulness,
Than preserve his prints to make   20
Every morn and eve an ache.

From the chair whereon he sat
Sweep his fur, nor wince thereat;
Rake his little pathways out
Mid the bushes roundabout;
Smooth away his talons' mark
From the claw-worn pine-tree bark,
Where he climbed as dusk embrowned,
Waiting us who loitered round.

Strange it is this speechless thing,   30
Subject to our mastering,

Subject for his life and food
To our gift, and time, and mood;
Timid pensioner of us Powers,
His existence ruled by ours,
Should—by crossing at a breath
Into safe and shielded death,
By the merely taking hence
Of his insignificance—
Loom as largened to the sense,   40
Shape as part, above man's will,
Of the Imperturbable.

As a prisoner, flight debarred,
Exercising in a yard,
Still retain I, troubled, shaken,
Mean estate, by him forsaken;
And this home, which scarcely took
Impress from his little look,
By his faring to the Dim
Grows all eloquent of him.   50

Housemate, I can think you still
Bounding to the window-sill,
Over which I vaguely see
Your small mound beneath the tree,
Showing in the autumn shade
That you moulder where you played.

■ 1. We might readily expect a poem on the death of a cat to sound
sentimental or insincere. Does this poem avoid such a sound, that is,
tone?

2. Consider the strategy by which visual, emotional, and reflective
materials are combined in the last six lines.

Nobody Comes

Tree-leaves labour up and down,
  And through them the fainting light
  Succumbs to the crawl of night.
Outside in the road the telegraph wire
  To the town from the darkening land
Intones to travellers like a spectral lyre
  Swept by a spectral hand.

A car comes up, with lamps full-glare,
That flash upon a tree:
It has nothing to do with me,
And whangs along in a world of its own,
Leaving a blacker air;
And mute by the gate I stand again alone,
And nobody pulls up there.

■   "Nobody Comes" is in some respects one of the simplest of Hardy's poems. A number of them involve the loneliness of old age or of disappointed love or of the mind that does not share common beliefs. Some involve grief for the dead, or man's predicament in a universe that is not adequate to his needs. In such poems the situations or attitudes which produce the loneliness are often given a central development or a strong emphasis, sometimes with entire success, and sometimes with such crudeness of irony and mechanical contrast that they mar the poem. But in "Nobody Comes" the loneliness is of the simplest kind— physical isolation. Despite the simplicity, however, the poem has subtleties and complexities which are lacking in poems of a more formidable intention. It is one of the poems which Blackmur would probably class among those that are not "violated" by any of Hardy's favorite ideas, and in which his sensibility was allowed to operate successfully.

Like so many of Hardy's poems, this one is dramatic in the sense that it is the utterance of an individual speaker—the first person singular is used. The poem may actually be personal with respect to the poet, but for this poem that is not important. Although there is no direct reference to the speaker in the first stanza, his existence is implied. For example, the light seen through the leaves, the road being "outside," and the telegraph wire leading "*to* the town"—all these details suggest the physical point of view from which the scene is being described. Consequently, the sensibility for which the scene produces an atmosphere attaches to an individual point of view, rather than to the anonymous and unplaced voice that speaks in some poems. The atmosphere *felt* is, of course, rendered by such words descriptive of sensibility as "labour," "fainting," "succumbs," and "crawl," and by the spectral image in which the telegraph wire is involved.

The point of view—that is, the individual speaking—becomes more precisely defined in terms of location and sensibility as the poem progresses. After the opening lines of the second stanza, the picture of the car's headlights on the tree, the speaker is directly introduced for the first time, with the line "It has nothing to do with me." Thus, for the first time, the note of loneliness is clearly introduced. In the closing lines of the poem the speaker's specific location is given, "by the gate"; and the sense of loneliness is confirmed by the word "alone" and by the statement of the last line.

This development, which moves toward an increasingly clear focus on the physical and psychological isolation of the speaker, is only one part of the poem's organization. The descriptive details function, in addition to their circumstantial reference, with symbolic reference to the theme of loneliness. Throughout the poem, the speaker's isolation (or loneliness) is symbolized by darkness, inactivity, and silence, and it is pointedly in contrast to its opposite—society or comradeship—for which the symbols are light, activity, and sound. The steady development toward a final clear image of isolation begins with the change from day to night. As we noticed above, the quality of the speaker's *felt* environment is expressed in the words "labour," "fainting," "succumbs," and "crawl." These are generally thought of as action words, but their action, in keeping with the speaker's attitude and the prevailing symbolism of the poem, is difficult, failing, and slow; it is negative compared to that of "intones" and "swept," later in the stanza.

The telegraph wire has a richly symbolic function. Although the eerie, spectral image in which it is presented is appropriate to the speaker's physical and emotional perspective, it involves a number of countersymbols. For example, the "darkening land" is identifiable with the speaker's loneliness, but the town to which the wire leads suggests human society, where there is light, activity, and sound. While the wire is, for the speaker, comparable in appearance and activity to a "spectral lyre," it intones not to him but to travelers. This intonation suggests, moreover, not only the sound which the wire makes in vibrating to the motions of the air, but the more spectral, inaudible *sound* of the communications which it conveys—again, *not* to the speaker. Thus the wire is spectral not only by its quality as a visual and auditory image but by its remoteness, since it symbolizes (and serves) an activity which is in contrast to the speaker's isolation.

The pattern of symbol and countersymbol becomes more explicit in the second stanza. The car, prepared for by "road" and "travellers" earlier in the poem, has "nothing to do" with the speaker. Unlike the tree in the glare of the lights, the speaker remains outside the scope of the car's activity. The person, or persons, inclosed by the car are not observed or mentioned. The car, speeding, lighted, and noisy, "whangs along in a world of its own," leaving the speaker in a world of *his* own. By emphatic contrast, he stands with an increased sense of isolation, in "a blacker air," "mute" and "alone." Just as the point of view emerges in a clear image of isolation, so do the descriptive details grow in symbolic meaning, until the final details are not only details of the scene but actually a statement of the meaning that has been emerging through the symbolic description.

The Darkling Thrush

I leant upon a coppice gate
    When Frost was specter-gray,
And Winter's dregs made desolate
    The weakening eye of day.
The tangled bine-stems scored the sky
    Like strings of broken lyres,
And all mankind that haunted nigh
    Had sought their household fires.

The land's sharp features seemed to be
    The Century's corpse outleant,   10
His crypt the cloudy canopy,
    The wind his death-lament.
The ancient pulse of germ and birth
    Was shrunken hard and dry,
And every spirit upon earth
    Seemed fervorless as I.

At once a voice arose among
    The bleak twigs overhead
In a full-hearted evensong
    Of joy illimited;   20
An aged thrush, frail, gaunt, and small,
    In blast-beruffled plume,
Had chosen thus to fling his soul
    Upon the growing gloom.

So little cause for carolings
    Of such ecstatic sound
Was written on terrestrial things
    Afar or nigh around,
That I could think there trembled through
    His happy good-night air   30
Some blessed Hope, whereof he knew
    And I was unaware.

William Butler Yeats

(1865–1939)

■■■■■■■■■■

W ILLIAM BUTLER YEATS was the son of the painter, John Butler Yeats. He was born in Dublin and in his early years was educated at home. He had three years of schooling in London during his family's residence there, and two additional years at Erasmus Smith High School in Dublin. But Yeats was a poor student and probably for this reason refused to follow the family custom of attending Trinity College, Dublin. All his life he was torn between his father's rationalism and skepticism and his mother's religiousness. He became an important figure in Irish literary movements, and much of his work has to be read in the light of his friendships with Irish contemporaries, both political and literary. He himself was a senator for four years. In a sense, Yeats is a transitional figure between the Victorian era and our own. His first book *Mosada: A Poem,* appeared in 1886. As a young man visiting or living for a period in London he belonged to the Rymer's Club, a group which included Arthus Symons, Oscar Wilde, and Ernest Dowson and which championed "art for art's sake." But gradually, especially because of his involvement with Irish politics and the Irish theater, he moved toward a literature with a more realistic psychology. He was also associated for a time with Ezra Pound, who had a strong influence on his critical principles. In 1923 he was awarded the Nobel Prize in Literature. His complete poetic works are available in *Collected Poems* (1951).

Suggested Readings

CLEANTH BROOKS, "Yeats: The Poet as Myth-Maker," in *Modern Poetry and the Tradition.* Chapel Hill: University of North Carolina Press, 1939. (Reprinted in Hall and Steinman, *The Permanence of Yeats.* New York: The Macmillan Company, 1950.)

EDMUND WILSON, "William Butler Yeats," in *Axel's Castle.* New York: Charles Scribner's Sons, 1931. (Also reprinted in *The Permanence of Yeats.*)

RICHARD ELLMAN, "Sailing to Byzantium," in *Yeats, the Man and the Masks.* New York: The Macmillan Company, 1948, pp. 240–256.

GRAHAM HOUGH, "Yeats," in *The Last Romantics.* London: Duckworth, 1949, pp. 216–262.

■■■■■■■■■■

The Song of the Happy Shepherd

The woods of Arcady are dead,
And over is their antique joy;
Of old the world on dreaming fed;
Grey Truth is now her painted toy;
But O, sick children of the world,
Of all the many changing things
In dreary dancing past us whirled,
To the old cracked tune that Chronos sings,
Words alone are certain good.
Where are now the warrior kings   10
Word be-mockers?—By the rood,
Where are now the old kings hoary?
They were of no wordy mood;
An idle word is now their glory,
By the stammering schoolboy said,
In the verse of Attic story
Chronicling chimaeras fled.
The very world itself may be
Only a sudden flaming word,
'Mid clanging space a moment heard   20
In the universe's reverie.
Then nowise worship dusty deeds,
Nor seek—for this also sooth—
To hunger fiercely after truth,
Lest all thy toiling only breeds
New dreams, new dreams; there is no truth
Saving in thine own heart. Seek, then,
No learning from the starry men,
Who follow with the optic glass
The whirling sways of stars that pass—   30
Seek then, for this is also sooth,
No word of theirs—the cold star-bane
Has torn and rent their hearts in twain,
And dead is all their human truth.
Go gather by the humming sea
Some twisted, echo-harboring shell,
And to its lips thy story tell,
And they thy comforters will be,
Rewording in melodious guile
Thy fretful words a little while,   40

Till they shall singing fade in ruth;
For ruth and joy have brotherhood,
And words alone are certain good.
Sing then, for this is also sooth.
I must be gone—there is a grave
Where daffodil and lily wave,
And downy bees have ambuscade,
And birdly iteration is
Through all the well-beloved glade.
Farewell! I must be gone I wis,   50
That I may soothe that hapless fawn
(Who's buried in the sleepy ground),
With mirthful songs till rise the dawn.
His shouting days with mirth were crowned,
And still I dream he treads the lawn,
Walking ghostly 'mong the dew,
Pierc'd by my glad singing through,
My songs of old earth's dreamy youth.
But ah! she dreams not now—dream thou!
For fair are poppies on the brow: 60
Dream, dream, for this is also sooth.

■ 1. Have you met the issue this poem attempts to face in earlier poets, especially in Blake and Coleridge? Explain.

2. Are the implications of the issue, the conflict between two kinds of truth, developed clearly? Consider the poet's treatment of "words," "dreams," and the "world."

In Memory of Major Robert Gregory

1

Now that we're almost settled in our house
I'll name the friends that cannot sup with us
Beside a fire of turf in th' ancient tower,
And having talked to some late hour
Climb up the narrow winding stair to bed:
Discoverers of forgotten truth
Or mere companions of my youth,
All, all are in my thoughts to-night being dead.

2

Always we'd have the new friend meet the old
And we are hurt if either friend seem cold,   10
And there is salt to lengthen out the smart

In the affections of our heart,
And quarrels are blown up upon that head;
But not a friend that I would bring
This night can set us quarreling,
For all that come into my mind are dead.

3

Lionel Johnson comes the first to mind,
That loved his learning better than mankind,
Though courteous to the worst; much falling he
Brooded upon sanctity   20
Till all his Greek and Latin learning seemed
A long blast upon the horn that brought
A little nearer to his thought
A measureless consummation that he dreamed.

4

And that enquiring man John Synge comes next,
That dying chose the living world for text
And never could have rested in the tomb
But that, long travelling, he had come
Towards nightfall upon certain set apart
In a most desolate stony place,
Towards nightfall upon a race
Passionate and simple like his heart.   30

5

And then I think of old George Pollexfen,
In muscular youth well known to Mayo men
For horsemanship at meets or at racecourses,
That could have shown how pure-bred horses
And solid men, for all their passion, live
But as the outrageous stars incline
By opposition, square and trine;
Having grown sluggish and contemplative.

6

They were my close companions many a year,
A portion of my mind and life, as it were,   40
And now their breathless faces seem to look
Out of some old picture-book;
I am accustomed to their lack of breath,
But not that my dear friend's dear son,
Our Sidney and our perfect man,
Could share in that discourtesy of death.

7

For all things the delighted eye now sees
Were loved by him: the old storm-broken trees
That cast their shadows upon road and bridge;
The tower set on the stream's edge;   50
The ford where drinking cattle make a stir
Nightly, and startled by that sound
The water-hen must change her ground;
He might have been your heartiest welcomer.

8

When with the Galway foxhounds he would ride
From Castle Taylor to the Roxborough side
Or Esserkelly plain, few kept his pace;
At Mooneen he had leaped a place
So perilous that half the astonished meet
Had shut their eyes; and where was it   60
He rode a race without a bit?
And yet his mind outran the horses' feet.

9

We dreamed that a great painter had been born
To cold Clare rock and Galway rock and thorn,
To that stern colour and that delicate line
That are our secret discipline
Wherein the gazing heart doubles her might.
Soldier, scholar, horseman, he,
And yet he had the intensity
To have published all to be a world's delight.   70

10

What other could so well have counselled us
In all lovely intricacies of a house
As he that practised or that understood
All work in metal or in wood,
In moulded plaster or in carven stone?
Soldier, scholar, horseman, he,
And all he did done perfectly
As though he had but that one trade alone.

11

Some burn damp faggots, others may consume
The entire combustible world in one small room   80
As though dried straw, and if we turn about
The bare chimney is gone black out

Because the work had finished in that flare.
Soldier, scholar, horseman, he,
As 'twere all life's epitome.
What made us dream that he could comb grey hair?

12

I had thought, seeing how bitter is that wind
That shakes the shutter, to have brought to mind
All those that manhood tried, or childhood loved
Or boyish intellect approved,   90
With some appropriate commentary on each;
Until imagination brought
A fitter welcome; but a thought
Of that late death took all my heart for speech.

The Second Coming

Turning and turning in the widening gyre
The falcon cannot hear the falconer;
Things fall apart; the centre cannot hold;
Mere anarchy is loosed upon the world,
The blood-dimmed tide is loosed, and everywhere
The ceremony of innocence is drowned;
The best lack all conviction, while the worst
Are full of passionate intensity.

Surely some revelation is at hand;
Surely the Second Coming is at hand.
The Second Coming! Hardly are those words out
When a vast image out of *Spiritus Mundi*
Troubles my sight: somewhere in sands of the desert
A shape with lion body and the head of a man,
A gaze blank and pitiless as the sun,
Is moving its slow thighs, while all about it
Reel shadows of the indignant desert birds.
The darkness drops again; but now I know
That twenty centuries of stony sleep
Were vexed to nightmare by a rocking cradle,
And what rough beast, its hour come round at last,
Slouches towards Bethlehem to be born?

■   If the reader of this poem knows something about Yeats's personal
beliefs and attitudes but does not happen to share them, he is likely to be
torn between two interpretations of this poem. Unlike most of his

contemporaries, Yeats was able to view a post-Christian world with a rather grim sense of satisfaction. (We may note the harsh irony of the title.) He held a cyclical view of history, in terms of which about every two thousand years an old civilization dies and a new one begins to take its place. The beginnings of the Christian era had meant painful destruction—the new belief had been "a fabulous, formless darkness" blotting out the beauties and rationality of the classical world. The poem is apocalyptic, a prophetic vision.*

For most readers, however, "The Second Coming" will seem to be concerned with the problem of belief, a problem fairly constant in the poetry of the nineteenth century. In Tennyson, Arnold, Clough, and Swinburne, for example, it is treated in terms of one's ability or inability to accept the supernatural order in Christian belief and its sanctions. Innocence is a Christian virtue. The symbols of Bethlehem, the rocking cradle, and the second coming are Christian. The image of the lion's body with the head of a man we think of as symbolizing a way of life alien to the Christian way, and holding for us an element of terror. The symbolism of the falcon, the gyre, and the drowning in blood, moreover, cannot be thought of as Christian.

The poem treats our time as the end of a cultural era, the end of the Western world whose values derived from the teachings of Christ. We associate the phrase "the second coming," of course, with the prophecy that Christ will return. (See, for example, Matthew 25, and Luke 21.) But Yeats envisions, not the coming of Christ, but some new world, bestial and violent. In other words, the poem says that Christianity as the dominant force in the Western world is spent and that a new force will succeed it. The new force will be similar to the world of "stony sleep" (the Egyptian world, say, which we conceive of as having been passive, slow moving, and without concern for individual personality). The poet sees the pre-Christian world as having been "vexed to nightmare" by the advent of Christ. After the two thousand years of Christianity, the new age will be like the rising of the Sphinx, a lion's body with the "head of a man," a world not knowing or respecting charity or pity or humaneness.

The reason for Yeats's envisioning this new world of violence and bestiality is given in the opening lines of the poem. We live, the poet says, in a time when no two groups believe quite, or at all, in the same things. The "best" people, those of a speculative nature and possessing

....

* We also know that although Yeats did not approve of the fascism of Germany and Italy he did not, on the other hand, advocate democracy. He apparently approved of a political order in which an aristocracy employed force to exert its will. It is likely therefore that, for Yeats, those filled with "passionate intensity" are the common run of humanity and that the "ceremonies of innocence" are the rituals of a dying aristocracy. Presumably he would deplore this decline. There would seem to be at least an element of contradiction between the grim satisfaction and such aristocratic sympathy.

good will, have no deep convictions, but those without the capacity for thought and lacking good will are "full of passionate intensity." In the opening lines of the poem, employing the figure of the falcon and the falconer, the poet says by implication that a society possesses in an understandable and meaningful way those values, like innocence, for example, that are a part of a coherent system. If we accept and live within the Christian realm of values we understand, respect, and tend to nurture innocence. If, however, we are committed, as in our time many are, to a realm in which self-interest is a dominant value, then innocence is to be seen as a vice.

The poem, then, is saying what Wallace Stevens has said in prose: "The spirit of negation" has been "active," "confident," and "intolerant." "All the great things have been denied and we live in an intricacy of new and local mythologies, political, economic, poetic, which are asserted with an ever-enlarging incoherence. This is accompanied by an absence of any authority except force, operative or imminent." The quotation from Stevens can be read as a gloss on "The Second Coming": The spirit of negation, of questioning all values, has destroyed for many in the twentieth century those virtues or values that are coherent if one accepts the Christian world view; if one does not accept it, one is likely to find his values or his orientation within a system of politics or economics or esthetics—not in a larger religious or philosophical view in which politics, economics, and esthetics are parts; force, which in Yeats's poem is the "rough beast," is likely to serve as the central discipline in lieu of a principle that is large enough and pervasive enough to control all the rest. Yeats, in other words, sees our age of skepticism and inability to accept a coherent system of values as a stage preceding a world of enforced order that will lack the humane virtues.

We may observe that the symbolism in this poem is powerful. The only difficulty we might face in reading it is in the use of the term "gyre," but in the context of the poem even this is fairly clear—the falcon flies in ever-widening circles, reaching finally a distance from the falconer so great that he cannot hear his master. Thus no highly specialized knowledge is necessary to read the poem. On the other hand, a certain amount of specialized knowledge may help us to see the relation of this poem to Yeats's view of history and the problems of the poet.

In Yeats's *A Vision*, a study devoted largely to explaining his understanding of cultural history, we are told that civilizations run through cycles, each roughly two thousand years in duration. At the beginning of the cycle there is a conflict with the waning civilization. Gradually the new civilization reaches its fullness, and then declines. A further complication is that each cycle of two thousand-odd years is divided into subcycles of one thousand-odd years each. Thus, for example, the high points in the subcycles within the two thousand years or so of the Christian cycle are the Byzantine civilization and the Renaissance. We, in our

me, are nearing the end of the second subcycle and the beginning of
new cycle, "The Second Coming." ("Leda and the Swan" is a represen-
ation of the beginning of the classical world. Byzantium, the symbol in
wo important poems, represented, for Yeats, an ideal state in the de-
elopment of a civilization. These are his own words: "I think that in
arly Byzantium, maybe never before or since in recorded history, re-
gious, aesthetic and practical life were one, that architect and artificers
–though not, it may be, poets, for language had been the instrument of
ontroversy and must have grown abstract—spoke to the multitude and
ae few alike.")

Yeats's system is not written as an abstract account; it employs such
mbols as the moon and the sun (the sun represents objectivity, the
ullness of the moon subjectivity), and interpenetrating gyres, whirring
round inside each other, representing antimonies or opposites such as
ubjectivity-objectivity, particular-universal, and quality-quantity. Ac-
ording to the system, history records the developments of civilization as
moves *toward* the full expression of subjectivity, favorable to growth
f individuality, or toward objectivity, favorable to mass movements and
npersonal expression. This is a greatly simplified account and merely
ints at the complexity of the views presented in *A Vision,* but it is
ecessary at least to sketch it in this fashion to understand its importance
Yeats. In "The Second Coming," the image of the gyrating falcon
mbolizes the culmination of one civilization and the imminent begin-
ing of another.

Yeats, like Blake, whom he admired, protested against the ration-
istic world that had been created by post-Renaissance science. "I am
ery religious," Yeats wrote in his *Autobiography,* "and deprived by
uxley and Tyndall, whom I detested, of the simple-minded religion of
y childhood, I . . . made a new religion, almost an infallible church,
poetic tradition." For a time he was involved with various spiritualistic
oups. Eventually, however, he turned to his own system, which had
rtain elements of the spiritualistic about it but which was largely an
count of cultural history in imaginative (symbolic) terms. Two of the
aracteristics of our world (Phase 23 of *A Vision*) are the absence of
neral principles (as pictured in "The Second Coming") and the ab-
actness of language.

Abstract language is a serious problem for the poet. The poet needs
mbols and images that can be understood by his reader because in writ-
g as a poet he creates a configuration, a little interrelated group of
mbols which have a great many implications, or ramifications in the
ind of the reader. If the poet finds relatively few such symbols available
him, then he must create them himself. And, if he does not succeed
incorporating in the poem itself the information necessary to under-
and the significance or all the connotations of the symbol, the reader
ill have to discover them outside the poem. Yeats often gives the reader

all the information necessary to read the poems themselves without any additional aid from *A Vision*. Critics of Yeats differ about whether it i necessary or unnecessary to refer to his system in order to appreciate th poems fully. The student can decide this matter for himself in examin ing some of these poems. For Yeats, the system was important. It helped him to organize his knowledge and, as he said, gave him metaphors fo his poetry. His search for a way to classify his knowledge and to find meaningful symbols to express it typifies in certain ways the problem of other modern poets. These poets have had to struggle to find ou what it is that they can believe and then to discover large symbols t hold or capture this meaning as T. S. Eliot did in *The Waste Lan* and as Hart Crone did in *The Bridge*.

Easter, 1916

I have met them at close of day
Coming with vivid faces
From counter or desk among grey
Eighteenth-century houses.
I have passed with a nod of the head
Or polite meaningless words,
Or have lingered awhile and said
Polite meaningless words,
And thought before I had done
Of a mocking tale or a gibe
To please a companion
Around the fire at the club,
Being certain that they and I
But lived where motley is worn:
All changed, changed utterly:
A terrible beauty is born.

That woman's days were spent
In ignorant good-will,
Her nights in argument
Until her voice grew shrill.
What voice more sweet than hers
When, young and beautiful,
She rode to harriers?
This man had kept a school
And rode our wingèd horse;
This other his helper and friend
Was coming into his force;
He might have won fame in the end,

So sensitive his nature seemed,
So daring and sweet his thought.   30
This other man I had dreamed
A drunken, vainglorious lout.
He had done most bitter wrong
To some who are near my heart,
Yet I number him in the song;
He, too, has resigned his part
In the casual comedy;
He, too, has been changed in his turn,
Transformed utterly:
A terrible beauty is born.   40

Hearts with one purpose alone
Through summer and winter seem
Enchanted to a stone
To trouble the living stream.
The horse that comes from the road
The rider, the birds that range
From cloud to tumbling cloud,
Minute by minute they change;
A shadow of cloud on the stream
Changes minute by minute;   50
A horse-hoof slides on the brim,
And a horse plashes within it;
The long-legged moor-hens dive,
And hens to moor-cocks call;
Minute by minute they live:
The stone's in the midst of all.

Too long a sacrifice
Can make a stone of the heart.
O when may it suffice?
That is Heaven's part, our part   60
To murmur name upon name,
As a mother names her child
When sleep at last has come
On limbs that had run wild.
What is it but nightfall?
No, no, not night but death;
Was it needless death after all?
For England may keep faith
For all that is done and said.
We know their dream; enough   70
To know they dreamed and are dead;

And what if excess of love
Bewildered them till they died?
I write it out in a verse—
MacDonagh and MacBride
And Connolly and Pearse
Now and in time to be,
Wherever green is worn,
Are changed, changed utterly:
A terrible beauty is born.   8

■ 1. This is a poem about revolution in Ireland and its effect on cer
tain people. What is the effect on them and on the observer of them
  2. How does the refrain release, as it were, the meaning of th
poem?

Sailing to Byzantium

1

That is no country for old men. The young
In one another's arms, birds in the trees,
—Those dying generations—at their song,
The salmon-falls, the mackerel-crowded seas,
Fish, flesh, or fowl, commend all summer long
Whatever is begotten, born, and dies.
Caught in that sensual music all neglect
Monuments of unageing intellect.

2

An aged man is but a paltry thing,
A tattered coat upon a stick, unless   I
Soul clap its hands and sing, and louder sing
For every tatter in its mortal dress,
Nor is there singing school but studying
Monuments of its own magnificence;
And therefore I have sailed the seas and come
To the holy city of Byzantium.

3

O sages standing in God's holy fire
As in the gold mosaic of a wall,
Come from the holy fire, perne in a gyre,
And be the singing-masters of my soul.   2

Consume my heart away; sick with desire
And fastened to a dying animal
It knows not what it is; and gather me
Into the artifice of eternity.

4

Once out of nature I shall never take
My bodily form from any natural thing,
But such a form as Grecian goldsmiths make
Of hammered gold and gold enamelling
To keep a drowsy Emperor awake;
Or set upon a golden bough to sing   30
To lords and ladies of Byzantium
Of what is past, or passing, or to come.

1. Paraphrase the first stanza.
2. What does the "golden bird" symbolize?
3. Explain the phrase "artifice of eternity."

Leda and the Swan

A sudden blow: the great wings beating still
Above the staggering girl, her thighs caressed
By the dark webs, her nape caught in his bill,
He holds her helpless breast upon his breast.

How can those terrified vague fingers push
The feathered glory from her loosening thighs?
And how can body, laid in that white rush,
But feel the strange heart beating where it lies?

A shudder in the loins engenders there
The broken wall, the burning roof and tower
And Agamemnon dead.
                          Being so caught up,
So mastered by the brute blood of the air,
Did she put on his knowledge with his power
Before the indifferent beak could let her drop?

1. What is the verse form of this poem?
2. Why is Agamemnon introduced?
3. Interpret the poem in relation to Yeats's theory of history.

Two Songs from a Play

I

I saw a staring virgin stand
Where holy Dionysus died,
And tear the heart out of his side,
And lay the heart upon her hand
And bear that beating heart away;
And then did all the Muses sing
Of Magnus Annus at the spring,
As though God's death were but a play.

Another Troy must rise and set,
Another lineage feed the crow,   10
Another Argo's painted prow
Drive to a flashier bauble yet.
The Roman Empire stood appalled:
It dropped the reins of peace and war
When that fierce virgin and her Star
Out of the fabulous darkness called.

2

In pity for man's darkening thought
He walked that room and issued thence
In Galilean turbulence;
The Babylonian starlight brought   20
A fabulous, formless darkness in;
Odor of blood when Christ was slain
Made all Platonic tolerance vain
And vain all Doric discipline.

Everything that man esteems
Endures a moment or a day.
Love's pleasure drives his love away,
The painter's brush consumes his dreams;
The herald's cry, the soldier's tread
Exhaust his glory and his might: 3
Whatever flames upon the night
Man's own resinous heart has fed.

■ 1. Point out the similarities in the phrasing of these lines and thos
in the chorus from Shelley's *Hellas* (p. 428).
   2. Who is the "staring virgin"? What is the "Magnus Annus"? T
what does the "fabulous darkness" refer?

3. Is the poet's view of the consequences of the cyclical movement of human history a pessimistic view? Justify your anwser.

The Apparitions

Because there is safety in derision
I talked about an apparition,
I took no trouble to convince,
Or seem plausible to a man of sense,
Distrustful of that popular eye
Whether it be bold or sly.
Fifteen apparitions have I seen;
The worst a coat upon a coat-hanger.

I have found nothing half so good
As my long-planned half solitude,
Where I can sit up half the night
With some friend that has the wit
Not to allow his looks to tell
When I am unintelligible.
Fifteen apparitions have I seen;
The worst a coat upon a coat-hanger.

When a man grows old his joy
Grows more deep day after day,
His empty heart is full at length,
But he has need of all that strength
Because of the increasing Night
That opens her mystery and fright.
Fifteen apparitions have I seen;
The worst a coat upon a coat-hanger.

Robert Frost

(1875–   )

■■■■■■■■■■

Frost, associated with the traditions of New England as no other modern poet is, was born in San Francisco. His father, a New Englander, died when the boy was ten. His mother, a schoolteacher, took him to the home of his paternal grandfather in Lawrence, Massachusetts, where he attended high school. He became devoted to Latin poetry, particularly Virgil, and decided he wanted to be a poet. He did not find college studies fully to his liking, and despite one year at Dartmouth and two years at Harvard he did not take a degree. At twenty he married Eleanor White. For eleven years he worked a small farm in New Hampshire; he also worked as a mill hand, teacher, and editor. In 1912, when the poetry movements in the United States were just getting under way, Frost took his family to England. *A Boy's Will* (1913) and *North of Boston* (1914) were well received in England, and by 1915 when he returned to the United States, he was well known and respected. Since that time his reputation has grown steadily. He has been much more widely read than Eliot or Stevens because readers usually have less difficulty understanding him. In 1924 he won a Pulitzer Prize and thereafter many other honors and awards. His *Collected Poems* (1939) include *A Boy's Will, North of Boston, Mountain Interval, New Hampshire, West-Running Brook,* and *A Further Range*. His other works include *The Witness Tree* (1942), *A Masque of Reason* (1945), and *A Masque of Mercy* (1947).

Suggested Readings

R. Thornton, ed., *Recognition of Robert Frost*. New York: Henry Holt & Co., 1937.

Lawrence Thompson, *Fire and Ice*. New York: Henry Holt & Co., 1942.

Malcolm Cowley, "Frost: A Dissenting Opinion," *New Republic*, 111 (September 11, 1944), 312–313.

Randall Jarrell, "The Other Robert Frost," *Nation*, 165 (November 29, 1947), 588, 590–591.

■■■■■■■■■■

It is customary, and also accurate, to describe the poetry of Robert Frost as traditional and popular. As used here, these descriptive terms are close to each other in meaning. Frost's poetry, unlike that of such contemporaries as Eliot, Stevens, and the later Yeats, shows no marked departure from the poetic practices of the nineteenth century. Those influences which have shaped modernism—such as the free verse movement, the French symbolists, the seventeenth-century metaphysicals—have left no trace on the work of Frost. The average reader of poetry in the early decades of the twentieth century, with tastes and preconceptions determined by nineteenth-century poetry, found Frost not only intelligible and familiar but frequently simple and homely. These qualities have, no doubt, contributed to Frost's popularity.

But Frost has been no mere continuator of the nineteenth-century traditions. While preserving certain basic features, he has brought them up to date with the prevailing principles of his own time. It is interesting to note that many of the modern characteristics of Frost's poetry are also appropriate to the literary personality and poetic role which Frost has chosen and within which he has worked, that of the New England rural character. This role has made it possible for him to blend successfully the traditional and the contemporary. Frost has put into blank verse, couplets, and a variety of stanzas the dry and pithy quality of Yankee speech. Except for a few instances of poetic license and echoes of nineteenth-century tone in his earliest volume, *A Boy's Will,* he remains faithful to the spoken language of his own time. Frost's Yankee manner, with its mixture of playfulness and seriousness, its skepticism and habit of understatement, has paralleled the contemporary tendency toward indirection and irony. And his regionalism, with its rich stock of images, situations, and anecdotes, has provided him with an abundant source of metaphor and symbol.

If Frost's poetry has the qualities of homeliness and simplicity, it has these, not because they are inevitable, but because Frost has achieved them. It is possible to be misled by these qualities into the notion that his poems are simple in all respects. Actually the simplicity is an effect achieved by a skillful and controlled craftsmanship, and it is related to the technique of understatement (a device for concentration and subtle shading of meaning). Beneath the simplicity can be found an intellectuality of attitude, a discernible structure, and a highly developed figurative technique.

A recurring pattern of development is to be found in many of the poems. Frost often begins a poem by presenting some actual detail or circumstance and exploring the features of this material. Then, with a sustained playfulness of tone, an imaginative whimsicality is mixed with or succeeds the realistic comment until the actual material with which the poem began, whether image or situation, yields a meaningful metaphor. Within this pattern Frost handles the central metaphors of his poems in a number of ways. At times he uses the metaphor as a transition to and in illustration of a general statement of idea, belief, or attitude. Examples of this procedure are "Birches" and "Two Tramps in Mud Time." At other times, usually in shorter lyrical poems, the shift into metaphor and then into statement is not obvious but rather a steady and uninterrupted development of the circumstantial materials until they take on a metaphorical or symbolical value. "Stopping by Woods on a Snowy Evening" and "For Once Then, Something" are examples of such development. It is in these shorter poems that Frost's use of realistic materials and metaphorical technique is most successful. In these poems the developed meanings seem to inhere inevitably in the realistic images and situations, in the actual thing. In poems like "Birches," however, the relationship between thing and meaning seems mechanically contrived for the sake of the meaning. Instead of becoming meaningful while it remains vivid in the fullness of its own individuality, the thing becomes covered over with abstract meaning and loses its vividness. In such poems an element of didacticism is not wholly avoided, despite Frost's carefully sustained qualities of casualness and humor. Significantly, in these poems the metaphorical relationship is often weak. Frost himself has said that every metaphor breaks down somewhere, and that with metaphor it is "touch and go." That breaking point, that point of departure, is too conspicuous in poems like "Birches."

Perhaps that is why Frost handles these metaphors in so playful a tone and so tentative a manner. If we grant the weakness of the metaphor, we must at least admire the skillfulness with which Frost avoids the worst consequences. And whether or not they succeed by one standard, Frost's metaphors usually have freshness and charm. Even in those poems which are diffuse and discursive, there is a positive stylistic achievement, an unwavering appropriateness of tone. Where there is looseness of structure, that looseness is often a device contributing to the achieved tone. However, there are marked limitations to the tonal range within which Frost works and has his successes. One does not find intensity of language in Frost's poetry. Intensity is not characteristic of the Yankee manner. It is not produced by understatement, whimsy, and casualness. But while Frost does not commit himself to intensity, he can achieve concentration of meaning.

Reluctance

Out through the fields and the woods
 And over the walls I have wended;
I have climbed the hills of view
 And looked at the world, and descended;

I have come by the highway home,
    And lo, it is ended.

The leaves are all dead on the ground,
    Save those that the oak is keeping
To ravel them one by one
    And let them go scraping and creeping
Out over the crusted snow,
    When others are sleeping.

And the dead leaves lie huddled and still,
    No longer blown hither and thither;
The last lone aster is gone;
    The flowers of the witch-hazel wither;
The heart is still aching to seek,
    But the feet question "Whither?"

Ah, when to the heart of man
    Was it ever less than a treason
To go with the drift of things,
    To yield with a grace to reason,
And bow and accept the end
    Of a love or a season?

This is one of Frost's earlier poems. What conventional poeticisms does it contain?

A Patch of Old Snow

There's a patch of old snow in a corner
    That I should have guessed
Was a blow-away paper the rain
    Had brought to rest.

It is speckled with grime as if
    Small print overspread it,
The news of a day I've forgotten—
    If I ever read it.

What is the effect of this poem? Does it do any more than present a lever and amusing comparison?

Birches

When I see birches bend to left and right
Across the lines of straighter darker trees,
I like to think some boy's been swinging them.
But swinging doesn't bend them down to stay.
Ice-storms do that. Often you must have seen them
Loaded with ice a sunny winter morning
After a rain. They click upon themselves
As the breeze rises, and turn many-colored
As the stir cracks and crazes their enamel.
Soon the sun's warmth makes them shed crystal shells   10
Shattering and avalanching on the snow-crust—
Such heaps of broken glass to sweep away
You'd think the inner dome of heaven had fallen.
They are dragged to the withered bracken by the load,
And they seem not to break; though once they are bowed
So low for long, they never right themselves:
You may see their trunks arching in the woods
Years afterwards, trailing their leaves on the ground
Like girls on hands and knees that throw their hair
Before them over their heads to dry in the sun.   20
But I was going to say when Truth broke in
With all her matter-of-fact about the ice-storm
I should prefer to have some boy bend them
As he went out and in to fetch the cows—
Some boy too far from town to learn baseball,
Whose only play was what he found himself,
Summer or winter, and could play alone.
One by one he subdued his father's trees
By riding them down over and over again
Until he took the stiffness out of them,   30
And not one but hung limp, not one was left
For him to conquer. He learned all there was
To learn about not launching out too soon
And so not carrying the tree away
Clear to the ground. He always kept his poise
To the top branches, climbing carefully
With the same pains you use to fill a cup
Up to the brim, and even above the brim.
Then he flung outward, feet first, with a swish,
Kicking his way down through the air to the ground.   40
So was I once myself a swinger of birches.
And so I dream of going back to be.
It's when I'm weary of considerations,

And life is too much like a pathless wood
Where your face burns and tickles with the cobwebs
Broken across it, and one eye is weeping
From a twig's having lashed across it open.
I'd like to get away from earth awhile
And then come back to it and begin over.
May no fate willfully misunderstand me   50
And half grant what I wish and snatch me away
Not to return. Earth's the right place for love:
I don't know where it's likely to go better.
I'd like to go by climbing a birch tree,
And climb black branches up a snow-white trunk
Toward heaven, till the tree could bear no more,
But dipped its top and set me down again.
That would be good both going and coming back.
One could do worse than be a swinger of birches.

1. Indicate the metaphors in the poem and discuss their function.
2. What details of the poem are especially productive of its tone?

Stopping by Woods on a Snowy Evening

Whose woods these are I think I know.
His house is in the village though;
He will not see me stopping here
To watch his woods fill up with snow.

My little horse must think it queer
To stop without a farmhouse near
Between the woods and frozen lake
The darkest evening of the year.

He gives his harness bells a shake
To ask if there is some mistake.
The only other sound's the sweep
Of easy wind and downy flake.

The woods are lovely, dark and deep,
But I have promises to keep,
And miles to go before I sleep,
And miles to go before I sleep.

"Stopping by Woods on a Snowy Evening," like Milton's sonnet on
is blindness and Arnold's "Dover Beach," seems to have established itself

permanently in anthologies and textbooks of poetry. It is one of Frost's best-known poems, and we might discover, if we had the means, that it is one of the best-known poems of the twentieth century. Its wide appeal like that of Frost's work in general, is not difficult to explain. With the clearest and simplest language, organized in a form that is catchy and easily remembered, Frost's poem evokes a common human experience of the beauty of nature. If one has not actually had such an experience it is at least of a kind that one can easily imagine. The quality of the experience is made available by the poem.

In other words, the poem produces an immediate and clear effect. Our description of this effect has been simple—indeed, too simple. When we dwell further on the poem and examine its several parts and aspects we discover that there is considerably more that can be said by way of interpreting it and of explaining its effect. We should notice, for example, that the poem is not primarily the description of natural scenery but the dramatic utterance of a person on the occasion of experiencing the scene, of being *in* the scene: the utterance is in the present tense. We may, in this respect, compare it with Wordsworth's poem about the daffodils (p. 370), which, for its own purposes, is in the past tense and thus lacks the dramatic quality of Frost's poem. Another significant difference between the two poems lies in the way each poem describes the natural scenery. In Wordsworth's poem there is the straightforward description of the "host of golden daffodils" and then a statement of the effect upon the poet of the scene and of his memory of the scene. Frost's poem gives us a scene, but it seems to be giving it to us only incidentally, not by direct and calculated description. We may assume that the indirection is calculated, however natural and casual the poem may seem as a statement.

Consider first the scene and then the means by which it is portrayed. The speaker is passing deep woods on a dark night. Across the road from the woods is a frozen lake. No houses are in sight. It is snowing heavily, and a gentle, soft sound is made by the wind and by the snow falling into the woods. And now consider how the scene emerges. The poem opens with immediate reference to the woods, but they are mentioned by way of observing that their owner is a certain man who lives in the village. Since he does live in the village, we are told, he will not see the speaker looking at his property. Whether or not he will see the speaker seems a pointless concern, certainly not a very interesting or serious one, yet natural and plausible enough—the sort of thought that might pass through anyone's mind under the circumstances. This thought is uttered, and as it concludes we learn about the snow. The second and third stanzas introduce in like manner the other details of the scene. In each of these stanzas the details are parts of the fond and whimsical speculations about the little horse. It is only in the last stanza that the speaker remarks directly, but briefly, upon the appearance and quality of the woods. They are "lovely, dark and deep." And in the closing lines the speaker says, or implies clearly, that he must leave the scene of the woods and be getting along. The indirect way in which the scene is described and the intermixture of casualness and whimsy are characteristic of the poetry of Frost and of the twentieth century. One can imagine a poem that might begin with the line, "The woods are lovely, dark and deep," and then proceed through a series of exclamatory appreciations to end with a general statement on nature and what it means to man, or to the poet. The climax and conclusion of such a poem would be an interpretation of what had gone before.

Frost's poem obviously contains no explicit interpretation. It may, nonetheless, be found significant beyond the scene and situation which it presents—that is, the poem is its own interpretation in that it implies some meanings in addition to those which are directly stated. We have already noticed that the poem has a particular kind of development. The scene is presented with some indirection. It is considered as someone's property and from the playfully imagined point of view of the little horse. That is, the speaker is not utterly absorbed in the scene. Although he responds to its loveliness, he is not so possessed by it that other thoughts, casual and whimsical, may not enter his mind. The implication is that the speaker does not forsake or forget all his other attitudes while he experiences the loveliness of the woods. His sensibility and appreciation exist among other attitudes and habits of mind, and they are therefore not put in the foreground of the poem.

These implications, which follow from the development of the poem, may be called immediate implications, for there are others less immediate. While the implications already mentioned qualify the speaker's act of contemplating the woods, there are implications which differentiate the several attitudes from which the woods may be regarded. From the first stanza we learn that they are the property of a man who lives in the village. The implication is that they represent an economic value and a practical purpose, as distinguished from their aspect as a lovely object to be watched, to be contemplated. In the second and third stanzas the playful remarks about the horse indicate that he is an animal that has been conditioned to a routine of purposeful behavior, and they thus imply that the speaker's behavior is not, in a sense, purposeful. He has stopped in order to watch the woods and the snow, and he watches toward no other end, but just for watching, for contemplating, for appreciating.

This implication is even clearer in the last stanza. The woods are unusually lovely, but the speaker must eventually be about his business and his responsibilities. There are still other implications in this stanza. The woods are symbolic of beauty in general, of esthetic value. This symbolism is enforced by the word *"but"* in the second line. If it were not for the promises and the miles, what would the speaker do? He might watch the woods indefinitely—he might devote his life to the experience of esthetic value. Or he might enter the woods, for it is their interior, their darkness and depth, which is lovely, and which thus suggests the peacefulness of death. In their fullest symbolic potentiality, then, the woods equate death with an exclusive commitment to esthetic value. The final lines of the poem have implications which are in accord with this interpretation. The speaker feels the urge to escape into loveliness, into the peacefulness of death, but he also acknowledges the fact that there are other values and other urges. He is committed to life, in all its diversity and complexity, and he wants to go on living, to fulfill that commitment, for death will come in time—"And miles to go before I sleep." The repetition of this last line, while it successfully closes the formal pattern of the poem, also emphasizes the symbolic function of the statement.

Considerable interpretive pressure has been put upon Frost's poem, but the poem can withstand this pressure. The ultimate meanings that are found, the less immediate implications, fit nicely with those which are more immediate and obvious. For example, the life-death tension (or dilemma) which is both raised and resolved in the last stanza is logically related to earlier parts of the poem—to the tension between the speaker's contemplation of the woods and his passing thoughts about their owner and the little horse. In its ultimate implication, the last stanza summarizes and generalizes some of the meanings of the foregoing stanzas. This development is marked also by the slight shift of tone which occurs with the last stanza, for the whimsy and playfulness of the earlier stanzas do not continue in the last.

For Once, Then, Something

Others taunt me with having knelt at well-curbs
Always wrong to the light, so never seeing
Deeper down in the well than where the water
Gives me back in a shining surface picture
Me myself in the summer heaven godlike
Looking out of a wreath of fern and cloud puffs.
Once, when trying with chin against a well-curb,
I discerned, as I thought, beyond the picture,
Through the picture, a something white, uncertain,
Something more of the depths—and then I lost it.
Water came to rebuke the too clear water.
One drop fell from a fern, and lo, a ripple
Shook whatever it was lay there at bottom,

Blurred it, blotted it out. What was that whiteness?
Truth? A pebble of quartz? For once, then, something.

■ Write an analysis of this poem.

Once by the Pacific

The shattered water made a misty din.
Great waves looked over others coming in,
And thought of doing something to the shore
That water never did to land before.
The clouds were low and hairy in the skies,
Like locks blown forward in the gleam of eyes.
You could not tell, and yet it looked as if
The shore was lucky in being backed by cliff,
The cliff in being backed by continent;
It looked as if a night of dark intent
Was coming, and not only a night, an age.
Someone had better be prepared for rage.
There would be more than ocean-water broken
Before God's last *Put out the Light* was spoken.

■ Compare this poem with Yeats's "The Second Coming."

Two Tramps in Mud Time

Out of the mud two strangers came
And caught me splitting wood in the yard.
And one of them put me off my aim
By hailing cheerily "Hit them hard!"
I knew pretty well why he dropped behind
And let the other go on a way.
I knew pretty well what he had in mind:
He wanted to take my job for pay.

Good blocks of oak it was I split,
As large around as the chopping block;
And every piece I squarely hit
Fell splinterless as a cloven rock.
The blows that a life of self-control
Spares to strike for the common good
That day, giving a loose to my soul,
I spent on the unimportant wood.

10

The sun was warm but the wind was chill.
You know how it is with an April day
When the sun is out and the wind is still,
You're one month on in the middle of May.   20
But if you so much as dare to speak,
A cloud comes over the sunlit arch,
A wind comes off a frozen peak,
And you're two months back in the middle of March.

A bluebird comes tenderly up to alight
And turns to the wind to unruffle a plume
His song so pitched as not to excite
A single flower as yet to bloom.
It is snowing a flake: and he half knew   30
Winter was only playing possum.
Except in color he isn't blue,
But he wouldn't advise a thing to blossom.

The water for which we may have to look
In summertime with a witching-wand,
In every wheelrut's now a brook,
In every print of a hoof a pond.
Be glad of water, but don't forget
The lurking frost in the earth beneath
That will steal forth after the sun is set   40
And show on the water its crystal teeth.

The time when most I loved my task
These two must make me love it more
By coming with what they came to ask.
You'd think I never had felt before
The weight of an ax-head poised aloft,
The grip on earth of outspread feet.
The life of muscles rocking soft
And smooth and moist in vernal heat.

Out of the woods two hulking tramps   50
(From sleeping God knows where last night,
But not long since in the lumber camps).
They thought all chopping was theirs of right.
Men of the woods and lumberjacks,
They judged me by their appropriate tool.
Except as a fellow handled an ax,
They had no way of knowing a fool

Nothing on either side was said.
They knew they had but to stay their stay
And all their logic would fill my head:
As that I had no right to play   60
With what was another man's work for gain.
My right might be love but theirs was need.
And where the two exist in twain
Theirs was the better right—agreed.

But yield who will to their separation,
My object in living is to unite
My avocation and my vocation
As my two eyes make one in sight.
Only where love and need are one,
And the work is play for mortal stakes,   70
Is the deed ever really done
For Heaven and the future's sakes.

■   1. Analyze the meter of the first two stanzas.
    2. Outline the development of the poem. How are stanzas 3
through 5 related to the rest of the poem?
    3. Comment on the effect of the last stanza.
    4. This poem is sometimes cited as an example of a regional poem.
What are its regional features?

Acquainted with the Night

I have been one acquainted with the night.
I have walked out in rain—and back in rain.
I have outwalked the furthest city light.

I have looked down the saddest city lane.
I have passed by the watchman on his beat
And dropped my eyes, unwilling to explain.

I have stood still and stopped the sound of feet
When far away an interrupted cry
Came over houses from another street,

But not to call me back or say good-by;
And further still at an unearthly height,
One luminary clock against the sky

Proclaimed the time was neither wrong nor right.
I have been one acquainted with the night.

Wallace Stevens

(1879–   )

■■■■■■■■■■

WALLACE STEVENS was born in Reading, Pennsylvania. As a student at Harvard he wrote some verse but apparently without serious literary ambitions. After graduation from the New York Law School he worked briefly for the *Herald Tribune*. In New York City he associated with young writers like William Carlos Williams, Carl Van Vechten, and Alfred Kreymborg. Greenwich Village was bustling with literary activities. During this period Stevens wrote some of his best poems, which appeared eventually in *Harmonium* (1923). In 1916 he moved to Hartford, Connecticut, to work as a lawyer for the Hartford Accident and Indemnity Company, and in 1934 he became a vice-president of the company. The first edition of Stevens' *Harmonium* sold less than one hundred copies. Since that time, however, his reputation has risen steadily. In 1929 Allen Tate called him "the most finished poet of the age." And in 1950 he was granted the Bollingen Award for Poetry. Between 1923 and 1930, when *Harmonium* was reissued, Stevens published little. Thereafter his work began to appear more steadily. His later books are *Ideas of Order* (1935), *Owl's Clover* (1936), *The Man with the Blue Guitar* (1937), *Parts of a World* (1942), *Notes toward a Supreme Fiction* (1942), *Transport to Summer* (1947), *Three Academic Pieces* (1947), *A Primitive like an Orb* (1948), and *Auroras of Autumn* (1950). Stevens' sole volume of prose, *The Necessary Angel: Essays on Reality and Imagination*, appeared in 1951.

Suggested Readings

R. P. BLACKMUR, "Examples of Wallace Stevens," in *The Double Agent*. New York: Arrow Editions, 1935, pp. 68–102.

WILLIAM VAN O'CONNOR, *The Shaping Spirit: A Study of Wallace Stevens*. Chicago: Henry Regnery Co., 1950, pp. 123–140.

■■■■■■■■■■

A High-toned Old Christian Woman[1]

Poetry is the supreme fiction, madame.
Take the moral law and make a nave of it
And from the nave build haunted heaven.

....

1. "A High-toned Old Christian Woman" is reprinted from *Harmonium*, by Wallace Stevens, by permission of Alfred A. Knopf, Inc. Copyright, 1923, 1931, by Alfred A. Knopf, Inc.

Thus, the conscience is converted into palms,
Like windy citherns hankering for hymns.
We agree in principle. That's clear. But take
The opposing law and make a peristyle,
And from the peristyle project a masque
Beyond the planets. Thus, our bawdiness,
Urged by epitaph, indulged at last,
Is equally converted into palms,
Squiggling like saxophones. And palm for palm,
Madame, we are where we began. Allow,
Therefore, that in the planetary scene
Your disaffected flagellants, well-stuffed,
Smacking their muzzy bellies in parade,
Proud of such novelties of the sublime,
Such tink and tank and tunk-a-tunk-tunk,
May, merely may, madame, whip from themselves
A jovial hullabaloo among the spheres.
This will make widows wince. But fictive things
Wink as they will. Wink most when widows wince.

1. Write a paraphrase of this poem.
2. Discuss the diction employed by the poet.
3. In what way or ways do the alliteration and sounds contribute to or support the sense or meaning of the poem?

The Emperor of Ice Cream[1]

Call the roller of big cigars,
The muscular one, and bid him whip
In kitchen cups concupiscent curds.
Let the wenches dawdle in such dress
As they are used to wear, and let the boys
Bring flowers in last month's newspapers.
Let be be finale of seem.
The only emperor is the emperor of ice cream.

Take from the dresser of deal,
Lacking the three glass knobs, that sheet
On which she embroidered fantails once
And spread it so as to cover her face.
If her horny feet protrude, they come

1. "The Emperor of Ice Cream" is reprinted from *Harmonium*, by Wallace Stevens, by permission of Alfred A. Knopf, Inc. Copyright, 1923, 1931, by Alfred A. Knopf, Inc.

To show how cold she is, and dumb.
Let the lamp affix its beam.
The only emperor is the emperor of ice cream.

1. What is the meaning of the line "Let be be finale of seem"?
2. Is the poem telling us that in accepting the products of imagination (as with the sheet on which the fantails are embroidered) we are free to ignore certain hard, difficult, or ugly aspects of our experience?
3. Are the living, as represented in this poem, disrespectful of the dead?
4. Is the title of the poem appropriate or inappropriate?

The Snow Man[1]

One must have a mind of winter
To regard the frost and boughs
Of the pine-trees crusted with snow;

And have been cold a long time
To behold the junipers shagged with ice,
The spruces rough in the distant glitter

Of the January sun; and not to think
Of any misery in the sound of the wind,
In the sound of a few leaves,

Which is the sound of the land
Full of the same wind
That is blowing in the same bare place

For the listener, who listens in the snow,
And, nothing himself, beholds
Nothing that is not there and the nothing that is.

1. "The Snow Man" is reprinted from *Harmonium*, by Wallace Stevens, by permission of Alfred A. Knopf, Inc. Copyright, 1923, 1931, by Alfred A. Knopf, Inc.

Thirteen Ways of Looking at a Blackbird [1]

I

Among twenty snowy mountains,
The only moving thing
Was the eye of the blackbird.

2

I was of three minds,
Like a tree
In which there are three blackbirds.

3

The blackbird whirled in the autumn winds.
It was a small part of the pantomime.

4

A man and a woman
Are one.
A man and a woman and a blackbird   10
Are one.

5

I do not know which to prefer,
The beauty of inflections
Or the beauty of innuendoes,
The blackbird whistling
Or just after.

6

Icicles filled the long window
With barbaric glass.
The shadow of the blackbird
Crossed it, to and fro.   20
The mood
Traced in the shadow
An indecipherable cause.

7

O thin men of Haddam,
Why do you imagine golden birds?
Do you not see how the blackbird

Walks around the feet
Of the women about you?

8

I know noble accents   30
And lucid, inescapable rhythms;
But I know, too,
That the blackbird is involved
In what I know.

9

When the blackbird flew out of sight,
It marked the edge
Of one of many circles.

10

At the sight of blackbirds
Flying in a green light,
Even the bawds of euphony   40
Would cry out sharply.

11

He rode over Connecticut
In a glass coach.
Once, a fear pierced him,
In that he mistook
The shadow of his equipage
For blackbirds.

12

The river is moving.
The blackbird must be flying.

13

It was evening all afternoon.   50
It was snowing
And it was going to snow.
The blackbird sat
In the cedar-limbs.

■   The following passage, from a brief article entitled "Leave Space
for the Birds to Fly," makes an interesting point about selectivity:

> At an exhibition of Chinese paintings we overheard a visitor tell
> the artist that she would like to buy one of his pictures—a bird on a
> bare branch. She explained to him, however, that she considered the

painting too empty and suggested he add a few more branches and leaves. "If I did that," the Chinese artist answered, "there would be no room for the bird to fly." It was the emptiness, the suggestion of in- finite space, that was the main feature of the picture.

Properly modified, this suggests a way of considering "Thirteen Ways of Looking at a Blackbird." Wallace Stevens knows what to leave out. The picture or image glows because it is not competing with trivial or irrele- vant detail. But by the same token it requires concentrated attention; the meaning is involved in the intensity, the compactness of the image. The poetry is obscure, insofar as it is, because it is suggestive—the meanings radiate into the space surrounding the bird, or, if one will, into the infinite space, the emptiness beyond it.

The poem may also seem obscure to those who do not read it against a background or knowledge of Stevens' other work. Undoubtedly there is something to the argument that most good writers constantly enlarge, qualify, and probe the same themes and subjects, coming at them from different directions but always in somewhat similar terms. The com- pleted work, viewed in perspective, has a homogeneity given to it by these persistent and pervasive themes. In one sense, then, the given poem is merely a part of one large, perhaps loosely organized but nonetheless cohesive body of poetry. This is true of the poetry of Wallace Stevens.

Perhaps not strictly necessary to an understanding of the poem but nevertheless useful in understanding Stevens' relationship to the poetry of his own time is the similarity between Japanese *haiku* and a number of the stanzas in "Thirteen Ways."* The *haiku* are strikingly imagistic verses; they are concise; general implications or thematic considerations can be inferred from the image or little patterns of images; the images are from scenes in nature; in most *haiku* a specific season is mentioned or to be inferred; and, in each, man is seen as a part of nature or as de- pendent upon nature. An examination of the second, third, fourth, fifth, and thirteenth stanzas in "Thirteen Ways of Looking at a Black- bird" reveal them to be good examples of *haiku*. But only one of these stanzas, the thirteenth, appears to have a parallel in Japanese *haiku*. The parallel is to "On a Leafless Bough," by the Japanese poet Bassho:

> In the darkening autumn dusk
> A crow has perched upon
> A leafless bough, alone.

This is Mr. Stevens' stanza:

> It was evening all afternoon.
> It was snowing

* Some of the following comments and information are borrowed from a University of Minnesota M.A. dissertation on the influence of Japanese *haiku* on British and American poetry. The author of the study is Earl Miner.

> And it was going to snow.
> The blackbird sat
> In the cedar limbs.

Probably it is not necessary to insist that Stevens got the idea for this stanza from Bassho. When he wrote "Thirteen Ways" the air was filled with theories about imagism and vorticism and even about *haiku*.

The title and organization of "Thirteen Ways" are obviously quite simple—the stanzas express and develop insights about the blackbird. In Stevens' poetry there are birds of many kinds: pigeons, starlings, grackles, and parakeets. And in each context the reason for the particular bird usually becomes clear. In this poem, "Thirteen Ways," he seems to have chosen the blackbird because it is beautiful but also small, somber, and even foreboding and portentous.

The first stanza is this:

> Among twenty snowy mountains,
> The only moving thing
> Was the eye of the blackbird.

Snow in Stevens' poetry—as in Frost's poetry or in Joyce's story, *The Dead*—symbolizes the negativism of a part of nature, the nothingness into which man will ultimately descend. In "The Snow Man" he has said,

> One must have a mind of winter
> To regard the frost and the boughs
> Of the pine-tree crusted with snow; . . .
>   and not to think
> Of any misery in the sound of the wind,
> In the sound of a few leaves. . . .

One must have faced the meaning of the snow before one is free to enjoy it disinterestedly as esthetic experience.

We can infer that the eye of the blackbird and the blackbird itself are intelligence and movement—the graces, the loves, or activities of humanity. And the blackbird—beauty, good, evil—must be the infinitesimal actions of human affairs against the infinity of the snowy mountains.

The second stanza of "Thirteen Ways" is

> I was of three minds,
> Like a tree
> In which there are three blackbirds.

In the light of Stevens' other poetry this suggests the elements of irrationality in any mind. Differing attitudes are in the same mind, each a blackbird, but the mind cannot be sure of what it believes. Each bird might go off at any moment in its own direction. And the separateness of the birds, the blackbirds being what they are, seems to suggest that one attitude is a little suspicious, at least wary, of the other two. Not that much should be made of the similarity, but the last two stanzas of "No Possum, No Sop, No Taters" seem to echo this second stanza:

> The crow looks rusty as he rises up.
> Bright is the malice in his eye . . .
>
> One joins him there for company,
> But at a distance, in another tree.

The imagery of the bird and tree is similar, of course, but there is also the suggestion of the individual's need for wariness and suspicion as well as for company.

The third stanza:

> The blackbird whirled in the autumn winds.
> 5   It was a small part of the pantomime.

A pantomime is a patterned and meaningful but soundless and entertaining movement. The movements of autumn are soundless (here at least) but meaningful. The blackbird's movement is described as "whirled"; it is caught in a force it cannot control. Autumn of course suggests dissolution, and there are a coldness and irrationality to the movements of autumn. But if one has previously faced its meanings—as one has faced the snow and developed a mind of winter—the pantomime can be exhilarating.

The fourth stanza:

> 8   A man and a woman
> Are one.
> A man and a woman and a blackbird
> Are one.

This stanza lacks the imaginative flourish, even the *gaudiness* (Stevens used this term about his "Emperor of Ice Cream") of some of the other stanzas, but it does have a little concentration of meanings. Among them there are these: man is born of woman, or, more specifically, man and woman depend on each other. Humanity, man and woman, also depend upon, or are, nature, the blackbird. And, since the blackbird, or nature, is beauty, goodness, *and* evil, therefore man is beauty, goodness, *and* evil.

The fifth stanza:

> I do not know which to prefer,
> The beauty of inflections
> Or the beauty of innuendoes,
> The blackbird whistling
> Or just after.

R. P. Blackmur, among others, has noted that the diction in Stevens' poems is usually employed in a precise way. In the word "inflections" we have a good example of Stevens' use of the proper word. "Inflections" connotes a shift in tone or pitch and a shift in gender or case, and therefore of meaning. It suggests sound, movement, and precision of meaning. The stanza is likely to recall Keats's lines:

> Heard melodies are sweet, but those unheard
> Are sweeter; therefore, ye soft pipes, play on;
> Not to the sensual ear, but, more endear'd,
> Pipe to the spirit ditties of no tone.

Keats tends to draw a firm line between the beauties of heard song and imagined song, and to favor the latter. Stevens makes the choice more difficult. To the beauty of melody he has added the beauty of specific and of hinted meaning (innuendo). And he further complicates the difficulty of choosing between heard and unheard melodies by suggesting that the unheard melody depends on recollection, on recalling the beauty of heard melodies. And it is also worth observing, probably, that Stevens' use of the blackbird—the blackbird whistling or just after—enables him to write with an economy of phrase that Keats, with his more determinedly expository manner, lacks or avoids.

The sixth stanza:

> Icicles filled the long window
> With barbaric glass.
> The shadow of the blackbird
> Crossed it, to and fro.
> The mood
> Traced in the shadow
> An indecipherable cause.

In this stanza there is the running together of an elegant, esthetic realm —the barbaric glass in the long window and the shadow of the blackbird crossing back and forth behind it—and the harsh or at least

unknown and inscrutable forces beyond the piercing of human intelligence. The two realms meet in the word "barbaric" as they do, for instance, in the sophisticate's awareness of the artisitic strength in primitive sculpture. Apparently the three final lines mean that the mood or
the aroused emotions find in the shadow itself the symbol of ultimate
mystery. Or, the "mood" of the artist or poet causes him to make a pat·
tern of the shadow, to create a work of art, but the ultimate meaning
of the pattern is indecipherable. The speech of poets, like the speech of
philosophers, is "the speech of clouds."

The seventh stanza:

> O thin men of Haddam,
> Why do you imagine golden birds?
> Do you not see how the blackbird
> Walks around the feet
> Of the women about you?

There is a town in Connecticut named Haddam. Therefore the
"thin men" might be the descendants of Puritans. But in the context
Haddam has an oriental sound. At any rate, the thin men of Haddam
are artists or thoughtful men. The general meaning, however, seems
clear enough. It is a theme Stevens developed in his review* of Marianne
Moore's poetry—what he called her "hybridization" of the real and the
unreal. "Moonvines are moonvines and tedious. But moonvines trained
on fishing twine are something else." All poets are romantic; if they are
not romantic they are not poets. But being romantic and being able to
see what is in front of one to be seen are not mutually exclusive. One
can be highly imaginative, capable of creating imaginary worlds, and at
the same time can have a firm sense of the actuality of the concrete
world.

In his verse play, *Three Travellers Watch a Sunrise*, Stevens early
developed another aspect of this theme. The play makes the point that
esthetic experience is deep and profound only if it involves human experiences—poverty, suffering, pity.

> It is the invasion of humanity
> That counts.

In an art object redness cannot be enjoyed impersonally—it has associations with the redness of blood, with violence. There is also the redness of the human eye in grief. To repeat, the point of the play is in the
lines:

---

* "A Poet That Matters," *Life and Letters Today* (December, 1935), XIII,
61–65.

> It is the invasion of humanity
> That counts.

To paraphrase what Stevens has said about moonvines and fishing twine, we can say that golden birds are romantic and tedious but that blackbirds are at once beautiful and involved with humanity. Golden birds live in the imagination. The blackbirds walk about the feet of the women of Haddam. And it is of the blackbirds the men or the poets of Haddam should write and to which they should give their imaginative powers.

The eighth stanza:

> I know noble accents
> And lucid, inescapable rhythms;
> But I know, too,
> That the blackbird is involved
> In what I know

Stevens knows the power of rhetoric, of language, of poetry. Nobility of accent and smooth, regular, and tremendous rhythms, however, can carry one too far from the world in which he is immediately involved, the tiny particularized world of the blackbird.

The ninth stanza:

> When the blackbird flew out of sight,
> It marked the edge
> Of one of many circles.

Esthetically the image is enjoyable, the circling of the blackbird until he reaches a distance into which the eye cannot follow. If we push against the image for a further meaning, we probably get something like this: human intelligence moves outward in concentric rings, but there is a circle beyond which it cannot go.

The tenth stanza:

> At the sight of blackbirds
> Flying in a green light,
> Even the bawds of euphony
> Would cry out sharply.

The "bawds of euphony" are those who refuse to admit abruptness and cacophony into their verses, but even they would exclaim sharply at the sight of the blackbirds in such a light.

The eleventh stanza:

> He rode over Connecticut
> In a glass coach.
> Once, a fear pierced him,
> In that he mistook
> The shadow of his equipage
> For blackbirds.

This stanza echoes a part of stanza VI, the shadow behind esthetic enjoyment. The glass coach in Connecticut is the world of artifact or, better, the world of elegant objects and decor created by civilization. Inside this elaborate little world the gentleman is at ease. Although the shadow cast by his equipage may be a little disturbing, he could get used to that. But there is no real defense against the fearsome, the portentous. The blackbirds intrude.

The twelfth stanza:

> The river is moving.
> The blackbird must be flying.

The river is moving again—it is spring. Nature is starting through another of its annual cycles. The blackbird, which is here beautiful movement as well as portentousness, is a part of the cycle. The bird is to spring in stanza XII what it was to autumn in stanza III, "a small part of the pantomime."

The thirteenth stanza:

> It was evening all afternoon.
> It was snowing
> And it was going to snow.
> The blackbird sat
> In the cedar-limbs.

The first line is of course a paradox: the darkness of evening pervades the afternoon light, as it does on certain days in winter. The snow, cold and impersonal, is present, and there will be more of it. The blackbird, the little margin of beauty or intelligence, is again present. And it does not sit in a starkly and cleanly beautiful tree; it sits in a cedar tree, with its gnarled, imperfect limbs and its rough, almost hemplike bark. The choice of the cedar tree as the appropriate setting for the blackbird recalls the section entitled "Approaching Carolina" of the long autobiographical poem, "The Comedian as the Letter C." The poet had studied in the book of moonlight and had come to know the romantic images traditional to poetry. But he wanted to get beneath the obviously poetic, the obviously romantic, to something that seemed more essentially real. He describes a little trip up a river in one of the Carolinas during which he learned to savor "emanations blown from warehouse doors, the gustiness of ropes, decays of sacks," and so forth, which helped him "round his rude aesthetic out." He wanted to write his poetry and see the world imaginatively but also honestly. He wanted, in a world filled with romantic falseness, to get close to the "essential prose" of things. On the integrity of the essential prose a poet can build more securely. The blackbird in the cedar limbs and against the backdrop of snow is such an image—the margin of the beautiful and the meaningful. The poetry is composed in terms of and out of the essential prose. And, finally, that is what the poem is about: the blackbird, beautiful and a little ominous but also involved with the everyday world, is an appropriate symbol for the poet.

No Possum, No Sop, No Taters[1]

He is not here, the old sun,
As absent as if we were asleep.

The field is frozen. The leaves are dry.
Bad is final in this light.

In this bleak air the broken stalks
Have arms without hands. They have trunks

Without legs or, for that, without heads.
They have heads in which a captive cry

Is merely the moving of a tongue.
Snow sparkles like eyesight falling to earth,

Like seeing fallen brightly away.
The leaves hop, scraping on the ground.

It is deep January. The sky is hard.
The stalks are firmly rooted in ice.

It is in this solitude, a syllable,
Out of these gawky flitterings,

Intones its single emptiness,
The savagest hollow of winter-sound.

----

1.   "No Possum, No Sop, No Taters" is reprinted from *Transport to Summer* by Wallace Stevens, by permission of Alfred A. Knopf, Inc. Copyright, 1942, 1947, by Wallace Stevens.

It is here, in this bad, that we reach
The last purity of the knowledge of good.

The crow looks rusty as he rises up.
Bright is the malice in his eye . . .

One joins him there for company,
But at a distance, in another tree.

Puella Parvula[1]

Every thread of summer is at last unwoven.
By one caterpillar is great Africa devoured
And Gibraltar is dissolved like spit in the wind.

But over the wind, over the legends of its roaring,
The elephant on the roof and its elephantine blaring,
The bloody lion in the yard at night or ready to spring

From the clouds in the midst of trembling trees
Making a great gnashing, over the water wallows
Of a vacant sea declaiming with wide throat,

Over all these the mighty imagination triumphs
Like a trumpet and says, in this season of memory,
When the leaves fall like things mournful of the past,

Keep quiet in the heart, O wild bitch. O mind
Gone wild, be what he tells you to be: *Puella*.
Write *pax* across the window pane. And then

Be still. The *summarium in excelsis* begins . . .
Flame, sound, fury, composed . . . Hear what he says,
The dauntless master, as he starts the human tale.

---

1. "Puella Parvula" (tiny little girl) is reprinted from *The Auroras of utumn*, by Wallace Stevens, by permission of Alfred A. Knopf, Inc. Copyright,)49, 1950, by Wallace Stevens.

T. S. Eliot

(1888–   )

■■■■■■■■■

THOMAS STEARNS ELIOT was born in St. Louis, Missouri, and lived there until he was eighteen. The Eliots were a New England family with strong religious and intellectual interests. His grandfather was one of the founders of Washington University, and his mother was a poet. At Harvard, where he took his B.A. in three years and his M.A. his fourth year, he came under the influence of Irving Babbitt and George Santayana. After a year at the Sorbonne he returned to Harvard to study philosophy, completing most of the requirements for the Ph.D. Later he traveled in Germany, studied at Oxford, and finally settled in England in 1915. There he worked in a bank, taught school, and was active as a literary figure. His first book was *Prufrock and Other Observations* (1917). In 1922 he founded *The Criterion*, a "little magazine" of limited circulation but wide influence, which he continued to edit for seventeen years. *The Waste Land* (1922) established him quite securely as an outstanding poet; *The Sacred Wood* (1920) had already established him as an outstanding critic. No other figure has had as great an influence on twentieth-century poetry and criticism. Increasingly his work has expressed his concern with religion and its relationship with the social order, as in the poetic drama *Murder in the Cathedral* (1935), *The Idea of a Christian Society* (1940), and *Four Quartets* (1943). Eliot was awarded the Nobel Prize in 1949, and his play, *The Cocktail Party* (1949) enjoyed a popular success on Broadway.

Suggested Readings

F. O. MATTHIESSEN, *The Achievement of T. S. Eliot*. New York: Oxford University Press, 1947.

LEONARD UNGER, ed., *T. S. Eliot: A Selected Critique*. New York: Rinehart & Co., Inc., 1948.

HELEN GARDINER, *The Art of T. S. Eliot*. New York: E. P. Dutton & Co., Inc., 1950.

■■■■■■■■■

However the future may evaluate the work of T. S. Eliot, it will have to admit that no other poet writing in English in the first half of the twentieth century had so penetrating and pervasive an influence on his own times. This is already a matter of history. Even as we move into the second half of the century, we find Eliot's name appearing in a variety of discussions as a familiar reference to a kind of poetry, to certain principles and problems of literary criticism, to certain attitudes toward social questions—and to the influence which Eliot has had, and continues to have, in all these matters. The amount of writing that is devoted to praising, attacking, and interpreting Eliot already far exceeds in volume Eliot's "complete works," and it grows steadily larger.

At the center of Eliot's writings, reputation, and influence are his poetry and his development as a poet. Insofar as any one person may be regarded as the leader of the movement which developed into "modern" poetry, that person is T. S. Eliot. The movement was already under way when Eliot began writing, but it was he who assimilated and consolidated its basic principles. While he was himself influenced by contemporary tendencies, especially by the poetry and theories of Ezra Pound, Eliot himself created the very atmosphere in which modernism was to achieve its fullest development.

Like other literary movements, modernism began as a reaction against the literature of the preceding period, against the tastes and standards of Victorianism. Poets attempted in a number of ways to free themselves from the traditions that had become established in the nineteenth century, and they sought this liberation by adopting new attitudes, practicing new techniques, and choosing new subjects. Until Eliot's appearance, however, the reaction was incomplete and fragmentary, or it was an obvious reversal of Victorian modes. For example, the pessimism of Housman and the estheticism of the early Yeats are both departures from the prevailing mood of the nineteenth century, but their work is in many respects continuous with that of their close predecessors, especially in language and literary forms. A complete technical revolution was attempted by the free verse writers of the imagist movement, but they inclined toward thinness of meaning and formlessness because they denied themselves the use not only of nineteenth-century conventions but of those practices and effects which are essential to the best poetry of all periods. Even Ezra Pound in much of his work sounds like a rebellious heir of the nineteenth century. Pound had, however, pointed the way toward escaping not only from Victorianism but also from a too obvious and exhausting rebellion against it. He had done this by calling attention to the literatures of other countries and of other periods, by indicating that the modern poet could legitimately and successfully avail himself of other traditions than those of nineteenth-century England.

Pound had pointed the way, but it was Eliot, more learned and more disciplined for such a venture, who made the great strides and arrived at a positive achievement. Pound never fully developed beyond being the anti-Victorian rebel and the virtuoso of a variety of styles and traditions. Eliot came clear of the nineteenth century and drew upon other traditions but succeeded in writing a poetry that represented and was appropriate to his own times.

Some of the older writers whom Eliot has admired and effectively studied are Dante, the metaphysical poets and Jacobean dramatists of seventeenth-century England, and the symbolist poets of nineteenth-century France. The French poets had, in some respects, the greatest influence on Eliot's development. One of the lesser-known symbolists, Jules Laforgue, contributed most to the tone and structure of Eliot's earlier poems. The irregular but dramatically appropriate metrical scheme, the mixture of plaintive despair and ironic wittiness, the use of psychological association for organizing the poem as a self-probing "interior" monologue—these are devices which Eliot found in Laforgue and perfected in his early poems, of which the best known is "The Love Song of J. Alfred Prufrock."

Throughout Eliot's development the essential technique of symbolism remains basic. The symbolists had avoided forthright statement and the elaboration of ideas in general terms. They used images and details of human experience as symbols of their attitudes and especially as a means of suggesting the feelings which attended their attitudes. In their poetry they attempted to isolate tone enriched and complicated to the fullest possible degree. The absence of explanatory statements and the emphasis on tone account in part for the difficulty of Eliot's poetry. For example, "Prufrock" and "Preludes" seem, on the surface, to lack coherence and the logical relationship of parts. Even before a close examination of these poems, however, one can readily observe that the poems have a distinct and firmly sustained tone. On closer examination it becomes evident that some materials of the poems, such as images and situations, are the symbols of ideas and attitudes, of *themes*, and that the poems have a thematic development which is quite logical and meaningful.

In the work that followed the period of "Prufrock," Eliot extended the symbolist technique beyond the characteristic practice of the French poets. He did this by following Pound in the use of quotations from other writers within his own poems. Eliot uses the other writers in a variety of ways. Sometimes there are phrases or lines borrowed or whole passages echoed which need not be recognized by the reader in order to gain the full meaning of Eliot's poem. To recognize such a passage gives the reader no more than an insight into one of Eliot's habits of composition. At other times, however, Eliot's borrowings need to be recognized as such in order to get the full benefit of the poem's meaning. An example of this is the quotation from the Gospel of John in "Mr. Eliot's Sunday Morning Service." This practice differs from the traditional use of allusions in that Eliot's references are often relatively unfamiliar and are rarely explained within the poem. His quotations and echoes function much like the images of French symbolism. They are meaningfully related to other parts of the poem by the tone and theme which they introduce and which they derive from their original contexts. They differ from the symbolist images in that they introduce an abundance of clearly definable ideas, an intellectuality never achieved or attempted by the French poets.

The intellectuality of Eliot's work often adds to its difficulty but at the same time gives it an exactness of meaning that is not available from the symbolists and many modern poets. The intellectuality is, moreover, closely related to Eliot's position as a critic of cultural and moral conditions. In his essay "The Metaphysical Poets," he first expressed the view that since the seventeenth century there has been a growing "dissociation of sensibility," a lack of meaningful relationship between man's habits of thought and his habits of feeling. This theory obviously has large implications, involving the psychological effects on man produced by the decline of traditional religious beliefs and their replacement by scientific explanations. Eliot has particularly deplored what he considers have been the effects on the course of poetry. His use of echoes and quotations has been one means by which he has attempted to combine thought and feeling in his own work.

Eliot's habit of borrowing and his use of echoes, allusions, and quotations as an extension of symbolist technique can be seen in his poems written in quatrains, as in the "Sunday Morning Service." In The Waste Land these devices are essential to the development of the poem. A distinguishing, remarkable and, also difficult feature of The Waste Land is that a large part of its meaning lies in its technique, as Eliot's notes to the poem clearly indicate. Eliot continues to use these devices in his later work. They are still habits of composition in Ash Wednesday and in Four Quartets, but their function is less prominent, and one does not have to "read" the technique so closely while reading the poems. But there is still a similarity of structure in all of Eliot's poems, from "Prufrock" to Four Quartets. I. A. Richards has described The Waste Land as "a music of ideas," and this description may aptly be applied to the other poems as well. Both tone and theme, in their musical significance, are peculiarly appropriate terms for referring to the method of Eliot's poetry, whether it be the symbolism of "Prufrock," the complex and copious allusiveness of The Waste Land, or the meditative discursiveness of Four Quartets. The last title obviously refers to the musical aspect of the poem's structure.

A question that has frequently been raised about Eliot's poetry is its apparent disparity with his insistence upon the revival and preservation of traditional values. But this disparity is only on the surface. True, in his poetry Eliot has deliberately broken with long-established literary traditions, not only those of the English nineteenth century. He has done this because he has been so profoundly concerned with the decay of cultural, moral, and especially religious values. The worn-out and abused literary traditions he regarded as inadequate for his purpose of criticizing this tendency, of recording its effect upon the individual, and of restoring the traditional values by adapting them to contemporary needs. It is not true, as some critics have argued, that Eliot has attempted to escape from the present into the past. Both the matter and the manner of Eliot's work show how conscientiously he has been involved in his own times. Few writers have felt so acutely the relationship between literary style and the civilization to which they belonged.

> We can only say that it appears likely that poets in our civilization, as it exists at present, must be *difficult*. Our civilization comprehends great variety and complexity, and this variety and complexity, playing upon a refined sensibility, must produce various and complex results. The poet must become more and more comprehensive, more allusive, more indirect, in order to force, to dislocate if necessary, language into his meaning.*

This passage implies that the poet's meaning is inseparable from his times, from his civilization. Whether or not we accept the implication as a general truth, we must grant that it is true of Eliot. His meaning is that of a man who has submitted himself to the variety and complexity, to the most serious and most painful aspects, of modern civilization.

The Love Song of J. Alfred Prufrock[1]

> *S'io credesse che mia risposta fosse*
> *A persona che mai tornasse al mondo,*
> *Questa fiamma staria senza piu scosse.*
> *Ma perciocche giammai di questo fondo*
> *Non torno vivo alcun, s'i'odo il vero*
> *Senza tema d'infamia ti rispondo.*[2]

Let us go then, you and I,
When the evening is spread out against the sky

---

* "The Metaphysical Poets," in *Selected Essays* (New York: Harcourt, Brace & Co., 1932), p. 248.

1. "The Love Song of J. Alfred Prufrock" is from *Collected Poems 1909-1935*, by T. S. Eliot, copyright, 1936, by Harcourt, Brace & Company, Inc. Reprinted by their permission and that of Faber & Faber Ltd.

2. "If I thought my answer were to a person who could ever return to the world, this flame would shake no more; but since no one ever returned alive from this depth, if what I hear be true, without fear of infamy I answer thee." *Inferno* XXVII, lines 61-66.

Like a patient etherized upon a table;
Let us go, through certain half-deserted streets,
The muttering retreats
Of restless nights in one-night cheap hotels
And sawdust restaurants with oyster-shells:
Streets that follow like a tedious argument
Of insidious intent
To lead you to an overwhelming question. . . .   10
Oh, do not ask, "What is it?"
Let us go and make our visit.

In the room the women come and go
Talking of Michelangelo.

The yellow fog that rubs its back upon the window-panes,
The yellow smoke that rubs its muzzle on the window-panes,
Licked its tongue into the corners of the evening,
Lingered upon the pools that stand in drains,
Let fall upon its back the soot that falls from chimneys,
Slipped by the terrace, made a sudden leap,   20
And seeing that it was a soft October night,
Curled once about the house, and fell asleep.

And indeed there will be time
For the yellow smoke that slides along the street,
Rubbing its back upon the window-panes;
There will be time, there will be time
To prepare a face to meet the faces that you meet;
There will be time to murder and create,
And time for all the works and days of hands
That lift and drop a question on your plate;   30
Time for you and time for me,
And time yet for a hundred indecisions,
And for a hundred visions and revisions,
Before the taking of a toast and tea.

In the room the women come and go
Talking of Michelangelo.

And indeed there will be time
To wonder, "Do I dare?" and, "Do I dare?"
Time to turn back and descend the stair,
With a bald spot in the middle of my hair—   40
(They will say: "How his hair is growing thin!")
My morning coat, my collar mounting firmly to the chin,

My necktie rich and modest, but asserted by a simple pin—
(They will say: "But how his arms and legs are thin!")
Do I dare
Disturb the universe?
In a minute there is time
For decisions and revisions which a minute will reverse.

For I have known them all already, known them all:
Have known the evenings, mornings, afternoons,   50
I have measured out my life with coffee spoons;
I know the voices dying with a dying fall
Beneath the music from a farther room.
   So how should I presume?

And I have known the eyes already, known them all—
The eyes that fix you in a formulated phrase,
And when I am formulated, sprawling on a pin,
When I am pinned and wriggling on the wall,
Then how should I begin
To spit out all the butt-ends of my days and ways?   60
   And how should I presume?

And I have known the arms already, known them all—
Arms that are braceleted and white and bare
(But in the lamplight, downed with light brown hair!)
Is it perfume from a dress
That makes me so digress?
Arms that lie along a table, or wrap about a shawl.
   And should I then presume?
   And how should I begin?

      .   .   .

Shall I say, I have gone at dusk through narrow streets   70
And watched the smoke that rises from the pipes
Of lonely men in shirt-sleeves, leaning out of windows? . . .

I should have been a pair of ragged claws
Scuttling across the floors of silent seas.

      .   .   .

And the afternoon, the evening, sleeps so peacefully!
Smoothed by long fingers,
Asleep . . . tired . . . or it malingers,
Stretched on the floor, here beside you and me.
Should I, after tea and cakes and ices,
Have the strength to force the moment to its crisis?   80
But though I have wept and fasted, wept and prayed,

Though I have seen my head (grown slightly bald) brought in upon
        a platter,
I am no prophet—and here's no great matter;
I have seen the moment of my greatness flicker,
And I have seen the eternal Footman hold my coat, and snicker,
And in short, I was afraid.

And would it have been worth it, after all,
After the cups, the marmalade, the tea,
Among the porcelain, among some talk of you and me,
Would it have been worth while,   90
To have bitten off the matter with a smile,
To have squeezed the universe into a ball
To roll it toward some overwhelming question,
To say: "I am Lazarus, come from the dead,
Come back to tell you all, I shall tell you all"—
If one, settling a pillow by her head,
    Should say: "That is not what I meant at all.
    That is not it, at all."

And would it have been worth it, after all,
Would it have been worth while,   100
After the sunsets and the dooryards and the sprinkled streets,
After the novels, after the teacups, after the skirts that trail along
        the floor—
And this, and so much more?—
It is impossible to say just what I mean!
But as if a magic lantern threw the nerves in patterns on a screen:
Would it have been worth while
If one, settling a pillow or throwing off a shawl,
And turning toward the window, should say:
    "That is not it at all,
    That is not what I meant, at all."   110

No! I am not Prince Hamlet, nor was meant to be;
Am an attendant lord, one that will do
To swell a progress, start a scene or two,
Advise the prince; no doubt, an easy tool,
Deferential, glad to be of use,
Politic, cautious, and meticulous;
Full of high sentence, but a bit obtuse;
At times, indeed, almost ridiculous—
Almost, at times, the Fool.

I grow old. . . . I grow old. . . .   120
I shall wear the bottoms of my trousers rolled.

Shall I part my hair behind? Do I dare to eat a peach?
I shall wear white flannel trousers, and walk upon the beach.
I have heard the mermaids singing, each to each.

I do not think that they will sing to me.

I have seen them riding seaward on the waves
Combing the white hair of the waves blown back
When the wind blows the water white and black.

We have lingered in the chambers of the sea
By sea-girls wreathed with seaweed red and brown   130
Till human voices wake us, and we drown.

■   1. What is the significance of the title of the poem?

2. Should the poem, for the most part, be considered a reverie or a narrative?

3. Notice that the poem is divided by spaces into a number of passages. Interpret the poem passage by passage, and in so doing explain the relationship of successive passages; that is, account for the transitions between the passages.

4. Compare your interpretation of the poem with that of Roy A. Basler in *Sex, Symbolism and Psychology in Literature*, (New Brunswick, N.J.: Rutgers University Press, 1948), pp. 203–221.

Preludes[1]

I

The winter evening settles down
With smell of steaks in passageways.
Six o'clock.
The burnt-out ends of smoky days.
And now a gusty shower wraps
The grimy scraps
Of withered leaves about your feet
And newspapers from vacant lots;
The showers beat
On broken blinds and chimney-pots,   10
And at the corner of the street
A lonely cab-horse steams and stamps.
And then the lighting of the lamps.

1. ....

1. "Preludes" is from *Collected Poems 1909–1935*, by T. S. Eliot, copyright, 1936, by Harcourt, Brace & Company, Inc. Reprinted by their permission, and that of Faber & Faber Ltd.

2

The morning comes to consciousness
Of faint stale smells of beer
From the sawdust-trampled street
With all its muddy feet that press
To early coffee-stands.
With the other masquerades
That time resumes,   20
One thinks of all the hands
That are raising dingy shades
In a thousand furnished rooms.

3

You tossed a blanket from the bed,
You lay upon your back, and waited;
You dozed, and watched the night revealing
The thousand sordid images
Of which your soul was constituted;
They flickered against the ceiling.
And when all the world came back   30
And the light crept up between the shutters
And you heard the sparrows in the gutters,
You had such a vision of the street
As the street hardly understands;
Sitting along the bed's edge, where
You curled the papers from your hair,
Or clasped the yellow soles of feet
In the palms of both soiled hands.

4

His soul stretched tight across the skies
That fade behind a city block,   40
Or trampled by insistent feet
At four and five and six o'clock;
And short square fingers stuffing pipes,
And evening newspapers, and eyes
Assured of certain certainties,
The conscience of a blackened street
Impatient to assume the world.
I am moved by fancies that are curled
Around these images, and cling:
The notion of some infinitely gentle   50
Infinitely suffering thing.

Wipe your hand across your mouth, and laugh;
The worlds revolve like ancient women
Gathering fuel in vacant lots.

■ 1. Explain the title.

2. Does "Preludes" have the unity and line of development of a single poem, or is it a collection of loosely related passages?

3. Notice the recurrence of a class of images that are a part of the human body: feet, hands, fingers, hair, eyes. What effects are produced by these images?

4. The imagery of "Preludes" obviously presents a picture of life in a modern city and, by implication, makes a comment upon it. What, in general, is this comment?

Mr. Eliot's
Sunday Morning Service [1]

Look, look, master, here comes two religious
caterpillars.—THE JEW OF MALTA.

Polyphiloprogenitive[1a]
The sapient sutlers[2] of the Lord
Drift across the window-panes.
In the beginning was the Word.

In the beginning was the Word.
Superfetation of $\tau\grave{o}$ $\ddot{\epsilon}\nu$,[3]
And at the mensual[4] turn of time
Produced enervate Origen.[5]

A painter of the Umbrian school
Designed upon a gesso ground
The nimbus of the Baptized God.
The wilderness is cracked and browned

But through the water pale and thin
Still shine the unoffending feet
And there above the painter set
The Father and the Paraclete.[6]

....

1. "Mr. Eliot's Sunday Morning Service" is from *Collected Poems 1909-1935*, by T. S. Eliot, copyright, 1936, by Harcourt, Brace & Company, Inc. Reprinted by their permission, and that of Faber & Faber Ltd.   1a. Loving many offspring.   2. One who follows an army and sells provision to the soldiers.   3. Greek for Being.   4. As measured by months   5. Church father of the third century.   6. The Holy Spirit.

• • •

The sable presbyters approach
The avenue of penitence;
The young are red and pustular[7]
Clutching piaculative[8] pence.   20

Under the penitential gates
Sustained by staring Seraphim
Where the souls of the devout
Burn invisible and dim.[9]

Along the garden-wall the bees
With hairy bellies pass between
The staminate and pistilate,
Blest office of the epicene.[10]

Sweeney[11] shifts from ham to ham
Stirring the water in his bath.   30
The masters of the subtle schools
Are controversial, polymath.[12]

■ There is, in the light of the poem, an obvious mockery in the title.
But is it in a sense also seriously intended? If so, in what sense?

....

7. Pimply.   8. A penitential offering.   9. Quoted from Henry Vaughan's
"The Night."   10. Having characteristics of both sexes or of neither sex
specifically.   11. Sweeney, appearing in several of Eliot's poems, is a character
of vulgar and confident sensuality. A product of civilization, like Prufrock, he is as
"uncivilized" as Prufrock is "overcivilized."   12. Extensively learned.

Geronion [1]

Thou hast nor youth nor age
But as it were an after dinner sleep
Dreaming of both.[2]

Here I am, an old man in a dry month,
Being read to by a boy, waiting for rain.[3]
I was neither at the hot gates[4]
Nor fought in the warm rain

....

1. "Geronion" is from *Collected Poems 1909–1935,* by T. S. Eliot, copyright, 1936, by Harcourt, Brace & Company, Inc. Reprinted by their permission,
and that of Faber & Faber Ltd. "Geronion" is Greek for "little old man."
2. From Shakespeare's *Measure for Measure,* Act III, scene i.   3. "Here he
sits, in a dry month, old and blind, being read to by a country boy, longing for
rain."—A. C. Benson's biography of Edward Fitzgerald.   4. Thermopylae
(literal translation: "hot gates") is where the Greeks successfully held back the
Persian invaders.

Nor knee deep in the salt marsh, heaving a cutlass,
Bitten by flies, fought.
My house is a decayed house,
And the jew squats on the window sill, the owner,
Spawned in some estaminet of Antwerp,
Blistered in Brussels, patched and peeled in London.　　　　10
The goat coughs at night in the field overhead;
Rocks, moss, stonecrop, iron, merds.
The woman keeps the kitchen, makes tea,
Sneezes at evening, poking the peevish gutter.
　　　　　　　　　I an old man,
A dull head among windy spaces.

Signs are taken for wonders. "We would see a sign!"
The word within a word, unable to speak a word,
Swaddled with darkness.[5] In the juvescence of the year
Came Christ the tiger　　　　20
In depraved May, dogwood and chestnut, flowering judas,[6]
To be eaten, to be divided, to be drunk
Among whispers; by Mr. Silvero
With caressing hands, at Limoges,
Who walked all night in the next room;

By Hakagawa, bowing among the Titians;
By Madame de Tornquist, in the dark room
Shifting the candles; Fräulein von Kulp
Who turned in the hall, one hand on the door.
　　Vacant shuttles　　　　30
Weave the wind. I have no ghosts,
An old man in a draughty house
Under a windy knob.

After such knowledge, what forgiveness? Think now
History has many cunning passages, contrived corridors
And issues, deceives with whispering ambitions,
Guides us by vanities. Think now
She gives when our attention is distracted
And what she gives, gives with such supple confusions
That the giving famishes the craving. Gives too late　　　　40

5.　These lines echo a passage from a sermon by the seventeenth-century Anglican bishop, Lancelot Andrewes. The passage is quoted by Eliot in his *Selected Essays* (1st ed.), p. 297.　6.　"Here and there a Negro log cabin alone disturbs the dogwood and the judas tree . . . . The tulip and the chestnut tree gave no sense of struggle against a stingy nature . . . . No European spring had shown him the same intermixture of delicate grace and passionate depravity that marked the Maryland May." *The Education of Henry Adams*.

What's not believed in, or if still believed,
In memory only, reconsidered passion. Gives too soon
Into weak hands, what's thought can be dispensed with
Till the refusal propagates a fear. Think
Neither fear nor courage saves us. Unnatural vices
Are fathered by our heroism. Virtues
Are forced upon us by our impudent crimes.
These tears are shaken from the wrath-bearing tree.

The tiger springs in the new year. Us he devours.
   Think at last   50
We have not reached conclusion, when I
Stiffen in a rented house. Think at last
I have not made this show purposelessly
And it is not by any concitation
Of the backward devils
I would meet you upon this honestly.
I that was near your heart was removed therefrom[7]
To lose beauty in terror, terror in inquisition.
I have lost my passion: why should I need to keep it
Since what is kept must be adulterated?   60
I have lost my sight, smell, hearing, taste and touch:
How should I use them for your closer contact?
These with a thousand small deliberations
Protract the profit of their chilled delirium,
Excite the membrane, when the sense has cooled,
With pungent sauces, multiply variety
In a wilderness of mirrors. What will the spider do,
Suspend its operations, will the weevil
Delay? De Bailhache, Fresca, Mrs. Cammel, whirled
Beyond the circuit of the shuddering Bear   70
In fractured atoms. Gull against the wind, in the windy straits
Of Belle Isle, or running on the Horn,
White feathers in the snow, the Gulf claims,
And an old man driven by the Trades
To a sleepy corner.

                 Tenants of the house,
Thoughts of a dry brain in a dry season.

◼   For an interpretative discussion of "Gerontion," see Chap. IV, Elizabeth Drew, T. S. Eliot: The Design of His Poetry (New York: Charles
Scribner's Sons, 1949).

7. "I that am of your blood was taken from you." Middleton's The Changeling,
Act V, scene iii; quoted by Eliot in Selected Essays (1st ed.), p. 148.

Marina[1]

Quis hic locus, quae
regio, quae mundi plaga? [2]

What seas what shores what grey rocks and what islands
What water lapping the bow
And scent of pine and the woodthrush singing through the fog
What images return
O my daughter.

Those who sharpen the tooth of the dog, meaning
Death
Those who glitter with the glory of the hummingbird, meaning
Death   10
Those who sit in the stye of contentment, meaning
Death
Those who suffer the ecstasy of the animals, meaning
Death

Are become unsubstantial, reduced by a wind,
A breath of pine, and the woodsong fog
By this grace dissolved in place

What is this face, less clear and clearer
The pulse in the arm, less strong and stronger—
Given or lent? more distant than stars and nearer than the eye   20

Whispers and small laughter between leaves and hurrying feet
Under sleep, where all the waters meet.

Bowsprit cracked with ice and paint cracked with heat.
I made this, I have forgotten
And remember.

....

1. "Marina" is from *Collected Poems 1909–1935*, by T. S. Eliot, copyright,
1936, by Harcourt, Brace & Company, Inc. Reprinted by their permission, and
that of Faber & Faber Ltd.

Eliot's "objective correlative" for the theme and attitude of this poem is the
recognition scene in Shakespeare's *Pericles, Prince of Tyre*, Act V, scene i, in
which the old king who lost his infant daughter at sea, after years of hopeless
search, finally discovers her, a gracious and beautiful young woman. In the moment of dawning recognition, Pericles says

> But are you flesh and blood?
> Have you a working pulse? and are no fairy?
> Motion! Well, speak on. Where were you born?
> And wherefore called Marina?

The daughter was named Marina because she was born at sea.   2. The Latin
epigraph, "What place is this, what region, what part of the world?" is spoken
by Hercules, just recovered from madness in Seneca's *Hercules Furens*.

The rigging weak and the canvas rotten
Between one June and another September.
Made this unknowing, half conscious, unknown, my own.
The garboard strake leaks, the seams need caulking.
This form, this face, this life   30
Living to live in a world of time beyond me; let me
Resign my life for this life, my speech for that unspoken,
The awakened, lips parted, the hope, the new ships.

What seas what shores what granite islands towards my timbers
And woodthrush calling through the fog
My daughter.

■   1. Explain how a formal quality is achieved in this poem without
the use of traditional versification.
     2. Of what is the girl Marina a symbol? See Unger's "T. S. Eliot's
Rose Garden," in *T. S. Eliot: A Selected Critique,* and relate your
interpretation of "Marina" to the persistent theme which that essay finds
in Eliot's work.

From *Four Quartets*
Section 2, "Little Gidding"[1]

Ash on an old man's sleeve
Is all the ash the burnt roses leave.
Dust in the air suspended
Marks the place where a story ended.
Dust inbreathed was a house—
The wall, the wainscot and the mouse.
The death of hope and despair,
     This is the death of air.

There are flood and drouth
Over the eyes and in the mouth,   10
Dead water and dead sand

....

1.   Section II of "Little Gidding" is from *Four Quartets,* copyright, 1943, by
T. S. Eliot. Reprinted by permission of Harcourt, Brace & Company, Inc., and
that of Faber & Faber Ltd.
     Each of the *Four Quartets* has for its title the name of a specific locality.
Little Gidding is the place in England where in the seventeenth century a religious
community was founded by Nicholas Ferrar, the friend and literary executor of
George Herbert. The community lasted only a short time, but the chapel at
Little Gidding has come to be regarded as an Anglican shrine.   2.   During
World War II Eliot served as an air raid warden in London. Notice that the event
related in the second part of the selection takes place soon after a night bombing
and ends with the all-clear signal at dawn.

Contending for the upper hand.
The parched eviscerate soil
Gapes at the vanity of toil,
Laughs without mirth.
    This is the death of earth.

Water and fire succeed
The town, the pasture and the weed.
Water and fire deride
The sacrifice that we denied.   20
Water and fire shall rot
The marred foundations we forgot,
Of sanctuary and choir.
    This is the death of water and fire.

In the uncertain hour before the morning²
  Near the ending of interminable night
  At the recurrent end of the unending
After the dark dove with the flickering tongue
  Had passed below the horizon of his homing
  While the dead leaves still rattled on like tin   30
Over the asphalt where no other sound was
  Between three districts whence the smoke arose
  I met one walking, loitering and hurried
As if blown towards me like the metal leaves
  Before the urban dawn wind unresisting.
  And as I fixed upon the down-turned face
That pointed scrutiny with which we challenge
  The first-met stranger in the waning dusk
  I caught the sudden look of some dead master
Whom I had known, forgotten, half-recalled   40
  Both one and many; in the brown baked features
  The eyes of a familiar compound ghost
Both intimate and unidentifiable.
  So I assumed a double part, and cried
  And heard another's voice cry: "What! are *you* here?"
Although we were not. I was still the same,
  Knowing myself yet being someone other—
  And he a face still forming; yet the words sufficed
To compel the recognition they preceded.
  And so, compliant to the common wind,   50
  Too strange to each other for misunderstanding,
In concord at this intersection time
  Of meeting nowhere, no before and after,
  We trod the pavement in a dead patrol.

I said: "The wonder that I feel is easy,
   Yet ease is cause of wonder. Therefore speak:
   I may not comprehend, may not remember."
And he: "I am not eager to rehearse
   My thought and theory which you have forgotten.
   These things have served their purpose: let them be.   60
So with your own, and pray they be forgiven
   By others, as I pray you to forgive
   Both bad and good. Last season's fruit is eaten
And the fullfed beast shall kick the empty pail.
   For last year's words belong to last year's language
   And next year's words await another voice.
But, as the passage now presents no hindrance
   To the spirit unappeased and peregrine
   Between two worlds become much like each other,
So I find words I never thought to speak   70
   In streets I never thought I should revisit
   When I left my body on a distant shore.
Since our concern was speech, and speech impelled us
   To purify the dialect of the tribe
   And urge the mind to aftersight and foresight,
Let me disclose the gifts reserved for age
   To set a crown upon your lifetime's effort.
   First, the cold friction of expiring sense
Without enchantment, offering no promise
   But bitter tastelessness of shadow fruit   80
   As body and soul begin to fall asunder.
Second, the conscious impotence of rage
   At human folly, and the laceration
   Of laughter at what ceases to amuse.
And last, the rending pain of re-enactment
   Of all that you have done, and been; the shame
   Of motives late revealed, and the awareness
Of things ill done and done to others' harm
   Which once you took for exercise of virtue.
   Then fools' approval stings, and honour stains.   90
From wrong to wrong the exasperated spirit
   Proceeds, unless restored by that refining fire
   Where you must move in measure, like a dancer."
The day was breaking. In the disfigured street
   He left me, with a kind of valediction,
   And faded on the blowing of the horn.

1. With special attention to rhythm and imagery, compare Eliot's
tyle here with the earlier style of "Prufrock" and "Gerontion."

Hart Crane

(1899–1932)

■■■■■■■■■

HART CRANE was a part of the poetic movement of the 1930's that brought a new maturity into our poetry. Crane was the victim of an oversolicitous mother and a businessman father who had almost no understanding of and very little sympathy for a son who wanted to be a poet. Crane suffered from emotional disorders and increasingly his life became a series of drunken and sexual orgies, wild enthusiasms and terrible depressions. He leaped into the sea on his way back to the United States from Mexico. (His story has been movingly told in *Life of an American Poet, Hart Crane,* by Philip Horton.) Crane himself had little in the way of academic learning, but he was a man of great sensitivity and was able to learn much that was necessary to him as a poet from the "little magazines" which he read and to which he contributed. And particularly after he moved to New York City from Cleveland he associated with men like Allen Tate, Waldo Frank, and Gorham Munson, who were able to help him. From the *Seven Arts,* edited by Frank, James Oppenheim, and Van Wyck Brooks, he learned about "America's coming of age" and was led to study Melville and Whitman very intensively. He also studied Marlowe, Shakespeare, and John Webster. Very laboriously he translated a few poems by Laforgue, but most of his knowledge of the poetic techniques of French symbolism he learned from studying translations. All Crane's work, including *White Buildings* (1926) and *The Bridge* (1930), is in *The Collected Poems of Hart Crane* (1933), edited by Waldo Frank.

Suggested Readings

R. P. BLACKMUR, "New Thresholds, New Anatomies," in *The Double Agent.* New York: Arrow Editions, 1935, pp. 121–140.

ALLEN TATE, "Hart Crane," in *Reactionary Essays.* New York: Charles Scribner's Sons, 1936, pp. 26–42.

WILLIAM VAN O'CONNOR, "The Influence of the Symbolists," in *Sense and Sensibility in Modern Poetry.* Chicago: University of Chicago Press, 1948, pp. 66–80.

■■■■■■■■■

Voyages II

And yet this great wink of eternity,
Of rimless floods, unfettered leewardings,
Samite sheeted and processioned where
Her undinal vast belly moonward bends,
Laughing the wrapt inflections of our love;

Take this Sea, whose diapason knells
On scrolls of silver snowy sentences,
The sceptred terror of whose sessions rends
As her demeanors motion well or ill,
All but the pieties of lovers' hands.

And onward, as bells off San Salvador
Salute the crocus lustres of the stars,
In these poinsettia meadows of her tides,—
Adagios of islands, O my Prodigal,
Complete the dark confessions her veins spell.

Mark how her turning shoulders wind the hours,
And hasten while her penniless rich palms
Pass superscription of bent foam and wave,—
Hasten, while they are true,—sleep, death, desire,
Close round one instant in one floating flower.

Bind us in time, O Seasons clear, and awe.
O minstrel galleons of Carib fire,
Bequeath us to no earthly shore until
Is answered in the vortex of our grave
The seal's wide sprindrift gaze toward paradise.

Hart Crane's "Voyages II" rewards careful study for at least two reasons; first, it is a fine poem in its own right, and, secondly, it exhibits the influence in modern poetry of the French literary movement called symbolism. Some of the characteristics of symbolist poetry, as they are found for example in Mallarmé (1842–1898) as well as in Crane, are these: finding unusual relationships between objects; making evocative statements as opposed to explicit statements; exploring the connotative meanings of words rather than relying on denotative meanings; exploring the range of associations, both personal and general, implicit in a coherent body of imagery; depending upon synaesthesia, or the unifying and interchanging of sense impressions; and moving from meaning to meaning within the poem by relying on association rather than strict logic. These generalizations will become clearer in examining "Voyages II," but they are made here because they are relevant not only to much of Crane's poetry but to that of other modern poets, such as T. S. Eliot, Wallace Stevens, Marianne Moore, Allen Tate, and Robert Penn Warren.

We may begin by stating the theme of "Voyages II," which each reader can verify or test for himself in studying the poem. The theme, quite simply, is that man is caught and lives in a universe of flux; in death he is reabsorbed into inanimate, unthinking nature. The sea is a symbol of eternity and flux which suggests man's relationship to nature. The poem is an investigation in imagistic language (a coherent body of imagery) of the sea as a symbol of eternity. The sea is, as a matter of fact, a good symbol of the "eternity" Crane was thinking about: life is believed to have originated in the sea; the sea is also vast, impersonal, powerful, annihilating; and its changing patterns, its tides, waves, appearances, its throwing up of life and taking it away in prodigal fashion, all suggest the idea of flux.

There are a number of words that may offer difficulty to some readers for either or both of two reasons: first, because their denotative (dictionary) meaning is unknown; second, because the poet has used them in a somewhat special way or at least in a specialized context. The following are some of these words: "samite" (a heavy silk fabric that is interwoven with gold or silver), "undinal" (from the noun "undine," meaning a fabled female water spirit who might receive a human soul by marrying a mortal), "diapason" (the entire compass of organ tones), "leewardings" (the side away from the wind; opposed to windward), "inflections" (changes or shifts in form, in tone, in pitch; a bend or curve), "spindrift" (the spray blown from waves at sea). These dictionary meanings are necessary or prerequisite to understanding their somewhat specialized usages in the poem. The word "leewardings" (line 2) offers no great difficulty—it helps us to see a vast expanse of smooth water running *with* the wind. "Samite" (line 3) is a little more difficult because we have, first, to think of the sea with a white smooth surface; only then can we think of it as shot through, like samite, with threads of gold or silver. The use of "undinal" (line 4) is even more specialized: the poet has made the sea feminine, in love with the moon, which controls the tides; if we recall that the undine, the water spirit, became human when she married a mortal, we have an ironic echo of this idea in remembering how many mortals the sea has taken, how many souls she has wedded. The word "inflections" (line 5) suggests not merely the changing and shifting of waves, but melodious patterns of laughter and the shifting levels of rapture in love. Again, "diapason" (line 6) is employed after the poet has made us think of the sea as laughing melodiously; "diapason" extends or deepens this idea by suggesting a tremendously powerful compass of sounds that would be appropriate to the vastness of the sea. Lastly, "spindrift" (line 25), in terms of the context of the poem, is made to describe man's aspiration toward heaven like the seal's gaze skyward through a windy spray of water.

Other words in the poem—"sessions," "demeanors," "adagios," "confessions," "bequeath"—are used in a specialized way, requiring that the reader experience them in a new context. They have to be read imaginatively. We may take these words one at a time in order to suggest something about the associations they arouse in our minds. The word "sessions" (line 8) suggests a parliament, the movement of dark-gowned figures legislating, acting in ways that may mean good or ill fortune for many people. The only force that may transcend the "sessions" is love—presumably because, whatever ill fortune befalls lovers, they have had a spiritual bond that somehow lifts them above misfortune or suffering. The word "sessions" is acceptable because we can imagine the waves to be figures in human parliaments. And several earlier words have prepared us for so conceiving the waves—the words "scrolls" "sentences" and "sceptred," all of which are associated with parliaments. The word "demeanors" (line 9) fits easily, too, because it means conduct or manners—and if we can think of the waves as sessions of parliamentarians we can apply the word "demeanor," usually thought of as grave or serious conduct, to the sea. The adagio is a slow tempo or movement in music. Thus *adagios of islands* (line 14) suggests a series of slow rhythmic movements of the tides. The islands, too, are mysterious, like the sentences spelled out by the salt and froth on the surface of the sea. Crane himself said, "The reference is to the motion of the boat through the islands." The "veins" or lines through the water spell out the "dark confessions" (line 15), obscure meanings, of the sea. Lastly, "bequeath" (line 23) is used in an unusual way in that the sea is requested not to allow the shore to inherit our bones until the inscrutable universe is made meaningful.

Like Mallarmé, Crane employed images which merge with one another, dissolve, and reappear in a different guise or form. First, the sea is thought of as a "great wink." In our usual perspective the sea is vast or "great," but in contrast to eternity it will, however large it seems or however long it endures, be only a wink. The suggestion for the comparison may have arisen in the poet's mind from the similar shape of the eyeball and the sea as we can perceive it. The juxtaposition of sea and wink is startling, but it is legitimate because it enables us to experience imaginatively, to some extent, the timelessness of eternity; it evokes a sense of eternity. (This startling kind of figure—in which unlike elements, the sea and a wink, meet on a common ground, time-in-relation-to-eternity—is, as we have said elsewhere, called a conceit.) This figure is dropped after the opening line.

The values of life, its beauties, love, and final peacefulness, are caught in the recurring flower imagery—"crocus lustres of the stars" (line 12), "poinsettia meadows" (line 13), and "floating flower" (line 20). This body of imagery, which associates readily with the riches and peacefulness of the islands, symbolizes "sleep, death, desire" (line 19).

The imagery concerned with the writing or sentences on the surface of the sea includes "scrolls of silver snowy sentences" (line 7), "veins spell" (line 15), and "superscription," or the raised printing on coins (line 18). It is as though the sea were writing out her meanings in the patterns of white foam and flecks that from shipboard look like written sentences.

Whiteness, a symbol of happiness and terror, is explicitly and implicitly employed. It occurs in "samite sheeted" (line 3); "moonward" (line 4); "scrolls of silver snowy sentences" (line 7); "sceptred terror," or the top of the wave shaped like a scepter (line 8); "crocus lustres of the stars," or the yellowish reflections of the stars in the water (line 12); "foam and wave" (line 18); and "spindrift" (line 25). Whiteness holds together much of the other imagery in that it is common to the other imagistic patterns.

Synaesthesia, or the interchanging of sense impressions, also helps to effect a unity of impression. The sea in its changing surfaces not only seems to write sentences but to laugh, and finally to give forth a full diapason of mournful sounds (line 6) and of bells (line 11). Synaesthesia, commonly employed by symbolist poets, suggests the unifying power of the mind. In "Voyages II" it is an especially useful device to suggest the nature of flux and change, not merely in the external universe but in man's mind.

The sea imagined as feminine affords another means of unifying the poem. She can love, laugh, write, change her demeanor, turn her shoulders (line 16) and hold the superscriptions as though in the palms of her hands (line 17). The seasons, too, are personified (line 21). They are asked to "bind us in time," that is, to give us our allotted time, but not to allow us to forgo or avoid a sense of "awe."

There is a paradox to be observed in the phrase "penniless rich palms." The palms of hands of the sea contain lavish riches but do not retain them. Nor are the riches monetary riches—the true riches are the human experiences of knowing "sleep, death, desire." The word "superscription" also suggests that the raised impressions on coins wash off that, in other words, wealth, like other human possessions, becomes a part of the flux.

It is true that many symbolist poems, like "Voyages II," are at first reading obscure. Yet if one grasps the general theme the obscurities yield themselves to the understanding. Most of the difficulties are, as we have seen, a result of a development by association of ideas and images, discovering new meanings in words, seeing resemblances where none were seen before, and depending on a generally imagistic language. The reader may ask at this point what the advantage is in using language in such fashion. The answer, which also applies to many of the techniques used by poets who have not written as symbolists, is that it makes a certain type of experience available esthetically which is not available in the ordinary prose language that emphasizes logical progression and immediately clear meanings. The idea of an inscrutable universe, of flux, in which men know love, desire, sleep, and other human feelings can be caught and felt in the language Crane employed. Other types of language would not at the same time be so economical and moving.

The Idiot

Sheer over to the other side,—for see
That boy straggling under those mimosas, daft
With squint lanterns in his head, and it's likely
Fumbling his sex. That's why those children laughed

In such infernal circles round his door
Once when he shouted, stretched in ghastly shape.
I hurried by. But back from the hot shore
Passed him again . . . He was alone, agape;

One hand dealt out a kite string; a tin can
The other tilted, peeled end clapped to eye.
That kite aloft—you should have watched him scan
Its course, though he'd clamped midnight to noon sky!

And since, through these hot barricades of green,
A Dios gracias, grac—I've heard his song
Above all reason lifting, halt serene—
My trespass vision shrinks to face his wrong.

1. What images especially bring home the idiocy of the boy?
2. Why does the passer-by shrink to face the idiot?

From *The Bridge*

The Tunnel

Performances, assortments, resumés—
Up Times Square to Columbus Circle lights
Channel the congresses, nightly sessions.

Refractions of the thousand theatres, faces—
Mysterious kitchens. . . . You shall search them all.
Some day by heart you'll learn each famous sight
And watch the curtain lift in hell's despite;
You'll find the garden in the third act dead,
Finger your knees—and wish yourself in bed
With tabloid crime-sheets perched in easy sight.   10

> Then let you reach your hat
> and go.
> As usual, let you—also
> walking down—exclaim
> to twelve upward leaving
> a subscription praise
> for what time slays.

Or can't you quite make up your mind to ride;
A walk is better underneath the L a brisk
Ten blocks or so before? but you find yourself   20
Preparing penguin flexions of the arms,—
As usual you will meet the scuttle yawn:
The subway yawns the quickest promise home.

Be minimum, then, to swim the hiving swarms
Out of the Square, the Circle burning bright—
Avoid the glass doors gyring at your right,
Where boxed alone a second, eyes take fright
—Quite unprepared rush naked back to light:
And down beside the turnstile press the coin
Into the slot. The gongs already rattle.   30

> And so
> of cities you bespeak
> subways, rivered under streets
> and rivers. . . . In the car
> the overtone of motion
> underground, the monotone
> of motion is the sound
> of other faces, also underground—

"Let's have a pencil Jimmy—living now
at Floral Park   4
Flatbush—on the Fourth of July—
like a pigeon's muddy dream—potatoes
to dig in the field—travlin the town—too—

night after night—the Culver line—the
girls all shaping up—it used to be—"

Our tongues recant like beaten weather vanes.
This answer lives like verdigris, like hair
Beyond extinction, surcease of the bone;
And repetition freezes—What

> "what do you want? getting weak on the links?   50
> fandaddle daddy don't ask for change—IS THIS
> FOURTEENTH? it's half past six she said—if
> you don't like my gate why did you
> swing on it, why *didja*
> swing on it
> anyhow—"

And somehow anyhow swing—

The phonographs of hades in the brain
Are tunnels that re-wind themselves, and love
A burnt match skating in a urinal—   60
Somewhere above Fourteenth TAKE THE EXPRESS
To brush some new presentiment of pain—

"But I want service in this office SERVICE
I said—after
the show she cried a little afterwards but—"

Whose head is swinging from the swollen strap?
Whose body smokes along the bitten rails,
Bursts from a smoldering bundle far behind
In back forks of the chasms of the brain,—
Puffs from a riven stump far out behind   70
In interborough fissures of the mind . . . ?

And why do I often meet your visage here,
Your eyes like agate lanterns—on and on
Below the toothpaste and the dandruff ads?
—And did their riding eyes right through your side,
And did their eyes like unwashed platters ride?
And Death, aloft,—gigantically down
Probing through you—toward me, O evermore!
And when they dragged your retching flesh,
Your trembling hands that night through Baltimore—   80

That last night on the ballot rounds, did you
Shaking, did you deny the ticket, Poe?

For Gravesend Manor change at Chambers Street.
The platform hurries along to a dead stop.

The intent escalator lifts a serenade
Stilly
Of shoes, umbrellas, each eye attending its shoe, then
Bolting outright somewhere above where streets
Burst suddenly in rain. . . . The gongs recur:
Elbows and levers, guard and hissing door.   90
Thunder is galvothermic here below. . . . The car
Wheels off. The train rounds, bending to a scream,
Taking the final level for the dive
Under the river—
And somewhat emptier than before,
Demented, for a hitching second, humps; then
Lets go. . . . Toward corners of the floor
Newspapers wing, revolve and wing.
Blank windows gargle signals through the roar.

And does the Daemon take you home, also,   100
Wop washerwoman, with the bandaged hair?
After the corridors are swept, the cuspidors—
The gaunt sky-barracks cleanly now, and bare,
O Genoese, do you bring mother eyes and hands
Back home to children and to golden hair?

Daemon, demurring and eventful yawn!
Whose hideous laughter is a bellows mirth
—Or the muffled slaughter of a day in birth—
O cruelly to inoculate the brinking dawn
With antennae toward worlds that glow and sink;—   110
To spoon us out more liquid than the dim
Locution of the eldest star, and pack
The conscience navelled in the plunging wind,
Umbilical to call—and straightway die!

O caught like pennies beneath soot and steam,
Kiss of our agony thou gatherest;
Condensed, thou takest all—shrill ganglia
Impassioned with some song we fail to keep.
And yet, like Lazarus, to feel the slope,
The sod and billow breaking,—lifting ground,   120

—A sound of waters bending astride the sky
Unceasing with some Word that will not die . . . !

.   .   .

A tugboat, wheezing wreaths of steam,
Lunged past, with one galvanic blare stove up the River.
I counted the echoes assembling, one after one,
Searching, thumbing the midnight on the piers.
Lights, coasting, left the oily tympanum of waters;
The blackness somewhere gouged glass on a sky.
And this thy harbor, O my City, I have driven under,
Tossed from the coil of ticking towers. . . . Tomorrow,   130
And to be. . . . Here by the River that is East—
Here at the waters' edge the hands drop memory;
Shadowless in that abyss they unaccounting lie.
How far away the star has pooled the sea—
Or shall the hands be drawn away, to die?

Kiss of our agony Thou gatherest,
                O Hand of Fire
                            gatherest—

1. Why is the tunnel a good organizing symbol in terms of what Crane has said in this section of *The Bridge?*
2. Why does he imagine the visage of Poe in the subway?

Wystan Hugh Auden

1907–   )

■ ■ ■ ■ ■ ■ ■ ■ ■

AUDEN WAS BORN in York, England, the son of a doctor. He attended Gresham's School, Holt, and later Christ Church, Oxford. From 1929 to 1934 he taught school. In the 1930's he was associated with poets like Louis MacNeice and Stephen Spender, who wrote from a leftist point of view and who helped to define a generation of poetry distinct in its way from the poetry of the generation of Eliot and Pound. In 1937 Auden drove an ambulance for the Loyalists in Spain. In the same year he was awarded the King George Gold Medal for poetry. Since 1939 he has lived in the United States, and in 1946 he became a citizen. His volumes of poetry include *Poems* (1930), *Look, Stranger!* (1936),

Selected Poems (1940), New Year Letter (1941), For the Time Being (1944), Collected Poems (1946), The Age of Anxiety (1945), and Nones (1951). Auden has also written a good deal of criticism. Alone and in collaboration he has also written plays and edited anthologies.

Suggested Readings

R. G. LIENHARDT, "W. H. Auden," in Eric Bentley, ed., The Importance of Scrutiny. New York: George W. Stewart, Inc., 1948, pp. 249–254.

JOSEPH WARREN BEACH, "The Poems of Auden and the Prose Diathesis," Virginia Quarterly, XXV, 23 (Summer, 1949), 364–385.

RICHARD HAGGART, Auden. New Haven: Yale University Press, 1951.

■ ■ ■ ■ ■ ■ ■ ■ ■ ■

Law like Love[1]

Law, say the gardeners, is the sun,
Law is the one
All gardeners obey
Tomorrow, yesterday, today.

Law is the wisdom of the old
The impotent grandfathers shrilly scold;
The grandchildren put out a treble tongue,
Law is the senses of the young.

Law, says the priest with a priestly look,
Expounding to an unpriestly people,   10
Law is the words in my priestly book,
Law is my pulpit and my steeple.

Law, says the judge as he looks down his nose,
Speaking clearly and most severely,
Law is as I've told you before,
Law is as you know I suppose,
Law is but let me explain it once more,
Law is The Law.

Yet law-abiding scholars write,
Law is neither wrong nor right,   2
Law is only crimes
Punished by places and by times,
Law is the clothes men wear

1.   "Law like Love," by W. H. Auden, is reprinted with the permission of Random House, Inc., and that of Faber & Faber Ltd. Copyright 1945, by W. H. Auden.

Anytime, anywhere,
Law is Good-morning and Good-night.

Others say, Law is our Fate;
Others say, Law is our State;
Others say, others say
Law is no more
Law has gone away.   30

And always the loud angry crowd
Very angry and very loud
Law is We,
And always the soft idiot softly Me.

If we, dear, know we know no more
Than they about the law,
If I no more than you
Know what we should and should not do
Except that all agree
Gladly or miserably   40
That the law is
And that all know this,
If therefore thinking it absurd
To identify Law with some other word,
Unlike so many men
I cannot say Law is again,
No more than they can we suppress
The universal wish to guess
Or slip out of our own position
Into an unconcerned condition.   50
Although I can at least confine
Your vanity and mine
To stating timidly
A timid similarity,
We shall boast anyway:
Like love I say.

Like love we don't know where or why
Like love we can't compel or fly
Like love we often weep
Like love we seldom keep.   60

All of us, probably, conceive of "law" as a great entity that controls
or influences our lives in various ways. Undoubtedly, too, we rarely con-
der the innumerable and even contradictory notions we hold about law.

Auden in this poem suggests not only the variety of attitudes and be
liefs the word "law" arouses but the half-mysterious reverence in which
we hold the law. The first part of the poem indicates our sense that the
law is as constant as the sun itself and also the ways in which we invoke
"the law" for our individual purposes; for the old, it is their sense of
knowing the right way to act, for the young it is following their own im
pulses, and for the priest it is his religious realm. Yet when obliged to
state the nature of law we retreat like the judge into verbiage or merel
beg the question—"Law is The Law." Again, we hear scholars, them
selves law-abiding, discuss the law, not as something in itself, perma
nent and immutable, but as custom, habits, and manners—as *mores*
Clearly, however, Auden is observing ironically that all the learned dis
cussion of relativism in law does not destroy "the law" itself, or respect
for it. Yet again, there are simplified or overly simplified views of law
such as "Law is our Fate" and "Law is our State," just as there is the
view of the angry group that their collective will is the law, and of the
individual that his personal feelings are the law.

The first half of the poem leaves no doubt in our minds that "the
law" is not readily or easily defined, despite the self-assurance with which
individuals, learned or ignorant, discuss it or invoke it in defense of
their actions. We might, at this point, expect the poet to conclude that so
much confusion makes any intelligent general discussion of the law ab
surd. But he does not conclude this. No more than the rest of man
kind can he, the poet, suppress his feelings about the law. He will, how
ever, try to state them modestly, with a minimum of self-assurance. H
would like to say that he sees a similarity between law and love. Ther
are, in fact, several similarities between them. We do not know wh
love is such a meaningful force in our lives, but we do know that it is
so with law. Love can neither be compelled nor fled from; similarly, law
Love, like the law, sometimes causes us grief. Finally, we break the law
just as we are too often false in love.

The poet maintains a distance from his subject, the law. He advo
cates no single-minded attitude toward it. In fact, he allows us to con
sider many of the somewhat foolish instances of single-mindedness with
regard to it, and permits us to see that even the judge, the professiona
expositor and interpreter of the law, is hard put to discuss it intelligently
But we know, just as we believe in a kind of reality we would find it har
to define, that we believe in the power and significance of the law. A
though he moves gingerly among attitudes toward the law, the poe
does not shy away from a commitment. He feels there are certain thing
he can and should say.

Certainly there is an irony in the fact that we all live with a sense of
the significance of the law, feeling in it a cohesive and helpful force
and yet we are not quite sure what it is we respect and accept. Aude
suggests the more amusing and the less amusing sides of this. But h

awareness does not cause him to recoil into some form of ironic bitterness from any view of the problem of living with respect for the law.

Musée des Beaux Arts[1]

About suffering they were never wrong,
The Old Masters: how well they understood
Its human position; how it takes place
While someone else is eating or opening a window or just walking
      dully along;
How, when the aged are reverently, passionately waiting
For the miraculous birth, there always must be
Children who did not specially want it to happen, skating
On a pond at the edge of the wood:
They never forgot
That even the dreadful martyrdom must run its course
Anyhow in a corner, some untidy spot
Where the dogs go on with their doggy life and the torturer's
      horse
Scratches its innocent behind on a tree.

In Brueghel's *Icarus,* for instance: how everything turns away
Quite leisurely from the disaster; the ploughman may
Have heard the splash, the forsaken cry,
But for him it was not an important failure; the sun shone
As it had to on the white legs disappearing into the green
Water; and the expensive delicate ship that must have seen
Something amazing, a boy falling out of the sky,
Had somewhere to get to and sailed calmly on.

1. What is the central irony behind this poem? List the incidental or specific ironies that support it.

2. Is the tone of the poem (consider all relevant aspects) appropriate to the irony?

1. "Musée des Beaux Arts," by W. H. Auden, is reprinted with the permission of Random House, Inc. Copyright, 1945, by W. H. Auden.

In Memory of W. B. Yeats[1]
(d. *January,* 1939)

He disappeared in the dead of winter:
The brooks were frozen, the airports almost deserted,
And snow disfigured the public statues;

1. "In Memory of W. B. Yeats," by W. H. Auden, is reprinted with the permission of Random House, Inc., and that of Faber & Faber Ltd. Copyright, 1945, by W. H. Auden.

The mercury sank in the mouth of the dying day.
O all the instruments agree
The day of his death was a dark cold day.

Far from his illness
The wolves ran on through the evergreen forests,
The peasant river was untempted by the fashionable quays;
By mourning tongues   10
The death of the poet was kept from his poems.

But for him it was his last afternoon as himself,
An afternoon of nurses and rumours;
The provinces of his body revolted,
The squares of his mind were empty,
Silence invaded the suburbs,
The current of his feeling failed: he became his admirers.

Now he is scattered among a hundred cities
And wholly given over to unfamiliar affections;
To find his happiness in another kind of wood   20
And be punished under a foreign code of conscience.
The words of a dead man
Are modified in the guts of the living.

But in the importance and noise of tomorrow
When the brokers are roaring like beasts on the floor of the Bourse,
And the poor have the sufferings to which they are fairly accustomed,
And each in the cell of himself is almost convinced of his freedom;
A few thousand will think of this day
As one thinks of a day when one did something slightly unusual.

O all the instruments agree   30
The day of his death was a dark cold day.

2

You were silly like us: your gift survived it all;
The parish of rich women, physical decay,
Yourself; mad Ireland hurt you into poetry.
Now Ireland has her madness and her weather still,
For poetry makes nothing happen: it survives
In the valley of its saying where executives
Would never want to tamper; it flows south
From ranches of isolation and the busy griefs,
Raw towns that we believe and die in; it survives,   4
A way of happening, a mouth.

3

Earth, receive an honoured guest;
William Yeats is laid to rest:
Let the Irish vessel lie
Emptied of its poetry.

Time that is intolerant
Of the brave and innocent,
And indifferent in a week
To a beautiful physique,

Worships language and forgives   50
Everyone by whom it lives;
Pardons cowardice, conceit,
Lays it honours at their feet.

Time that with this strange excuse
Pardoned Kipling and his views,
And will pardon Paul Claudel,
Pardons him for writing well.

In the nightmare of the dark
All the dogs of Europe bark,
And the living nations wait,   60
Each sequestered in its hate;

Intellectual disgrace
Stares from every human face,
And the seas of pity lie
Locked and frozen in each eye.

Follow, poet, follow right
To the bottom of the night,
With your unconstraining voice
Still persuade us to rejoice;

With the farming of a verse   70
Make a vineyard of the curse,
Sing of human unsuccess
In a rapture of distress;

In the deserts of the heart
Let the healing fountain start,
In the prison of his days
Teach the free man how to praise.

■   1. List all the characteristics of this elegy which give it its contemporaneity.

2. Compare Auden's view of the social role of poetry with that expressed in Tennyson's "The Poet."

3. In what sense is part 3 of this poem ritualistic?

Look, Stranger[1]

Look, stranger, on this island now
The leaping light for your delight discovers,
Stand stable here
And silent be,
That through the channels of the ear
May wander like a river
The swaying sound of the sea.

Here at the small field's ending pause
When the chalk wall falls to the foam and its tall ledges
Oppose the pluck
And knock of the tide,
And the shingle scrambles after the suck-ing surf,
And the gull lodges
A moment on its sheer side.

Far off like floating seeds the ships
Diverge on urgent voluntary errands,
And the full view
Indeed may enter
And move in memory as now these clouds do,
That pass the harbour mirror
And all the summer through the water saunter.

■   Discuss the sensory effects of this poem.

As I Walked Out One Evening[1]

As I walked out one evening,
    Walking down Bristol Street
The crowds upon the pavement
    Were fields of harvest wheat.

....

1. "Look Stranger, on This Island Now," and "As I Walked Out One Evening," by W. H. Auden, are reprinted with the permission of Random House, Inc., and that of Faber & Faber Ltd. Copyright, 1945, by W. H. Auden.

And down by the brimming river
   I heard a lover sing
Under an arch of the railway:
   "Love has no ending.

I'll love you, dear, I'll love you
   Till China and Africa meet,   10
And the river jumps over the mountain
   And the salmon sing in the street.

I'll love you till the ocean
   Is folded and hung up to dry,
And the seven stars go squawking
   Like geese about the sky.

The years shall run like rabbits,
   For in my arms I hold
The Flower of the Ages,
   And the first love of the world."   20

But all the clocks in the city
   Began to whirr and chime:
"O let not Time deceive you,
   You cannot conquer Time.

In the burrows of the Nightmare
   Where Justice naked is,
Time watches from the shadow
   And coughs when you would kiss.

In headaches and in worry
   Vaguely life leaks away,   30
And Time will have his fancy
   Tomorrow or today.

Into many a green valley
   Drifts the appalling snow;
Time breaks the threaded dances
   And the diver's brilliant bow.

O plunge your hands in water,
   Plunge them in up to the wrist;
Stare, stare in the basin
   And wonder what you've missed.   40

The glacier knocks in the cupboard,
    The desert sighs in the bed,
And the crack in the tea-cup opens
    A lane to the land of the dead.

Where the beggars raffle the banknotes
    And the Giant is enchanting to Jack,
And the Lily-white Boy is a Roarer,
    And Jill goes down on her back.

O look, look in the mirror,
    O look in your distress;   50
Life remains a blessing
    Although you cannot bless.

O stand, stand at the window
    As the tears scald and start;
You shall love your crooked neighbor
    With your crooked heart."

It was late, late in the evening,
    The lovers they were gone;
The clocks had ceased their chiming,
    And the deep river ran on.   60

1. What is the central irony of this poem?
2. Explain the major shift in the tone.
3. Is the lyricism of the poem affected by the shift in tone?

September 1, 1939[1]

I sit in one of the dives
On Fifty-second Street
Uncertain and afraid
As the clever hopes expire
Of a low dishonest decade:
Waves of anger and fear
Circulate over the bright
And darkened lands of the earth,
Obsessing our private lives;
The unmentionable odour of death   10
Offends the September night.

....
1. "September 1st, 1939," by W. H. Auden, is reprinted with the permission of Random House, Inc., and that of Faber & Faber Ltd. Copyright, 1945, by W. H. Auden.

Accurate scholarship can
Unearth the whole offence
From Luther until now
That has driven a culture mad,
Find what occurred at Linz,
What huge imago made
A psychopathic god:
I and the public know
What all schoolchildren learn,   20
Those to whom evil is done
Do evil in return.

Exiled Thucydides knew
All that a speech can say
About Democracy,
And what dictators do,
The elderly rubbish they talk
To an apathetic grave;
Analysed all in his book,
The enlightenment driven away,   30
The habit-forming pain,
Mismanagement and grief:
We must suffer them all again.

Into this neutral air
Where blind skyscrapers use
Their full height to proclaim
The strength of Collective Man,
Each language pours its vain
Competitive excuse:
But who can live for long   40
In an euphoric dream;
Out of the mirror they stare,
Imperialism's face
And the international wrong.

Faces along the bar
Cling to their average day:
The lights must never go out,
The music must always play,
All the conventions conspire
To make this fort assume   50
The furniture of home;
Lest we should see where we are,
Lost in a haunted wood,

Children afraid of the night
Who have never been happy or good.

The windiest militant trash
Important Persons shout
Is not so crude as our wish:
What mad Nijinsky wrote
About Diaghilev   60
Is true of the normal heart;
For the error bred in the bone
Of each woman and each man
Craves what it cannot have,
Not universal love
But to be loved alone.

From the conservative dark
Into the ethical life
The dense commuters come,
Repeating their morning vow;   70
"I *will* be true to the wife,
I'll concentrate more on my work,"
And helpless governors awake
To resume their compulsory game:
Who can release them now,
Who can reach the deaf,
Who can speak for the dumb?

All I have is a voice
To undo the folded lie,
The romantic lie in the brain   80
Of the sensual man-in-the-street
And the lie of Authority
Whose buildings grope the sky:
There is no such thing as the State
And no one exists alone;
Hunger allows no choice
To the citizen or the police;
We must love one another or die.

Defenceless under the night
Our world in stupor lies;   90
Yet dotted everywhere,
Ironic points of light
Flash out wherever the Just
Exchange their messages:

May I, composed like them
Of Eros and of dust,
Beleaguered by the same
Negation and despair,
Show an affirming flame.

■   1. Fill in some of the historical details appropriate to the date of this
poem.
    2. Are the ironies aside from or related to the major theme?

SUPPLEMENTARY POEMS:
A CHRONOLOGICAL SEQUENCE

Anonymous (16th century)

Mary Hamilton

Word's gane to the kitchen,
    And word's gane to the ha',
That Marie Hamilton gangs wi bairn[1]
    To the hichest Stewart of a'.

He's courted her in the kitchen,
    He's courted her in the ha',
He's courted her in the laigh[2] cellar,
    And that was warst of a'.

She's tyed it in her apron
    And she's thrown it in the sea;   10
Says, Sink ye, swim ye, bonny wee babe!
    You'l neer get mair o me.

Down then cam the auld queen,
    Goud tassels tying her hair:
"O Marie, where's the bonny wee babe
    That I heard greet[3] sae sair?"

"There was never a babe intill my room,
    As little designs to be;
It was but a touch o my sair side,
    Come oer my fair bodie."   20

"O Marie, put on your robes o black,
    Or else your robes o brown,
For ye maun gang wi me the night,
    To see fair Edinbro town."

"I winna put on my robes o black,
    Nor yet my robes o brown;
But I'll put on my robes o white,
    To shine through Edinbro town."

When she gaed up the Cannogate,
    She laughd loud laughters three;   30
But whan she cam down the Cannogate
    The tear blinded her ee.

....
1. Child.   2. Low.   3. Grieve.

When she gaed up the Parliament stair,
 The heel cam aff her shee;
And lang or she cam down again
 She was condemnd to dee.

When she cam down the Cannogate,
 The Cannogate sae free,
Many a ladie lookd oer her window,
 Weeping for this ladie.   40

"Ye need nae weep for me," she says,
 "Ye need nae weep for me;
For had I not slain mine own sweet babe,
 This death I wadna dee.

"Bring me a bottle of wine," she says,
 "The best that eer ye hae,
That I may drink to my weil-wishers,
 And they may drink to me.

"Here's a health to the jolly sailors,
 That sail upon the main;   50
Let them never let on to my father and mother
 But what I'm coming hame.

"Here's a health to the jolly sailors,
 That sail upon the sea;
Let them never let on to my father and mother
 That I cam here to dee.

"Oh little did my mother think,
 The day she cradled me,
What lands I was to travel through,
 What death I was to dee.   60

"Oh little did my father think,
 The day he held up me,
What lands I was to travel through,
 What death I was to dee.

"Last night I washd the queens feet,
 And gently laid her down;
And a' the thanks I've gotten the nicht
 To be hangd in Edinbro town!

"Last nicht there was four Maries,
   The nicht there'l be but three;   70
There was Marie Seton, and Marie Beton,
   And Marie Carmichael, and me."

■   What are the *particulars,* the concrete details, that help to give this ballad its emotional force?

■■■■■■■■■

Henry Howard, Earl of Surrey (1517?–1547)

Vow to Love Faithfully Howsoever He Be Rewarded

Set me whereas the sun doth parch the green,
Or where his beams may not dissolve the ice,
In temperate heat, where he is felt and seen;
With proud people, in presence sad and wise,
Set me in base, or yet in high degree;
In the long night, or in the shortest day;
In clear weather, or where mists thickest be;
In lusty youth, or when my hairs be gray;
Set me in earth, in heaven, or yet in hell;
In hill, in dale, or in the foaming flood;
Thrall, or at large,—alive whereso I dwell;
Sick or in health, in ill fame or in good;
Yours I will be, and with that only thought
Comfort myself when that my hap is naught.

Brittle Beauty

Brittle beauty that nature made so frail,
Whereof the gift is small, and short the season,
Flow'ring today, tomorrow apt to fail,
Tickle treasure, abhorrèd of reason,
Dangerous to deal with, vain, of none avail,
Costly in keeping, passed not worth two peason,[1]
Slippery in sliding as an eelès tail,
Hard to attain, once gotten not geason,[2]
Jewel of jeopardy that peril doth assail,

---
1. Old plural form of "pea."   2. Scarce, unusual.

False and untrue, enticèd oft to treason,
Enemy to youth (that most may I bewail!),
Ah, bitter sweet! infecting as the poison,
Thou farest as fruit that with the frost is taken:
Today ready ripe, tomorrow all too shaken.

■ ■ ■ ■ ■ ■ ■ ■ ■ ■

Anonymous (early 16th century?)

Tom o' Bedlam's Song

From the hag and hungry goblin
That into rags would rend ye,
   All the spirits that stand
   By the naked man
In the book of moons, defend ye,

That of your five sound senses
You never be forsaken,
   Nor wander from
   Yourselves with Tom
Abroad to beg your bacon.　　　　　　　　　　10

With a thought I took for Maudlin,
And a cruse of cockle pottage,
   With a thing thus tall,
   Sky bless you all,
I befell into this dotage.

I slept not since the Conquest,
Till then I never wakèd,
   Till the roguish boy
   Of love where I lay
Me found and stript me naked.　　　　　　　　20

The moon's my constant mistress,
And the lonely owl my marrow;
   The flaming drake
   And the night-crow make
Me music to my sorrow.

I know more than Apollo,
For oft, when he lies sleeping,

I see the stars
  At mortal wars
In the wounded welkin weeping,   30

The moon embrace her shepherd,
And the queen of love her warrior,
    While the first doth horn
    The star of morn,
And the next the heavenly farrier.

With an host of furious fancies,
Whereof I am commander,
    With a burning spear
    And a horse of air
To the wilderness I wander;   40

By a knight of ghosts and shadows
I summoned am to tourney
    Ten leagues beyond
    The wide world's end—
Methinks it is no journey.

1. What sort of person is revealed by the imagery?
2. What are the two sources of imagery in the poem?
3. Is there a connotative as well as denotative meaning to "Bedlam"?
4. Are there any examples of synecdoche in this poem?

George Gascoigne (1525?–1577)

Gascoigne's Lullaby

Sing lullaby, as women do,
Wherewith they bring their babes to rest,
And lullaby can I sing too
As womanly as can the best.
With lullaby they still the child,
And if I be not much beguiled,
Full many wanton babes have I
Which must be stilled with lullaby.

First, lullaby, my youthful years,
It is now time to go to bed,   10

For crooked age and hoary hairs
Have won the haven within my head;
With lullaby, then, youth be still,
With lullaby, content thy will,
Since courage quails and comes behind,
Go sleep, and so beguile thy mind.

Next, lullaby, my gazing eyes,
Which wonted were to glance apace.
For every glass may now suffice
To show the furrows in my face;   20
With lullaby, then, wink awhile,
With lullaby, your looks beguile,
Let no fair face nor beauty bright
Entice you eft with vain delight.

And lullaby, my wanton will,
Let reason's rule now reign thy thought,
Since all too late I find by skill
How dear I have thy fancies bought;
With lullaby, now take thine ease,
With lullaby, thy doubts appease;   30
For trust to this, if thou be still,
My body shall obey thy will.

And lullaby, my loving boy,
My little Robin, take thy rest;
Since age is old and nothing coy,
Keep close thy coin, for so is best;
With lullaby, be thou content,
With lullaby, thy lusts relent,
Let others pay which have more pence,
Thou art too poor for such expense.   40

Thus lullaby, my youth, mine eyes,
My will, my ware, and all that was!
I can no more delays devise,
But welcome pain, let pleasure pass;
With lullaby, now take your leave,
With lullaby, your dreams deceive,
And when you rise with waking eye,
Remember Gascoigne's lullaby.

Sir Edward Dyer (1540?–1607)

My Mind to Me a Kingdom Is

My mind to me a kingdom is;
    Such present joys therein I find
That it excels all other bliss
    That earth affords or grows by kind.
Though much I want which most would have,
Yet still my mind forbids to crave.

No princely pomp, no wealthy store,
    No force to win the victory,
No wily wit to salve a sore,
    No shape to feed a loving eye;   10
To none of these I yield as thrall—
For why? My mind doth serve for all.

I see how plenty surfeits oft,
    And hasty climbers soon do fall;
I see that those which are aloft
    Mishap doth threaten most of all;
They get with toil, they keep with fear—
Such cares my mind could never bear.

Content to live, this is my stay;
    I seek no more than may suffice;   20
I press to bear no haughty sway;
    Look, what I lack my mind supplies.
Lo, thus I triumph like a king,
Content with that my mind doth bring.

Some have too much, yet still do crave;
    I little have, and seek no more.
They are but poor, though much they have,
    And I am rich with little store.
They poor, I rich; they beg, I give;
They lack, I leave; they pine, I live.   30

I laugh not at another's loss;
    I grudge not at another's gain;
No worldly waves my mind can toss;
    My state at one doth still remain.
I fear no foe, I fawn no friend;
I loathe not life, nor dread my end.

Some weigh their pleasure by their lust,
  Their wisdom by their rage of will;
Their treasure is their only trust;
  A cloakèd craft their store of skill.   40
But all the pleasure that I find
Is to maintain a quiet mind.

My wealth is health and perfect ease;
  My conscience clear my chief defense;
I neither seek by bribes to please,
  Nor by deceit to breed offense.
Thus do I live; thus will I die;
Would all did so as well as I!

■   1. Is the situation upon which the poet prides himself a paradoxical
one?
      2. What are some of the examples of unhappiness in "happy" situa-
tions to which he points?

■■■■■■■■■■

Chidiock Tichborne (1558–1586)

On the Eve of His Execution

My prime of youth is but a frost of cares,
  My feast of joy is but a dish of pain,
My crop of corn is but a field of tares,
  And all my good is but vain hope of gain;
    The day is past, and yet I saw no sun,
    And now I live, and now my life is done.

My tale was heard and yet it was not told,
  My fruit is fallen, yet my leaves are green,
My youth is spent and yet I am not old,
  I saw the world and yet I was not seen;
    My thread is cut and yet it is not spun,
    And now I live, and now my life is done.

I sought my death and found it in my womb,
  I looked for life and saw it was a shade,
I trod the earth and knew it was my tomb,
  And now I die, and now I was but made;

My glass is full, and now my glass is run,
And now I live, and now my life is done.

■   Restate this poem in your own language, avoiding any paradoxes.
What is lost in terms of poetic effect?

■ ■ ■ ■ ■ ■ ■ ■ ■ ■

Christopher Marlowe (1564–1593)

The Passionate Shepherd to His Love

Come live with me and be my love,
And we will all the pleasures prove
That valleys, groves, hills, and fields,
Woods, or steepy mountain yields.

And we will sit upon the rocks,
Seeing the shepherds feed their flocks,
By shallow rivers to whose falls
Melodious birds sing madrigals.

And I will make thee beds of roses
And a thousand fragrant posies,
A cap of flowers, and a kirtle
Embroidered all with leaves of myrtle;

A gown made of the finest wool
Which from our pretty lambs we pull;
Fair linèd slippers for the cold,
With buckles of the purest gold;

A belt of straw and ivy buds,
With coral clasps and amber studs:
And if these pleasures may thee move,
Come live with me, and be my love.

The shepherds' swains shall dance and sing
For thy delight each May morning:
If these delights thy mind may move,
Then live with me and be my love.

Is the metrical pattern of this poem appropriate or not? Explain.

Thomas Nashe (1567–1601)

In a Time of Pestilence

Adieu, farewell earth's bliss.
This world uncertain is;
Fond are life's lustful joys,
Death proves them all but toys.
None from his darts can fly;
I am sick, I must die.
Lord, have mercy on us!

Rich men, trust not in wealth,
Gold cannot buy your health;
Physic himself must fade;   10
All things to end are made;
The plague full swift goes by.
I am sick, I must die.
Lord, have mercy on us!

Beauty is but a flower
Which wrinkles will devour;
Brightness falls from the air;
Queens have died young and fair;
Dust hath closed Helen's eye.
I am sick, I must die.   20
Lord, have mercy on us!

Strength stoops unto the grave,
Worms feed on Hector brave;
Swords may not fight with fate;
Earth still holds ope her gate;
Come, come! the bells do cry.
I am sick, I must die.
Lord, have mercy on us!

Wit with his wantonness
Tasteth death's bitterness;   30
Hell's executioner
Hath no ears for to hear
What vain art can reply.
I am sick, I must die.
Lord, have mercy on us!

Haste therefore each degree
To welcome destiny;

Heaven is our heritage,
Earth but a player's stage.
Mount we unto the sky.   40
I am sick, I must die.
        Lord, have mercy on us!

■ ■ ■ ■ ■ ■ ■ ■ ■ ■

Thomas Campion (1567–1620)

There Is a Garden in Her Face

There is a garden in her face,
    Where roses and white lilies grow,
A heavenly paradise is that place,
    Wherein all pleasant fruits do flow.
There cherries grow, which none may buy
Till "Cherry ripe!" themselves do cry.

Those cherries fairly do enclose
    Of orient pearl a double row;
Which when her lovely laughter shows,
    They look like rose-buds filled with snow.
Yet them nor peer nor prince can buy,
Till "Cherry ripe!" themselves do cry.

Her eyes like angels watch them still;
    Her brows like bended bows do stand,
Threatening with piercing frowns to kill
    All that attempt with eye or hand
Those sacred cherries to come nigh,
Till "Cherry ripe!" themselves do cry.

My Sweetest Lesbia

My sweetest Lesbia, let us live and love;
And though the sager sort our deeds reprove,
    Let us not weigh them. Heaven's great lamps do dive
Into their west, and straight again revive;
But, soon as once set is our little light,
Then must we sleep one ever-during night.

If all would lead their lives in love like me,
Then bloody swords and armor should not be;
No drum nor trumpet peaceful sleeps should move,
Unless alarm came from the camp of love.
But fools do live and waste their little light,
And seek with pain their ever-during night.

When timely death my life and fortunes ends,
Let not my hearse be vexed with mourning friends;
But let all lovers rich in triumph come,
And with sweet pastime grace my happy tomb.
And, Lesbia, close up thou my little light,
And crown with love my ever-during night.

■■■■■■■■■

Richard Corbet (1582–1635)

The Fairies' Farewell

Farewell, rewards and fairies,
    Good housewives now may say,
For now foul sluts in dairies
    Do fare as well as they.
And though they sweep their hearths no less
    Than maids were wont to do,
Yet who of late, for cleanliness,
    Finds sixpence in her shoe?

Lament, lament, old Abbeys,
    The fairies' lost command;   10
They did but change priests' babies,
    But some have changed your land!
And all your children sprung from thence
    Are now grown Puritans,
Who live as changelings ever since,
    For love of your domains.

At morning and at evening both
    You merry were and glad;
So little care of sleep or sloth
    These pretty ladies had;   20
When Tom came home from labor,
    Or Ciss to milking rose,

Then merrily went their tabor
    And nimbly went their toes.

Witness those rings and roundelays
    Of theirs, which yet remain,
Were footed in Queen Mary's days
    On many a grassy plain;
But since of late, Elizabeth
    And, later, James came in,   30
They never danced on any heath
    As when the time hath been.

By which we note the fairies
    Were of the old profession;
Their songs were *Ave-Maries*,
    Their dances were procession.
But now, alas! they all are dead,
    Or gone beyond the seas;
Or farther for religion fled;
    Or else they take their ease.   40

A tell-tale in their company
    They never could endure;
And whoso kept not secretly
    Their mirth, was punished sure;
It was a most just Christian deed
    To pinch such black and blue:
Oh, how the Commonwealth doth need
    Such justices as you!

Now they have left our quarters,
    A register they have,   50
Who can preserve their charters,
    A man both wise and grave.
A hundred of their merry pranks,
    By one that I could name
Are kept in store; con twenty thanks
    To William for the same.

To William Churne of Staffordshire
    Give laud and praisés due;
Who every meal can mend your cheer
    With tales both old and true.   60
To William all give audience,
    And pray you for his noddle;

For all the fairies' evidence
Were lost if it were addle.

■   1. If Corbet associates the world of the fairies with the "Ave Marias" of Catholics, with what does he associate the Puritan spirit? Answer in considerable detail. What historical situation is at the center of the poem?

2. William Churne of Staffordshire was the old servant of Corbet's father-in-law, Leonard Hutten. He is called both wise and grave by the poet. Does Corbet so refer to him solely in ironic terms and out of his own sense of his superior knowledge that there are no fairies, or does he suggest that William Churne has something that his contemporaries would do well to understand?

■ ■ ■ ■ ■ ■ ■ ■ ■ ■

Henry King (1592–1669)

Sic Vita

Like to the falling of a star,
Or as the flights of eagles are,
Or like the fresh spring's gaudy hue,
Or silver drops of morning dew,
Or like a wind that chafes the flood,
Or bubbles which on water stood:
Even such is man, whose borrowed light
Is straight called in, and paid to night.
The wind blows out, the bubble dies;
The spring entombed in autumn lies;
The dew dries up, the star is shot;
The flight is past—and man forgot.

From The Exequy

Sleep on, my love, in thy cold bed,
Never to be disquieted!
My last good-night! Thou wilt not wake
Till I thy fate shall overtake;
Till age, or grief, or sickness must
Marry my body to that dust
It so much loves, and fill the room

My heart keeps empty in thy tomb.
Stay for me there, I will not fail
To meet thee in that hollow vale.
And think not much of my delay;
I am already on the way,
And follow thee with all the speed
Desire can make, or sorrows breed.
Each minute is a short degree,
And every hour a step toward thee.
At night when I betake to rest,
Next morn I rise nearer my west
Of life, almost by eight hours' sail
Than when sleep breathed his drowsy gale.   20

Thus from the sun my bottom steers,
And my day's compass downward bears;
Nor labor I to stem the tide
Through which to thee I swiftly glide.

'Tis true, with shame and grief I yield,
Thou like the van first tookst the field,
And gotten hath the victory
In thus adventuring to die
Before me, whose more years might crave
A just precedence in the grave.   30
But hark! my pulse like a soft drum
Beats my approach, tells thee I come;
And slow howe'er my marches be,
I shall at last sit down by thee.

■ Explain how the poet sustains the imagery of a journey, giving special consideration to "sleep breathed his drowsy gale" and "my pulse like a soft drum."

■ ■ ■ ■ ■ ■ ■ ■ ■ ■

Thomas Carew (1595?–1645?)

The Spring

Now that the winter's gone, the earth hath lost
Her snow-white robes, and now no more the frost
Candies the grass, or casts an icy cream

Upon the silver lake or crystal stream;
But the warm sun thaws the benumbèd earth,
And makes it tender; gives a sacred birth
To the dead swallow; wakes in hollow tree
The drowsy cuckoo and the humble-bee.
Now do a choir of chirping minstrels bring
In triumph to the world the youthful spring.
The valleys, hills, and woods in rich array
Welcome the coming of the longed-for May.
Now all things smile, only my love doth lour;
Nor hath the scalding noonday sun the power
To melt that marble ice, which still doth hold
Her heart congealed, and makes her pity cold.
The ox, which lately did for shelter fly
Into the stall, doth now securely lie
In open fields; and love no more is made
By the fireside, but in the cooler shade
Amyntas now doth with his Chloris sleep
Under a sycamore, and all things keep
Time with the season; only she doth carry
June in her eyes, in her heart January.

A Song

Ask me no more where Jove bestows,
When June is past, the fading rose;
For in your beauty's orient deep
These flowers, as in their causes, sleep.

Ask me no more whither do stray
The golden atoms of the day;
For in pure love heaven did prepare
Those powders to enrich your hair.

Ask me no more whither doth haste
The nightingale when May is past;
For in your sweet dividing throat
She winters, and keeps warm her note.

Ask me no more where those stars light,
That downwards fall in dead of night;
For in your eyes they sit, and there
Fixed become as in their sphere.

Ask me no more if east or west
The phoenix builds her spicy nest;
For unto you at last she flies,
And in your fragrant bosom dies.

■   1. Describe the tone of this poem.
     2. What do diction, imagery, and rhythm contribute to the tone?

■■■■■■■■■■

Abraham Cowley (1618–1667)

Drinking

The thirsty earth soaks up the rain,
And drinks and gapes for drink again;
The plants suck in the earth, and are
With constant drinking fresh and fair;
The sea itself (which one would think
Should have but little need of drink)
Drinks twice ten thousand rivers up,
So filled that they o'erflow the cup.
The busy sun (and one would guess
By's drunken fiery face no less)
Drinks up the sea, and when he's done,
The moon and stars drink up the sun:
They drink and dance by their own light,
They drink and revel all the night.
Nothing in nature's sober found,
But an eternal health goes round.
Fill up the bowl, then, fill it high!
Fill all the glasses there—for why
Should every creature drink but I?
Why, man of morals, tell me why?

Are there any instances of overstatement in these lines?

Love

Five years ago (says story) I lov'd you,
For which you call me most inconstant now;
Pardon me, madam, you mistake the man;

For I am not the same that I was then;
No flesh is now the same 'twas then in me,
And that my mind is chang'd yourself may see.

The same thoughts to retain still, and intents,
Were inconstant far; for accidents
Must of all things most strangely inconstant prove,
If from one subject they t'another move:
My members then, the father members were
From whence these take their birth, which now are here.
If then this body love what th'other did,
'Twere incest, which by nature is forbid.

■■■■■■■■■■

Sir John Suckling (1609–1642)

Why So Pale and Wan?

Why so pale and wan, fond lover?
　　Prithee, why so pale?
Will, when looking well can't move her,
　　Looking ill prevail?
　　Prithee, why so pale?

Why so dull and mute, young sinner?
　　Prithee, why so mute?
Will, when speaking well can't win her,
　　Saying nothing do 't?
　　Prithee, why so mute?

Quit, quit for shame! This will not move;
　　This cannot take her.
If of herself she will not love,
　　Nothing can make her.
　　The devil take her!

■■■■■■■■■■

Richard Lovelace (1618–1658)

To Amarantha

That She Would Dishevel Her Hair

Amarantha, sweet and fair,
  Ah, braid no more that shining hair!
    As my curious hand or eye
Hovering round thee, let it fly!

Let it fly as unconfined
  As its calm ravisher the wind,
    Who hath left his darling East
To wanton o'er that spicy nest.

Every tress must be confest,
  But neatly tangled at the best;
    Like a clue of golden thread
Most excellently ravelled.

Do not, then, wind up that light
  In ribbands, and o'ercloud in night,
    Like the Sun in's early ray;
But shake your head, and scatter day!

■ 1. What is the meaning of the final line?
2. Does "its calm ravisher the wind" (line 6) add an element of
indirectness to the poem?

To Althea, from Prison

When Love with unconfinèd wings
  Hovers within my gates,
And my divine Althea brings
  To whisper at the gates;
When I lie tangled in her hair
  And fettered to her eye,
The birds that wanton in the air
  Know no such liberty.

When flowing cups run swiftly round
  With no allaying Thames,
Our careless heads with roses bound,
  Our hearts with loyal flames;

10

When thirsty grief in wine we steep,
  When healths and draughts go free,
Fishes that tipple in the deep
  Know no such liberty.

When, like committed linnets, I
  With shriller throat shall sing
The sweetness, mercy, majésty,
  And glories of my king;   20
When I shall voice aloud how good
  He is, how great should be,
Enlargèd winds, that curl the flood,
  Know no such liberty.

Stone walls do not a prison make,
  Nor iron bars a cage;
Minds innocent and quiet take
  That for an hermitage;
If I have freedom in my love
  And in my soul am free,   30
Angels alone, that soar above,
  Enjoy such liberty.

■   1. Which images in this poem are purely descriptive? Which images occur in similes and metaphors?
    2. Point out examples of wit and paradox.

■ ■ ■ ■ ■ ■ ■ ■ ■ ■

John Wilmot, Earl of Rochester (1647–1680)

A Song

Absent from thee I languish still;
  Then ask me not, when I return.
The straying fool 'twill plainly kill,
  To wish all day, all night to mourn.

Dear, from thine arms then let me fly,
  That my fantastic mind may prove
The torments it deserves to try,
  That tears my fixed heart from my love.

When wearied with a world of woe,
    To thy safe bosom I retire,
Where love and peace and truth does flow,
    May I contented there expire.

Lest, once more wand'ring from that heaven,
    I fall on some base heart unblest;
Faithless to thee, false, unforgiven,
    And lose my everlasting rest.

■ 1. Write a paraphrase of this poem.
   2. Does the poem present any special difficulties for paraphrase?

■ ■ ■ ■ ■ ■ ■ ■ ■ ■

Thomas Chatterton (1752–1770)

Last Verses

Farewell, Bristolia's dingy piles of brick,
Lovers of mammon, worshippers of trick!
Ye spurned the boy who gave you antique lays,
And paid for learning with your empty praise.
Farewell, ye guzzling aldermanic fools,
By nature fitted for corruption's tools!
I go to where celestial anthems swell;
But you, when you depart, will sink to hell.
Farewell, my mother!—cease, my anguished soul,
Nor let distraction's billows o'er me roll!
Have mercy, Heaven! when here I cease to live,
And this last act of wretchedness forgive.

■ ■ ■ ■ ■ ■ ■ ■ ■ ■

George Crabbe (1754–1832)

From The Village

Thus groan the old, till, by disease oppress'd,
They taste a final woe, and then they rest.
    Theirs is yon house that holds the parish-poor,
Whose walls of mud scarce bear the broken door;
There, where the putrid vapors, flagging, play,   230

And the dull wheel hums doleful through the day;—
There children dwell who know no parents' care;
Parents who know no children's love, dwell there!
Heartbroken matrons on their joyless bed,
Forsaken wives, and mothers never wed,
Dejected widows with unheeded tears,
And crippled age with more than childhood fears;
The lame, the blind, and, far the happiest they!
The moping idiot and the madman gay.
Here too the sick their final doom receive,   240
Here brought, amid the scenes of grief, to grieve,
Where the loud groans from some sad chamber flow,
Mix'd with the clamors of the crowd below;
Here, sorrowing, they each kindred sorrow scan,
And the cold charities of man to man:
Whose laws indeed for ruin'd age provide,
And strong compulsion plucks the scrap from pride;
But still that scrap is bought with many a sigh,
And pride embitters what it can't deny.
    Say ye, oppress'd by some fantastic woes,   250
Some jarring nerve that baffles your repose;
Who press the downy couch, while slaves advance
With timid eye, to read the distant glance;
Who with sad prayers the weary doctor tease,
To name the nameless ever-new disease;
Who with mock patience dire complaints endure,
Which real pain and that alone can cure;
How would ye bear in real pain to lie,
Despised, neglected, left alone to die?
How would ye bear to draw your latest breath,   260
Where all that's wretched paves the way for death?

■ How does the poet's holding to descriptions of actual situations
rather than developing imaginative extensions of them contribute to the
tone?

The Whistling Boy

The whistling boy that holds the plough
    Lured by the tale that soldiers tell,
Resolves to part, yet knows not how
    To leave the land he loves so well.
He now rejects the thought, and now
    Looks o'er the lea, and sighs "Farewell!"

"Farewell!" the pensive maiden cries.
   Who dreams of London, dreams awake—
But when her favorite lad she spies,
   With whom she loved her way to take,
Then doubts within her soul arise,
   And equal hopes her bosom shake.

Thus, like the boy, and like the maid,
   I wish to go, yet tarry here,
And now resolved, and now afraid:
   To minds disturbed old views appear
In melancholy charms arrayed,
   And once, indifferent, now are dear.
How shall I go, my fate to learn—
And, oh! how taught shall I return?

■■■■■■■■■■

Matthew Prior (1664–1721)

The Secretary

While with labour assiduous due pleasures I mix,
And in one day atone for the business of six,
In a little Dutch chaise on a Saturday night,
On my left hand my Horace, a nymph on my right:
No memoire to compose, and no postboy to move,
That on Sunday may hinder the softness of love;
For her, neither visits, nor parties at tea,
Nor the long-winded cant of a dull refugee.
This night, and the next shall be hers, shall be mine,
To good or ill fortune the third we resign:
Thus scorning the world, and superior to fate,
I drive on my car in processional state.
So with Phia through Athens Pisistratus rode:
Men thought her Minerva, and him a new god.
But why should I stories of Athens rehearse,
Where people knew love, and were partial to verse;
Since none can with justice my pleasures oppose,
In Holland half drowned in interest and prose?
By Greece and past ages what need I be tried,
When the Hague and the present are both on my side?
And is it enough for the joys of the day,
To think what Anacreon or Sappho would say?

When good Vandergoes and his provident Vrow,
As they gaze on my triumph, do freely allow,
That, search all the province, you'll find no man there is
So blest as the Englishen Heer Secretaris.

■ Discuss any characteristics, especially the little verbal twists, which
distinguish these lines from what one expects ordinarily in prose.

■■■■■■■■■■

John Pomfret (1667–1702)

From *The Choice*

If Heaven the grateful liberty would give
That I might choose my method how to live,
And all those hours propitious fate should lend
In blissful ease and satisfaction spend:

1. *The Gentleman's Retirement*

Near some fair town I'd have a private seat,
Built uniform, not little nor too great;
Better if on a rising ground it stood,
Fields on this side, on that a neighbouring wood.
It should, within, no other things contain
But what are useful, necessary, plain.   10
Methinks 'tis nauseous, and I'd ne'er endure
The needless pomp of gaudy furniture.
A little garden, grateful to the eye,
And a cool rivulet run murmuring by,
On whose delicious banks a stately row
Of shady limes or sycamores should grow;
At th' end of which a silent study placed
Should with the noblest authors there be graced:
Horace and Virgil, in whose mighty lines
Immortal wit and solid learning shines;   20
Sharp Juvenal and amorous Ovid too,
Who all the turns of love's soft passion knew.

In some of these, as fancy should advise,
I'd always take my morning exercise;
For sure no moments bring us more content
Than those in pleasing, useful study spent.

2. *His Fortune and Charity*

I'd have a clear and competent estate,
That I might live genteelly, but not great;
As much as I could moderately spend;
A little more sometimes t' oblige a friend.

.   .   .

A frugal plenty should my table spread
With healthy, not luxurious, dishes fed;
Enough to satisfy, and something more
To feed the stranger and the neighb'ring poor.

■   Discuss this excerpt from the poem which Dr. Johnson said was more often read than any other in the eighteenth century in terms of its subject matter and the ideals it expresses. Discuss its manner and language in terms of their appropriateness to the subject matter and ideals.

■ ■ ■ ■ ■ ■ ■ ■ ■

Oliver Goldsmith (1728–1774)

Song

When lovely woman stoops to folly,
    And finds too late that men betray,
What charm can soothe her melancholy?
    What art can wash her guilt away?

The only art her guilt to cover,
    To hide her shame from every eye,
To give repentance to her lover,
    And wring his bosom, is—to die.

■ ■ ■ ■ ■ ■ ■ ■ ■

William Cowper (1731–1800)

The Castaway

Obscurest night involved the sky,
    The Atlantic billows roared,
When such a destined wretch as I,
    Washed headlong from on board,

Of friends, of hope, of all bereft,
His floating home forever left.

No braver chief could Albion boast
    Than he with whom he went,
Nor ever ship left Albion's coast
    With warmer wishes sent.   10
He loved them both, but both in vain,
Nor him beheld, nor her again.

Not long beneath the whelming brine,
    Expert to swim, he lay;
Nor soon he felt his strength decline,
    Or courage die away;
But waged with death a lasting strife,
Supported by despair of life.

He shouted: nor his friends had failed
    To check the vessel's course,   20
But so the furious blast prevailed,
    That, pitiless perforce,
They left their outcast mate behind,
And scudded still before the wind.

Some succor yet they could afford,
    And such as storms allow,
The cask, the coop, the floated cord,
    Delayed not to bestow.
But he (they knew) nor ship nor shore,
Whate'er they gave, should visit more.   30

Nor, cruel as it seemed, could he
    Their haste himself condemn,
Aware that flight, in such a sea,
    Alone could rescue them;
Yet bitter felt it still to die
Deserted, and his friends so nigh.

He long survives, who lives an hour
    In ocean, self-upheld;
And so long he, with unspent power,
    His destiny repelled;   40
And ever, as the minutes flew,
Entreated help, or cried "Adieu!"

At length, his transient respite past,
   His comrades, who before
Had heard his voice in every blast,
   Could catch the sound no more;
For then, by toil subdued, he drank
The stifling wave, and then he sank.

No poet wept him; but the page
   Of narrative sincere,
That tells his name, his worth, his age,   50
   Is wet with Anson's[1] tear;
And tears by bards or heroes shed
Alike immortalize the dead.

I therefore purpose not, or dream,
   Descanting on his fate,
To give the melancholy theme
   A more enduring date;
But misery still delights to trace
Its semblance in another's case.   60

No voice divine the storm allayed,
   No light propitious shone,
When, snatched from all effectual aid,
   We perished, each alone:
But I beneath a rougher sea,
And whelmed in deeper gulfs than he.

....

1. The subject of this poem was suggested by an account of a drowning in Anson's *A Voyage Round the World.* Cowper thought of his insanity as a kind of drowning.

■ ■ ■ ■ ■ ■ ■ ■ ■ ■

Robert Burns (1759–1796)

To a Mouse

*On Turning Her Up In
Her Nest With The Plow*

Wee, sleekit, cowrin, tim'rous beastie,
O, what a panic's in thy breastie!
Thou need na start awae sae hasty,
   Wi' bickering brattle!

I wad be laith to rin an' chase thee,
   Wi' murd'ring pattle.[1]

I'm truly sorry man's dominion,
Has broken Nature's social union,
An' justifies that ill opinion,
   Which makes thee startle   10
At me, thy poor, earth-born companion,
   An' fellow-mortal!

I doubt na, whiles, but thou may thieve;
What then? poor beastie, thou maun live!
A daimen icker in a thrave[2]
   'S a sma' request;
I'll get a blessin wi' the lave,[3]
   An' never miss't!

Thy wee bit housie, too, in ruin!
It's silly wa's the winds are strewin!   20
An' naething, now, to build a new ane,
   O' foggage[4] green!
An' bleak December's winds ensuin,
   Baith snell[5] an' keen!

Thou saw the fields laid bare an' waste,
An' weary winter comin' fast,
An' cozie here, beneath the blast,
   Thou thought to dwell—
Till crash! the cruel coulter past
   Out thro' thy cell.   30

That wee bit heap o' leaves an' stibble,
Has cost thee mony a weary nibble!
Now thou's turned out, for a' thy trouble,
   But house or hald,
To thole[6] the winter's sleety dribble,
   An' cranreuch cauld! [7]

But, Mousie, thou art no thy lane,[8]
In proving foresight may be vain;
The best-laid schemes o' mice an' men
   Gang aft agley,[9]   40

....
1. Plow stick.   2. An odd ear of corn in two shocks of grain.   3. Re-
mainder.   4. Coarse grass.   5. Bitter.   6. Endure.   7. Sharp hoar-
frost.   8. Not alone.   9. Often go wrong.

An' lea'e us nought but grief an' pain
    For promised joy!

Still thou art blest, compared wi' me;
The present only toucheth thee:
But och! I backward cast my e'e,
    On prospects drear!
An' forward, tho' I canna see,
    I guess an' fear!

■   Characterize the tone of this poem, and then indicate what factors
contribute to it.

■ ■ ■ ■ ■ ■ ■ ■ ■

William Cullen Bryant (1794–1878)

Thanatopsis[1]

To him who in the love of Nature holds
Communion with her visible forms, she speaks
A various language; for his gayer hours
She has a voice of gladness, and a smile
And eloquence of beauty, and she glides
Into his darker musings, with a mild
And healing sympathy, that steals away
Their sharpness, ere he is aware. When thoughts
Of the last bitter hour come like a blight
Over thy spirit, and sad images   10
Of the stern agony, and shroud, and pall,
And breathless darkness, and the narrow house,
Make thee to shudder and grow sick at heart;—
Go forth, under the open sky, and list
To Nature's teachings, while from all around—
Earth and her waters, and the depths of air—
Comes a still voice—
                        Yet a few days, and thee
The all-beholding sun shall see no more
In all his course; nor yet in the cold ground,
Where thy pale form was laid with many tears,   20
Nor in the embrace of ocean, shall exist

----

1. The word *thanatopsis* is made up of two Greek words, Θάνατος, death,
and ὄψις, view, hence a view of death.

Thy image. Earth, that nourished thee, shall claim
Thy growth, to be resolved to earth again,
And, lost each human trace, surrendering up
Thine individual being, shalt thou go
To mix forever with the elements,
To be a brother to the insensible rock
And to the sluggish clod, which the rude swain
Turns with his share, and treads upon. The oak
Shall send his roots abroad, and pierce thy mold.   30

Yet not to thine eternal resting-place
Shalt thou retire alone, nor couldst thou wish
Couch more magnificent. Thou shalt lie down
With patriarchs of the infant world—with kings,
The powerful of the earth—the wise, the good,
Fair forms, and hoary seers of ages past,
All in one mighty sepulcher. The hills
Rock-ribbed and ancient as the sun,—the vales
Stretching in pensive quietness between;
The venerable woods—rivers that move   40
In majesty, and the complaining brooks
That make the meadows green; and, poured round all,
Old Ocean's gray and melancholy waste,—
Are but the solemn decorations all
Of the great tomb of man. The golden sun,
The planets, all the infinite host of heaven,
Are shining on the sad abodes of death
Through the still lapse of ages. All that tread
The globe are but a handful to the tribes
That slumber in its bosom.—Take the wings   50
Of morning, pierce the Barcan wilderness,
Or lose thyself in the continuous woods
Where rolls the Oregon, and hears no sound,
Save his own dashings—yet the dead are there;
And millions in those solitudes, since first
The flight of years began, have laid them down
In their last sleep—the dead reign there alone.
So shalt thou rest, and what if thou withdraw
In silence from the living, and no friend
Take note of thy departure? All that breathe   60
Will share thy destiny. The gay will laugh
When thou art gone, the solemn brood of care
Plod on, and each one as before will chase
His favorite phantom; yet all these shall leave
Their mirth and their employments, and shall come

And make their bed with thee. As the long train
Of ages glides away, the sons of men,
The youth in life's green spring, and he who goes
In the full strength of years, matron and maid,
The speechless babe, and the gray-headed man—   70
Shall one by one be gathered to thy side,
By those, who in their turn shall follow them.

    So live, that when thy summons comes to join
The innumerable caravan, which moves
To that mysterious realm, where each shall take
His chamber in the silent halls of death,
Thou go not, like the quarry-slave at night,
Scourged to his dungeon, but, sustained and soothed
By an unfaltering trust, approach thy grave,
Like one who wraps the drapery of his couch   80
About him, and lies down to pleasant dreams.

■ 1. There are in this poem a number of expressions that might be
considered clichés. What are some of these?

    2. Are specific clichés appropriate or inappropriate to the style of
the poem?

■ ■ ■ ■ ■ ■ ■ ■ ■ ■

Thomas Moore (1779–1852)

The Time I've Lost in Wooing

The time I've lost in wooing,
In watching and pursuing
    The light that lies
    In woman's eyes,
Has been my heart's undoing.
Though Wisdom oft has sought me,
I scorn'd the lore she brought me,
    My only books
    Were woman's looks,
And folly's all they've taught me.   10

Her smile when Beauty granted,
I hung with gaze enchanted,
    Like him, the Sprite,
    Whom maids by night

Oft meet in glen that's haunted.
Like him, too, Beauty won me,
But while her eyes were on me;
  If once their ray
  Was turn'd away,
Oh, winds could not outrun me.   20

And are those follies going?
And is my proud heart growing
  Too cold or too wise
  For brilliant eyes
Again to set it glowing?
No, vain, alas! th' endeavor
From bonds so sweet to sever;
  Poor wisdom's chance
  Against a glance
Is now as weak as ever.   30

■ Does there seem to be an unintended pun in line 3? What effect
does the line have on the tone of the entire poem?

■ ■ ■ ■ ■ ■ ■ ■ ■ ■

John Clare (1793–1864)

Clock-o'-Clay

In the cowslip pips I lie,
Hidden from the buzzing fly,
While green grass beneath me lies,
Pearled with dew like fishes' eyes,
Here I lie, a clock-o'-clay,
Waiting for the time o' day.

While the forest quakes surprise,
And the wild wind sobs and sighs,
My home rocks as like to fall,
On its pillar green and tall;
When the pattering rain drives by
Clock-o'-clay keeps warm and dry.

Day by day and night by night,
All the week I hide from sight;
In the cowslip pips I lie,

In the rain still warm and dry;
Day and night, and night and day,
Red, black-spotted clock-o'-clay.

My home shakes in wind and showers,
Pale green pillar topped with flowers,
Bending at the wild wind's breath,
Till I touch the grass beneath;
Here I live, lone clock-o'-clay,
Watching for the time of day.

■   1. What figure of speech is "clock-o'-clay"?
    2. Is the phrase effective by virtue of connotations?
    3. Is the phrase intimately related to the rest of the poem?

■ ■ ■ ■ ■ ■ ■ ■ ■

Ralph Waldo Emerson (1803–1882)

Concord Hymn

By the rude bridge that arched the flood,
    Their flag to April's breeze unfurled,
Here once the embattled farmers stood,
    And fired the shot heard round the world.

The foe long since in silence slept;
    Alike the conqueror silent sleeps;
And Time the ruined bridge has swept
    Down the dark stream that seaward creeps.

On this green bank, by this soft stream,
    We set to-day a votive stone;
That memory may their deed redeem,
    When, like our sires, our sons are gone.

Spirit, that made those heroes dare
    To die, and leave their children free,
Bid Time and Nature gently spare
    The shaft we raise to them and thee.

Days

Daughters of Time, the hypocritic Days,
Muffled and dumb like barefoot dervishes,
And marching single in an endless file,
Bring diadems and fagots in their hands.
To each they offer gifts after his will,
Bread, kingdoms, stars, and sky that holds them all.
I, in my pleached garden, watched the pomp,
Forgot my morning wishes, hastily
Took a few herbs and apples, and the Day
Turned and departed silent. I, too late,
Under her solemn fillet saw the scorn.

The Snow-Storm

Announced by all the trumpets of the sky,
Arrives the snow, and, driving o'er the fields,
Seems nowhere to alight: the whited air
Hides hills and woods, the river, and the heaven,
And veils the farm-house at the garden's end.
The sled and traveller stopped, the courier's feet
Delayed, all friends shut out, the housemates sit
Around the radiant fireplace, enclosed
In a tumultuous privacy of storm.

Come see the north wind's masonry.
Out of an unseen quarry evermore
Furnished with tile, the fierce artificer
Curves his white bastions with projected roof
Round every windward stake, or tree, or door.
Speeding, the myriad-handed, his wild work
So fanciful, so savage, nought cares he
For number or proportion. Mockingly,
On coop or kennel he hangs Parian wreaths;
A swan-like form invests the hidden thorn;
Fills up the farmer's lane from wall to wall,
Maugre the farmer's sighs; and at the gate
A tapering turret overtops the work.
And when his hours are numbered, and the world
Is all his own, retiring, as he were not,
Leaves, when the sun appears, astonished Art
To mimic in slow structures, stone by stone,
Built in an age, the mad wind's nightwork,
The frolic architecture of the snow.

Elizabeth Barrett Browning (1806–1861)

How Do I Love Thee?

How do I love thee? Let me count the ways.
I love thee to the depth and breadth and height
My soul can reach, when feeling out of sight
For the ends of Being and ideal Grace.
I love thee to the level of everyday's
Most quiet need, by sun and candle-light.
I love thee freely, as men strive for Right;
I love thee purely, as they turn from Praise.
I love thee with the passion put to use
In my old griefs, and with my childhood's faith.
I love thee with a love I seemed to lose
With my lost saints—I love thee with the breath,
Smiles, tears, of all my life!—and, if God choose,
I shall but love thee better after death.

■ ■ ■ ■ ■ ■ ■ ■ ■ ■

Henry Wadsworth Longfellow (1807–1882)

Hymn to the Night

I heard the trailing garments of the Night
    Sweep through her marble halls!
I saw her sable skirts all fringed with light
    From the celestial walls.

I felt her presence, by its spell of might,
    Stoop o'er me from above;
The calm, majestic presence of the Night,
    As of the one I love.

I heard the sounds of sorrow and delight,
    The manifold, soft chimes,
That fill the haunted chambers of the Night,
    Like some old poet's rhymes.

From the cool cisterns of the midnight air
    My spirit drank repose;
The fountain of perpetual peace flows there—
    From those deep cisterns flows.

O holy Night! from thee I learn to bear
    What man has borne before.
Thou layest thy finger on the lips of Care,
    And they complain no more.

Peace! Peace! Orestes-like I breathe this prayer!
    Descend with broad-winged flight,
The welcome, the thrice-prayed for, the most fair,
    The best-beloved Night!

Divina Commedia

2

How strange the sculptures that adorn these towers!
    This crowd of statues, in whose folded sleeves
    Birds build their nests; while canopied with leaves
    Parvis and portal bloom like trellised bowers,
And the vast minster seems a cross of flowers!
But fiends and dragons on the gargoyled eaves
    Watch the dead Christ between the living thieves,
    And, underneath, the traitor Judas lowers!
Ah! from what agonies of heart and brain,
    What exaltations trampling on despair,
    What tenderness, what tears, what hate of wrong,
What passionate outcry of a soul in pain,
    Uprose this poem of the earth and air,
    This mediaeval miracle of song!

Excelsior

The shades of night were falling fast,
As through an Alpine village passed
A youth, who bore, 'mid snow and ice,
A banner with the strange device,
    Excelsior!

His brow was sad; his eye beneath,
Flashed like a falchion from its sheath,
And like a silver clarion rung
The accents of that unknown tongue,
    Excelsior!

In happy homes he saw the light
Of household fires gleam warm and bright;
Above, the spectral glaciers shone,
And from his lips escaped a groan,
        Excelsior!

"Try not the Pass!" the old man said;
"Dark lowers the tempest overhead,
The roaring torrent is deep and wide!"
And loud that clarion voice replied,
        Excelsior!

"O stay," the maiden said, "and rest
Thy weary head upon this breast!"
A tear stood in his bright blue eye,
But still he answered, with a sigh,
        Excelsior!

"Beware the pine tree's withered branch!
Beware the awful avalanche!"
This was the peasant's last Good-night;
A voice replied far up the height,
        Excelsior!   30

At break of day, as heavenward
The pious monks of Saint Bernard
Uttered the oft-repeated prayer,
A voice cried through the startled air,
        Excelsior!

A traveler, by the faithful hound,
Half-buried in the snow was found,
Still grasping in his hand of ice
That banner with the strange device,
        Excelsior!   40

There in the twilight cold and gray,
Lifeless, but beautiful, he lay,
And from the sky, serene and far,
A voice fell, like a falling star,
        Excelsior!

Edward Fitzgerald (1809–1883)

From The *Rubáiyát of Omar Khayyám*

1

Awake! for Morning in the Bowl of Night
Has flung the Stone that puts the Stars to Flight:
    And Lo! the Hunter of the East has caught
The Sultan's Turret in a Noose of Light.

7

Come, fill the Cup, and in the fire of Spring
Your Winter-garment of Repentance fling:
    The Bird of Time has but a little way
To flutter—and the Bird is on the Wing.

64

Strange, is it not? that of the myriads who
Before us pass'd the door of Darkness through,
    Not one returns to tell us of the Road,
Which to discover we must travel too.

99

Ah Love! could you and I with Him conspire
To grasp this sorry Scheme of Things Entire,
    Would not we shatter it to bits—and then
Re-mould it nearer to the Heart's desire!

■ ■ ■ ■ ■ ■ ■ ■ ■ ■

Arthur Hugh Clough (1819–1861)

The Latest Decalogue

Thou shalt have one God only; who
Would be at the expense of two?
No graven images may be
Worshipped, except the currency;
Swear not at all; for, for thy curse
Thine enemy is none the worse:
At church on Sunday to attend
Will serve to keep the world thy friend:
Honour thy parents; that is, all
From whom advancement may befall;

Thou shalt not kill; but need'st not strive
Officiously to keep alive:
Do not adultery commit;
Advantage rarely comes of it:
Thou shalt not steal; an empty feat,
When it's so lucrative to cheat:
Bear not false witness; let the lie
Have time on its own wings to fly:
Thou shalt not covet, but tradition
Approves all forms of competition.

■   1. What is the theme of the poem?
2. Why is this form, contrasting ironic commandments with the
commonly accepted Christian commandments, a method of indirection?

■ ■ ■ ■ ■ ■ ■ ■ ■ ■

George Meredith (1828–1909)

From *Modern Love*

In our old shipwrecked days there was an hour,
When in the firelight steadily aglow,
Joined slackly, we beheld the red chasm grow
Among the clicking coals. Our library-bower
That eve was left to us; and hushed we sat
As lovers to whom Time is whispering.
From sudden-opened doors we heard them sing;
The nodding elders mixed good wine with chat.
Well knew we that Life's greatest treasure lay
With us, and of it was our talk. "Ah, yes!
Love dies!" I said (I never thought it less).
She yearned to me that sentence to unsay.
Then when the fire domed blackening, I found
Her cheek was salt against my kiss, and swift
Up the sharp scale of sobs her breast did lift.—
Now am I haunted by that taste! that sound!

■   Discuss the shift in imagery in this poem. Does the shift affect the
tone?

Lucifer in Starlight

On a starred night Prince Lucifer uprose.
Tired of his dark dominion swung the fiend
Above the rolling ball in cloud part screened,
Where sinners hugged their spectre of repose.
Poor prey to his hot fit of pride were those.
And now upon his western wing he leaned,
Now his huge bulk o'er Afric's sands careened,
Now the black planet shadowed Arctic snows.
Soaring through wider zones that pricked his scars
With memory of the old revolt from Awe,
He reached a middle height, and at the stars,
Which are the brain of heaven, he looked, and sank.
Around the ancient track marched, rank on rank,
The army of unalterable law.

1. What is the theme of the poem? Does the imagery adequately support the theme?

2. There are romantic and prosaic images in the poem. How do they function thematically?

■■■■■■■■■■

Dante Gabriel Rossetti (1828–1882)

The Ballad of Dead Ladies

From François Villon

Tell me now in what hidden way is
    Lady Flora the lovely Roman?
Where's Hipparchia, and where is Thais,
    Neither of them the fairer woman?
Where is Echo, beheld of no man,
Only heard on river and mere—
    She whose beauty was more than human?—
But where are the snows of yester-year?

Where's Héloïse, the learned nun,
    For whose sake Abeillard, I ween,
Lost manhood and put priesthood on?
    (From Love he won such dule and teen!)
And where, I pray you, is the Queen

Who willed that Buridan should steer
  Sewed in a sack's mouth down the Seine?—
But where are the snows of yester-year?

White Queen Blanche, like a queen of lilies,
  With a voice like any mermaiden—
Bertha Broadfoot, Beatrice, Alice,
  And Ermengarde the lady of Maine—
  And that good Joan whom Englishmen
At Rouen doomed and burned her there—
  Mother of God, where are they then?—
But where are the snows of yester-year?

Nay, never ask this week, fair lord,
  Where they are gone, nor yet this year,
Except with this for an overword—
  But where are the snows of yester-year?

■ In what sense is the refrain an indirection? Why is it effective?

■ ■ ■ ■ ■ ■ ■ ■ ■ ■

Christina Rossetti (1830–1894)

Song

When I am dead, my dearest,
  Sing no sad songs for me;
Plant thou no roses at my head,
  Nor shady cypress-tree:
Be the green grass above me
  With showers and dewdrops wet;
And if thou wilt, remember,
  And if thou wilt, forget

I shall not see the shadows,
  I shall not feel the rain;
I shall not hear the nightingale
  Sing on, as if in pain:
And dreaming through the twilight
  That doth not rise nor set,
Haply I may remember,
  And haply may forget.

Up-Hill

Does the road wind up-hill all the way?
  Yes, to the very end.
Will the day's journey take the whole long day?
  From morn to night, my friend.

But is there for the night a resting-place?
  A roof for when the slow, dark hours begin.
May not the darkness hide it from my face?
  You cannot miss that inn.

Shall I meet other wayfarers at night?
  Those who have gone before.
Then must I knock, or call when just in sight?
  They will not keep you standing at that door.

Shall I find comfort, travel-sore and weak?
  Of labor you shall find the sum.
Will there be beds for me and all who seek?
  Yea, beds for all who come.

■   Consider whether or not this poem is objectionably didactic.

■ ■ ■ ■ ■ ■ ■ ■ ■ ■

Arthur O'Shaughnessy (1844–1881)

From Ode

We are the music-makers,
  And we are the dreamers of dreams,
Wandering by lone sea-breakers,
  And sitting by desolate streams;
World-losers and world-forsakers,
  On whom the pale moon gleams:
Yet we are the movers and shakers
  Of the world for ever, it seems.

With wonderful deathless ditties
We build up the world's great cities,
  And out of a fabulous story
  We fashion an empire's glory:
One man with a dream, at pleasure,
  Shall go forth and conquer a crown;

And three with a new song's measure
    Can trample an empire down.

We, in the ages lying
    In the buried past of the earth,
Built Nineveh with our sighing,
    And Babel itself with our mirth;
And o'erthrew them with prophesying
    To the old of the new world's worth;
For each age is a dream that is dying,
    Or one that is coming to birth.

■ What is the effect on the tone of this poem of the phrases "it seems,"
and "deathless ditties"?

■■■■■■■■■

Gerard Manley Hopkins (1844–1889)

Spring and Fall: [1]

To a Young Child

Márgarét, are you grieving
Over Goldengrove unleaving?
Leáves, líke the things of man, you
With your fresh thoughts care for, can you?
Ah! ás the heart grows older
It will come to such sights colder
By and by, nor spare a sigh
Though worlds of wanwood leafmeal lie;
And yet you wíll weep and know why.
Now no matter, child, the name:
Sórrow's spríngs áre the same.
Nor mouth had, no nor mind, expressed
What heart heard of, ghost guessed:
It ís the blight man was born for,
It is Margaret you mourn for.

■ 1. The accents indicated are Hopkins' own. Do they make for the
best reading of the poem?
    2. Do any of the rhyme endings make significant contributions to
the quality of the poem?
....

1. "Spring and Fall" is from Collected Works, published by Oxford University Press.

W. E. Henley (1849–1903)

Margaritae Sorori

A late lark twitters from the quiet skies;
And from the west,
Where the sun, his day's work ended,
Lingers as in content,
There falls on the old, gray city
An influence luminous and serene,
A shining peace.

The smoke ascends
In a rosy-and-golden haze. The spires
Shine, and are changed. In the valley
Shadows rise. The lark sings on. The sun,
Closing his benediction,
Sinks, and the darkening air
Thrills with a sense of the triumphing night—
Night with her train of stars
And her great gift of sleep.

So be my passing!
My task accomplished and the long day done,
My wages taken, and in my heart
Some late lark singing,
Let me be gathered to the quiet west,
The sundown splendid and serene,
Death.

■   This poem is in free verse. Are the line arrangements arbitrary, or do they contribute to a particular effect?

■■■■■■■■■■

Robert Louis Stevenson (1850–1894)

Romance

I will make you brooches and toys for your delight
Of bird-song at morning and star-shine at night.
I will make a palace fit for you and me,
Of green days in forests and blue days at sea.

I will make my kitchen, and you shall keep your room,
Where white flows the river and bright blows the broom,
And you shall wash your linen and keep your body white
In rainfall at morning and dewfall at night.

And this shall be for music when no one else is near,
The fine song for singing, the rare song to hear!
That only I remember, that only you admire,
Of the broad road that stretches and the roadside fire.

1. Is there any inconsistency in the imagery of the first stanza?
2. Would the poem be improved if it ended at line 8?

Requiem

Under the wide and starry sky,
    Dig the grave and let me lie.
Glad did I live and gladly die,
    And I laid me down with a will.

This be the verse you grave for me:
Here he lies where he longed to be;
Home is the sailor, home from sea,
    And the hunter home from the hill.

A. E. Housman (1859–1936)

To an Athlete Dying Young[1]

The time you won your town the race
We chaired you through the market-place;
Man and boy stood cheering by,
And home we brought you shoulder-high.

Today, the road all runners come,
Shoulder-high we bring you home,
And set you at your threshold down,
Townsman of a stiller town.

1. "To an Athlete Dying Young," is from *A Shropshire Lad,* by A. E.
Housman. Used by permission of Henry Holt and Company, Inc., and of The
Society of Authors, literary representative of the Trustees of the estate of the late
A. E. Housman, and Messrs. Jonathan Cape Ltd., publishers of A. E. Housman's
Collected Poems.

Smart lad, to slip betimes away
From fields where glory does not stay,
And early though the laurel grows
It withers quicker than the rose.

Eyes the shady night has shut
Cannot see the record cut,
And silence sounds no worse than cheers
After earth has stopped the ears:

Now you will not swell the rout
Of lads that wore their honors out,
Runners whom renown outran
And the name died before the man.

So set, before its echoes fade,
The fleet foot on the sill of shade,
And hold to the low lintel up
The still-defended challenge-cup.

And round that early-laureled head
Will flock to gaze the strengthless dead,
And find unwithered on its curls
The garland briefer than a girl's.

■■■■■■■■■■

Rudyard Kipling (1865–1936)

Danny Deever

"What are the bugles blowin' for?" said Files-on-Parade.
"To turn you out, to turn you out," the Color-Sergeant said.
"What makes you look so white, so white?" said Files-on-Parade.
"I'm dreadin' what I've got to watch," the Color-Sergeant said.
   For they're hangin' Danny Deever, you can 'ear the Dead March play,
   The regiment's in 'ollow square—they're hangin' him today;
   They've taken of his buttons off an' cut his stripes away,
   An' they're hangin' Danny Deever in the mornin'.

"What makes the rear-rank breathe so 'ard!" said Files-on-Parade.
"It's bitter cold, it's bitter cold," the Color-Sergeant said.
"What makes that front-rank man fall down?" says Files-on-Parade.
"A touch of sun, a touch of sun," the Color-Sergeant said.

They are hangin' Danny Deever, they are marchin' of 'im round.
They 'ave 'alted Danny Deever by 'is coffin on the ground:
An' 'e'll swing in 'arf a minute for a sneakin' shootin' hound—
O they're hangin' Danny Deever in the mornin'!

"'Is cot was right-'and cot to mine," said Files-on-Parade.
"'E's sleepin' out an' far tonight," the Color-Sergeant said.
"I've drunk 'is beer a score o' times," said Files-on-Parade.
"'E's drinkin' bitter beer alone," the Color-Sergeant said.   20
    They are hangin' Danny Deever, you must mark 'im to 'is place,
    For 'e shot a comrade sleepin'—you must look 'im in the face;
    Nine 'undred of 'is county an' the regiment's disgrace,
    While they're hangin' Danny Deever in the mornin'.

"What's that so black agin the sun?" said Files-on-Parade.
"It's Danny fightin' 'ard for life," the Color-Sergeant said.
"What's that that whimpers over'ead?" said Files-on-Parade.
"It's Danny's soul that's passin' now," the Color-Sergeant said.
    For they're done with Danny Deever, you can 'ear the quickstep play,
    The regiment's in column, an' they're marchin' us away;   30
    Ho! the young recruits are shakin', an' they'll want their beer today,
    After hangin' Danny Deever in the mornin'.

■   1. How does the rhyme scheme contribute to the sense of marching
men and disciplined formations? Are there any imperfect rhymes?
    2. What is the effect of the slant rhyme in lines 1 and 2?

■■■■■■■■■■

Ernest Dowson (1867–1900)

Non Sum Qualis Eram Bonae sub Regno Cynarae

    Last night, ah, yesternight, betwixt her lips and mine
    There fell thy shadow, Cynara! thy breath was shed
    Upon my soul between the kisses and the wine;
    And I was desolate and sick of an old passion,
        Yea, I was desolate and bowed my head:
    I have been faithful to thee, Cynara! in my fashion.

    All night upon mine heart I felt her warm heart beat,
    Night-long within mine arms in love and sleep she lay;
    Surely the kisses of her bought red mouth were sweet;

But I was desolate and sick of an old passion,
　　When I awoke and found the dawn was gray:
I have been faithful to thee, Cynara! in my fashion.

I have forgot much, Cynara! gone with the wind,
Flung roses, roses riotously with the throng,
Dancing, to put thy pale, lost lilies out of mind;
But I was desolate and sick of an old passion,
　　Yea, all the time, because the dance was long:
I have been faithful to thee, Cynara! in my fashion.

I cried for madder music and for stronger wine,
But when the feast is finished and the lamps expire,
Then falls thy shadow, Cynara! the night is thine;
And I am desolate and sick of an old passion,
　　Yea, hungry for the lips of my desire:
I have been faithful to thee, Cynara! in my fashion.

■　Attempt to describe the rhetorical quality of this poem. Is it justified? Explain your answer.

■■■■■■■■■

Edwin Arlington Robinson (1869–1935)

Eros Turannos[1]

She fears him, and will always ask
　　What fated her to choose him;
She meets in his engaging mask
　　All reasons to refuse him;
But what she meets and what she fears
Are less than are the downward years,
Drawn slowly to the foamless weirs
　　Of age, were she to lose him.

Between a blurred sagacity
　　That once had power to sound him,
And Love, that will not let him be
　　The Judas that she found him,

10

---

1. "Eros Tyrannos" (the tyrant love) is from *Man against the Sky*, by Edwin Arlington Robinson. Reprinted with the permission of the publishers, The Macmillan Company.

Her pride assuages her almost,
As if it were alone the cost.
He sees that he will not be lost.
    And waits and looks around him.

A sense of ocean and old trees
    Envelops and allures him;
Tradition, touching all he sees,
    Beguiles and reassures him;   20
And all her doubts of what he says
Are dimmed with what she knows of days—
Till even prejudice delays
    And fades, and she secures him.

The falling leaf inaugurates
    The reign of her confusion;
The pounding wave reverberates
    The dirge of her illusion;
And home, where passion lived and died,
Becomes a place where she can hide,   30
While all the town and harbor-side
    Vibrate with her seclusion.

We tell you, tapping on our brows,
    The story as it should be,
As if the story of a house
    Were told, or ever could be;
We'll have no kindly veil between
Her visions and those we have seen,—
As if we guessed what hers have been,
    Or what they are or would be.   40

Meanwhile we do no harm; for they
    That with a god have striven,
Not hearing much of what we say,
    Take what the god has given;
Though like waves breaking it may be,
Or like a changed familiar tree,
Or like a stairway to the sea
    Where down the blind are driven.

■■■■■■■■■■

Ezra Pound (1885–

Portrait d'une Femme

Your mind and you are our Sargasso Sea,
London has swept about you this score years
And bright ships left you this or that in fee:
Ideas, old gossip, oddments of all things,
Strange spars of knowledge and dimmed wares or price.
Great minds have sought you—lacking someone else.
You have been second always. Tragical?
No. You preferred it to the usual thing:
One dull man, dulling and uxorious,
One average mind—with one thought less, each year.   10
Oh, you are patient, I have seen you sit
Hours, where something might have floated up.
And now you pay one. Yes, you richly pay.
You are a person of some interest, one comes to you
And takes strange gain away:
Trophies fished up; some curious suggestion;
Fact that leads nowhere; and a tale or two,
Pregnant with mandrakes, or with something else
That might prove useful and yet never proves,
That never fits a corner or shows use,   20
Or finds its hour upon the loom of days:
The tarnished, gaudy, wonderful old work;
Idols and ambergris and rare inlays,
These are your riches, your great store; and yet
For all this sea-hoard of deciduous things,
Strange woods half sodden, and new brighter stuff:
In the slow float of differing light and deep,
No! there is nothing! In the whole and all,
Nothing that's quite your own.
                    Yet this is you.   30

Taking Leave of a Friend

Blue mountains to the north of the walls,
White river winding about them;
Here we must make separation
And go out through a thousand miles of dead grass.
Mind like a floating wide cloud,

Sunset like the parting of old acquaintances
Who bow over their clasped hands at a distance.
Our horses neigh to each other
    as we are departing.

■■■■■■■■■

Marianne Moore (1887–   )

A Grave[1]

Man looking into the sea,
taking the view from those who have as
    much right to it as you have to it
    yourself,
it is human nature to stand in the middle of
    a thing,
but you cannot stand in the middle of this;
the sea has nothing to give but a well
    excavated grave.
The firs stand in a procession, each with an   10
    emerald turkey-foot at the top,
reserved as their contours, saying nothing;
repression, however, is not the most
    obvious characteristic of the sea;
the sea is a collector, quick to return a rapacious look.
There are others besides you who have
    worn that look—
whose expression is no longer a protest; the
    fish no longer investigate them   20
for their bones have not lasted:
men lower nets, unconscious of the fact
    that they are desecrating a grave,
and row quickly away—the blades of the oars
moving together like the feet of water-
    spiders as if there were no such
    thing as death.
The wrinkles progress upon themselves in a
    phalanx—beautiful under networks   30
    of foam,
and fade breathlessly while the sea rustles in
    and out of the seaweed;
the birds swim through the air at top speed,
    emitting cat-calls as heretofore—

----

the tortoise-shell scourges about the feet of
  the cliffs, in motion beneath them;
and the ocean, under the pulsation of
  lighthouses and noise of bell-buoys,
advances as usual, looking as if it were not   40
  that ocean in which dropped things
  are bound to sink—
in which if they turn and twist, it is neither
  with volition nor consciousness.

■ ■ ■ ■ ■ ■ ■ ■ ■

John Crowe Ransom (1888–   )

Philomela[1]

Procne, Philomela, and Itylus,
Your names are liquid, your improbable tale
Is recited in the classic numbers of the nightingale.
Ah, but our numbers are not felicitous,
It goes not liquidly for us.

Perched on a Roman ilex, and duly apostrophized,
The nightingale descanted unto Ovid;
She has even appeared to the Teutons, the swilled and gravid;
At Fontainbleau it may be the bird was gallicized;
Never was she baptized.   10

To England came Philomela with her pain,
Fleeing the hawk her husband; querulous ghost,
She wanders when he sits heavy on his roost,
Utters herself in the original again,
The untranslatable refrain.

Not to these shores she came! this other Thrace,
Environs barbarous to the royal Attic;
How could her delicate dirge run democratic,
Delivered in a cloudless boundless public place
To an inordinate race?   20

1. "Philomela" is reprinted from *Selected Poems,* by John Crowe Ransom
by permission of Alfred A. Knopf, Inc. Copyright, 1924, 1945, by Alfred A.
Knopf, Inc.

I pernoctated with the Oxford students once,
And in the quadrangles, in the cloisters, on the Cher,
Preciously knocked at antique doors ajar,
Fatuously touched the hems of the hierophants,
Sick of my dissonance.

I went out to Bagley Wood, I climbed the hill;
Even the moon had slanted off in a twinkling,
I heard the sepulchral owl and a few bells tinkling,
There was no more villainous day to unfulfill,
The diuturnity was still.   30

Up from the darkest wood where Philomela sat,
Her fairy numbers issued. What then ailed me?
My ears are called capacious but they failed me,
Her classics registered a little flat!
I rose, and venomously spat.

Philomela, Philomela, lover of song,
I am in despair if we may make us worthy,
A bantering breed sophistical and swarthy;
Unto more beautiful, persistently more young,
Thy fabulous provinces belong.   40

■■■■■■■■■■

Allen Tate (1899–   )

The Mediterranean[1]

Quem das finem, rex magne, dolorum?

Where we went in the boat was a long bay
A slingshot wide, walled in by towering stone—
Peaked margin of antiquity's delay,
And we went there out of time's monotone:

Where we went in the black hull no light moved
But a gull white-winged along the feckless wave,
The breeze, unseen but fierce as a body loved,
The boat drove onward like a willing slave:

---

1. "The Mediterranean" is reprinted from *Poems—1922–1947*, by Allen Tate; copyright, 1932, 1948, by Charles Scribner's Sons; used by permission of the publishers.

Where we went in the small ship the seaweed
Parted and gave to us the murmuring shore,   10
And we made feast and in our secret need
Devoured the very plates Aeneas bore:

Where derelict you see through the low twilight
The green coast that you, thunder-tossed, would win,
Drop sail, and hastening to drink all night
Eat dish and bowl to take that sweet land in!

Where we feasted and caroused on the sandless
Pebbles, affecting our day of piracy,
What prophecy of eaten plates could landless
Wanderers fulfil by the ancient sea?   20

We for that time might taste the famous age
Eternal here yet hidden from our eyes
When lust of power undid its stuffless rage;
They, in a wineskin, bore earth's paradise.

Let us lie down once more by the breathing side
Of Ocean, where our live forefathers sleep
As if the Known Sea still were a month wide—
Atlantis howls but is no longer steep!

What country shall we conquer, what fair land
Unman our conquest and locate our blood?   30
We've cracked the hemispheres with careless hand!
Now, from the Gates of Hercules we flood

Westward, westward till the barbarous brine
Whelms us to the tired land where tasseling corn,
Fat beans, grapes sweeter than muscadine
Rot on the vine: in that land were we born.

■ ■ ■ ■ ■ ■ ■ ■ ■ ■

Robert Penn Warren (1905–   )

Pursuit[1]

The hunchback on the corner, with gum and shoelaces,
Has his own wisdom and pleasures, and may not be lured
To divulge them to you, for he has merely endured

1.   "Pursuit" is from *Selected Poems,* by Robert Penn Warren, copyright,
1944, by Harcourt, Brace and Company, Inc. Reprinted by permission.

Your appeal for his sympathy and your kind purchases;
And wears infirmity but as the general who turns
Apart, in his famous old greatcoat there on the hill
At dusk when the rapture and commonade are still,
To muse withdrawn from the dead, from his gorgeous subalterns;
Or stares from the thicket of his familiar pain, like a fawn
That meets you a moment, wheels, in imperious innocence is
      gone.   10

Go to the clinic. Wait in the outer room
Where like an old possum the snag-nailed hand will **hump**
On its knee in murderous patience, and the pomp
Of pain swells like the Indies, or a plum.
And there you will stand, as on the Roman hill,
Stunned by each withdrawn gaze and severe shape,
The first barbarian victor stood to gape
At the sacrificial fathers, white-robed, still;
And even the feverish old Jew stares stern with authority
Till you feel like one who has come too late, or improperly clothed, to a
      party.   20

The doctor will take you now. He is burly and clean;
Listening, like lover or worshiper, bends at your heart;
But cannot make out just what it tries to impart;
So smiles; says you simply need a change of scene.
Of scene, of solace: therefore Florida,
Where Ponce de Leon clanked among the lilies,
Where white sails skit on blue and cavort like fillies,
And the shoulder gleams in the moonlit corridor.
A change of love: if love is a groping Godward, though blind,
No matter what crevice, cranny, chink, bright in dark, the pale
      tentacle find.   30

In Florida consider the flamingo
Its color passion but its neck a question;
Consider even that girl the other guests shun
On beach, at bar, in bed, for she may know
The secret you are seeking, after all;
Or the child you humbly sit by, excited and curly,
That screams on the shore at the sea's sunlit hurlyburly,
Till the mother calls its name, toward nightfall.
Till you sit alone: in the dire meridians, off Ireland, in fury
Of spume-tooth and dawnless sea-heave, salt rimes the lookout's
      devout eye.   40

Till you sit alone—which is the beginning of error—
Behind you the music and lights of the great hotel:
Solution, perhaps, is public, despair personal,
But history held to your breath clouds like a mirror.
There are many states, and towns in them, and faces,
But meanwhile, the little old lady in black, by the wall,
Who admires all the dancers, and tells you how just last fall
Her husband died in Ohio, and damp mists her glasses;
She blinks and croaks, like a toad or a Norn, in the horrible light,
And rattles her crutch, which may put forth a small bloom,
                    perhaps white.   50

■   1. State the theme of this poem.
     2. Discuss the metrical pattern of the third stanza in terms of tone.
     3. There are different sorts of images in this poem ranging from
the poor hunchback to the figure of Ponce de Leon, or the snag-nail
to the small white blossom. What effect does this range of images have on
the tone?

■ ■ ■ ■ ■ ■ ■ ■ ■ ■

Stephen Spender (1909–   )

I Think Continually of Those [1]

I think continually of those who were truly great.
Who, from the womb, remembered the soul's history
Through corridors of light where the hours are suns,
Endless and singing. Whose lovely ambition
Was that their lips, still touched with fire,
Should tell of the spirit clothed from head to foot in song.
And who hoarded from the spring branches
The desires falling across their bodies like blossoms.

What is precious is never to forget
The essential delight of the blood drawn from ageless springs
Breaking through rocks in worlds before our earth.
Never to deny its pleasure in the simple morning light
Nor its grave evening demand for love.
Never to allow gradually the traffic to smother
With noise and fog the flowering of the spirit.

Near the snow, near the sun, in the highest fields
See how these names are fêted by the waving grass,
And by the streamers of white cloud,
And whispers of wind in the listening sky;
The names of those who in their lives fought for life,
Who wore at their hearts the fire's center.
Born of the sun they traveled a short while towards the sun,
And left the vivid air signed with their honor.

INDEXES

INDEXES

Topic Index

■■■■■■■■■■

Index of Authors, Titles, and First Lines

. . . .

Titles marked with an * are discussed at some length, and an * before the name of an author indicates that his work as a whole is discussed.

I

N

O

P